Communications In Business

Walter Wells
California State University
Dominguez Hills

COMMUNICATIONS IN BUSINESS

Third Edition

Kent Publishing Company

A Division of Wadsworth, Inc.
Boston, Massachusetts

Production Editor: *Nancy J. Crow*
Book Designer: *Armen Kojoyian*
Cover Designer: *Steve Snider*
Production Coordinator: *Linda Card*

Kent Publishing Company
A Division of Wadsworth, Inc.

Printed in the United States of America
3 4 5 6 7 8 9 — 85 84 83

Library of Congress Cataloging in Publication Data
Wells, Walter.
Communications in business.
Includes index.
1. Commercial correspondence. 2. Business report writing. I. Title.
HF5721.W36 1981 651.7′4 81-657
ISBN 0-534-00934-3 AACR2

To
A. Earl Manville — teacher, prophet
and Ben Siegel — colleague, friend

And to all the teachers across the nation and beyond,
who, by their efforts, not only raise the quality of communication
in business, but advance the causes of literacy and language
sophistication. Those efforts make life a little better for
all of us.

About the Author

WALTER WELLS has taught, lectured, and consulted in business communications since 1962. In addition to *Communications in Business* (here in its Third Edition) he is the author of several books on American writers, and numerous articles. He is a frequent contributor to the *Los Angeles Times Book Review*.

A native New Yorker, he holds the B.S. Degree in marketing and the M.A. in English from New York University. He took his D.Phil. Degree in American Studies at the University of Sussex. After serving as a media buyer for Grey Advertising in New York, and as a market research analyst for the National Dairy Corporation, he joined the faculty at the California State Polytechnic College at Pomona, teaching business and technical writing there for three years.

Since 1967, Dr. Wells has been at the California State University's Dominguez Hills campus where, besides his regular courses, he conducts the annual summer Writer's Craft Workshop and is Chairman of American Studies. In 1970, he was a member of the California Governor's Panel on Higher Education. He is also University representative to the Rhodes Scholar program.

Dr. Wells's accomplishments have earned him entries in *Who's Who in the West, The Directory of American Scholars, Contemporary Authors,* and *The Dictionary of International Biography.*

Preface To The Third Edition

I've been extremely pleased by the reception of the first two editions of this text — especially the Second, which seems to have caught the spirit, and found the preferences, of so many of the growing ranks of business communications teachers. Those to whom I've spoken call consistently for a book that enlivens a student's interest in the subject as well as teaching it. This is the spirit in which the book has been written. This Third Edition, revised and updated for the 1980s, aims to provide its readers a continuous combination of fresh understanding and enjoyable reading.

New to this edition are chapters on business proposal writing and formal speaking; a section on "scouting the territory" for job searchers; and what I think is the most thorough attack in print on the major malady of business writing today — the ponderous bureaucratic style. I'm calling the malady "CorpSpeak" (with a nod to George Orwell), and treating it as Number One on the F.B.I.'s (fearless business instructors') Most Wanted List. You'll see the approach in Chapter 2.

Like the earlier editions, the Third maintains its interest in writing style throughout — not fancy writing or formal writing, but "how best to say it" in any situation. Besides its several chapters on style, there are abundant style exercises and frequent notes on specific ways of fitting language to circumstance. While some of the ideas are new, I think that even the more conventional concepts are approached originally, and more productively. Some points are returned to several times to explore their different ramifications. (*Parallelism,* for example, is first discussed in Chapter 2 as a basic need; then in Chapter 3 as a flexible tool; and again in Chapter 4 as a connective technique.) Thus reinforced, the concept is I'm convinced better taught.

The Third Edition also remains behavioral in its approach. Its only "givens" are the communicator's needs to satisfy those who must act upon the information they receive, and to shape the behavior of those to whom the information flows. All principles, strategies and tactics are flexibly aimed at those needs. I've de-emphasized the more categorical distinctions between types of business writing — distinctions between *sales* and *promotion* letters, *complaints* and *claims, credit* and *adjustment* writing. They are less important, I think, from a writer's point of view than differences between *persuasion* and *conciliation,* between the delivery of *bad news* and the delivery of *good,* between memos that must effectively *request* and those that must *demand.* These are behavioral distinctions. And inasmuch as business writers seek to shape human behavior, they seem to me the more significant. Once defined behaviorally, each function suggests certain strategies that I've tried to describe in detail. And from the strategies flow tactics.

On sensitive matters — like dealing with one's past most persuasively on a resume, asking delicate questions, or removing some of the masculine bias of the language — the Third Edition tries to deal sensitively, realizing that there are as yet no perfect answers to people's preferences in these matters.

Like the previous edition, the Third is subdivided into five major parts, an arrangement that hopefully facilitates any approach to the subject the instructor prefers. The following flow-chart suggests some of the options:

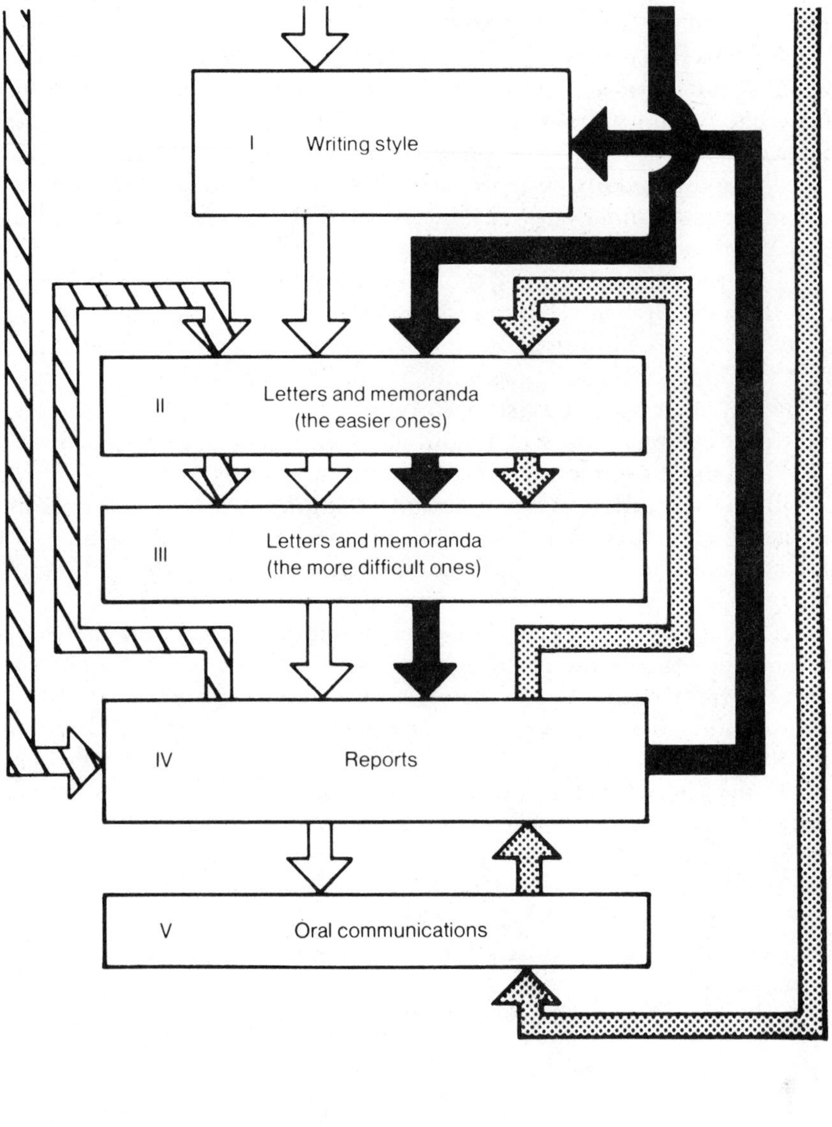

Acknowledgments

Among the many debts I've incurred in writing this book are the thanks I owe to those who have so carefully and expertly reviewed it in manuscript and helped to give it final shape: In the First Edition, Clifford V. Horn, College of San Mateo; Norman F. Kallaus, University of Iowa; Alton B. Parker Liles, Georgia State College; John D. Minch, Cabrillo College; Ruth Wallace, Foothill College. And in the Second Edition, Lois J. Bachman, Community College of Philadelphia; Mrs. Stanley Boulee, Kankakee Community College (Kankakee, Illinois); Martha Brown, Virginia Western Community College; Thomas A. Burdick, California State Polytechnic University (Pomona); Carol Hanggee, Lee College (Baytown, Texas); and Thelma Radding, Evergreen Valley College (San Jose, California). And in the Third Edition, Lydia Brunton, Mount San Antonio College, (Claremont, CA); Jacqueline K. Vines, Davenport College of Business, (Grand Rapids, MI); Charlene Lucken, North Dakota State University, (Fargo, ND). To Tom Burdick go my extra thanks for his constant support as a friend and colleague.

Dave McEttrick and Dick Crews of Kent Publishing Company will see their much appreciated influence on this Third Edition.

As before, Joan, Tony, Chris and Evan belong here too.

Contents

INTRODUCTION

Not long ago, the personnel director of a giant corporation said, "Show me a person who can communicate effectively, and I'll show you a future Vice-President!" The speaker, a well-paid executive, had spent many years in the thick of corporate activity, and he meant what he said. Another businessman — this one a local grocer in Cedar Rapids, Iowa — recently boasted of success in the face of heavy chain store competition. "With customers I can communicate," he said, "and the supermarket cannot!" He too spoke from years of experience.

Two remarks made by two very different kinds of business people, yet their points are essentially the same. True, both of them exaggerated a bit; not every competent communicator can become a corporate vice-president, nor is every supermarket a totally impersonal operation. Nevertheless, both were stating one of the basic facts of business life: *the ability to communicate is vital!*

One could almost argue that business *is* communication. Try, if you can, to imagine business being transacted without it. Impossible. History's very first business transaction was probably brought off by a series of grunts and gestures between two cave dwellers, each seeking benefit through some exchange. No doubt they grunted and gestured until agreement was reached, then exchanged

The birth of business communications.

their wares, and ambled away content. The trade may have involved just a jagged stone for a scrap of hide, but on that day business was born — and with it, *business communication.*

We've come a long way since that first primeval bartering session (though grunts and gestures haven't disappeared entirely from the marketplace). The most significant advance — at least until the Computer Revolution — was the development of the written communication. It did not supplant the oral message but vitally augmented it. The written message, of course, has one tremendous advantage over the oral — it lasts. An oral message, unless recorded, is lost beyond capture once it is uttered. A written message can be retained, duplicated, circulated, pondered, and reconsulted long after its contents are first expressed.

With the written communication, the world of business had its ticket to the modern age. An organization could coordinate the efforts of scattered workers toward a single objective. Strategies, plans, and agreements could become complex and sophisticated, with much less fear of being forgotten or confused. Many matters could be carried on concurrently. In short, written communication allowed the world of business to mature.

But communication in business is much more than simply putting ink to paper, as the bankruptcy courts can well attest. Not all business communications do their job well. Every day the business community sees its time, its energies, and its potential profits wasted by communications that don't effectively communicate. It's a frustrating sight. From the outside looking in, modern business may seem to whir with the intricate precision of a dynamo. On the inside, however, any executive can recall (usually in a cold sweat) instances of near chaos caused by breakdowns in communications. As a corporate executive lamented recently, "It's a sin. The thing our employees do *most* on the job is the thing they do *most poorly* . . . I mean communicate!" An oil company supervisor recently put it this way: "We can't do anything with their engineering if they can't *explain* it to us. I don't have the time to fiddle around with their ideas unless they've worked them into shape." An official of the American Society for Training and Development goes even further, insisting that poor writing has contributed to the relative decline of American productivity.

And don't believe the skeptic who says that good writers are born and not made. As a skill, communications has something in common with other skills: it can be learned. The ability to communicate effectively is not something that comes gift-wrapped in the chromosomes. Many companies, with great success, conduct seminars, workshops, and training programs to improve the communications skills of their employees. Industry also depends increasingly on colleges and universities to offer communications training to tomorrow's executives — the kind of training you're probably embarking upon as you read the first pages of this book.

The communications skill is also vital from the standpoint of the individual, the young man or woman planning a business career. No matter how bright, dynamic, or perceptive you may be as a newcomer in a business organization, those who sit in judgment can learn of your talents *only* through your ability to communicate. The written communications of young staff members are scrutinized, not only for what they say about their subjects, but for what they indicate about their authors' intelligence, ability, and insight. You can stand or fall on the strength of what you write. One of our recent graduates at Cal State put it his own way in a letter to a student of mine in "252" — our business communications class. The letter appears in Figure 1.

Figure 1
Letter From a Graduate

Mobil Oil Corporation

3655 SOUTH SOTO STREET
LOS ANGELES, CALIFORNIA 90058

December 19, 19____

Dear Lee:

Three years ago, I was sitting exactly where you are sitting now, in Business Communications at Cal State Dominguez.

Today I have an exciting marketing position with Mobil Oil Corporation. So as one Dominguez business student to another, I'd like to pass along something important I've learned.

Nothing in business determines how fast or how far you will advance more than your ability to write clear and effective messages.

This is true whether you're in accounting, computers, finance, marketing, management, or any other area. Don't kid yourself that you won't have to write, or that your secretary will do all the writing for you. If your secretary can write better than you, the day will come when she or he will be your boss. I am shocked at the amount of writing required in business. Even accountants are expected routinely to produce reports.

Your employer, of course, will expect you to know the technical side of business. You learn that in the School of Management. But if you cannot communicate in writing, your knowledge will do you little good. And you learn communication in your 252 class.

While you have the opportunity, learn every skill you can in Business Communication. Before long you'll discover that in business the ladders are all made of paper. You can write yourself into a vice-presidency . . . or out of a job.

Hang in there,

Blake

Blake Heinemann
Marketing Representative

The Variety of Written Business Communications

What kinds of communications must the businessperson write? For the most part, there are three: *letters, memoranda,* and *reports.* These three forms make everyone in business a business writer. There are other types of business writing, however; so before we focus on the three mainstays, let's briefly survey the entire spectrum of written communications in business.

In the broadest sense, anything that concerns business, and is written to be read, is a business communication. Handbills, house organs, prospectuses, package copy, annual reports, advertisements, leaflets, catalogs, contracts, letters, manuals, memoranda — all these and more are written business communications. At first glance, the variety seems overwhelming. But if, instead of worrying about the differences between them, we concentrate on their similarities, our survey becomes much less formidable. Actually, we can grasp the entire range of written communications by making two significant distinctions.

The first distinction is that between:

a *direct* communication, which is addressed to, and intended for, a specific person or group of people, all of whom will read it, (and)

an *indirect* communication, which, instead of being specifically addressed, is made available to a large number of people, some of whom will read it as they have the time and the inclination.

This distinction is similar to that between a rifle and a shotgun. The rifle fires a single projectile aimed carefully at a target point; the shotgun simultaneously discharges many projectiles aimed only in a particular direction.

The second vital distinction is that between:

an *expository* communication, which is intended primarily to provide information and objective interpretation for its recipient, (and)

a *reaction-evoking* communication, which is intended primarily to bring about a specific reaction in, or to evoke a particular response from, its reader.

Expository communications are mainly concerned with the facts; reaction-evoking communications are mainly concerned with the reader, and how he or she will react upon receiving the facts. Of course, expository communications don't ignore the reader; nor are reaction-evokers unconcerned with facts; but they have different primary objectives. Expositors are written to convey the facts. Reaction-evokers *use* the facts to shape people's thinking and behavior — openly or subtly.

With these two distinctions in mind, we can classify any business communication as either *direct* or *indirect,* and as either *expository* or *reaction-evoking.* We have, then, four kinds of written communications (as represented in the diagram opposite): *indirect expositors, indirect reaction-evokers, direct expositors,* and *direct reaction-evokers.*

Let's look at some examples.

Articles in business journals and trade magazines are clearly indirect expositors. Their primary purpose is to present information about business to a large and widespread audience. Magazine advertisements, store displays, and the promotional copy on food packages are, just as clearly, indirect reaction-evokers. Their audience is also broad, but their primary purpose is not so much to transmit information as to bring about specific reactions — purchases — from that audience. Even those ads that don't promote immediate purchase are reaction-evokers because they attempt to turn readers' minds toward the ultimate act of purchase. Their goal is psychological rather than overt reaction, but it's just as important in the long run for the advertiser.

Certain other communications, such as company house organs, employee handbooks, and newsletters, are indirect and usually expository; but to the

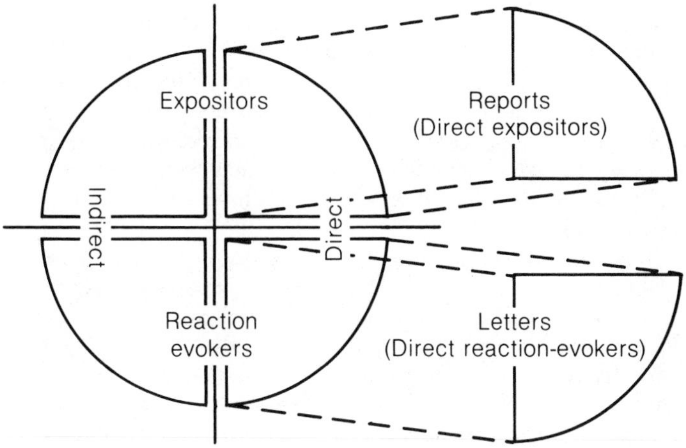

extent that they aim to develop company spirit among employees and pride in one's work, they take on an obviously reaction-evoking function.

The corporate annual report, often artistically designed in glossy four-color reproduction, is an example of an indirect communication whose real function is easily overlooked. Although it does carry fact, its primary purpose is usually to sing the corporation's praises and create the impression of a strong fiscal position. Thus, annual "reports" produced for the public are usually indirect reaction-evokers.

Of the different kinds of *direct* communications (those directed to specific recipients), two of the most important in business are the *letter* and the *report*. Apart from their differences in format, there is one important distinction: reports are essentially expository; letters are essentially reaction-evoking. A report is written to transmit facts; it also often interprets those facts. Its task is one of objective disclosure for the benefit of the reader. A letter, while it too contains facts, is written primarily to get its reader to do something, or to feel a certain way, or to think along certain lines. Realistically speaking, letters are usually written for the benefit of the writer: they are self-serving.

So too are *formal proposals*, a form of business writing that has become increasingly important to anyone intent on climbing the business ladder. Proposals try, quite openly, to get the reader to do what the writer wants.

When a report attempts to do something other than objectively transmit facts and interpretations, it ceases (by definition) to be a report (even if it looks like one). It has entered the realm of persuasion, propaganda, or special pleading. And when the writer of a business letter cares little about the reader's reaction (other than his getting the needed facts), the writer is no longer writing a letter (except in format), but rather a letter-report. In practice, of course, these sharp distinctions are often blurred. Nonetheless, they're important for they determine in large measure how a communication is to be written.

Another kind of direct communication in business — probably the most common — is the *memorandum*. The "memo" (as it's often called) is used for communication *within* an organization. It's the bread-and-butter communication of big business. The memo may be several lines or several pages long, and it may contain anything from the most casual reminder to top-secret information. Its format, a relatively simple matter, will be discussed in Chapter 6. Its function can be either expository or reaction-evoking. When written solely to communicate information, it becomes, in essence, a memo-report, one of several kinds of direct expository communication used within a company. When aimed at evoking a particular response or reaction from someone within the company, it becomes an internal letter, and follows the same principles and strategies as any business letter.

In this text we will focus on the most common forms of direct communication: letters, memoranda, and reports. That focus is dictated by a simple reality. Indirect communications, such as ads, magazine articles, house organs, and promotional copy are usually written by specialists — the highly paid copywriter, the public relations person, the acknowledged business expert. Direct communications, however, are written by everyone. The young trainee, while not expected to write first-rate advertisements or brilliant technical articles for publication, *is* expected, from the very first day on the job, to write effective memos and letters.

So as you proceed through this text, keep this fact in mind: business people who write well, regardless of the type of communication, have a tremendous edge over those who do not.

Where the Text Is Going

Where to from here? This text in written business communications has five main parts and several appendices.

No matter what kind of communication you want to write (and the confident business writer takes advantage of *every* writing opportunity), there are certain basic things you must remember. For one thing, you must be precise: precise in handling the facts you want to disclose, precise in selecting the words that make up the message, and precise in controlling the rules and mechanics of your language. In addition, you should write with style. By "style" I don't mean mere embellishment. On the contrary, I mean putting language on paper so that it's clear, fluent, and interesting to its reader, and says exactly (and not just approximately) what you want to say. These two vital concerns, precision and style, are discussed in Part 1 (Chapters 1 through 4).

Part 2 examines in detail the writing of *direct reaction-evokers:* letters and memoranda. Many sophisticated techniques are involved in evoking predetermined reactions from your readers. After all, you're literally shaping their behavior. Part 2 (Chapters 5 through 9) systematically takes you through these techniques.

So does Part 3, on a different level. This section (Chapters 10 through 14) is devoted to the more difficult reaction-evokers — communications that must effectively demand, those that must conciliate, those that must deliver bad news, and those that must persuade. One of the three chapters on persuasion is specifically devoted to writing formal proposals, and another to writing effective job applications.

In Part 4, we shift our attention to planning and writing effective business reports. This section (Chapters 15 through 18) explores *direct expository* communications in all their diversity: what they do (and don't do); how they're defined, researched, organized, and put together; and how they serve their objectives.

Finally, Part 5 (Chapters 19 and 20) briefly explores the oral side of business communication: speaking and listening, nonverbal communication, using the telephone, interview technique, and (with a chapter all its own) the formal speech.

The book concludes with several appendices on such matters as dictation, international business communications, business nomenclature, grammar, spelling, capitalization and punctuation.

The book attempts much in its over five hundred pages, but it expects no miracles. It simply sets down, in the plainest terms possible, the techniques practiced by the best business writers. It also discusses the problems that arise when those techniques are neglected. With this exposure and practice, you will unquestionably become a better business writer than you are at the outset. Being better at it, you'll find the task more enjoyable. And from that point on, success and confidence reinforce each other as your skill increasingly strengthens.

An ever-strengthening skill . . . *that* is the book's objective.

PROBLEMS

1. Select a business executive or the owner of a small business and interview this person regarding the function and importance of written communications in the firm's operations. Report your findings either orally or in writing, as your instructor directs.

2. Recall a situation in which it was necessary for you to evoke a specific reaction from someone (preferably not a member of your immediate family or a very close friend). How did you go about evoking that reaction? Would you alter your approach if you faced that situation again?

3. "I don't write too well," said an ambitious young salesperson, "but it doesn't matter. When I've got something to say to somebody — a client, a supplier, a hot prospect, anybody — I just pick up the phone or knock on their door. It's quicker and more to the point. The ability to write well is overrated!"

It's a point of view you hear expressed every so often. And it's worth assessing. Consider the variety of messages that a salesperson has to put into words during an average workweek, and comment on the wisdom of this contention.

4. Identify each of the following written business communications as either an indirect expositor, an indirect reaction-evoker, a direct expositor, or a direct reaction-evoker:

a. A highway billboard
b. A collection letter (dunning letter)
c. A memorandum announcing a department meeting
d. A letter of reference for a job
e. The script for a radio commercial

f. A Sears-Roebuck catalog
g. An article in the *Wall Street Journal*
h. An engraved invitation to an industrial exhibit
i. A legal brief
j. A recruitment pamphlet
k. A eulogy for a deceased former chairman of the board
l. A chemical report on a competing company's new rust inhibitor
m. A joint communique hammered out by management and labor to announce the signing of a new three-year contract
n. A project proposal seeking grant money from the U.S. Department of Commerce
o. A letter of thanks for a favorable recommendation

5. Peter Cooper wants to start a business (whatever kind of business you wish to assume). He hates paperwork and thinks that most of the paperwork in business is unnecessary and time consuming. He vows that with the exception of financial records (journals, ledgers, accountant's reports, etc.) he will outlaw paperwork in his new firm. Trace him through the early stages of his new enterprise and determine how long he'll be able to keep his vow.

6. In what ways, if any, have recording devices such as the tape recorder and the dictating machine reduced the need for written communications in business? How has computer technology reduced it? How about rapid-speed word processing machines?

7. The Introduction to this text notes the importance of effective communications to the independent businessperson, the corporate executive, and the aspiring young employee. But what of employees of a government agency or bureau — will the ability to write effective communications be of any use to them? And what of the woman who, instead of a career, plans to marry and raise a family?

8. Obtain a copy of a corporate annual report and read it carefully. Determine which of its elements, if any, make the annual report reaction-evoking in function, despite its title, which implies that it is mainly expository. Present your findings either orally or in writing, as your instructor directs.

9. It might be helpful for you at this early stage in the course to look over the problems that appear at the end of each chapter. They are typical of the problems that confront people in business every day. Although each draws on skills and techniques that you will develop as you progress through the book, you might try your hand at one or more of them. Then, when you return to these problems later, you can measure the growth in your ability to handle them successfully.

PART ONE

THE BASICS OF BUSINESS WRITING

CHAPTER 1

THE THREE PRECISIONS

No matter what its purpose, anything you write must possess certain qualities that are common to all good writing. Most important among these qualities are the *three precisions:* factual precision, mechanical precision, and verbal precision. Each is fairly easy to master, but only if you pay it careful attention. *Factual precision* allows a reader to grasp the content of your message immediately, completely, and with absolute clarity. *Verbal precision* results from using the best, most precise words to convey that content. *Mechanical precision* means writing that obeys accepted rules — rules that exist for some very good reasons. So, to these three important kinds of precision, let's turn our attention. First —

FACTUAL PRECISION

A piece of writing is factually precise only when it conveys *all* the necessary facts, ideas and background, down to the smallest pertinent detail, *with immediate clarity* to its reader. There should not be the slightest doubt or confusion over what's been said, not even for a second. Sounds simple enough, but it's a quality often missing in business writing. The problem is rarely that the writer doesn't know the facts. (If you don't know your facts, you shouldn't be writing!) The problem is getting all those facts transferred from your mind onto the paper, and from there into the mind of your reader. Here's an example of the problem:

Dear Mrs. Livermore:

Mr. Conroy has told our agent Harris that the mistake was his. As a result, his insurer has acquiesced. We shall be repaid the full amount of our subrogation interest in this matter.

If this and the reasons for it are satisfactory to you, please sign the release and forward it along with your notarized pink slip, affidavit, etc.

In due course, your deductible interest will be remitted.

Yours truly,

H. Mudderman

This letter is, unfortunately, typical of many a business letter — something's wrong. One can't be sure with a single reading exactly what it says. After grappling with it for three or four readings, Mrs. Livermore may be able to decipher most of its meaning, but it's a struggle.

Now, compare Mudderman's letter to this one:

Dear Mrs. Livermore:

Mr. Conroy, the driver whose 1978 Datsun collided with you last December 10, has admitted his blame for the accident. As a result, his insurance company, Park Forest Indemnity, has agreed to repay us the full amount ($680.50) for repairing your collision damage. We are quite pleased at Park Forest's willingness to settle out of court.

If their offer is acceptable to you, please sign the enclosed release and return it to me, along with your notarized pink slip, the original affidavit, and our transcript of the accident report.

As soon as the check from Park Forest arrives, we'll return your $50 deductible payment to you.

Respectfully,

Donna Clarendon

What a difference factual precision makes! One easy reading is now all Mrs. Livermore will need to understand the letter — and to act upon it. Clarendon has told her clearly who has done what, how much money is involved, what the company wishes her to do, what it plans to do in return, and when it will do it. Nothing is hazy; nothing is left to figure out or puzzle over.

What makes the difference? For one thing, Clarendon has obviously kept an eye on the *five W's and an H*. She has asked herself, "Am I making clear to my reader, in every important detail, *who, what, when, where, why,* and *how?*" Indeed she is! (There will be more to say about the *five W's and an H* later on. For now, it's enough that you see how important they are to factual precision.)

Beyond that, Clarendon avoids certain common blunders that victimize many business messages. These are the blunders of *omission, contradiction, ambiguity, imprecise wording,* and *plain laziness.* Let's consider them more closely.

The Enemies of Factual Precision

Omission Clarity suffers when anything the reader ought to be told is omitted. And such omission is probably the easiest mistake for a writer to make. When you're writing, you have all the facts and details in your head (or at least you should have). It's easy to think that whatever's in your head is being put on paper. Often it's not. You should protect against such omissions.

In the first of the two letters above, for example, Mudderman forgot to indicate that Park Forest Indemnity would be paying the $680.50 in damages, and he also omitted requesting that Mrs. Livermore return the transcript of the accident report. He had those facts in mind, but they never reached the paper.

A sales writer is guilty of omission if he informs a customer of "additional charges" but neglects to indicate how much, or even worse fails to mention the charges at all. A job applicant commits the same "sin of omission" (and probably fatally) if she writes "I am graduating from school this year" without indicating what kind of school, or when exactly during the year. The writer of this sentence:

```
All applicants for this year's Golden Gloves Tournament must
register at the Los Angeles YMCA.
```

would also be guilty of omission if he did not also indicate the precise address, the duration of the registration period, and the hours during which one could register.

Apparent Contradiction Though you know perfectly well what you mean to say, you'd be guilty of apparent contradiction if you wrote:

```
Rain hit the Eastern Seaboard today. In the South it was
clear.
```

Some areas — Florida, Georgia, South Carolina — are both southern and eastern. Did it rain or shine there? The social service worker who wrote the following sentence was also guilty of contradiction:

```
We do not advocate violence, but we feel it's the only way for
minority members to get their rights.
```

Contradictory too was the nutritional expert who wrote this pair of sentences:

> The belief that food is more important to your health than good housing was expressed by Dr. C.B. Smith at the Bridgeport convention. This is certainly not to say that housing is not of the first importance but. . . .

Notice that the contradiction needn't be actual; presumably each writer had some distinction clearly in mind. The statements *appear* to contradict themselves, however, and that's enough to destroy the factual precision of a message.

Such apparent contradiction also ruins sentences like these, simply because they employ the wrong conjunction:

> The structure of the atom is very complicated and it may be described in a few words.
>
> (The *and* must be replaced by a conjunction like *yet, still, but,* or *although,* one that acknowledges the discrepancy between the two clauses.)

> Jenkins wasn't very bright, but he didn't impress anyone.
>
> (Here the misused conjunction *but* implies a discrepancy which does not exist. The writer may mean *and,* or he may mean *so* or *therefore,* but *but* simply doesn't fit.)

Ambiguity Ambiguity is the capacity of a statement to be interpreted in more than one way. It's useful to poets, but it's a curse to business writers. In a business communication each word, phrase, and statement should have one, and only one, possible meaning.

One kind of ambiguity — the kind that results from the *careless use of a pronoun* — was the downfall of Mudderman's first sentence. He wrote:

> Mr. Conroy has told our agent Harris that the mistake was his.

To whose mistake does the *his* refer? Was it Conroy's, or Harris's? This flaw is often referred to as "squinting reference" — the reader's mind has to squint in search of the pronoun's intended referent.

When she rewrote Mudderman's letter, Donna Clarendon cleared up the ambiguity (by getting the name to which the *his* did not refer out of the sentence altogether):

> Mr. Conroy, the driver whose 1978 Datsun collided with you last December 10, has admitted his blame for the accident.

Careless pronoun ambiguities are also evident in these sentences taken from business reports:

> We added the oil to the mixture when it reached 175°.
>
> (When what reached 175°? The oil? Or the mixture?)

Don't make your reader squint to find your pronoun's reference.

```
Gilligan often compares Smith and Devereaux to Hitler and
Stalin, saying he doesn't know whom he hates more.
```

(Hates Smith or Devereaux more? Hates Smith *and* Devereaux or Hitler *and* Stalin more?)

The key distinctions in both sentences are lost because the pronouns are carelessly used.

The meanings of sentences can also be thrown into doubt by *ambiguous modifiers,* words or phrases that don't clearly attach themselves to the things they are meant to modify. Here are two examples:

```
The photograph was identified as the one snapped during the
crime by the student.
```

(Did the student snap the photo or commit the crime?)

```
The ban on cyclamates will affect about ten percent of the
soft-drink industry, estimated at more than $3 billion
annually.
```

(Is $3 billion the size of the soft-drink industry? Or the size of ten percent of it?)

Ambiguity can also result from a word which has *more than one possible meaning in a given context,* as in this sentence:

```
Children usually shrink from being washed.
```

When a London newspaper recently headlined a story on American foreign policy, *America's Friendship Offensive,* readers couldn't be sure if the story was about America's campaign to build international good will, or about British distaste for America. Mark Twain once showed his readers how silly, as well as confusing, ambiguity could be by writing of "an attractive young lady standing behind a desk with narrow legs and no drawers."

Ambiguities can crop up even if you watch all your pronouns, carefully place all your modifiers, and avoid words with double meaning. A sentence as simple as this one can be ambiguous:

> The County Commission proposed a new plan to build inexpensive housing for migrant farm workers.

Will the housing be inexpensive for the county to build, or inexpensive for the workers to rent, or both? Just as ambiguous is this sentence:

> One cannot devote too much effort to securing the rights of others.

Is the sentence warning its readers not to devote too much effort? Or is it encouraging them to devote more?

Ambiguity is always difficult to catch when you're writing because you know what you're trying to say. You should try to put yourself in your readers' place and read what you've written through their eyes, not your own. Only then can you catch and cure ambiguity.

Imprecise Wording Much of the vagueness in Mudderman's letter was caused by his poor selection of words, a weakness shared by many business writers. His word choice was unnecessarily high-flown when, in the second paragraph, he used the word *acquiesced* instead of a more natural word like *consented.* His letter was riddled with *jargon* (trade language which you shouldn't expect outsiders to be familiar with): he used terms like *subrogation, insurer,* and *deductible interest,* which Clarendon avoided in her revision. (Much more will be said about imprecise word choice in the latter part of this chapter.) Mudderman's use of the passive voice (which we'll discuss further in Chapter 3) also weakened his clarity. "We shall be repaid" is not as factually clear as Clarendon's: "Park Forest Indemnity has agreed to repay us. . . ."

Lazy Phrasing Finally, factual precision can be undermined by phrasing that is simply lackadaisical. In his letter to Mrs. Livermore, Mudderman ended his first paragraph by referring to "our subrogation interest in this matter." Apart from the technical term *subrogation,* what does *in this matter* mean? Nothing earlier in the letter clarifies that phrase. It's just a lazy way of saying what he's thinking, and it takes its toll on clarity. He has the same problem with the phrase *In due course* at the beginning of the final paragraph — it's a lazy phrase.

Mudderman also clouds the meaning of his letter with the word *etc.,* which he uses at the end of his second paragraph. He knows all the items he wants Mrs. Livermore to send him, and he carelessly assumes she knows them too. She probably doesn't. As a general rule, never use *etc.* (or its equivalents *and so on, and the like*) to abbreviate a series of items unless you're sure your reader knows exactly what items you're referring to.

Another form of verbal laziness is the *misused absolute.* The lazy writer might use the sentence on page 18.

> You can find Johnson's Bargain Stores <u>everywhere</u> in Los Angeles.

What he really means is that there are sixty-three Johnson's Bargain Stores in Los Angeles, and you should be able to reach the nearest one — if you know where it is — within fifteen minutes from anywhere inside the city limits. The absolute word *everywhere* is misleading. The lazy writer might also write:

> Nobody uses Hepperson's Vegetable Tonic any more.

but mean, in truth, that relatively few people still use it. Again, an absolute term (in this case, *nobody*) gives rise to a misleading assertion.

Exceptions to the Rule of Factual Precision

Having said all this, let's hasten to add that there are times — not often, but occasionally — when factual precision is either impossible or unwise. In these instances, you should use *strategic generalization.* When do you strategically generalize?

1. You might generalize if you're not sure of a particular detail that isn't crucial to your message. For example, you might write:

> I have learned that the Birdwell Company is opening a new <u>unit</u> in Des Moines . . .

using the general word *unit* because you're not sure whether it's a factory, warehouse, or retail outlet that's being opened.

2. You might avoid factual precision in order to be diplomatic. Collection writers do this when they write "It's been a while since we've heard from you about your payment . . ." instead of "It's been ninety-four days since. . . ."

3. You should also avoid being factually precise if that precision wouldn't mean anything to your readers, or might perhaps even confuse them. As a wise man once said, "A little inaccuracy can sometimes save tons of explanation." It would, for instance, be overly precise, and useless, to tell the average person, "You scored 934.7 on your Clerical Multi-Perceptive Index Test, putting you in the second quartile . . . ," if the only relevant fact were "You passed the test."

4. You would avoid factual precision if you wanted your reader to read his own meaning into what you've said. Instead of writing "In your eight years as a patron of our store, we have been pleased to . . . ," you might write, "In your many years as a patron of our store . . . ," because you want the duration of that patronage to sound as long as possible. To most people, *many* sounds like more than *eight*. For the same reason, you might write, "Holman's prices are substantially less than those at competing stores . . . ," instead of, "Holman's prices are nine percent less than . . . ," because the general term *substantially* is more appealing than the specific term *nine percent*. Beware, however, of using this kind of strategic generalization on sophisticated readers — it can backfire. The sophisticated reader looks skeptically upon such generalizations as "Shady Acre Homes are priced from $91,000" or " . . . as low as $91,000."

5. You might be forced to generalize when writing a *form letter*. When any single letter must apply to a number of different situations (as form letters

must), factual precision to the last detail becomes impossible. Form-letter writers often must write "Thank you for your cooperation," because the different kinds of cooperation they've gotten are too varied for more specific acknowledgement. (More will be said about form letters in Chapter 8.)

An Important Principle

One more principle must be stressed. The clarity of your writing must be immediate, not eventual. Have you ever been told, "Your language is unclear at this point," only to reply, "I know. But keep reading. It gets clearer"? Perhaps it does. But subsequent clarification does not overcome the problem of earlier imprecision. For one thing, confusion, no matter how fleeting, distracts readers. Even momentary gaps in understanding are dissatisfying. Furthermore, when readers are unclear at any one point, you can't be sure that they'll read on — as you want them to — to clear up the confusion. They may stop instead to ponder your intent, or may go back several lines thinking that they're missing something. In either case, you've fouled them up.

Your rule should be this: Although anything you write can stand in need of elaboration, it must, at the very least, make clear sense the instant it's read.

MECHANICAL PRECISION

Not only your facts, but your mechanics as well, must be handled precisely. Sloppy typing, obvious erasures, crossouts, and inky smudges will ruin a communication. So too will violations of the basic rules of written language — bad grammar, misspellings, poor punctuation.

Of course, there's always the fool who'll argue that mechanical details are the secretary's job. Although such details *are* part of the secretary's job, if they're handled badly, the fault is the writer's. A negative impression of the writer, not the secretary, is guaranteed if that writer okays a mechanically imperfect communication by signing it.

Proficient business writers know not only what to say, but how to prepare a communication mechanically once it's said. This ability also comes in handy when, in the rush to get things done, you have to type a letter yourself.

And even the most fastidious of writers must beware of accidental sloppiness. Some older typewriters can't go two lines without jumping a space or two. Electric typewriters will bedevil the inexperienced user with double strikings. Not all stationery takes erasure equally well, nor do all so-called typewriter erasers erase clearly. To overcome the problem of erasures, some writers used a lightly glazed, erasable stationery; this stationery tends to smudge, however, as soon as fingers touch the print.

In the long run, your best assurance of neatness is to strive for mechanical perfection, and to insist upon it when others do your typing. When an error is made, start over again, unless time absolutely won't permit. Erasures, when necessary, must be done carefully. In no event should a mistake be merely crossed out.

Three Reasons to Avoid Errors in Mechanics

Violations of mechanical rules can destroy an otherwise strong communication in any of three ways: they can confuse the facts, corrupt a communication's character, or disrupt the reader's flow of thought.

They Can Confuse the Facts Mistakes in grammar, spelling, or punctuation can blur the meaning of what you say. The question *Did you call, Mr. Grigsby?* is changed completely by the accidental omission of the comma: *Did you call Mr. Grigsby?* The meaning of the sentence *Her actions affected the result* is altered sharply if you misspell *affected* and write *Her actions effected the result.* If you mean to write *Only Mr. Jackson took his secretary to lunch* and you misplace the *only,* you can end up with *Mr. Jackson took only his secretary to lunch,* or *Mr. Jackson took his secretary only to lunch.* In either case, the meaning conveyed is not the one intended.

They Can Corrupt a Communication's Character Mechanical mistakes, even if they don't disrupt meaning, can ruin the character of a communication. They stand out like a cross-eyed albatross. Most readers, having learned the so-called rules of the language, can't help lowering their estimate of a writer who seems unable to handle those rules. While there are no logical reasons for preferring *Jim and I saw it* to *Me and Jim seen it,* there are very powerful social reasons. To burden your writing with mechanical error is simply to insult many readers. And have you ever tried to communicate effectively with someone you've just insulted?

They Can Disrupt the Reader's Flow of Thought Even if your reader is one of the rare ones who really don't mind a writer's errors, those errors will still cripple a communication by disrupting the flow of that reader's thought. Consider this hypothetical case: You write a letter to Mrs. Harwood to convince her to take a certain course of action. Success depends upon Mrs. Harwood's being won over by your ideas; she must be able to follow them clearly, one by one, as you advance them. If at any point in her reading she is distracted from those ideas, their effect upon her will be weakened, at least temporarily. The *vehicle* of communication (your words and sentences), if flawed, will call attention to itself, and away from the ideas it's transporting. Such distractions can't help but reduce the communication's chances of total success.

The Importance of Proofreading

The answer to mechanical errors is, of course, careful proofreading — but only when it's time to proofread. That time is not during the first draft. When you're in the midst of shaping your thoughts into words, and putting those words onto paper, never stop to question the mechanical correctness of what you're writing. Such self-interruption is as harmful to your writing as the errors themselves. When you sense, as you're first drafting a message, that you may be misspelling a word, misusing a verb tense, or using the wrong punctuation, just draw a quick circle around it and go right on composing your thoughts. When your thoughts are completely down on paper, that's the time to return to check the mechanical precision of the things you've circled.

When proofreading for misspellings, many writers find it useful to read their drafts backward. Silly as it sounds, starting with the last word and reading backward has a purpose. When you proofread forward from the beginning, you get mentally reinvolved with the thoughts you've written, and tend to slip blindly past the very mistakes you're looking for. By reading backward, you divorce yourself from the content of the message and force your attention upon the spelling of every word. Unless you're one hundred percent sure that a word is spelled correctly (ninety-eight percent won't do), circle it. When you've finished reading through the draft, return to those circles with a dictionary in hand and check every one of them. Backward reading won't catch every mistake, but it should catch those you missed when proofreading forward.

Interestingly, instructors of writing find that the words most frequently misspelled are everyday words. Most writers using words like *baccalaureate* or *ophthalmologist* will look them up, not trusting themselves to spell them correctly. But words like *receive, convenient,* and *occurred* are often misspelled because writers think they know how to spell them.

Finally, you might keep a careful eye out for the occasional problem that results from word-splits at the end of a line. There's nothing wrong with words like *pacifist* and *figurine,* when they appear whole. But if you split them thus — paci/fist, fig/urine — the second half of each word, standing alone at the beginning of a line, will probably cause your readers some distraction

(Appendix F at the back of the book provides a broad review of the rules of grammar, spelling, and punctuation. Use it as reference whenever necessary.)

Remember no one was ever born proficient in the mechanics of language — especially the English language. Proficiency is gained only through trial and error, hard work, and a never-ending commitment to self-improvement. And careful proofreading. Mistakes made in the privacy of a rough draft make no difference. The problems arise when those mistakes still appear in a final draft.

VERBAL PRECISION

More difficult to achieve than factual or mechanical precision is verbal precision, the ability to select exactly the right words to communicate an idea. To be verbally precise, you ought to command a healthy vocabulary; but that can come gradually if you give it some effort. Even more importantly, you must understand what words really are, and how they transmit meaning to your readers.

What Words Are

Words are symbols. Like a musical notation or a storm-warning flag, a word is a thing used to represent something else. (That something else is, of course, a word's *meaning.*) As with any kind of symbol, you have no guarantee that other people will understand its meaning. They may not. Worse yet, they may mistakenly think they do. Thus, one of the major problems in writing effective communications is to select words that will allow the reader to understand your meanings precisely and fully.

The quest for verbal precision encounters two major complications. First, the relationship between words and their meanings is not one-to-one. Many words have more than one meaning, and many meanings are expressible by more than one word. Words also have different *kinds* of meaning: they have *denotation* (the explicit dictionary meaning of a word, the one agreed upon by most people who use the language), and they have *connotation* (the feelings and impressions that the word evokes). The total meaning a reader gets from a word is a combination of the word's denotation (provided he knows it) *and* its connotation.[1]

[1]The formula $M = D + C$ is useful to emphasize this important concept. A word's *total meaning* equals its denotation plus its connotation.

Denotation and Connotation

Suppose that you, as a managing supervisor, wish to describe someone who never gives up in the face of adversity. In your report, you might use the word *persevering*, or *persistent*, or *tenacious*, or *obstinate*, or *stubborn*, or *pigheaded*, depending on how you wanted your reader to feel about the person you're describing. Each of these words has essentially the same *denotation:* "staying with a task, no matter how difficult, until it is done." But the words are not interchangeable. They differ substantially in connotation. Hence, their total meanings are different. You'd use the word that carried both the denotation and the connotation you wanted.

Consider the words *slender, slim, thin, skinny* and *scrawny*. They also mean the same thing denotatively; but their connotations, and hence their total meanings, differ sharply. A phrase like *periodic wage increases obtained by labor unions* would probably, in the hands of an anti-labor writer, be transformed into *continued wage grabs by Big Labor*. What is *open space* to the conservationist is often *undeveloped* or *unimproved land* to real-estate people. *Substantial corporate profits paid out in dividends to investors* might become, in the hands of a socialist, *inflated profits handed over to non-working coupon clippers*. In each of these pairs of phrases and sentences, the denotations are essentially the same. It's the connotations that differ.

Suppose that you use the word *brochure* in a letter to John Doe. The word evokes no particular feeling in him (that is, he gets no connotational meaning from it), so its total meaning is simply its denotation — "a promotional pamphlet." Or suppose you use a word like *ethnophilologist*. If Doe (like most of us, until we look it up) doesn't know the word's denotation, its meaning to him will consist entirely of the fuzzy connotative value it has for him — perhaps "something scholarly sounding and awfully complicated." Suppose that elsewhere you use the word *caviar*. Doe knows its denotation — "a food made from fish eggs" — but its total meaning for him is more than that: it includes the connotation that the word has for him — "a smelly and repulsive food that some people manage to swallow and say they like." If another of your readers happens to feel that *caviar* is an expensive and delightful delicacy, your intended meaning will differ from the meaning Doe gets when he reads the word. It's conceivable that a breakdown in communication over this single word could cost you the overall reaction you seek from Doe.

There's a story that went the rounds several years ago about a young man fresh from the University who went to work for a local company. On his first day there, the boss asked him casually to replace a burned-out lightbulb in the reception room. The young man sputtered and stammered, "But, but I'm a college grad!" to which his boss, suddenly realizing what he'd done, said, "Oh I'm so sorry. I forgot. Here, let me show you how." Need it be said? — the phrase *college grad* had very different connotations for the two of them.

Connotation is always a personal matter. The total meaning of any word — its denotation plus its connotation — can vary from person to person. Your readers, each of them, will react entirely as they wish to any word you use. You must anticipate what those reactions will be, and choose your words accordingly.

Purr Words and Snarl Words

S. I. Hayakawa, the senator and noted semanticist, coined the terms *purr word* and *snarl word* to refer to words commonly used to sway people's emotions in predictable directions. Purr words such as *freedom, liberty, sovereignty, distinc-*

tive, superb, motherhood, and *the home* are words we usually respond to warmly; they have strong connotations of goodness.[2] Snarl words — *treason, fraud, cheap, malignant, death, hideous, festering* — are words that make us angry or uneasy; their connotations are distasteful. Purr words and snarl words are staples in the rhetoric of many advertisers, politicians, and propagandists as they seek to win our dollars, our votes, and our minds.

But not everyone is moved by these loaded words. More and more, people are able to distinguish between logical persuasion and purely emotional appeals. To the intelligent reader (whose numbers in business are legion), any obvious indulgence by a writer in empty "purrs" and "snarls" is insulting. From the writer's standpoint, the use of such language then becomes counterproductive. Intelligent readers simply don't take that kind of writing seriously.

Euphemism

Writers must sometimes discuss negative situations. Yet in trying to win certain reactions from their readers, they want to avoid using negative words. Words like *vomit, toilet, corpse,* and *syphilis* are harsh enough to offend some readers and "gross" enough to evoke a smirk from others. In either case, they're distracting. They turn the reader's attention momentarily away from the central idea of the communication and onto the word itself. To avoid the distracting negativity of such words, writers use *euphemisms.*

A euphemism is a word or phrase used in place of another word or phrase to avoid (or soften) a negative connotation. The substitute word is rarely as precise or as expressive as the original, but it's preferable because the reader understands it without reacting adversely to it. Instead of *vomit,* you might use the less offensive term *throw up.* Instead of *corpse,* you'd probably refer to *the body,* or *the remains.* Through the process of euphemism, *toilets* become *rest rooms* or *powder rooms,* and *syphilis* becomes a *social disease.* In our national distaste for the aging process, we now seem to use the term *middle-aged* for anyone under sixty-five who still gets around under his own steam. After that, he becomes a *senior citizen.* If someone is throwing a party but wants you to pay for your own drinks, you'll be told it's *a no-host cocktail party.*

[2] The connotative impact of the word *sovereignty* was actually measured in a survey by Elmo Roper. In his report, Roper stated that

> one of the biggest barriers to changes in our relations with other nations is a word — and that magic word is *sovereignty.* When we asked people, "Do you feel the world situation is going to make it necessary to give up some of our national sovereignty, or do you feel we should hold on to our national sovereignty at all costs?" 67 percent said they wanted to hold on at all costs. A softer version of the question which spoke of "merging our sovereignty with other free nations," asked of a split half of the sample, still yielded a 60 percent vote for holding on.
>
> It is evident that the *words* "national sovereignty" have become a sanctified cliché that draws an automatic, stereotyped response. But this doesn't stop people from favoring any number of specific steps which would in fact transfer a considerable amount of "national sovereignty" to supernational institutions. For 52 percent of those who stoutly declared they wouldn't part with a smidgin of national sovereignty favored an Atlantic Court, 37 percent favored a legislative Congress, and 23 percent actually came out for an Atlantic union — now or at some future time.

When a euphemism becomes entrenched in the language — as they so often do — and takes on the same negative connotations the original word had, it's usually reeuphemized. *Graveyard* became *cemetery* and then, in time, *cemetery* became *memorial park*. *Prisons* became *penitentiaries* (places for doing penance), and later *penitentiaries* became *correctional institutions*.

As a business writer, you should be sensitive to the process of euphemism and the need for it. Occasionally, you'll have to search hard for a euphemism to avoid a displeasing and distracting term — but the effort will be well worth it. (A list of some of our commonly used euphemisms appears below). You also want to be careful not to euphemize unnecessarily. The writer who seems to euphemize his way around every unpleasantry, no matter how slight, usually conveys a tone of insincerity.

More will be said about the avoidance of negative connotation in our discussion of "tone" in Chapter 7.

Some Common Euphemisms

THE UNPLEASANT TERM	*THE EUPHEMISM*
periodic payments	premiums
cheap	inexpensive
expensive (but not extremely so)	affordable
false teeth	dentures
armpits	underarms
mole	beauty mark
pregnant	expecting
hit in the testicles	hit below the belt
gastric pains	distress
diarrhea	looseness
the cheapest wine	table wine
second-grade beef	"choice" cut
third-grade beef	"good" cut
cooked calf pancreas and thymus glands	sweetbreads
raised in a poor neighborhood	raised in modest surroundings
slums	urban blight
the poor	the needy
garbage collector	sanitation worker
toilet	restroom, ladies' room, powder room, water closet (British)
to urinate	to relieve oneself
spying	intelligence gathering
propaganda	information
prison	correctional institution
war prison	detention center, concentration camp*
neurotic	sensitive, high strung
psychopathic	unbalanced
a dying patient	a terminal case
committed suicide	took his own life
to punish bodily	corporal punishment

to kill (for legal punishment)	capital punishment
to kill an animal out of mercy	to put to sleep
to kill a human being out of mercy	euthanasia
to kill (an enemy in war)	terminate with extreme prejudice
one's grave	one's final resting place
failure of the radar in an airport control tower	unscheduled computer outage (official F.A.A. term)
unintended civilian victims of bombing raids	collateral damage, circular error probability (official Defense Department terms during the Vietnam War)
repairmen** (for the Trane Air Conditioning Company)	Trane Comfort Corps
to fire someone	to terminate, to deselect
ladies' dresses: size 16 and up	fashions for the generous figure
to raise prices in a government-controlled economy	to make a price correction

*Notice that *concentration camp,* which itself now has negative connotation for most people, means literally just *a place where people are concentrated.*

**Repair isn't really a negative word, but it can convey negative suggestions — we'll discuss this kind of negativity in Chapter 7.

Synonyms?

We're in the habit of calling words that mean the same thing *synonyms.* But are there really such things as perfect synonyms? If the total meaning of a word can vary from person to person, can we depend on any two words being interchangeable? No, we cannot. Do *teenager* and *adolescent* mean the same thing? Denotatively they do; but if you're under twenty, no doubt you'd rather be called one than the other. Do *student* and *pupil* mean the same thing? *Intellectual* and *egghead? Politician* and *statesman? Childlike* and *childish?* Do the terms *capitalism* and *free enterprise* mean the same? Do the phrases *to associate with* and *to consort with?* Is *Thank you for your business* precisely the same as *Thank you for your patronage?* A large retail merchant, acutely aware of such differences in connotation, headlined his recent display ads:

Inexpensive Does Not Mean Cheap!

No, synonyms are, at best, approximate. Only when their connotational differences are insignificant can two denotatively identical words be used interchangeably. The careful business writer not only selects words carefully, but weighs very closely any possible substitution of one word for another.

Levels of Diction

Another factor that limits the interchangeability of words is their *level of diction.* The verbs *buy* and *purchase,* for example, have the same denotation, and no identifiable connotations except that one sounds more formal than the other. In a memo to the corporate president, you would probably write *we purchased,* while in a note to a fellow worker you would write *we bought.* The word *purchase* stands at a higher level on the dictional stairway that exists in our language. We can envision this stairway as shown on page 26.

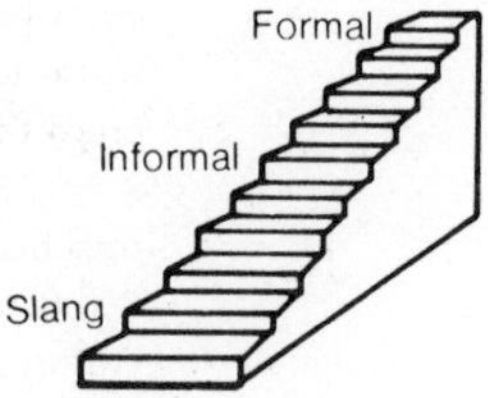

While the verb *purchase* belongs at a higher level than the more informal *buy*, the slang verb *pick up* (as in "Go to the store and pick up some bread") belongs at a lower.

The difference between the verbs *to depart, to leave, to go,* and *to scram* can likewise be arranged on the dictional stairway. Your instructor might insist that your work *improve, get better,* or *shape up,* depending on the level of diction at which he or she wants to address you. I might say about a friend that *her equanimity is inviolable,* that *she's always even-tempered,* or that *she never blows her cool;* each clause denotatively says the very same thing, but differs in level of diction. The illustration on page 27 shows several groups of denotative synonyms; the words in each group are arranged in proper order on the dictional stairway.

No level of diction is naturally better than any other. What matters is *appropriateness.* For every communication you write, you must at the outset determine the level of diction most appropriate to it, then maintain that level throughout the communication. Any sudden shift in dictional level, either up or down (unless you do it for laughs), will make your writing sound silly and destroy its effectiveness. That's what happens when the dictional level suddenly shifts at the end of each of these two sentences:

> As the fifth plenary session convened, the delegates, all cognizant of the impending confrontation, looked down in the dumps.

> Teddy got the kind of job he was looking for -- with a small outfit, great working conditions, lots of room to climb, and a most superior remuneration.

Many business writers mistakenly try to write more formally than a situation requires, and they end up sounding unduly stuffy. They deprive themselves of the natural vitality of informal language. You might take a look at problem 10 on page 91 for an example of how informal diction can help make business writing more lively and interesting to read.

Exactness of Meaning

Nothing is sillier in a business communication than a misused word: a word like *decimate* when you mean *disseminate,* or *epitaph* when you mean *epithet.*

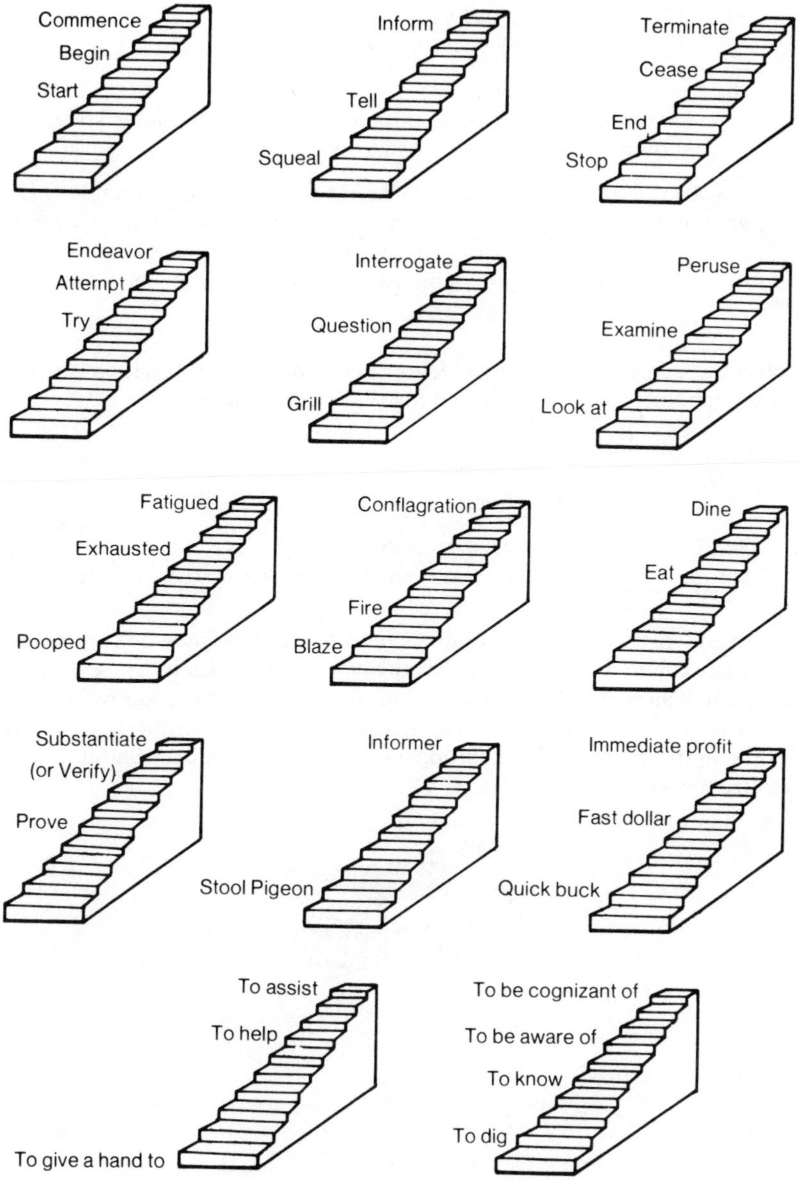

They are words which simply have the wrong denotation (they're called *malapropisms,* after Sheridan's Mrs. Malaprop, who knew all the words but had trouble with their meanings). Recently, a young woman in Phoenix confused the word for her weekly welfare check and wrote to her board. "Please send my elopement as I have a four-month-old baby. . . . Unless I get my husband's money soon, I will be forced to lead an immortal life." Good for laughs, but not very effective in a reaction-evoking communication.

Less funny than the wrong word — but just as harmful — is the *inexact word,* the word that doesn't quite say what the writer thinks, or hopes, it says. The underlined words in the sentences on page 28 are examples of inexactness.

He's a man of great culture.
(What exactly does *culture* mean here?)

This showroom is nice.
(Says almost nothing about the quality or characteristics of the showroom.)

The Board of Supervisors submitted a fabulous (or tremendous, or marvelous, or fantastic, or great) plan for constructing a new civic center.
(These words simply communicate an emotion. They say nothing, really, about the plan.)

Each of these sentences becomes clearer in meaning if words with more precisely limited denotation are substituted for those underlined:

He's a man of great dignity.

This showroom is appealingly simple.

The Board of Supervisors submitted an exciting yet economical plan for constructing a new civic center.

Even words whose meanings seem unmistakable may be communicating less clearly than you think. Consider the word *surrounded* in the sentence: "The warehouse was surrounded by a ten-foot fence." The writer knows the physical relationship of the fence to the warehouse, has a clear mental picture of it. But does the sentence make that relationship clear to the reader? Should the reader visualize a scene like this:

or one like this?

The word *surrounded,* by itself, doesn't make it clear. More words are necessary if the verbal picture is to be complete.

Vividness in Word Choice

Another criterion in your selection of words should be their *vividness*. Some words have the ability to make a reader almost see, or hear, or feel, or taste, or smell what you are talking about. And when a reader's senses become involved, you can be sure he or she is fully involved in what you're saying.

Instead of writing . . .	*the good writer will write . . .*
The intruder approached Baxter.	The intruder crept up on Baxter.
	or
	The intruder strode toward Baxter.
	or
	The intruder raced after Baxter.

The constructions at right turn the simple fact expressed at left into a mental "picture." Here's another example

The crowd reacted when Stevenson entered.	The crowd murmured when Stevenson entered.
	or
	The crowd roared when Stevenson entered.
	or
	The crowd hissed, booed, and stamped their feet when Stevenson entered.
	or
	The crowd surged forward when Stevenson entered.
Our soups are made of the finest farm ingredients available.	The juice of tender, sun-ripened tomatoes; chunks of rich, aged beef; fresh country butter — all are blended into . . .

Words like *crash, shriek, click,* and *roar* appeal to the reader's sense of hearing. Words like *scratchy, fuzzy, sweltering, milky,* and *lump* can make him or her almost feel a texture or sensation. Words like *acrid, pungent, sugary,* and *sour* call the senses of taste and smell into play. To say an animal *salivated* is to inform your reader what happened, but to say the animal *drooled* is to make that event come alive.[3]

[3]Of course, if the word *drool* is inappropriately low on the dictional ladder for your audience, you'd probably want to sacrifice its vivid quality and use a more formal substitute.

Get in the habit of using words that appeal to the senses. Your writing will become more vivid and, consequently, more effective.

Concrete, Relative, and Abstract Denotations

Another problem confronting you in the quest for verbal precision is that different words have different *kinds* of denotation. Words like *typewriter* and *newspaper*, for example, have tangible meanings; they refer to things you can see and feel and describe precisely if you have to. *Typewriter* and *newspaper* are *concrete* words, usable in a communication with little fear that a reader will misinterpret them.

(Another kind of concrete word is one like *unique*, or *gallon*, or *seventeen*, or *infinite*. These are words whose meanings are an absolute measure, precise and unmistakable.)

Not all words, though, have concrete denotations. The word *quickly*, for example, has a meaning which a reader, though familiar with the word, may not clearly understand when he reads it. It's a *relative* word, susceptible to measurement and to varying interpretation. For example, if you write "I need the charts quickly," you may leave your reader wondering "How quick is *quickly*?" Right away? In an hour? Today? Within a week? In the sentence "Baxter's son scored high on his college entrance exams," the word *high* is relative. Out of a possible eight hundred points, did he top five hundred? six hundred? seven hundred? We can't tell. There are hundreds of relative words in the language — words like *big, heavy, hot, ample, far, shortly, awhile*, to list just a few — and they all pose the same problem for the user.

As a rule of thumb, never use a relative word when you can substitute a more exact word or phrase — for example, "I need the charts by noon today" or "Baxter's son scored 635 on his college entrance exams — a very high score." If you do allow a relative word to stand alone in your writing, be absolutely sure your reader will read its value exactly as you intend.

A third kind of word, the *abstract* word, has a denotation that is neither tangible nor measurable, but is purely conceptual — the word *art*, for example. Everyone has a general idea of what *art* is, but there's great disagreement over its specifics (some will even say it doesn't have specifics). In a letter to someone who shares my aesthetic values, I can safely use the word *artistic*. But when writing to someone whose background and tastes may be different from mine, I'll take pause, fearing that this person will read into the word a different meaning than I intend. I must be similarly cautious in using words like *socialism, leadership, freedom*, and *discrimination*, all of which are abstractions.

Certainly, abstract words are necessary. Intangibles exist and we've got to be able to refer to them. But you've got to be extremely careful in using abstractions. Use them only when necessary, and be sure to accompany them with whatever concrete details you need to bring their meanings into sharp focus. *Never allow an abstract word to stand alone*, unelaborated upon by relative and concrete words that can bring the abstraction's meaning into focus for the reader.

That's how the writer handles the key abstraction in this paragraph (taken from a proposal for an overseas construction project):

> For family life as we know it, conditions on the island of San Felipe are insufferable. It is hot and humid, with

temperature and humidity both over ninety on most days. Mosquitoes abound. No plumbing exists. And the only road within twenty miles of the coastal village is mud in the winter and submerged in the summer.

The writer uses an abstraction (the word *insufferable*) in the opening sentence to state a general fact, and then follows it up with several sentences of relative and concrete elaboration. There remains no question what the abstraction refers to. The concrete and relative details that follow it make its meaning clear. Always amplify your abstractions with specific details.

One further example of the way good writers support their abstractions with concrete detail is the following paragraph by George Orwell, called by some the greatest reporter of his generation. Here he describes the housing that British coal miners lived in during the 1930s. You'll notice that each of his first four sentences is confined to abstractions. But from the fifth sentence on, it's concrete detail after concrete detail to bring those earlier abstractions into vivid focus:

I found great variation in the houses I visited. Some were as decent as one could possibly expect in the circumstances, some were so appalling that I have no hope of describing them adequately. To begin with, the smell, the dominant and essential thing, is indescribable. But the squalor and the confusion! A tub full of filthy water here, a basin full of unwashed crocks there, more crocks piled in any odd corner, torn newspaper littered everywhere, and in the middle always the same dreadful table covered with sticky oilcloth and crowded with cooking pots and irons and half-darned stockings and pieces of stale bread and bits of cheese wrapped round with greasy newspaper! And the congestion in a tiny room where getting from one side to the other is a complicated voyage between pieces of furniture, with a line of damp washing getting you in the face every time you move and the children as thick underfoot as toadstools!

Building a Vocabulary

Make no mistake — if you are consistently to choose your words well, you must develop an ample vocabulary. Only with a good vocabulary can you make sharp distinctions, make them concisely, and control your connotations.

It takes time, and commitment, to build such a vocabulary. There are no thirty-day shortcuts. The most natural way to develop your store of words is to read at every opportunity. Read as broadly as your interests allow (occasionally even further), and read writers who are widely acknowledged to be good. And don't ever let a word whose meaning you're not sure of get by you. Look it up, and learn it.

Mark Twain, who saw himself not only as a writer but as a businessman, insisted that "the difference between the right word and the almost right word is the difference between lightning and the lightning bug." Remember that as you work to develop your ever-increasing verbal precision.

A CONCLUDING WORD

There is a common objective underlying your quest for each of the *three precisions:* factual, mechanical, and verbal. Ideally, your reader will move easily through what you've written, reading smoothly, without interruption, from beginning to end, allowing your facts and ideas to build upon one another and taking from them, at the end, whatever message you fully intend.

Anything, therefore, that impedes your reader's smooth movement through what you've written hurts its effectiveness. Any obvious imprecision — a factual fuzziness, a mechanical blunder, or an ill-chosen word — calls attention to itself. And when an imprecision does this, the reader's attention is diverted momentarily *away* from the ideas your language is intended to convey. Once interrupted, the mind of the reader must find its way back into the message — perhaps only to be distracted again, and yet again, by subsequent imprecisions.

As a business writer, you must — and our entire text is devoted to this necessity — carefully write each communication in the way best suited to serving its ultimate objective. Every word and every sentence must be aimed at the objective. If, along the way, you burden the communication with imprecisions, you make its job all the harder.

PROBLEMS

1. Here are some sentences taken from business letters and memos. None of them is as clear as it could be. Rewrite them (inventing any details you might need) to improve their factual precision.

   a. The new Clearox 1220 makes copies a lot faster than the older 880.
   b. Margate Doors can be installed on any normal-sized garage.
   c. Send us everything you have on your accident, Mrs. Kagen, and we'll see that your claim is expedited immediately.
   d. I am graduating from school this year, and would like to apply for a job with your company.
   e. We would appreciate your sending that book on war you advertised in last week's paper.
   f. Kramer's is down Elm Street, past the post office.
   g. Tom, send the following letter to all our regular customers.
   h. All large orders must be approved by the head buyer.
   i. Please send me a few copies of your pamphlet at my old address.
   j. We thank you for your request for the pamphlet.

2. The following sentences are ambiguous or contradictory. Rewrite each so that its meaning is immediately clear.

   a. Tomkins arrived in time to tell Baxter he'd won the award.
   b. They are fellowships awarded by colleges that are heavily endowed.
   c. The *Times* printed Baxter's picture even.
   d. My grandfather often spoke of Andrew Carnegie's concise and fragmentary memos.
   e. It's about ten minutes before six, maybe less.
   f. The purpose of this letter is to secure your acceptance of the Cartwright proposal by returning the enclosed card prior to July 1.
   g. The office party was dull and we were exhausted, but we went home.

h. My religious beliefs were formed like so many young people, at their father's knee.
i. Baxter followed his secretary as she went to the file cabinet with a leer.
j. These resources could never have been found, except at prohibitive cost.
k. American citizens are overburdened by taxes on incomes that grow larger every year.

3. In a memorandum to your instructor, describe three instances in your own experience when "strategic generalization" was necessary. You may, of course, draw fully on the discussion of "Exceptions to the Rule of Factual Precision" on pages 18–19, but the examples must be your own.

4. Write an article of approximately one thousand words entitled "Clarity in Business Writing: An Elusive Quality." The article is to appear in the magazine *Promotion*, a monthly which is subscribed to primarily by junior executives in all fields of American industry.

5. Proofread the following paragraph for spelling errors, and submit a corrected version to your instructor. Underline every word you find necessary to respell.

> A corperation, like a state, needs faith. Most people gain comfert from the feeling that they are in someway doing good, helping mankind, leaveing the world a better place, serving a nobel ideal. A corperation which enables its employees to feel that there doing all these things by virtue of their jobs is clearly on to a good thing. Just as soldeirs fight much better for a great caws like Christianty or Liberty or Democrasy then for the protection of trading interests, so insurence firms can put more presure on salesmen who feel they are spreding protection and securety and piece of mind among their fellow citizens then ones who simply beleive they are being paid to increase the companys' return on employed capitol and the annual dividends of shareholders.

6. The following is a four-paragraph excerpt from Hal Higdon's book, *The Business Healers* (with its lines numbered for easy reference). After the excerpt appear a number of questions about Higdon's use of punctuation marks and his capitalization. If you can answer all of these questions, you have a pretty fair grasp of the rules governing punctuation and capitalization. (If any of the questions cause you difficulty, you might find help in Appendix F.)

> As part of its continuous effort to attract business school graduates into the consultant ranks, McKinsey & Company several years ago produced a record entitled ''Career Opportunities in a New Profession.'' The LP record, which the firm has distributed to college radio stations, features two consultants talking informally with three university students -- one from Harvard, one from New York University, and one from the University of

Chicago — about consulting as a career. Richard F. Neuschel, a director, and James T. Bartlett, an associate, represented McKinsey. Midway through the interview the Harvard student asked about the amount of travel involved in consulting.

Neuschel responded to the question: ''The amount of travel varies enormously from near zero, if one is serving a client or clients in his home-based city, to fairly extensive travel. We have a policy of always bringing our men home to their families on weekends unless they are so far that the amount of travel would make this impractical, and then we arrange for them to come home every other weekend.''

''Let me add just one point to that,'' commented Bartlett. ''It's been our experience that if an individual has the interest and skills and is dedicated to the professional life, he will not find the travel that he is required to do a real problem for him.''

This record received distribution only among college students through their radio stations. If it had been mailed to ex-consultants (and present ones), the resulting moans of dismay might have reverberated loud enough to shatter windows from New York to the firm's office in Melbourne, Australia. The major reason why men leave the consulting field is travel: their apparent unwillingness to spend most of their time in some city other than their home. ''The average amount of traveling a consultant does is no more than that done by the average member of middle or top management in corporations,'' insists Philip W. Shay, executive director of ACME, but many would challenge that statement.

The First Paragraph

line 3 — Could the comma after *ranks* be omitted? Why(not)?

line 3 — When would you use the ampersand (i.e., the symbol &), instead of spelling out the word *and*?

lines 4-5 — Could the quotation marks be omitted and the title put into italics instead? Why(not)?

line 5 — Shouldn't the period be placed outside the quotation mark rather than inside?

line 5 — Is the abbreviation *LP* in good usage, or would you have spelled out the word *long-playing*?

lines 5-6 — Why the commas around the phrase *which the firm has distributed to college radio stations*?

lines 8-10 — Shouldn't the dashes have been parentheses?

lines 10-11 — Why the commas around the phrases a *director* and *an associate*? Shouldn't the words *director* and *associate* have been capitalized?

The Second Paragraph

line 15	Shouldn't the colon have been a semicolon? a dash? a period?
line 16	Why the comma after *zero*?
line 17	Why not commas around the phrase *or clients*?
line 21	Shouldn't the comma have been a period and the word *and* capitalized to begin a new sentence?

The Third Paragraph

line 24	Why the comma after *that*?
line 25	Shouldn't the word *It's* have been spelled out *It is*?
line 26	Shouldn't there be a comma after *skills*?

The Fourth Paragraph

line 31	Shouldn't the *c* in *college* have been capitalized?
line 32	Is the hyphen in the word *ex-consultants* necessary?
lines 32-33	Are the parentheses around *and present ones* necessary? Wouldn't just a comma after *ex-consultants* have been enough?
line 35	Is the apostrophe in *firm's* necessary? Is the comma after *Melbourne* necessary?
line 37	Can you justify the colon after *travel*? Couldn't it just as well have been a dash? a semicolon? a period (with the next word capitalized to begin a new sentence)?
lines 39-41	Since it is a simple statement of fact, does the statement require the quotation marks that appear around it? Why(not)?
line 41	Shouldn't the comma after *corporations* fall outside the quotation mark rather than inside? Is that comma necessary at all?
line 42	Are the commas around *executive director of ACME* necessary?

7. The following paragraph has its clarity threatened and its character certainly ruined, by grammatical errors. With some careful reading past those errors, you should be able to understand what the paragraph says. Study it carefully, and rewrite it, correcting those errors.

> Like the steam railroad from 1840 to 1880, the automobile has changed the face of the nation in the first half of the twentieth century. Because of automobiles, not only did people travel and sent goods different, but lived and thought different too. Aside from war, the motor industry became the greater stimulant to American capital investment. Directly it draws private capital into rubber, glass, the making of electrical equipment, steel and other metals. Indirectly it had been responsible for millions of new suburban homes, stores, offices and factories, and expending massive government funds on highways, bridges, tunnels. During the twenties, government constructing roads for automobiles, except for buildings, was the largest type of investment. By 1940, the network of paved highway represents a capital outlay as big, if not bigger than, railroads, and larger than in public utilities. Following World War II again building construction becomes the great

consumer of capital, but much of the new investment were in locations which was only made accessible by automobiles and trucking.

8. Each line in the following groups contains a list of words whose meanings differ, but not by much. Using your dictionary for whatever help you need, distinguish among the words in each line.

Group 1

a. Minimize, belittle, disparage, deprecate
b. Infidel, atheist, agnostic, unbeliever
c. Unstable, capricious, fickle, flighty
d. Amenable, obedient, tractable, docile, easy
e. Old, antique, old-fashioned, passé, antiquated

Group 2

a. Religion, faith, belief, creed
b. Wise, smart, sagacious, shrewd, sharp
c. Enjoyment, satisfaction, pleasure, gratification
d. Outdo, surpass, excel, transcend, exceed
e. Allow, approve, permit, sanction

Group 3

a. Probable, likely, plausible, imminent
b. Suffering, pain, grief, anguish
c. Deceive, mislead, fool, defraud
d. Diversity, contrast, difference, disparity
e. Insolence, impertinence, audacity, impudence, temerity

Group 4

a. Theory, hypothesis, conjecture, supposition
b. Predict, prophesy, prognosticate, divine
c. Unaware, ignorant, uninformed, unknowing
d. Similarity, likeness, analogy, homogeneity
e. Descend, decline, drop, fall, plummet

9. Suppose you are being interviewed for a job you want very much. The interviewer is attempting to assess your intelligence, your personality, and the breadth of your interests by asking you the following wide-ranging questions. Each of the questions poses a problem of "meaning." Identify that problem of meaning, and indicate how it would affect your answer to the question.

a. Do you consider writing a profession?
b. What, to your way of thinking, is intelligence?
c. Do you feel that television scripts are literature?
d. Do you consider the President a great man?
e. Do you think censorship should be permitted?
f. Do you believe in beating around the bush on matters of personnel discipline?
g. In your opinion, is bullfighting really a sport?
h. Do you believe that campaigning politicians should spend a lot of money and time digging up dirt about their opponents?

10. The following sentences have all been taken from written business messages. Each sentence contains a key abstract term, the interpretation of which affects one's understanding of the sentence. Identify the key abstraction in each sentence and discuss its effect on the meaning of the sentence.

a. You've got to admire any person who has character.
b. I don't want him working for us unless he can communicate.
c. The trouble with young trainees today is their lack of discipline.
d. As an employee of this firm, I have a right to be told about any new company policy.
e. Either we get some *real* art on our showroom walls, or we don't get any at all!
f. There is something unwholesome about O'Reilly's new secretary.
g. Corwin treats all his employees with equality, from his department heads down to his janitors.
h. Livingston is a better supervisor than either Baxter or Levy.
i. Thompson says that from now on our department will be run democratically.
j. We've got some real poets in our copywriting department.
k. All coffeehouses should be required to have cabaret licenses.

11. Using *vivid* descriptive terms, write one sentence describing each of the following:

a. Your trip to school (or to work) this morning
b. Your last date
c. The last book you read
d. Your favorite food
e. Your favorite instructor (or supervisor)
f. An accident scene you came upon
g. Your favorite painting (or other art work)
h. A vehicle taking a turn too sharply
i. A person suddenly changing mood
j. A showroom on opening day

12. With pencil and notepad at the ready, pay a visit to a stockbrokerage, or an auction, or a newspaper office, or an outdoor market, or any other place where business is being conducted dynamically. Take on-the-spot notes, and write a description of the place at least several paragraphs long that is strongly oriented towards sense impressions. Your objective is to make your reader vicariously undergo the experience you're writing about. (You might reconsult pages 29–31 before embarking upon the project.)

13. In a memo to your instructor, list all the euphemisms you can think of for

a. Jail
b. Toilet
c. Drunk
d. Failure (as in *Baxter is a failure.*)
e. Insane
f. Die (or death)
g. An act of violence
h. Various "private" parts of the human body

14. In memorandum format, submit to your instructor a comprehensive semantic analysis (that is, analysis of the meaning) of each of the following terms often heard in the business world:

a. Capitalism
b. Socialism
c. Laissez-faire
d. Big business
e. Free enterprise
f. Market economy

Remember, you want to analyze *total* meanings $(M = D + C)$.

15. Select a piece of advertising copy twenty to thirty words long and, in a memo to your instructor, write a thorough semantic analysis of it. Analyze all the connotational possibilities, levels of diction, and degrees of abstraction in the words used; discuss the possible effects these will have on the readers of the ad. Point out purr words, snarl words, and euphemisms.

16. On pages 531–536 you'll find a list of words frequently confused with each other. Taking those pairs (or groups) of words your instructor points out, write clear definitions for each of the words, definitions which show clearly the differences in meaning between them. For every word you define, imagine an appropriate business context for the word and write a sentence that uses the word correctly.

CHAPTER 2

"CORPSPEAK" AND OTHER AILMENTS

When we talk about "style" in business writing, we're not talking about the mere embellishment or ornamentation of language. Style is the way your writing "sounds" to its reader, for better or for worse. It is an unavoidable characteristic of your writing. Your style may be lively, vital, and interesting for your reader (which is, of course, what we're aiming at), or it may be tiresome, long-winded, or clumsy. Unfortunately, a weak writing style makes the message itself seem dull and unimaginative, no matter what its importance. So when we talk about improving your business writing style (and whose style can't use *some* improving?), what we're really aiming at is making your language a more effective servant of the messages it carries.

In Chapters 3 and 4, we'll examine effective writing style and look at ways of achieving it. First, though, we must examine the habits that threaten and damage style by making it dull or awkward to read.

OVERCOMING "CORPSPEAK"

The greatest obstacle to lively, interesting, and perfectly clear writing in business today is the almost universal tendency toward *CorpSpeak*.

To one extent or another, CorpSpeak affects the writing style of more than ninety percent of those people who regularly put pen to paper in the course of their jobs. At its worst, it's deadening. Everyone recognizes the result. And few people (when they stop to think about it) really like to read it — even the worst offenders themselves. Yet every day, managers, executives, administrators, engineers, educators, lawyers, you name them — *and* the young people who emulate them — slip into that telltale bureaucratic drone every time they write, and with it almost challenge their readers to stay awake.

Here's just a brief example of CorpSpeak, taken from the preliminary report of a select committee:

> Fad-spreading is a commonly observed syndrome in those of adolescent age and in persons detached from the stable aspects of society. C.S.A.B.M. is desirous of making a determination regarding the distribution and frequency of this phenomenon in the Memphis SMA, and of establishing a comprehensive conceptual model as a valid description of that phenomenon within our geographical area at the present point in time.

What the writer seems to mean (in clearer language) is this:

> As a rule, fads spread more rapidly among teenagers and those who are not strongly attached to home or family. We want to determine the present extent of this behavior in Greater Memphis, and develop a conceptual model to describe it.

A number of theories can be advanced about the prevalence of CorpSpeak in organizational language, especially the written language: it creates a sense of self-importance, it sounds more dignified, that's the way you're expected to write, one does as the boss does, and other theories more complex. But theories don't solve the practical problem. That's our purpose here. And make no mistake — CorpSpeak *is* a problem. Writers who can intelligently avoid it and impress their readers with a clear, straightforward style will quickly gain the edge that Blake Heinemann speaks of in his pep-talk letter back on page 00.

Avoiding CorpSpeak is tough primarily because it isn't a single problem: it's the result of a number of bad writing habits, each of which must be overcome separately before the cure is complete. So we'll approach it symptom by symptom. We'll look at its root causes: jargon, wordiness, piled-up adjectives, and noun addiction.

Jargon

Jargon is "specialized" language — the words and phrases and language devices common to business and technical writing. Besides being vague — and more than a bit pompous — to outsiders, jargon tends toward dullness even for those who most readily understand it.

In part, jargon consists of a lot of *professional pet-words* like *syndrome* and *aspects* (which we saw in the excerpt we looked at), and others like *finalize, implement, input, time-frame, interface* — words we see in so many business letters and reports. Most of them are simply unnecessary in the effort to make meaning clear.[1]

[1]Some specialized language is, of course, necessary. Medical people, for example, need phrases like *topical application, pruritas,* and *myocardial infarction* to say precisely and economically what they mean. Such phrases still run the risk, however, of being unclear to laymen and should be avoided (unless explained) in commu-

Here's a list of some of the pet-words of business jargon, along with some straightforward equivalents:

SOME OF THE JARGONEER'S PET-WORDS	*SOME STRAIGHTFORWARD EQUIVALENTS*
ameliorate	improve
assimilate	absorb, digest
cognizant of	aware of, know
consolidate	combine, unite
delineate	describe
designation	name, title
effectuate	carry out, do
enumerate	count, list
expedite	speed up, do promptly
facilitate	make easy, simplify
finalize	finish, end, complete
initiate, institute	begin, start
interface	meet with
modification	change
optimum	best, most ______
subsequent to	after, later, next
termination	end, quit, fired

Jargon also consists of *acronyms,* initials like the *C.S.A.B.M.* (Committee for Studying Adolescent Behavior in Memphis) and the *SMA* (standard metropolitan area) we saw in the excerpt. Generally speaking, words can have style, but initials don't. *S.O.P.* or *T.G.I.F.* may be well known to most of us, but they remain stylistically clumsy ways of saying *standard operating procedure* or *Thank God, it's Friday.*

Jargon is also characterized by *circumlocution* — the long-way-around of saying something: *those of adolescent age* rather than *teenagers*; *at the present point in time* rather than *now* or *presently*; *sufficient fiscal resources* instead of, simply, *enough money*. Jargoneers will habitually refer to *low confidence factors* rather than *pessimism*, and write sentences like *Jones has achieved baccalaureate status* instead of *Jones has graduated from college.*

Finally, jargon is marked by tendencies toward more formal diction than is necessary, and by consistently abstract word-choice. (Recall our discussions of dictional level and abstract words in Chapter One: on pages 25-26 and 30-31.) And as you work to keep jargon from turning your writing into tedious CorpSpeak, remember (a) to keep your language at a level likely to be most comfortable to your particular reader, and (b) to accompany each abstraction you use with concrete elaboration.

Wordiness

One of the obvious differences between the clumsy CorpSpeak sample we began with and its clearer counterpart was their difference in length. The shorter, more direct version, in 41 words, said everything that it took the longer one 64

nicating with them. One specialist in the problem, Lois DeBakey, professor of scientific communication at the Baylor College of Medicine, argues that such technical jargon (which she calls "medicant") not only alienates patients but also masks fuzzy thinking among doctors themselves.

words to say. To write CorpSpeak is usually to write more wordily than you need to — and this is more than a mere problem of quantity.

Writers who use more words than they need create a burden for their readers. Every word in a business communication should contribute to the meaning, or to the intended attitude, of the message. Words that don't contribute are simply deadwood. They waste their readers' time by slowing their intake of meaning, and readers very quickly sense that waste. You must learn to convey your business messages *completely but in the fewest words necessary for that completeness.*

This point is worth stressing: *Conciseness* (which is the quality we're aiming at) consists of a balance between brevity and completeness. It's a balance that can be disrupted by using either too many words to say what you mean, or too few to get your meaning across completely. (We looked at the problem of *omission,* a lack of completeness in Chapter One. Here we deal with the other half of the virtue.) You want to use enough words to get your meaning completely on paper . . . then make sure you've been as brief as you can be, while preserving that completeness.[2]

There are so many ways to express a single thought that the briefest way isn't always apparent. Let's look at the problems that get in the way.

Redundancy Learn to avoid using words whose meanings are clearly implied by other words you are using. This flaw is called *redundancy*. Here are some examples (the redundant words are in italics):

[2]On page 40 you saw the 64-word CorpSpeak excerpt brought down to an economical 41 words. It would have been possible to trim even more words from the original. Perhaps —

> Fads spread rapidly among teenagers and those detached from stable homes. We aim for a conceptual model to describe this in Memphis.

the month of December	permanently disabled *for life*
green *in color*	to combine *together*
visible *to the eye*	a *complete* monopoly
his *personal* opinion	*absolutely* essential
a pair of twins	in *the state of* Montana
sufficient *enough*	in *a state of* shock
surrounded *on all sides*	a *necessary* prerequisite
consensus *of opinion*	a *new* innovation
when *first* begun	we are invited *to go* to
many *different* reasons	he was *originally* born in
to rule *over*	a similar *type of* argument

Redundant words and phrases can be removed with no loss in meaning.

Worthless Couplets You should also avoid using worthless couplets, those compound phrasings which really don't compound the meaning of what you say. For example:

The value and importance of this project . . .

Any help or assistance you can give us . . .

His capacity to understand and his ability to explain computer programming. . .

(If he can *explain* computer programming, he certainly *understands* it. Obviously one can understand something without being able to explain it; but the ability to explain something clearly implies the capacity to understand it.)

We went through the bills and separated them into four piles.

(You certainly had to *go through* the bills in order to *separate* them.)

In this business there are daily crises which must be met and dealt with.

(If a crisis has been *dealt with*, it obviously has been *met*.)

In each case, one of the terms in the couplet would have said it all.

Phrases and Clauses with One-Word Equivalents Another cause of cumbersome style is the phrase or clause that has a one-word equivalent.

Instead of writing . . .	*Just write . . .*
during the time that	while
a large number of	many

Now it's down to 22 words. But something's wrong. Too much has been cut from the original. It has become somewhat vague. The excerpt now lacks the quality of completeness.

a small number of	few
in the same way	similarly
at an early date	soon
in the near future	soon
at the present time	now (*or* presently)
due to the fact that	because
most of the time	usually
leaving out of consideration	disregarding
without making any noise	noiselessly
as a result of	consequently
there is no doubt that	doubtlessly
it cannot be denied that	undeniably
not as good in quality	poorer, inferior
in the event that	if
prior to the start of	before, preceding

Unnecessary Pronouns Unless they're used for a specific purpose (and we'll discuss such purposes in Chapter 3), relative pronouns — *who, that, which* — can also contribute to wordiness. For example:

Instead of writing . . .	*You might more concisely write . . .*
Dr. DeBakey, who is a well known heart surgeon, . . .	Dr. DeBakey, the well known heart surgeon, . . .
The company that manufactures this product . . .	The company manufacturing this product . . .
The Lake Pontchartrain Bridge, which is twenty-four miles long, . . .	The twenty-four-mile Lake Pontchartrain Bridge, . . .

The indefinite pronoun *one* can also clutter up your prose. Why write *This year has been a successful one,* when you can write more concisely *This year has been successful*?

Two other unnecessary "fatteners" of written language are the indefinite pronouns *It* and *There* used as sentence openers.

Unless you have special reason for opening a sentence like this . . .	*Drop the opening* It *or* There, *and more concisely write . . .*
It is quite possible that we will lose the Livermore contract . . .	We may lose the Livermore contract . . .
There are certain circumstances prohibiting the sale of . . .	Certain circumstances prohibit the sale of . . .

It is unfortunate that there are so few people who care about . . .	Unfortunately, few people care about . . .

Unnecessary Articles If you have a choice between using the singular or the plural, use the plural. It eliminates unnecessary articles (*a, an, the*).

Instead of writing . . .	*Use the plural . . .*
A gimmicky headline usually means a dull story.	Gimmicky headlines usually mean dull stories.

Neglecting the Possessive Form Wordiness also results when you forget that the language contains possessive adjectives. Don't neglect the "apostrophe *s*" form.

Instead of writing . . .	*Why not write more concisely . . .*
one of the most beautiful resorts in the world	one of the world's most beautiful resorts
the most exciting campaign of the year	the year's most exciting campaign
the advice given to him by his doctor	his doctor's advice

Neglecting the Infinitive Some writers also seem to neglect infinitive verbs in favor of much wordier equivalents. Avoid this tendency.

Instead of writing . . .	*Use the infinitive . . .*
In order that sufficient time be allowed . . .	To allow sufficient time . . .
He is here for the purpose of working.	He is here to work.

Multiple Hedging Another cause of deadwood is the need to hedge on a statement. Business writers will use such phrases as *this seems to prove, he appears to be,* or *it is said that* to absolve themselves from the greater responsibility of absolute statements. It's often necessary. The overly cautious writer, however, will use more hedges than necessary, thereby developing an excessively wordy (as well as a seemingly timid) style. The following sentence for example, contains one assertion and *three* hedges:

```
I believe that Smith's background seems to show that he
appears capable of the job.
```

Such multiple hedging makes a writer seem afraid to make an assertion. And it makes him or her unnecessarily wordy. Only one hedge was necessary in this case:

> I believe Smith's background shows him capable of the job.
>
> or
>
> Smith's background seems to show that he is capable of the job.
>
> or
>
> Smith's background shows him to be apparently capable of the job.

Self-Evident Statements Another thing to avoid are self-evident statements, assertions so obvious they need not have been made. Consider this sentence from a student's evaluation of an article in a business magazine:

> Chapman begins his article with an idea which, in my opinion, he develops throughout the rest of the article.

The statement may indeed reflect the student's belief — but is it worth making? Doesn't just about every well-written article focus, from the beginning, on its central idea? The reader's response to this sentence will probably be — *Okay, but so what?* This sentence too:

> All of us, no matter who we are, will someday die.

will strike most readers as wordage wasted on the wholly self-evident. The statement is a *truism* — it's true, but in most contexts it's so obvious that it hardly needs mention.

Aren't each of the following three sentences also so self-evident as to waste a busy reader's time?

> The profound social changes of the 1920s influenced life in subsequent decades.
>
> (Don't the profound changes of *any* decade always influence subsequent decades? That's what makes them *profound!*)
>
> If it weren't for improvements in cameras and film and the inception of sound tracks and color processing, the film industry would be back where it was in the 1920s.
>
> (Isn't this much like saying if it weren't for cars and highways, we would have no traffic jams?)
>
> From the facts I was able to uncover about the period, a generalization can be drawn.
>
> (Isn't it possible to draw a generalization from almost any set of facts? Just go ahead and draw it.)

Overlooking the Perfect Word A final and always exasperating cause of wordiness is the inability to find that one right word that expresses an idea. There's nothing unclear about a sentence like:

`Baxter was cleared of involvement in the conspiracy.`

But with the right word, this eight-word sentence can be rendered more succinctly:

`Baxter was cleared of complicity.`

The following nine-word assertion —

`Hargrove smugly and ostentatiously shows off his art collection`

can, with the benefit of the one right word, be reduced to a much crisper five words:

`Hargrove flaunts his art collection.`

Finding that one right word is another reason for working hard to develop your vocabulary.

Piled Up Adjectives

As schoolchildren, we learn very early that, in English, the adjective usually comes before the noun. *Red balloons, dignified executives, an efficient method, the difficult situation* — in each of these common noun-phrases the adjective comes before the noun. We learn that lesson so well that it later comes back to haunt our writing. We try — many of us do — to put *every* adjective we use in front of the noun it modifies, no matter how many adjectives we're using. It doesn't work. The result can be an awkwardly long noun-phrase like:

`. . . the much-delayed Presidential Advisory Committee meeting.`

a phrase that forces the reader to gather and store all those adjectives before the noun finally arrives to make some sense of them. The sentence suffers from piled up adjectives — a major tendency of CorpSpeak.

Notice how much easier the phrase is to read if the noun (*meeting*) comes earlier in the phrase with some of its adjectives allowed to trail behind it:

`. . . the much-delayed meeting of the Presidential Advisory Committee`

Even a short noun-phrase like:

`a commonly observed pattern in accounting`

becomes more fluent — that is, more easily read by the reader — if its noun (in this case *pattern*) is placed in front of its modifying adjective (see page 48).

a pattern commonly observed in accounting

Whenever you want to modify a noun with more than a one-word adjective, consider bringing the noun up front of at least some, maybe all, of its adjectives. Avoid a pile-up of adjectives in front of the noun.

Instead of	*Write*
societally stable characteristics	the characteristics of a stable society
a loud, glass-shattering sound	a sound so loud it could shatter glass or a sound so loud it shattered glass
a smugly and ostentatiously displayed art collection	an art collection, (that was) displayed smugly and ostentatiously

Noun Addiction

Even more basic a problem than the way nouns are handled is the surrender of many business writers to *noun addiction*. At bottom, that dull droning quality of CorpSpeak comes from its preponderance of nouns, noun-phrases, noun-substitutes and noun-modifiers — and a corresponding lack of active verbs and verb-modifiers. CorpSpeakers (whether they're speaking or writing) seem addicted to noun forms, and repelled by verbs.

The difference is more than just grammatical. Consider what nouns and verbs are. Nouns give names to things; they are labels, and essentially static. Verbs (except the various forms of *to be*) indicate action. It may be internal action or external action; but whichever it is, verbs are action words. Nouns tend to make writing static. Verbs give it a dynamic quality.

Yet for some strange reason, many writers — perhaps you're among them — seem more comfortable with static nouns than with action verbs. They would rather write *After his arrival* (in which the preposition *After* is followed by a two-word noun phrase) than write *After he arrived* (in which the *After* is followed by a pronoun, then a verb).

A CorpSpeaker would be likely to write:

He dances in an awkward way . . .

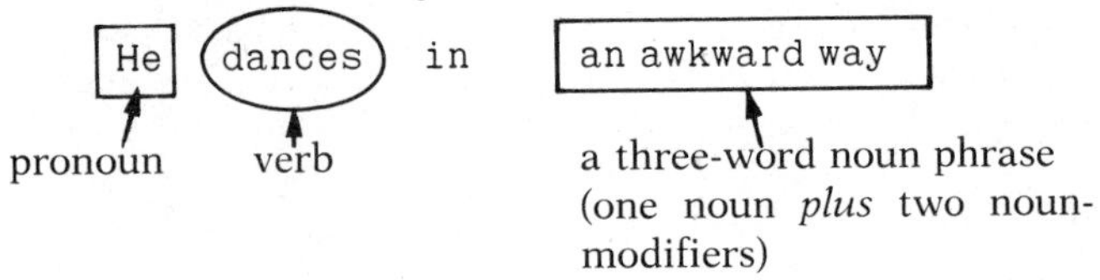

in which four of the six words function "nominally" (that is, in noun roles), rather than:

He dances awkwardly. . .

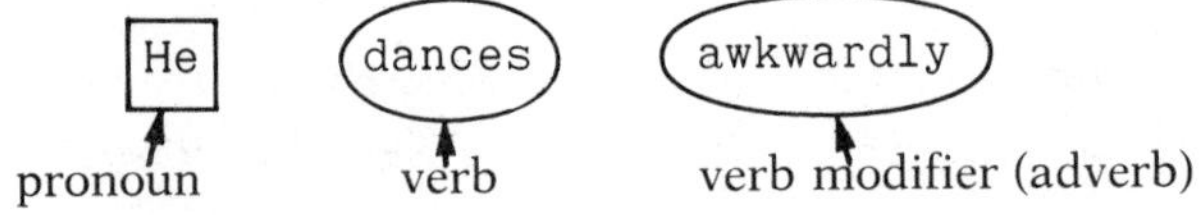

in which two of the three words function "verbally." The first sentence is noun-heavy; the second more verbal. And the verbal sentence is much more "alive." (It is also more concise, a virtue we'll be discussing shortly.)

Let's look at a pair of longer sentences and consider their "nominal" and "verbal" makeup:

```
We are desirous of making
a determination of guilt
or innocence regarding
street gang members.
```

```
We wish to determine the
guilt or innocence of
those who belong to
street gangs.
```

Most of us would agree, I think, that the sentence at right reads more smoothly and with greater vitality than the one at left. The left one is stilted. It's CorpSpeak. It has that bureaucratic ring, largely because of its excessive noun-heaviness. Let's look at "nominal/verbal" makeup:

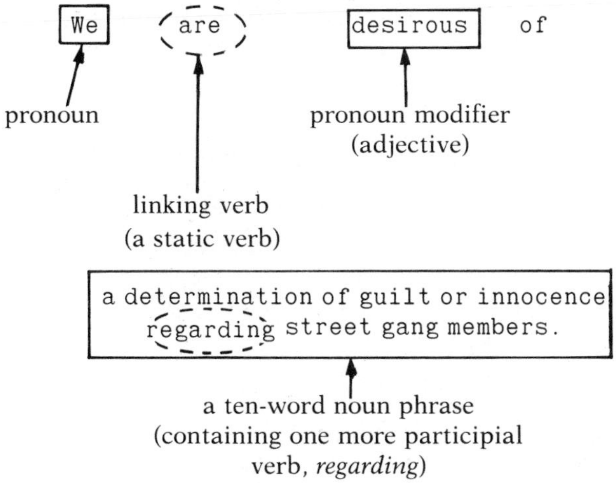

In this fifteen-word construction only three words function "verbally" (*are, making,* and *regarding*) and none of them is an active verb (that is, a verb that can stand alone in conveying an action). Now look at the makeup of the sentence on the right.

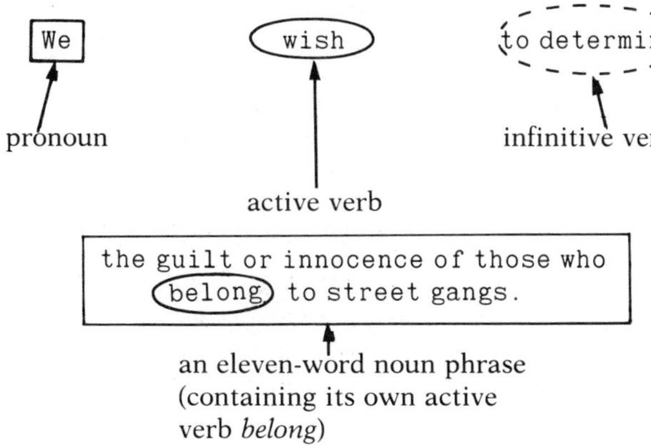

Here, in a fifteen-word construction, four words function verbally, and two of them (*wish* and *belong*) are active verbs. Although both sentences contain more "nominal" than "verbal" phrasing, the one on the right (with its two active verbs) is unquestionably livelier.

Here are several more side-by-side examples of noun-heavy CorpSpeak sentences rewritten in livelier, more "verbal" form. Note carefully in each of them the specific conversions of noun and noun-phrase into verb and verb phrase.

Noun-Heavy CorpSpeak . . .	The Livelier "Verbal" Style . . .
Norcroft Aviation is a manufacturer of military and commercial aircraft.	Norcroft Aviation manufactures military and commercial aircraft.
There has been a substantial increase in the number of government contracts.	The number of government contracts has substantially increased.
We are hopeful that the acquisition of the coastal ranch property by the State will take place.	We hope the State will acquire the coastal ranch property.
The necessity for exceeding the old ratio is justified on the basis of efficiency.	Efficiency requires that we exceed the old ratio.

There's one more thing you want to note: Obviously, every sentence, to be complete, needs a main verb. Knowing this, writers can try to find precisely the right verb — or (and here's where the trouble starts) they can take the lazy way out and simply use a linking verb (that is, some form of the verb *to be*). Once the linking verb is used, the rest of the sentence will usually fall very "nominally" into place — and dull prose results because linking verbs do not convey action. They merely attach subjects to predicates. One unmistakable symptom of CorpSpeak is the predominance of linking verbs.

Look at the four sentences at left above. There's not an active verb in the lot. Their main verbs, respectively, are *is, has been, are* and *is.* If most of your sentences depend on linking verbs, you too may be guilty of noun addiction — and of putting your readers to sleep with your business prose.

A Postscript on CorpSpeak

The dull and pompous language we've been attacking since the beginning of the chapter once prompted a U.S. congressman to coin the term *gobbledygook* — it all sounded to him like the gobbling of a Texas turkey. It also prompted an ingenious Public Health Service official named Philip Broughton to invent a "machine" to save writers the trouble. The machine consists of three columns of carefully chosen words:

The sin of CorpSpeak often begins with "innocent" writers reaching for the temptingly easy linking-verb instead of trying to find the most precise verb.

Column 1	*Column 2*	*Column 3*
0. integrated	0. management	0. options
1. total	1. organizational	1. flexibility
2. systematized	2. monitored	2. capability
3. parallel	3. reciprocal	3. mobility
4. functional	4. digital	4. programming
5. responsive	5. logistical	5. concept
6. optional	6. transitional	6. time-phase
7. synchronized	7. incremental	7. projection
8. compatible	8. third-generation	8. hardware
9. balanced	9. policy	9. contingency

The procedure is simple. The business writer just thinks of any three-digit number, then chooses the corresponding words from each column. For example, the number 257 produces "systematized logistical projection." Number 931 gives you "balanced reciprocal flexibility." "These are phrases," says Broughton, "that can be dropped into virtually any report to give it that ring of decisive, knowledgeable authority. No one will have the faintest idea of what you're talking about — but they're not about to admit it."

Broughton's "machine" works so dreadfully well because its results embody virtually every characteristic of CorpSpeak at its worst. Many of its component words are the professional pet-words so common to business jargon. Many of them are also dictionally quite formal, and most are abstract. The resulting phrases are, in most cases, wordier than they have to be to express what they mean (whatever they mean!). And in every case the result is a solid clot of noun-work that suffers from adjective pile-up.

OTHER CAUSES OF DULLNESS

As much of a problem as CorpSpeak can be, it isn't the only cause of dullness in business writing. There are other traps you should avoid. Let's look at them: *hackneyed phrasing, clichés, repetitious wording, overworked intensifiers,* and *unnecessary compound constructions.*

Hackneyed Phrasing

Although their numbers are fortunately dwindling, some people still feel that business writing has its own peculiar style, one that sounds like this:

```
Dear Sirs:

Yours of the 12th gratefully received and contents duly
noted. We humbly beg to inform your office that pursuant to
the matter in question, you will find enclosed, herewith,
disputed document.

Thanking you in advance for your consideration tendered in
its regard, we remain,

Yours truly,
```

It might as well be signed by the Chief Assistant to the Emperor Julius Caesar, it sounds that ancient! This is *not* effective business writing. The letter is loaded with hackneyed phrases — *yours of the 12th gratefully received, contents duly noted, we humbly beg, enclosed herewith* — phrases which first saw daylight long ago; stilted, stuffy, time-wasting phrases. They ought to be turned into plain, straightforward English.

Here is a list of some hackneyed phrases you'll see in business letters, along with some suggestions for enlivening them:

`We wish to advise that . . .`

(It's obvious that you *wish* to say what you're about to say. And don't say *advise* if you mean *inform.* Just delete this phrase if you catch yourself using it, and simply express the idea you wish to express.)

`We beg to acknowledge`

(Begging has no place in the modern business letter. Just write *Thank you for* or *Thanks for. . . .*)

`We are in receipt of . . .`

(Sounds too pompous. Why not simply *We have received* or *Thank you for?*)

`I have your recent letter at hand . . .`

(To say you have *received* something conveys a sense of action; to simply *have* it is static. The phrase *at hand* is superfluous; omit it. Once again, the expressions *We have received* and *Thank you for* are simpler, and much better.)

`As per your report . . .`

(Write more naturally: *According to your report.*)

`Permit me to say that . . .`

(Permission is irrelevant. Simply say what you want to say.)

`Yours of the 12th . . .`

(Be specific. Write *Your memorandum of June 12,* or *Your inquiry of June 12.*)

`And contents duly noted . . .`

(Superfluous. If you're answering a communication, obviously you've noted it.)

`Re your claim . . .`

(This is stiff and legalistic. Write instead *About your claim* or *Regarding your claim.*)

`Pursuant to . . .`

(This too sounds stiff and legalistic. You probably mean *According to, Complying with,* or *Following upon.*)

`In reference to said contract . . .`

(*Said* as an adjective is also quite stiff.)

`Attached herewith . . . Attached please find . . . ,`
`Enclosed herein . . . Please find enclosed . . .`

(These are stuffy ways of saying *We have attached* or *Enclosed is.*)

`Anticipating your favor, I remain . . . (or) Awaiting your reply, we are . . . (or) Trusting we shall receive your favor, I am, Yours truly . . .`

(These *-ing* endings have been old-fashioned for years. Get rid of the opening participle — *anticipating, awaiting, trusting* — and rewrite the closing as a self-contained sentence: *We look forward to hearing from you soon.*)

`In due course . . .`

(A vague and stuffy way of saying *Within* ——— *weeks* [or *days,* as the case may be].)

Under separate cover . . .

(Just write *separately*, and, if you can, add the mode of dispatch: *by air mail, by parcel post.*)

Allow me to express . . .

(Another high-flown and superfluous opening. Just say whatever you wish to say.)

In response to same . . .

(This is another carry-over from legal documents — which for the most part are hideously written. You're better off using the pronoun *it* or the appropriate noun: *In response to it, In response to your recent inquiry.*)

That letter from Caesar's chief assistant, when purged of its hackneyed style, would probably sound more like this:

Gentlemen:

We thank you for your thoughtful note of June 12, and enclose with this letter a copy of the disputed brochure for you to examine. Incidentally, we'd also like to express our appreciation for your allowing the brochure's early publication.

Sincerely,

Clichés

Another bad habit of many business writers is an unwitting dependence upon clichés. Clichés are phrases that we've heard so often they make a communication seem stale. Clichés submerge the significance of a message by making it sound like a thousand other messages the reader has received.

Some clichés are old quotations from literature, phrasings that were once original but have now grown stale through endless repetition:

Birds of a feather flock together.
Blood is thicker than water.
Hope springs eternal in the human breast.
Better late than never.
A rolling stone gathers no moss.
Variety is the spice of life.
All work and no play makes Jack a dull boy.
Necessity is the mother of invention.
Life is but a stage.
Absence makes the heart grow fonder.

Other clichés are carry-overs from windbag oratory:

To make a long story short . . .
To coin a phrase . . .
In closing I would like to say . . .
First and foremost . . .
We earnestly hope and trust . . .

And last but not least . . .
A man who needs no introduction . . .
Gone but not forgotten.

Some clichés are nothing more than overworked comparisons:

happy as a lark
light as a feather
hard as nails
sober as a judge
quick as a flash
cool as a cucumber
busy as a bee
pretty as a picture
selling like hotcakes
dry as a bone
bald as a billiard ball
easier said than done
pure as the driven snow
a fate worse than death
slept like a log
sadder but wiser
as phony as a three-dollar bill

Still others consist of adjectives and nouns which have been linked together so often that their lack of originality has become embarrassing:

guiding light
primrose path
striking example
budding genius
acid test
almighty dollar
watery grave
hard facts
bone of contention
clinging vine
hasty retreat
bitter end

And there are numerous other common expressions, once original, that have degenerated into tiresome clichés:

a legend in his own time
on the spur of the moment
another day, another dollar
keep your nose to the grindstone
lay your cards on the table
beyond the shadow of a doubt
got up on the wrong side of the bed
got off on the wrong foot in life
by leaps and bounds
a step in the right direction
the calm before the storm
the bigger they are, the harder they fall
bite off more than you can chew
let the chips fall where they may
cut off your nose to spite your face
in the twinkling of an eye
call a spade a spade
the blind leading the blind
raining cats and dogs
pass with flying colors
you bet your bottom dollar
let's get the show on the road
a shot in the dark
crying over spilt milk
explore every avenue
a chip off the old block
keep the ball rolling
by hook or by crook
let's get on the ball
in all walks of life
keeping a low profile
that's the bottom line

You may be quite competent at your job, but your memos are going to bore a lot of people (and cost your reputation some points) if you persist in clichéd writing like this:

> And last but not least, the recent recession has made serious inroads into our sales figures, and our profit margins have been cut to the bone. I needn't remind you that a dollar saved

```
is a dollar earned. Therefore, I am asking each of you to keep
the ball rolling and . . .
```

I am not suggesting that clichés be avoided altogether. Sometimes they can't be, or shouldn't be. There is the story of an executive who, determined to avoid using clichés, crossed out the sentence *Where there's smoke, there's fire* in an early draft and rewrote it as follows: *Carbon-bearing emittances are usually found in a cause-and-effect relationship with conflagratory phenomena.* Out went the cliché, and in came CorpSpeak. It was no improvement! Clichés should, however, be avoided whenever there is a more original or more direct way of saying what you want to say — as there usually is. Most sophisticated readers find clichés tiresome.

Repetitious Wording

Occasionally, a skillful writer will repeat a word or phrase for emphasis (a technique we'll examine in the following chapter). But unless repetition is skillfully done, the result will be tedious for the reader.

In the following excerpts, notice the dullness that begins to seep in with repetitious wording:

```
We are happy to receive your letter of January 7. We always
like to have our customers suggest ways in which we can
improve our home-delivery service.
```

This tiresome repetition of the pronoun *we* can be remedied by alternating the subjects of successive clauses and combining those clauses that need not stand alone, as follows:

```
We were happy to receive your letter of January 7 suggesting
improvement in our home-delivery service. Such suggestions
always help us serve you more efficiently.
```

A tiresome style is also created by unnecessarily repeating nouns, as in this sentence:

```
The contract shall be considered a valid contract if the
terms of said contract are not made retroactive to the date
on which the contract is signed.
```

We can avoid this kind of tiresome repetition with pronouns:

```
The contract shall be considered valid if its terms are not
made retroactive to the date of signing.
```

Another example of tedious repetition — this time of a prepositional phrase — occurs in this sentence:

```
So that we may fill your order on credit, will you please send
us the names of two companies who sell to you on credit.
```

You can avoid repeating the phrase *on credit* by altering the end of the sentence:

```
So that we may fill your order on credit, will you please send
us the names of two companies with whom you have a credit
account.
```

Overworked Intensifiers

The style of enthusiastic business writers can suffer from *overintensification.* In trying to emphasize ideas, they overuse adverbs and superlatives. Instead of writing *the latest fashions,* for example, they write *the very latest fashions.* Instead of *thank you very much,* they write *thank you so very much.* Instead of *we will be happy to,* it's *we will indeed be more than happy to.*

There's nothing wrong with an occasional intensifier to give emphasis to a special idea; but unless you use them sparingly, intensifiers can make you sound gushy and insincere.

Consider this paragraph. It's loaded with intensifiers (the underlined words):

```
We are extremely proud to offer you a position on our staff of
highly trained and exceptionally talented professionals.
The position provides extraordinary benefits which I would
be very eager to fully extend to you.
```

How much more effective — and, in fact, more intense — the writer's style becomes when the intensifiers are deleted and the descriptive words allowed to speak for themselves.

```
We are proud to offer you a position on our expert staff. The
position provides benefits I would be eager to extend to you.
```

Unnecessary Compound Constructions

Because the thoughts in our heads often run together as we attempt to get them on paper, many writers develop the tiresome habit of running those thoughts together on paper, creating unnecessary compound constructions. Overuse of the conjunction *and* is the most frequent offense. Mechanically, there's nothing wrong with the sentence:

```
There's a 5:30 plane leaving for Los Angeles tomorrow, and
I'd better be on it if I'm to address the convention.
```

But its style is clearly improved if each of the ideas is given its own separate sentence:

```
There's a 5:30 plane leaving for Los Angeles tomorrow. I'd
better be on it if I'm to address the convention.
```

The longer each separate idea becomes, the more its style is impaired by unnecessary compounding. Both of the following sentences can be greatly improved by dropping the *and* and turning the single sentence into two.

Ideas Unnecessarily Compounded	*Improved*
In the nineteenth century, a woman was expected to remain in the home, and she was not encouraged to aspire to a career.	In the nineteenth century, a woman was expected to remain in the home. She was not encouraged to aspire to a career.
After testing the Maxwell conveyor system, I find it completely suited to our requirements and I think we should install it.	After testing the Maxwell conveyor system, I find it completely suited to our requirements. I think we should install it.

This unnecessarily compound sentence:

> Michaelson grabbed his coat and next he kissed his wife, and then he rushed for the office.

can be improved by using *one* subject (instead of three — *Michaelson, he, he*), and confining the compounding to the predicate of a simple sentence:

> Michaelson grabbed his coat, kissed his wife, and rushed for the office.

The following sentence is also unwisely compounded:

> The Warren Report was probably the world's most publicized report, and many people felt that its findings were dubious.

It is markedly improved by grammatically subordinating the less important idea (the report's publicity). Instead of giving it the first of two independent clauses in a compounded sentence, the writer can relegate that less important idea to a simple noun phrase placed next to its subject:

> The Warren Report, at the time the world's most publicized report, presented findings that many people felt to be dubious.

We'll have more to say in Chapter 3 about compounding and grammatical subordination. For now, let's put the rule most simply: Unless there is clear-cut justification for bringing a set of ideas into compound construction, either keep them separate or subordinate the less important ones.

PREVENTING AN AWKWARD STYLE

Finally, among the various problems that plague business writing style, there is plain awkwardness. Awkward style, like mechanical error, calls attention to itself, interrupting the reader's absorption of ideas and destroying the smooth flow of the communication. Awkwardness has many causes. All we can do here is briefly examine some of the more common ones: *fractured parallelism, dangling modifiers,* various *illogical constructions, awkward back-pointers,* and *violations of euphony.* Watch for them — and avoid them.

Fractured Parallelism

When you present your reader with two or more parallel ideas in a single sentence, good style demands that you aid the reading by putting those ideas into parallel form. Failure to do so results in a *fractured parallelism,* a jarring awkwardness of style. Consider this sentence:

> Baxter neither wrote a report nor a speech to the finance committee.

It contains two parallel ideas (writing a report and making a speech), two things which Baxter didn't do. But they aren't presented in parallel form. Since the first idea, *wrote a report,* is expressed as a verb phrase in the past tense, the second idea should also be expressed as a verb phrase in the past tense, not just as a noun. The sentence should be revised to read:

> Baxter neither wrote a report nor made a speech to the finance committee.

or

> Baxter neither wrote a report, nor spoke to the finance committee.
>
> (*spoke,* an intransitive verb, does not need an object to complete its meaning.)

Here's another sentence with fractured parallelism:

> When Carson retired, he was admired by his colleagues, respected by his adversaries, and his staff members loved him.

It contains three parallel ideas. The first two begin with past participles *(admired, respected);* so should the third, but it doesn't. The sentence should be revised to read:

> When Carson retired, he was admired by his colleagues, respected by his adversaries, and loved by the members of his staff.

Or, if the writer wants to convey a somewhat different implication, he can build his parallelism around the original structure of the third idea, and write:

> When Carson retired, his colleagues admired him, his adversaries respected him, and his staff members loved him.

Parallel construction is important because the human mind sees relationships more quickly when presentation reflects those relationships. And because your communications in business must be grasped immediately if they're to be effective, it's vital that you learn to avoid fractured parallelisms.

Dangling Modifiers

A modifier (as you know) is an element that adds to, alters, or limits the meaning of something else in a sentence. *Dangling* modifiers, as the term implies, are modifiers given nothing to modify. Usually a writer's intended modification is obvious, in spite of dangling construction; but the foolishness of the dangling element, particularly with a sophisticated reader, usually evokes a chuckle and not much respect. Here are some danglers taken from actual business letters:

> While walking down Madison Avenue, a bright idea popped into my head.
>
> (When readers get halfway through this sentence, they are hit with the picture of a bright idea strolling down Madison Avenue.)
>
> Knowing Baxter's preference for scotch, three bottles were ordered for dinner.
>
> (Sounds as though it's the three bottles that know Baxter's preference.)
>
> By constantly practicing, your ability to close a sale is bound to improve.
>
> (Who is doing the constant practicing — you or your ability?)
>
> At the age of eighteen, my father suggested that I enter the family business.
>
> (An eighteen-year-old father making such a suggestion?)

Remedying a dangling modifier is usually easy. The first of the danglers above can be cured with either of two revisions:

> While I was walking down Madison Avenue, a bright idea popped into my head.
>
> While walking down Madison Avenue, I suddenly had a bright idea.

The other danglers above are just as easily remedied:

> Knowing Baxter's preference for scotch, we ordered three bottles for dinner.
>
> By constantly practicing, you are bound to improve your ability to close a sale.
>
> When I was eighteen, my father suggested I enter the family business.

Illogical Constructions

To violate logic in your use of language, even though a reader can see past the violation, is to distract and cause an awkward reading. Let's look at some of these common illogicalities.

Illogical Comparisons Illogical comparisons can plague your writing if you're not on the lookout for them. A sentence like this one:

> Columbia salmon is far superior to any fish on the market.

will jar most readers with the illogic of its comparison, even though its meaning is clear. *Columbia salmon* and *any fish on the market* are not comparable because they aren't mutually exclusive ("any fish on the market" *includes* "Columbia salmon"). What is meant of course — and what must be said — is:

> Columbia salmon is far superior to any <u>other</u> fish on the market.

Here's another sentence made awkward by illogical comparison:

> As you might expect, the reflexes of an athlete are, on the average, much quicker than the average man.

The sentence seems to compare apples with oranges — it compares *reflexes* with *the average man.* Logically, it must compare *reflexes* with *reflexes:*

> As you might expect, the reflexes of an athlete are, on the average, much quicker than <u>those of</u> the average man.
>
> or
>
> . . . much quicker than the average man<u>'s</u>.

Illogical Couplets Awkward too are illogical couplets, pairs of items that don't logically pair up. This sentence for example:

> The streets are lined with large trees in Atlanta and most southern cities

stands upon an illogical couplet. Atlanta itself is a southern city. What the writer meant to say was

> The streets are lined with large trees in Atlanta and most <u>other</u> southern cities.
>
> or
>
> The streets are lined with large trees in Atlanta, <u>as in</u> most southern cities.
>
> or
>
> The streets are lined with large trees in Atlanta, <u>in fact in</u> most southern cities.

Illogical Parallelisms Here, awkwardness results from putting together into parallel structure items that are not parallel in meaning to each other. This construction for example:

> In Meecham's biology lab, there were kept all sorts of experimental animals: herbivorous, carnivorous, rodents . . .

is awkward because the word *rodents* is not parallel to *herbivorous* or *carnivorous,* which are designations of food preference. This next sentence, too, stumbles over the illogic of its parallelism:

> During the war, the Army Corps of Engineers found itself designing not only bridges and fortifications, but living quarters, food service facilities, hospitals, recreation centers, and buildings of all kinds.

Aren't *living quarters, food service facilities, hospitals,* and *recreation centers* themselves kinds of *buildings?*

Illogical Shifts Awkwardness also occurs when shifts in grammatical function — shifts in verb tense, person, or number — occur without apparent reason. Here, for example, is an illogical shift in *verb tense:*

> We had known for some time that a tax surcharge is on its way.

The second verb in the sentence, *is* (a present tense verb), is inconsistent with the first verb, *had known* (which is in the past perfect tense). The present tense refers to now; the past perfect refers to a time prior to some point in the past (see the chart on page 524). They do not logically go together. Either the surcharge is already here:

> We <u>had known</u> for some time that a tax surcharge <u>was</u> on its way.

or it's still to come:

> We <u>have known</u> for some time that a tax surcharge <u>is</u> on its way.

In the following excerpt, the awkwardness stems from a careless shift in grammatical *person:*

> Each applicant must have his forms approved by both his prospective supervisor and the Personnel Officer. Without these two approvals you will not be allowed on the job site.

In the first sentence the writer refers to the subject in the *third person* (*Each applicant, his*); then in the second sentence the writer shifts, without apparent reason to a *second-person* reference (*you*). The inconsistency can be alleviated either by using the more formal third person throughout:

```
Each applicant must have his forms approved by both his
prospective supervisor and the Personnel Officer. Without
these approvals, he will not be allowed on the job site
```

or by consistently using the more empathetic and less formal second person:

```
As an applicant, you must have your forms approved by both
your prospective supervisor and the Personnel Officer.
Without these approvals you will not be allowed on the job
site.
```

We'll discuss the use of *you* more fully in Chapter 5.

Careless shifts in grammatical *number* (from singular to plural, or vice versa) also cause awkwardness. If, for example, the sentences above had begun with a plural subject instead of a singular one (*All applicants* instead of *Each applicant*), they would have had to maintain that plural reference throughout:

```
All applicants must have their forms approved by their
prospective supervisors and by the Personnel Officer.
Without these approvals, they will not be allowed on the job
site.[3]
```

Awkward Back-Pointers

To save words, or perhaps out of laziness, business writers sometimes use expressions like the following to point the reader's attention backward on the page:

the former	the aforementioned
the latter	the above captioned
respectively	as mentioned above

An executive might, for example, write in a memo:

```
Uniforms for salaried employees and volunteers are
distributed by the Personnel Department and the Staff
Office respectively.
```

The back-pointer at the end of this sentence *(respectively)* is a device for establishing the proper relationship between items in a sentence. The difficulty, however, is that the reader must jump back to the beginning of the sentence to interpret its meaning. And anything that makes the reader stop, even momentarily, and scramble backward through the message is a style flaw that should be avoided. The back-pointer in our sentence is easily avoided:

```
Uniforms for salaried employees are distributed by the
Personnel Department; those for volunteers, by the Staff
Office.
```

[3]Regarding grammatical number, remember that some organizations have plural names: *United Auto Workers, United Nations, Associated Foods.* These organizations should be treated as singular in sentence construction. Rather than "The United Nations *are* convening today," for example, you should write "The United Nations *is* convening today."

Back-pointers can occasionally save you a few words in a letter, but they should never be used at the expense of a smoothly flowing message.

Violations of Euphony

Euphony is the pleasing and agreeable "sound" we get from someone's writing when it's well written. To disrupt the euphony in your prose (even when what you write isn't read out loud) is to ruin your style. The most common violation, the careless repetition of similar sounds, can make you sound less like a business writer and more like Mother Goose. You don't have to be a poet to catch the disturbing rhyme in the following sentences:

> The satisfaction of the liberal faction was merely a reaction against the prevailing conservative attitude.
>
> Our examination this evening concerns the relation of racial integration to primary education.

Nor is anyone likely to miss the distracting repetition of consonants in this sentence:

> Oliver Christopher created the world's first crumple-proof crinoline in a crash program right after Christmas.

Exaggerated, perhaps. But it gives you some idea of what the violation of euphony can do to your style. Beware of it.

IN SUMMARY

It probably seems, by the time you reach the end of this chapter, that there are a hundred problems that can undermine your writing. The truth is, there are more. We've looked only at the most obvious of them. Lively, direct writing that's easy and pleasurable to read, unfortunately, isn't easy to write. Even avoiding all the problems won't get it for you. But learning to recognize them (and their remedies) is a long first step toward achieving what so few business people have achieved — a really effective writing style.

The second step must be a personal commitment to work at avoiding those problems. As you proofread your early drafts, be on the lookout for them. Give at least one full proofreading, maybe two, to the problem of CorpSpeak alone. Devote another to removing any hackneyed or clichéd phrasing that may have slipped into your initial draft, and still other proofreadings to the other problems we've discussed in the chapter. At first the task will be time-consuming, to say the least. But gradually it gets easier, and in time becomes second nature. You'll know what you're looking for, and get rid of it fast whenever you spot it.

In the next two chapters, we'll move beyond writing problems to look at the characteristics of effective style — for effective style is more than just avoiding problems. Remember, though, unless you learn to avoid the pitfalls we've looked at, no amount of effective technique will help.

PROBLEMS

1. Here's a passage of business prose that smacks unmistakably of jargon — and hence CorpSpeak. See if you can rewrite it in a crisper, clearer, more direct way.

> During the decades of the development of intensive market research methodology, industry found, in the techniques of area sampling and depth interviewing, two great functional additions to its analytic procedures. At the present point in time, an equal commitment to and application of computer programming techniques is absolutely essential for intelligent functioning in the field of market research.

2. The following letter from Kayval Company was written in answer to an inquiry about the availability of Kayval distributorships. While its tone is friendly, this letter has more than twice the number of words it needs to communicate its message fully. Read it through, then rewrite it. Eliminate every unnecessary word, but be sure to retain its friendly tone.

> Dear Mr. McGillicuddy:
>
> We wish to thank you very much for your recent inquiry into the possibility of being made a distributor for Kayval Products in your immediate area. It has, for quite a long time, been the policy of the Kayval Company to make its distributorships exclusive in cities which have a population of 30,000 or fewer inhabitants. This policy allows our appointed distributors in those areas a more potentially lucrative market for Kayval Products, while at the same time providing us with the opportunity of assuring an efficient and high quality distribution.
>
> We are absolutely sure that as a Kayval distributor you would offer the kind of service which consumers have come to associate with the product line, but as we already have one distributor in Rivervale, and since the city's population is still under the 30,000 mark, we are unable to grant a Kayval distributorship to you at this time.
>
> We will certainly keep your name and address on file, so that if we should find the need at some time in the future to establish a new distributorship in your city of Rivervale, we will surely be in touch with you further to discuss the matter.
>
> Yours sincerely,
>
> Kasia Bartkowiak
>
> The Kayval Company

3. The following sentences are all too long for what they say. Rewrite them more concisely.

a. We wish therefore to inform you that we will pay to Mrs. Cavanaugh the sum of $45.

b. We have made a complete and thorough review of your records.

c. It seems as though we might be unable to agree to some of the terms you are posing here.

d. We are now in a position to make an evaluation of Dr. Johnson's claim.

e. We ask that you do not present the check for payment until after all the bids have been mailed back to us.

f. Regardless of what were the contributory causes, Baxter was fired.

g. Your primary job — and it is a continuing one — is always to plan things in advance.

h. Both Bolshevism and Fascism are two false dreams.

i. He got a job working in a foundry.

j. Every member of this staff must learn to anticipate ahead at all times.

k. The chief arbitrator insisted that the word should be removed.

l. For instance, the industrial psychologist may try to determine why a person who lives in the decaying parts of the inner city might tend to become an alcoholic.

m. Tom Levering is responsible for the safe movement of all hazardous and dangerous materials within the warehouse.

4. Here's a simple exercise in avoiding redundancy. Rewrite each of the phrases below (exactly as shown). Then, draw a line — a bold cross-out line — through the word or words in each phrase that contribute nothing to its meaning.

a. the actual number of pieces

b. stunted in growth

c. in a state of shock

d. cylindrical in shape

e. a similar type of argument

f. streamlined in appearance

g. not actually true

h. the conclusive proof

i. small in size

j. quite impossible

5. The following is an excerpt from a report entitled "Student Activism in the 1960s," written in the early 1970s for a broad readership of business people, educators, civic officials, and other "opinion leaders." Though well researched, the report had an obvious inclination toward wordiness. Probably forty to fifty percent of its words could have been eliminated (through deletion or compression) with no loss in meaning and with a net gain in the quality of writing.

See what you can do to make this paragraph more concise.

Ever since the student ''rebellion'' occurred at the University of California at Berkeley in 1965, the general conception which the public has had of the politically oriented student has not been a positive or a flattering one. Our present study shows us that this feeling of the public is without justification however. It shows us that a very large majority of today's college students are resentful of being smeared with the brush of student activism. One female student in a campus interview made a very typical remark when she told us, ''These radicals are a minority, not the majority — they're a small minority who grab control of student government and the campus newspaper and make themselves seem stronger than they really are.'' It is our finding in this report that the consensus of opinion among the faculty members that we interviewed as a part of the study concurred with this girl's observation and statement. It would appear that many of today's students, who have full college workloads and spend a great deal of time leading busy social lives, just seem not to have a great deal of time to devote to, nor the inclination for, political activism.

6. Each of the following constructions taken from actual business documents suffers from the piling up of adjectives. Without changing its meaning, rewrite each item so that its pile of adjectives in front of the noun is broken up, allowing it to read with ease.

a. a not easily determined amount

b. a valid, retroactively binding contract

c. the newly enacted emission-control bill

d. a severe, cool, extraordinary, efficient and pleasant secretary

e. The Supervisor requests an intensive, six-month on-the-job, error-proof training program for new recruits.

7. The following sentences are all *noun addicted.* Each suffers from a heaviness of noun-structures and an absence of active verbs and verb phrases. They are vintage CorpSpeak.

Without changing their meanings, rewrite each of these sentences in a livelier, more "verbal" style.

a. The West Texas Gas Company has a great need for a new billing system.

b. This sales message is of vital concern to all our personnel.

c. General Motors offered an apology to Baxter.

d. The vertical water pump is currently inoperative.

e. I am responsible for the consolidation and removal of all recyclable materials to the Reclamation Salesyard.

f. The purpose of this document is to provide identification for the recovered objects.

g. The procurement of widgets is mandatory for the manufacture of engine mountings.

h. It is not possible to make an accurate forecast regarding the President's intention to sign the new labor bill.

i. It is our objective to have the efficiency of the new delivery system achieve a higher level.

j. A *review* is a report on some other published work, sometimes a simple description of that work, at other times an evaluation of it.

k. He was the originator of the new information system that is being developed under my supervision.

l. After eight months of operation, there is a belief in this committee that we have a means for the solution of our problem.

m. All business students should have knowledge about the operation of a computer.

8. The following passage by Thorstein Veblen about academic administration has a valuable point to make. But its style is so cramped and cumbersome, so affected by CorpSpeak, that nine readers out of ten will be asleep (or elsewhere) by the time that point is fully made. Rewrite the passage for clarity, without altering its meaning.

> The salesmanlike abilities and the men of affairs that so are drawn into the academic personnel are, presumably, somewhat under grade in their kind, since the pecuniary inducement offered by the schools is rather low as compared with the remuneration for office work of a similar character in the common run of business occupations, and since businesslike employés of this kind may fairly be presumed to go unreservedly to the highest bidder. Yet these more unscholarly members of the staff will necessarily be assigned the more responsible and discretionary positions in the academic organization; since under such a scheme of standardization, accountancy, and control, the school becomes primarily a bureaucratic organization, and the first and unremitting duties of the staff are those of official management and accountancy. The further qualifications requisite in the members of the academic staff will be such as make for vendability, — volubility, tactful effrontery, conspicuous conformity to the popular taste in all matters of opinion, usage and conventions.
>
> The need of such a businesslike organization asserts itself in somewhat the same degree in which the academic policy is guided by considerations of magnitude and statistical renown; and this in turn is somewhat closely correlated with the extent of discretionary power exercised by the captain of erudition placed in control. At the same time, by provocation of the facilities which it offers for making an impressive demonstration, such bureaucratic organization will lead the university management to bend its energies

with somewhat more singleness to the parade of magnitude and statistical gains. It also, and in the same connection, provokes to a persistent and detailed surveillance and direction of the work and manner of life of the academic staff, and so it acts to shut off initiative of any kind in the work done.

— from *The Higher Learning in America*

9. Here's an honest-to-goodness one-sentence excerpt from a report of the General Accounting Office in Washington. It's the epitome of CorpSpeak! Wade through it a few times, then rewrite the sentence in direct, straightforward English.

It is important to understand the various aspects relating to all factors in order to achieve a general feel for the classification mode of thinking as well as to be able to explain to staff why factors addressed on a position description have not necessarily been addressed on an assignment complexity evaluation.

10. Read the following letter carefully:

16th March, 19__

Mrs. Bessie Leatherwood
120 South Temple Street
Los Angeles, California

My dear Madame:

We beg to acknowledge receipt of yours dated 12th March, and your inquiry therein of the whereabouts of your recent order. Please be advised that our records indicate your order for two (2) prs. teakwood bookends was mailed some time ago (in 2 pks.). We feel certain that you have received same by this date; however, if you have not, please renotify. We shall initiate search pursuant to that notice. Permit us to extend our regrets over your not having received said bookends, and our assurances that same will be forthcoming upon discovery of cause.

Hoping to retain your esteemed favor, we remain.

Yours truly,

Mark Gabor

The Ram Sales Co.

If you read this letter carefully, you can probably figure out what it says, but it's a bit of a chore. The letter is loaded down with hackneyed jargon of the kind that was stylish (though no clearer) around the turn of the century. Rewrite this letter in modern and effective style.

11. Here's a short reply letter written in a hackneyed, whiskered style. Rewrite it, making it sound more natural.

Dear Mr. Bigelow:

Yours of the 22nd received and contents duly noted. Enclosed please find one copy of ''Natural Redwood Fencing,'' as per your request.

We are glad to be able to provide you with same.

Yours,

I. Hobbins

Ichabod Hobbins
Customer Service

12. The following sentences taken from business communications are all weakened by cliché. Rewrite them in fresher, more original language.

a. He showed his true colors when it came to actually doing the work for the committee.

b. She swallowed the excuse hook, line, and sinker; so we were able to make it a real surprise party.

c. It stands to reason that if you stay in shape, you'll be none the worse for wear after strenuous exercise.

d. The Conroys' home is just loaded with antiques, and Baxter is like a bull in a china shop whenever he visits them.

e. Mary is a borderline candidate for admission at State, but where there's a will there's a way.

f. Mrs. Herbert fought tooth and nail to get the new school bill passed.

g. I told Canby what we needed, and it was no sooner said than done.

h. He was up at the crack of dawn every morning because the early bird always gets the worm.

i. Good marriages these days are few and far between.

j. Baxter really burned the midnight oil: for seven straight days last week he worked until the wee small hours.

k. Making ends meet is rough sledding in this day and age.

l. For all intents and purposes, people who really care about their jobs are as scarce as hen's teeth.

m. While some of his assistants were stealing to their hearts' content, Oscar Adams remained as honest as the day is long.

n. Tickets for Lowenthal's new musical are selling like hot cakes, even though the show itself leaves much to be desired.

o. Peter Tremaine is just one of those people who got off on the wrong foot in life.

13. Each of the following sentences contains a fractured parallelism. Rewrite each sentence more effectively.

a. Baxter's plan is not only remarkable both because it's shrewd, and more importantly fills a real company need.

b. Both candidates were in their twenties, had college degrees, single, and with no work experience.

c. His closest friends told him that he was silly and to remember his responsibilities.

d. Let's not forget what race he belongs to, and discrimination in employment.

e. Amalgamated has established neither a liberal pay scale nor does it have a meaningful retirement plan.

f. To study hard and doing all the assignments are a student's main responsibilities.

14. Each of the following excerpts contains an illogical construction of one kind or another. Spot the illogicality in each sentence and rewrite the sentence more effectively.

a. Technique is very important to the professional salesman. He should capture his prospect's attention completely, then make the presentation quickly and logically, and finally answer all the prospect's questions. Do not argue with the prospect.

b. Mrs. Michaels does not do justice to Baxter by calling him a fool. She brought up only his failures and ignored his successes!

c. Any executive should be sensitive to the feelings of their employees.

d. All employees can use the new third-floor lounge. You need not have a pass.

e. Last June, the President spoke about what has happened in the 1960s to bring about the energy crisis.

f. First push the red button; then, if there's no response, the emergency switch should be tripped.

g. When I have chosen the field in which I want to excel, I would be happy.

h. Many men never take their wife on business trips.

CHAPTER 3

MAKING YOUR SENTENCES COME ALIVE

"Face to face," said an executive recently, "my people communicate skillfully . . . with warmth and persuasiveness. But when they write, they come across as bland, a bit dull, and utterly unimpressive." We probably all recognize the description. It fits countless business people and administrators, as well as students who aspire to those ranks. The proverbial Martian, encountering this situation for the first time, would suspect that speaking and writing demanded different languages, one of them much more complex and difficult to use than the other — which, of course, is not so.

What is it, then, that makes writing so different from, and for most of us, so much more difficult than, speaking? It is certainly not grammar: writers and speakers both operate under the same grammatical rules. Nor is it word choice. Writers and speakers both rely upon the same abundant English vocabulary to convey their intended denotations and connotations. (The difference between *buy* and *purchase,* for example, is the same whether you speak the words or write them.) It would even seem that writers have an advantage over speakers: they can reconsider their words during proofreading and change them before any harm is done. No, the difference is elsewhere.

EMPHASIS AS THE KEY TO LIVELY WRITING

What we lose when we move from speaking to writing is a whole arsenal of techniques for generating *emphasis.* When we speak, we can give greater relative importance to (that is, we can emphasize) certain words or phrases in a variety of ways. By slowing down or pausing, raising our voice, lifting an eyebrow, jabbing a finger, banging a fist, smiling, scowling, or by any of a hundred other gestures, inflections, or facial expressions, we can impart emphasis precisely where we want it. But when we turn to writing, we lose all of these familiar nonverbal means of apportioning emphasis among our words. All a writer can give the reader are words on a page — no vocal inflections, no thumps or gestures, no overt means of controlling the reader's pace or intake of the message. This is why so many people who speak with vitality become dull and unimpressive when they write.

What the skillful writer realizes, however, is that the written language provides almost as many ways to emphasize key words and phrases as the spoken language. They just aren't as obvious. In fact, different kinds of emphasis are inherent in the written language, and can't be avoided. As a writer, you either put them to work for you, or you risk their working against you.

As a consequence, the skillful shaping of sentences is, in a sense, a search for lost property. It's the attempt to reestablish on paper what is lost from the language when you shift from speaking to writing. The ultimate shape of each of your sentences should be determined by your finding that precise arrangement of words that gives you the emphases that most accurately reflect the message you wish to convey.

A writer might, for instance, write:

    Henry Ford perfected the techniques of mass production.

and the information in the sentence would be clear. But can a reader tell whether the writer means to emphasize that:

    Henry Ford perfected the techniques of mass production.
    (that is, not Thomas Edison or Andrew Carnegie or anyone else . . . but Henry Ford.)

or whether he means:

    Henry Ford perfected the techniques of mass production.
    (he didn't invent them, he didn't develop them . . . he perfected them.)

or:

    Henry Ford perfected the techniques of mass production.
    (not the principles . . . but the techniques.)

or:

    Henry Ford perfected the techniques of mass production.
    (not any other kind of production . . . but mass production.)

No, the reader can't be sure. It's up to the writer to write the sentence in such a way as to make its total meaning unmistakable to the reader — and that requires the ability to control emphasis.[1]

[1]Occasionally, a writer can indicate emphasis as I have above, in the four "Henry Ford" sentences, by underlining (or *italics*). But that technique very quickly grows stale. You can't do it very often. More intelligent techniques for emphasis must be found.

So, in this chapter on sentence making, our focus will be on the specific sources of emphasis in the written language, and on how they are used. We'll look at each of these sources separately, but keep in mind that on paper they operate simultaneously. These sources of emphasis are:

1. Emphasis by WEIGHT (by *bulk weight* and by *grammatical weight*).
2. Emphasis by POSITION (by *subject position*, by *initial* and *terminal positions*, and by *periodic position*).
3. Emphasis by SEPARATION and ISOLATION.
4. Emphasis by INTERRUPTION.
5. Emphasis by REPETITION (by *verbal repetition* and by *structural repetition*).
6. Emphasis by RHYTHM.
7. Emphasis by OMISSION.

Emphasis by Weight

Two kinds of "weights" are available for emphasizing ideas: *bulk* weight and *grammatical* weight.

Bulk Weight The first of these, *bulk weight*, is simple: The greater the number of words you devote to an idea, the more important (or emphatic) that idea seems within its context. Take this sentence, for example:

> Henry Ford, a brilliant innovator, singlehandedly converted the making of automobiles from cottage industry to industrial colossus.

If we change that three-word modifying idea, *a brilliant innovator*, into a five-word modifier, the relative importance of that idea within the sentence seems to increase correspondingly.

> Henry Ford, <u>an innovator of great brilliance</u>, singlehandedly converted the making of automobiles . . .

If we give that idea even greater bulk weight, it assumes an even greater relative importance:

> Henry Ford, <u>an innovator of great and unquestioned brilliance</u>, singlehandedly converted the making of automobiles. . . .

It may seem, at first glance, that the principle of bulk weight violates our quest for conciseness. But it doesn't. Remember that conciseness is not just brevity; it is the *complete* expression of an idea in the fewest words. Any idea that lacks the emphasis it deserves is an idea expressed incompletely, not concisely.

As you study writing more, you'll often hear advice to vary the lengths of your sentences, to mix short sentences with long ones and medium-sized ones in order to bring your style alive. It's good advice. Consider how the varied sentence lengths in this memorandum contribute to its vitality:

```
The Hanscombe project, which you are about to undertake,
will require a quick mind, sharp reflexes, and more than a
normal amount of courage. Others have tackled it, and
failed. Many of them came to it with the same confidence you
feel, only to be frustrated quickly by its difficulties.
They underestimated the project's requirements. I'm
confident you won't.
```

Five sentences — first a fairly long one, then a short one, another long one (though not as long as the first), then two short ones in a row. The style is lively. You can, of course, strive directly for length variation in your sentences. But the truth is, if you give every fact within a sentence the number of words it needs to do its job — no more, no less — you will automatically find yourself varying the lengths of your sentences.

Grammatical Weight The other kind of emphasis by weight is just as simple a concept: the larger the grammatical unit you devote to an idea, the more emphatic that idea becomes. In our original sentence, the idea we focused on (Ford's innovative brilliance) was first expressed, grammatically, as a noun phrase:

```
Henry Ford, a brilliant innovator, singlehandedly
converted . . . .
```

Its relative importance can be modulated upward not only by increasing its bulk weight, but by giving it greater grammatical weight. The following sentence does so by turning the idea into a dependent clause (in this case, a relative clause, or *who*-clause):

```
Henry Ford, who was a brilliant innovator, singlehandedly
converted . . .
```

It becomes even more important if we give it the status of an independent clause (a clause capable of standing alone as a sentence):

```
Henry Ford was a brilliant innovator who singlehandedly
converted . . . .
```

And more important still if we give the idea a sentence all its own:

```
Henry Ford was a brilliant innovator. He singlehandedly
converted . . . .
```

If we combine this additional grammatical weight with added bulk weight, we can make that "brilliant innovator" idea even more emphatic:

```
Henry Ford was one of history's most brilliant innovators.
He singlehandedly converted . . . .
```

Clauses are grammatically weightier (and hence more emphatic) than phrases. Independent clauses are weightier than dependent clauses. And separate sentences are weightier than either kind of clause. The principle is simple. All it needs is practice to become a valuable part of your arsenal of writing techniques.

Another kind of grammatical weight can be observed in the verbs we use. Consider the following two sentences:

> The people coming out of the room talked about the possible merger.

> The people came out of the room talking about the possible merger.

The only difference, essentially, between these two sentences is the grammatical weight of their several verbs. In the first sentence, the main verb (that is, the verb without which the sentence could not function as a sentence) is *talked*. The other verb, *coming*, is subordinate; it could not, in its present form, function as a main verb.[2] As a result, in that first sentence, the ongoing conversation about the merger seems more significant (that is, more emphatic) than the movement out of the room. In the second sentence, the grammatical weight of those verbs is reversed: *coming* is turned into the main verb (*came*), and *talked* is reduced to the subordinate *talking*. Now it's the movement out of the room that seems the more significant of the two activities. Which sentence is better? Whichever one more accurately conveys the impression the writer wishes to convey! In these two sentences, manipulation of grammatical weight in the verbs makes the difference.

Emphasis by Position

Position, like weight, can help to determine the emphasis an idea gets within a sentence. Some positions naturally give emphasis to ideas. Let's examine them.

Subject Position The position of the grammatical subject in a sentence provides natural emphasis, an emphasis some writers ignore — at their peril. The subject of a sentence is, after all, what the sentence is about — at least it should be. But inexperienced writers often have trouble finding (or don't take the trouble to find) the appropriate subject for each sentence. They thereby misplace some of the sentence's natural emphasis. Look again at this sentence:

> Henry Ford, a brilliant innovator, singlehandedly converted the making of automobiles from cottage industry to industrial colossus.

Here, *Henry Ford* takes subject emphasis. The sentence is a statement about Henry Ford. Even if the structure of the sentence is changed to read:

[2]This is further discussed in the section on "Verbals," page 526 .

```
A brilliant innovator, Henry Ford singlehandedly converted
the making of automobiles . . .
```

subject emphasis still goes to *Henry Ford.* He remains the grammatical subject. But, if the sentence is rewritten:

```
The making of automobiles was converted singlehandedly by
Henry Ford from . . .
```

the subject shifts from *Henry Ford* to *The making of automobiles*. The sentence is now not about Henry Ford; it's about automobile making. Change the sentence's subject again, and the emphasis shifts to the new subject:

```
Innovative brilliance like Henry Ford's was necessary to
convert the making of automobiles from . . . .
```

Now the sentence is about innovative brilliance.

As you proofread and revise your first-draft sentences, make sure that what each sentence is really about is made its *grammatical* subject, thereby giving it the emphasis it deserves.

There's a bonus when you do so. If you carefully select the subject of each sentence, you'll never be plagued by the unvarying passive voice that some business writers seem to develop. Consider the difference between the *active* and *passive* voices: a sentence is in the active voice when its subject does the acting:

```
Baxter delivered the dedication speech.
(subject)
```

It's in the passive voice when the subject is being acted upon:

```
The dedication speech was delivered by Baxter.
    (subject)
```

But these sentences are not merely in different "voices." The change in voice has brought about a change in grammatical subject. The first sentence is a statement about Baxter; the second is about the dedication speech. Rather than worrying whether your sentences are in the active or passive voice, just be sure that you've selected the right subject for each sentence — the subject that deserves subject emphasis — and let verb-voice follow naturally from it. In the process, you will find that you are varying your active and passive constructions just as you vary your sentence lengths — to give your sentences the patterns of emphasis you want them to have.

Initial and Terminal Positions This second kind of emphatic position is well known to professional writers. It's the emphasis which naturally resides in the first and last positions in a sentence — initial and terminal emphasis. The unskilled writer, unaware of it, often lets it go to waste or misapplies it. Suppose, for example, you wrote the following sentence in the first draft of a report:

> No one can deny that the computer has had a great effect upon the business world.

It's not a bad sentence. But does it use its initial and terminal positions as well as it could? Let's assume that you intend two main points in this sentence: (1) that computers have affected business *greatly*, and (2) that this great effect cannot be denied. Your key words in the sentence, then, are *great* and *No one can deny that*. First, try to recast the sentence so that the single word *great* comes at the beginning or the end. It can be done fairly easily, as follows:

> No one can deny that the computer's effect upon the business world has been great.

As for the clause *No one can deny that*, its five-word length carries it past the emphatic opening position. But it has a one-word equivalent, the word *undeniably*, that can be put in the opening position and make the sentence read:

> Undeniably, the computer's effect upon the business world has been great.

The sentence now takes full advantage of the natural emphasis positions at beginning and end. It now stresses exactly what you want it to stress.

Notice how each of the original sentences below is revised to take advantage of these emphasis positions:

Original	He finally left after what seemed like hours of tedious pleading.
Better	After what seemed like hours of tedious pleading, he finally left.

(By placing the modifying clause first, we get one of the key words in this sentence, *left*, into an emphasis position.)

Even Better	Finally, after what seemed like hours of tedious pleading, he left.

(By moving the other key word, *finally*, to the beginning of this sentence, we have an even more effective sentence.) Here's another example:

Original	I will never vote against Hoolihan.
Better	Never will I vote against Hoolihan.

(This is as far as we can effectively revise this sentence. Any attempt to get the other key word, *against,* into an emphasis position would result in a misshapen sentence.) Two more examples ought to suffice:

Original	The decision in Reynolds v. Sims makes it compulsory that population be the sole criterion for the apportionment of all state legislatures.
Better	The Reynolds v. Sims decision makes it compulsory that state legislatures be apportioned solely on the basis of population.
Original	Cashmere goods have sold quite poorly this summer. However, woolens have sold exceptionally well.
Better	Cashmere goods have sold quite poorly this summer. Woolens, however, have sold exceptionally well.

Periodic Positioning This type of emphasis — emphasis by *periodic* positioning — depends simply on the position of the main clause within a sentence. A *loose* sentence (so-called by generations of grammarians) is one in which the main clause is stated early, followed by modification and supporting detail:

> Mathews resumed his presentation after standing silently before the committee for a full minute with a look of tired frustration on his face.

The first four words in this sentence, *Mathews resumed his presentation,* are its main clause; they make the basic assertion. The remaining nineteen words are modification. Now let's look at essentially the same sentence recast in *periodic* construction (in which the main clause follows, rather than precedes, the modification):

> After standing silently before the committee for a full minute with a look of tired frustration on his face, Mathews resumed his presentation.

In this periodic construction, the reader is forced to give heightened attention because his mind must gather and retain all that modification while anticipating the main assertion. A loose construction, by delivering the main idea early, allows for a more relaxed, less emphatic reading of the rest of the sentence.

Here's another example of an idea expressed in both loose and periodic construction:

Loose	*Periodic*
`Both these applicants are superb, even though it's hard to find good secretaries nowadays.`	`Even though it's hard to find good secretaries nowadays, both these applicants are superb.`

For effective style, the majority of your sentences should be *loosely* constructed. It's unwise to make your reader's mind work harder than it has to. But for those sentences that state your most important assertions, consider using periodic construction — that is, positioning of the main clause at or near the end. Your reader's mind will be made to focus more attentively on these assertions, and thereby emphasize them.

Emphasis by Separation and Isolation

This principle is simple enough, though too few business writers take advantage of it: Put some distance between key ideas, and the significance of each of them will stand out more clearly. In this sentence, for example:

```
Samuelson's memos are clear and concise.
```

the two qualities of Samuelson's memos — their clarity and their conciseness — don't seem as distinct from one another as they do in this sentence:

```
Samuelson's memos are clear, and they are concise.[3]
```

Now we have a sentence in which each quality is isolated in its own independent clause, putting a greater separation between them. By going one step further and giving each its own sentence — an even greater separation — these two qualities can be made to seem even more distinct from one another:

```
Samuelson's memos are clear. They are also concise.
```

An entire report or letter confined to such brief sentences would, of course, be choppy and primer-like. But occasionally, separate short sentences like these can provide just the emphases you need.

Emphasis by separation also makes this sentence:

```
Man has the brains, the imagination, and the skill to
overcome the problems which stand before him . . .
```

a better one than this briefer version of the same idea:

```
Man has the brains, imagination, and skill to overcome
the problems which stand before him.
```

[3]This "separation" and the next one can also be seen, of course, as examples of added *grammatical weight.*

The repeated *the*'s in the first version put added distance between these three attributes of man, allowing the reader's mind to focus on each of them a bit longer.

The next passage also demonstrates the advantages of the use of the principle of emphasis by separation:

> Last month's fire completely ruined Patterson. He lost his house, his car, his boat, all his personal effects, and hundreds of irreplaceable documents.

The insertion of *his* before each of the listed items sets them farther apart from one another, making each seem a little more important.

Emphasis by Interruption

This is one of the least appreciated and most valuable of all writing techniques — emphasis by interruption. The principle is simple: anything that interrupts something else calls attention to itself by doing so. You can, at times, interrupt the normal flow of a sentence by injecting a related idea into its midst. By appearing unexpectedly, the injected idea — the interrupter — receives emphasis. Furthermore, it can be injected at precisely the right moment for maximum impact. For example, there's nothing wrong with this sentence:

> Uncle Tom's Cabin was one of the great successes in American publishing, and one of the most immediately influential books ever to have appeared in this country.

But when its author, Edmund Wilson, wanted to express these ideas — and wanted also to emphasize that the book's influence was immediate rather than long-term — he turned that key idea into an interrupter:

> Uncle Tom's Cabin was one of the great successes in American publishing, and one of the most influential books -- immediately influential at any rate -- ever to have appeared in this country.

Interrupters also provide a bonus for the writer. They create a conversational tone, a sense of the spoken voice, that adds vitality to writing. When we speak, we constantly violate the normal subject-verb-object pattern in our sentences: we inject ideas, shift direction, often correct ourselves midway. (Listen closely to most speakers; you'll see what I mean.) An interrupter on paper, besides providing useful emphasis, imitates our natural speech.

Consider this two-sentence excerpt from a business memo:

> In preparation for the upcoming conference, Bailey and I went to four lectures. Every one of them was dull.

Now watch it come alive when that second sentence is turned into an interrupter:

> Bailey and I went to four lectures last week -- every one of them dull -- in preparation for the upcoming conference.

In the following sentence, a clarifying detail is given emphasis by being injected into the heart of the sentence it elaborates upon:

> The extraordinary number of topics discussed at last night's meeting -- seventeen by my secretary's count -- speaks poorly of the committee's desire for prudence and deliberation.

And here we see an interrupter used emphatically to qualify a toughly put question.

> You are not then -- if I understand your argument -- prepared to accept the ultimatum?

If used carefully, and with restraint, interruptive emphasis can be put to good advantage in just about any business writing situation.

Emphasis by Repetition

Not all repetition causes repetitiousness. Anything that is repeated in a piece of writing — a word, a phrase, an entire clause, a grammatical structure — receives emphasis from that repetition. If what is emphasized *deserves* the emphasis, then the repetition is certainly useful.

Repeating Key Words I would not, for example, tell the writer of the following passage to avoid using the same word so often:

> Around the turn of the century, ministers began reminding industrialists that Christians had duties to their fellow men, that Christian morality detested the slum and the sweatshop and that Christian values abhorred the exploitation of human beings. They argued, in fact, that big business owed one of its greatest debts to Christianity.

The word *Christian* (in several forms) is used four times in the passage, but that word is at the heart of the writer's meaning. Repetition gives only the emphasis it deserves.

Notice, in the following excerpt from a training-department memo, how the writer implants a key idea in the reader's mind by repeating an entire clause:

> You will begin by learning the company's general organization. You will learn the difference between line and staff functions. You will learn the attributes of an effective United Foods manager. And you will learn how to spot the problems that plague a company like ours and head them off at the start.

Certainly Lincoln, one of our greatest writer-executives, realized the importance of repeating key ideas for emphasis. If mere brevity were the goal, he would no doubt have shortened his "government of the people, by the people, for the people," to simply "government of, by, and for the people" — and the people in turn may well have forgotten that address at Gettysburg.

Repeating Grammatical Structures Another useful source of emphasis is the repeated grammatical structure — a technique called *parallelism.* (Many students think of *parallelism* as one of those rules that lurk in the hearts and handbooks of English teachers, ready to pounce on the unwary violator; but the experienced writer knows what a boon it can be.) Parallelism is used to emphasize the similarity between things. In this sentence, which we looked at in Chapter 2:

> When Baxter retired, he was admired by his colleagues, respected by his adversaries, and loved by the members of his staff . . .

the parallel past-participles — *admired, respected, loved* — simply stress the fact that each was a group emotion directed at Baxter.[4]

Parallel structures are useful in other ways as well. They can be used to bestow emphasis on key words. In the following sentence, for example, parallel structure was used by the writer to emphasize a certain feeling:

> After nine years of fighting to little purpose, after the loss of over forty thousand men, we at last began to disengage ourselves from the seemingly endless war.

The parallel phrases, both beginning with the preposition *after,* help to emphasize a sense of the war's awful protractedness, a sense that would have been diminished had the sentence been written without those parallel *after*'s:

> After nine years of fighting to little purpose and the loss of over . . .

Parallel grammar can also be used to emphasize contrasts. There's nothing wrong with writing:

> Many things which are easy to do can be taught only with difficulty.

But a balanced parallel construction makes the contrast between these two clauses much more emphatic:

> Many things which are <u>easy</u> <u>to</u> <u>do</u> prove quite <u>difficult</u> <u>to</u> <u>teach</u>.

Instead of writing:

> Baxter is an unpredictable man. He will flatter his enemies, but his friends will often be disappointed by him . . .

you should put the two contrasting ideas in that second sentence into parallel construction:

[4]*Parallelism* actually works by giving each item in the series the same *grammatical weight* as the others.

> Baxter is an unpredictable man. He will flatter his enemies but often disappoint his friends.

Parallel structure is also the only practical way of underscoring the continuity of an action through time and space. Witness this sentence from Rachel Carson:

> Strontium 90, released through nuclear explosions into the air, comes to earth in rain or drifts down as fallout, lodges in soil, enters into the grass or corn or wheat growing there, and takes up its abode in the bones of a human being, there to remain until his death.

Had any of the underlined verbs been taken out of parallel with the rest, the sense of the continuous movement of those Strontium 90 particles would have been broken.

Emphasis by Rhythm

The most elusive kind of emphasis in the written language is emphasis through rhythm. So let's look at a single example — just to suggest its potential.

The principle of emphasis through rhythm is tied to several fairly obvious facts about the language: (1) that stressed syllables are more emphatic than unstressed syllables (on paper as well as in speech) and (2) that *successive* stressed syllables tend to slow down the reader, giving emphasis to the words over which the reader has slowed. A normal reading of the following sentence should demonstrate this second effect:

> Standing in back of us were all six board chairmen scheduled to testify before the committee.

While the first six words of the sentence reflect a normal random pattern of stressed and unstressed syllables:

> Stándĭng ĭn báck ŏf ŭs wĕre . . .

the next four words create an unusual run of four successive stressed syllables:

> . . .áll síx bóard cháirmĕn . . .

after which the sentence resumes a more normal rhythmic pattern:

> . . . schédulĕd tŏ téstĭfy̆ bĕfóre thĕ cŏmmíttĕe.

To most readers, whose minds are sounding the words as they read them, the sentence slows down during those successive stresses and the six board chairmen seem to loom with an almost physical presence in the sentence. Watch the effect disappear if we revise the sentence and break that string of successive stresses:

> Standing in back of us were all six of the board chairmen scheduled to . . .

Emphasis by Omission

The principle of *omission* helps not only in our quest for conciseness, but in our search for emphasis as well. Not only should we leave out superfluous words and phrases; we can also omit words that seem grammatically called for, if those words are clearly implied in the preceding structure:

In this sentence, for example:

```
Martyn's trademark is yellow; Kerner's trademark is blue.
```

we can omit from that second clause, not only the noun:

```
Martyn's trademark is yellow; Kerner's is blue . . .
```

but its linking verb as well;

```
Martyn's trademark is yellow; Kerner's blue.
```

or, less formally punctuated

```
Martyn's trademark is yellow, Kerner's blue.
```

Omission by itself doesn't emphasize anything, but by omitting the words *trademark* and *is* from the second clause, we keep them from being emphasized through repetition (as they would have been), and allow the reader to focus on the words that actually make the comparative point of the sentence — *Kerner's* and *blue.*

Omission also allows a writer to use what some textbooks call "an acceptable sentence fragment." Here's an example:

```
The high school years, in America anyway, are surely the
worst time in a young man's life -- the most awkward,
uncomfortable, inept and embarrassing of years. And the most
fruitless.
```

That final "sentence," which technically lacks both a subject and a verb, allows the writer to retain grammatical parallelism (*awkward, uncomfortable, inept, embarrassing,* and *fruitless* are all parallel adjectives), while at the same time isolating one of them — the one he felt was most important — in its own sentence structure at the end for emphasis.

Omission allows "Adam Smith" the same kind of emphasis in this passage from *The Money Game:*

```
''Skeptics, yes,'' said my friend the Gnome of Zurich. ''We
stand for disbelief. We are basically cynical about the
ability of men to manage their affairs rationally for very
long. Particularly politicians.''
```

Technically the last sentence should have to read: *We are particularly cynical about politicians.* But omission allows him to trim away all that is implied in the previous sentence, leaving only the artfully emphatic fragment.

A CONCLUDING WORD ON SENTENCE MAKING

This brief survey of emphasis techniques by no means exhausts their possibilities. Each technique lends itself to individualized use, and you'll probably find some of them more to your liking than others. But they're all there in the written language to help you reestablish those emphases you lose when you switch from speaking to writing. At the very least, try each of them in your early drafts.

When taken hand in hand with effective word choice (which we looked at in Chapter 1), the techniques of emphasis allow you to do the following kind of sentence revision, revision which is clearly for the better. Suppose, for instance, that you want to express the following two ideas, here constructed in the two simplest of sentences:

```
He may be bright. His work is mediocre.
```

Upon rereading them you see that they need (among other things) an appropriate connector. (We'll look more closely at connectors in Chapter 4.) So you add one:

```
He may be bright. However, his work is mediocre.
```

Then you look again at the second of your sentences. Maybe you feel it's a bit too strong. So you give it a qualifier:

```
He may be bright. However, sometimes his work is mediocre.
```

Then you wonder whether the qualifier needs greater emphasis; so you try it at the front of the sentence:

```
He may be bright. Sometimes, however, his work is mediocre.
```

No, the rhythm is wrong, and the qualifier stands out too much. You try again:

```
He may be bright. However, his work is sometimes mediocre.
```

Better. But maybe the *however* doesn't need the added emphasis it gets by being set off with a comma. You take it out:

```
He may be bright. However his work is sometimes mediocre.
```

That's even better. You then ask yourself whether these two ideas really belong in separate sentences, whether they need that degree of separation and isolation from one another and deserve the grammatical weight of separate sentences. Perhaps one compound sentence would more accurately indicate their close relationship:

```
He may be bright; however his work is sometimes mediocre.
```

And *however* might sound too formal for the tone you wish to create. If so, revise again, using a less formal connector:

```
He may be bright, but his work is sometimes mediocre.
```

Now the level of diction is right, but maybe something's still wrong. You may feel that the first idea is actually less important than the second and should be grammatically down-weighted (or subordinated to it). So you rewrite your sentence giving the second idea an independent clause while the first idea takes a dependent clause (grammarians call this a *complex sentence,* but it's really not very "complex"):

`Even though he may be bright, his work is sometimes mediocre.`

Too many words? You may not need *Even:*

`Though he may be bright, his work is sometimes mediocre.`

Now you notice that you still haven't used your emphasis positions to best advantage. So you juggle your words and discover that you can very neatly get the two most important ones at the beginning and the end:

<u>Bright</u> though he may be, his work is sometimes <u>mediocre</u>.

Now you ask yourself a final question: Do *bright* and *mediocre* express exactly what you mean? Might *intelligent* or *perceptive* be a better word than *bright*? Might *average* or *unexceptional* be better than *mediocre*? If so, then make the change.

Our revision of this particular sentence might have gone in any number of directions. What's more important is that this kind of revision represents a knowledge of writing technique, and the self-questioning of your own intended meanings, that eventually will make you an effective business writer.

PROBLEMS

1. Obtain copies of two business letters and, in a memorandum to your instructor, analyze the stylistic differences between them (that is, differences in word selection and use of emphasis). Speculate on how the style of each contributes to its effectiveness or ineffectiveness. Attach the two letters to your memorandum when you submit it.

2. Compare the differences in style between the sentences in each of the following groups:

Group 1
a. There are four important points in this report.
b. Four important points are made in this report.
c. Four points in this report are of importance.
d. This is a report in which four important points are made.
e. Important in this report are four points.
f. This report makes four important points.

Group 2
a. Harmon McGillicuddy was swindled out of ten thousand dollars.
b. Someone has swindled Harmon McGillicuddy out of ten thousand dollars.
c. Somebody's swindled Harmon McGillicuddy out of ten thousand dollars.
d. Ten thousand dollars Harmon McGillicuddy was swindled out of.
e. Someone has swindled ten thousand dollars from Harmon McGillicuddy.

Group 3

a. The blue chips of yesterday aren't always the blue chips of today.
b. The blue chips of yesterday are not necessarily the blue chips of today.
c. Yesterday's blue chips aren't necessarily today's blue chips.
d. Yesterday's blue chips are not always blue chips today.
e. Today's blue chips aren't always yesterday's blue chips.
f. Today's blue chips aren't always yesterday's.

3. Reread "A Concluding Word on Sentence Making" on pages 85–87. Take each of the following groups of simple sentences through a process of combining and revising similar to the one illustrated in that discussion. Don't stop until you have found the construction that you imagine might be the best possible for its purpose.

a. The process is lengthy.
It is also costly.
Its results are worth the price.
b. Give me a call.
I'll bring the samples.
I'll also bring the pricesheets.
c. There is a hamburger.
It is off to one side.
It is half-eaten.
Flies are around it.
d. Their car is gassed up.
It is ready for the night's patrol.

4. This exercise is intended to have you practice using the various modes of emphasis available to you as a business writer. Let's start with this basic sentence:

```
Spector is sitting in a little cream room in his office
suite at 440 East 62nd Street with his back to a window
that is practically on top of the East Side Drive.
```

Now see if you can, by revising this sentence in the ways directed, achieve the desired changes or shifts in emphasis that are indicated:

a. By manipulating *bulk weight* alone:
(1) increase the emphasis on the color of the room
(2) increase the emphasis on the size of the room
(3) reduce the importance of the window's proximity to the East Side Drive
b. Through *grammatical weight*:
(1) increase the emphasis on the fact that Spector's back is to the window
(2) decrease the importance of his being seated
c. By employing *separation*:
(1) increase the importance of the fact that it is Spector's *office suite* where the scene takes place
(2) increase the importance of his back's being toward the window
d. By shifting them into the *subject position* of the sentence:
(1) give the office suite greater importance
(2) give Spector's back greater importance

e. By shifting them into the *initial* or *terminal positions* in the sentence:
   (1) increase the significance of the scene's taking place in the little cream-colored room
   (2) make the fact that Spector is *seated* more important
   (3) make the fact that the window is behind Spector more important
f. Through *periodic emphasis*:
   (1) heighten the importance of the fact that is given us by the base clause: that Spector is sitting there
g. By employing an *interruptive structure*:
   (1) highlight the fact that Spector's back is to the window
   (2) highlight the fact that the room is cream-colored
h. Through *verbal repetition*:
   (1) make more emphatic the fact that the scene takes place on the *east* side of town
   (2) make more important the fact that Spector's office is a *suite*

5. The following sentences are all probably too long (though conciseness is, of course, more than mere brevity). Without altering the ideas they convey, rewrite each sentence in more effective style. (If you think a sentence should be broken up into several smaller ones, you should by all means do so.)

a. In reference to the transmission damage you reported to your automobile on November 9, 19__, this is to advise, after making a thorough inspection of your automobile and after talking with Mr. Jones, the service manager at Smith's Garage, that we have determined that the pump inside your transmission was bad, causing this damage, and that it was not caused from any hole in the pan.
b. You will recall that I wrote you on October 26, 19__, regarding the above-captioned matter placing you on notice of our subrogation rights and including certain documents along with that letter.
c. We are therefore attaching our settlement draft drawn to your order for $5.00, reimbursing you for the road service charge, and trust you will find same satisfactory.
d. If you move or will be away from this address, please notify this office exactly where you may be reached, so that we or the attorney can contact you promptly with respect to any part of the lawsuit which may require your personal attention, including date and place of trial.

6. From the standpoint of style, the following paragraph is poorly written:

Advertising agencies supply the talent necessary for companies to have effective advertising campaigns. The service which agencies provide the companies costs less than if the companies did their own advertising. The companies pay for copywriting and artwork. This they would have to pay for anyway if they did their own advertising. Probably they would have to use freelance talent and pay more for it than the agencies pay their own talent to work on any one company's advertising. The companies don't pay one red cent more for space in the print media or for the time which broadcast media have for sale than if they did their own advertising. Here is an example. It would cost a manufacturer $10,000 to purchase a full page of advertising space in Women's Week Magazine. Women's Week Magazine charges an advertising agency $8,500 for a full page. This is the discount all media allow advertising agencies. The advertising agency charges the manufacturer $10,000 for the space. The advertising agency keeps $1,500. It is no wonder that companies are glad to have agencies to do their advertising for them. It is no wonder, also, that agencies compete quite hard for the advertising business of companies.

Without altering its sequence of ideas, rewrite this paragraph in more effective style. Keep in mind all the bad style habits discussed in Chapter 2 (several are evident in this paragraph) and the techniques of emphasis discussed in this chapter.

7. Without changing or adding to its basic ideas, rewrite each of the following sentences in as many ways as you can (including ways that entail more than one sentence). Then, alongside each version, indicate under what circumstances it would be the most effective way to write the sentence.

a. You have been under my supervision for over a year and I feel you are one of the most conscientious people in my department.
b. This report on business bankruptcies must be in by August 10; the chairman has scheduled a press conference on it for August 12.

8. Write the first draft of a paragraph describing your average day at school or on the job. Make the paragraph *at least* seven sentences long.

After you've finished the first draft, make a copy of it and set the copy aside. Then go to your first draft and experiment with its style, using most (if not all) of the emphasis techniques we discussed in this chapter.

When you finally settle on the most effective revision of your original paragraph, turn that revision into a clean, final copy and submit to your instructor: (1) the unmarked copy of your first draft, (2) the clean copy of your final draft, and (3) a memo describing *why* you made each of the changes you made as you went from first to final draft.

9. *Omission* is a style technique that does double-duty for a writer: it aids in the quest for conciseness while making way for effective emphasis. In a memo to your instructor explain how this technique has been used in the following two examples, and how each would have to be written if *omission* weren't employed.

a. Bennington's copywriters have long been among the industry's finest; their artists among the worst.
b. With Wilson, it was simply a case of frustration with his work. So too with Kramer.

10. In one of the problems of Chapter 2 you were asked to explain the style problems that made an excerpt by Thorstein Veblen so difficult to read. Here is an excerpt from Perrin Stryker's book *The Character of the Executive* that you will probably find as easy to read as Veblen's was hard. It's an entry in the diary of a hypothetical business executive. Read it, and in a memo to your instructor, carefully point out the features that give it its readability. (You might also comment on the style's limitations if you feel there are any.)

Thursday, July 19

Since yesterday I've been puzzling over Delucci's ideas about initiative. He seemed content to play his part quietly under Maddox and, for my money, seemed much too calm about the fact that Royt is favored to cop the v.p.'s job. So I went back and talked to Delucci again this afternoon, and now I'm inclined to give him an A plus for ''controlled aggressiveness.'' Delucci disclosed his strategy to me only after he seemed convinced that I was friendly and not sold on Royt. He knew I might change sides, but he was willing to take this risk, which in itself is a nice symptom of initiative.

Briefly, Delucci said he intended to stick close to his patron, Maddox, who is practically certain to succeed Outerbridge as president. Then Delucci hopes to become the president's assistant and as nearly indispensable as he can make himself. Delucci not only figures Maddox will depend on him to handle all personnel matters, just as he'd handled union negotiation and personnel grievances in the shop; Delucci also expects to guide Maddox through the sales and marketing jungles, which are now almost unknown territory to him. By the time his patron's retirement date rolled around, Delucci thinks his own qualifications will be clearly recognized by the directors.

But meanwhile what about Royt? Delucci isn't worried. He says he calculates that Royt will wind up the way a friend of his at the Mitral Plastic Co. did. This fellow, Delucci says, ''always has both elbows out'' and his aggression overshadowed all possible rivals. He spent money wildly and continually irritated associates, but the top brass forgave this because they liked his aggressive salesmanship and kept promoting him right on up to be assistant to the general manager. But when this bull in a china shop started to make big decisions for the general manager, the general manager finally said he couldn't take it any more. The company still didn't want to lose him, so the fellow was sent out to Chicago, as a special divisional vice president, but it was really a dead-end staff job.

Delucci's gamble looks good. These fellows like Royt usually thrash around, take charge, make decisions—right or wrong—until they are moved up or out. They look hot for a while, but I've seen many of them burnt out in their fifties. I'm generally inclined to bet on quiet, foresighted planners like Delucci, who don't continually need their egos pampered. Delucci is no fireball, and both his initiative and ambition are now rather narrowly centered on his promotion strategy. But he's got the kind of lasting drive and personal flexibility that Royt obviously lacks.

CHAPTER 4

SHAPING PARAGRAPHS, BUILDING CONNECTIONS, AND USING IMAGINATION IN BUSINESS WRITING

Three last matters of style will concern us in this chapter: making paragraphs, connecting ideas, and using figurative language to inject imagination into your business writing. Paragraphs are one of the least appreciated and most helpful of style devices; like sentences, they give shape to our meanings and help control how a reader understands those meanings. Connections are necessary to assure a reader's smooth movement through a message. Figurative language — language used imaginatively in appropriate situations — gives your writing vitality and sets it apart from the ordinary run of business writing — and that's no small advantage! Let's look first at the shaping of paragraphs.

SHAPING PARAGRAPHS

Think of the break at the end of a paragraph simply as another kind of punctuation — as a *super period,* a period that ends not just a single sentence, but several sentences that all help to develop the same idea. The paragraph break gives unity to that sentence group, and it gives a heightened importance to the sentence that begins the next paragraph.

As punctuation, paragraph-breaks (or "super-periods") are as flexible in their usage as periods are. That's what a lot of writers don't realize about them: they see them as clumps of writing tightly determined by rules, or as mere ways of getting more white space on the page. They are more than that, and much more useful.

The Paragraph and Its Main Parts

To see how paragraphs — and the breaks between them — function, let's look at the different roles that sentences can play within a paragraph. (By defining the roles of sentences *within* paragraphs we can best come to understand the roles of paragraphs themselves.)

The Head Sentence The *head sentence* is the paragraph's key sentence. It introduces the idea to be developed by the rest of the paragraph, or it points out the direction the rest of the paragraph will take.[1] Usually — though not always — the head sentence stands at the head of a paragraph. If, for example, we begin a paragraph with the following sentence:

> Most of today's economists confine themselves to reinterpreting the past. . .

we signal our reader that the rest of the paragraph will develop this idea. The sentences that follow this head sentence will expand the idea, make it more specific, give it historical context, provide examples for it, or in some other way *elaborate* upon its meaning.

Coordinate and Subordinate Elaborators What differs from paragraph to paragraph is the *pattern of elaboration* that follows the head sentence. When you're doing the writing, it can be virtually any pattern you want it to be.

Consider this paragraph (I've numbered its sentences for easy reference):

> (1) Economic historians saw capitalism as having moved through a series of stages. (2) The mercantile stage, in which America had grown up, was characterized by the import and export merchant being the most important type of entrepreneur. (3) Then, in the early 19th century, came ''industrial capitalism,'' with independent small-scale factory proprietors as the most dynamic influence. (4) After that, as business grew larger and more corporate, the need for capital brought the investment banker into prominence, so that by 1900 he was the most important figure in a stage we now refer to as ''finance capitalism.''

The paragraph opens with its head sentence. Then come three more sentences, each of which, in parallel fashion, elaborates on that head sentence. (Each of

[1]The *head sentence* of a paragraph is commonly referred to as the "topic sentence," but I'm avoiding this term because the head sentence often stops short of fully expressing the paragraph's "topic." It is often only a signpost, indicating the paragraph's direction of movement.

them defines one of the "stages" of capitalism introduced in the head sentence.) The paragraph's pattern is one of *coordinate* elaboration. It functions like this:

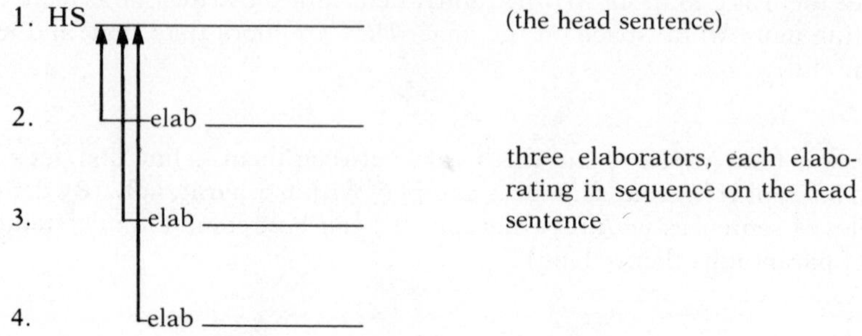

In another paragraph, we see a different pattern of elaboration:

> (1) This is not to say that a faculty, or anyone else in a university, can have absolute power. (2) Almost every group in a university has some veto power over the actions of other groups. (3) For example, it has always been within the power of students to strike. (4) What held them back for so long was the notion that a college degree was all important, and that nothing should impede their progress toward it.

In this paragraph, the pattern is one of *subordinate* elaboration. Each sentence elaborates, not upon the head sentence, but upon the sentence that immediately precedes it. The paragraph functions this way:

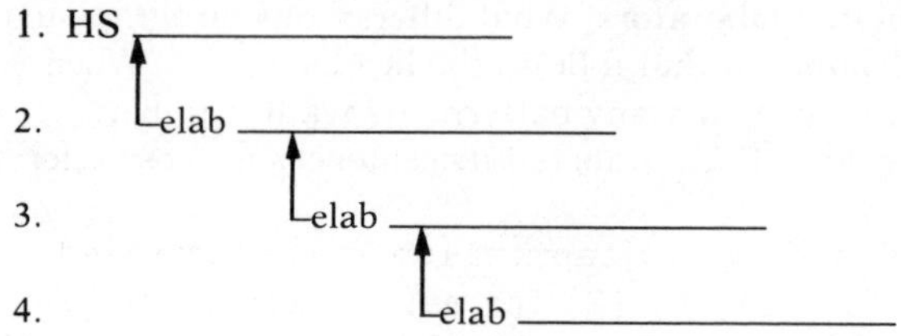

Actually, both these patterns of elaboration — the purely coordinate and the purely subordinate — are less frequently used than *mixed* patterns of elaboration. Some mixed patterns are illustrated in the following paragraphs (each with its elaborative pattern diagrammed for easy analysis). Read the paragraphs, then consider closely their patterns of elaborations.

> (1) On any person who desires it, New York will bestow the gift of privacy -- and loneliness. (2) The city is filled with people whose main concern is the pursuit of their own private grails. (3) That pursuit doesn't leave much time for attention to others. (4) It consumes most of an ambitious person's time and energy. (5) It fosters self-concern. (6) And it isolates those others who, in less frenetic circumstances, could turn to the grail pursuers for human companionship.

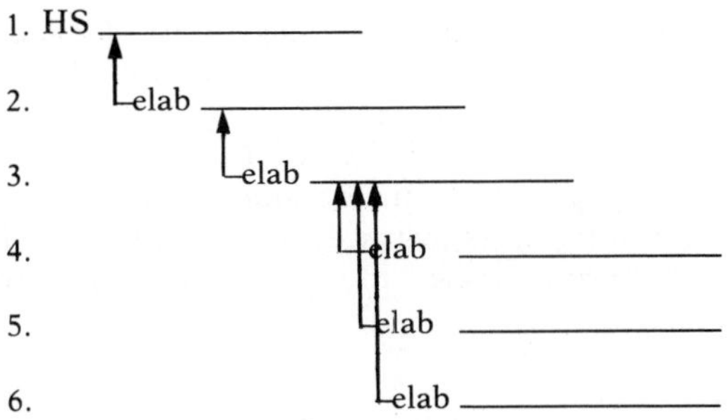

(1) London is also a large and heterogeneous city. (2) It is larger than New York, by several million in fact. (3) Its urban sprawl extends even further than New York's. (4) And its people come from an even wider variety of homelands in search of what home could not provide. (5) But while involved in his own personal grail search, the Londoner somehow manages to maintain human contact with other people. (6) Other people are more to him than customers for his product, competitors for his seat on the commuter express, or victims for his everyday plots and schemes for greater profit.

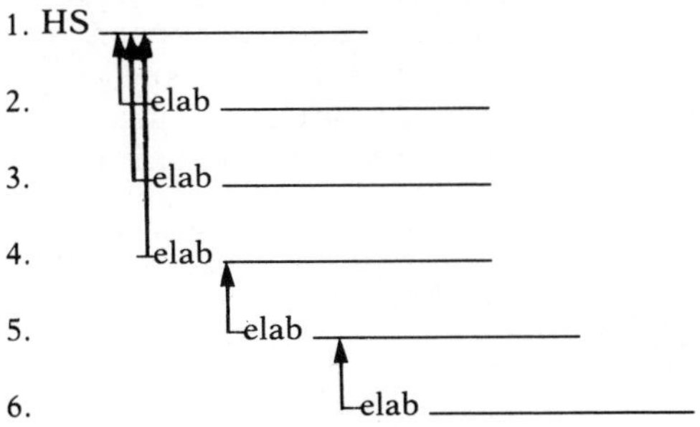

(1) The devastation of the Kafati Exchange during the war kindled the deepest and most surprising human emotions. (2) And the historian has every reason to take such emotions seriously. (3) They are the impulse without which great collective efforts of reconstruction could not take place. (4) In Kafati, that emotion took on even larger proportions than one might expect. (5) Nowhere else on earth had people developed such deep and abiding attachments to the commercial system created by their ancestors.

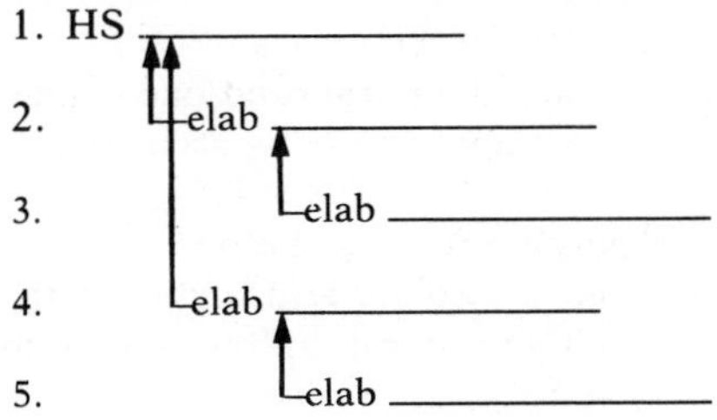

In these three paragraphs, we just begin to see the variety of elaborative patterns that paragraphs can assume. In the "New York" paragraph, elaboration begins subordinately, then becomes coordinate. In the "London" paragraph, it begins coordinately, then becomes subordinate halfway through. In the "Kafati" paragraph, the pattern begins subordinately, then doubles back for a second sequence of subordinate elaborators. In its own way, each paragraph gives a sense of unity to the ideas the writer wished to unify. That is the primary function of paragraph structure.

The Flexibility of the Paragraph Break

Notice, too, that in each of the three paragraphs above, the paragraph break could have been employed differently. Had the writer of the "New York" paragraph wished to give greater emphasis to his belief that New Yorkers don't have time for other people, he could have imposed a paragraph break at the end of sentence 2, and thereby made sentence 3 the head sentence (and controlling idea) of its own separate paragraph:

> (1) On any person who desires it, New York will bestow the gift of privacy — and loneliness. (2) The city is filled with people whose main concern is the pursuit of their own private grails.
>
> (3) That pursuit doesn't leave much time for attention to others. (4) It consumes most of an ambitious person's time and energy. (5) It fosters self-concern. (6) And it isolates those others who, in less frenetic circumstances, could turn to the grail pursuers for human companionship.

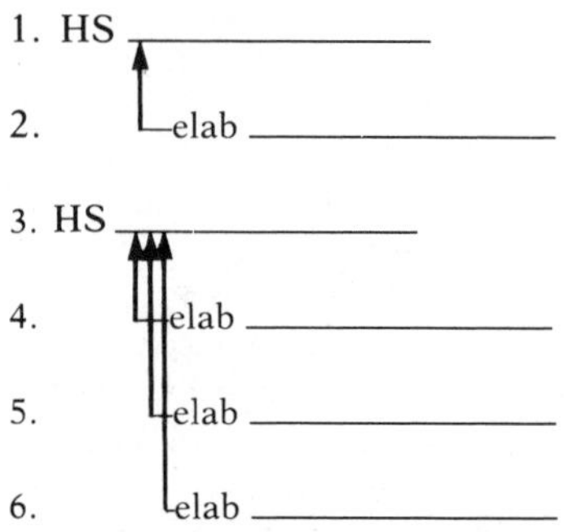

Similarly, in the "London" passage, a paragraph break (or "super period") could well have been employed between sentences 4 and 5, thereby rearranging its emphasis. Take another look at it in that light. The "Kafati" paragraph, too, in the hands of another writer, might have been turned into two separate paragraphs with a break between its third and fourth sentences.

It is this flexibility in shape that makes the paragraph one of the most adaptable — though somehow one of the least appreciated — style tools for the business writer.

Even the occasional one-sentence paragraph (like the one that just preceded this sentence) can be used effectively to isolate and highlight the idea carried by that single sentence. The one-sentence paragraph is an extreme use of the "super period", and if overused, becomes gimmicky and self-defeating. But used with restraint, it can work very well.

Occasionally, writers will use *fewer* paragraph breaks than might seem called for — again for the purpose of highlighting precisely the relationships they wish to highlight. Here's one example:

> (1) Franklin Roosevelt, who would have been lost without the press, revived the press conference and brought it to new heights of influence and public interest. (2) Any certified journalist was admitted to the conference, and questions were asked and answered ''from the hip.'' (3) Roosevelt maintained the rule first laid down by President Wilson that he was not to be quoted directly without specific permission, but otherwise the conference became a wonderful game of give-and-take, with the President, a genius at sarcasm, doing most of the giving. (4) Harry Truman, despite some lapses in his first term, carried forth the press conference practices of Mr. Roosevelt. (5) He gets the credit and the blame -- and both are deserved -- for shifting the conference from the Oval Office to the old State Building auditorium, and thus putting it on a much more formal basis.

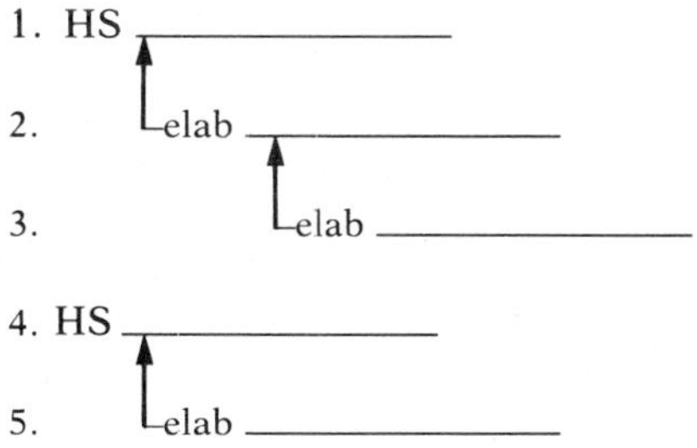

This paragraph really has *two* head sentences, and develops *two* ideas — the presidential press conference under Roosevelt, and under Truman. So why not a paragraph break between sentences 3 and 4? There's no break because the writer wants to highlight the point (stated in an earlier paragraph) that the press conference had become a more important means of public communication under Roosevelt *and* Truman than it had been under earlier presidents. So he sets Roosevelt and Truman off *together* in a single paragraph, separated from the previous paragraph in which he'd discussed those earlier presidents. Again, we see a well-structured paragraph giving unity to precisely what the writer wants to give unity to, and separating its contents from precisely what the writer *wants* them separated from. The flexibility of paragraphs can be wonderful to behold.

Other Kinds of Sentences

Within a paragraph, sentences can serve functions other than those of head sentence or elaborator. Let's look at them.

Groundlayers One such sentence is a *groundlayer,* a sentence that expresses neither the paragraph's controlling idea nor an elaborative idea, but instead lays the groundwork for one or the other. The most typical groundlayer in a paragraph is one that *precedes* the head sentence, and prepares the reader for that head sentence. Here's a paragraph with an opening groundlayer:

> (1)It was predictable. (2) Man's conquest of the Moon has set industry to thinking of all the raw materials that might be available there. (3) Lunar exploration has fed the imagination at U.S. Gypsum every bit as much as at NASA or JPL . . . .

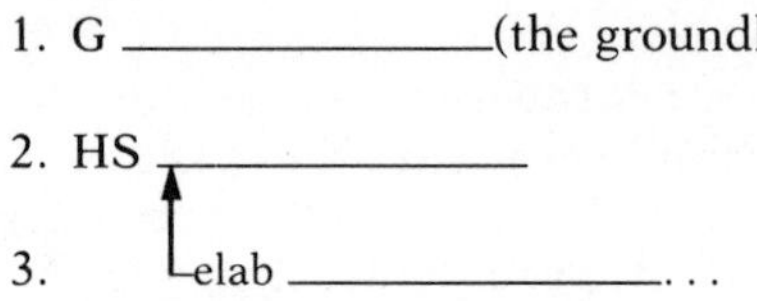

In this partial paragraph, the second sentence is the head sentence. The first sentence is used to lay the groundwork for it.

Summary Sentences A paragraph can also employ a *summary sentence,* a sentence at the end that sums up, and sometimes comments on, the contents of the paragraph. Here's an example:

> (1) Elementary education in America, for all its complexity and variety, is a giant boondoggle. (2) Oh, our kids do learn a few things, like the alphabet and words; but they certainly don't learn how to read. (3) They learn numbers and arithmetic signs too; but nothing resembling a true numerical concept. (4) Dates and names, kings and queens, presidents and generals, all are marched endlessly before them; but few kids learn the most simple of those ''lessons that history can teach us.'' (5) Grade schoolers have even started to learn foreign languages, everything about them except how to speak them, read them, write them, or understand them. (6) Yes, this largest of all our industries -- educating the young -- has failed us miserably.

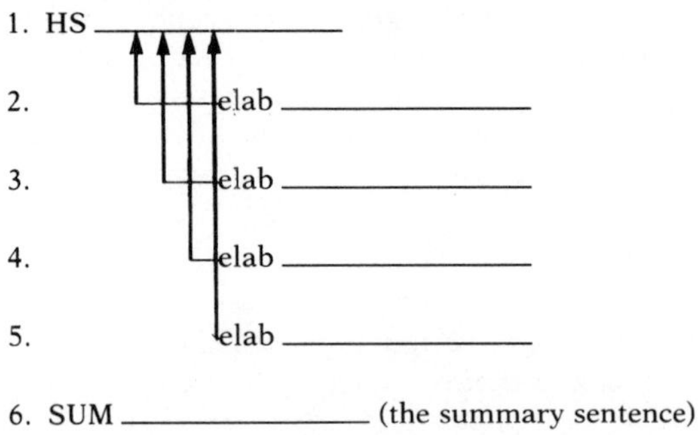

Transitional Sentences Within a paragraph, a sentence can also be used as a *transitional sentence.* A transitional sentence is a sentence used to build a smooth bridge from one paragraph to the next. It can be placed at the beginning to build a bridge from the preceding paragraph, or at the end to build its bridge into the following paragraph. Here are examples of each. First, a paragraph with an opening transitional:

> (1) We come then to a crucial question. (2) What, if anything, is to be done to assure the survival of companies that can't compete in the world market? (3) Many solutions to the problem have been proposed . . . .

1. T ________(transitional sentence)
2. HS ________
3. elab ________ . . . .

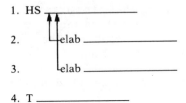

And here's a paragraph with a closing transitional sentence:

> (1) For the longest time, I feared the idea of having to sell a product -- any product -- to a wary customer. (2) I felt that no product was perfect, and that I'd be caught trying to sell imperfections. (3) I also lacked confidence in my own ability to put words together coherently. (4) I hadn't always been this unsure of myself, but when did it start -- and why?

1. HS ________
2. elab ________
3. elab ________
4. T ________

A Final Word About the Making of Paragraphs

Here, then, are the points you want to remember about paragraphing:

1. A given sentence can play any of a number of roles within its paragraph. It can function as head sentence, as a coordinate *or* subordinate elaborator, as a groundlayer, a transitional sentence, or a summary sentence. This variety of roles gives you some structural flexibility that many business writers don't exploit.

2. The sentences that make up a paragraph can assume a wide variety of patterns, as long as those sentences — whatever pattern you give them — all serve the paragraph's controlling idea in one way or another. This, too, gives you greater structural flexibility than many writers feel they have.

3. The paragraph *break* should be treated as another — and very useful — kind of punctuation. It's really a *super-period,* to be used to give unity to the

paragraph it ends, *and* to give heightened importance to the sentence that follows it. You can use the super-period anywhere you wish, as long as it doesn't violate the meanings of the sentences and paragraphs it separates. If you carefully consider the order of your sentences, and the way they relate to one another, your paragraph breaks can be used — however you choose —to reflect precisely the unities and emphases you want your reader to understand. Again, flexibility is the key.

BUILDING CONNECTIONS TO ASSURE SMOOTH FLOW

Even if your sentences are well written, and your paragraphs well shaped, they must still be linked together to create a *smooth flow* of facts and ideas for your reader. The reader should never be left with a sense of gaps.

The transitional sentences we just looked at in the previous section are only one of the ways of assuring yourself this smooth connection. Other linking devices — repeated words, demonstratives, pronouns and pronominal adjectives, enumerators, various connective words and phrases, and parallel sentence patterns — are available to help build those connections and assure smooth flow. Let's examine them.

Repeated Words

Repeated words not only provide emphasis (as we saw in Chapter 3), they also help to connect the clauses and sentences that contain them. It is connection by echo. Notice how the sentences in the following excerpt are smoothly connected by the repetition of key words in successive statements:

> A major steel corporation, realizing that its marketing abilities had outstripped its administrative capacity, decided within the last few years to reorganize. The corporation had three divisions, each selling to the same market. Each division had as its head a capable and tough-minded manager, and each of the three managers had developed an extremely loyal staff.

The repeated words are what establish the linkages:

1st sentence:	...corporation...		
	↕		
2nd sentence:	...corporation...	...divisions...	
		↕	
3rd sentence, (1st clause):		...division...	...manager...
			↕
3rd sentence, (2nd clause):			...managers....

Demonstratives

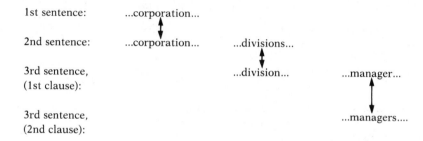

Demonstratives are words that point to things: *this, that, these, those.* As either adjectives or pronouns, they can be used to connect successive statements. You do this by beginning a second statement with a demonstrative that clearly points back to the first. Here's an example:

> Instead of politely requesting, the chairman demanded that all the board members attend the meeting. This lack of tact cost him their support in the election.

The demonstrative adjective *This* points back to the previous assertion, while at the same time beginning the next. A smooth connection between the two ideas is created.[2]

Pronouns and Pronomial Adjectives

Other pronouns and pronomial adjectives are also useful as connectors. As every writer knows, a pronoun needs an antecedent (something it obviously refers to) if it's to be clear. If a pronoun and its antecedent are in different sentences (close enough, of course, for the relationship to be clear), that relationship serves to connect the two sentences. A reader can't miss the pronoun linkage in the following pairs of sentences:

> Leadership, to Baxter, required that every branch office be treated as a separate business. He was really expressing a new philosophy of management.

> One can't help but question the wisdom of political anarchists. Most people revile them, and think that. . .

> Hitler had been brought up as a Catholic and was impressed by the organization and power of the Church. Its hierarchical structure, its skill in dealing with human nature, and the unalterable character of its creed, were all features from which he claimed to have learned.

Enumerators

Sentences or paragraphs can also be linked to one another by *enumerators* (or *sequence signals*). The most obvious enumerators are the numbers with which some business writers list their points (the second paragraph of the letter on pages 174-175 is an example). Short of actual numbers, you can use enumerative words to link ideas into a sequence, as the writer here does:

[2]Notice that if the phrase *lack of tact* were dropped, the demonstrative *This,* as a pronoun, would still serve as a connector. It would lack precision, however.

> Among his assumptions, at least three appear to be doubtful. One is that all employees will understand the operation of the company. Another is the assumption that purely technical knowledge, even when they have it, will enable them to reach sound decisions. And the third is the assumption that managers elected by employees will be mere rubber stamps for their constituents' wishes.

After the head sentence, the writer begins each of his coordinate elaborators with an enumerative phrase: *One is . . . . Another is . . . . the third is . . . .* The technique is a common one. Throughout this text, you will notice ideas being linked together with such phrases as *one way to . . . another way to . . .* or *first you . . . then you . . . after that you . . . finally you . . . .*

Connective Words and Phrases

Many words and phrases in the language exist primarily to connect successive clauses or sentences, helping the reader's mind to move smoothly from idea to idea. Such connectors as *and, also, plus, what is more,* and *in addition to* are used to connect parallel ideas. Others, like *meanwhile, presently,* and *subsequently,* relate two statements *in time,* as this excerpt illustrates:

> The steno pool worked strenuously on into the night. Meanwhile, the executive committee was meeting.

Without the connector *meanwhile,* there would be no smooth transition from the first idea *(the steno pool worked strenuously on into the night)* to the second idea *(the executive committee was meeting).* The connector relates the two statements as simultaneous events.

Other connectors, like *consequently, therefore,* and *that is why,* relate statements in terms of cause and effect. Still others, like *but, however, yet, nevertheless,* and *on the other hand,* connect ideas by setting them into contrast with one another.

As a business writer, you ought to cultivate all the connective words and phrases the language provides you. Here's a list of some of them, catalogued by function:

a. connectors that add assertions to one another in coordinate relationships:	*and, also, too, moreover, or, nor, furthermore, so too, then too, similarly, likewise, besides, in addition*
b. connectors that bring assertions together in contrast, opposition, or contradiction to one another	*but, yet, however, though, on the contrary, at the same time, on the other hand, in contrast, instead*
c. connectors used when summing up the consequences or the results of a series of assertions or minor points	*therefore, thus, and so, so, hence, consequently, all in all, in short, on the whole, as a result, in brief, in general, in other words, in summary*
d. connectors used to introduce an illustration for an assertion	*for example, for instance, for one thing, illustratively, to illustrate*

e. connectors that introduce a reason or a justification for an assertion	*because, inasmuch as, since*
f. connectors that introduce an amplification or elaboration upon an assertion	*frequently, occasionally, usually, specifically, especially, in fact, as a matter of fact, in particular, actually, indeed, even*
g. connectors for conceding a point that does not support a generalization	*it is true that, of course, no doubt, understandably, to be sure, granted that*
h. connectors for reasserting a generalization after making an exception to it	*despite, still, nevertheless, notwithstanding*
i. connectors used to build toward a climax	*more important(ly), more significant(ly), what is more*
j. connectors to help narrow your focus toward a specific point	*specifically, more to the point, looking more closely at*
k. connectors to indicate a forward movement in time	*then, later, next, after that, finally, at last, at long last, in time, in a while, eventually, subsequently, thereafter*
l. . . . a backward movement in time	*previously, earlier, before that, prior to that, formerly*
m. connectors that shift a reader's focus in space	*above, below, ahead, behind, to the right, to the left*
n. connectors that indicate simultaneity	*meanwhile, in the meantime, simultaneously, at the same time*

Notice too that these connectors need *not* be placed directly between the ideas they connect. For example:

> The getaway car was parked in a narrow blind alley with its engine off. The front wheels, moreover, were not in the position they should have been.

The connective word *moreover,* which links the two sentences, appears three words into the second sentence. The writer wanted connection, but also wanted *The front wheels* in the initial position of that second sentence. So the connector, *moreover,* was placed immediately after that subject phrase, *The front wheels.*

Parallel Sentence Patterns

When a string of ideas is given a series of parallel sentence structures (recall our discussion of parallel structures in Chapters 2 and 3), those parallel sentences also give a strong sense of connection to the ideas within them. For example, this paragraph:

> John Grabowski is obviously the best man for the job. When rushed, he works efficiently and never makes a mistake. In a crisis, he always performs coolly. In debate, he is invariably a winner ''hands down.''

The paragraph begins with its head sentence; then, in parallel sentences, it follows with three coordinate elaborators. The parallel sentence structures themselves are sufficient to link the ideas. No connective words or phrases are needed for smooth connection.

FIGURATIVE LANGUAGE: THE USE OF IMAGINATION IN BUSINESS WRITING

Metaphor, or figurative languge, is one of a writer's richest resources — and one sorely undervalued by most business writers.[3] From earliest times, metaphor has been used to make language a more effective tool for informing, affecting, and persuading others — for the very things, in fact, that business people must do with their writing: inform, and evoke reactions.

Don't be taken in by a common misconception: figurative language isn't simply embellishment or ornament hung onto sentences to make them different. Figurative language reflects a basic working of the human mind — the detection of significant similarities. When a journalist writes that two countries have *severed diplomatic relations,* the phrase is figurative. It likens the discontinuance of ambassadorial exchange to the act of slicing. When a bankruptcy attorney (if not bogged down in legalistic jargon) writes that the Metropolax Company *drowned in its own red ink,* he too writes metaphorically, likening a corporate failure to the act of drowning and substituting for water the appropriate liquid. Through metaphor, both these writers have communicated effectively *and* with some imaginative appeal.

Here are several more examples of metaphor at work:

> The <u>death of</u> the World Journal Tribune left New York with only three metropolitan dailies.
>
> At Fieldcroft, children were as <u>thick underfoot as toadstools after a rainstorm</u>.
>
> Legal fees <u>siphoned off</u> most of Amalgamated's 1980 profits.
>
> The American Indian was, for the most part, <u>left to rot</u> on his reservation.
>
> Yesterday's board meeting was one of the <u>stormiest</u> in months.

[3]We'll use the term *metaphor* in its broad sense, that is, to refer to any figure of speech that likens two essentially dissimilar things. The technical distinctions between similes, metaphors, personifications, and the rest — although very real — need not concern us here.

Blacks will have to learn to refuse crumbs from big city political machines and steadfastly demand a fair share of the loaf. -- Martin Luther King

Other kinds of figurative language can also enliven a writing style. You can superimpose different sense impressions upon one another:

Kids, tell Mom to buy you Boomo – the extra loud-tasting breakfast cereal.

Listen to the luscious strings of the Brandenberg Quartet.

Cooperman's so-called art show was a putrid display.

You can endow inanimate things with animate characteristics:

Probably no American corporation of substantial size escaped the committee's scrutiny.

The commissioner's decision posted a warning sign for any enterprise flirting with organized crime.

One generation abandons the enterprises of another like stranded vessels. -- Henry David Thoreau

You can use *allusions* (that is, references to other sources of "authority" or information):

In today's political campaigning, you simply cannot win on shoe leather, nor can you count on previous friendships. As ''Professor'' Harold Hill said in ''The Music Man,'' you've got to know the territory -- the political subdivisions, their voting records, and their liberal or conservative leanings.

You can play on words:

Stop kidding! Join the Planned Parenthood Association.

A reputable company will get you where you're going. Without taking you. -- Bekins Moving & Storage

London Fog goes to great lengths for a short coat.

Figurative language can also be used in longer stretches — as long as you don't make the imaginative part seem more important than the literal idea it's intended to serve. In the following passage, Antony Jay uses a metaphor from the family refrigerator to enliven a discussion about executive promotion:

The cream always rises to the top. This happy domestic metaphor can be a great comfort to good corporation men, and

> the nearer they are to the top, the more comforting they will find it. But not all corporations are milk bottles: Some (if we are to stay in the larder) can be jugs of salad dressing, in which the oil rises to the top and the vinegar stays at the bottom -- even if the corporation would be better run by the vinegary executives than by the oily ones. It is, in fact, by no means inevitable that the best men will go to the top of the firm. And even if you pursue the milk metaphor, you will find that cream has another property as well as rising to the top: it also goes sour quickest.

In the next excerpt, Jay uses an extended *analogy,* an imaginative comparison between two things, to help him clarify his major point:

> A corporation, like a state, needs a faith . . . . Just as soldiers fight much better for a great cause like Christianity or Liberty or Democracy than for the protection of trading interests, so insurance firms can put more pressure on salesmen who feel they are spreading protection and security and peace of mind among their fellow citizens than ones who simply believe they are being paid to increase the company's return on employed capital and the annual dividends of the shareholders.

The point is not that you ought to imitate this kind of prolonged metaphoric writing, but rather that you keep your mind open to metaphoric possibilities. An ability to use figurative language — to draw imaginative comparisons, and with them to clarify and enliven your meanings — is a primary attribute of effective writing. As our examples have tried to demonstrate, it's as helpful to business writers as to any others.

As you write your first drafts, leave the mental door open for your imagination. Make metaphoric comparisons of the kind we've just looked at. If, upon rereading the drafts, you feel that they're forced or ineffective, you can always eliminate them in your rewrites. But if you never try them, your writing cannot possibly be as enlivened as it might be.

A CONCLUDING WORD ON STYLE AND THE BUSINESS WRITER

To be sure, a truly effective writing style isn't easy to achieve. The effort is time consuming, and the rewards aren't quickly evident. One way to develop your own style is to *read* good writing, and seriously contemplate what makes it good. You might also try carrying a pencil and paper with you at all times. Many effective ways of saying things pop suddenly into mind, and in the strangest places. Be ready to capture them. Whenever you know in advance of a communication you must write, start thinking about it, and drafting it, early. Give yourself as much time as you can for the vital process of revision and stylistic tightening.

In the long run, good style will pay off. Your writing will increasingly impress your readers, and you'll be impressed yourself at how enjoyable your business writing has become.

PROBLEMS

1. Using subjects that you're familiar with, perhaps from your own major, see if you can write original paragraphs that conform to each of the following paragraph patterns:

```
a. HS ________
       elab ________
       elab ________
       elab ________
           elab ________

b. HS ________
       elab ________
           elab ________
       elab ________
           elab ________
   SUM ________

c. G ________
   HS ________
       elab ________
           elab ________
           elab ________
           elab ________

d. HS ________
       elab ________
   HS ________
       elab ________
           elab ________

e. T ________
   HS ________
       elab ________
           elab ________
               elab ________

f. HS ________
       elab ________
           elab ________
           elab ________
               elab ________
   T ________

g. HS ________
       elab ________
         elab ________
           elab ________
             elab ________

h. HS ________
       elab ________
   SUM ________
```

2. In its original state, the 24-sentence paragraph below consisted of a number of separate paragraphs. Those original paragraphs have been run together into one. Read the paragraph carefully.

> (1) Diffusion of economic power is indispensable to a society that aspires to be responsive to the rightful social and economic claims of free citizens. (2) This does not mean a return to the backyard foundry, any more than diffusion of political power contemplates a return to the township as the ideal unit of government. (3) But it does mean that the giant corporation must be broken up. (4) Neither the giant corporation nor giant government should be the regulator of the economy; competition should be, almost always. (5) But it cannot be so long as the corporation is permitted to exercise sovereign power. (6) There is nothing sacred about the corporation. (7) No process of God or nature controlled the evolution which produced it. (8) Rather, it developed as a method for accumulating capital and for shielding the user of that capital from individual liability. (9) Thus, it is a mere legal device. (10) And what the law has created, the law must be free to control. (11) The corporation cannot be permitted to be above the law, just as the citizen cannot.

(12) For too long, the corporation, as a device for doing business, has exploited and manipulated the very society that gave it life. (13) A corporation exists because one or the other of the fifty states has granted it a charter that, under the Constitution, must be honored throughout the land. (14) This is absurd. (15) The modern corporation operates in several states, or in all of them, and in many countries. (16) Yet, the laws of the single state that incorporated it govern its operations. (17) Often the corporation chose that state as its legal home because its management could have maximum freedom from legal strictures. (18) Early in the American experience, the states kept a relatively tight rein on corporations. (19) They limited total capitalization, conditioned charters on fairness of business operations, and restricted the scope of those operations. (20) During the nineteenth century, however, significant expansion occurred in the nature and range of commerce. (21) Single corporations began to operate on a national scale. (22) They raised capital in one state. (23) They took raw materials from a second state and processed them in a third. (24) Then they sold the finished products everywhere.

a. As an exercise in paragraphing logic, see if you can determine how many paragraphs the original version consisted of, and between which sentences the paragraph breaks (or "super periods") appeared. Justify your analysis by identifying the idea or concept around which each of the paragraphs was unified.
b. Comment upon the effects (good or bad, logical or illogical) that a paragraph break would cause at each of the following points:

   (1) between sentences 2 and 3
   (2) between sentences 3 and 4
   (3) between sentences 8 and 9
   (4) between sentences 11 and 12
   (5) between sentences 16 and 17
   (6) between sentences 19 and 20

3. Read the following two-paragraph excerpt carefully. After you have studied the makeup of each of these paragraphs, do the following exercises:

a. for both paragraphs 1 and 2 draw a diagram of the paragraph's sentence pattern, like the diagrams on pages 94-99.
b. identify each of the connective devices used in the paragraphs;
c. point to places in paragraph 2 where additional paragraph breaks might have been employed, explain what their effects would have been, and speculate as to why they were not employed;
d. ascertain whether sentence 3 (in paragraph 1) might have been moved into paragraph 2, and what the effect of such a shift would have been.

(1) Whenever an American moves abroad, he suffers from an affliction known as "culture shock." (2) In his new location, there is an absence or distortion of many of the old familiar cues he is used to, and in their place appear many strange new cues. (3) Some examples of these new cues that cause culture shock are

evident in the ways different cultures use and organize space. (4) Houses in Latin America, for example, are often built around a patio that is next to the sidewalk, but hidden from passers-by behind a wall. (5) How do such small but significant differences in architecture affect outsiders? (6) Many American technicians on assignment in Latin America used to complain that they felt "left out of things," that they were "shut off." (7) Looking at other people's houses, they often wondered what was "going on behind those walls." (8) In the States, close proximity is the basis for many relationships. (9) We tend to consider our neighbors as close to us. (10) Being a neighbor gives one certain privileges, as well as responsibilities. (11) You can borrow food or drink or lawnmowers, but you must also be ready to take your neighbor to the hospital in an emergency. (12) Your neighbor has almost as much claim on you, in this respect, as a cousin, maybe more. (13) As another consequence, Americans usually pick their neighborhoods very carefully, knowing that they'll be thrown into fairly intimate contact with the people next door. (14) There is another consequence, we fail to understand — when we move abroad — why the people who live next door to us, sharing that adjacent space, don't conform to our own "neighborly" patterns. (15) In England and France, for example, relations between neighbors tend to be cooler than in the U.S. (16) Mere proximity does not tie people together. (17) In England, children living next door to one another don't play together as they do in our neighborhoods. (18) When they do, it's usually by arrangement that's been made by parents weeks in advance, as though they had to come clear across town.

4. Examine the paragraph structure of each of the following pieces of business writing, and indicate: the idea around which each of its paragraphs is unified, the wisdom of each of its paragraph breaks (or "super periods") in establishing those unities, and the connective devices used to assure smooth flow.

a. the letter on page 217
b. the memorandum on pages 275-276
c. the memo-report on page 431
d. the memorandum on pages 249, 251
e. the letter on pages 255-256
f. the letter on page 352
g. the memorandum on page 335
h. the letter on page 301

5. Obtain three business letters or magazine advertisements that use metaphor or other figurative language. Circle all figures of speech on these communications, and in a memorandum to your instructor, explain the contribution of figurative writing to the effectiveness of those communications. Attach the three examples to your memo.

6. It is often said that clichés are only "metaphors that have gone stale." Re-read the discussion of clichés (back in Chapter 2, on pages 54-56), and con-

sider it alongside the discussion of figurative language in this chapter. In a brief article (suitable for publication, say, in the campus newspaper or in a business journal), lay out as many useful guidelines as you can for when a business writer should and shouldn't use figurative language. Be sure your guidelines contain examples, and that your examples are drawn not only from this text, but from your reading elsewhere and from conversations you've had in school, on the job, or socially.

PART TWO

THE FUNDAMENTALS OF BUSINESS LETTERS AND MEMORANDA

CHAPTER 5

WRITING TO SHAPE BEHAVIOR

One expert, a man who has taught and analyzed business writing for many years, feels that only one person in fifty can write consistently effective business letters — a sad commentary on the state of the art. And probably true. Though many people in business speak effectively, it is the exceptional person who has learned to write well enough to shape other people's reactions as desired. And that, after all, is the purpose of most business letters and memos: to evoke specific reactions from other people.

So for the man or woman who plans a career in business — and wants the advantage of being that one in fifty — the question looms large: *What makes a business letter effective?* (As a convenience, let's use the term *letter* to refer to both letters and memos that are reaction-evoking, as we explore the answer.)

CHARACTER AS WELL AS CLARITY: THE FIRST IMPORTANT PRINCIPLE

Every business letter you write communicates in two distinct ways: by *what* it says, and by *how* it says it. Don't ever forget that. This kind of double-barreled message isn't limited to the written word. In face-to-face conversations, the tone of a person's voice, its sense of urgency or calm, the manner of speaking, the smile or frown on the speaker's face — all tell you something beyond what the words are saying. Sometimes, this "secondary" message reinforces the speaker's words. At other times, it may seem to contradict them.

Business letters have the same double dimension.

For now, let's refer to all the characteristics of this "secondary" message with the word *character.* Look closely at any business letter and you'll see it has as much character — good, bad or indifferent — as an oral communication.

It has a literal message, plus a manner in which it delivers that message. The combination of these two dimensions is the *total message* you get from reading that letter.

What importance does this concept of a double message have when we write business letters? Simply this: since with every letter we are trying to evoke some specific reaction from the reader, we must make sure that the letter's clarity (that is, *what* the letter says) *and* its character (*how* the letter says it) both help to evoke those reactions. Character cannot be ignored. It's there on the page whether you like it or not. In business letters, you either put character to work for you, or you risk its working against you. And because a letter's character is susceptible to so many flaws (flaws we'll examine closely later on), that risk can be great.

EMPATHY: THE SECOND IMPORTANT PRINCIPLE

Also crucial to any business letter's success is its *empathy* with its reader. Empathy is the ability to identify yourself, emotionally and intellectually, with other people's situations: to put yourself in their shoes, to see things through their eyes — and make it evident to them that you're doing so. Without empathy, your business letters and memos are likely to fail.

Being empathic in your business letters can make strong demands on you as a writer. You've got to sharpen your sensitivity to the interests, the motives, the capabilities, the biases, and the possible reactions of anyone with whom you're communicating. If you're dealing with a retailer who is victimized by shortages in supply, your letter must reflect an understanding of that plight. If you're writing to home buyers caught in a high-interest mortgage market — and want to win their favor — your letter must show that you know what the world looks like from that *disad*vantage point. If your reader is a student, a truckdriver, a milliner, a schoolteacher, a physician or a homemaker, then from each of these points of view must you be able to write. You can win the reactions you seek only by writing in terms of your readers' own interests and motives — and in a way that they most readily understand.

Empathy was long ago nicknamed the "you-attitude," a reminder to build your letters and memos around your reader's point of view, not your own. It reminds you, among other things, that the pronouns *you* and *yours* should, when possible, predominate — instead of *I, me, ours,* or *we.* Instead of writing "We are shipping your order immediately," you create more empathy by writing "*Your* order is being shipped immediately and should reach *you* no later than Friday, May 3." No matter what facts your message contains, or what their purpose, those facts must project a you-attitude.[1]

[1]Although the you-attitude is much more than simply using the pronoun "you," one way of evaluating the you-attitude in a letter is by counting the number of first- and second-person references in it, and then calculating its *empathy index.* When you've finished the first draft of a letter, count all its second-person references (pronouns, possessive adjectives, and proper nouns that refer to your reader) and subtract from that the number of first-person references (*I, we, ours, me,* and so on). The result is your empathy index. The higher its positive value, the more likely it is that your letter possesses the you-attitude. A negative index might indicate more of a me-attitude or a we-attitude than a you-attitude, and suggest that you do some revising.

CHARACTER AND EMPATHY: A CASE IN POINT

With these two principles in mind — the need for character and for empathy — let's take a look at a hypothetical situation. It involves a bright but rather brash young college graduate who went to work for the Fitwell Uniform Company of Los Angeles as an assistant sales correspondent. His boss told him how to fill orders: "You check both the chest size and the sleeve size," the boss said, "and make sure the boys in the warehouse send the right sizes." Things went smoothly, until the first order came across the young man's desk. To his dismay, it did not indicate the desired sleeve sizes. A bit perturbed, he fired off a reply to the customer. Both letters, the customer's order and the young correspondent's reply, are shown in Figure 2.

The results of the reply were predictable. The customer complained and took his business elsewhere. And the young man became an ex-sales correspondent.

As poorly written as this reply was, it wasn't unique. Thousands of business letters every day are equally ineffective, and for much the same reasons: they lack clarity, they lack appropriate character, and they lack empathy. They might as well read like the young correspondent's letter, for they fail just as dismally to get the reactions they seek.

But criticizing bad letters is easy. What isn't so easy is writing a good one. Look back at the problem the young correspondent faced when he opened Fred Fox's order letter. Let's handle it for him.

After reading it, we have to write an effective reply to Fred Fox, one that gets him to send us the sleeve sizes he wants. Before writing a single word, we must *define every objective* of that reply. Exactly what reactions do we want from Fred Fox? (Notice that we want *more* than one simple reaction. This is usually the case.)

1. We want Fred Fox to send his desired sleeve sizes.

2. We want him to send them *right away.* The sooner he sends that information, the sooner we can fill his order satisfactorily — and that is *our* constant objective.

3. We want him *not* to be disappointed or annoyed by our reply, as he might possibly be. Remember, he is expecting the jackets. Instead, he is getting only a letter asking him for more information. It's up to us to make our request in terms of *his* best interests (i.e., to state it empathetically). If he's not made to feel that our request is in *his* best interests, it may be just an annoyance to him, and he may send his order elsewhere.

Our objective, then, is more complicated than it first seemed. We seek both an overt reaction (his sending us the sleeve sizes) and a psychological reaction (his continued confidence in Fitwell). Only after we've defined our objectives this carefully should we begin to draft the letter to Fox.

Once a rough draft is written, we begin proofreading and revising. Is the draft as clear as it can be? If not, we must revise it for maximum clarity. Will its character work to achieve the reactions we seek? (Realize that part of a letter's character is its freedom from mechanical error.) Has the letter been written with as much empathy as possible? Put yourself in the position of the recipient. Ask yourself if *you'd* react in the desired way after reading the letter. Not until you have a draft that satisfies each of the requirements should it be typed and sent.

Figure 2

Hoagy's Restaurant
El Centro, Calif.
Sept. 20, 19—

Fitwell Uniforms, Inc.
1818 Evergreen Avenue
Los ~~Ang~~ Angeles, Californa

Gentlemen:

I would like to purchase six of your black, Prince Raymond Waiter's jackets, with narrow lapels (3@ size 40, 3@ size 42) at $22.95 as advertised by you in the L.A. Times. The enclosed check for $137.70 should be just right to cover the cost.

Very truly yours,
Fred Fox
Manager

THIRD NATIONAL BANK
MIDWAY SHOPPING CENTER BRANCH, EL CENTRO, CALIFORNIA

Sept. 20, 19- NO. 145

PAY TO THE ORDER OF Fitwell Uniforms Inc. $ 137.70

One hundred thirty-seven and 70/100 —— DOLLARS

Fred Fox

FITWELL UNIFORMS, INCORPORATED
1818 EVERGREEN AVENUE, LOS ANGELES, CALIFORNIA

Dear Fred
What's the matter?
Ain't your waiters got arms?
Yours truly,
John Sands

A word about dictation is appropriate here. Why do all that revising? Why not just call in a stenographer, and dictate the letter? Sounds great . . . until you've tried it. Dictating a really effective letter — one that needs no improvement whatsoever — is possible only after months of practice. Anyone can dictate words as they come to mind, but only the trained business writer can dictate a letter that will evoke precisely the right reactions from its reader. And such a writer will never dictate until all the letter's objectives have been carefully analyzed. (Appendix A provides a more detailed look at the process of dictation.)

For now, let's look at one good solution to the Fitwell reply problem:

Dear Mr. Fox:

Thank you very much for your order of September 20 for six black Prince Raymond waiter's jackets with narrow lapels. Your check for $137.70 is also gratefully acknowledged.

As we were about to fill your order, we discovered that although we have the desired chest measurements — 3 @ size 40, 3 @ size 42 — we have no record of the desired sleeve sizes. Because we want to assure your maximum satisfaction with your new Prince Raymonds, we'd like you to jot down the precise sleeve sizes on the enclosed postcard and return it to us.

Your order will be filled as soon as we hear from you; and your jackets will, in the Fitwell tradition, be tailored perfectly to your needs.

Sincerely yours,

Fitwell Uniforms, Inc.

This solution isn't the only way to handle the problem, but it faithfully follows the principles we've just discussed. It is clear in its request, and in its details. Its character is congenial. And its entire orientation is empathetic — Fred Fox's point of view predominates throughout the letter. The writer makes sure that everything is aimed at getting the desired reactions from Fox. Though you can never be sure how someone will react, you could hardly do more than this writer has to encourage the desired reactions.

Some of the special techniques used by the writer should also be noted. They are pointed out in the marginal comments in Figure 3.

LOOKING FURTHER INTO THE EFFECTIVE BUSINESS LETTER

So far so good. Our search for ways to make a business letter effective is off to a fast start, but only a start. Now we move further into these basic principles. It may be evident that the success of any letter depends on both its clarity and its character. But what makes a letter clear? And what gives it appropriate character? With the aid of the quality analysis chart in Figure 4, let's examine the qualities that determine a letter's *clarity* and give it *character.* The chart

Figure 3
Detailed analysis of an effective solution to the Fitwell–Fred Fox problem.

Dear Mr. Fox:

Thank you very much for your order of September 20, for six black Prince Raymond waiter's jackets with narrow lapels. Your check for $137.70 is also gratefully acknowledged.

As we were about to fill your order, we discovered that although we have the desired chest measurements -- 3 @ size 40, 3 @ size 42 -- we have no record of the sleeve sizes you desire. Because we want to assure your maximum satisfaction with your new Prince Raymonds, we'd like you to jot down the precise sleeve sizes on the enclosed post card and return it to us.

Your order will be filled as soon as we hear from you, and your jackets will, in the Fitwell tradition, be tailored perfectly to your needs.

Sincerely yours,

"Thanks" is always appropriate in the opening of any letter which acknowledges a customer's order.

Any time a request is made, good reason for it should be given. And this reason should be in the reader's interest, as in this case —"to assure your maximum satisfaction."

Note the continuing "you-attitude" in closing.

We not only acknowledge the customer's order, but we do it with explicit reference to the details of the order. This assures the customer that his order has been clearly received.

Here we've given separate acknowledgment to the remittance Fred Fox included with his order. His check should be considered a gesture of confidence toward Fitwell. He is paying us for the goods before receiving them. This gesture deserves our recognition in the form of a separate acknowledgment.

Here is clear indication of exactly how he can comply with our request. The postcard makes it easy for him to respond immediately. If Fox were left unclear as to exactly how to comply, he might not comply at all.

Note that nowhere are there mistakes in spelling, punctuation, or grammar. Nor is there any trace of sloppiness.

The empathy index of this letter is +3. There are twelve second-person references and only nine first-person references. (See footnote on page 113)

Note that nowhere do we accuse Fred Fox of "omitting" or "neglecting" or "forgetting" inclusion of the sleeve sizes in his order letter. We're not seeking to intimidate him, even in the mildest way. From his point of view, it is significant *only* that we do not have those sizes.

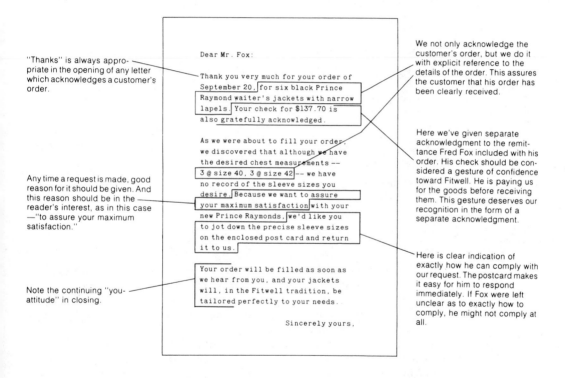

Figure 4
The effective business letter: a quality analysis chart.

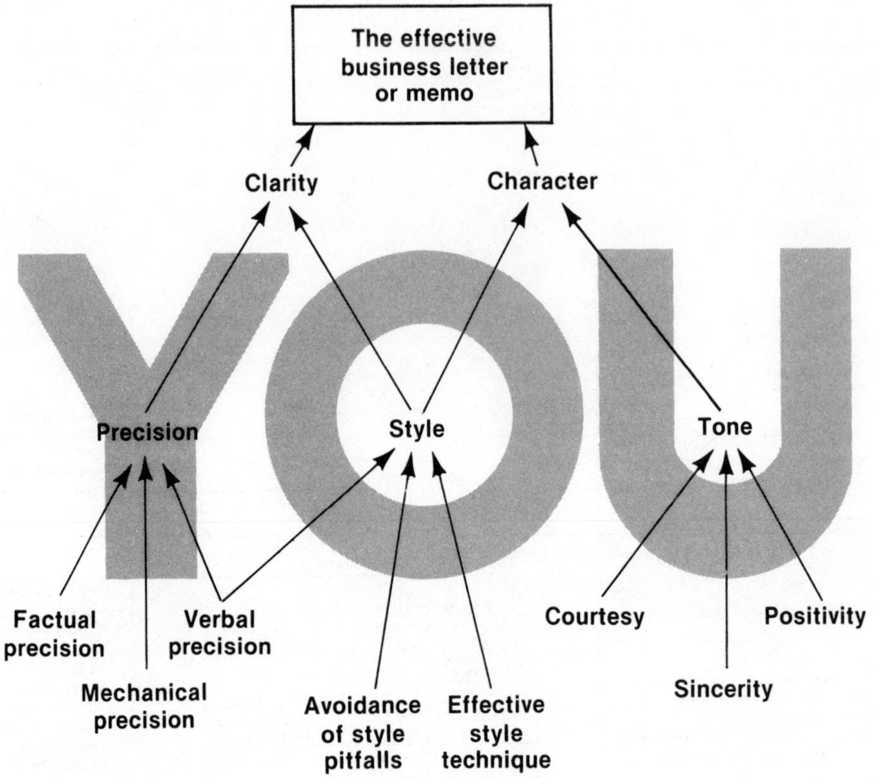

identifies each of the qualities of an effective letter and shows how each of them contributes, in combination with the others, to make a letter effective.

As the chart indicates, three major qualities give a letter its *clarity* and *character* — they are its *precision,* its *style,* and its *tone.* Two of these qualities we've already discussed in detail: precision and style. In Chapter 1 we examined the "three precisions," and in Chapters 2, 3, and 4, the avoidance of bad style and the achievement of good style. Precision and style are characteristics of *all* effective business writing. The third quality, *tone,* is the one we've still to look at. It's particularly important in reaction-evoking communications. Good tone is itself the result of three strong traits — *courtesy, sincerity,* and *positivity* —all of which we'll discuss in Chapter 7.

As the chart also shows, these qualities and their components are all superimposed upon the word YOU. Empathy, or the you-attitude, pervades *every* quality of an effective business letter. A letter's precision, style, and tone must all be adapted to the viewpoint of its recipient. Without empathy, all other qualities are severely diminished.

A WORD IN CLOSING

Before we go on to consider more closely the writing of effective business letters, I want to repeat — and emphasize — a rule that holds true no matter what kind of reaction-evoking communication you're writing. It is this. Before a single word is written, you must carefully determine the reactions you want from the recipient. I say *reactions*, in the plural, because rarely do you want (when you stop to think about it) just a single reaction to a business letter. (Remember the three desired reactions in the Fitwell problem.) And wanting several reactions from your reader, you've got to build into your letter phrases and sentences designed to capture each of them. There are as many business letters and memos ruined by saying too little as too much. (As we saw in Chapter 2, conciseness isn't mere brevity alone, but brevity balanced with completeness.)

Once you've fully determined the reactions you want from your reader, you're ready to write, and rewrite, the letter and bring it to final form.

PROBLEMS

1. On the basis of your own business experiences, write a memo to your instructor briefly outlining what you feel are the advantages and disadvantages of the *business letter* (or *memo*) as compared with other forms of business communication such as face-to-face discussion, telephone, and telegram.

2. What's wrong with this letter?

Dear Mr. Castronovo:

We can certainly understand your request for credit to sustain your firm through the introductory period of its new product line. Unfortunately, we are unable to grant it.

At present, we are handling as many accounts on credit as we possibly can. Two of our credit customers were recently victimized by foreclosures, resulting in partial losses to us. Our margin of profit is so relatively narrow that we cannot, at this time, accept further risk, no matter how excellent your rating. We know you will understand our position.

Our products have, as you know, been rated above all the competition. Our guarantee is the most comprehensive, and our prices are amongst the lowest in the industry. We would consider it a pleasure to supply your needs on a C.O.D. basis.

Sincerely,

Nigel Winkler

Nigel Winkler

3. Tone is an important characteristic in both letters and reports. One point of view, however, sees tone as more important to a letter than to a report. Based on your own experiences, write a one-page statement agreeing or disagreeing with the viewpoint and stating the reasons for your opinion.

4. The following little "business" dialogue takes place regularly in the offices of college professors. Speculate on its outcome and on the reason(s) for that outcome.

STUDENT (entering):	Er, uh, excuse me, sir.
PROFESSOR:	Yes, Mr. Phillips?
STUDENT:	I was absent from your class the day before yesterday . . .
PROFESSOR:	Yes, I recall.
STUDENT:	. . . and I wanted to ask you if I missed anything important.

5. The *empathy index* (described in the footnote on page 113) is not the only way of determining the empathy of a business letter, but it's usually one good indicator. Read the business letters and memos indicated below, and calculate the empathy index of each of them. If the empathy index for a letter is on the minus side, determine whether (and how) it could be improved.

a. Victor T. Evans' letter on page 182
b. Sylvia Weatherby's memo on page 208
c. T. B. Comerford's memo on page 235
d. Conrad Jones's letter on pages 265-266
e. Niven Campbell's letter on pages 289–291

6. You've been at work for several weeks with the Carlson Upholstery Cleaning Service, a long-established firm with branches all over the city. One evening you met a couple, Mr. and Mrs. Don Harris, who recently used the Carlson service to have their sofa and two upholstered chairs cleaned. They said they'd been happy with the service, but that a week after the cleaning they'd received a card from the firm which they thought "a little pushy." You asked to see it, and they showed it to you. It was a card sent as a follow-up expression of gratitude for the customer's patronage. It also attempted to elicit from the customer some specific opinions about the cleaning job, and the names of friends who might also be interested in using the Carlson service. Nothing wrong with the purposes of the card, but upon reading it, you agreed with the Harrises; it did seem a little aggressive and self-concerned. Here it is:

Dear Folks,

This card is to express our utmost and sincere thanks to you. We really appreciate the fact that you called upon us to clean your furniture — and we want you to know it. We also want to be sure that our service was satisfactory to you — because only by satisfying you can our business grow.

Take just a moment to answer the few questions on the reverse and mail the card to us. It may seem like just a little thing, but it's important to us — we will appreciate it.

We look forward to serving you again in the future, and to serving your friends as well.

Rex Mixon
Rex
Customer Service

See if you can rewrite the card so that it still serves its purposes, but with a more appealing tone.

7. You have become the Customer Relations Director of Melody Crystalware, Inc., a large manufacturer of quality glass and crystal products. Yesterday your company received the following letter, which was forwarded to your office:

32 Cactus Avenue
Chandler, Arizona
March 29, 19–

Melody Crystalware
1800 Market Street
San Francisco, California

Gentlemen:

I saw your advertisement in last month's Sunset Magazine and would like you to send me 1/2 dozen of those lovely Starlight Sherry glasses. My check for $27.00 is enclosed.

Very truly yours,
Sarah Jones

The ad to which Ms. Jones refers did run last month in *Sunset Magazine*, and it did announce the price of your Starlight Sherry glasses at $4.50 apiece. The ad also indicated, however, that Starlight glasses are available at department stores throughout the West, but Ms. Jones apparently overlooked this last bit of copy. The letter came to the desk of one of your young staff members. To inform Ms. Jones that the company does not fill consumer orders, he jotted off the following letter to her, subject to your approval;

Dear Ms. Jones:

We received your order for glasses, but unfortunately we cannot send them to you. We manufacture these glasses. We do not sell them to customers. They are distributed by us to wholesalers who sell them to retail stores. Your local store is where you should go. A careful reading of our recent ad would have prevented your mistake, and eliminated the necessity of our having to return your check.

Yours truly,

Tom Cutter

Thomas Cutter
Service Department

Wisely, you did not allow this letter to be mailed, for its tone is almost sure to alienate a customer. The letter lacks empathy in both its attitude and its explanation. At the least, it could have informed Ms. Jones that the Melody distributor nearest her is William Wellborn & Sons, at 100 Ocotillo Avenue in Tempe, Arizona. As it stands, this letter will lose not only the eventual sale, but also some of your company's hard-earned goodwill. Rewrite this reply to Ms. Jones, showing your young staff member how to achieve maximum effectiveness in this kind of situation.

8. Assume that you have gone to work for the Hillcrest Resort Hotel, in Angel's Ridge, Colorado, as a customer-relations correspondent. The management has asked you to prepare a business promotion letter to be sent at Christmas time to each guest of Hillcrest this past summer. The letter should contain the following ideas:

> Thanks to the guest for patronizing Hillcrest and for allowing the hotel to make its resort facilities available.
>
> Mention of the new facilities the hotel will be able to offer next summer — sauna baths, a color television in every room, and a delicious Sunday brunch — with no increase in rates.
>
> A statement that the hotel looks forward to serving the guest next summer.

In writing the letter, compose these thoughts in whatever order you feel appropriate. Remember that your letter should be perfectly clear and should convey the appropriate tone (one of sincere desire to extend quality service to the patron). Remember, too, the need for empathy when developing this letter. Foremost among the reactions you want from each recipient is a definite disposition toward returning to Hillcrest next summer.

9. Assume that you are the assistant vice-president of Regal Foods, a large manufacturer of canned goods. It has just come to your attention that some ineffective letters have been sent out by your employees to consumers, suppliers, and, in one instance, to a state inspection agency.

Write a memorandum to your staff (the heads of departments, junior executives, and secretaries) stressing the importance of the communications they write. You want to keep the memo fairly brief (to avoid sounding like you're preaching a lesson), but you want them to get the message and act on it.

10. Everyone is constantly exposed to business communications of one sort or another. Take note of all the business writing that comes to your attention during a twenty-four-hour period, and write your instructor a relatively brief memo-report (five hundred to a thousand words) discussing the effectiveness or ineffectiveness of those business communications. In discussing their qualities and deficiencies, use the concepts and the terminology you've learned in the preceding chapters.

11. Collect two examples of what you consider to be well-written business letters, and three examples of good memos. Examine them closely and point out to your instructor any significant differences in:

a. their factual precision and detail
b. their levels of diction
c. their character (i.e., the way they say what they say)

12. Three students at Valhalla University, all of them experienced masons, decided to start a business to help put themselves through college and graduate school. They placed a classified ad in the "Professional Services" section of the local newspaper. The ad read as follows:

CONCRETE WORK

by
The Starving College Students
Call: 288-8767

Does the ad appeal to you? Explain why, or why not, in a brief memo to your instructor.

13. Mr. Joe Belli, of the Belli Gymnastic Equipment Company (in Gardena, California), sent the following request letter to one of his competitors:

UCS, Inc.
155 State Street
Hackensack, New Jersey 07601

Gentlemen:

Please mail our company one current catalog of the gymnastics equipment and matting your company manufactures.

Sincerely,

Joe Belli

In reply, someone at UCS, Inc. simply scribbled the following message across the bottom of Belli's letter and sent it back to him:

Why should we? You make your own gym equipment. Catalogs are expensive and so are stamps. Besides that, our prices should not concern you.

This is not a fictional situation. It actually happened. And when you think about it, what the reply says is true. The Belli Company *is* a competitor. And catalogs *are* expensive. So is postage. UCS, Inc. obviously doesn't want to provide any help to the competition.

In a memo to your instructor, discuss in detail the wisdom (or folly) of the UCS reply.

CHAPTER 6

WHAT PROPER LETTERS AND MEMOS LOOK LIKE

It's as true in business as anywhere else in life: *first impressions count heavily.* And when you receive a written business communication, its first impression comes, not from what it says, but from the way it looks.

Like it or not, the people you expect to read what you've written will almost always notice, before they read it, what your letter or memo *looks* like. If its format is in any way odd or unconventional, your reader will anticipate oddness or unconventionality in its message. Send out a sloppy letter — one with smudges, crossouts, erasures or obvious errors — and its recipient will find it hard to take you or your message seriously. Greet your reader by saying something that offends him or her (even unintentionally), and you'll end up either on a grudge-list or in a wastebasket. That prejudgment (or prejudice) on the reader's part may be erroneous. It may even be unfair. But as the writer, you're stuck with it.

So it pays to know, beyond mechanical precision, what makes letters and memos look good. That's our primary concern in this chapter. We'll consider the formats of letters and memos — that is, their physical layouts — and we'll examine each element in those formats to see what it does, and how it should be constructed. (For a corresponding look at the formats of business reports, see Chapter 18.)

THE FORMAT OF A BUSINESS LETTER

There are several different business letter formats, but they follow pretty much the same rules, rules with good reasons behind them. The recipient of a letter should be able to tell *at a glance* when it was written, where it was written, exactly for whom it's intended, and how the writer should be addressed in reply.

Having this information where it belongs is vital to a letter's clarity. A neat and accurate format also contributes to a letter's character: it implies that the writer knows how to correspond in a professional manner.

The Modified Block and Full Block Formats

The formats most frequently used for business letters are the *modified block* and *full block* formats, illustrated in Figures 5 and 6 respectively. Figure 5 identifies each of the format elements in a typical business letter, elements that we'll discuss as the chapter progresses.

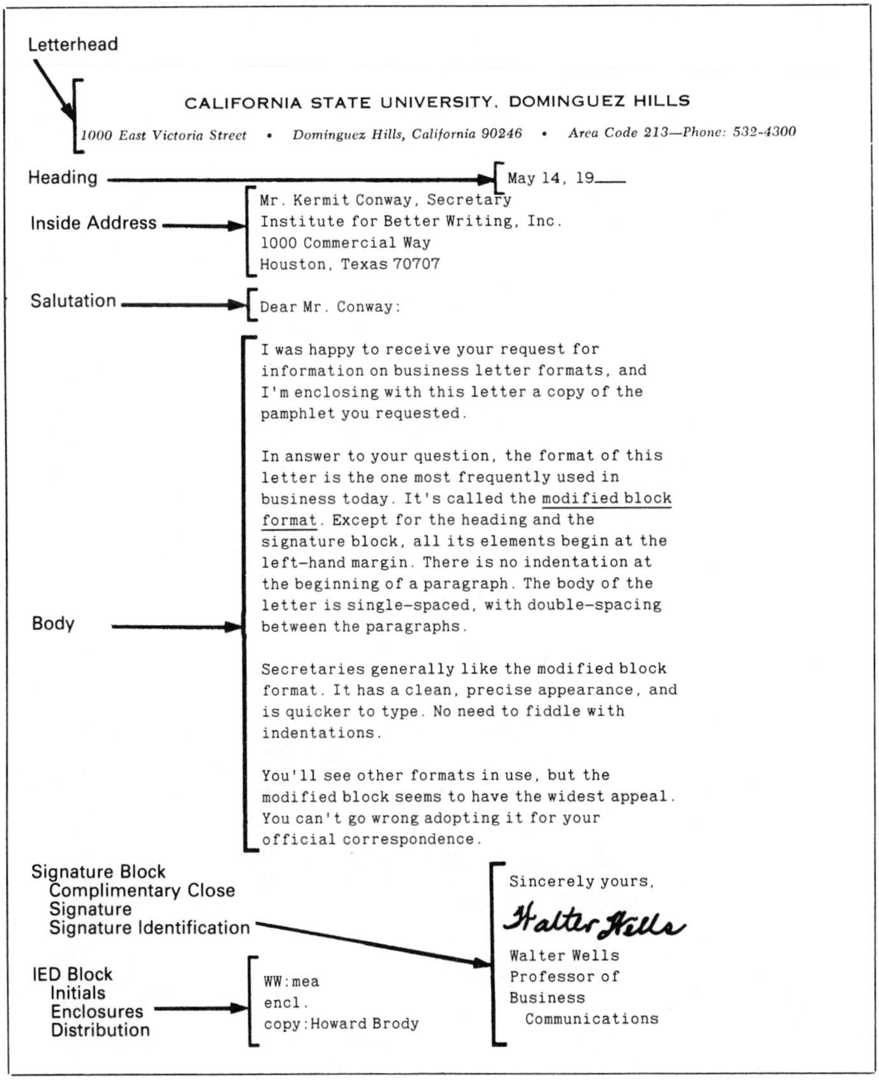

CALIFORNIA STATE UNIVERSITY, DOMINGUEZ HILLS
1000 East Victoria Street • Dominguez Hills, California 90246 • Area Code 213—Phone: 532-4300

May 14, 19__

Mr. Kermit Conway, Secretary
Institute for Better Writing, Inc.
1000 Commercial Way
Houston, Texas 70707

Dear Mr. Conway:

I was happy to receive your request for information on business letter formats, and I'm enclosing with this letter a copy of the pamphlet you requested.

In answer to your question, the format of this letter is the one most frequently used in business today. It's called the modified block format. Except for the heading and the signature block, all its elements begin at the left-hand margin. There is no indentation at the beginning of a paragraph. The body of the letter is single-spaced, with double-spacing between the paragraphs.

Secretaries generally like the modified block format. It has a clean, precise appearance, and is quicker to type. No need to fiddle with indentations.

You'll see other formats in use, but the modified block seems to have the widest appeal. You can't go wrong adopting it for your official correspondence.

Sincerely yours,

Walter Wells

Walter Wells
Professor of
Business
Communications

WW:mea
encl.
copy:Howard Brody

Figure 5
A business letter in modified block format. All typed elements in this format, except the heading and the signature block, begin at the left-hand margin. This saves the secretary from having to make different margin settings on the typewriter.

Other Formats

Like longer hair and beards, the traditional *indented* format (as diagrammed in Figure 7) has made a come-back, and can be seen in a number of business letters today. In this format, the first line of each paragraph is indented from seven to ten spaces.

In some business organizations, the *simplified format* is used. In the simplified format (shown in Figure 8), the writer omits both the salutation and the complimentary close. A *subject line* in place of the salutation announces the subject of the letter. Advocates of the simplified format claim that salutations and complimentary closes add nothing to a message, and that they waste the time of both reader and typist. Other writers are reluctant to give up the *tonal* qualities of these two elements, and hence resist the simplified format.

When in Rome, do as the Romans do — unless, of course, Caesar gives you a choice. Then you can make up your own mind which format to use.

Figure 6
THE FULL BLOCK FORMAT. Some companies carry the time-saving logic of the block format one step further and use a *full block* format. Here, even the heading and signature block are brought to the left-hand margin.

Figure 7
THE TRADITIONAL INDENTED FORMAT. For those companies and business writers who prefer traditional paragraph indentations and are willing to spend the slight extra time it takes to do the indenting.

The Elements of a Business Letter Format

Using Figure 5 as a guide, let's briefly examine each of the elements in the business letter format.

Letterhead The most obvious element in a company's business letter is its letterhead. A letterhead's two functions are to identify and to look good: it identifies where the letter came from, and it gives the recipient his first impression of the letter, the writer, and the writer's organization.

Letterhead design has become a job for specialists. Letterheads are designed to be attractive, and periodically *re*designed to keep their attractiveness up to date. We see as old-fashioned those letterheads that take up a lot of space with corporate slogans, pictures, and a roll call of the company's officers. The

Figure 8
A business letter in simplified format.

CALIFORNIA STATE UNIVERSITY, DOMINGUEZ HILLS

1000 East Victoria Street • Dominguez Hills, California 90246 • Area Code 213—Phone: 532-4300

May 21, 19--

Institute for Better Writing, Inc.
1000 Commercial Way
Houston, Texas 70747

THE SIMPLIFIED FORMAT IN BUSINESS LETTERS

As a follow-up to my letter of May 14, I'm writing this letter to illustrate the simplified format in action.

The simplified format, with its subject line in place of a salutation, makes it easy for the reader to identify the subject. But if that subject is negative, the writer may want to find some phrasing that avoids a negative impression at the outset.

Some teachers now teach the simplified format exclusively. Others are holding out for one or the other of the more traditional forms. As usual, all the alternatives have their advantages and their drawbacks.

Walter Wells

Walter Wells

WW:mea

modern look is uncluttered and less ornate. (Notice the style of the various letterheads illustrated in this chapter and thereafter.)

A letterhead should always contain the name and address of the company and (unless there is reason for omitting it) the telephone number. Sometimes a trademark or brief slogan is used effectively. Many large companies add departmental identification to their letterheads, and companies doing business internationally usually add their cable address.

Heading On letterhead stationery, the heading consists simply of the date of writing (as in Figure 5). The date should be written in standard form: *April 10, 1981, without* the ordinal suffixes (*-st, -nd, -rd, -th*) which are often tacked on to date numbers. Don't abbreviate the month; the letter's character is enhanced slightly if its heading is spelled out. Avoid the military/bureaucratic form of date writing — *10 April 81* — unless your company demands it. And stay away from the all-number forms (like 4/10/81); they confuse some readers, and are not used consistently throughout the English-speaking world.[1] Always consider the reader's possible reaction, even to something as minor as the way the date is written. It's a good habit to develop.

As a rule of thumb, on letterhead stationery, type the date a double space below the last line in the letterhead, or two inches below the top edge of the paper, whichever places the date in the lower position. In the full block format, type the date at the left margin. In the modified block, the date may begin at the center of the paper.

When a letter is written on stationery without a letterhead (as it usually is when a private individual writes a business letter), the writer's address becomes part of the heading, preceding the date:

```
22 Vermilion Drive
Price, Utah 88307
April 8, 198_
```

The writer's name does not belong in the heading; it appears in the signature block.

Inside address Preceding the body of the letter is a complete designation of the letter's destination — the *inside address*. Why include the address in the letter when it already appears on the envelope? Because the envelope is usually thrown away. The letter itself must clearly indicate for whom the message was intended.

The inside address can direct a letter to:

an individual	Mr. Joseph T. Pender 16 Oak Hill Road Chappaqua, New York 10514
several individuals:	Messrs. William Craft and John Simon 2650 North Dixie Boulevard Savannah, Georgia 38652

[1]For example, the date *August 1, 1981* — which Americans would write *8-1-81* — is written *1-8-81* in Great Britain.

to a section or department within a company:	Public Relations Department Splitsilver Copper Company, Inc. 700 Main Street Minesboro, Pennsylvania 32682
or to an entire organization:	The Four Star Company, Inc. 12420 West Sunset Boulevard Hollywood, California 90082

When you address a letter to an individual, show him or her the courtesy of a title, even if it's only the usual *Mr., Ms., Miss* or *Mrs.* — unless you're addressing someone whose sex you don't know and can't easily learn. When addressing a woman, use *Ms.* (pronounced *Miz*) unless she has previously identified herself to you as *Miss* or *Mrs.*

If your addressee has earned some other title — for example, *Dr.* Marion MacDonald, *General* John M. Taylor, *Reverend* Edwin P. Foster, *Professor* Barbara L. French, *Senator* Paul Laxalt — that title should always be used in the inside address. Note, too, that except for *Mr., Mrs., Ms.,* and *Dr.,* titles of respect are spelled out.

Also be sure to include in your inside address the organizational title of the person being addressed, if you're addressing him in that capacity:

```
Mr. Berry Gordy, President
Motown Industries, Inc.
6255 West Sunset Blvd.
Los Angeles, California 90025
```

If the job title is too long to fit neatly after the name, devote a separate line to it:

```
Dr. Saundra Washington
Associate Dean of Student Activities
District of Columbia Polytechnic
900 Avenue E, N.W.
Washington, D.C. 20025
```

If your addressee's title is a departmental one, the name of the department also becomes part of the address:

```
Ms. Edith B. Morris, Director
Personnel Department
Northwest Productions, Inc.
680 Timberline Drive
Seattle, Washington 99050
```

Check to be sure that all titles are accurate and that your addressee's name is spelled correctly. It's worth the extra effort to avoid the discourtesy or unconcern that such mistakes inevitably imply. Be sure, as well, to write department and company names and addresses correctly.

A note of caution: avoid duplicating titles in writing your addressee's name. You'd be guilty of duplication if you write *Dr. Harry M. Brown, Ph.D.*, because the *Ph.D.* says *"Doctor."*

There is a modern trend toward the U.S. Postal Service's abbreviations of state names (NY for New York, CA for California, GA for Georgia, etc.— Figure 9 provides a complete list.) But some writers feel you enhance the character of your letter by spelling out state names, as well as words like Company, Avenue, Street and Boulevard. (Again, company policy may make this decision for you.)

Figure 9
Two letter abbreviations of state names.

Alabama: AL
Alaska: AK
Arizona: AZ
Arkansas: AR
California: CA
Colorado: CO
Connecticut: CT
Delaware: DE
District of Columbia: DC
Florida: FL
Georgia: GA
Hawaii: HI
Idaho: ID
Illinois: IL
Indiana: IN
Iowa: IA
Kansas: KS
Kentucky: KY
Louisiana: LA
Maine: ME
Maryland: MD
Massachusetts: MA
Michigan: MI
Minnesota: MN
Mississippi: MS
Missouri: MO
Montana: MT
Nebraska: NE
Nevada: NV
New Hampshire: NH
New Jersey: NJ
New Mexico: NM
New York: NY
North Carolina: NC
North Dakota: ND
Ohio: OH
Oklahoma: OK
Oregon: OR
Pennsylvania: PA
Rhode Island: RI
South Carolina: SC
South Dakota: SD
Tennessee: TN
Texas: TX
Utah: UT
Vermont: VT
Virginia: VA
Washington State: WA
West Virginia: WV
Wisconsin: WI
Wyoming: WY

You can also spell out numbers, if they're only one word long:

```
Two Fifth Avenue
New York, New York 10010
```

```
908 West Eleventh Street
Los Angeles, CA 90025
```

Be sure to include any apartment or unit number in the street address:

```
1810 Crenshaw Drive, Apt. 215
```

And include the ZIP CODE number after the state — unless you don't know it *and* can't find it. (Remember, though, the wrong zip code can be worse than no zip code at all.) As this edition of the book goes to press, the U.S. Postal Service is planning to change from a five-digit to a nine-digit Zip Code system. The new nine-digit numbers promise speedier and more efficient mail delivery — so be watching for them.

Salutation The traditional greeting in a letter is its *salutation,* the verbal gesture that salutes your reader. It is the salutation that injects the first "human element" into a letter. Instead of saying "Hi" (or the equivalent), as you would face to face, you write a salutation.

Theoretically, your letter will always be received by its designated addressee — that is, the person, the group, the department, or the company whose name appears on the first line of your inside address. So you salute that addressee. If you're addressing:

```
Mr. Joseph T. Pender
16 Oak Hill Road
Chappaqua, New York 10514
```

your salutation would be, simply:

```
Dear Mr. Pender:
```

If you're addressing an organization, for example —

```
The Four Star Company
12420 West Sunset Boulevard
Hollywood, California 90082
```

the traditional salutation would be:

```
Gentlemen:
```

But that traditional salutation will get you into trouble with many readers who dislike its masculine bias. More and more, teachers are recommending that *Ladies and Gentlemen* be used to salute organizations and companies. To some writers, *Ladies and Gentlemen* smacks too much of platform oratory, and they look for other ways around the problem of implied "sexism." Some people are using the salutation *Greetings* to avoid the problem of gender altogether. It's no doubt best, when fashion is so much in flux, to seek the advice of your nearest expert — your classroom teacher or a current secretarial handbook.

If the name of an organization tells you it consists entirely, or mostly, of women:

```
Butte Chapter
Montana Women's Auxiliary
123 Horner Street
Butte, Montana 81919
```

the traditional salutation would be

```
Ladies:
```

The trend in modern business letters has been away from the more formal salutations like *Dear Sir* and *Dear Madam*, and toward the warmer, more cordial salutation that greets the addressee by name. It is certainly not disrespectful to salute John Jennings as *Dear Mr. Jennings* or Barbara Revere as *Dear Ms. Revere;* if they're like most of us, they enjoy being greeted by name.

The old-fashioned salutation *Dear Sirs* is also out of style. And the very formal *My dear Sir* and *My dear Madam* are inappropriately stuffy — they sound to some people like a tight-lipped smile before an outburst of wrath.

On the other hand, you want to avoid being too informal in your salutations. You would not, for instance, do what the brash young correspondent in Chapter 5 did, and salute your customer — *Dear Fred.* First names should be used in saluting only those people you know on a first-name basis. When writing personal business letters on a first-name basis, some writers employ a format that brings the inside address down *below* the body of the letter.

There are other appropriate business letter salutations. If you're addressing a husband and wife:

```
Mr. and Mrs. Hugo Waters
92 Boulder Avenue
Laramie, Wyoming 70694
```

the correct salutation is the most natural one:

```
Dear Mr. and Mrs. Waters:
```

When you answer a classified ad that gives only a box number for an address, salute the box number as if it were the name of the company:

```
Box 85642
Los Angeles Times
Times-Mirror Square
Los Angeles, California 90052

Ladies and Gentlemen:
```

If you are writing a formal letter to someone of high position, certain rules for salutations are generally followed. The rules are spelled out in Appendix B on pages 504-509.

The correct punctuation for most business letter salutations is a *colon.* If your addressee happens to be a personal friend, someone you're saluting on a first-name basis, you can use a comma; but for most business salutations, the comma is too informal. Never punctuate the salutation with a semicolon.

Body of the letter Several comments should be made regarding format *within the body* of a letter. The lines within a paragraph should be single-spaced, with double-spacing between paragraphs (except for very short letters, which can be double-spaced). Be careful not to type the body of a letter so far down the page that there isn't enough room for the signature block and some blank space. If the letter won't fit comfortably onto one page, use a second. When you use a second page, make sure it contains at least the last three lines of the letter's body; a second page that carries nothing but a signature block looks silly. For a second page (and a third, if necessary), use plain stationery of the same grade as the first page, but without a letterhead. Second and third pages have their own headings (in either of the following two formats) that indicate the addressee's name, the page number, and the date:

Mr. Joseph T. Pender —2— July 30, 198—

Mr. Joseph T. Pender
Page 2
July 30, 198—

Signature block There are three separate elements in a letter's signature block: the *complimentary close,* the *signature,* and the *signature identification.*

The *complimentary close* ends the letter's message in a congenial way, just as *good-bye* or *so long* ends a conversation. Some of the most frequently used complimentary closes are:

Yours truly,	Cordially,	Warmest regards,
Very truly yours,	Best regards,	With warmest regards,
Respectfully,	Sincerely yours,	Best wishes,
Respectfully yours,	Sincerely,	

Notice that each of these complimentary closes conveys a slightly different tone. When closing a letter, select the one most appropriate to the tone and level of formality of your communication. Complimentary closes can even be given a unique flair, like that at the end of letters sent out by a large chain of travel agencies:

Yours for travel convenience and economy,

or that used by the United States Playing Card Company:

Recreationally yours, . . .

The correct punctuation for the complimentary close is a comma. Notice also that only the *first* word in a complimentary close is capitalized.

The *signature* and the *signature identification* complete the signature block. When typing a letter, leave five blank lines below the complimentary close, and on the sixth, directly beneath the complimentary close, type your signature identification. Your signature goes into the space between these two typed lines. The typewritten identification tells neatly and legibly who wrote the letter. The signature itself, apart from its legal ramifications, adds a personal touch.

When a letter is sent on letterhead stationery, the signature block indicates who in the company has written the letter and what his or her position is. On the Acme Corporation letterhead, signature blocks might read:

Respectfully yours,	Yours truly,
J. Williams	Susan Kipling
Joseph Williams Comptroller	Susan Kipling, Director Market Research Department

If the Acme letterhead also included the designation *Market Research Department*, Susan Kipling's signature block would read simply:

Yours truly,

Susan Kipling

Susan Kipling
Director

Because a signature makes a letter official and gives it a look of completeness, any letter in which the signature is omitted or rubberstamped seems to say either "I, the author, care little about this communication," or "this letter is just part of my everyday routine." However unintended these feelings might be, they can ruin an otherwise skillful reaction-evoking communication. Always sign a business letter by hand.

When letters are signed by someone other than the person shown in the signature block (e.g., Lois Griffith signing her boss's name to a letter in his absence), the signature should be followed by the initials of the surrogate signer:

Sincerely yours,

Michael Wilson (l.g.)

Michael Wilson

The IED Block. The IED block (*i*nitials, *e*nclosures, and *d*istribution list) appears at the left-hand margin two lines below the signature block, as shown in Figure 5. The first line of the IED block, giving the initials of the writer and the secretary, should appear, as follows, on all but the most personal business letters:

Sincerely,

Betty Kavanaugh

Betty Kavanaugh
Executive Vice President

BK:mr

When a letter is accompanied by a brochure, document, check, photocopy, or any other enclosure, a second line is used to say to the recipient, in effect, "Look out, don't miss the rest of this communication!" This *enclosure indicator* appears immediately beneath the initials, usually (but not always) abbreviated; and it indicates the number of enclosures accompanying the letter.

```
JBW:las     JBW:las      JBW:las
encl.       encls.: 2    encls.: Check ($17.82)
                                 Copy of Invoice #18903
```

The third line in the IED block is used to inform the recipient that copies of the letter have been distributed to third parties. When included, *a distribution list* usually looks like this:

```
JBW:las
encl.
copies: A. L. Baxter
        C. M. Walsh
```

If copies are directed to more than one individual, list the individuals according to rank. If the individuals are equal in rank, or ranking is unimportant, alphabetize the list.

Ranked distribution list:

```
copies: R. F. Sillham, President
        T. L. McMillan, Vice-President
        F. S. Timpkins, General Manager
```

Alphabetized distribution list:

```
copies: Marcus L. Brendero
        Joanne Langville
        David M. Silverman
```

When you don't want to show a copy notation on the original letter, use a *blind copy* notation to route the copies. Type this distribution notation on the copies only.

```
bc: Dave McEttrick
    Jon Thompson
```

Attention line, subject line, and postscript Besides the basic format elements we've already discussed, business writers will occasionally employ an *attention line,* a *subject line* (even without the simplified format), or a *postscript* in their letters.

An attention line, placed between the inside address and the salutation, may be used to facilitate the handling of a letter addressed to a company:

```
Major Electric Company
9900 Lincoln Highway
St. Paul, Minnesota 60402

Attention: Mr. Paul Dixon

Greetings:
```

(In a letter using the traditional indented format, the attention line would also be indented.) Legally, a letter's addressee has the sole right to open it. If the letter were addressed to Dixon (rather than merely directed to him by an attention line), no one else, technically, could open the letter; whereas a letter addressed to the company, and directed to the *attention* of Dixon, can be opened by anyone in Dixon's absence. Because this technicality is not often observed, many writers don't use the attention line; they feel it is too impersonal. Instead, they address the person they want to handle the letter. Notice that when an attention line is used, the salutation still salutes the letter's addressee — in this case, the Major Electric Company.

Some writers and companies — even those who don't use the simplified format — use a subject line in their letters, following the salutation. Others avoid it, preferring to have their readers learn the subject of a letter, and its key points, less quickly. When it's used, a subject line announces what the letter is about. For example:

```
Drew, Pastor & Lubbock
Attorneys at Law
201 South San Leandro Street
Dallas, Texas 69015

Gentlemen:

Subject: Proposed Delay of the Thomson Trial
```

Sometimes a subject line is used to refer to an account number or invoice number. And sometimes, instead of the word *Subject,* the Latin *Re* is used at the head of a subject line.

One other use for subject lines and attention lines has recently come into play. Some writers use one, or the other, *to avoid a salutation that might offend the reader.* If you're writing to someone whose name isn't clearly male or female — say, L. T. Morgan or Lee Kramer — do you write *Mr.* or *Ms.* in your salutation? You can sidestep the problem (and a possibly embarrassing mistake) by using an attention line:

Instead of	*You can write*
L. T. Morgan Accounting Department Cresswell, Inc. 400 Fortune Street Phoenix, Arizona 82073 Dear ?	Accounting Department Cresswell, Inc. 400 Fortune Street Phoenix, Arizona 82073 Attention: L. T. Morgan Ladies and Gentlemen:

Some writers who aren't comfortable with the salutation *Ladies and Gentlemen,* but still wish to avoid the traditional *Gentlemen* (which offends some readers), use a subject line *in place of* the salutation:

Accounting Department
Cresswell, Inc.
400 Fortune Street
Phoenix, Arizona 82073

Subject: Credit Account of Mr. Peter Boggs, #34-2197

I have just received my April invoice, and wish to . . .

The postscript (P.S.) is almost never used in business letters to do what it traditionally has done — that is, to include an idea omitted earlier. It is used instead as a device to emphasize the idea it expresses. If readers thought a postscript really represented something the writer forgot to say in the body of the letter, they might react skeptically toward the apparent poor planning. The modern reader knows, however, that postscripts are used not to remedy omissions but to highlight ideas — as in the case of the young man who ends a letter to his sweetheart with "P.S. I love you." Writers of sales letters often withhold one last convincing argument for emphatic inclusion in a postscript. And some executives, to add a personal touch to their typewritten letters, occasionally add a handwritten postscript:

to see you at our final meeting of the year at the Statler-Hilton on July 12.

Sincerely,

Robert Jackson

Robert Jackson
Sales Manager

P.S. They're serving that delicious prime rib, Tom

Other physical characteristics The stationery generally used for business letters is $8\frac{1}{2}$-inch by 11-inch, twenty-weight, plain white bond. As an economy measure, some organizations (especially government agencies) have gone to a lighter bond. Some executives use heavier-than-average stationery for its prestige value. One national van line, whose gold-colored vans are widely recognized on the highways, carries the color motif into its letters by using gold-colored stationery.

Margins contribute substantially to a letter's visual impression. They should create the effect of a well-framed picture. Both left- and right-hand margins should be at least $1\frac{1}{4}$ inches wide — more, if a letter is fairly short. A letter with a relatively brief body can have margins as wide as two inches or more. The right-hand margin should be made as nearly regular as possible,

Figure 10
A business letter layout guide.

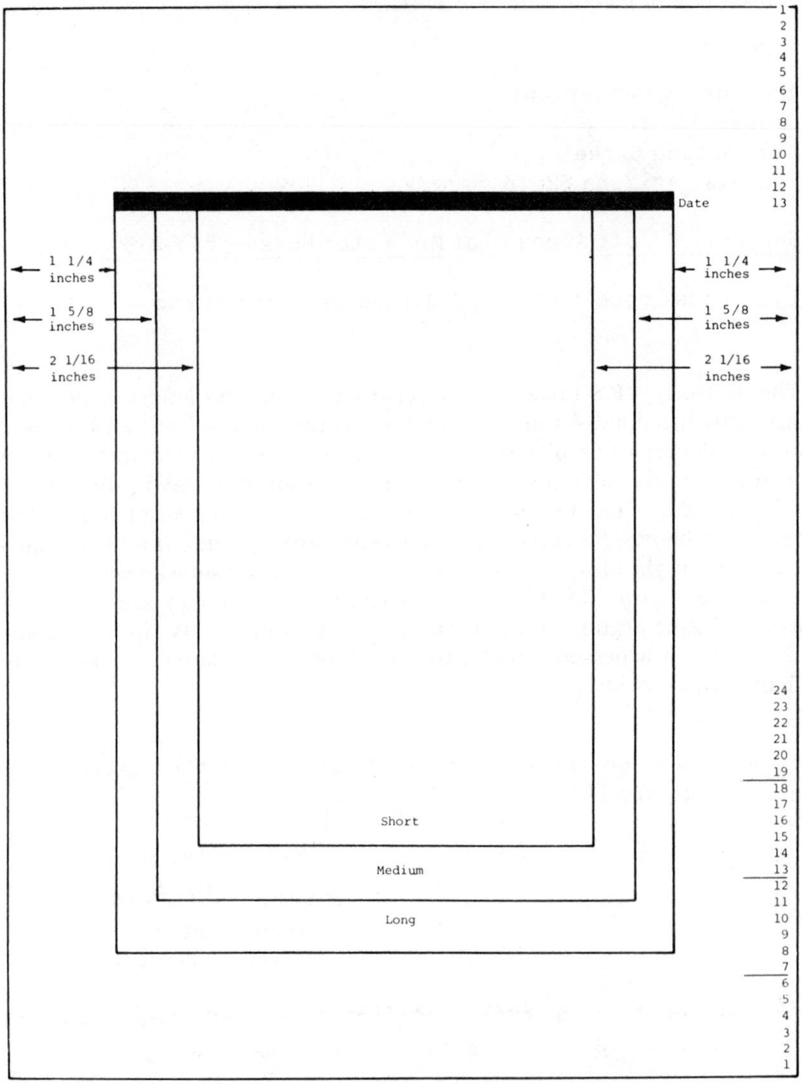

without too many breaks in multisyllabled words. (A recent innovation in electric typewriters allows for completely uniform right-hand margins — "justified" margins. Many typewriters, however, lack this capability.) The amount of white space at the top and bottom of the letter should be in proportion to the vertical margins, creating a "picture frame" effect — as shown in the layout guide in Figure 10.

The Envelope We cannot ignore the envelope that carries the business letter to its destination. A well-designed, well-typed business envelope should look like those in Figure 11. The recipient's address, identical to the inside address, is centered on the front side of the envelope. The return address is usually located in the upper left-hand corner, though some companies use the glue flap on the other side. Most companies imprint their names and addresses attractively, not only for the benefit of the post office in case of return, but also to make a handsome first impression on the recipient. Attention lines are repeated on the face of the envelope, usually in the position shown in Figure 11.

Figure 11
Well-designed business envelopes.

FIRST FEDERAL SAVINGS
1020 Plaza Drive
Mountain View, Ca. 94040

Attention: Peter Bishop

Carson Industrial League
1717 Novotny Way
Neander, Idaho 87102

Severin Security Corporation
200 Post Street
Willow, N. Y. 10026

Confidential

Mr. Bruce L. Lee, Manager
Acme Tool Company
101 Memorial Drive
Santa Susanna, CA. 94403

Type-of-mail notations (such as *Special Delivery, Certified,* or *Registered Mail*) are usually placed about a half-inch below the stamp — as shown here:

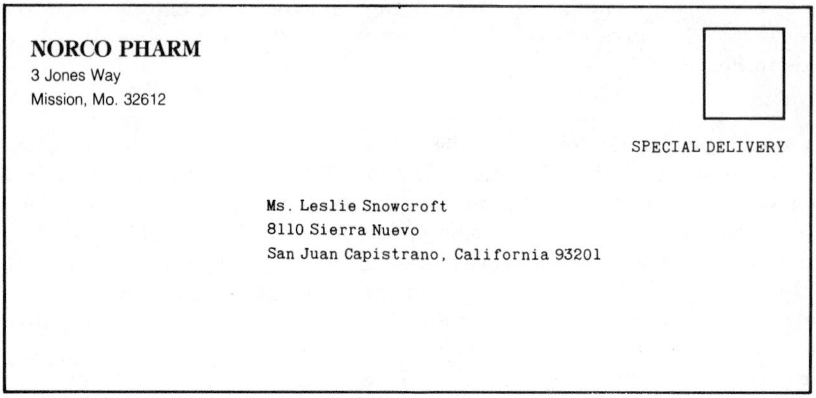

There is only one correct place for the stamp — the upper right-hand corner. Most large organizations use metered postage as an expedient, but for that very reason there is something impersonal about it. When you do use a stamp, get it on straight. And if a letter must be especially impressive, make sure there is nothing out of date about its stamp — as there is when a Christmas commemorative is used on a letter in February.

People react even to the way a letter is folded — so fold carefully. For insertion into a regular business envelope, the $8\frac{1}{2} \times 11$ letter is folded horizontally, almost into thirds, its typed side inward:

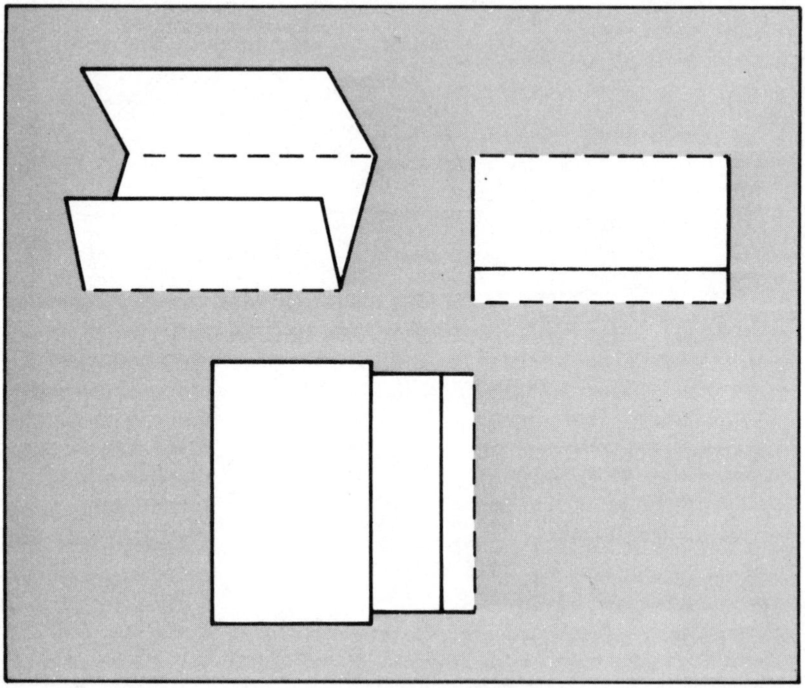

For a smaller envelope, the same letter is folded horizontally in half, then vertically into near-thirds, and inserted in the same way.

THE FORMAT OF A MEMORANDUM

The format of a memorandum is quite different from that of a letter, because it's a format designed to serve a different purpose — communication *within* an organization.

As a company's stationery bears a letterhead, so its memo stationery bears a "memo-head," a briefer imprint consisting simply of the company name and the designation *Memorandum* (or *Interoffice Communication*), as in Figure 12.

Figure 12
A sample business memorandum.

CONTINENTAL MANUFACTURING COMPANY
MEMORANDUM

To: Teresa Wright
cc: Ben Siegel
Patricia Newman
Angela Millel

Date: March 21, 19--

File No: 0010

From: Walter Wells

Subject: A Word About Memorandum Format

Memos can serve either an expository or a reaction-evoking function. They can be long or short as need demands; but they must be clear, have an appropriate character, and be as impressive in format as any letter.

Memo format is, of course, more tightly determined by its imprinted memo-head, as at the top of this memo. Memo-heads come with minor variations, but this one is typical. Sometimes the From and To lines are positioned more closely together, and the "distribution" indicator is placed after the body of the memo rather than before it. But in its essentials, this model is as good as any.

As with your letters, you will be measured to a great extent by the memos you write. So be sure to write them neatly, and write them well.

ms

Instead of an inside address, a salutation, and a signature block, the memo format employs a *To* line and a *From* line to identify its recipient and its writer. Within a company's walls there is no need for addresses, and the character-creating functions of the salutation and complimentary close are not considered necessary. (This does not mean, however, that character is unimportant in a memorandum.) A distribution indicator is used to indicate who receives copies of the memo; sometimes it appears at the end, as in a letter; at other times (as in Figure 12) it appears immediately beneath the *To* line. Its placement is usually a matter of company policy. The *date* line, at upper right, speaks for itself; it's useful (and sometimes vital) to know when any communication was written. The *file number* line helps simplify filing. A *subject* line, though not often used in business letters, always appears in a memo head. It's not easy to write precise subject lines, but the necessary pains should be taken; vague titles are irritating to the hurried businessperson who wants to know immediately what the message is about.

Like letters, memos are written on several sizes of stationery — full size ($8^1/_2 \times 11$ inches) for memos of several paragraphs or several pages, half size ($5^1/_2 \times 8^1/_2$) for brief notes. Pages beyond the first in a multi-paged memo are typed on plain bond paper and carry the same kind of "page 2" heading that letters do.

PROBLEMS

1. Using correct form, type the following headings for letters to be written on stationery without a letterhead:

a. Your own home address and the current date.
b. 5348 213 st bayside new york 11364 july fourth 19_
c. june 23 19_ 890 waverly road clinton mississippi 24663.
d. 12 feb 19_ costa mesa california 6274½ vallejo road zip 91832
e. 8/11/8_ 4317 D st n.e. wash 20017 dc.

2. For each of the following inside addresses, write the appropriate salutation:

a. Dr. John Holloway, Director
The Institute of Graphic Design
400 La Salle Boulevard
Chicago, Illinois 42901

b. The Retlaw Company
9817 Kemptown Road
Flushing, New York 11350
Attention: Mr. Banks

c. Mr. and Mrs. Carl Bewley
12 Oak Knoll Drive
Chester, Pennsylvania 26321

d. Box D9302, The Times
Los Angeles, California 90017

e. E. T. Driver
Customer Relations
AfroNational Bank
1000 Fifth Avenue
New York, N.Y. 10028

f. Daughters of the American Revolution
7200 Avenue L (Suite 400)
Washington, D.C. 20004

3. Companies spend a lot of money creating modern and attractive letterheads. In a memo to your instructor, write a relative evaluation of the following five letterheads:

a. The Armstrong Cork letterhead on page 280.
b. The Industrial Motivation letterhead on page 304.
c. The Trane Company letterhead on page 272.
d. The *Western Horseman* letterhead on page 278.

4. After giving some solid thought to the problem, write a letter to your instructor stating whether you think salutations and complimentary closes serve useful functions in business letters. Remember, this letter should clearly present your opinions, and its tone should be appropriate to the student-teacher relationship.

Address your letter properly, using your instructor's correct title and exact school address. If this takes a little research, it's just the kind of research that professional business correspondents do every day.

5. In a well-written memo to your instructor, discuss the differences in tone among the following complimentary closes:

```
Very truly yours                Best wishes
Cordially yours                 Respectfully yours
                     Sincerely
```

6. Obtain copies of three business letters sent out by three different companies. Make a comparative analysis and evaluation of their formats, concluding with your opinion on which letter is the most attractive. Your analysis should not be wordy; but neither should it be superficial. After writing a rough draft of your analysis, transcribe it into a well-written memorandum to your instructor. Attach the three letters to your memo.

7. Let's assume that after you successfully complete your course in business communications you become the office manager of Hastings-Arrow, Inc. Before you took this position, letters sent out on company stationery maintained no particular format. But to your way of thinking, consistency in business letter format is one important way of building a company image. As the new office manager, write a memorandum directed to all of Hastings-Arrow's secretaries and stenographers, establishing a consistent format for all company letters. Tell them which format to use (making sure they understand what you mean). And, because you don't believe in sounding arbitrary, tell them *why* as well.

Your memorandum will obviously be a reaction-evoking communication. Not only do you want to inform the secretarial staff of a new policy, but you want enthusiastic compliance from them.

Don't forget to "have a copy of the memo go to" Clyde Harris, Hastings-Arrow's executive vice-president.

8. One of your company's salesmen, John Fuller, asked a temporary stenographer to write, and prepare for mailing, a letter he was anxious to get out. The stenographer did, and what a mess! It appears below, containing more than twenty errors in format and mechanics.

First, fire the temporary steno. Then proofread the letter carefully for mistakes in spelling, grammar, punctuation, and format. Finally, rewrite the letter for Fuller, eliminating all the errors you've found.

May 12th '81

The Eastside Corpor.
120 Park Avenue
San Francisco, 95462 Calif.

Attention, (Mr.) Morris Murphy,

My Dear Mr. Murphy;

We wish to extend our congradulations to you on you're recent promotion into the Vice presidency of one of the most sucessful and most friendliest ~~business~~ concerns with who we do business. Knowing what a honor this is for you, the news of it was received with great pleasure by our staff.

Respectively Yours . . .

Mr. John Fuller
Sales Representive

9. On your new job as assistant to the comptroller at the Delta Water Company (1250 Fogcutter Avenue, Eastport, Maine), you receive the note on page 145 from your boss, Comptroller Walt Ridgeway.

Prepare the three announcements for mailing. Select the format you think looks best, and the forms of address and salutation you feel most appropriate.

10. Only fifteen years ago, all letters addressed to organizations (rather than to an individual) bore the salutation *Gentlemen.* Any woman whose marital status wasn't evident was addressed as *Miss,* and women-correspondents were expected to indicate their marital status in the signature block. A married woman was always addressed by her husband's first name rather than her own (e.g. *Mrs. William T. Perkins* rather than *Mrs. Patricia Perkins* or *Ms. Patricia Perkins).* Things have changed, however. (The chapter you've just read has tried very hard to stay current with the changes.)

Reflect upon your own feelings about these changes, and upon anyone else's that you're aware of regarding how women are addressed and saluted in business letters. In a carefully written memo to your instructor (remember, he or she will have opinions on the matter too) discuss your feelings about these changes, the need for them (or otherwise), and your own inclination to do things the old way or the new.

Just realized my secretary forgot to send out 3 last announcement letters to our upcoming stockholder's convention. She's at home with a cold so would you please get them for me. They should read as follows - We are glad to announce that Delta's 20th Anniversary Stockholder's Convention will be held on Sat., May 15, at the Shore Country Club in Eastport.

Send them to Peter Quince (M.D.) 316 Grayrock Drive, Eastport; 9th National Reserve Bank (make that attention Miss Kay Brooks) 33 Lake Blvd., Lakehurst, N.J.; and President Salvatore Deems of Keystone Products, Inc., 4 Scotchmoor Ave., Phila. Pa. (zip # 20401).

Better send the last two air mail.

Thanks —

WR

CHAPTER 7

TONE: THE WAY WE SOUND ON PAPER

COURTESY
The Courtesy Balance
The Courtesy Blunders
SINCERITY
The Importance of Sincerity
The Causes of Insincerity
POSITIVITY
Neutrality and Unnecessary Conditionality
The Vital Principle of the "Positive Sandwich"

Never forget that the recipients of your business letters and memos are human beings, prey to all the feelings, whims and foibles of human nature, no matter how humble or exalted their positions. They will react not only to what you say, and to your fluency, but to the *tone* of what you've written — the attitude they sense in that voice on the page.

People will always respond better when they feel they matter to you. Your tone should convey that feeling. They will react adversely to apparent indifference or insult. Your tone must never, even accidentally, fall into these traps. On the contrary, your tone must make readers feel that you value their interests and their points of view, that you respect their time and their abilities, that you know the full worth of their cooperation or their patronage.

Your tone, then, like everything else in the letter or memo, must be oriented toward your reader — it must be empathetic. If that tone is to do its job in helping evoke the desired reactions, it must be *courteous,* it must be *sincere,* and it must be *positive.*

COURTESY

Courtesy is something we learn to recognize and to display in our dealings with other people early in life. As children, we learn to say "please" when asking for something, and "thank you" when it's granted. Most of us are taught to respond quickly, fully, and graciously when something is asked of us. And we learn to show respect to people when we address them. All in all, courtesy is one of those things that become second nature to us by the time we reach maturity.

But most people get little experience at showing courtesy in their writing. They grow up feeling that written language is something apart from everyday speech. They think it's more formal than speech, and are much less at home with it. The courtesy they show so naturally in their day-to-day encounters does not pervade their writing. Letters to friends are usually inadequate indicators of the warmth of a friendship. Fortunately, friends don't mind because they're fond of the writer (and because their own letters are usually just as bad).

But a person in business writes to people who do *not* overlook the lack of courtesy. Discourteous tone in writing (though unintended) has ruined many a business relationship.

The Courtesy Balance

Courtesy in writing is more than just a well-timed "please" or "thank you." Courtesy results from a balance between *cordiality* and *tact:* cordiality being the warmth and friendliness you show toward your reader, tact, the sensitivity and discretion. When writing a letter or a memo, you should carefully measure your relationship to your reader; then make sure that your communication strikes the balance between cordiality and tact appropriate to that relationship. The tone of a memo to a fellow employee will differ from the tone of a memo to the company president. But if both those memos are to succeed, they must achieve the balance that makes for courtesy.

Any one of a number of blunders can disrupt the courtesy balance and ruin your communication. And most of these blunders are accidental. Writers don't realize most of their discourtesies. Simply becoming *aware* of the pitfalls should help you avoid them.

The Courtesy Blunders

Courtesy is destroyed in business letters if your readers feel that you are curt, sarcastic, peevish, angry, or suspicious of their motives. Your chances of favorable reaction are also ruined if they feel you've insulted them, accused them of something, talked down to them, or been overly familiar or presumptuous toward them. The catalog of courtesy blunders is numerous; let's briefly survey them.

Curtness *Curtness* results from inordinate brevity, brevity that's uncalled-for, brevity that implies to a reader that you don't care very much about his ideas or predicament. Curtness is being *too brief* for the situation. Certainly you shouldn't waste your reader's time by saying more than necessary. But neither should you be so brief as to imply a lack of concern. It *is* necessary to avoid that feeling. Curtness can result either from carelessness, or from attempting too strenuously to be concise. In either case, its effect on the reader is that of an ice cold shoulder.

For instance, how do you think Mrs. Clemens felt after she wrote a long and detailed letter to the Tru-Val Company expressing her approval of its recently introduced product — and received this reply?

```
Dear Mrs. Clemens:

Thank you for your recent letter. We always appreciate
hearing from our customers.
                                  Yours truly,
                                  The Tru-Val Company
```

The writer did not mean to offend Mrs. Clemens. But he did — by being too brief. His letter was curt. Her effort in writing her long letter — no matter what its recipient thought of it — deserved a more substantial reply.

Sarcasm Seldom is a letter or memo helped by *sarcasm,* that special kind of wit which, by saying the opposite of what is meant, is used to ridicule. Sometimes a writer will be sarcastic to give vent to ill feeling; at other times, just to make a point with emphasis. But most people dislike being on the receiving end of sarcasm, and they respond poorly to it.

Consider, for example, the following memorandum written by a department store supervisor to his staff of twenty-five saleswomen. He wanted to tell them emphatically that they had fallen short of their sales quota, and he wanted to chide them into stronger effort. So he wrote:

> Congratulations, ladies. I'm proud to announce that, as a result of your sterling and tireless efforts last month, we fell only $1,700 short of our sales quota. Be sure to pick up your trophies on the way out this evening.
>
> J. P. Gallagher

Instead of motivating the sales staff to increased effort, the memo raised tempers and created resistance to working any harder for "that creep Gallagher." In short, the memo failed because of its sarcasm.

Peevishness Another courtesy blunder that has ruined many a business letter is that tone of petty irritation we call *peevishness.* Nobody likes whining, even if the whining is typed on a piece of paper. Here's a case in point taken from an interoffice memo. Imagine the reaction it got from its recipient:

> How do you expect the steno pool to do its job correctly if you don't fill out Form 211F in triplicate like you're supposed to? You ought to know better!

The peevish tone is certainly no inducement to enthusiastic compliance by the reader.

Anger If peevishness sounds like whining in a business letter, anger sounds like a roar. And there are very few people who, when roared at, don't roar back — even if they have to roar under their breaths.

Here's part of a letter written by an irate customer to an auto mechanic shop. What do you think the response was?

> As mechanics you guys are genuine butchers. I'm bringing my 280Z back in on Tuesday. This time, kindly expel the carbon monoxide from between your ears — and fix that damn carburetor!

The writer was probably justified in his complaint, but the letter's angry tone is just as likely to result in a "four-letter" brush-off as in compliance.

No one can tell you not to get angry. Those situations do arise in business. But when you're angry, leave your pen on the desk and the dictaphone off. The only thing evoked by communicated anger is reciprocal anger, and if that's your only objective in a letter, you don't need a textbook to tell you how to write it.

Suspicion Whether you mean to or not, you can make yourself seem suspicious of your reader's motives by using phrases like "If, as you state . . . " and "If what you say is true. . . . " These phrases could be uttered harmlessly and inoffensively in a face-to-face conversation. But in a letter or a memo, where your vocal inflections and facial expressions are left to the reader's inference, such phrases can make it seem as though you doubt his integrity — not a very good way to evoke a favorable reaction.

Suppose you received a letter which said, in part,

> If the mixer was defective at the time of purchase, as you allege, we will definitely replace it with a new one. We do think it strange, however, that you waited so long to inform us because. . . .

The writer is doing what you want — replacing your mixer. But how stupidly he announces it! Instead of your feeling satisfied (which, after all, should be the writer's major objective), you would resent the letter, the writer, and the company — all because of the ridiculous tone of suspicion. It destroys the letter.

Insult Intentional insult is rare in business letters. When it occurs, it obviously destroys any chance the writer might have of evoking a desired reaction. Frequently, however, writers insult their readers accidentally. The most common cause of accidental insult is the *unflattering implication,* the statement that unintentionally demeans the reader.

Consider, for example, this excerpt from a product promotion letter mailed to office managers:

> All wise office managers around the country order LightNing — the quickest yet mildest of all industrial detergents.

The businesswoman who wrote this wanted to persuade her readers to purchase LightNing, but instead she insulted many of them by implying that their wisdom was in question.

And consider this sentence from a letter turning down an applicant for a summer job:

> Without Senior Red Cross certification, you are not qualified to be a lifeguard.

Technically, the writer is correct about the applicant's qualifications. But in this context, the word *qualified* has broader connotations. The sentence can be read as an insult to the applicant's ability. (You can easily avoid the implied insult in this case by writing "Regulations require that all our lifeguards have Senior Red Cross qualification.")

Even less obvious to the well-meaning writer, but equally unflattering to the reader, is the implication of this sentence from a job rejection letter:

> We have received so many applications from excellent candidates that we are unable to consider yours.

It might as well call the applicant "incompetent."

Accusation Another way to destroy courtesy is to point an accusing finger at your reader. Even if the reader *has* done something wrong, it's not your job to reprimand or even remind him of that wrongdoing — particularly if, at the same time, you wish to evoke a favorable reaction. Even the mildest accusation or reprimand may provoke the reader's irritation. And you're certain to offend with any remark as accusing as this one:

> You obviously ignored our request that you return the report by messenger.

The same idea would be much more courteously and effectively written:

> We did request that you return the report by messenger.

Even worse is the finger of accusation when no one really is at fault. Recall the letter written by the Fitwell Uniform Company to Fred Fox back on page 115. Its writer might have said to Fox: "you forgot to include the sleeve sizes" or "you neglected to include the sleeve sizes." But there was no reason whatsoever to imply that Fox was at fault, even mildly at fault. All that mattered was that the Fitwell Company didn't know the desired sleeve sizes, and needed them to fill the order.

Any time you find yourself using phrases like *you neglected, you omitted, you forgot to,* or *if you'd done it differently,* you risk offending your reader with a tone of accusation.

Talking down No one likes to feel talked down to. Yet some executives, administrators, and correspondents build an irritating tone of superiority into their memos and letters. The tone of condescension — of "talking down" — is usually unintentional, but its effects are nonetheless destructive.

This foolish and discourteous tone of superiority is evident in the phrasing used by a department store manager in a letter to a customer:

> In an establishment as large as ours, Mrs. Harris, we seldom have cause to . . .

A tone of pretentious superiority is also evident in the following extract from a letter written by a senator's assistant to a constituent.

When you receive as much correspondence as Senator Dilworthy does every day, it is of vital importance that . . .

In both cases, the recipient's reaction will probably be "Now who's he trying to impress?" Even a common remark:

Please do not hesitate to call upon us whenever we may be of service . . .

can sound pretentious because, to some, it suggests that the writer is so puffed up with self-importance that he or she feels others *would* hesitate to call. No matter what the rest of the letter has to say, such a self-aggrandizing tone often destines the communication for the nearest wastebasket.

Equally offensive is the out-and-out braggart, like the promotion writer who writes:

Our dictionary costs more than competing ones because it's worth more than competing ones . . .

or the job applicant who writes:

I possess a distinguished record.

How much more appealing the same remarks are, if only slightly modified:

Our dictionary costs more than competing ones because we honestly believe it offers more than competing ones.

I possess what my present supervisor has called a distinguished record.

You also seem to talk down to your reader when you sound like you're *instructing* or *teaching*. It's always best to avoid this *didactic* tone. The writers of the following two sentences did not:

It will soon be time to renew your credit privileges. You'll be needing them in the summer months ahead.

The best way for you to increase your turnover would be to use point-of-purchase displays.

There are times when instruction must be given, but you've got to be circumspect in giving it. The two sentences above would have been much more effectively written as follows:

Just a reminder, with summer on its way, that your Margate Credit Card is soon due for renewal.

Problems of turnover similar to yours have been solved in the past by the increased use of point-of-purchase displays.

Be careful, too, to avoid the tone of *paternalism* that crept into the following sentences in a letter from a personnel director, to a job candidate:

> You must realize that you are starting a very important phase of your career. . . . We know you will make this decision wisely.

The tone, though well-intended, is condescending and unbusinesslike.

Some readers are even offended when a writer — with no didactic or paternal trace in his tone — informs them of things they already know. "Does this writer think I'm a dope or something?" is a typical oversensitive reaction. Clever writers, when they suspect their readers *might* already know a key fact, but *aren't sure,* often preface their assertions with the phrases:

> You will recall that . . .
> As you already know, . . .
> As you're probably well aware, . . .

Finally, to avoid talking down to your readers, avoid using sentence openers like "You may call me at . . ." or "We shall allow you to . . ." These ideas are much better when phrased "Please call me at . . ." or "We will be glad to . . ."

Overfamiliarity Recent years have seen a trend toward less formality in business letters. No longer do most business people write the stuffy letters of days gone by. But some writers make the mistake of becoming *too* friendly and familiar. Instead of building rapport, they offend their readers.

As a general rule, don't refer to anything the reader might consider personal or embarrassing. And don't let your diction become more informal than it should be.

One other sure way of creating an offensive overfamiliarity is to use your reader's name repeatedly throughout a communication. Some writers have this habit, mistakenly feeling that the way to readers' hearts is through their names. They write communications that sound like this:

> Dear Mr. Lowe:
>
> I am happy to have had the chance to serve you and your family. You see, Mr. Lowe, we here at Updike's have been in business for seventy-eight years. No company stays in business that long without learning how to serve its customers well.
>
> As you and your wife know, Mr. Lowe, the value that . . .

This technique of calling your reader by name somewhere in the letter can be helpful in creating rapport, but only if used very sparingly — no more than once in a lengthy letter or memo.

Presumption Most people are offended by a writer who openly *presumes* they will do something before they've made up their minds to do it. The presumptuous tone usually backfires. Consider the reactions probably evoked by the following memo (sent to employees of the Harmon Company by the corporate comptroller):

> The Comptroller's Office is proud to announce the introduction of a new Harmon stock-option plan. The plan will be made available to all employees beginning on July 1. The small additional deduction from your weekly paycheck will provide you with . . .

and on it went, describing the benefits of the new stock-option plan. But, the tone of the third sentence — "The . . . deduction . . . *will* provide" — made the employee feel his mind had been made up for him. The tone was sufficiently presumptuous to turn some employees against the plan.

Presumptuous too is any statement, like the following, that ascribes a preference to its reader, a preference the reader may not have:

> You would of course rather serve your guests with fine silver and crystal. . . .

Similarly presumptuous are some letters of job offer. They irritate their readers by sounding too sure the offer will be accepted.

Even the common ploy of thanking someone in advance for something annoys many readers.

A confident attitude won't hurt a business letter, but a presumptuous one — one that sounds more confident than it should — will hardly ever help.

SINCERITY

"Faked feelings!" said one writer years ago, "The world is all gummy with them." And things haven't changed much. Because some areas of the business world are so "gummed up" with fakery, a sense of sincerity has become a vital requirement for the effective communicator.

The Importance of Sincerity

The courteous attitude we've been discussing is one of the greatest assets your writing can have — but only if it is believed. A person reading your letter must feel that your courtesy is sincere, not just a tool for self-gain like the artificial smiles we see every day on the faces of so many business people. Not only your message, but its tone as well, must strike your reader as genuine. If it doesn't, the message will fail.

The Causes of Insincerity

To *sound* sincere in a communication, it helps to *be* sincere when you write it. Insincerity very quickly shows through. As in our quest for courtesy, however, there are blunders that can — quite by accident — make even the most sincere writer sound like a gold-plated phony.

Overhumility A little humility is appropriate in certain kinds of business messages: those you write to company superiors, prospective employers, people in positions of respect. But if your attitude is *overly* humble, you risk sounding insincere. People do not respect — more often they don't believe —the attitude of a letter that virtually drips with humility, like this one:

> Gentlemen:
>
> Our most sincere apologies for the foolish error we made in handling your last order. Our distribution coordinator, our driver, and myself, all wish to say we're extremely sorry.
>
> We are so very thankful, too, for the renewed opportunity your good company is giving us to serve your needs. We shall continue trying, to the limits of our ability, to justify your faith in our efforts.
>
> Obediently yours,
>
> *Richard Riverspill*
>
> Richard Riverspill

There's nothing wrong with an apology if it's warranted, nor with a compliment if it's justified. But Riverspill overdoes both, and downgrades his company in the process. His expressed humility overshoots the mark. His tone is obsequious. Could he possibly mean it?

Obvious flattery Flattery, like humility, can occasionally help the effectiveness of a business letter. But most readers are wary of the writer whose flattery is obvious:

> Only you, Mrs. Owen, can handle this difficult assignment for us . . .

or

> We ask your advice, Dr. Jacobs, because of your widely acknowledged reputation in this field.

Assertions like these are so obviously intended to flatter that they cast doubts on the writer's sincerity.

If you feel you *should* flatter, use *implied flattery* — the kind of flattery inherent in statements like:

> As you have often said. . . .

> We thought we should come to you in this matter because. . . .

Exaggeration Exaggeration is usually easy to detect, and very easy to dislike. Television commercials that tell a housewife how much she'll enjoy her washdays after switching to Super Sudzo are guilty of obvious exaggeration. Hardly anyone takes them seriously.

Control any tendency you have to use words like *sensational, amazing, unique, fantastic, revolutionary,* or any of the overworked intensifiers that we discussed back on page 57. And unless you're providing hard evidence, avoid making extraordinary statements. Even if true, they're difficult to believe, and they create a tone of exaggeration that makes many readers doubt your sincerity.

Consider the following excerpt from the *Jet Setters Newsletter.* It was intended to stimulate patronage of the nationwide chain of posh Jet Setter Clubs. But its tone is so obviously exaggerated (even by "Jet Set" standards) that it more likely evoked a "ho hum" from most of its readers:

> The club is your castle -- even miles from home. So take your new Jet Setters Key along whenever you roam -- include Jet Setter Clubs in your planning. Then the fun's even finer!
>
> Top talent appears in all the Club showrooms. And you'll find the fabulous food, the man-sized ounce-and-a-half drinks, the beautiful Stewies, the super service and our famed atmosphere of conviviality and comfort wherever you go.
>
> Heading sunward? Head funward. The posh New Orleans Club welcomes you in the heart of that city's historic French Quarter where the Mardi Gras spirit prevails year-round. In Phoenix, play in a penthouse for top-level times. California boasts two Clubs -- one in Los Angeles, a veritable Disneyland for adults, and the other in the elegant Bay City of San Francisco.
>
> Or try our mile-high-plus Club in Denver. Everything about it's new and now -- the Living Room's stainless steel dance floor is the smoothest ever and Disco Stewies spin the big beat in tune with an electric light show.
>
> Chicago, home of the Jet Setter Clubs, began it all . . . stop by on your way to the magnificent new $30,000,000 Jet Setter Hotel, just 90 minutes down the road in Lake Au Claire, Wis., a 365-day-a-year paradise for sports!
>
> Travelers east often enjoy the Detroit Club, in the heart of the city's fine dining district. And Jet Setter in New York is the world's most lavish and successful club!

Who's kidding whom?

POSITIVITY

The third dimension of tone in a business letter is the letter's outlook on its subject. Effective letters and memos usually possess the quality of *positivity.* This quality is called "positive statement" by some, and by others "positive thinking put into words." Still others refer to it as "looking at the bright side of things."

Whatever its definition, positivity is the knack of *presenting an idea in its most positive and most favorable light.* Achieving positivity in a business message is similar to what photographers achieve when they select the correct angle and the best exposure for a picture. In no way do they alter the nature of the subject. They simply make sure they capture the most favorable view of that subject, the view that will be best appreciated — and best responded to.

Here are some examples of how the skilled business writer achieves positivity in communications:

Instead of writing . . .	*With "positivity" the skilled writer will write . . .*
Because of recent heavy demand, we will not be able to deliver your goods before August 12.	Although recent demand has been heavy, we will be able to deliver your goods by August 20.
Your order will be filled without further delay.	Your order will be filled immediately (or right away).
The only work experience I have is two summers as a camp counselor.	I have had supervisory responsibility as a camp counselor for two full summers.
You will never regret purchasing this fine reference book.	You will always be grateful that you own this fine reference book.
This unfortunate incident will not recur.	Future transactions will be serviced with the utmost care.
The barrel is half-empty.	The barrel is half-full.
We do not have any black convertibles in stock.	At present, we have (only) one blue, one gray, and two green convertibles in stock.[1]
We are withholding your shipment until we receive payment.	We will forward your order to you as soon as payment is received.[2]
We can no longer change the name on your policy because you've allowed it to lapse.	We will be happy to change the name on your policy as soon as it's put back into force.[3]
This medicine is not dangerous for children.	This medicine is absolutely safe for children.

[1] Not only is this construction more positive than the one at left, its bad news is softened even further by the opening "At present." Consider also the word *only*; it may or may not be necessary here — to protect the writer's tone of sincerity; but if it isn't, it can just as well be omitted to maximize the sentence's positivity.

[2] A style note: Notice that this sentence could have read "We will forward your order to you as soon as we receive payment." But the writer wanted to get the word *payment* out of the emphatic end position, so he used the passive construction "payment is received."

[3] A style note: Notice that, once again, a passive construction ("as soon as it's put back in force") is used instead of the active ("as soon as *we* put . . ."). Here the passive construction avoids explicitly placing the burden of the action onto the writer's company.

We will sponsor a golf tournament for you, to be limited to 100 guests.	We will sponsor a golf tournament for you for up to a hundred guests.
At Standard Investments, Inc., we free you from having to make decisions on market data you don't understand.	At Standard Investments, Inc., we free you from having to make decisions on market data with which you may not be familiar. *or* . . . on market data that may be foreign to your background.
WARNING: Section 333B of the State Penal Code makes it a felony to present a false or fraudulent claim to an insurer.	For your protection, the State asks us to point out that Section 333B of the Penal Code makes it a felony to present a false or fraudulent claim to an insurer.

The sentences at the right carry the same information as those at the left, and they carry it with equal clarity. The only difference is in perspective. The ones at right have been phrased as positively as possible.

Remember these four basic rules for achieving positive tone in your business letters:

1. Make sure that you stress what things *are,* what they *have,* or what they *will be,* rather than what they aren't, what they lack, or what they won't be. And stress what you *have* done, what you *can* do, or what you *will* do, rather than what you haven't done, can't do, or won't do.

2. Avoid using words with negative connotations. Even though statements like:

```
I'm sorry we blundered on your order . . .
```

or

```
We regret the inconvenience you've been caused by the broken
mixer . . .
```

are intended to be positive expressions of apology, their highly negative wording — *blundered, regret, inconvenience, broken* — is vivid reminder of the unfortunate situations underlying those apologies. Such statements have a *negative reminder value.* The two sentences above would be much more effectively written as follows:

```
I want to apologize for the order we delivered.

We're truly sorry about the experience you had with your
Keithman mixer.[4]
```

Always avoid a *negative reminder value.*

3. Be aware of any negative implications that may be read into something you write, no matter how positively you think you've phrased it. When a district sales manager told his executive vice president in an intercity memo:

[4] Notice the euphemistic quality of the word *experience* in this sentence.

Sales out here are suddenly starting to perk up, for some unaccountable reason.

he was not only giving the good news, but implying his own inability to analyze the existing market — not a very good image to project to the boss back in the home office. And when a customer-relations officer writes a sentence like this: "So that we may better serve you in the future . . . ," the reader will get the clear impression that past service has been less than perfect.

4. Finally, your quest for positivity will be affected, strongly, by your frame of mind when writing the communication. If you have to write to someone, don't resent that necessity as another burden upon your time. Welcome it as an opportunity to establish or enhance a positive relationship between you and your reader.

A word should be said here about positivity in *government correspondence* — or the usual lack of it. Many people — once they go to work for local, state or federal government offices — seem to assume that, with the law behind them, their tone doesn't matter. When, for example, the Federal Trade Commission mails a routine form-letter to mail-order houses that says, in part: "In order to avert possible action by the FTC, you should immediately insure that you are not engaged in any of the practices proscribed" — the tone is insulting! Most business owners resent the implication that they may be out to cheat consumers, and they come to view the government antagonistically. (If you doubt the cumulative effect of such messages, ask ten or twenty business owners what they think of government regulation.) Ironically, much of the problem results from simply insensitive and authoritarian tone in communications — a problem easily avoided with a little care.

Neutrality and Unnecessary Conditionality

Although the most obvious violations of positivity are a negative attitude and negative wording, there are other ways in which to fall short of positivity. If you write from a *neutral* perspective, or from an *unnecessarily conditional* one, you will also lose the advantage of positive statement.

The following pairs of sentences will illustrate the relative weakness of a neutral attitude:

Neutral wording	*Positive wording*
We have received your letter of February 18.	We thank you for your letter of February 18. *or* We were glad to receive your letter of February 18.
Your car can be picked up on Thursday at noon.	Your car will be waiting for you on Thursday at noon.[5]
We are sending the charts to you by Air Express.	We are rushing the charts to you by Air Express.
Call me in the evening between 8 and 10.	I'd be glad to have you call any evening between 8 and 10.

[5] A style note: Notice the figurative language here. The writer not only writes more positively, but enhances the style by treating the car as though it had a personality.

I hereby appoint you . . .	I take great pleasure in appointing you . . .

The neutrally phrased sentences at left are not seriously flawed. They are just less effective than the positive ones at right.

The following pairs of sentences should illustrate the relative weakness of an unnecessarily conditional attitude:

Conditional wording	*Positive wording*
If you will submit your bid right away, you will be able to . . .	By submitting your bid right away, you will be able to . . .
If your references prove satisfactory, we shall . . .	As soon as your references are checked, we shall gladly. . . .
If you would like us to send you a sample . . .	We would be happy to send you a sample . . .
Should you wish to make a statement concerning . . .	We will appreciate any comment you'd like to make . . .
We hope you find this adjustment satisfactory.	We are glad to offer you this adjustment.
It appears that Walker may be the man we need.	Walker may be the man we need. *or* Walker appears to be the man we need.

In the first three sentences at left, the word *if* gives the assertion its conditionality ("If you will submit your bid . . . ," "If your references prove satisfactory . . . ," "If you would like us to . . . "). What they each imply, unnecessarily, is that the reader *might not* submit a bid, that his references *might not* prove satisfactory, that he or she *might not* want the writer to send a sample. The revisions on the right show the same ideas expressed without implying these negative possibilities.

In the fourth sentence, the revision at right shifts the focus from the possible to the positive — from the possible desire of the reader to make a statement, to the positive appreciation that any such statement would meet.

In the fifth sentence, the word *hope* suggests that the reader *might not* find the adjustment satisfactory. Why let the power of suggestion work against you when (as the revision at right clearly shows) the tone of conditionality can be eliminated?

And in the sixth sentence, it is multiple hedging that causes unnecessary conditionality. (Recall our discussion on page 45 of multiple hedging as a cause of wordiness). The writer apparently feels it is necessary to hedge. But once is enough, as demonstrated by revisions at the right. Two phrases implying possibility (*It appears* and *may be*) create too much conditionality.

Remember this. You cannot always avoid conditionality. The words *hope* and *if* cannot be eliminated from your business vocabulary. Sometimes you need them. Nor can you always dispense with hedging. There are times when a conditional tone is necessary to avoid sounding presumptuous. (Rather than writing "Please give us the names of friends who would benefit from our service," you'd probably want a more conditional phrasing like "We'd appreciate knowing about any friends who *might* be interested in our service.") All too often, however, the words and phrases of conditionality are used unnecessarily. When they are, they cost a letter its positivity and weaken its chances of getting the reaction you want.

The Vital Principle of the "Positive Sandwich"

In studies of people's reactions to communications, psychologists have recognized an interesting pattern. Communicators, regardless of whether they're speaking or writing, usually make the strongest impressions on their audiences with what they say at the *beginning* of their message, and what they say at the *end*. Not that people forget what's said in the middle — they don't. But what comes in the middle of a message doesn't make as strong an impression as what comes first and last.

Clever writers and speakers, especially those who seek specific reactions, put this principle to work in their communications. Because the success of your letter or memo depends, in large part, on the reader's favorable disposition toward the message and toward you, you should use these positions of maximum impression to help create that favorable disposition. You should create a "positive sandwich."

Give your reader a "positive sandwich."

No matter what the basic content of your message, put that message between two slices of positive attitude. Begin with a tone as positive as the situation will allow, and end the same way. Obviously, some messages are more difficult than others to open and close congenially (for instance, letters that make a complaint or those that try to collect money). But to the extent that it's possible to construct a positive opening and closing without sounding unnatural, you should. It's a powerful technique.

Here's how the "positive sandwich" works: if you've received an order from a customer, don't begin your acknowledgment with a neutrally phrased construction like "We received your recent order for . . . . " And don't close it with a neutrally worded sentence like "Your order will be delivered shortly." Instead, build a "positive sandwich" around your acknowledgment:

Dear Ms. Evans:

We thank you for your recent order for . . .

(The body of
your message)

Your order will be packaged immediately, and delivered to you as soon as possible.

If you're sending a copy of a research report to someone who has requested it, your accompanying letter should avoid a bland opening like:

Dear Mr. Jones:

Enclosed is a copy of . . .

Use the "positive sandwich," and make your reply look like this:

Dear Mr. Jones:

We are happy to enclose a copy of . . .

(The body of
your message)

Your interest in our research is certainly gratifying.

If your letter is intended to satisfy a complaint made by a customer, its structure should not read like this:

Dear Ms. Rankin:

Your letter about the broken chinaware arrived today. We will send you . . .

(The body of
your message)

Let us know if this adjustment is satisfactory to you.

Instead, put the "positive sandwich" to work:

Dear Ms. Rankin:

We appreciate your contacting us so quickly about the breakage of your chinaware. As soon as we received your letter, we . . .

(The body of your message)

Your replacement china will be rushed to you as soon as we receive your go-ahead.

Of course there's nothing you can do to guarantee success in a reaction-evoking communication. The "positive sandwich" won't perform miracles. But by wisely exploiting those positions of strongest impression at beginning and end, you will increase the likelihood of the success of any letter or memo you write. So you'll see much more of the "positive sandwich" in the next few chapters.

PROBLEMS

1. The following letter was sent to the office of Coldbar Publications:

857 Prairie Parkway
Bismarck, North Dakota
April 25, 198_

Coldbar Publications, Inc.
201 Madison Avenue
New York, New York 10086

Gentlemen:

I've searched all around my city for a place that sells the Weekly Forum, but to no avail. Can you tell me if the periodical is distributed in Bismarck? If it isn't, can it be subscribed to? What is the annual subscription rate? And where should I send my subscription order?

Yours truly,

Thomas Yancy

Thomas Yancy

This is the reply Yancy got:

Dear Mr. Yancy:

The Weekly Forum is sold on newsstands only in larger cities. Subscriptions are available at $19.75 yearly, payable in advance. We trust you will continue enjoying this extraordinary magazine.

Sincerely,

Frances Kapp

Frances Kapp
Circulation Manager

An informative reply — but not very courteous or congenial! Your tasks are two:

a. Identify *all* the courtesy blunders this reply letter makes.

b. Rewrite the letter so that its tone will encourage (rather than discourage) Yancy's subscribing.

2. Here's a written reply to a customer's complaint. Evaluate its courtesy, and if you think it could be more courteous, rewrite it.

Mrs. Roberts:

We really find it difficult to understand your stated cause for complaint. As far as we know, you have not yet paid your bill for $17.50. If, as you say, you remember writing the check, perhaps you forgot to mail it, or misaddressed it. Such things do happen.

Unless you receive a cancelled check from your bank, you have nothing to worry about. In the meantime, we're sure you will understand why, in a business as large as ours, it is impossible for us to credit your account merely on your say-so.

Don't worry though. Everything will be all right.

Very truly yours,
Kay Kenny
Hepperson's

3. Doris Caswell wrote to cancel her auto insurance policy because she was selling her car. Here's the way one of the insurance company's staff drafted a reply:

Dear Madam:

As per your request, we are cancelling herewith your policy #B 71-328. Enclosed please find a check in the amount of $148.80, the refund owing to you.

Very truly yours,

Associated Mutual

What a dim-witted way to end a business relationship! Ms. Caswell had been a policy holder for six years, without a single claim made by or against her; but this letter seems unaware of her record or of the possibility she might buy another car in the future. Rewrite it with more positive tone.

4. The following sentences have been lifted from actual business letters. Each is unnecessarily negative in tone. Without adding or deleting any factual details, rewrite these sentences more positively.

a. Your own carelessness in completing the order form has been the cause of this unfortunate delay.
b. We cannot comprehend why you deducted $12 from your payment of May 3.
c. What you failed to notice was the thirty-day limit on our standard guarantee.
d. The alterations you have requested should not present too much of a problem.
e. Why have you ignored our four letters?
f. Since you mailed your application too late, we regret that we cannot enter your display in the trade show.

5. Your firm, the wholesale house of Mackintosh, Inc., on May 23 sold $681.90 worth of goods to Peter Krumpett, a retail appliance dealer. Terms were 2/10, net 30 (that is, two percent off if paid within ten days, net due within thirty days). June 22 passed without a check from Krumpett. On July 9, the company sent a letter to Krumpett reminding him of his overdue account. On July 17 came a letter from Krumpett, one in which he explained that heavy expenditures on store repairs had kept him from paying his bill. He asked for a thirty-day extension on payment. The company has decided to honor his request.

Below are four possible ways of replying to grant Krumpett's request. In a memo to your instructor, evaluate these replies and rank them according to their effectiveness. If your instructor requests, write a fifth reply which is better than any of the four.

[Dear Mr. Krumpett:]

a. Thank you for your prompt reply to our letter regarding your delinquent account of $681.90. We are granting your request for an extension of thirty days. Now we *do* expect payment by August 20.
b. We have received your request for an extension of thirty days on your account of May 23. Although we can't usually grant such extensions, your case does seem justifiable. Hence, we ask that full payment of $681.90 be made by August 20.

c. Your prompt reply to our recent inquiry regarding your account for $681.90 is sincerely appreciated. In accordance with your request, we are extending the due date to August 20.

d. Your request for an extension on your account for $681.90 is granted. Payment is now due on August 20.

[Sincerely yours,
Mackintosh, Inc.]

6. The writer of the following letter has obviously not learned the lesson of positivity. Sincere though he probably is in his regret over not being able to provide better service for the customer, he will probably evoke only a perplexed or angry response from her when she receives this letter. Its point of view is completely negative.

November 15, 19__

Mrs. Philip Fiedler
13 Blackfoot Drive
Lodi, New Jersey 13469

Dear Mrs. Fiedler:

It seems that nothing is turning out quite the way we had planned. It's not our fault. It's just that some of these hotels and carriers don't want to maintain any flexibility in their service.

First of all, Desert Airways says it can't book passage for two in tourist class until two weeks from tomorrow take it or leave it. And as if that weren't bad enough, the Sand Dune Hotel can't provide a room looking out on the swimming pool. They'll have to put you around the corner from it. That's the best we can do.

It's too bad we had to go to work on these reservations so late in the season. Next year, if we can start early, you won't have to get stuck with what's left.

Yours for travel convenience,

Ms. Paula Pessimiz

Rewrite this travel agent's letter from a positive perspective. Mrs. Fiedler has said she'll accept whatever accommodations she can get, but you must make her feel as good as possible about these arrangements *and* make her feel that your travel agency is still the best one to do business with.

7. Often, slight differences in the phrasing of a letter can make a difference tonally. If, for example, you were writing to a long-time customer who was having difficulty paying her current bill, would you prefer any one of the following phrases over the other?

When you pay your bill, . . .
When your bill is paid, . . .
When your payment is received, . . .
When we receive your payment, . . .
As soon as we receive your payment, . . .
As soon as your payment is received, . . .

Explain your choice.

8. The following letter (with attached questionnaire) was sent recently by the District School Superintendent in Los Irvinos, California, to all parents of school-age children in the district. Its intent is clear. But some of the implications it conveys may not have been intended by its author.

Put yourself in the position of a parent receiving this letter. You have one or more school-age children whose personal and educational well-being is extremely important to you. What are your reactions to the letter? Explain them in detail.

Dear Parents,

In response to proposals made to the District during the past two years, we are conducting this survey to determine the interest of parents in the implementation of a Basics Plus Program in Los Irvinos. If implemented, the program would be installed at several elementary and intermediate schools in the District; and parents would have the option of keeping their children in a neighborhood school, or transferring them into a Basics Plus Program. Transportation will be provided for all students who are transferred.

What Is Basics Plus?

The Basics Plus Program is predicated upon the belief that the school's primary objective and responsibility is to provide students with a sound basic academic education. This foundation in basics should allow the student to successfully pursue a course of higher education or to gain productive employment. Other curricular areas, such as Fine Arts and Foreign Languages, while considered important, should not detract from the attainment of specific, predetermined objectives in the basics.

What Are the Characteristics of Basics Plus?

- Solid foundation in the basic subjects
- Regularly assigned homework at all levels

- Discipline which assures self-respect, respect for property, accountability for personal behavior, respect for others, and obedience to the established rules
- Promotion of good citizenship
- Controlled learning environments
- Effective home-school communication
- Defined level of achievement for each grade level

How Is Basics Plus Different?

- Greater attention paid to attendance and discipline
- Fewer elective subjects with increased emphasis on achievement and performance in basic subjects
- Consistent emphasis and methods from grade to grade
- End-of-year promotion contingent upon explicit levels of performance
- Statement accepting program philosophy and regulations signed by both parent and child

The Basics Plus Program is expected to begin next September, pending the availability of facilities and sufficient enrollment. If you are interested in enrolling your son or daughter in the Basics Plus Program, please complete the accompanying questionnaire, and return it to the District Office in the enclosed postage-paid envelope. Remember, it is your responses that will determine the implementation of Basics Plus in Los Irvinos.

Sincerely,

B. Sidney Corman

B. Sidney Corman
Superintendent

9. Back in the 1950s, when the airlines came to Dr. Ernst Dichter, the famous motivational researcher, they were in the midst of ad campaigns stressing the safety of flying. They were trying to cure the public of a still widespread fear of going up in airplanes. After looking at the problem, Dichter recommended that the airlines abandon the "safety" theme, and concentrate instead on selling, to men, the "speed and convenience" of air travel, and to women the idea that airplanes would get their husbands home faster when they were traveling.

Was Dichter's advice an application of the principle of positivity? If so, why? And if not, where does it depart from that principle?

10. On page 168, in capsule form, is an intellectual quarrel over the concept of positivity: First is the advice of a writer as it appeared several years ago in a general circulation magazine. Second, we have the opinion of a language expert about that writer's advice. Read them both carefully.

Words that sound happy put your reader in the right frame of mind to say "yes" to your request. Remember that a negative word or an unfriendly expression should never be used if there is a positive way to express the same thought. You might say: "We regret that we are unable to supply you with the item ordered. Is there another item which we may send you on the same subject?"

But your reader-reaction will be 100 percent improved if you rephrase that sentence to read: "Fortunately for you, although the specific item you ordered is out of print, we have another which might serve your purpose."

vs.

Nothing could be plainer than that this change of style is a radical change in meaning. None of us would countenance such a bland invitation to write "words that sound happy" in order to con the subnormal reader into the appropriate "reader-reaction" — so that he gets the impression that you are practically doing him a favor by not sending him the item he ordered. But we encourage this sort of confusion when we speak of style as though it *were* detachable and manipulable independent of meaning . . . That is what encourages people to entertain the *absurd idea* that, as this writer puts it, there is both a "positive" and a "negative" . . . way to express the same thought."

In whatever format your instructor suggests, present your own critique of this "argument" between the magazine writer and the language expert. State your own opinions clearly, and carefully spell out the reasoning behind them.

11. The following letter was written by the Office of Economic Planning of the City of Harborside, New Jersey:

Board of Directors
Woodstock Corporation
400 Park Avenue
New York, New York 10022

Gentlemen:

We have learned that the Woodstock Corporation is interested in the possibility of a new plant site in northern New Jersey. Business people have found many reasons for giving special consideration to our rapidly growing and dynamic community of Harborside. We believe you should know about them. Our taxes are still low. We have a plentiful labor supply. Industrial utility services are readily accessible. And there remains a wide variety of sites from which to choose. These considerations are vital ones to any company contemplating expansion.

The Office of Economic Planning can prepare a confidential survey of selected locations for a new Woodstock plant in Harborside. This report would not be an undigested list of real estate listings, nor a merely generalized statement of available sites. If you tell us how much space and land you need, how many personnel, what kind of buildings, transportational requirements, etc., etc., we can go to work on a special survey.

If this offer is of interest to your company, we will allow time for you to meet with us and discuss plans for a study.

Very truly yours,

This letter did not create much interest among the directors of the Woodstock Corporation. The reasons for its failure are obvious. The letter has a certain lack of clarity. Even more significantly, it lacks a character appropriate to promotion letters of this type. It is nonempathetic in its viewpoint. Its ideas lack a positive perspective; some of them are stated conditionally, others are plainly negative. In spots, the letter is tactless. It sounds rather like a form letter not particularly well-adapted to Woodstock's specific problems. In general, the letter lacks enthusiasm. As a result, it fails to generate any enthusiasm in its readers.

Rewrite this letter more effectively.

CHAPTER 8

ROUTINE MESSAGES: A NOT-SO-ROUTINE SKILL

The groundwork has been laid. In our quest to understand what makes a business letter succeed, we looked (in Chapters 1 through 4) at the attributes of all good business writing. Then (in Chapters 5 through 7) we examined those added qualities common to all well-written, direct reaction-evokers (that is, letters, memos, and other direct communications that seek primarily to evoke specific reactions).

Now, let's begin to distinguish among the different types of direct reaction-evokers, and among the different functions each of them must serve. Each function makes its own special demands on your ability as a business writer. Some of these demands are fairly easy; others are difficult, even brutal. Every time you write a letter or a memo, you've got to recognize which of these functions you must serve, then shape your strategy accordingly.

DISTINGUISHING THE FUNCTIONS OF DIRECT REACTION-EVOKING COMMUNICATIONS

How many different functions can a direct reaction-evoker serve? Although every letter or memo you write will be unique in some way, there are, generally speaking, seven functional categories:

1. *Routine Communications* — those everyday letters and memos that either *initiate* some exchange of information or ideas, or *reply* to someone else's initiating communication.

2. *Good-Will Communications* — those letters and memos written primarily to enhance the recipient's good feeling toward the writer or the writer's organization.

3. *Good-News Communications* — those letters and memos that convey information the recipient will be happy to read.

4. *Demand Communications* — those letters and memos that demand, rather than just ask for, something.

5. *Conciliatory Communications* — those letters and memos that are written to repair the recipient's ill feeling toward the writer or the writer's organization.

6. *Bad-News Communications* — those letters and memos that convey information displeasing or disappointing to their recipients.

7. *Persuasive Communications* — those letters and memos that must induce a new way of thinking in the recipient's mind, or bring about a previously unanticipated action from the recipient.

In the next five chapters, we'll examine each of these types of direct reaction-evoker, in the order listed, from the easiest to the most complex. In this chapter we look at routine letters and memos.

ROUTINE INITIATORS

Consider the following letter. It makes a simple (if not quite clear) inquiry.

Gentlemen:

What happens if my car gets into an accident with somebody else behind the wheel? I have looked all over my policy and you haven't got it anywhere.

I hear some people say I'm covered and then some say I'm not. Reply as soon as possible.

Yours,

Gary Gammerman

Gary Gammerman

Now compare Gammerman's letter with the following one, which makes the same inquiry. Which is more effective?

Ladies and Gentlemen:

I would appreciate your clarifying a point regarding my auto insurance policy (No. A21-64). Does my coverage protect me from liability if an accident should occur while my nineteen-year-old nephew is driving my car? I've searched through the policy but am unable to find the answer.

Could you please let me know as soon as possible.

Sincerely yours,

Roger Richardson

Roger Richardson

Gammerman's letter may be typical of many a muddled business inquiry, but Richardson's is by far the more effective.

For one thing, Gammerman's letter lacks the *clarity* of Richardson's. After reading it, the poor clerk at the insurance office will wonder exactly what Gammerman wants to know. Even if the clerk finally figures out that Gammerman's third sentence is about limitations in his coverage, an accurate reply won't be possible, for it probably makes a difference who that "somebody else" behind the wheel is.

Secondly, the *character* of Gammerman's letter will not encourage a prompt and specific response. His tone sounds demanding. His letter lacks a "positive sandwich." His second sentence sounds like an accusation. By comparison, Richardson is courteous. His letter avoids the tone of accusation, and it opens and closes positively. In both clarity and character, Richardson's letter is far superior.

No doubt Gammerman's letter will get a response. He is, after all, a paying customer. But because of his letter's inexactness, the response might well fail to tell him exactly what he needs to know. He may have to write a second time. And with its crude tone, the clerk may just slip it to the bottom of the mail pile, a spite-reaction that occurs in business every day. If Gammerman writes the same kind of inquiries to people who can't profit by answering him, chances are he waits and waits for replies that never come. On the other hand, Richardson's precision, his style, and his tone will assure him, over the long run, replies that are prompter and more satisfactory.

Routine Requests and Inquiries

Let's take a look at a few more examples of well-written requests and inquiries. Here is one written by a "camera bug" after she spotted an interesting advertisement:

Gentlemen:

I would appreciate your sending me further information about the Soundamatic Home Movie Kit you advertised in the recent May 12 edition of Newsweek.

Sincerely,

Martha Faust

Martha Faust

The letter is brief, yet complete. Because the advertiser expects such requests, Martha Faust has said everything she needed to say to be sure of getting her desired reaction. Notice, too, that she injects a positive attitude (one of appreciation) into the beginning of the letter.

A request memorandum can also be brief and still effective:

TO: M. Foster, Staff Librarian
FROM: T. Bradshaw
SUBJECT: Request for Library Delivery

Marge, when you have a chance, would you please send up Volume 13 of the Consumer's Home Annual.

Tom

Because library delivery is a standard part of Marge Foster's job, nothing more is necessary in Tom Bradshaw's memo. Yet notice the way he phrases his request. Instead of using a declarative sentence, like:

I would like Volume 13 of the Consumer's Home Annual

or an imperative sentence, like:

Send up Volume 13 of the Consumer's Home Annual.

Bradshaw uses a *rhetorical question* — that is, an *interrogative* sentence that really doesn't ask a question — to make his request:

. . . would you please send up Volume 13 of the Consumer's Home Annual.

Rhetorical questions are the warmest, least demanding way of requesting action from your reader. (Note that rhetorical questions don't even need a question mark; a simple period is enough.)

Notice, too, that Bradshaw includes other little touches — her name at the beginning (even though a memo requires no salutation), the phrase "when you have a chance" (to add a touch of courtesy), and a personal first-name signature. All contribute to the memo's warm tone and make the recipient glad to respond.

Warm tone becomes all the more vital when an inquiry asks someone to go out of his or her way to provide something, as the following letter does. Its recipient will in no way profit by replying; his reply will simply be a favor to the writer. Realizing this, the writer tries carefully to build rapport by creating a friendly tone. The writer is also careful to spell out, in clear detail, precisely what she wants, thereby making the request as easy as possible to respond to. Jenny Cantwell shows effective technique in this request, making it as difficult as possible for the editor, Godfrey Bliss, to ignore her. Not to answer a letter like this one would weigh heavily upon Bliss's conscience. Read it carefully, then take a close look at the analysis of this effective request in Figure 14.

Some business people, those engaged in the credit field for example, spend much of their time writing inquiries. Typical of the credit manager's job are

January 20, 19--

Mr. Godfrey Bliss
Managing Editor
The Muse
Valhalla University
Kent, Ohio 40405

Dear Mr. Bliss:

Largely because of the success of The Muse, your new campus literary magazine, we at Colfax feel the time is right for a similar publication on our own campus. Your help on a few vital questions would get us rolling in the right direction.

We would like to know:

1. How you went about soliciting manuscripts for your first edition.

2. How you decided upon the proportions of space to devote to fiction, poetry, criticism, reviews, and advertising.

3. Whether you use university or commercial printing facilities.

4. What mailing list you used to solicit charter subscriptions.

5. Why you decided to price The Muse at $1.25.

Our enthusiasm runs high over the possibility of a literary review at Colfax. Target date for the first issue is October 1 of this year. We've got the administration's green light, and adequate student-body funding. The faculty is solidly behind us. With your aid, we can be that much closer to realizing our goal: a first-rate campus publication capable of standing beside the best from the larger schools -- The Muse most certainly among them.

Sincerely,

Jennifer Cantwell

Jennifer Cantwell
Student Body
Vice-President

the following two letters (on pages 174 and 176), both of them well written. The first asks a prospective credit customer for information about himself.

Dolman Brothers, Inc.
125 South Orange Street
Daytona Beach, Florida

Subject: Your Order of May 12, 198_

We are happy to have your order of May 12 for three Model 12C amplifiers.

Figure 14
Detailed analysis of the inquiry letter from Jennifer Cantwell to Godfrey Bliss.

January 20, 19—

Mr. Godfrey Bliss
Managing Editor
The Muse
Valhalla University
Kent, Ohio 40405

Dear Mr. Bliss:

Largely because of the success of The Muse, your new campus literary magazine, we at Colfax feel the time is right for a similar publication on our own campus. Your help on a few vital questions would get us rolling in the right direction.

We would like to know:

1. How you went about soliciting manuscripts for your first edition.

2. How you decided upon the proportions of space to devote to fiction, poetry, criticism, reviews, and advertising.

3. Whether you use university or commercial printing facilities.

4. What mailing list you used to solicit charter subscriptions.

5. Why you decided to price The Muse at $1.25.

Our enthusiasm runs high over the possibility of a literary review at Colfax. Target date for the first issue is October 1 of this year. We've got the administration's green light, and adequate student-body funding. The faculty is solidly behind us. With your aid, we can be that much closer to realizing our goal: a first-rate campus publication capable of standing beside the best from the larger schools — The Muse most certainly among them.

Sincerely,

Jennifer Cantwell

Jennifer Cantwell
Student Body
Vice-President

Adhering to the principle of the "positive sandwich," Cantwell phrases her opening in the most positive, most empathetic way she can.

Style note: Cantwell could have written "we need help on ..." Instead she made the phrase "your help" the subject of this key sentence giving that phrase subject emphasis.

To make sure that Bliss attends to each of these crucial questions, Cantwell uses an openly enumerative construction (1,2,3, . . .).

Notice, too, that Cantwell is careful to use *parallel* grammatical construction for all her questions.

Notice how the phrase *this year* is given terminal emphasis in this sentence, to stress the urgency with which Cantwell needs the information she's asking for.

Cantwell plans to ask Bliss for a lot of private information. So, to assure that Bliss won't say "none of your business," Cantwell devotes her whole first paragraph to associating Bliss with the plight of the Colfax student body.

Notice Cantwell's somewhat *informal* level of diction. It aids her attempt to develop rapport in this student-to-student communication.

Are these sentences vital to Cantwell's purpose? Factually, no. But their implication *is*. They imply "everybody's on the bandwagon, now we need only you" — a hard appeal for Bliss to resist.

Cantwell continues to identify Bliss with the success or failure of the forthcoming Colfax magazine.

Again, in maintaining the "positive sandwich" — an emphatically positive closing idea.

So that we can fill your order on account as quickly as possible, will you please send us the names of three firms from whom you purchase on a credit basis. Enclosed is a form for your convenience in submitting this information.

Three Model 12C's are being held aside to assure your quick delivery. We enjoy the opportunity of being able to serve you, and will process the information you provide immediately.

Very truly yours,

Patrick Gibson

Patrick Gibson
Credit Manager

The warm, positive tone in this letter is repeated by Gibson when he pursues one of the credit references supplied by Dolman Brothers.

Miami Supply Company
7110 Trewsdale Boulevard
Miami, Florida 33171

Subject: Request for Credit Information

So that we can fill an initial order on account for Dolman Brothers, a Daytona Beach firm we believe you supply, would you kindly assist us with some information.

We would like to know how long Dolman Brothers has had an account with you, how promptly they pay their invoices, and if any credit limit has been placed on their account.

Your cooperation will allow us to speed their order to them. We will, of course, be more than happy to reciprocate if ever we can.

Sincerely,

Patrick Gibson

Patrick Gibson
Credit Manager

Pat Gibson is obviously concerned with both the clarity and character of every inquiry he writes.

Some businesses use inquiry letters like the following one to recover lost patronage. It, too, is effectively composed.

Dear Mrs. Fisher:

Is everything all right?

We have noticed that your Langdon's Charge Card has not been used recently.

If perchance you have misplaced it, just give us a call and we'll rush a new one to you.

Or, if this letter has been forwarded to you at a new out-of-town address, remember we stand ready to continue serving you through our Total Delivery Mail Order Service.

On rare occasions, customers receive service they feel not up to par. If this has happened we would certainly like to know about it. We'll do everything in our power to provide the remedy.

We at Langdon's have always welcomed, and shall continue to welcome, the opportunity of serving you.

Sincerely,

Edith Terwilliger
Customer Service Department[1]

The writing of inquiries often involves the asking of questions. And there are right ways and wrong ways (that is, wise and unwise ways) to ask any question. In Chapter 16 you'll find a discussion on "framing your questions," on pages 402–404.

Routine Order Letters

Another kind of routine initiator is the order letter. Although most purchase orders are made on order forms or by contracts that specify the purchase terms, you will still occasionally need to write a letter to place an order. Order letters can be as brief as this one:

[1] In Edith Terwilliger's first draft of this letter, her final sentence read as follows: "We at Langdon's have always welcomed the opportunity to serve you, and we shall continue to welcome it." But she wasn't happy with that closing. Too many *we's*, she felt, and not enough empathy. She revised and revised until she came up with the excellent sentence that now ends the letter: "We at Langdon's have always welcomed, and shall continue to welcome, the opportunity of serving you." In that revised sentence, the significant clause *and shall continue to welcome* was converted to an emphatic interrupter (see pages 81-82); and the phrase *serving you*, with its empathetic overtones, was put in the sentence's emphatic terminal position.

Kay-Nine Publications, Inc.
13 Grosvenor Place
Pittsfield, Massachusetts 03622

Ladies and Gentlemen:

Please send two copies of your new publication, The Long-Haired Boxer, to me at the above address. My check for $4.50 is attached.

Yours truly,

Dolores Pender

Dolores Pender

The two principal strengths of this order letter are its clarity and its conciseness. Note, too, that whenever a prepayment check is included with the order, the order letter should refer to it.

Occasionally, order letters must be longer and more detailed, like this one:

Huntington Decorative Supply Company
Eight East Clay Street
Atlanta, Georgia 32822

Gentlemen:

Please ship the following prepaid order via freight express on the Gulf, Mobile & Ohio:

6 Early American Tank Trays @ $3.50	$ 21.00
8 Early American Solid Brass Spittoons @ $5.00	40.00
6 Wrought Iron Butcher's Racks @ $1.75	10.50
24 Cross-stitch Pillows (8 red, 8 blue, 8 olive) @ $2.50	60.00
12 Antique Copper Kettles @ $6.50	78.00
6 Early American Johnny Seats @ $6.50	39.00
6 15″ × 5″ Decorated Butter Molds @ $3.25	19.50
Total	$268.00

My check for $284.50 is attached to cover both the goods ($268.00) and the freight charges ($16.50). I would very much appreciate your sending out this order in time to reach me by December 5.

Yours very truly,

Lee Cosgrove

Lee Cosgrove
Manager

Both of these order letters are effectively written. Responding to them will be easy.

Giving Instructions

Among their many tasks, supervisors in business must routinely write instructions to their subordinates. Well-written instructions not only clearly describe the tasks to be done; they also motivate their recipients to do the job well. The following memo is a case in point. Its writer, Tony Rowan, is a senior management consultant whose firm has agreed to investigate a personnel problem at a Georgia factory. Rowan is writing to Chris Allen, a junior associate in the firm, who has just been dispatched to Georgia to do the early spadework in the investigation.

TO: Chris Allen (Confidential)
Hotel Sheridan Plaza
Augusta, Georgia

DATE: April 8, 198__

FILE: 612

FROM: Tony Rowan

SUBJECT: The Obereddy Corporation Project

Just a brief follow-up, Chris, to our meeting over lunch yesterday about the unhappiness at Obereddy's Augusta plant, and our upcoming investigation of it.

The problem there appears to be real, and some changes would seem to be necessary — though, as I said yesterday, I think Obereddy's president, Max Morrison, overestimates its importance. He got a head full of ''participation training'' at a university conference last fall, and has gone overboard on this business of ''interpersonal skills.'' During the project, we've got to live with these new biases of his; but we do not have to defer to them in our final report.

You will, I'm sure, find plenty of friction at the plant. There are a lot of stiff-necked oldtimers down there who don't care much for Morrison's pressure for ''cooperation.'' I think you'd better poke around the plant for a day or so, sizing up the general situation before you begin to look at the particular sore spots we've discussed.

As this is your first project of this sort, let me suggest that you send me short daily reports on your findings. I'll try on this end to help with any comments or suggestions that seem useful. It might also be a good idea (unless your recollection of such things is better than mine) to brush up quickly on terms like ''participation,'' ''group work,'' ''viscidity,'' and the like. Meyer Raymond's book, Groups in Industry, would probably be your best single source. Morrison might ask you somewhere along the line about the plant's ''hedonic tone,'' and you'll want to know what he's talking about. Don't worry about the technicalities though; definitions ought to be quite enough to handle it.

As I told you yesterday, I'm confident that with those quick perceptions of yours, and your sound judgment, we'll uncover the source of Obereddy's problem in Augusta. We can discuss solutions later. Good luck.

Tony

Notice the overriding empathy of this memo, and its candid but conversational tone. It employs a "positive sandwich," reiterates all the necessary background, and lays out clearly what it wants done. Rowan gives Allen specific instructions, but at the same time makes him feel like a full-fledged professional participant in the Obereddy project — even though it is Allen's first problem of this sort. It is an uncommonly good memorandum of instruction, far better than the average one, which in this case might have read:

TO: Christopher Allen

FROM: Anthony W. Rowan

SUBJECT: The Obereddy Account

In view of background as discussed by us yesterday, you are hereby instructed to:

1. Examine the general situation at Obereddy's Augusta plant before beginning study of particular problem areas.
2. Brush up on concepts of ''participation training,'' ''interpersonal skills,'' ''hedonic tone,'' and the like,, which Max Morrison, Obereddy president, feels are relevant to the present difficulty (see: Meyer Raymond, Groups in Industry)
3. Submit to me daily reports on your findings.

AWR

If you were Chris Allen, to which of these memos would you respond more enthusiastically?[2]

Letters of Introduction

Business people, usually those in management or supervisory positions, write letters of introduction to help others gain the advantage of being formally introduced to some third party. Here's a good example of such a letter:

> Mr. Paul Barrymore, Executive Secretary
> League for Consumer Protection
> 14 Rockefeller Plaza
> New York, New York 10038
>
> Dear Paul,
>
> I'm happy to introduce a man who will be calling you next week: Mr. Dean Phillips, a bright young trial attorney with whom we have worked for the past three years.
>
> Mr. Phillips is moving to New York and is anxious to continue his work in consumer protection. His record of prosecutions in the field is already impressive. I felt you would be the best person for him to see about affiliation in the East.
>
> I'm confident you'll find Phillips an articulate and perceptive man quite destined for eminence.
>
> My best wishes,
>
> Timothy B. Carlberg
>
> Timothy B. Carlberg
> Attorney at Law

Three things must be included in any effective introduction letter. You want to indicate the relationship between you and the person you're introducing, state the reason for the introduction, and give pertinent praise for the person being introduced. And (it almost goes without saying), positive tone is vital —lest the letter seem not to mean what it says.

Routine Reminders

Even routine reminders — which are vital in business — can be well or poorly written. Consider this one sent by an insurance company to one of its policyholders:

[2] Allen received the first of these memos from Rowan, and responded with a series of daily memo-reports, the first of which you can take a look at on page 431.

Dear Ms. Jones:

On March 3, we sent you medical forms and requested that you complete said forms and return to this office. To date, we have received no reply from you.

Unless we hear from you within fourteen days regarding this matter, we assume that you have no claim to present, and will close our file accordingly.

Very truly yours,

Chester Crochett

Chester Crochett

It's a reminder letter that neglects its own tone. It is cold, antagonistic, self-concerned, and guaranteed to make Miss Jones dislike the company, perhaps enough to take her insurance business elsewhere. A good writer would write the same inquiry like this:

Dear Ms. Jones:

In reviewing your file, I see that we haven't yet received the medical forms we sent you on March 3.

I don't want to rush you, but if you do wish to make a claim, it is advisable for us to process these forms within the next fourteen days.

As soon as your forms arrive, we will go ahead with the claim on your behalf.

Yours sincerely,

Victor T. Evans

Victor T. Evans

This letter says the same thing as Crochett's, but much more effectively. It avoids Crochett's heavy-handedness. Evans does not accuse Ms. Jones (as Crochett does) of neglecting to return the forms. He simply says, "We haven't yet received them." The word *yet* is used to imply very clearly that "we know it's only a matter of time before we do receive them." In his second sentence, Evans uses a conditional construction ("*if* you do wish to . . .") to imply to Ms. Jones that she is in control of the situation; the next step is hers entirely.[3]

[3] This is *not* an example of unnecessary conditionality. Evans uses his conditional phrasing intentionally, as a tool. And notice that he still adds a positive ring to that intentionally conditional phrasing: he writes "if you do wish" rather than "if you wish" or "if you don't wish."

Crochett, on the other hand, makes his request for the medical forms sound like an ultimatum, one which says in effect, "Hurry up, woman, or you'll pay the consequences!" Ironically, only Crochett's employers will pay the consequences, in lost patronage, if the reader is offended.

In Summary

We can sum up our discussion of routine initiators, then, with some general rules. These rules can be used as guidelines for writing any inquiry, request, order letter, instruction, or reminder you have to write:

1. Begin and end your communication as *positively* as you can. Rapport between you and your respondent will induce a more satisfactory response. This is the "positive sandwich" concept (as discussed on pages 160–162).
2. Unless it is self-evident, make clear early in the communication *who* you are (what position you hold, or what situation you are in that has caused you to write).
3. State specifically and completely *what* you want.
4. Unless self-evident, state *why* you want it. The reason(s) you give make it easier for the respondent to provide precisely what you need.
5. Unless self-evident, indicate why you are writing *to the person* you're addressing. People like to know why requests or inquiries are being made of them.
6. Provide as much information as your reader will need in order to react as you desire. Don't force your reader to "read your mind" in order to comply with what you want.
7. Ask for as little information as you have to. It is annoying to be asked for information that is readily available elsewhere or that is obviously superfluous.
8. Make your request or desire, in every way, as easy to satisfy as possible.
9. If possible, time your requests, inquiries, and order letters to coincide with your respondent's least busy period.
10. Write with as much empathy as you can, injecting the everyday courtesies into your communications.

ROUTINE REPLIES

In business, you not only write routine initiators, you reply to them as well. To reply effectively requires the same skill and technique.

On page 184 there's a letter from Sparco Electronics. Read it as though you had actually received it. What do you think of it?

This letter is not bad, but it could be better. It does provide information, probably all that Ted Locke asked for. But what of its tone? If Locke is easily offended (as many people are), the letter's tone is likely to damage his good will and perhaps even lose his patronage. The first paragraph is entirely negative in its attitude. The whole letter is didactic: it sounds as though it's giving Locke (the "amateur") a profound lecture. And it lacks empathy. It's almost completely self-centered.

How might this reply be improved? Here's one way:

Dear Mr. Locke:

We were most pleased to receive your inquiry regarding reprocessed sound tape. Many customers have expressed curiosity as to its quality.

SPARCO ELECTRONICS
888 Lincoln Boulevard
St. Louis, Missouri

January 10, 19--

Mr. Ted Locke
72 Sequoia Park Road
South Bay, Oregon 97022

Dear Mr. Locke:

In answer to your inquiry, we wish to inform you that we do not market reprocessed magnetic sound tape, of any length. Its quality is wholly substandard, and we advise that you do not use it if you want satisfactory results on your home tape recorder. Reprocessed tape is usually nothing more than outdated tape or the ends of tape used at professional sound studios. The studios would not think of using it, and it is certainly not suited to the needs of the amateur.

We suggest for satisfactory results that you use our Sparco Magna-Luxe 4T sound tape. It is available at your local dealer for only $9.95--actually not much more than reprocessed tape. It is fully guaranteed.

Very truly yours,

Horace Cruishank

Horace Cruishank
Customer Service Dept.

After carefully investigating the different kinds of reprocessed tape, Sparco has decided not to market any of them. We want to be able to guarantee fully any product we put on the market. Because reprocessed tape usually consists of outdated tape or the scrap ends of tape used professionally, we are unable to guarantee the quality of its reproduction. Some of our customers have tried reprocessed tape because of its low cost. But they've been dissatisfied with it.

Actually, the tape we recommend -- Sparco Magna-Luxe 4T Sound Tape -- costs little more than reprocessed brands. It is widely available and we fully guarantee it. We are anxious to provide you with only the best in recording supplies because we know how much their dependability can mean to you.

Sincerely,

John Wordsworth

John Wordsworth
Customer Service Department

This letter is a great improvement over Cruishank's original. Take a look at the reasons why in Figure 15.

Figure 15
Detailed analysis of a well-written and informative reply letter.

Dear Mr. Locke:

We were most pleased to receive your inquiry regarding reprocessed sound tape. Many customers have expressed curiosity as to its quality.

After carefully investigating the different kinds of reprocessed tape, Sparco has decided not to market any of them. We want to be able to guarantee fully any product we put on the market. Because reprocessed tape usually consists of outdated tape or the scrap ends of tape used professionally, we are unable to guarantee the quality of its reproduction. Some of our customers have tried reprocessed tape because of its low cost. But they've been dissatisfied with it.

Actually, the tape we recommend -- Sparco Magna-Luxe 4T Sound Tape -- costs little more than the reprocessed brands. It is widely available and we fully guarantee it. We are anxious to provide you with only the best in recording supplies because we know how much their dependability can mean to you.

Sincerely,

John Wordsworth

John Wordsworth
Customer Service
Department

Wordsworth uses a "positive sandwich" to very good effect in this letter. Notice the tonally positive opening.

Notice how this sentence avoids the arbitrary tone of Cruishank's "we feel that its quality is wholly substandard, and we advise that you do not use it . . ."

Note that the writer avoids that old style bugaboo —the "split infinitive."

Though mentioned only once, the product name is mentioned *emphatically* as an appositive interrupter. Notice too how the word *Actually* functions as a connector between 2 paragraphs.

As a persuasive technique — the kind we'll discuss more fully in Chapter 12 — the writer points out that it is not only himself and his company who feel this way about reprocessed tape.

Notice this highly positive and empathetic closing. . .

. . . a closing which puts the word *you* in the emphatic terminal position.

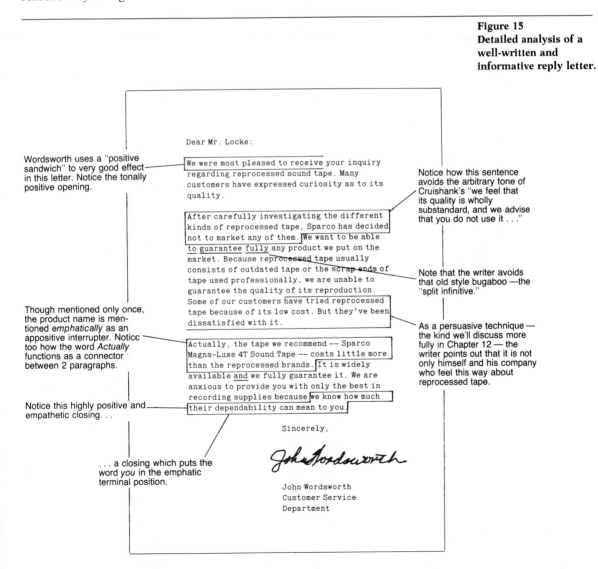

COASTAL CRUISE LINES
New York, N. Y. 10010

March 22, 19--

Mr. and Mrs. William Mumma
90 Main Street
Landisville, Pennsylvania

Dear Mr. and Mrs. Mumma:

We were pleased to receive your request for information regarding this year's Tropical Sunshine Cruises, and are happy to enclose complete brochures with full details of these marvelous voyages.

You may, of course, select from a number of attractive itineraries. There's a length and tempo of cruise for every taste. As to your question regarding Trinidad, you can certainly stay as long as you like and return on a later ship.

Any voyage in the planning stages raises scores of questions; we'll be more than happy to answer them for you. As you know, you can reserve at any time--no need to pay 'til later. Just let us know which cruise you'd enjoy most, and we'll put together your complete accommodations.

Very truly yours,

Maria Michaels

Maria Michaels
Customer Service

On this page and next are two more examples of routine reply letters, each of them serving the double function common to all good replies. They provide the recipient with the information desired, *and* they enhance the recipient's feeling for the writer and his or her organization. The first of these letters was written to convince Mr. and Mrs. Mumma that Coastal Cruise Lines is *the* cruise line to deal with. The second was written to increase Cynthia Forbes' enthusiasm over applying to Valhalla University. Both letters do their jobs well.

Corporations as well as colleges must frequently reply to requests for information. Many corporations, as a policy, not only send the information, but accompany it with a short and effective reply letter like the following:

VALHALLA UNIVERSITY
KENT, OHIO

October 29, 19__

Miss Cynthia Forbes
88 Anthracite Lane
Johnstown, Pennsylvania

Dear Miss Forbes:

Thank you for your inquiry about admission to Valhalla University. We were pleased to hear of your plans for furthering your education.

We've enclosed with this letter a preliminary application form. We will also be sending you, as soon as it's off the press, a copy of the new Valhalla Bulletin. It should reach you within three weeks.

After you've had a chance to study the Bulletin, just complete the application form and return it to us. It will be reviewed, and you will hear from us shortly thereafter.

Should the Bulletin leave any of your questions unanswered, we will be glad to answer them for you.

Sincerely yours,

Carl Doberman
Admissions Officer

Dear Mr. Young:

I was quite pleased to receive your request for the brochure, "The American Growth Environment in the 1970s." The enclosed copy should prove as interesting for you to read as it was for us to compile.

[4] A note on word selection: In his first draft of this letter, Doberman wrote, "Should the *Bulletin* fail to answer any of your questions, we will be . . . ." But upon rereading it, he asked himself, "why put the onus of 'failure' on our *Bulletin* even if the 'failure' is only a manner of speaking?" So he revised his last sentence to its present form.

Your interest in our company's research is sincerely appreciated.

Very truly yours,

Paul Thomaseau

Paul Thomaseau
Executive Secretary

Had Mr. Young mentioned any specific points of interest in his request, Paul Thomaseau's reply would have spoken directly of them, or told Young where in the brochure those points were discussed.

The credit manager, whose inquiries we looked at earlier, must also be able to write effective replies when information is requested of him. Those replies must exhibit a delicate balance: they must be informative enough to help the inquirer, yet not so informative as to violate the customer's confidence by divulging too much. The following letter is a well-written reply to Patrick Gibson's request for credit information (a request we examined on page 176).

Mr. Patrick Gibson, Credit Manager
Amplitronics, Inc.
190 South Market Street
Philadelphia, Pennsylvania 17101

Dear Mr. Gibson:

We are happy to supply the information you requested about our customer -- Dolman Brothers of Daytona Beach, Florida.

The company has purchased from us regularly for the past nine years. They are an all-purpose department store, with a remarkably fast turnover in electronic supplies and components. We have placed no limit upon their credit purchases. Seldom in the past nine years have they failed to qualify for the discount on our regular terms of 2/10, net 30. They never pay late.

We're confident this information will be helpful to you in qualifying Dolman Brothers for a credit account.

Very truly yours,

John Teague

Miami Supply Company

Notice the writer's technique in replying. He answers all of Gibson's questions, and provides some additional information he feels pertinent (that Dolman Brothers is an all-purpose department store with a brisk trade in electronic supplies). He does *not* specify precisely how much business his firm does with the company; he uses relative terms — *regularly, seldom* — to answer Gibson's inquiries. (Often, when a credit manager must divulge a customer's *poor* credit record, he avoids putting *any* remarks on paper and uses the telephone instead.)

Still another example of an effective reply to a request for information is the letter from the American Meat Institute appearing in Figure 16. It provides a lot of detailed information and does so with a tone that is consistently congenial.

The principles of the effective reply letter hold equally true for internal memoranda. In the following example, the writer provides the requested information in clear detail and a congenial tone, and even offers some additional information that is pertinent to the reply:

Date: Dec. 13, 198_

To: L. A. Carter
From: M. B. Bugliose
Re: The Proposed EDP Installation

Fred Livsey in the Controller's Office has completed those rough estimates you asked for on the proposed electronic data-processing installation. His estimates on the major items are as follows:

Programming	$ 350,000
Coding data	220,000
Site preparation	150,000
Computer	2,225,000
Monthly operating costs	90,000

Fred tells me that these figures, which he phoned down to me yesterday afternoon, are provisional. He thinks they're a little high, but in line with the costs he's heard quoted by other controllers on similar installations. He also feels that renting a big computer would cost approximately the same as the amortization charges on an outright purchase.

With enthusiasm, he also asked me to tell you that the installation might eventually save the company as much as $50,000 a month in reduced personnel costs.

MBB

AMI AMERICAN MEAT INSTITUTE

59 EAST VAN BUREN STREET CHICAGO, ILLINOIS 60605 WAbash 2-4686

July 5, 19__

Mr. R. G. Conner
208 Olsen Way
Marshalltown, Iowa

Dear Mr. Conner:

Thank you for your recent letter in which you asked for information on training programs and career opportunities in the meat industry.

The American Meat Institute is the national trade, educational and research association of the meat packing and processing industry. Since your letter indicated you may be interested in opportunities at retail as well as packer level, you probably would be able to get suitable information by writing to any of the retail organizations. Three that come immediately to mind are:

National Association of Food Chains
1725 "I" Street, N.W.
Washington, D.C.

National Association of Retail Grocers
of the United States
360 North Michigan Avenue
Chicago, Illinois 60601

Super Market Institute, Inc.
200 East Ontario Street
Chicago, Illinois 60611

I am happy to enclose material about career opportunities that exist in the meat packing and processing industry. Enclosed are a copy of our booklet,

onner - 2 -

"Opportunities for You," and copies of our pamphlets that describe home-study courses available through our AMI Center for Continuing Education.

There are a number of privately operated meat trade schools in operation in the United States, and I am enclosing a list of seven of them. Naturally, I am not in a position to endorse or recommend any of these schools. I enclose the list so you may contact as many of them as you wish to request additional information.

We appreciate your interest and we hope you will contact us again if we can be of further service.

Sincerely,

DEPARTMENT OF MEMBERSHIP
AND PERSONNEL RELATIONS

Cholm G. Houghton

CGH/kb
Enclosure

Cholm G. Houghton, Director

Figure 16
A detailed and well-written reply to a request for information.
(Reproduced with the kind permission of American Meat Institute)

Routine Confirmations and Acknowledgments

Another kind of business reply is the letter that confirms a customer's order. The effective confirmation letter conveys the essential facts, *and* it expresses appreciation for the customer's patronage. Here's a good example:

> **HILLCREST RESORT HOTEL**
> **Angel's Ridge, Colorado**
>
> May 20, 19--
>
> Mr. Jonathan Foster
> 891 Golden Gate Avenue
> San Francisco, California 96004
>
> Dear Mr. Foster:
>
> We are delighted to confirm the following accommodation for you here at Hillcrest:
>
> Double bedroom, with bath and separate dressing area, for two weeks beginning July 3. Charge $42 per day.
>
> We look forward to your visit and promise the utmost in service to make it a memorable one.
>
> Yours truly,
>
> *Samuel Kraft*
>
> Samuel Kraft
> Reservations Manager

Hillcrest's confirmation is short but detailed. And it's highly positive. Notice how the "positive sandwich" principle is put to work: positive opening, then the confirmed details, then a positive closing. If the service at the Hillcrest is as good as its confirmation letters, repeat patronage is almost assured.

The confirmation letter at the top of page 192 serves a slightly different purpose. It was written to avoid any possible confusion over the terms of an oral agreement, as well as to convey a friendly attitude.

Dear Cynthia,

Just to confirm our agreement over lunch this afternoon: We will ship ten thousand ball point pens, in royal blue and white, with the slogan ''Winchester for Senator,'' at $3^{1}/_{4}$ cents apiece. The shipment is to arrive at Winchester campaign headquarters not later than Friday morning, April 20.

Again, my thanks for your order. You have not only my sincere gratitude — but my vote as well.

Yours,

Hank

Confirmations can be written even when they aren't absolutely necessary. They thus become *acknowledgments*. Many suppliers, upon receiving orders from regular customers, write brief acknowledgments, mostly to strengthen good will. For example:

Dear Ms. Virgil:

We appreciate your order of March 13 for two additional AK4 file cabinets. They will be fitted with Style C slide locks, as you requested, and sent out right away.

As always, it is a pleasure to serve you.

Sincerely,

William Peterson

William Peterson
Sales Supervisor

If a customer includes a remittance with his order, the acknowledgment letter should refer to it explicitly. First-time orders should always be acknowledged, preferably with a well-developed letter like the following:

Victory Department Store
14 East First Street
Birmingham, Alabama 38652

Ladies and Gentlemen:

Just a note of thanks for your recent order, and for your check for $387.10 in prepayment. We've already shipped your sixty cartons of Purvelle Paper Towels. They should reach you within a few days.

We feel sure you'll find the same rapid turnover that other dealers have found with Purvelles. Consumers find their multipurpose value and easy disposability hard to resist, to say nothing of the attractive package.

Needless to say, for you there is Purvelle's handsome retail profit margin.

Enclosed is a handy Purvelle order form for your convenience at reordering time.

Sincerely,

Donald Bostwick

Donald Bostwick
Distribution Manager

This acknowledgment is written positively from beginning to end, and its tone is excellent. Notice, as well, two stylistic choices Bostwick makes to increase his letter's effectiveness. He uses the brand name *Purvelle* repeatedly (four times, once in each paragraph) to build product identification in the reader's mind. And he emphasizes the most appealing idea by isolating it in a single-sentence paragraph, the third.

Effective acknowledgments must also be written by nonprofit institutions that receive gifts and donations. For obvious reasons, these acknowledgments must maintain and even strengthen their recipient's good will, as the letter in Figure 17 (on page 194) does.

Stopgap Replies

Another kind of reply often necessary in business is the *stopgap* reply. If, for instance, you get a request for information that will take you awhile to compile, *don't* remain silent until you do so. Send a stopgap reply, like the following:

MEMORANDUM --

Date: July 1, 198_

To: J. B. Perkins
From: Research Department (T. LaGuardia)
Subject: Your Request for Data on Mountain-States Markets

We have begun compiling, for cross-reference, the data on mountain-states markets that you requested in your memo yesterday.

The data are not as accessible as we thought. Because of last year's marketing reorganization, four different sources will be necessary. But we've located each of them and the staff is busy on the compilation. I expect to have it on your desk by Friday morning at 9.

T. LaG.

Figure 17
A well-written acknowledgment letter sent by a nonprofit institution to one of its benefactors.

TAYLORVILLE MEMORIAL HOSPITAL
Taylorville, Iowa

August 17, 19—

Mr. Joseph L. Griffith
97 Oak Park Way
Cedar Rapids, Iowa 56039

Dear Mr. Griffith:

You have our grateful thanks for your recently renewed contribution to our hospital development fund. Because of the support of friends like you, Taylorville Memorial has grown in the last several years in both size and excellence.

We appreciate your generosity and confidence in the Hospital, and shall do our utmost to continue deserving it.

Very truly yours,

Ernest K. Rogers

Ernest K. Rogers
Secretary-Treasurer

LaGuardia saw that he could not immediately comply with the boss's request, so as soon as he determined when he could, he wrote a stopgap reply. His memo is precisely informative, and it carries a tone of brisk efficiency.

Some Routine Problems with Routine Replies

Sometimes business replies are complicated by minor problems. A writer will ask for information that you cannot reveal, or perhaps ask a question you don't know the answer to. When this happens, that old cliché "honesty is the best policy" still holds true. Explain *why* you cannot provide the information, and perhaps offer to help in some other way. Admit that you don't know the answer and suggest, if you can, where it can be found.

Another difficulty in replying arises when a request or order letter isn't completely clear. Your reply may have to request clarification. The Fitwell Uniform Company effectively wrote this kind of reply to Fred Fox back on page 116.

Perhaps the customer has remitted a check with his order without realizing the price has gone up, or perhaps an order cannot be filled because of a supply shortage. You must state the facts *and* avoid displeasing the customer with the news — a vital double objective.

Here are two such replies that should successfully avoid disappointing the customer:

Mr. Simon Black, Office Manager
Silver Way Express Company
981 Ninth Avenue
New York, New York 10044

Dear Mr. Black:

We appreciate your recent order for one hundred gross of Barker No. 966 hexagonal red pencils, and your check for $360. The pencils are in stock and will be prepared for delivery to you by the middle of next week.

Owing to a recent rise in the cost of materials, and a year-end wage hike, a small increase in price -- from $3.60 to $3.75 per gross -- has been necessary. The invoice accompanying your order will reflect this slight change, but we wanted you to be aware of it before the order reaches you.[5]

You will find absolutely no change in the durability of Barker pencils, nor in their quality.

Yours truly,

Oscar Burne

Oscar Burne
Sales Manager

Both the tone and the underlying assumption of this letter are positive. The writer does not make the price increase sound like something to be suffered. He simply conveys the news, with a reasonable explanation, and assumes that the customer, in a time of inflation, will understand.

This second letter concerns a supply shortage:

[5] Note how the writer uses *strategic generalization* in this sentence. Instead of being as precise as he could have been by writing "The invoice . . . will reflect this $15 increase" he referred to the increase with the phrase "this slight change."

Gentlemen:

Our many thanks for your order of November 12. We are proud to be able to offer you such a wide line of hand-crafted utensils.

So that you may receive the exact styles you desire — styles which aren't on our shelves at the moment — we have requested that a special shipment be made to you directly from the manufacturer.[6] He assures us that your order will be shipped within the next ten days.

Again, our thanks.

Sincerely,

Harriet M. Bowen

Harriet M. Bowen
Wholesale Director

Nowhere in this letter does Harriet Bowen treat the delay in shipment as undesirable. She explains it in terms of benefit to the customer. Many less skilled business writers would have ruined this letter by writing "We are sorry but your order will be delayed because . . ."

In Summary

As with routine initiators, we can post some general rules for writing good routine replies:

1. Read the communication you're replying to very carefully. As you read it, you might even circle all the points you want to be sure to answer. An incomplete reply is a bad reply.

2. The "positive sandwich" principle is once again important. Begin and end every routine reply as positively as possible to establish a congenial tone.

3. If the communication you're replying to contains significant particulars, be sure to acknowledge those particulars. For example, when acknowledging a purchase order, be sure to restate the details of the order (unless those details are so long they'll make your reply clumsy). Restatement is a courtesy which assures your reader that his communication has been fully understood.

4. If the communication contains a remittance, acknowledge it.

5. If your reply does not answer all the questions that were put to you, explain why those questions are unanswered.

6. If necessary to make a reply complete, give *more* information than requested. If your reply contains enclosures, be sure it tells the reader *where* in the enclosed material his or her questions are answered.

[6] The principles of bulk and grammatical weight for emphasis are brought into play in this first sentence of the second paragraph. (Recall our discussion of them in Chapter 3.) The potentially disappointing idea (phrased as unnegatively as possible) is made into a 9-word phrase and sandwiched between a 10-word dependent clause and a 15-word independent clause both of which are completely positive and empathetic in outlook. These positive ideas are made to dominate and outshine the less-than-positive fact of a temporary shortage.

7. When your reply is potentially disappointing (for instance, when a price has risen or there is a shortage) treat the situation as positively as you can, and with empathy.

8. Always reply as empathetically as you can, keeping the recipient's point of view uppermost in your message. If you read the initiating communication carefully, there's a lot you can learn about the writer and his or her interests.

9. Always reply as promptly as you can — if possible, immediately. Promptness is not only a courtesy, it can keep your recipient from losing interest or thinking you are slow.

A WORD IN CLOSING ABOUT FORM LETTERS

Many of a company's routine communications tend to be recurrent. So to save time and money, some companies use *form letters*. Everyone knows what form letters are. They eliminate having to write a new reply and expend additional stenographic time each time a reply is necessary.

But all too often, the economy of form letters is a false economy. Most recipients don't like the impersonality of form letters, and don't react to them very well.

Consequently, any time you contemplate using a form letter, you're faced with a major decision. Is that inevitable loss of appeal worth the dollar savings? If it is, then use the form letter. If it isn't — don't!

One alternative to the "pure " form letter is the *prototype letter*. Business writers construct ready-written replies that they keep on file. Each time such a letter is needed, it is typed anew from the file-model and made to include whatever specific information is called for. Carefully composed, a prototype letter can provide distinctive, original-sounding letters at a fraction of the usual cost in time. But unless the prototype is carefully composed and freshly typed for each usage, it's as likely as a form letter to displease its recipient by its apparent impersonality. Good examples of effective letters from prototypes are the Valhalla University letter on page 187 and the Hillcrest Resort Hotel letter on page 191.

In recent years, some business communicators have relied on *computer letters* to gain the economy of form letters while avoiding their impersonality. A computer letter is a prototype letter programmed for multiple reproduction, with each copy bearing the name of its recipient and one or two individualized references to that recipient's situation in the letter's body. Computer letters tend to work well the first few times someone receives them; but after a while, unless they're very well written and carefully programmed, the technique wears thin.

PROBLEMS

1. Assume that you are writing a term report on modern advertising techniques. Select an advertisement from any current magazine, one that you feel is particularly original and effective. Then, write a letter to the advertising department of the company whose ad you've selected, asking them for information you can use in your report. You might ask for such information as how the central idea of the advertisement was originated, what kind of audience the advertisement is aimed at, why the magazine in which you found the ad was

used as the advertising medium, and if and how the company will be able to measure the ad's effectiveness. You can also ask any other questions about the ad you might feel significant.

This is not an easy letter to write well. You are asking a busy office for a lot of information solely as an aid to your education. But most companies are inclined to answer such requests, if the requests are well stated.

2. You and two of your friends plan to fly to the Canadian Rockies for a two-week vacation. Each of you has saved around five hundred dollars for the trip. You are interested in getting low-cost but clean and comfortable accommodations, and you want to visit as many interesting spots as possible.

Write to Vacations, Inc., a large travel agency in your city (or the large city nearest you), requesting pertinent information and specific suggestions on stretching your vacation dollars. Some of the questions you might ask are: What are tourist air fares? What are rates at hotels and lodges in the area? What are some of the best spots to visit? And there are no doubt other questions.

3. Compose a well-written letter to your representative in Congress or to your state legislator, requesting him or her to vote a certain way on an impending bill that is of interest to you, or to introduce legislation you think is really needed. Be sure to make clear the nature of the legislation you favor, and the reasons why you favor it.

4. You have gone to work as a credit correspondent for Williams & McGillicuddy, a large retail clothing store. This morning, you received the following letter:

114 Peacock Avenue
Scarsdale, NY 19432
January 8, 198_

Williams & McGillicuddy
1901 Madison Avenue
New York, NY 10091

Gentlemen:

After purchasing from your store for the last eighteen months, I would like to open a charge account in my name. Please sent the charge-a-card to me at the above address.

Very truly yours,

Maybelle Radcliffe

Maybelle Radcliffe

The store would very much like to open a charge account for Ms. Radcliffe, but first it must look into her credit rating. Your job is to write her a letter enclosing the store's standard credit inquiry form, which asks questions about her employment or other sources of income, her banking affiliations, and other charge accounts presently held.

In the letter, you should request that Ms. Radcliffe complete the form and return it to you as soon as possible. It's not a difficult letter to write, but if you imply in any way that Ms. Radcliffe's credit record might not be satisfactory, you may offend her, and instead of gaining a credit customer you'll lose a cash one.

5. Assume that four weeks have passed since you sent a letter to The Halaby Press (490 Furman St., Philadelphia, Pa.) ordering a copy of the book *The American University in the Twenty-First Century* by Carl I. Newhouse. You had attached a check for $6.95 to your order letter in full payment of the book. You have gotten no response to that order. Write a letter to The Halaby Press inquiring into the delay.

6. Thumb through a national magazine or your local newspaper and locate a mail-order advertisement for some relatively low-priced item you would like to own. When you find one, write a letter ordering that item. Assume that you are enclosing a check in payment for it. Clip the ad and attach it to your letter when you submit it to your instructor.

7. Harold Cox, the midwestern regional representative of the Continental Manufacturing Company, is a personal acquaintance of yours. He learns that you are writing a term report for your business communications class entitled "Big Business and Its Communications Problems," and tells you that Continental has a training manual for its correspondents that discusses the very problems you plan to consider in your report. He suggests that you write to Continental's home office (8800 Raritan Blvd., Caldwell, New Jersey 14801) for a copy of the manual. Write the letter.

8. Assume that you are the manager of the mail order department at the Huntington Decorative Supply Company of Atlanta, Georgia. You received Lee Cosgrove's order letter, which appears on pages 178–179, and have just filled the order and shipped it via freight express as Mr. Cosgrove requested. Now, because it's your policy to acknowledge all orders with a letter, write an effective letter of acknowledgment to Mr. Cosgrove. This is the first order you've received from him. Remember to acknowledge the check he included with his order.

9. You're the new public relations staff assistant for the Chamber of Commerce in the city of Cocoanut Beach, Florida. In hiring you, the city has chosen someone they feel is talented enough to initiate and sustain an effective public relations program for Cocoanut Beach.

During your first day on the job, your office receives the following postcard from someone who is probably suffering through a cold northeastern winter:

Gentlemen,

My family and I are moving to the southern part of Florida in two months, and we are interested in knowing about Cocoanut Beach, its job opportunities, housing, etc.

Yours truly,

Blanton Beale

321 12th St.
Bridgeport, Conn.

Before you went to work for the Chamber, all such requests were answered by sending out an illustrated brochure describing the city's climate, historical background, educational institutions, recreational opportunities, economic factors (including a list of employers), housing, population, taxes, transportation facilities, and utilities. Everyone who inquired got the same brochure, and the Chamber thought it was doing its job.

Now, however, you have decided to enhance the image of Cocoanut Beach by accompanying the standard brochure with a well-written letter. And you want this letter to say more than just, "Here's the information you requested." Have the letter introduce Mr. Beale to the brochure. You want him, of course, to read the whole brochure, but as a matter of courtesy you indicate in your letter where the brochure discusses the two matters he specifically inquired into ("Economic Opportunities," pp. 15-18 and "Housing," pp. 22-23). Remember to use a "positive sandwich" in the letter, and be as empathetic and congenial as you can.

10. You are on the job at Worthington, Bachelor, Inc., the large mail-order house. The following letter from Howard Carruthers (2 Piltdown Square, Bethany, Mo.) comes to your attention:

Gentlemen:

Please send me 3 pale green, Marlboro dress shirts, size 16, with short sleeves.

Yours truly,

Howard Carruthers

You'd like to fill the order right away, but Carruthers' letter does not indicate whether he wants *tab, regular,* or *button-down* collars.

Write a reply to Carruthers that requests this additional information without disappointing him over the delay.

11. You are personnel manager of United Steel (executive offices: 1300 Thunder Parkway, Pittsburgh, Pa.). Tom Blanding, a sophomore at Valhalla University, has written you inquiring about jobs at United Steel for college graduates. More specifically, Blanding wants to know what kind of curriculum (and extracurricular activities) would best prepare him for a position in United Steel's sales department two years hence, when he graduates.

You must answer his letter. Tell Blanding that it doesn't really matter what field he majors in; United Steel selects sales trainees with a wide variety of academic majors. Some course work in economics is helpful, but United Steel is *more* interested in academic attainment no matter what the major. Serious extracurricular activities are also a plus as far as United Steel is concerned.

One thing to remember in writing this letter. You don't want to give the impression that Blanding now has the inside track on a job in two years. But you do respect a young man who seems to be planning his future so seriously.

12. The Armstrong Cork Company prepared the prototype acknowledgment letter below as a promotional aid for its retailers. Whenever one of the retailers installed a new Armstrong floor in a customer's home, the letter (addressed specifically to the customer by the store manager) was sent out shortly after the installation.

Drawing upon all that you know about the writing of effective acknowledgment letters, write a thorough and detailed critique of this one — citing its strengths *and* weaknesses. Submit the critique in whatever format your instructor requests.

Dear Mr. and Mrs. ________

Please accept this quart of Armstrong Linogloss Wax as our token of appreciation for the privilege of installing an Armstrong Vinyl Corlon floor in your family room. As we mentioned earlier, you can't beat Armstrong Vinyl Corlon material for beauty, long wear, and easy maintenance. If you will follow the simple rules left by our flooring craftsmen and occasionally wax your floor with Armstrong Linogloss, we know that you will have no trouble keeping your floor beautiful and spotless.

If perchance there is some installation detail in which you are not perfectly satisfied, please call us and we will correct it immediately.

It was a pleasure to install the Armstrong floor in your home, and again we wish to thank you for your patronage and look forward to the time when we can serve you again.

Yours very truly,

John Doe
Store Manager

CHAPTER 9

CONVEYING GOODWILL AND GOOD NEWS

In this chapter, we look at two more types of direct reaction-evoker — the *goodwill* communication and the *good news* communication. The primary purpose of the goodwill letter or memo is to convey warm tone, and with that tone to create a stronger bond between the writer and the recipient. The purpose of the good news letter or memo is, in effect, to say "yes" to something the reader is hoping for, and to say it with the greatest effect. Let's look at them.

LETTERS AND MEMOS OF GOOD WILL

Some letters and memos in business are written simply to make their recipients feel good. Human beings that they are, business executives and merchants will often write such communications just to express sincere feelings. And business people that they are, they will write such communications because people tend to like those who make them feel good. There are practical as well as spiritual benefits to being liked.

When used as an instrument of business advantage, the goodwill communication is intended to create or strengthen the reader's good feeling for the writer and the writer's organization. The following letter is an example:

THE DESMOND NATIONAL BANK
& TRUST COMPANY
Main Street
Desmond, Iowa

February 27, 19__

Mr. Pierre Cartier
Route Four
Desmond, Iowa 61027

Dear Mr. Cartier:

This seems an especially appropriate time to express our appreciation for your patronage, which began one year ago this week. It has been a pleasure serving your account, and we look forward to continuing this service to you in the years to come.

The officers and staff join me in this expression of gratitude, and in the wish that you'll feel free to consult us whenever our counsel might be helpful.

Cordially yours,

T. Willard Drummond

T. Willard Drummond
President

Notice what Drummond has done. He has found a factual hook — in this case, the first anniversary of the customer's patronage — and hung a goodwill message on it. The purpose of the message is obvious: to enhance the reader's feeling toward Desmond National. The letter contains fact, but the facts aren't vital. It's the feeling that's important. An anniversary of patronage is the occasion for the letter, but the writer could have chosen any justifiable occasion to send such a message — perhaps after one month's patronage, or at the end of the first interest period, or after a particularly large deposit.

In the goodwill letter, the "positive sandwich" again comes into play. In fact, the positive opening and closing of Drummond's letter virtually join to become the entire message.

Goodwill messages shouldn't be very lengthy, but neither should they be too brief. You don't need many words to create good feeling; but you must say enough — and with a "you-attitude" — to avoid any hint that your message might be self-centered, or that you are merely discharging an obligation to say something nice. The following "goodwill" letter fails because it is both abrupt and self-centered:

> Dear Mr. Crabbe:
>
> This is to acknowledge your unblemished record in paying your bills over the last five years. All our other customers should be so prompt. Thank you.
>
> Simon La Rue

There are many kinds of goodwill communication in business, and numerous "hooks" upon which to hang them. In the next few pages, we'll examine some of these "hooks."

Messages of Thanks

Gratitude can be expressed for virtually anything in business with a written "thank you." In addition to gratitude, of course, the motive of business promotion underlies many a thank-you letter. Here's an example:

> Dear Mr. Silverman:
>
> Your consistent promptness in paying your invoices has earned for you that invaluable asset -- a strong credit standing. As your supplier, we really appreciate it. In many businesses, accounts like yours go unnoticed and seemingly unappreciated, while most of the attention goes to those who are slow in discharging their debts. This ought not to be.
>
> So we'd like you to consider this letter a sincere expression of our thanks for the splendid handling of your account. We are proud to serve you.
>
> Sincerely yours,
>
> Christopher C. Thompson
> Regional Manager

Other letters of thanks are written, not for sales promotion as such, but to strengthen a working relationship between two people. That's the intent of the following note from a salesman to a prospective customer's secretary:

Dear Miss Field:

Just a brief note of thanks for your help last week in getting me in to see Mr. Carnavale. It was important that I speak to him, and climbing through twelfth-floor windows is not my forte. Once in conference, he and I had what I feel was a very productive meeting.

If I can ever return the favor, I'd be more than happy to. Thanks again.

Joe Halbe

Star Products

Within an organization, occasions for thank-you messages are just as abundant. Here's a memo of gratitude from an account executive to a member of another department. Notice that it not only conveys thanks to its recipient; it also, via copies, informs supervisors up the line of his contribution to the company effort.

TO: R. C. Tillman	DATE: Sept. 9, 19__
cop: E. V. Muldoon	FILE: Cramwell 381
J. B. Christopher	
T. L. Underwood	

FROM: Diana Raymond

CONCERNING: The Recent Cramwell Request for Revised Layouts

My thanks to you, Bob, for coming through when the pressure was on.

It's safe to say that without your willingness to labor on into the night, we would not have satisfied the Cramwell people and perhaps have lost their account. Oscar Gustafson, chief liaison for Cramwell, liked the layouts you produced and was fully aware of the crisis conditions under which you produced them.

Again, my thanks for a splendid job.

Diana Raymond

Account Executive

Messages of Welcome

People are usually more comfortable, and more productive, if they're made to feel at home when new to a job or community. The welcome message is written to instill that feeling. On page 206 is a good example of an effective welcome.

NATIONAL MOTORS
INTEROFFICE COMMUNICATION

TO: John Farrington DATE: April 1, 19--

FROM: Lester M. Bornstein, Executive Vice-President

SUBJECT: Your Recent Appointment to National Motors

Welcome aboard, John.

If your first several days on the job have been anything like mine were eight years ago, you'd probably appreciate the relative tranquility of Kennedy Airport at rush hour.

I just want you to know that we in the Executive Office are happy to have you at National Motors. Judging by the credentials you bring with you, the corporation certainly stands to benefit from your talents. I feel sure you'll find your work -- and your career at National Motors -- stimulating and rewarding.

Lester M. Bornstein

In the letter at the top of page 207 — a welcome to someone new in the community — notice how the writer combines a promotional appeal with an expression of good will. This technique can be very successful if the promotional content is kept subordinate to the welcome.

Messages of Congratulation

A well-written message of congratulation can be an effective goodwill builder. Its appeal goes straight to the reader's ego. And there are many "hooks" upon which congratulatory messages can be hung — births, birthdays, engagements, marriages, promotions, awards — any special event or occasion.

Here are several examples of effectively written congratulations. Each is short and warm without being gushy. The first, to Mr. Timothy Ramsey, is written by a wholesaler to one of his regular customers:

MAYWOOD BROTHERS

"Your Local Strongwell Flooring Dealer"
Jamestown, Minnesota

September 20, 19--

Mrs. James L. Simpson
8912 Seventh Street
Jamestown, Minnesota 45920

Dear Mrs. Simpson:

Welcome to Jamestown. We hope that by now you've reached most of the things the movers probably left in the middle of your kitchen floor.

Jamestown isn't big, but there's a lot to it. We've enclosed a map of the city and a list of its restaurants, shops, and professional services. They are all within five minutes of the Civic Center by car. For any information about the city, please feel free to call on us.

We have been in business here for twenty-five years, and would like to be of service to you in selecting fine flooring products as the years go by. We handle the complete line of Strongwell flooring materials, for professional installation and for the do-it-yourselfer. And we're open all day, Monday through Saturday.

Our best wishes to you and your family in these hectic first days of establishing a home. It will be worth it, though. You'll like Jamestown.

Very truly yours,

Bob Maywood

Mr. Timothy Ramsey
Cranston's Department Store
555 Fifth Avenue
New York, New York 10012

Dear Tim,

I just heard the great news about the birth of your grandson. The first person who said ''grandchildren are all the joys without the headaches'' sure knew what he was talking about. It's a wonderful experience.

Next time we have lunch, we'll have to limit debate on prices to ten minutes. I know you'll have at least two hours' worth to report on the newest member of the Ramsey dynasty.

My best wishes,

Morris Schapp

Morris Schapp

This next message was sent when its writer learned that a colleague had been promoted.

TO: R. Cargill
FROM: S. Weatherby
SUBJECT: A Job Well Done

Congratulations, Bob,

I just learned of your promotion to the Executive Office. I'm delighted at the recognition the Board has shown one of the most deserving men at Amalgamated.

You have my very best wishes in your new position. I for one will miss you in Marketing.

Sylvia

The next one is a letter of congratulations from a manufacturer to a retail dealer who has just opened a new and larger store.

Dear Mr. Marder:

We congratulate you on the opening of your fine new shop. I guess you just can't keep a good businessman small.[1]

You have our sincere good wishes for the continued success your efforts so richly deserve.

Yours truly,

Jerome Fitzpatrick

Jerome Fitzpatrick
Distribution Coordinator

[1] Style note: Clichés are usually something to be avoided. But if you can give a *fresh twist* to an old cliché, the result can be quite satisfying. That's what the writer tries here when he turns that old chestnut: "You can't keep a good man down" into "You can't keep a good businessman small."

If all goes well with Marder's new store, Fitzpatrick will probably be writing the following kind of goodwill message five years from now:

Dear Mr. Marder:

Success is a wonderful feeling -- but it's hectic. So hectic at Marder's that you may not have realized your present store is five years old next Tuesday. Judging from what we've heard in the industry, you've become a landmark on Madison Street.

We just wanted to say ''happy birthday'' to the store -- and ''congratulations'' to you on your continuing success.

Sincerely,

Jerome Fitzpatrick
Assistant Vice-President

One of the most effective congratulatory messages is the message of commendation written by a boss to a staff member. Such messages not only boost an employee's morale, but they make that employee more receptive to constructive criticism if it's ever necessary. Here's an example, written by a marketing vice-president to an award winning sales rep:

Dear Roberta,

I know that it was a real source of satisfaction for you to receive the annual First-Place Sales Award last week -- all the more, I suspect, after coming so close last year.

Reaching 109% of quota, after a change of territory and with a tough, new assignment, is an achievement of which you can be proud. I have a feeling that this year in the same territory will prove an even more successful one for you.

I want to thank you again for all the energy you have devoted to the company, and for the cooperation you have always shown the executive office. We're proud to have you as a member of the team.

Sincerely,

Roger Walston
Vice-President, Marketing

Messages of Seasonal Greeting

Everyone is familiar with messages of seasonal greeting, most commonly seen during the Christmas holidays. Some business people also send greetings at other holidays, when there's less competition in the recipient's mailbox.

The goodwill generated by a seasonal greeting card can be increased if the message is personalized with a brief letter, like this one from Ridley's Furniture Market:

> Dear Mr. Donaldson,
>
> Among our things-to-be-thankful-for here at Ridley's during this time of Thanksgiving are the opportunities you have given us during the past year to serve you.
>
> Let me tell you how much we appreciate your patronage. You and your family have our warmest wishes for the upcoming holiday season.
>
> Sincerely,
>
> Michael Turner
> President

Unexpected Messages of Apology

In business, whenever you cause inconvenience to someone — no matter how slight — you ought to apologize. Major blunders, of course, demand an apology. But even when an incident is slight, and apology probably unexpected, a well-written letter or memo of apology can not only set things straight, but develop added goodwill for the writer.

State highway departments use this strategy when they put up signs at construction sites apologizing for inconvenience to motorists. Here's a good example of an unexpected apology written by the manager of a downtown office building to all its tenants; management was not really at fault in the matter, but it seized the opportunity to apologize anyway:

> Dear ___________:
>
> We want to apologize for Tuesday's drop in water pressure. It was as surprising to us as it must have been to you.
>
> We phoned the water district office immediately after the drop, and they told us that a feeder pipe that supplies us and ''250'' next door had broken. The District Manager now assures us that the break has been repaired and that precautions against recurrence have been taken. He promises us that the precious liquid will flow dependably from now on. We're keeping our fingers crossed.
>
> Yours very truly,
> The Preston Company

Much more will be said about the technique of apology when we discuss effective conciliation in Chapter 10.

Messages Preventing Ill Will

When business people find they must do something that might engender ill will, they can often head off that ill will with a letter announcing and explaining the action. Such messages are often written to warn stockholders of forthcoming dividend decreases. Businesses often forewarn their customers of renovations or upcoming price rises. In Figure 18, we see an "open letter" of this sort, written by the management of an international hotel chain and posted at its reception desks to explain its policy of first-night prepayment and to head off customers' objections to it. Even as an impersonal "open letter," this message conveys a feeling of concern for the hotel's clients. It effectively prevents ill will.

Figure 18
A message designed to prevent ill will.

GRAND CAY HOTEL

Nottingham-Darby Stockbridge Lane NG 12 5 FQ
Telephone: (06362) 04183
Telex: 585746

Dear Traveller,

In attempting to provide the best service possible for our guests, we've been faced with a problem. More and more often, it seems, people are engaging hotel accommodations without prior booking, and leaving without settling their accounts.

These "silent departures" have caused us--and other hotels as well--substantial cash losses. So far, at Grand Cay we've been able to absorb these losses without passing their cost on to our guests in the form of increased prices. But we're approaching our limit.

So, in order to prevent further losses of this sort, and to keep our prices as low as possible in this time of inflation, we are asking that--

ANY PERSON SEEKING OVERNIGHT ACCOMMODATION WITHOUT A PRIOR CONFIRMED BOOKING, PLEASE PAY IN ADVANCE THE FULL COST OF THE ACCOMMODATION.

Only by the introduction of such safeguards can the problem be alleviated. Please understand our position, and know that the service we will provide you will continue to be the best we can humanly offer.

Many thanks,

Godfrey Billingham

Godfrey Billingham
General Manager

Inquiries Designed to Generate Good Will

Another way of building goodwill is to show someone you care about his or her ideas and opinions. That's the principle underlying the letter in Figure 19. Basically, it's a letter of inquiry. An elected official is asking his constituents for their opinions on a variety of political issues. Those opinions will be valuable to him as he decides how to vote on pending legislation. But even more valuable, come Election Day, will be the goodwill he is building by showing his constituents that he cares about their views. Notice the timing of Assemblyman Mencken's letter. The mails are generally flooded with this kind of letter as Election Day approaches, and voters are rightly cynical about the motives of such "eleventh-hour" inquiries. But the timing of Mencken's letter, only three

Figure 19
An inquiry used to generate good will.

THE ASSEMBLY

STATE OF NEBRASKA
LINCOLN

WALTER L. MENCKEN
ASSEMBLYMAN, FIFTH DISTRICT
FEDERAL BUILDING
MONROE, NEBRASKA

COMMITTEES:
COMMERCE
JUDICIARY
ROADS

January 19, 19--

Dear Mr. Knox:

I want to thank you, along with other residents of the Third District, very much for your generous support in the recent election. I sincerely appreciate it.

During the upcoming Assembly session, many issues and problems will, as you know, be up for consideration. As your assemblyman, I plan to develop a legislative program that will earn your continuing support. To this end, I would very much like to hear your views on the key issues confronting us as Nebraskans, as farmers, and as law-abiding citizens.

I have had my staff compile, on the enclosed questionnaire, a list of the issues that seem to bear directly on the everyday lives of our constituents. I'd be pleased to have you indicate, alongside each of them, your feelings and your opinions. Please also feel free to comment upon any other issues you consider important.

It has long been my aim to bring state government home closer to the people, and to increase their participation in the making of law and public policy. This post-election questionnaire seems one way to ensure that your views will be heard in the Legislature.

Very truly yours,

Walter L. Mencken

Walter L. Mencken

encl.

months after his election, strongly implies a genuine concern for the opinions of his constituency. The letter effectively generates goodwill.

One of the most valuable things about the goodwill messages we've just considered is their enormous range of application. They can be used by businesses to create or enhance goodwill with their customers, their employees, their stockholders, the communities in which they are located, and the industries in which they compete. Once a year, for example, a company named TRW in Los Angeles conducts a systematic search through its workforce — which runs to many thousands of employees — to determine who among them ought to be formally recognized by the company for doing volunteer community work of one kind or another. If you're in a supervisory position, the number of possibilities for such messages is limited only by your imagination and your desire to please people. We have sampled only a few.

LETTERS AND MEMOS OF GOOD NEWS

Next among the types of direct reaction-evoker, let's consider the *good-news* message. In simple terms, the good news communication is one that says "yes" to something its recipient is hoping for. The granting of credit to a credit applicant, the acceptance of a college applicant, the awarding of a prize or scholarship, the appointment of job candidates to positions they sought, the announcement of a raise or a promotion, the acceptance of a proposal — these are just a few of the situations that call for a good-news message.

On the face of it, good-news communications would seem easy to write. How hard can it be to say "yes"? The truth is, however, that good-news messages in business are a "land of lost opportunity." Good-news letters and memos give a writer an unbeatable opportunity to build goodwill. And far too many writers, thinking that all they have to do is state the good news, unknowingly throw that opportunity away. Consider the following letter:

Dear Sir:

Enclosed is our draft in the amount of $381.90, which is the amount over your deductible for which Smith Motors, the garage of your choice, agreed to repair your automobile. You will also find enclosed a copy of the estimate on the basis of which they agreed to repair.

Yours truly,

Norris Sedzlick

Norris Sedzlick
Claims

The facts are clear, and the news is good. The reader is $381.90 richer. But there's something missing from the letter. Compare it to the following letter written in the same situation:

> Dear Mr. Jones:
>
> I'm happy to enclose our draft for $381.90 to pay for damages to your 1979 Camaro. The sum represents the entire amount of the claim in excess of the $100 deductible called for in your policy.
>
> We were glad to have Smith Motors in Dalhart submit the estimate, as you requested, and we're confident they'll get your car back in perfect order.
>
> For our part, we at Mutual are pleased as always to be able to serve you.
>
> Cordially yours,
>
> Charles Golden
> Claims Officer

Both letters bear the same good news, but Golden's does it better. You feel after reading Sedzlick's letter that his company begrudges the settlement. It lacks positivity, and its tone is dull. Golden, on the other hand, has the knack for writing good news. He takes advantage of a naturally positive situation. He presents the check to the client, and he sounds glad that his company is able to lift part of the burden of repair from the client's shoulders.

Golden's letter illustrates the way a good-news message should be written. First, the *positive sandwich* principle is put to work: the letter opens with positive tone ("I'm happy to . . ."), and it closes with positive tone (" . . . are pleased as always to be able to serve you.") And notice this: because the central message itself is positive (in this case, "here's your check for $381.90"), that fact is delivered at the beginning, as part of the letter's opening. The good news itself *becomes* the positive opening. No need to keep the reader in suspense.

Then, after opening positively by revealing the good news, the writer devotes the middle of the letter to the accompanying details, the details that are a necessary part of the good news. And here's where so many good news messages in business fall short of the mark. The details should be presented as positively, and with as much empathy, as the good news itself. Don't make the mistake of following your positive opening with a mere routine recitation of detail. The reader is pleased with the good news you've brought. So use the rest of the letter to *sustain* that pleasure, and thereby convert it, instantaneously, into goodwill for you, the writer.

Here is the recommended strategy pattern for good-news letters and memoranda:

Recommended Strategy Pattern for Letters and Memos of Good News

First,	write a positive opening, including delivery of the good news right at or near the beginning;
then,	give all the necessary accompanying details (as *positively* and *empathetically* as possible);
finally,	write a tonally positive closing (one that is relevant to the good news that's been conveyed).

Notice how this pattern is used consistently in all of the following good-news communications. The first is a letter granting credit to a retail customer:

Dear Ms. Leftler:

We are extremely happy to honor your request for a credit account at Martin's. From now on, all you need say is ''Charge it to my account!''

As part of our special service to you as an account holder, you will be able to take advantage of all price reductions before they are advertised to the public. You may also, whenever the need arises, use your account by phone. Just tell the Order Department what you want and give them your account number. Early calls mean same-day delivery anywhere in the Springfield area. You will also find in the enclosed booklet many time-saving, dollar-saving services available to you as an account holder at Martin's.

You have our immediate thanks. Our appreciation for your patronage over the long term can best be shown by the courteous and efficient service we're proud to provide you.

Sincerely yours,

Charles Morrison

Charles Morrison
Credit Manager

Take a look at the close analysis of this good-news letter in Figure 20.

The good-news pattern is also evident in the letter on page 217 to Cynthia Forbes, who applied for University admission back on page 187. The writer

Figure 20
Detailed analysis of a well-written good-news letter.

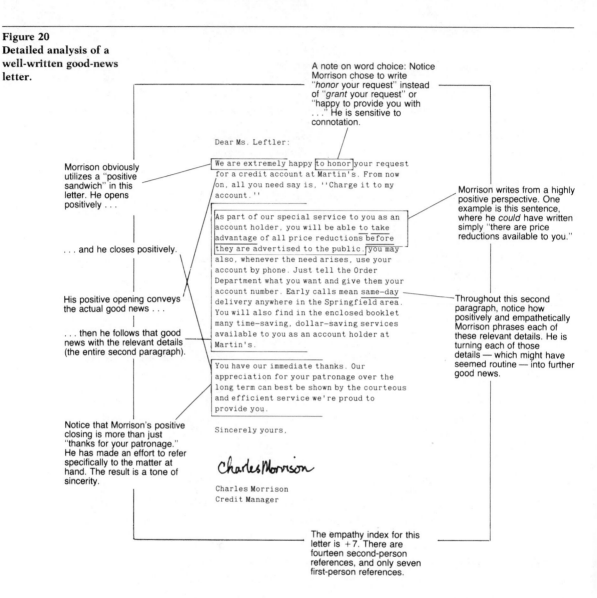

A note on word choice: Notice Morrison chose to write "*honor* your request" instead of "*grant* your request" or "happy to provide you with . . ." He is sensitive to connotation.

Morrison obviously utilizes a "positive sandwich" in this letter. He opens positively . . .

. . . and he closes positively.

His positive opening conveys the actual good news . . .

. . . then he follows that good news with the relevant details (the entire second paragraph).

Notice that Morrison's positive closing is more than just "thanks for your patronage." He has made an effort to refer specifically to the matter at hand. The result is a tone of sincerity.

Morrison writes from a highly positive perspective. One example is this sentence, where he *could* have written simply "there are price reductions available to you."

Throughout this second paragraph, notice how positively and empathetically Morrison phrases each of these relevant details. He is turning each of those details — which might have seemed routine — into further good news.

Dear Ms. Leftler:

We are extremely happy to honor your request for a credit account at Martin's. From now on, all you need say is, ''Charge it to my account.''

As part of our special service to you as an account holder, you will be able to take advantage of all price reductions before they are advertised to the public. You may also, whenever the need arises, use your account by phone. Just tell the Order Department what you want and give them your account number. Early calls mean same-day delivery anywhere in the Springfield area. You will also find in the enclosed booklet many time-saving, dollar-saving services available to you as an account holder at Martin's.

You have our immediate thanks. Our appreciation for your patronage over the long term can best be shown by the courteous and efficient service we're proud to provide you.

Sincerely yours,

Charles Morrison

Charles Morrison
Credit Manager

The empathy index for this letter is +7. There are fourteen second-person references, and only seven first-person references.

opens with highly positive tone, revealing the good news right at the beginning. Then he proceeds with the necessary details, stating them positively and with empathy for the pleasure and anticipation the good news has no doubt created. Then he closes positively. The occasion for this letter may be quite routine for its author (after all, the Dean of Admissions may send hundreds of such lettters every year). But he knows that the news is very special for Cynthia Forbes, and he does nothing to diminish its special impact.

Still another example of an effectively patterned good-news letter is the following one, sent by a philanthropic organization to Ted Benson, a successful candidate for a fellowship:

VALHALLA UNIVERSITY
KENT, OHIO

February 14, 19--

Ms. Cynthia Forbes
88 Anthracite Lane
Johnstown, Pennsylvania

Dear Ms. Forbes:

After a thorough evaluation of your record and your transcripts, I am happy to announce your acceptance to freshman standing at Valhalla this September. We're pleased to welcome you.

Orientation Week for new students will begin on Monday, September 15. On that day, you will be assigned a freshman advisor, and have your first opportunity to consult about your goals and your program of studies. Please be sure to bring the enclosed forms with you, completed, on that day. Classes will begin the following Monday, September 22.

We also ask that the enclosed intent-to-register card be returned to us as soon as possible, and in any event in time to reach us by July 1.

On behalf of the trustees, the faculty, and the student body, I wish you every success as a member of the Class of '85. We look forward to greeting you in September.

Sincerely yours,

Herbert A. Riddle
Dean of Admissions

Dear Mr. Benson:

We take pride in awarding you a Goodnoy Fellowship for the school year beginning this September. This award is being granted to you after a careful screening of over three hundred qualified applicants. You have our congratulations.

Your stipend of $3,200 will be paid promptly by mail in ten monthly installments beginning September 1. When you register at the Valhalla Graduate School, all you need to do is submit the enclosed form 102A to the Registrar. That

office will send your tuition bill to us, where it will be paid. If we can answer any further questions regarding your Goodnoy Fellowship, we will be more than happy to. Just give us a call.
We wish you every success during this coming year and in all your future pursuits.

Yours truly,

Joseph M. Hurley
Awards Coordinator

Next is a letter to a college graduate offering him the job he's been seeking. Unquestionably, it's a good-news letter, but one with a necessary modification. The writer is quite happy to offer the job, and she wants to convey enthusiasm; but she does not want the successful candidate to feel that the company is chasing him. The company must retain its prestigious image. A delicate balance between enthusiasm and reserve is needed. Let's see how the writer does it.

Dear Mr. Tydings:

We're very pleased to offer you the position of Management Trainee here at Consolidated. Your academic preparation, your work experience, and your excellent showing during your recent interview all promise a successful managerial career. After meeting you, Mr. Langston, Mrs. Peterson and Mr. Cardozo all felt you were the best candidate for the job.

As we agreed, your beginning salary will be $1200 per month, with all contingency allowances and personnel benefits as spelled out in your discussion with our Assistant Personnel Officer, Mr. Davey. You will be assigned, at first, to Mr. Cardozo's Production Department for approximately three months, where you will work with every phase of the production process. From there, subsequent assignments will take you through the entire Parmco operation, providing you with the most thorough managerial training available in our industry.

I would appreciate your calling or writing me as soon as possible regarding this offer. Personally, I am confident that both you and the company stand to gain immeasurably from your acceptance.[2]

Sincerely yours,

Ethel A. Butterworth

Ethel A. Butterworth
Personnel Manager

After Tydings is with the company for a while, he may receive a memo like the following. It too is a good-news message, but without the reserve necessary in Butterworth's letter.

TO: Darrell Tydings DATE: February 14, 19___
FROM: Rod Schultz
SUBJECT: Your Work on the Shady Farms Account

In recognition of your tireless efforts and your unqualified success with the Shady Farms account, I am happy to promote you to the position of Associate Account Executive, effective immediately.

As you well know, the Shady Farms account has more than tripled in size during your tenure as Account Aide. Ken Dippolito of Shady Farms Advertising Department has, upon numerous occasions, praised you as being the man most responsible for the success of their recent magazine campaign. Your supervisor, Jeanne Peterson, concurs enthusiastically.

So please accept my congratulations upon your climbing one more step up the ladder. We are happy to have you on the job.

Rod

Occasionally, a company executive will have to write a "blanket" good-news communication, like the following memo to every member of the company's art department. Though briefer than the preceding good-news communications, it still follows the appropriate pattern:

[2] A note on positivity: In her first draft, Butterworth ended this letter with the sentence "Personally, I am confident that both you and the company will gain if you accept." But upon rereading, she felt that closing clause, *if you accept*, was unnecessarily conditional in tone, implying that Tydings might not accept. So she revised it until she came up with the sentence that now closes this letter, a sentence that sounds neither overly confident nor overly conditional.

To: All Members of the Art Department
From: F. Tolstoy
Subject: Salary Increase

The Comptroller's Office is happy to inform all members of the Parmco Art Department of a 6% increase in salary beginning October 1. Raises will be first reflected in your October 15 pay checks. We honestly feel that there is no department in the company more deserving of this increase.

Fred Tolstoy
Frederick Tolstoy
Comptroller

Finally, let's look at a good-news message that expresses acceptance of a business proposal. The letter, which follows, notifies its recipient that the book he has begun to write seems like a good one; the publisher to whom he submitted the idea along with some sample chapters wants to put the book under contract. Once again, we see the good news first; then a detailed and *extremely empathetic* highlighting of the conditions the publisher wants to impose on the project (which will be spelled out further in the contract); and, in closing, a warm and positively worded encouragement that the work proceed full speed ahead.

Dear Mr. Dunnaway:

We were most pleased to receive the prospectus for your projected book on board room politics, and we are equally happy to give you a contractual ''go-ahead'' on the project. A formal contract will be sent out to you within ten days.

As outlined and begun, your book seems very promising. It's the kind of manuscript -- solid and well researched, yet irreverent -- that we're especially interested in publishing. With ten more chapters on a par with those you've submitted, the book is bound to become a best seller in its field.

Let me touch upon a few points that I think will give the book its strongest possible appeal:

1. I like the sample illustrations by Max Groman that you submitted, and am pleased to have Mr. Groman working with you on the book. As you plan your subsequent illustrations, remember to keep them as functional as possible. Make every illustration illuminate one or more of your concepts. Art that is merely decorative can, in this field, give a book that ''micky mouse'' feeling -- and hurt it badly.

2. Of the two chapters we already have, I think Chapter One opens more effectively. Its anecdotal opening, which

drops the reader into the midst of a high-powered board meeting, works better than the ''talkier'' opening of Chapter Two. Can we make Two, and subsequent chapters, more immediately appealing through anecdote or some other device? I leave the method up to you.

3. Our resident lawyer has had a look at your chapters and thinks he recognizes much too easily the real-life models behind your ''Homer Hanratty'' and ''J. P. Windover.'' I think we're going to have to alter the backgrounds and physical descriptions of these two ''power wielders'' enough to assure us that we won't be hit by lawsuits.

4. To get the book on the market by next year's Fall season, I think November 1 ought to be our outside time limit. If you can finish by October 1, as you suggested, all the better.

Everything else seems quite in order. Please let me know your reactions to these suggestions as soon as you have a chance. And know that we look forward very much to getting your manuscript through production and into the market. With some strong reviews and the right publicity, the book will be, I am sure, the best of all publications -- the book that simultaneously enlightens and entertains.

Yours sincerely,

Martin L. Royster

Martin L. Royster
Senior Editor

Notice especially in this letter how positively and empathetically the details are handled. It would have been very easy to make them sound like obstacles, or even warnings — *You must make every illustration functional. . . . Chapter Two doesn't open as well as Chapter One. . . . Unless you do some altering, we will be vulnerable to lawsuit. . . .* But that would undermine one of the very purposes the letter must serve: to motivate Dunnaway and keep his enthusiasm at a maximum during the arduous process of finishing a first-rate book.

It's a very good good-news letter!

IN SUMMARY

As a perceptive businessperson, you want to remain alert to those situations that allow you to enhance someone's favorable feeling toward you, and toward your organization. They occur more often than you may realize. Failure to seize such opportunities with a goodwill letter or memo is a waste of business resource just as surely as throwing money or talent down a drain. Look for those occasions, or "hooks," onto which you can hang messages of thanks, congratulations, welcome, greeting, or unexpected apology.

And always take maximum advantage of any situation that sees you granting someone's wishes. While it's easy to say "yes," it requires real care — and a continuing concern for tone and empathy —to turn that "yes" to your best advantage.

Goodwill and good-news communications are not the most difficult kinds of business message you will write — but they can be, and often are, the most productive.

PROBLEMS

1. One theory of management — that of "management by exception" — holds that the primary task of the business manager is to solve problems that cannot be solved by subordinates. As a business executive (so the theory goes), you delegate responsibility and authority to those below you on the corporate hierarchy, and you keep your own desk free of all problems except those that cannot be handled at a lower level. You instruct your subordinates to handle all the problems they can and simply keep you informed of what they (and their subordinates) are doing, so you can coordinate all their efforts, and account for them to top management.[3] When followed faithfully, this theory sees you, the manager, staying *un*involved with matters until they become problems.

What likely effects will such a management theory have on the wide range of efforts described in this chapter as goodwill communications?

2. "Goodwill letters are a good idea," said one businessman recently, "but who's got the time to write them all?" He went on to say, "What the smart executive does is go to his nearest Hallmark Card Shop. They've got all you'll ever need in the way of goodwill messages right there on the card racks."

Comment on the pros and cons of this executive's idea.

3. Assume that you are in business (in any capacity you wish). In a memo to your instructor, indicate the position you're in, and list all the "hooks" onto which you could hang a useful goodwill message (that is, all the situations you can think of in which it would be smart business for you to send a goodwill communication). Don't forget that your concern for goodwill doesn't stop with your customers or prospective customers. Relations with your suppliers (if you have suppliers) and relations with your fellow employees should also be cultivated both superiors and subordinates.

Quite obviously, your list won't be a short one.

4. Looking back on your college work, pick the course you now feel provided the greatest amount of useful career preparation, and write the teacher of that course a letter of thanks. The letter needn't be long, but it should refer to at least one or two specific examples of that usefulness.

5. John Michaels, a data analyst in your division, responded very promptly to your request and compiled data on last year's sales in the Philadelphia market, submitting them to you in a memorandum that you received

[3] This "thumbnail" theory is, of course, a bit too simply stated — but it is a simplification to which many executives in both industry and government nonetheless subscribe.

this morning. You, as Division Director, need to incorporate these figures into the semi-annual Divisional Director's Report for submission to R.D. Markingham, your company's Executive Vice-President. Thanks to Michaels' quick work, you'll be able to complete the report before the day is out. First, though, you ought to write a brief memo of thanks to Michaels, expressing your appreciation for his prompt and good work. Write the memo.

6. Assume that you are the manager of Merchants-Plus, a drug wholesale house located at 420 Broadhurst Avenue, Baltimore, Maryland. You serve many of the retail druggists in North Baltimore. One day in the *Baltimore Star-Telegram* you see the following announcement:

> NEWLY MARRIED -- Barbara Josephs, daughter of Mr. & Mrs. Robert P. Josephs of 12 Sunrise Lane, North Baltimore, became the bride of Herbert Fielding, son of Dr. and Mrs. Roger Fielding of Tucson, Arizona, in a ceremony performed last Saturday at All Souls Episcopal Church in North Baltimore. A reception followed at the Thunderbird Manor. The couple will reside in Tucson after a three-week honeymoon.

You recognize the bride as the only daughter of a customer of yours, Bob Josephs, a pharmacist who has his own store at 1213 Main Street in North Baltimore. Write a short goodwill letter to Josephs in recognition of his daughter's wedding.

7. On page 207, there's a letter of welcome sent by Maywood Brothers to Mrs. James L. Simpson, a newly arrived resident. Assume that you own and manage a clothing store in your own home town (men's or women's clothing, whichever you wish). Compose a letter, similar to Maywood Brothers', which you could sent out to welcome newcomers to your town.

8. You are the personnel manager at United Foods in Philadelphia, Pennsylvania. You and the management of United Foods decide that it might be an effective goodwill gesture for the company to begin paying recognition to the outside activities of your employees.

Marvin Oakes, a clerk in the Billing Department, just last week guided the Little League team he manages to victory in the South Philadelphia Little League Finals. Now his team moves into the Pennsylvania District Elimination Tournament.

Write a memorandum to Oakes commending him on this service to the community.

9. Bland's Novelty Store, at 14 Foster Street in Augusta, Georgia, is one of the retail stores that your company — Nixon Novelty Wholesalers, in Atlanta — regularly supplies. Unfortunately, Bland's had a fire last week. The store was not totally burned out, but Tim Bland's office at the back of the store was severely charred.

Write a goodwill letter to Bland conveying your sympathy over the fire, your confidence that he can overcome the temporary hardship, and your willingness to replace any Nixon samples, brochures, or price lists that may have been destroyed. You would also be quite willing to duplicate for Bland any records of transactions he has had with you.

10. Yesterday, you were elected to the City Council, getting fifty-two percent of the total vote cast in your district. Your success would not have been

possible without the thirty-five campaign workers who gave tirelessly of their time, ringing doorbells, making telephone calls, and handling correspondence in your behalf.

Write an effective letter of thanks which can be individually addressed to each of your campaign workers. In addition to being genuinely grateful to them, remember—you'll be up for reelection in a short two years and needing campaign help once again.

11. Upon your graduation, you apply for a top-flight starting position with a very good firm. The competition for that job, as you would expect, is quite keen. You ask Professor Jones, one of your college teachers, to write a letter of recommendation for you. He does, and rather than keep his letter to the firm strictly confidential, he sends you a copy of it — and it is glowing. He has praised your achievements, your abilities, your general intelligence, your motivation, and your character very highly.

You have your interviews with the firm; but, unfortunately, you do not get the job. The personnel manager at the firm tells you cordially but frankly that you were, as a result of all their screening, their third choice out of twenty-nine serious applicants. But their first-choice candidate accepted the job.

It would now seem that you have several good reasons to write a goodwill letter to Professor Jones. If you agree, write the letter. If you don't agree, write a memo to your instructor explaining why you feel it is unnecessary.

12. The computer letter opposite was sent out as a goodwill gesture by ExConn Gas to credit-card holders who consistently paid their bills on time. In a memo to your instructor, evaluate whatever strengths and weaknesses you feel the letter has, and comment on what you feel its overall effectiveness was.

13. In your capacity as personnel manager for United Foods, Inc., in Philadelphia, Pennsylvania, you write a lot of letters, some of them good-news letters. Here's one such case: You've received an application from Adam Pierce, a senior at Valhalla University in Kent, Ohio. His well-written letter and resumé show the following information about him.

> He is twenty-three years old, single, and free to relocate geographically.
>
> He is graduating with a humanities major and a business-administration minor, in the top five percent of his class.
>
> He seeks a position as a management trainee with United Foods.

You are impressed with his application and wish to have him fly to Philadelphia at the company's expense for an interview. Write a letter to Pierce acknowledging his application and expressing your interest in seeing him during the first half of March. In the letter, ask him to call you collect to inform you exactly when he'll be able to come for an interview.

14. Read the situation in problem 13 above. Assume that Pierce came in for the interview and was approved by everyone who spoke to him. Now you want to write a letter to Pierce formally offering him the position.

The starting salary, as indicated during the interview, is to be $1400 a month. The job entails serving the first four weeks at United Foods' regional

ExConn
PETROLEUM PRODUCTS

TRAVEL CARD CENTER

ExConn Inc.
885 WILCOX BOULEVARD
P. O. BOX 304
LOS ANGELES, CALIF 90060

November 12, 19-- 75-291-5213-9

W. Wells
1944 Sierra Nuevo
Los Irvinos, CA 92864

Dear Friend:

In today's business world, many times it's the good credit customers, like you, who go unnoticed and seemingly unappreciated.

Your account deserves special recognition for the prompt manner in which it has been paid since its opening on November 1, 1974.

We also note your purchases totaled $968.40 over the last twelve months and the confidence you have shown in our products is appreciated.

Thank you for your friendship. We will continue in our efforts to deserve it.

Very truly yours,

Brenda Ann Roberts

Manager - Travel Card Center

BAR:cb

packing plant in Birmingham, Alabama, then returning to the Philadelphia home office to continue training.

If Pierce accepts the job and can meet the schedule you have in mind, he will begin work on Monday, June 20, in Birmingham. He will take his preemployment physical and complete all the necessary paperwork in Philadelphia on Friday the 17th, and fly down to Birmingham on the 18th.

In the letter, you want to sound confident that Pierce will accept your offer, but not presumptuous. And you don't want Pierce to feel that the path to success at United Foods is going to be easy. But you do want to sound enthusiastic about having him join the company, and you do want your letter to reflect your awareness that this decision he's about to make is one of those important ones in life.

15. The following letter was written by a businesswoman who was convinced she knew how to deliver good news. Though it isn't a completely bad letter you'll probably find some weak points in it. Prepare a full critique of this good-news letter, discussing both weaknesses and strong points.

John Doe
3619 Seeley Avenue
Rockford, Illinois 75432

Dear Sir:

It is with genuine pleasure that we have opened a charge account for you, and we sincerely hope that you will find it a source of satisfaction in your purchases whenever you see the Remaco sign. You have a right to expect that all of us here at Remaco, and our associated dealers, do all in our power to please you in every phase of our merchandise and service.

You will receive an itemized statement every month showing all transactions of the preceding month. We are on a cycle billing, and your statement is mailed on the 1st of each month. Payment should be made within 10 days to protect and further enhance your splendid credit record standing.

If at any time any one of us should fall short of your expectations, as humans sometimes do, we would consider it a favor of you to let us know.

Cordially yours,

Mina Webster

Mina Webster
Credit Manager

16. From a department store or some other large retail outlet which provides customers with charge-account cards, obtain a copy of the letter sent to customers informing them that their request for credit privileges is being granted. In a memorandum to your instructor, analyze in detail that letter's effectiveness as a good-news business message.

17. You are this year's chairman of FAIR (The Foundation of American Industrial Relations). This year's FAIR Award for the Executive of the Year will be going to John C. Merriwether, vice-president of National Motors, Inc. (Deerfield, Michigan), for his outstanding efforts in mediating a price dispute last spring between the automotive industry and the American Association of Electrical Suppliers. As FAIR chairman, you must write a letter to Merriwether,

informing him of the award and inviting him to come to New York on October 15, at FAIR's expense, for the annual awards banquet.

18. You are the shipping manager for the Seven Seas Lines, a steamship company based in Mobile, Alabama. One of the smaller loads carried on the last trip of your ship the S.S. Waterbury, from Le Havre to Mobile, was a shipment of six trunks of personal effects belonging to Mr. Ed Roy Palmer of Carlisle, Alabama. Four of Mr. Palmer's six trunks were damaged en route—damage which your agent was able to confirm when Palmer picked up the luggage in Mobile. Palmer has written a claim to the Seven Seas Lines for $575, the replacement value of the damaged goods.

Now you want to write a letter to Palmer accepting the claim, apologizing for the damage and the inconvenience, assuring him that such occurrences are rare on Seven Seas ships, and informing him that your insurance company will settle his claim as filed. Tell Palmer that he'll be receiving his check, probably within two weeks.

19. Assume that you are credit manager for Carter Electronics. On May 14, your firm received an order for three Model 12C Carter Amplifiers from Dolman Brothers, Inc., of Daytona Beach, Florida. The amplifiers are priced at $272.50 apiece; Dolman Brothers has requested credit terms of sixty days. You acknowledged the order by letter, and requested that Dolman Brothers supply you with three credit references (see the letter on page 176). You pursued the references they supplied (see the following letter, on page 188) and learned that their credit rating was "good." Now you can grant credit terms. Write to Dolman Brothers telling them their order is being filled as requested. Make it a really effective good-news letter. This is the first order that Carter has received from Dolman Brothers, and you certainly don't want it to be the last.

PART 3

SOLVING PROBLEMS WITH LETTERS AND MEMOS

CHAPTER 10

THE ARTS OF DEMANDING AND CONCILIATING

Now we move on to direct reaction-evokers that are more difficult than the routine, good-will, and good-news messages discussed in the last two chapters. In this chapter, we'll consider those communications that must effectively *demand*, and those that must successfully *conciliate*. They're harder because they both arise out of some form of disturbance. You don't usually demand something unless you've been disturbed. And you don't need to conciliate (that is, win back good feeling) unless someone else has been disturbed. First, let's look at demands.

LETTERS AND MEMOS THAT MAKE DEMANDS

Letters and memos of demand are written when you feel that someone owes you something, and you want "delivery." Of course, the recipient won't always agree with you, or will, for other reasons, resist the demand. This complicates your problem.

Among the more familiar kinds of business demands are *claims letters, collection letters, complaints* (which are demands for satisfaction of some sort), and *reprimands* (demands that someone's performance improve). On the surface, each kind of demand has a different objective. Basically, though, they're much the same: the response you're demanding (be it overt or psychological) must be evoked, and it must be evoked *without losing the goodwill or good feeling of the recipient.* Effective demands are difficult to write, for two reasons: (1) Most people naturally resist demands. (2) Good will is easily lost when demands are made.

Here's the way a clumsy writer might write a letter of demand:

Dear Sirs:

Just what kind of outfit are you people running? We place a simple order, delivery takes forever, and when it finally gets here, half the pieces are broken. To top it all off, in the same day's mail we get your bill. Some joke!

We feel we can do without this kind of rotten service. There's no time left for us to place an order with a decent company (although we'd like to), so get on the ball and send us a replacement order right away.

Yours truly,

Nathaniel Schroog

Nathaniel Schroog

Put yourself in the recipient's shoes. Your company is probably successful; you usually take the utmost care in preparing orders for shipment; and you wouldn't be seriously hurt by losing one customer. How would you respond to Nathaniel Schroog?

Now compare Schroog's letter with this one, written in the same situation:

Gentlemen:

On January 10, we placed an order with you for 500 pieces of glassware in various patterns. Yesterday the order arrived, much to our dismay, with only 234 pieces in salable condition. All the rest were chipped or broken.

You can understand our disappointment, I am sure! Customers have been requesting your glasses, and we've been promising them a prompt supply. Now some of them will probably go elsewhere -- their faith in us destroyed, and our potential profit lost -- unless you can do something for us immediately.

We ask that you send us an immediate duplicate order, and allow us to adjust our payment to cover only the salable glassware. We are confident that you will be able to get this shipment to us as soon as possible.

Respectfully yours,

Lucille Dunbar

Lucille Dunbar

Obviously, this letter is more courteous and much less antagonistic than the first. Unlike Schroog's letter, its details are specific and its *demand* on the reader is clear. Everything about it is aimed at the objective: speedy replacement of the damaged order without destroying the business relationship.

The antagonizing tone of Schroog's demand would probably have angered the recipient into saying, "Who needs this crude loudmouth's business anyway?" Business people will do that. They're made of flesh and blood, with the same feelings and emotions as everyone else.

Look closely at Dunbar's letter. Given the disturbing situation, her opening is as positive as it can be. (Were it any more positive, it would sound artificial and insincere; after all, she has been badly inconvenienced by the breakage, and she wants the reader to realize it.) But Dunbar's opening carefully avoids an angry tone. Anger would probably breed reciprocal anger and work against her objective. Schroog, on the other hand, opens inflamingly with, "Just what kind of outfit are you people running?" Schroog's reader will be angry by the end of the first sentence and, as a result, unable to sympathize with what follows.

The next thing Dunbar does is state her case — that is, why she is writing, and why the reader should respond as she wishes. The argument, in Dunbar's case, is simple: she has promised her customers patterned glassware, and she must have it quickly to make good on that promise. She doesn't clutter her argument with extraneous and offensive remarks like "in the same day's mail we get your bill. Some joke!" or "we can do without this kind of rotten service."

Only after fully revealing the situation does Dunbar make her demand. She states it without antagonism, clearly and specifically: "We ask that you send us an immediate duplicate order, and allow us to adjust our payment to cover only the salable glassware."[1] It's a demand much more likely to evoke prompt compliance than Schroog's tart insistence that his reader "get on the ball and send us a replacement order right away."

After making her demand explicit, Dunbar closes by expressing confidence in her reader's ability to remedy the situation. This ending gives the letter a "positive sandwich," the resulting tone doing much to insure the reader's prompt cooperation. It's easy to be blunt, as Schroog is; but effectiveness is measured by results, not by angry self-righteousness.

The pattern of Dunbar's letter is best followed in writing almost any communication of demand:

[1] Style note: Dunbar wants to indicate that she needs a replacement order immediately. But she felt that to write: "We ask that you immediately send us . . ." or "We ask that you send us a duplicate order immediately . . ." might sound somewhat intimidating. So instead she asks for "an immediate duplicate order." As an adjective, the word *immediate* is just as explicit, without being quite as emphatic.

Recommended Strategy Pattern for Letters and Memos of Demand

First,	write an opening as *positive as it can reasonably be* under the circumstances, one that avoids an angry tone; ↓
next,	state your case — describe in detail the situation that has necessitated your communication: that is, the reasons why a demand is in order. ↓
then,	make the *demand* itself: state it clearly, specifically, and completely (obviously, the demand must be reasonable in light of the revealed situation); ↓
finally,	write a tonally positive closing, one that expresses confidence (but not cocksuredness) that the demand will be met.

Let's look at several other examples of effectively written demands. The following one was written by Kenneth Darwin, a young man who applied to graduate school at the state university several years after graduating from there. The admissions office replied with a request that Darwin provide transcripts from every school he'd previously attended. Darwin was annoyed. He felt the request unjustified, since he had already supplied these documents when he came to State as an undergraduate transfer student. So he wrote this letter explaining his situation and "demanding" that the requirement be waived:

Ladies and Gentlemen:

I was a bit surprised to receive your recent request for more transcripts to complete my application to the Graduate School. I will, of course, have them sent if absolutely necessary, but I do feel your request penalizes me.

Upon coming to State as a transfer undergraduate in 1974, I paid two dollars, for transcripts-in-duplicate, to each of the three institutions I'd previously attended. At that time, you informed me that all my papers were in order, and you admitted me. Now you request the very same transcripts in support of my graduate application.

Would it not be possible for you to refer to the transcripts already in your possession? Or if copies must be sent to the graduate advisor, could you not duplicate my transcripts and send me the bill? In either case, you would save me the time of recontacting each institution, and perhaps protect against delays in their responding.

I trust this request is in no way unjustified. It should help us both in the processing of my application.

Sincerely yours,

Kenneth Darwin

Kenneth Darwin

A week later, Kenneth Darwin received a letter from the Admissions Office informing him that his file would be reconsulted and the necessary records would be duplicated. Darwin's "demand" was met. He did not need to recontact the three institutions, nor did he receive a bill for duplicating charges. Several weeks later, he received another letter admitting him to the Graduate School.

Before moving on in the chapter, consider closely the analysis of Darwin's demand technique shown in Figure 21.

Figure 21
Detailed analysis of an effective "demand" letter.

Ladies and Gentlemen:

I was a bit surprised to receive your recent request for more transcripts to complete my application to the Graduate School. I will, of course, have them sent if absolutely necessary, but I do feel your request penalizes me.

Upon coming to State as a transfer undergraduate in 1974, I paid two dollars, for transcripts-in-duplicate, to each of the three institutions I'd previously attended. At that time, you informed me that all my papers were in order, and you admitted me. Now you request the very same transcripts in support of my graduate application.

Would it not be possible for you to refer to the transcripts already in your possession? Or if copies must be sent to the graduate advisor, could you not duplicate my transcripts and send me the bill? In either case, you would save me the time of recontacting each institution, and perhaps protect against delays in their responding.

I trust this request is in no way unjustified. It should help us both in the processing of my application.

Sincerely,

Kenneth Darwin

Kenneth Darwin

It's difficult to open positively when you're making a demand. But Darwin tries to be as positive in tone as he can be in beginning his letter. He betrays no anger, and he even assures his reader of his willingness to comply.

After his as-positive-as-possible opening, Darwin describes the situation as he sees it, providing the justification for the demand he will make in the next paragraph.

In this paragraph, Darwin makes his "demand"—phrasing it as a well-meaning and business-like *request.* He's in no position to sound more threatening.

Notice how Darwin adds more justification. He does so from the viewpoint of benefit to his reader. He puts "empathy" to work.

Darwin is careful to stress cost as well as inconvenience in justifying his point of view. It's a highly believable appeal coming from a student.

Notice how Darwin very clearly describes what he believes to be the inconsistency of the admissions office, but *without* being insulting or antagonistic.

Notice Darwin's technique in making his "demand." He suggests alternatives . . .

. . . and he phrases them as *questions* to avoid sounding like he's making a demand. It's the technique of the "rhetorical question" (discussed on page 173).

Darwin closes as positively as he can. The first sentence of his last paragraph is a subtle attempt to convey *sincerity.* The second sentence conveys an outlook which is both positive and empathetic.

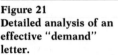

Constructive Criticism

Constructive criticism is another kind of "demand" often necessary in business, a demand that improvement in performance be shown. Executives and supervisors are responsible for remedying deficiencies in the work of their staffs. The task requires the ability to criticize effectively, *without harming morale or lowering initiative.* Again, we have that delicate double objective common to most demands — evoking reaction and preventing ill will. Ultimately, of course, many bosses have the power to fire their subordinates for incompetence. (The amount of "clout" possessed by the writer is always an implied factor in any demand.) But the manager who repeatedly fires people, without raising his staff's productivity, will be seen as a failure.

The following memo is a good example of how to write constructive criticism:

To: P. Jacobson
From: T. B. Comerford, Sales Manager
Subject: The Sales Calls We Made Together on Tuesday, March 13

Paul, after traveling with you last Tuesday, I must say you perform an excellent demonstration. It's obvious why your ratio of sales over demos is 56%, second highest on the staff. Realizing this, you are probably more troubled than I over your low standing in ''total sales.''

In checking last month's field reports from each of the territories, I found that our people were having great success with the new Drop-Off Kit. Over three-quarters of the prospects who received the kit called the sales-rep back in. Many of those prospects were subsequently sold. Your report, on the other hand, shows only occasional use of the Drop-Off Kit. I think this is our key to getting your results up over quota where they belong.

Whenever your prospect is out, leave a Kit with the secretary or the assistant, no matter how unreceptive they might seem. If you get only as far as the receptionist, leave it with her, and phone back later to remind her about delivering it to your prospect. I'm willing to bet that with the increased use of Drop-Off Kits, your total sales will increase by at least 25%.

Once more, the suggested pattern for written demands is put to use. Comerford, the sales manager, opens positively with praise for his reader — praise that is deserved, and that keeps Jacobson from reading the memo in a defensive frame of mind. The positive opening disarms him. Comerford wants to make him receptive to the criticism that follows.

After opening positively (which in this memo takes up two full sentences), Comerford reveals the deficiency (of which Jacobson is no doubt aware), and he analyzes its cause.

Then, in his third paragraph, Comerford states explicitly what he'd like done. Finally, he closes by completing his "positive sandwich" with the optimistic belief that his suggestion will succeed. It's a memo written by a true supervisor.

Demanding with Humor

Occasionally, a writer can depart from some of the accepted principles and still write an effective demand. In the following letter, the writer depends on a wry sense of humor and the sympathy of his reader to achieve his goal. His opening is mellow, his description vivid. He saves his demand for the very end, then makes it emphatically, but disarmingly, by posing it as a question:

June 8, 198_

State Compensation Insurance Board
1120 South Main Street
Salem, Oregon

Subject: Compensation Case No. P81702

I was happy to hear so promptly from you, but dismayed that you felt it necessary to reduce my bill for treating Bobby Phillips' broken arm.

This brittle-limbed young Olympian has been the curse of my existence. He goes swimming in his cast. He uses it for a softball bat. He even hammers nails with it. In general, he applies every stress to it frowned upon by medical science.

He even ruined my wedding anniversary last Saturday night when he fell into a pit barbecue and half scorched his cast off. He keeps me awake nights worrying how large a malpractice suit I will face if his antics cause a separation or a deformed wrist. This, gentlemen, is the case of my patient, Bobby Phillips.

The initial fee for setting the young man's arm would have been $200 in private practice -- maybe more Add to this the additional charges the boy would have incurred for repeated castings. My humanitarian instincts and my fidelity to the spirit of Hippocrates told me to bill his father only $175.

So imagine, if you can, what a nightmare it was to receive your letter which, in hauntingly purple jargon, reduced my bill to $118.60. Your explanation of that reduction was like a painting by Jackson Pollock -- artistic, and incomprehensible.

I am an honest, hard-working, and God-fearing servant of mankind. Why can't I have my measly $56.40?

Yours very truly,

Arnold Johnson, M.D.

An effective letter — but only because its sense of humor is more pronounced than its mild insults.

Collection Letters

The last kind of demand we'll look at is familiar to everyone. It's the collection letter, the letter that tries to get its recipient to pay an overdue debt. For various reasons — forgetfulness, procrastination, fear of financial depletion — people often fail to pay when they should. The enormous expansion of credit in the last few decades has increased the collection problem. Creditors are frequently forced to write letters that "demand" remittance.

Collection letters (or dunning letters, as they're sometimes called) are a special breed of business demand. The nature of the collection problem often requires the writer to send more than one of them. Many people who are slow in paying their debts tend to ignore "one shot" collection attempts. Consequently, most companies plan a series of messages in order to collect delinquent accounts. A series of communications, one demand after another, creates a sense of insistence that usually brings about payment.

In a collection series, each element (let's call the separate messages "elements" — they're not all letters) is a request that payment be made. The assumption underlying each collection element is that the recipient will respond with payment, and that no further demand will be necessary. From experience, however, the businessperson knows he or she will often have to send out the next element, and perhaps the next, and so on. Each successive element is somewhat stronger in its demand for payment, until finally, if payment isn't made, the account is turned over to an attorney or a collection agency, and the company's collection effort is terminated.

Every collection element, whether it's a "one shot" letter, or whether it comes early or late in a series, has a double goal (as most demands do). It tries to collect, and it tries to retain good will. Why should you worry about the good will of delinquent customers? For the same reason that you send them collection letter after collection letter. Even though they're delinquent at present, they are prospects for future business once the present bill is paid. Unless you would rather not sell any more to a customer who presently is slow in paying, any collection message you send should have a good-will objective. Of course, the further along in a collection series, the more difficult it becomes to retain good will because the demand must be more strongly stated. But the skillful writer can retain good will right up to the end of a collection series.

Here for example is a poor collection letter, especially bad because it was the first collection attempt the customer received. The debt, a small one, had honestly slipped this person's mind. Only a reminder was needed. Instead, the customer got this heavy-handed demand:

> Dear Customer:
>
> This is to inform you, herewith, that you have not paid your bill of Dec. 13, for $12.75.
>
> We hope this delinquency will soon be remedied. If it is not, you will force us to take action which will be as displeasing to ourselves as it will be repugnant to you.
>
> Cordially yours,
>
> Blake Bros.

Straight out of the "sledgehammer" school of debt collection! Compare it to the following letter. Which of them is more likely to attain both goals: remittance and continuing goodwill?

> Dear Mr. Johnson:
>
> Just a note to remind you that payment on your bill of December 13, for $12.75, hasn't reached us yet. If you've already mailed your remittance, just disregard this note, and accept our sincere thanks.
>
> Yours for better service,
> Coplins, Inc.

The differences between these two letters are so obvious, no analysis is necessary.

Now let's take a look at a skillfully written collection series. Keep in mind that these samples are by no means the only way to write a good collection series. But they are good examples of effective collection writing. The Cooper Office Supply Company is requesting payment from one of its customers. (Read through all seven elements of Figure 22 on the following pages, then return here for a discussion of them.)

This sample series happens to have seven elements. Some series have fewer; often they have more. It's largely a matter of cost efficiency.

Almost five months were allowed to pass before Benjamin, the credit manager, invoked an ultimatum. This time lapse raises the tricky question of timing in a collection series. A creditor must decide not only how to phrase each collection effort, but also how long to wait before sending the first element, how much time to allow between elements, and how long to keep writing before finally giving up the effort.

How is this timing determined? —

First (an obvious principle), the greater the number of messages you can afford to send, the less time need elapse between elements. Frequent messages

"I've been getting 30 percent more money from home since I took this course!"

Figure 22
A typical collection series.

COOPER OFFICE SUPPLY COMPANY INC.
12345 EAST COLORADO, PASADENA, CALIF.

ACCOUNT: MR. LIONEL R. BAKER
B682 821 CENTRAL AVENUE
CHINO, CALIFORNIA

MAY 4, 19__

	CHARGES	CREDITS	BALANCE
APRIL 1, 19__	$425.00		$425.00

ELEMENT NUMBER 1
In this sample collection series, the first element is simply a monthly statement indicating the date on which the transaction was made, and the amount owed. The assumption underlying this first collection attempt is that the recipient needs only to be reminded of the bill; there is no question of his intentionally withholding payment.

Figure 22 (continued)

COOPER OFFICE SUPPLY COMPANY
INC.
12345 EAST COLORADO, PASADENA, CALIF.

ACCOUNT: MR. LIONEL R. BAKER
B682 821 CENTRAL AVENUE
CHINO, CALIFORNIA JUNE 2, 19_

	CHARGES	CREDITS	BALANCE
APRIL 1, 19_	$425.00		$425.00

PLEASE REMIT
THIS ACCOUNT IS OVERDUE

ELEMENT NUMBER 2
The second element is another monthly statement, this time bearing a special stamp to call the recipient's attention to the tardiness of payment. Its underlying assumption as a collection message is that the customer only needs to be reminded once more that payment is overdue.

ELEMENT NUMBER 3
The third element is a brief form note. Its underlying assumption is that the customer has again forgotten the debt, but needs a more direct reminder that payment is due. Its tone is cordial and completely positive. Its closing sentence serves two purposes — besides its explicit purpose of tentative thanks, it gives the writer a closing with positive tone. The "positive sandwich" principle is at work even in this short note.

June 24, 19_

Dear Mr. Baker:

Just a friendly reminder that payment on your invoice #B682 for $425.00 is still due.

If you have already sent your check, please disregard this notice, and accept our thanks for your patronage.

Yours very truly.

Cooper Office Supply

ELEMENT NUMBER 4
The fourth element is a brief but more personal sounding note than number 3. Its underlying assumption is that the customer needs some prodding. Its tone is still quite positive, but just a little less cordial. The writer is controlling his tone to imply that while the tardiness in payment is not yet regarded as serious, the company is starting to become a little concerned.

July 15, 19_

Dear Mr. Baker:

We'd like to remind you once again that payment on your invoice #B682 for $425.00 is still due.

We would very much appreciate receiving your check as soon as possible. The enclosed envelope is for your convenience in remitting.

Very truly yours,

Cooper Office Supply

Figure 22 (continued)

July 29, 19__

Mr. Lionel R. Baker
821 Central Avenue
Chino, California

Dear Mr. Baker:

I trust this letter finds your new office prospering, and all the problems of business expansion about solved. Quite a few years ago, when our business was new, we swore our creditors outnumbered our customers by at least four to one. We understand your situation.

If the pressure of initial expenses is still heavy, perhaps you would find your account for $425 more easily settled in periodic payments. If so, you need only drop us a line, or call, and we'll be happy to make a mutually convenient arrangement.

Cordially yours,

Keith Benjamin

Keith Benjamin
Credit Manager

ELEMENT NUMBER 5
This fifth element is a personal letter. By now, it's obvious that Baker's failure to pay is more than just oversight. The letter is friendly in tone, and empathetic in its outlook. Its underlying assumption is that Baker is undergoing some financial hardship. Rather than adding to his woes, this letter offers to relieve him of some of his burden by arranging terms for payment. Benjamin clearly had a double goal in this letter — to evoke payment (or at least a response) and to generate good will.

August 12, 19__

Mr. Lionel R. Baker
821 Central Avenue
Chino, California

Dear Mr. Baker:

We're at a loss. We can't understand why we haven't heard from you in response to our recent letter. As you know, your bill of April 1, for $425.00, is still outstanding. We have been as fair as we can be, I think, in offering a way of easing the burden of payment for you. But so far, you've ignored us.

We must ask that you send us a check this week, or get in touch with us promptly.

Sincerely,

Keith Benjamin

Keith Benjamin
Credit Manager

ELEMENT NUMBER 6
This sixth element is another personal letter, less friendly in tone than the fifth (though not unfriendly), and more direct. It goes to the heart of the matter in the very first sentence. Having offered to ease Baker's burden in the last letter, and gotten no response, Benjamin here appeals to Baker's sense of fairness. He implies, for the first time, a sense of urgency.

Figure 22
(continued)

August 22, 19__

Mr. Lionel R. Baker
821 Central Avenue
Chino, California

Dear Mr. Baker:

So far, four reminders and two letters have not been able to bring forth a response from you regarding your unpaid bill. Payment on your invoice of April 1, for $425.00, is now long overdue. As much as we appreciate your patronage, we can no longer afford to carry this unpaid account on our books.

Believe me, we don't like to think in terms of action against you. We're here to serve customers, not summonses; and it does us no good to see your credit rating destroyed. This is, of course, the inevitable outcome.

So we ask that you save both you and us the trouble. We will wait another seven days before seeking legal assistance, in collecting your account, hopeful as always that you will remit the payment owed us.

Respectfully,

Keith Benjamin

Keith Benjamin
Credit Manager

ELEMENT NUMBER 7
Still getting no response, Benjamin makes this seventh element a letter of ultimatum. The ultimatum itself, stated in the last paragraph, still reflects hope of making the collection. (Without such hope, there is no reason for writing the letter.) The action that Benjamin plans to take if payment is not forthcoming, is clearly laid out for Baker to contemplate, but the tone is more forthright than angry.

allow the creditor to appear insistent before his appeals become severe. If messages are frequent, the time lapse between them must, nevertheless, still be long enough to allow for compliance with the earlier appeal.

Second, *who* the debtor is can determine timing. If at the time of purchase his or her credit rating was excellent, you'd be wise to allow liberal timing. If, on the other hand, it was only fair or moderate, timing would probably be shorter.

Third, the nature of your business helps determine timing. A luxury department store will pursue delinquent accounts more slowly and tactfully than a high-interest, short-term loan agency will. (If you happen to be a national government granting loans to other nations or bankrupt cities or corporations, repayment may conceivably take years.)

Finally your competition will help determine your collection timing. If your three major competitors all wait twelve months before taking action, you'd be unwise to insist upon turning your delinquent accounts over at sixty days.

A closing word should be said about gimmickry in collection writing. In place of straightforward notes and letters, many business people inject gimmick messages into their collection efforts to stimulate remittance. They feel that devices like rhymes, cartoons, and studio cards, if used early, induce cooperation and effect payment. Figure 23 illustrates several such collection devices. Some collection gimmicks are effective. Others fall flat. If you use gimmicks at all, don't let them lose sight of the primary goal — collecting the debt.

Figure 23
Some gimmick collection messages.

MEMO

from the
Maxwell Press

Just a brief note to repeat our thanks for your continuing interest in the Jersey Journal and its comprehensive "same day" coverage of regional news. We are confident you'll find your Journal subscription the best way to keep abreast of events.

And may I add further thanks—in advance—for your taking care of the enclosed bill as soon as possible. I've enclosed this duplicate invoice in case the original was overlooked or mislaid.

All of us at Maxwell are glad to have you aboard, and proud to provide you with what we believe to be the very best in regional reporting.

TED NEVINS, DIRECTOR
SUBSCRIPTIONS SERVICE

Figure 23 (continued)

With our compliments...

. . . a ditty from Foster's,
who are here to serve you.

You've no doubt heard about the bugs
Who have little ones which bite 'em –
An entomological chain reaction
That goes on ad infinitum.

Well, we at Foster's form a link
In the same kind of bug-like chain.
The cash must flow both in and out,
For the chain to work again.

From you to us at Foster's,
Then on to our purchasing crew.
They spend it at the wholesaler's
And in turn he spends it too.

So you're a link within this chain
And we happily count on you.
Your patronage is vital if
The chain is to work anew.

(Just a little bit of poetry
Giving us a chance to say
We'd very much appreciate your check
If you could forward it today.)

THE FUNCTIONAL DOWN-SHIFT

Since Chapter 8, we have been looking at communications that serve increasingly difficult functions. First we looked at routine letters and memos, then at goodwill and good-news communications, now at demands. From here on in, the functions get even harder.

Realizing this, you should develop an "eye" for a strategy that many business writers overlook — the strategy of the *functional down-shift.* At first glance, a problem confronting you may seem to require a certain functional solution. Someone, for example, may have done you wrong in business; so your instinct immediately tells you, "Write a *demand.*" But is the situation viewable *only* as a demand situation? If you can possibly view it in another light, and write your communication as though it were serving a less difficult function, the communication becomes easier to write, and its chances of success correspondingly rise. You *down-shift* your function for strategic advantage.

Here's a case in point: The MacDonald Aircraft Company has been struck by the International Union of Machinists (I.U.M.). Members of the Western Engineers Guild (W.E.G.), who also work at MacDonald, are in sympathy with the striking machinists, but cannot join them in the strike because the engineers' own contract with MacDonald is still in force. So at the engineers' request, the president of the I.U.M. grants picket-line passes to the engineers, allowing them to cross the machinists' picket line unmolested.

Problems arise however. Some rank-and-file machinists, unaware of the engineers' sympathy, ignore the passes and jeer, harass, and even threaten the engineers as they seek to cross the picket line. One engineer even gets punched in the nose. This turn of events understandably angers the W.E.G. president, Ned Hoffman, whose first impulse is to demand that the I.U.M. pickets honor the passes.

Second thoughts, however, point him toward a wiser and more effective course of action. Instead of treating the situation as one befitting a demand — which he has every right to — Hoffman decides to turn his letter into a *goodwill* communication. He strategically down-shifts his function. He realizes that a demand, however justified, would probably cause ill will and divide the two groups whose interests, in the long run, will be better served by solidarity. So he writes instead the following letter of *thanks*:

Mr. Kevin Grady, President
International Union of Machinists
6000 Sawtelle Boulevard
Los Angeles, California 90001

Dear Mr. Grady:

Let me take this opportunity to thank you again for the picket-line passes you supplied to our members. We know the inconvenience that such passes create for your men on the picket line, and we hope they all understand that the terms of our present contract with MacDonald require us to continue working during this labor dispute.

I want to assure you that our members are steadfastly avoiding struck work. We are behind you one hundred percent.

We know that you and your members are ''going to the line'' for all of us, in both our present and future contract negotiations with the MacDonald Company.

Your strength and determination in fighting for the rights of your membership will be a guide and inspiration to others who find it necessary to act against companies who refuse to bargain in good faith with unions in the aerospace industry.

I'm sure your actions will result in better working conditions and higher standards being written into all future contracts between MacDonald and its employees.

Yours sincerely,

Ned Hoffman

Ned Hoffman

If things happen as Hoffman expects (and he does know pretty much what to expect), his letter will be read to the striking machinists at their daily strike-meeting. The machinists will be reminded of the engineers' sympathy, and of their own president's having granted the passes. They will willingly step aside and allow engineers to cross the picket line. And what's more, they will strongly support the engineers a year from now when the W.E.G. negotiates its own new contract with MacDonald Aircraft. That's a lot of benefit to be had from one business letter whose function was carefully *down-shifted*. We'll see more of the functional down-shift in later chapters.

CONCILIATORY COMMUNICATIONS

We've looked at writing demands. Now let's look at how to *respond* to them. You can safely assume, if you receive a demand, that the demander's confidence in you has been impaired. Perhaps he or she feels that you have acted irresponsibly or performed unsatisfactorily. For some reason, that person is disturbed at you. Your task — and it's not an easy one — is to alleviate the distress and, if possible, to remedy its cause. In other words, you must conciliate.[2]

Conciliation can take various forms. If, for example, a customer makes a legitimate complaint over poor service, damaged merchandise, or an overcharge, your conciliatory effort should include an offer of adjustment — that is, an attempt to *repair* the deficiency. First, ask yourself what can be done to satisfy the complaint. Can you provide new merchandise? reservice the customer? make an acceptable cash settlement? If so, then offer to do so.

But not all demands, even the most justifiable, can be adjusted. If you've made an irreversible decision and someone complains about it, all you can do to conciliate is *explain* why you decided as you did. Or if someone demands that

[2] If a customer's complaint is not legitimate, or if it's unjustified, you'll probably want to turn it down. That's an even stickier communication to write — we'll consider it in the next chapter.

you pay a bill, and for the time being you cannot, you'll need a good explanation to avoid a lawsuit. In these instances, explanation must carry the entire burden of conciliation.

Finally, there are demands — usually reprimands or petty complaints — that no explanation can satisfy. When this is the case, *apology* alone must bear the burden of conciliation.

Conciliating with Apology, Explanation, and a Remedy

Usually, all three kinds of conciliatory tactic are employed in a single conciliatory message — apology, explanation, and offer of remedy. For example, put yourself in the shoes of John Jones, sales manager for a large furniture outlet. Jones received this note one morning:

> My dear Sir,
>
> To put it bluntly, you sure screwed up delivery on my Dreameze Hide-a-Bed. If I told you guys once, I told you five times you should deliver it to my weekend place on Mt. Moran, not to my regular address. So up there I sat, with my in-laws who were going to sleep in the thing, while you tried to deliver it to the regular address. If the neighbors hadn't seen your delivery man with the bed, we still wouldn't know what happened. I've got a good mind to cancel my charge account and take my business someplace where they've got ears!!!
>
> Disgustedly yours,
>
> Carl Teasdale

The problem was obvious. Jones had to write a conciliatory reply to an old customer, a reply that would soften Teasdale's anger, and offer him an adjustment sufficient to retain his patronage. Teasdale had to be conciliated. A tall order! Here's what Jones wrote:

> August 3, 198_
>
> Mr. Carl Teasdale
> 16 Avenida de Rancho
> Fresno, California 94807
>
> Dear Mr. Teasdale:
>
> Please accept our most sincere apologies for the delivery mix-up on your Dreameze Daybed. Upon receiving your letter this morning, I checked the delivery slip and found that, in completing it, our shipping department had copied the address straight from your account folder. When your neighbor told our delivery man that you were on vacation, he

brought the daybed back to the store assuming he would redeliver it as soon as you got back. We in the sales department assumed delivery had been made to your summer residence. Both departments are indeed embarrassed.

Having purchased from us for many years, you know that we do our best to avoid these slip-ups in communications. Somehow, this one got away from us.

What we'd like to do is deliver your Dreameze to you at either address you wish. And, because it didn't get to you in time for your vacation, we'd like to pay for your not having had it by delivering it at a thirty percent discount. By doing this, we can say we're sorry and still provide you with the finest in Dreameze quality for your many summer vacations to come.

Mr. Carter, our shipping manager, will call you for your ''OK'' on a delivery time that will meet your earliest convenience.

Very truly yours,

John L. Jones

John L. Jones
Sales Manager

This letter has all the attributes of effective conciliation. Everything in it is aimed at achieving Jones's objectives. Its tone is appropriately conciliatory, yet positive; its explanation and adjustment are clearly stated.

Note its technique: Jones opens, as positively as he can, with the vital apology. (People expect and like apologies; apology doesn't become negative until it's overdone.) After apologizing, he fully explains the cause of the misdelivery. This explanation, while detailed, avoids blaming anyone for the mishap; it simply relates the facts. Jones is counting on this explanation to make Teasdale see how an honest mistake occurred and, in so doing, alter his attitude from anger to understanding. Teasdale must undergo this shift in attitude if the subsequent adjustment offer is to be acceptable to him. (People are much less likely to accept solutions if they're still angry and fuming.) When Jones feels his explanation is thorough enough to win at least Teasdale's sympathy, he then offers adjustment, attempting at the same time to justify the merits of his offer.[3] Then Jones concludes with an empathetically worded suggestion of how Teasdale should respond.

[3] One precaution to be kept in mind: it is *un*wise to offer *carte blanche* (or "blank check") adjustment — that is, an adjustment that says essentially, "We'll do anything you say to remedy this problem." For the timid complainant, a carte blanche adjustment offer simply poses another problem — not knowing what to ask for. For the greedy one, it's an invitation to take you for all he can get, raising the likelihood that you'll have to disappoint him a *second* time by not complying with his wishes.
Decide what adjustment you can, or wish to, make. And offer it expressly.

Like good-news and demand messages, conciliatory communications have an advisable pattern of composition, a pattern obvious in Jones's letter:

Recommended Strategy Pattern for Letters and Memos of Conciliation

First,	make the opening as positive as it can reasonably be, making whatever *apology* might be necessary; ↓
then,	(in most cases) follow with a complete *explanation* of what has happened to cause the circumstance; ↓
then,	(if remedy or reassurance is feasible) make a statement of what will be done for the writer; that is, offer a *remedy*; ↓
finally,	develop a tonally positive closing. (If the reader is to respond, it should be a closing that indicates clearly *how* he or she should respond). The "positive sandwich" concept is once more put to work.

Before we look at further examples of conciliation, a closer look at Jones's adjustment letter should be helpful. Consider the detailed analysis of it in Figure 24.

The need for conciliation also arises within an organization. When internal complaints occur, they threaten the smooth operation of a business, and must be promptly conciliated. That's the task of the following memo. Its author, a division chief named Hal Abbot, is replying to a complaint by J.B. Donald, another division head, that Abbot's staff has been "lax in performing project follow-ups." Abbot's memo seeks to conciliate, but without any loss of self-esteem. It apologizes, tries courteously to "set the record straight," then (as a "remedy") offers assurances about future follow-ups. It's a strong attempt to reestablish a smooth working relationship. It's effective conciliation.

TO: J.B. Donald DATE: April 5, 198_

FROM: H. Abbot

SUBJECT: Your Memo of April 3 on Project Follow-Ups

I appreciate your memo and want to apologize for the circumstances that necessitated it. There have, indeed, been several lapses in communication between our divisional staff and the laboratory. And I think that bringing them to light is the best assurance against their recurring.

Figure 24
Detailed analysis of an effective letter of conciliation.

Although Mr. Teasdale does not now have the bed, the writer maintains psychological identification between Teasdale and the bed by using the possessive adjective.

Dear Mr. Teasdale:

Please accept our most sincere apologies for the delivery mix-up on your Dreameze Daybed. Upon receiving your letter this morning, I checked the delivery slip and found that, in completing it, our shipping department had copied the address straight from your account folder. When your neighbor told our delivery man that you were on vacation, he brought the daybed back to the store assuming he would redeliver it as soon as you get back. We in the sales department assumed delivery had been made to your summer residence. Both departments are indeed embarrassed!

Having purchased from us for many years, you know that we do our best to avoid these slip-ups in communications. Somehow, this one got away from us.

What we'd like to do is deliver your Dreameze to you at either address you wish. And because it didn't get to you in time for your vacation, we'd like to pay for your not having had it by delivering it at a thirty-percent discount. By doing this, we can say we're sorry and still provide you with the finest in Dreameze quality for your many summer vacations to come.

Mr. Carter, our shipping manager, will call you for your ''OK'' on a delivery time that will meet your earliest convenience.

Very truly yours,

John L. Jones
Sales Manager

This letter is a response to a *justified* complaint. The only appropriate opening is an explicit apology.

An attempt to euphemize: It could have been called an "error" or a "mistake," but why build in a negative reminder?

Note the avoidance of any phrasing in this paragraph which might have "negative reminder value."

Notice the intentionally *in*explicit phrasing here. The writer could have been factually precise and stated the number of years, but he preferred to let the connotative value of this phrase act upon Teasdale.

Instead of giving a "yes or no" alternative, the writer gives Teasdale two *positive* alternatives — delivery at one address, or delivery at the other.

Opening a sentence with a conjunction gives rhetorical emphasis to that conjunction. That's just what the writer wants here — emphasis on the compound (or double) nature of the adjustment.

Here the writer risks a slightly hackneyed phrase to get this highly empathetic idea into the emphatic last position in the letter.

This phrase is used not only because it's true, but because of the sense of immediate action it will convey to Teasdale.

The same suggestion of "immediacy" is the purpose underlying this phrase.

An appeal to an emotion which everyone has known. The writer wants Teasdale to empathize with him, though to say so directly would be tactless.

Instead of *telling* Teasdale of the store's continuous efforts, the writer assumes he is already aware of them. It is psychologically much more difficult for Teasdale to deny this statement when it is phrased in this way.

Another attempt to euphemize.

Here the writer appeals to a widely accepted philosophy — "an eye for an eye . . ."

Notice the writer *implicitly* assumes that Teasdale will accept the adjustment, rather than asking. He does *not*, however, make this assumption overtly. Teasdale knows he is still to be given the chance to refuse when Mr. Carter calls. He is not made to feel "pushed into a corner."

The empathy index for this letter is + 5, not bad for a letter in which the writer must explain his company's actions.

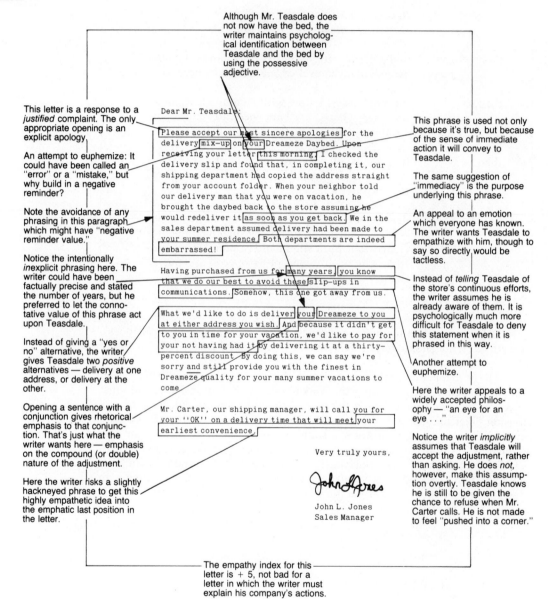

Having shared many hours of task-force work with you, I know we also share the belief that the efficiency of an entire operation cannot be condemned by a few exceptions. By the Controller's own count, those lapses cost us an approximate follow-up of 3% on last month's projects. I fully agree that it takes only one overdue project to stall the efforts of other departments. On the other hand, in this league, where we're depending upon the total cooperation of scores of high-powered lab scientists, who are often going in their own directions, a .970 batting average isn't bad. In addition, over 40% of our projects last month were completed a week or more before they were due. The record's pretty good.

So I make no excuses. We do need closer controls in our liaison with the lab, and we're convening the project leaders next Monday to come up with ways to establish them. I'm confident that out of that meeting will come new procedures that will benefit the company as a whole and our two divisions in particular.

As soon as the meeting ends, I'll apprise you of its results.

H Abbot

Here's another example of effective conciliatory writing — this one much shorter. The Heritage Book Club has received a complaint from a new member, Paul O'Brian, that one of the books he ordered arrived in battered condition. He immediately returned it, demanding a replacement. The tone of his letter very strongly implied disappointment and frustration at the service. His goodwill and continued membership were clearly in jeopardy. So, as soon as his letter was received, the Heritage Book Club sent him this note:

Dear Mr. O'Brian:

We want to thank you for writing us so quickly about the condition of Volume 3 of your new Civil War Encyclopedia. Please accept our apologies.

A new copy of Volume 3, in mint condition, has just been shipped out to you to complete your set, and we're enclosing with this letter the 42¢ postage it cost you to return the original.

We want you to keep only excellent copies of any books we send you. Again, our thanks for your so quickly allowing us to satisfy you completely on this order.

Sincerely yours,

Trudi Elman

Trudi Elman
Secretary

Conciliating Without a Remedy

The letter by Jones, the daybed sales manager, and the memo by Abbot, the division chief, were able to use all three means: *conciliatory apology, explanation,* and the *offer of a remedy.* Trudi Elman, the book club secretary, chose not to explain: she simply apologized and adjusted. But often when conciliation is necessary, remedy is not possible. Conciliation must then be effected by apology and explanation alone. This is the situation underlying the following letter. The Taywin Company had erroneously told a customer that her recent payment was insufficient to cover her invoice. She promptly complained. Taywin checked, found the customer was right, and wrote her the following conciliatory letter:

> Dear Mrs. Kennedy:
>
> We sincerely apologize. Upon receiving your letter, we rechecked your invoice of December 10. You are correct. Your check for $420.50 does cover the charges fully. Shipping costs incurred by another customer had been mistakenly added to your account.
>
> You have our assurance that, however bleary-eyed from overtime our bookkeepers may become, our policy is still to make your bills as low as we possibly can.
>
> Cordially yours,
>
> Mark L. Taywin
>
> Mark L. Taywin
> Vice-President

The pattern used in this letter is apology-explanation-closing. No adjustment, or remedy (in the tangible sense) was necessary. The tone, however, had to be delicately conciliatory. Though he could have blamed his bookkeepers for the mistake, Taywin would have been wrong to, just as Jones would have been unwise to tell Mr. Teasdale that the shipping department was to blame for the misdelivery of the daybed. "Passing the buck" would be a simple approach to take, but not one likely to conciliate. The Chevron Asphalt Company of San Francisco, in a letter to its district managers, warns against buck passing:

> With our customers' accounts now billed and handled, to a great extent, in San Francisco by use of electronic data processing, a tendency could develop to ''pass the buck'' to that far-off point instead of responding promptly and positively to a customer's question or misunderstanding regarding his account. Actually, the customer is dealing with our Company and, usually, is not particularly interested in what division or section of our total Company is responsible for any differences that may develop. He

merely wants the courtesy he is accustomed to from our people: correction if something is wrong; or an explanation if there is a misunderstanding. Courteous, prompt, business-like handling of a customer's question or complaint can quickly eliminate a possible source of future irritation.

To reinforce this advice, Chevron encloses for posting on bulletin boards, this simulated IBM punch card:

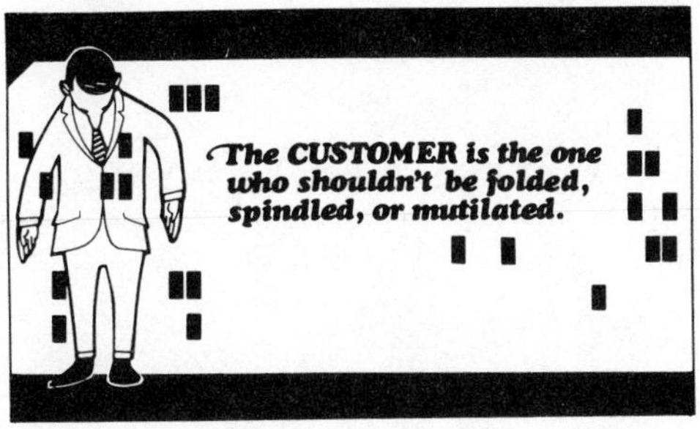

Card and letter are reproduced with the permission of Standard Oil of California.

A similar problem — conciliation without possible remedy — confronts television networks and stations whenever substitutions in programming are made. Any such change inevitably incurs the displeasure of some viewers. When viewers complain, media people must conciliate — as station WBTV does effectively in the following letter:

Dear Mr. DiCarlo:

We genuinely appreciate your letter regarding the recent changes in our ''Six O'Clock News'' format. The decision to replace anchorman Roger Foster with the team of Brinkman and Harvey -- we can assure you -- was not made lightly. Our admiration for Roger and his perceptive news analyses remains unbounded.

Nevertheless, our primary responsibility is to provide you, the viewer, with the broadest, swiftest, most complete coverage possible. Increasingly in the past few years, such service has meant coverage from two major news centers -- hence, our new double-anchor format with Ted Brinkman in New York and Frank Harvey in Washington. Mr. Foster, who retains a key role on the ''Six O'Clock News'' staff, feels as we do that the switch is a wise one.

Do give us the chance to prove it to you by keeping your dial set at Channel 8, where the WBTV staff is committed -- 'round the clock -- to serving you.

Very truly yours,

Philip L. Simmons
Vice President in Charge of Programming

Since no actual "remedy" is possible in such situations, the entire burden of conciliation in this letter rests upon WBTV's explanation of the change, and their tone in explaining. The letter does its job exceedingly well.

Conciliating Without an Explanation

Not only are there conciliatory situations that don't lend themselves to tangible remedy; there are also those in which even an explanation is unnecessary or meaningless. In this brief letter, conciliation is brought about with just an apology (and the right tone, of course):

Dear Mrs. Theobald:

Please excuse our sending you that second renewal notice. You were completely right; it was a mistake on our part.

And thank you for calling our attention to this slip-up. Your note will help us avoid such double notifications in the future.

Cordially,

Deborah Charlemagne

The following letter also conciliates simply with an apology — and some chat.

Dear Mrs. Zenobia:

My apologies! I know personally how it feels when someone misspells my name -- they usually reverse the i-e.

Please forgive the stenographer's mistake. The intention of our letter -- to say <u>thanks</u> for your patronage -- still stands. We appreciate it.

Sincerely yours,

Kenneth Siegel, Manager

It would be worthless to try to explain stenographical errors. They simply happen. Yet Mrs. Zenobia complained, so she had to be *conciliated* (some people would say *humored*). Had Siegel written only

Dear Mrs. Zenobia:

We're sorry we misspelled your name.

Yours truly,

he would have been guilty of compounding his "offense" with abruptness. So he wrote a light and friendly apology with some "padding" to give the message an effective character. This "chat" is *not* a violation of conciseness; it was necessary to Siegel's purpose.[4]

IN CONCLUSION

The two problems we've discussed in this chapter — how to *demand* and how to *conciliate* effectively in business — will test the mettle of any business writer. While routine, goodwill, and good-news communications require you to make the most of pleasant situations or everyday circumstances, the need to demand or conciliate involves disturbance. Demands are themselves the potential disturbers; if they're to succeed, they must minimize that disturbance while, at the same time, getting what they demand. Conciliation, the effective handling of demands or anger, is accomplished only when the disrupted goodwill of the demander is restored, and relations brought back to normal. Both situations are far more delicate than the ones we looked at earlier, and the strategies for meeting them are more imperative.

The difficulty of effectively demanding or conciliating also makes it advisable (to put it mildly) that you "functionally down-shift" anytime you can — that is, that you treat a difficult situation, if possible, as though it were a less difficult one, and write accordingly.

Review these strategies for effective demands and conciliation, and the technique of the functional down-shift, and make them part of your repertoire of business writing abilities.

[4] A note on positivity: Notice how Siegel avoids negativity. He could have written: "I know how *annoying* it is . . ." or "I know how *irritating* it is when someone misspells my name . . ." But why remind Mrs. Zenobia of her own annoyance? Her silly reaction is much better forgotten than brought up again.

PROBLEMS

1. Think back to the last time you were dissatisfied with a product or service you purchased, and told yourself you were going to write a stiff letter of complaint to the appropriate higher-ups. Now is your chance. Write that letter.

Besides expressing your discontent with tactful firmness, you might also mention that you are active in a number of organizations and will gladly pass along the news of your dissatisfaction to your friends and fellow members to protect them from the same kind of dissatisfaction. If you don't remember the name and address of the company you're complaining to, make them up.

2. Assume that you recently purchased four Avondale Permano-Press shirts from the Globe Department Store in Passaic, New Jersey. You purchased this particular brand because they are advertised as being "100% permanent pressed — all you need do is wash and drip dry!" You wore three of the shirts and, following the manufacturer's instructions, washed them in cold water and hung them on the line. They dried all right, but with more wrinkles than the regular kind of shirt ever had. Write an effective complaint letter to the Avondale Manufacturing Company, 16 West 32nd Street, New York, New York, stating your problem and demanding your money back.

3. El Toreador Restaurant is an expensive but highly recommended restaurant, the recipient of a number of international awards for its cuisine. So you decided to have an engagement party at El Toreador for a close friend. At the party, you and all fifteen of your guests ordered the Prime Rib of Beef Deluxe at $12.75. To your surprise, the meat was fatty, and the vegetables were a little dry. To say the least, you were disappointed, especially at having to pay the $204 check. Write a letter of complaint to El Toreador.

4. Last Sunday you purchased a quart of Dairy Maiden butter pecan ice cream. You brought it home, and your family had it for dessert. Everything about the ice cream was as expected — the flavor was delicious, the pecans were good and crunchy — until you bit down on what you thought was a pecan, only to cut your inner gum on what proved to be a pecan shell. Actually, the pain lasted only for about half an hour. Write a letter to the Dairy Maiden Ice Cream Company (6000 LaSalle Street, Brooklyn, New York) complaining about your injury.

5. Obtain samples of the collection letter series used by two competing companies (perhaps department stores, gasoline companies, or magazine publishers). Write a comparative analysis of these two collection series. Analyze how they both attempt to meet the double collection goal of remittance *and* good will retention, and analyze the different appeals made to the recipient, the timing of each series, and how each series gradually increases pressure for payment. Present this analysis to your instructor in the form of a well-written memo-report.

6. Assume that you are the advertising credit manager at *Women's Week Magazine*. Six weeks ago, your publication sold a quarter page of advertising space to Nouveau Notions, Inc. (9800 Nether Way, Miami Beach, Fla. 36102). Nouveau's president and general manager is Mr. Jack Sprey. His firm is small and only two years old. The Downtown Credit Association of Miami Beach rates

Nouveau Notions as a "fair to good" credit risk because, although their assets are merely adequate for their present level of business, their growth potential is excellent.

You received copy from Nouveau Notions and ran it, as contracted, in your edition of four weeks ago. According to that contract, full payment ($450) was to be made immediately upon error-free publication of the ad. Although your proofreaders assure you that the ad was run without error, no payment has been received.

Two weeks ago, you sent Nouveau Notions a duplicate invoice stamped "payment due," but payment was still not forthcoming.

a. Today, you want to send a reminder note to Nouveau Notions — a cordial and brief note explicitly calling their attention to the overdue charge. Write this note.
b. Assume that by two weeks from today, you still have not received payment. You want to write a second reminder note with a somewhat different and more persuasive approach. Write this second reminder note.
c. Assume that by four weeks from today, you still have not received payment. You now want to write what may have to be the first of several personal letters — perhaps addressed directly to Sprey — appealing for payment. Write it.
d. Assume that by six weeks from today, still no payment has arrived. You must write a second letter in your attempt to collect this account.

Your instructor may want to give you additional instructions regarding how many more letters will be sent before action is taken against Nouveau Notions. If not, make this decision on your own and indicate it at the bottom of communication *d*.

7. You have just been hired by the California Department of Fish and Game to aid in its new ocean conservation program. The first problem that comes across your desk is one that has occurred before — it has, in fact, become more frequent in the last few years — but it has never been as well handled as the Department would like it to be.

It seems that Mr. Anthony Owens, owner of the power cruiser "Half Wit," was observed by officers of the Department harassing several California Grey Whales with his boat as their southward migration took them near the Dana Point Yacht Harbor where the Half Wit is anchored. Such conduct is obviously unsafe — for boaters and whales alike. Several injuries to humans and whales, and some boat damage, have already resulted from such behavior in the last two years. But this is the first time Owens has been observed in the practice.

Up to the present, the Department has been empowered only to issue warnings to offenders. But as of January 1 of next year, when the new State Senate Bill 123 becomes law (it "prohibits power boats from harassing, chasing or otherwise interfering with the migration of whales along the California coastline"), the Department will be able to issue citations to first offenders, and to suspend the boating licenses of repeat offenders.

Your job is to write a letter to Anthony Owens (a letter which will become a standard first communication to boaters observed harassing the whales) warning that such behavior must be stopped. You don't want to try to intimidate

Owens — it is important that the Department not be viewed as attempting to limit the freedom of boat owners to enjoy their pastime. But you want him to get the message clearly and stop bothering the whales.

8. You are the Assistant Vice President in charge of the Student Loan Department at the United Federal Bank in Kent, Ohio. One of your clients is a student at Valhalla University named Jackie M. Drake, to whom you have made a loan of $800 through the University's Financial Aids Office.

On November 26, you received a letter from Mrs. Carole Winter, the University's Financial Aids Officer, stating that Jackie Drake had, back in mid-October, repaid the loan and that the University would be forwarding the money to you shortly to close out Ms. Drake's account.

Apparently, though, the University then misplaced Jackie Drake's file, and did not send the funds to you until January 15, by which time additional interest of $9.30 had accrued on the loan. Since Ms. Drake had repaid the money to the University well before the new interest charge, you do not feel that she should be held responsible for the additional payment. But you do not want to lose the money either since it is United Federal's money and it was outstanding until January 15. So you must write a letter to the Financial Aids Office at Valhalla asking that they — who failed to forward the funds on time — pay the additional $9.30 in interest charges.

Write the letter.

9. Sometimes reprimands must be given more than once. When this is necessary, the pressure for compliance must increase, but the tone must remain positive if a good relationship between writer and recipient is to continue. Here's an example.

Hal Harkness, a field engineer for Sparco Electronics, has been stationed abroad on a long-term work assignment. He is one of the firm's most talented young engineers, and is doing a good job fulfilling the firm's contract at a U.S. Navy installation in Naples, Italy. But Hal Harkness has a penchant for submitting heavy expense reports. As the Division Head and Hal's boss, you have to get this habit of his back in line. More specifically, the facts are these:

a. Sparco's present contract with the Navy calls for a food-and-rent allowance of $40 a day for the field engineer.
b. During Hal's first two weeks in Naples, when he stayed in a hotel, you allowed him to declare more than the $40 a day, but made it clear that he would have to cut back to this limit once his wife and two children joined him in Naples and they moved into an apartment.
c. His wife and children arrived three weeks ago, they took their apartment, and Hal continued to submit per diem expense claims of $46 to $54.
d. You wrote him last week reminding him that he had to keep his claims at or under $40 a day.
e. His latest weekly expense report continues to claim an average of $50.25 a day, and to that report, Hal has added a comment — which you know to be true — about the brutal inflation that Italy is experiencing.
f. Sparco is presently renegotiating the Navy contract, and there is some hope that within several months the per diem allowances may be raised. But for now, the present contract remains in force; the Navy is auditing all expenses that are claimed; and the $40 a day limit *must* be enforced.

Write another letter to Hal Harkness "demanding" that he comply with the limit.

10. You are in charge of the Automotive Customer Service Dept. at C. J. Fenney's in San Leandro. A customer, Mr. Tom Brewer (of 8887 Evanston Way, San Leandro) has ordered four chrome Apache wheel rims, style #57136. As you don't have the rims in stock, you place a rush order for them with the manufacturer, Car Chrome, Inc. (963 Carson Blvd., Wilmington, California).

Car Chrome, Inc. ships the rims to you right away, and within four days you drop a card to Mr. Brewer telling him to come and pick up his order. Unfortunately, you forget to open the cartons and check the rims. Brewer picks them up from one of your sales clerks, still in their cartons, takes them home, and within an hour is hollering at a clerk over the phone that two of the rims have chrome burns on them, a third is chipped, and the fourth one isn't the style he ordered.

You now have two letters to write, and very quickly:

a. a conciliatory letter to Mr. Brewer that offers the best adjustment you can reasonably offer.
b. a letter to Car Chrome, Inc. demanding that they speedily make good their shipment to you.

11. Analyze the probable effect of the following conciliatory letter upon its recipient, and the reasons for that effect.

Terrelli Manufacturing Company
7500 Damrot Boulevard
Hope, Indiana
43290

November 12, 19__

Solomon Lincoln, Inc.
2341 East Third Street
Indianapolis, Indiana

Attention: J. L. Black

Gentlemen:

We were quite surprised to read your letter of last week in which you state that you wrote "Rush" on your order blank. There was no such notation on the order form we worked from. So we sent your order by rail freight just as we usually send all orders.

We have a policy here at Terrelli that says the customer is always right. So we are certainly sorry for any inconvenience you might have been caused.

Sincerely yours,

Hugo Terrelli

Hugo Terrelli

12. Assume that you have received the letter written by Lucille Dunbar, on pages 231–232. Answer it, taking any reasonable steps that you feel necessary to effect complete conciliation.

13. Put yourself in the place of salesman Paul Jacobson, who just received the memo on page 235 from T. B. Comerford, the sales manager. Write an effective conciliatory reply — one that apologizes, explains, and offers assurance about the future.

14. Here's an example of an adjustment letter written by a poor business writer. He gets his point across, but the general tone of the letter is not likely to endear him to its recipient. Considering the fact that the recipient has complained, this unappealing and uninformative reply will probably result in his taking his business elsewhere.

Mr. Kenneth Porfirio, Purchasing Manager
The MacReedy Corporation
217 Gulf Boulevard
Houston, Texas 51502

Dear Sir:

We were shocked to read in your recent letter that the imprinted ball point pens we shipped were unsatisfactory to you.

You claim that most of them were tarnished and that many of them would not write. In the event this is true, we cannot understand how such deterioration could have occurred. We observe very strict quality control procedures, and these pens were manufactured only last month.

But since you have been a customer of ours for such a long time, we will take back the pens and send a replacement order to you soon. I hope this solution will be satisfactory to you.

Yours truly,

Wm. Limpson

Wm. Limpson
Sales Manager

What actually happened (and Limpson never took the trouble to track down what *had* happened) was that a warehouse assistant, upon being asked to bring five thousand blue retractable pens to the imprinting room, knew there was a case of five thousand old pens which had been sitting around for three years and took it upon himself to "finally get them out of the way."

With these facts in mind, rewrite Limpson's conciliatory letter to Mr. Porfirio. You want to keep him as a customer, get him to accept your adjustment offer, and assure him that the quality of your product remains high.

15. Assume that you are the public relations consultant for El Toreador, the famous restaurant mentioned in problem 3. The restaurant has received a letter from a disenchanted customer accusing the restaurant of "trading on its reputation." It seems that the customer and his party of fifteen guests had Prime Rib of Beef Deluxe last Friday night and found it "terribly fatty." He also said "the vegetables were all dried out." El Toreador has never received a complaint like this before, and unless this disappointed customer is effectively conciliated, he could really hurt the restaurant's reputation.

The management has asked you to write the customer a letter. "Do anything within reason for him," they say, "just make him happy." Make him happy.

16. Your company, the Dandee Candy Company, is faced with a public relations problem which at some time affects almost every manufacturer of consumer products. You've dropped a product from your line, and made a certain portion of your public unhappy by doing so.

For the last three years, sales of your previously popular Jupiter Bar had been declining steadily. Last month you dropped it from your product line of five candy bars. Inevitably, some people who had come to love the Jupiter Bar were unhappy enough to write letters of complaint.

Your task, as a writer for the company's public relations department, is to write an effective conciliatory letter to those who complained. To explain your action in dropping the Jupiter Bar strictly from the company standpoint (declining sales) will not make many of the complainers happy. You'd be wiser to write empathetically. You might reveal how losses on the Jupiter Bar would curtail your company's effort to develop new and even better flavors. Actually the company is presently at work on two new bars, one of which will have basically the same ingredients as the discontinued Jupiter Bar.

This letter isn't easy to write, but without it, you will not be able to retain the goodwill of the complaining customers.

17. Your office, the public relations department of the Totspride Toy Company, this morning received the following letter:

Gentlemen:

Last Monday, I bought my seventeen-month-old son one of your Fearsome Fido push toys. Before purchasing this toy, I asked the salesgirl at Mayne Brothers about this toy and she assured me that your company was one of the most reliable of all the toy manufacturers. Some laugh!

After playing with Fearsome Fido for only two days, my son broke the handle off the toy. I found him running around the room with the broken stick in his hand. As if the loss of the toy (and my $11.98) weren't enough, the broken handle had a jagged point which was lethal. It could easily have put my son's eye out.

I don't know how a company with such a supposedly fine reputation can manufacture such an inferior and dangerous toy. I have considered reporting this to the Better Business Bureau, and I will certainly never buy another Totspride Toy again.

Jean Manning

(Mrs.) Jean Manning

Your job is obvious. You must conciliate Mrs. Manning. Send her a check for $11.98, and send her another Fearsome Fido if you think it wise. Salvage whatever goodwill you can.

18. You are the General Editor of Charmley Publishing Company's Textbook Division. One of your publications, a moderately successful textbook in business communications published in 1975, is scheduled for republication in a revised edition this coming year. You have been working closely with its author, Dr. Hillard McGinnis of Valhalla University, and the process of revising the book is proceeding smoothly. Both you and McGinnis, as well as Charmley's Board of Directors, look forward to a successful revised edition that will be adopted by even more colleges and universities than the first edition.

Then one day you receive the following letter:

June 2, 19_

Charmley Publishing Co.
1000 Indigo Parkway
San Francisco, CA 98765

I am writing regarding a textbook you published in 1975 entitled The Business Communicator by Hillard McGinnis. I wish to protest the publication of this book on the grounds of sexism.

I am aware that this book is used at California Technical College in San Rafael and by Mount Sebring Community College in Dateville for classes in business communications. It is no doubt also used elsewhere.

Every single example shown in the book for letters of employment and resumes has either a man applying for an executive position or a woman applying for a clerical position. I highly resent this discriminatory and sexist attitude, and have written those two colleges about their use of this book.

Mr. McGinnis's book was published many years ago. I believe it is time for an updated, more modern edition.

Karen Cedarholm

Ms. Karen Cedarholm
720 Evergreen Avenue
Dateville, CA 98173

No matter what your personal feelings about the women's rights movement, you must treat this complaint as a serious matter. The accusation in Karen Cedarholm's third paragraph is factually accurate. She may be responsible for having two institutions drop their adoption of the text (public institutions are very sensitive to this kind of accusation). And her complaint may well reflect the feelings of many other users of the text, and of potential adopters who may be refusing to order the text because of the "bias" to which Karen Cedarholm refers.

Upon reading the letter, you hurriedly consult with Hillard McGinnis over the phone. He assures you that the "sexist imbalance" of the first edition is being remedied in the revised edition. Now you want to write an effective letter of conciliation to Karen Cedarholm assuring her that the book, in its new edition, will have overcome the problem.

CHAPTER 11

DELIVERING BAD NEWS (AND STAYING FRIENDS)

Not surprisingly, the communication that business people least like to write is the one that recipients least like to receive — the one that conveys bad news. Rejections, refusals — anything likely to displease the reader constitutes a bad-news message. To write one well takes skill and practice.

A freshman once asked me why I thought refusals and rejections were difficult to write. "They're simple," he insisted. "Just spin your stationery into the typewriter and type *n-o,* no!" Fortunately, he had three years to go before putting his theories into practice.

Sure it's easy to write a letter or memo that merely says *no.* We'd be wasting time and space to discuss a communication with so simple a function. What the freshman didn't see is that bad-news messages (like demands and conciliatory messages) have double-barreled objectives. They must deliver the bad news *and* retain goodwill. They must say "no" — yet not alienate the recipient. Again, it's the double goal that creates the problem.

When communicating bad news, you must express that news with unmistakable clarity. But you must also soften its impact on the recipient. If a client company makes a request you cannot grant, a tactless refusal is likely to lose their account. If the requests of your employees are callously denied, their efficiency and morale inevitably suffer. If cash customers with bad credit ratings nevertheless apply for credit (as they often do), you must turn them down without sacrificing their patronage, if possible. If someone applies to you for a job, or a loan, or a grant, or simply asks a favor — and you must refuse — your refusal must be clear, yet it must not alienate.

So the problem is difficult. But it's not impossible. Some business writers face it every day, and with great success. Let's take a look at a well-written bad-news letter, one quite likely to achieve its double goal. It was written by a manufacturer's customer-service manager to a small hardware dealer, Ray Rilling, who sought to purchase goods on credit. Upon checking with the regional credit bureau, the customer-service manager learned that Rilling had been slow in paying his bills during the last eighteen months, and that during that time two new shopping centers had opened right outside of Rilling's town, with a third scheduled to open in three months. The shopping centers were obviously drawing trade away from the downtown area where Rilling's store is located.

There was no alternative. Credit had to be refused. Yet the manufacturer (the Appleton Appliance Company) wanted to do everything possible to retain Rilling's patronage on a cash basis. After all, he might well survive his difficulty and become a good repeat customer.

Here's the customer-service manager's letter to Ray Rilling.

May 10, 19--

Mr. Ray Rilling
Rilling Hardware Company
884 Main Street
Carthage, Wisconsin 50478

Dear Mr. Rilling:

Thank you very much for your May 6 order for 6 rotisserie cookers, 18 toasters, 18 irons, and 12 electric can openers. We appreciate your interest in the Appleton line and feel that -- in both quality and price -- the items you ordered are among the best values in the small appliance market.

We're also interested in the Carthage market area. In the past year, as you know, two new suburban shopping centers have opened near Carthage, with a third scheduled to open in several months. Among the results has been a substantial readjustment of retail buying patterns in the county. It's a situation we see in many areas across the country.

The public's increased patronage of these new shopping complexes has seemingly affected a number of older established retailers in Carthage and elsewhere, resulting in losses of revenue and a sharply reduced ability to meet credit commitments on schedule. The most recent report of the Five Counties Credit Bureau confirms this trend. As a result, it has become inadvisable for us, until the marketing picture stabilizes, to enter into new credit arrangements in downtown Carthage.

There is an answer however. Although we're unable, at this time, to extend credit, we are confident that we can work successfully around any cash-flow problem and deliver the goods you need. Because of the general growth in county commerce, our deliveries to the Carthage area have been increased to three times a week. This provides the advantage. If you can cut your order by half or more -- and consent to delivery on a C.O.D. basis -- we can get the appliances to you right away, and at a 2% discount for cash. Thereafter we can, within 48 hours or less, deliver the other half, or more, as soon as you need them. In effect, we can serve as warehouse for all the additional Appleton inventory you can sell. Your cash flow is minimal. And, with the cash discount, your profit margin is larger. All we need is your approval.

Just call or wire us, collect, and we'll have the goods immediately on their way to you. And please know that, both now and in the future, we look forward to the opportunity of serving you.

Yours sincerely,

Conrad Jones
Customer Service Manager

It's a well conceived, well executed bad-news letter, especially when you see how poorly it *could* have been written. Too many bad-news communications in business sound like this:

Dear Sirs:

We regret to inform you that we cannot grant you credit as per your request. We will, however, fill your order C.O.D. if you wish. Wire us collect if this suits you.

Yours truly . . . .

(Remember how poorly the same kind of letter was written back in problem 2 on page 119.)

The rule is this: A bad news communication does not succeed unless it achieves both parts of its double goal. In the letter to Rilling, success requires that Rilling learn clearly that he cannot have credit *and* that his patronage be retained. If handled tactfully and empathetically (as he is in Conrad Jones's letter) Rilling will probably respond by "okaying" the C.O.D. terms. That's success!

The letter written by Conrad Jones clearly demonstrates four techniques of successful bad-news writing: (1) the "positive sandwich" construction (which we've been using all along), (2) the empathetic reason-first rule, (3) the complex-sentence technique for stating the actual refusal, and (4) the well developed positive alternative to soften the impact of the bad news.

THE "POSITIVE SANDWICH" CONSTRUCTION IN BAD-NEWS COMMUNICATIONS

The "positive sandwich" structure is vital in writing bad-news messages. You must prevent the disappointing news from turning your reader against you; so you try to make that reader as favorably disposed toward you as possible before you assert the bad news. Of course your reader's feeling toward you will be partly determined by prior dealings between you. But in the message itself, the opening — which always sets the tone — should be used to strengthen whatever good feeling exists. Certainly if you put the bad news at the beginning, you'd be giving it far too much emphasis, and jeopardizing goodwill.

How do you phrase the opening of a bad-news message positively? It isn't easy. In his letter to Rilling, Jones opened with a thankful acknowledgment of Rilling's order. (And note that the order is acknowledged in detail.) Consider, for just a moment, other bad-news messages. If you must refuse a request for information, you can still begin by being thankful for the request; after all, it was to *you* that your reader turned for help. If someone's ideas must be rejected, you can still, in opening your message, express appreciation for having had the chance to consider them. In almost any situation, you can find something for which to express your thanks or appreciation. Use your opening sentence or two to convey that positive idea —and *don't* do it so briefly that it seems perfunctory and insincere.

Equally vital to a bad-news message is the other half of the "positive sandwich": a positive ending. If the opening and the body of the communication have done their job, the reader will have been informed of the bad news, yet his disappointment will have been softened by the writer's explanation and obvious empathy. The reader's feeling for the writer (and his inclination to continue a satisfactory relationship) hang in the balance. A positive closing — a positive idea expressed positively at the end — can tip the scale toward retaining of the reader's goodwill.

Note the positive closing Jones wrote in his letter to Rilling: " . . . please know that, both now and in the future, we look forward to the opportunity of serving you."

THE EMPATHETIC REASON-FIRST RULE

The act of refusal or rejection is always potentially offensive to the person who's being refused or rejected. The only way to avoid such offense is to show *why* rejection was necessary. Without a reason, any refusal seems arbitrary; and an arbitrary refusal is guaranteed to shatter good will. You must explain your refusals — as Jones explained his to Rilling.

Furthermore, the explanation you give must be *empathetic*. You cannot, for example, hope to retain the good will of a steady customer if you refuse to grant her a requested adjustment by telling her you don't believe her story. Nor can you hope to keep the good will of an unsuccessful job applicant by telling him: "your test results show you're incapable of holding the position" — or the morale of an employee by telling her: "you don't deserve a raise." Conrad Jones would have ruined his letter had he told Rilling his credit record was horrible, or had he given him a self-serving explanation like: "Our profits would be hurt . . . . " It is even unwise to invoke "company policy" as a reason for refusal: your saying "company policy disallows our helping you" may be a fact, but it's not an explanation.

And understand this — not only must you give a reason for your refusal, and make it empathetic; you must also, whenever possible, give the reason *before* the refusal. This is the *reason-first* method of communicating bad news: the logical way to tender a refusal (and "tenderize" it as well). You want your reader to read that reason in a totally objective frame of mind — not a frame of mind already jaundiced by a refusal. Most people cannot read (or listen) with an open mind *after* they've been inexplicably refused. So, put the reason first.

In addition, your reason for refusal should be written so that the actual statement of refusal flows from it logically and naturally. Notice how Jones did this in his letter to Rilling. He developed his reason for refusing credit, fully and empathetically, in the second and third paragraphs, then made his actual statement of refusal emerge naturally from it in the fourth.

Caution should be taken in your explanation not to say anything that will lead the reader to infer that his desires are about to be granted. That only makes the ultimate bad news harder to swallow — and goodwill even harder to retain.

Here's how Standard Oil of California advises its employees about the reason-first technique in writing rejections and refusals:

> The ability to say *NO* and still keep the reader in a friendly mood is a real task in the Standard Oil Company of California, because we are besieged every day with ideas or propositions which we must reject.
>
> Yet, the reader's viewpoint must be maintained. He feels that he is offering us a real opportunity when he presents his proposition to us. If we say *NO* at the very beginning of our letters, he will miss the warmth and sincerity of purpose behind our reasons for declining his ideas.[1]

Other letters and memos later in the chapter will illustrate the reason-first rule.

THE COMPLEX-SENTENCE TECHNIQUE FOR BUSINESS REFUSALS

One major problem remains. When you reach the point in your communication (as Jones does early in paragraph three) where the actual refusal must be stated, how do you say it? How do you phrase the actual refusal or rejection so that your chances of retaining good will are maximized? Your refusal must be unmistakable, but de-emphasized so that it doesn't spoil the tone of the communication and alienate its recipient. The necessary *no* must be cushioned.

One way to do it — perhaps the best way — is to use grammatical weight. (Recall our discussion of grammatical weight back on pages 75–76.) In a complex sentence — that is, a sentence with an independent clause *and* a dependent clause — emphasis falls upon the contents of the independent clause. It's grammatically weightier. To soften the impact of a refusal, while clearly stating it, skillful writers often put the actual refusal into the less emphatic dependent clause of a complex sentence, and use the more emphatic independent clause to develop a related, positive idea. In refusing Rilling's credit request, Conrad Jones could simply have written:

```
We cannot, at present, offer you credit terms.
```

[1] Reproduced with permission from the Correspondence Handbook of the Standard Oil Company of California.

In such a sentence, the refusal is clear, but it's also emphasized. And that's the last thing Jones wants to emphasize. Instead he builds that statement of refusal into the dependent clause of a complex sentence, and devotes the more emphatic independent clause to the positive alternative he's offering:

> Although we're unable, at this time, to extend credit, we are confident that we can work successfully around any cash-flow problem and deliver the goods you need.

Notice how that handy word *although,* which opens the dependent clause, helps make the transition from negative to positive a smooth one.

Even a sentence that contains both a refusal and the reason for that refusal can be improved with a complex sentence. This sentence isn't awful:

> Because our main offices are now in Chicago, we will be unable to service you directly.

But with the complex-sentence technique, it can be improved substantially:

> Although our new Chicago location precludes[2] our servicing you directly, we are asking McGill Associates in New York, the most reliable agent we know, to continue your regular service calls.

or more informally:

> Although our move to Chicago now keeps us from servicing your account directly, we are asking McGill Associates in New York, . . .

The refusal and the reason are both built into the dependent clause, while the grammatically weightier independent clause, with its natural emphasis, conveys a related and highly positive idea.

There is, of course, no guarantee that you'll be able to retain good will in all bad-news situations. But the complex-sentence technique, like the "positive sandwich" structure and the reason-first method, will immeasurably strengthen your chances of retaining it.

THE WELL-DEVELOPED POSITIVE ALTERNATIVE

After the actual statement of refusal and the quick transition into a more positive outlook, Jones in his letter to Rilling does precisely what the writer of bad news should do: he *develops* the positive alternative as fully and as empathetically as he can. His purpose is to make the bad news (in this case, the refusal of credit) seem less significant than it is; and to make the positive prospect—the added profits, the reduced cash flow problem — seem more significant by comparison. In a sense, the positive alternative is made to outweigh — and even

[2] A note on word selection: In his first draft of this sentence, the writer wrote: "Although our new Chicago location *prevents* our servicing you directly . . ," but upon rereading the draft, he felt that *prevents* was unnecessarily negative in tone and replaced it with *precludes.*

overwhelm, if possible — the preceding bad news. Jones makes sure that every feature of his alternative plan is spelled out persuasively, so that Rilling will be convinced that Appleton Appliance does want his patronage and does care about his plight in Carthage.

Even though positive alternatives aren't always this readily available in bad-news situations, there is usually some positive outlook or possibility that can be included to counterbalance the bad news. A scheduled guest speaker who must cancel her appearance might suggest a worthy substitute. A scholarship officer might assure an unsuccessful applicant that his academic record is nevertheless strong and not the reason a scholarship was denied. A research director, after turning down an interesting but unusable proposal, might suggest other places to which that proposal could be submitted. Some positive counterweight can almost always be found — and should be — to offset the burden of refusal.

So, as with our previous types of direct reaction-evokers, there is also an advisable pattern for writing bad-news messages — the strategy pattern used by Conrad Jones in his bad-news letter to Ray Rilling:

Recommended Strategy Pattern
for Bad-News Letters and Memos

First, create a positive opening, one which expresses thanks or appreciation for something the reader has done relative to the situation you're writing about. In the absence of thanks or an expression of appreciation, some statement designed to please the reader should open the message;

↓

next, develop empathetically the reason for the bad news you are about to deliver; perhaps implying, but *not actually expressing*, the bad news itself;

↓

then, deliver the bad news itself, phrased clearly but without emphasis; and follow it with a quick shift into whatever positive alternative or positive outlook you can offer;

↓

then, develop that positive alternative or outlook as fully and as empathetically as you can to make it seem just as important as — and maybe even more important than — the bad news itself was;

↓

finally, construct a *tonally positive closing*. If you want the reader to respond (as Jones wanted Ray Rilling to respond), the closing should also clearly suggest how the response should be made.

Before moving on to other examples of effective bad-news writing, let's take a closer look at the techniques used by Jones in his letter to Rilling, Consider the point-by-point analysis of it in Figure 25.

Figure 25
Analysis of a well-written bad news letter

October 10, 19--

Mr. Ray Rilling
Rilling Hardware Company
884 Main Street
Carthage, Wisconsin 50478

Dear Mr. Rilling:

Thank you very much for your May 6 order for 6 rotisserie cookers, 18 toasters, 18 irons, and 12 electric can openers. We appreciate your interest in the Appleton line and feel that -- in both quality and price -- the items you ordered are among the best values in the small appliance market.

We're also interested in the Carthage market area. In the past year, as you know, two new suburban shopping centers have opened near Carthage, with a third scheduled to open in several months. Among the results has been a substantial readjustment of retail buying patterns in the county. It's a situation we see in many areas across the country.

The public's increased patronage of these new shopping complexes has seemingly affected a number of older established retailers in Carthage and elsewhere, resulting in losses of revenue and a sharply reduced ability to meet credit commitments on schedule. The most recent report of the Five Counties Credit Bureau confirms this trend. As a result, it has become inadvisable for us, until the marketing picture stabilizes, to enter into new credit arrangements in downtown Carthage.

There is an answer however. Although we're unable, at this time, to extend credit, we are confident that we can work successfully around any cash-flow problem and deliver the goods you need. Because of the general growth in county commerce, our deliveries to the Carthage area have been increased to three times a week. This provides the advantage. If you can cut your order by half or more -- and consent to delivery on a C.O.D. basis -- we can get the appliances to you right away, and at a 2% discount for cash. Thereafter we can, within 48 hours or less, deliver the other half, or more, as soon as you need them. In effect, we can serve as warehouse for all the additional Appleton inventory you can sell. Your cash flow is minimal. And, with the cash discount, your profit margin is larger. All we need is your approval.

Just call or wire us, collect, and we'll have the goods immediately on their way to you. And please know that, both now and in the future, we look forward to the opportunity of serving you.

Yours sincerely,

Conrad Jones

Conrad Jones
Customer Service
Manager

Note the opening half of the "positive sandwich" at work here. Jones wants to build as much rapport with Rilling as he can in beginning.

Notice the empathetic view with which Jones begins the "reason-first" step of his letter.

Jones includes this phrase to prevent the sentence from sounding didactic: from sounding as if it's telling Rilling something that Jones thinks he doesn't know yet.

Here Jones uses the "complex-sentence" technique: the actual refusal goes into the dependent clause (beginning with although), while the more emphatic independent clause (or main clause) introduces a positive alternative.

Look at how substantially Jones develops the positive alternative. He wants to persuade Rilling to accept it — not just create a "take it or leave it" feeling about it.

Note the closing half of the "positive sandwich." The letter ends on a totally positive note.

Notice that Jones acknowledges Rilling's order in detail. It's a conventional courtesy and Jones wants to do nothing that would imply that the details of Rilling's order are unimportant (even though credit will be denied).

Jones could have said "There's been a sharp decline in downtown business." But why inject negative-reminder-value (N.R.V.) when the letter's ultimate purpose is positive?

It's very easy, in stating a reason for refusal, to insult or disparage the person you're refusing. Notice how carefully Jones avoids any such disparagement of Rilling's financial condition.

Notice how Jones adds this interruptive phrase to avoid implying a "no, never" tone. It's the same reason he inserted "Until the marketing picture stabilizes," two sentences earlier.

Every detail here is phrased as positively as Jones can phrase it.

Jones has created throughout this paragraph a tone of confidence that Rilling will accept the C.O.D. terms. This sentence is added to protect against sounding overly confident.

Notice the phrase that is put in the emphatic terminal position of the letter.

Notice how the word "collect" is isolated by optional commas here, giving it greater emphasis than it would get without the commas.

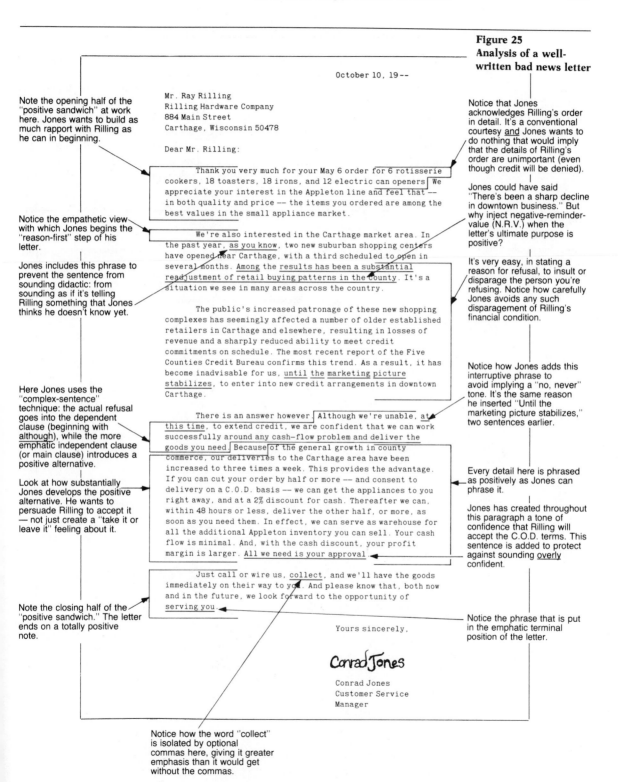

FURTHER EXAMPLES OF BAD NEWS EFFECTIVELY DELIVERED

The form letter used by the Trane Company for turning down unsuccessful job applicants follows the same strategic pattern as the letter to Rilling — creating a tone most likely to retain good will. Consider the letter in Figure 26. Notice, among other things how the writer has carefully manipulated the burden of responsibility for the bad news. Instead of telling the applicant (in the second paragraph) that his "experience and abilities do not fit the position," he shifts the burden by saying that "the requirements of the position . . . do not match your experience and abilities." It's a clever manipulation of *subject emphasis* (which we looked at on pages 76–77) here to deliver bad news with as little negative impact as possible.

Figure 26
A letter used to turn down job applicants.
(Reproduced by permission of the Trane Company.)

MANUFACTURING ENGINEERS OF AIR CONDITIONING • HEATING • VENTILATING AND HEAT TRANSFER EQUIPMENT

THE TRANE COMPANY

GENERAL OFFICES, LA CROSS, WISCONSIN, U.S.A.

September 14, 19--

Mr. Charles A. Brown
1537 Hamilton Avenue
Tulsa, Oklahoma 74100

Dear Mr. Brown:

Thank you for your recent inquiry concerning employment possibilities with The Trane Company. We are pleased to have this expression of your interest in us.

We have reviewed your background very carefully. The requirements of the position in which you have expressed interest do not match your experience and abilities as closely as do those of several other candidates we are currently considering. For that reason, we will not be able to proceed in your behalf.

With the qualifications you have, it seems certain that you will find the kind of assignment you seek. To that end, I wish you every success. Again, thank you for the thought which prompted your inquiry.

Sincerely,

THE TRANE COMPANY

Frank Pryor

Manager
Staff Employment

Frank Pryor: ram

The following bad-news reply, to a student's attempt to get his old summer job back, also does its task effectively:

Dear Mr. Dixon:

We appreciate your interest in reemployment this summer with the Carter Corporation.

The contracts and subcontracts we are presently at work on have lowered our projected manpower requirements for the rest of the year. As a consequence, all our regular summer spots must be filled by full-time, permanent employees -- leaving us without a position to offer you this summer.

This reply is certainly no reflection upon your qualifications or abilities. We were quite pleased with your performance last summer, and we hope to be able to open spots for college men like you again a year from now.

Our thanks once more for your interest in Carter. We wish you every success during the coming academic year.

Sincerely,

Doris Grendola

Doris Grendola
Personnel Manager

The letter's strategy is this: first, a positive opening; then, reasons (in the first five lines of paragraph 2); following that, the actual refusal (at the end of that second paragraph); and finally, two concluding paragraphs of positive assurance and positive close. Notice once again the careful phrasing of that actual refusal — "leaving *us* without . . ." rather than "leaving *you* without . . ."

Here's another interesting bad-news situation. The board-chairman of Douglas Steel, Inc., a well known corporate executive, has accepted an invitation to speak at a prestigious, hundred-dollar-a-plate dinner to be held by the National Chamber of Commerce in Washington. But a week before the luncheon, a crisis erupts in Douglas Steel's International Division. The board-chairman must travel abroad, and probably won't be back in time to fulfill his speaking engagement. Here's the bad-news message he writes to the National Chamber to inform them that he must cancel:

August 25, 198_

Mr. Dale Anderson, Chairman
National Chamber of Commerce
2332 12th Street, S.W.
Washington, D.C. 20029

Dear Mr. Anderson:

For several months I have been looking forward to an upcoming speaking engagement at your luncheon in Washington. An opportunity to speak before the National Chamber of Commerce is an honor and a pleasure.

A complication has arisen, however, involving last weekend's coup d'etat in Ibana. The overthrow vitally concerns Douglas Steel inasmuch as we have investments of over a hundred million dollars in smelting and processing facilities there.

As of this morning, negotiations between our local management and the new Ibanese government have broken down. Our Board of Directors, in concurrence with the State Department, feel that my presence in Ibana is of the utmost importance. And subsequent negotiations there could last for weeks.

It is best then, I think, to protect against a last-minute unavailability, that I forego the engagement. If a recommendation is in order, I would suggest that my dear friend, the eminent Mr. Raymond Haymaker, would be an excellent substitute. He has informed me that he could clear his schedule for the engagement.

As President of Orion Motors, Mr. Haymaker possesses great insight into the problems of multinational corporations and their effect on American politics. His recent position as Chairman of the President's Select Committee on International Relations would also be of particular relevance to this year's luncheon program.

Let me repeat my regret that the situation in Ibana has necessitated my fullest attention, and let me again express my esteem for the Chamber's ongoing work and my thanks for your kind invitation.

Sincerely,

Leonard R. Leslie
Chairman of the Board

Note how the recommended strategy-pattern for bad-news messages is put to work here: the letter begins with a brief paragraph whose purpose is to open positively, nothing more. Then, in the next two paragraphs, the writer describes the situation that has arisen: he establishes his *reason first,* before the actual statement of cancellation. At the beginning of the fourth paragraph, the bad news is then stated, followed by a well developed suggestion (in the fourth and fifth paragraphs) about a substitute speaker — that is, a positive alternative. Finally, the letter closes as positively as it can under the circumstances. It's a well written letter.

Notice as well how the actual statement of cancellation is made (at the top of the fourth paragraph). A note of empathy is brought right into the sentence along with the bad news: obviously a last-minute cancellation would hurt the National Chamber even more than this earlier one. And instead of using an openly negative verb like *cancel* or *quit,* the writer uses the "softer" verb *forego.* He's sensitive to connotation. Most top executives are.

The need for another kind of bad-news letter arises whenever a request for information must be denied. Here's a letter that effectively does the job without losing the good will of the requester:

Gentlemen:

We certainly appreciate your interest in our company's method of remunerating its local distributors.

Because each of the distributors deals with us under individual contract, we have no one standard method of remuneration. Each has agreed that it is beneficial to them, as well as to the company, to keep these terms under strict confidence. So although we would like to provide the information for you, please understand why we cannot.

We would be happy to provide you with any other assistance possible.

Very truly yours,

Rena Spellman

Rena Spellman
Distribution Director

The tone in this letter is positive and friendly throughout. The basic attitude is not: "No, you cannot have it because . . ." It is rather: "We would be glad to let you have it if we could." This difference in attitude makes an enormous difference in tone.

It is bad news, too, when a company executive has to turn down an employee's idea or proposal. The following memo does this, while at the same time it works to keep the employee's morale and enthusiasm high.

TO: Ed Bellow DATE: August 22, 19--
FROM: Jason Martin
SUBJECT: Your Project Proposal of August 10

I very much appreciate the proposal outlined in your memo of August 10. I've examined it carefully and passed it on to appropriate members of my staff for further review.

My own questions about it center on its cost. As you've indicated, the materials for the project would cost us $1300, and distribution approximately $1000. This along with the cost of supervision, and the now exorbitant service charges, would bring the total to almost $3000.

The projected saving, if I understand correctly, would be somewhere around the same figure, perhaps slightly less. In view of this, I don't think the project can be justified at present. If my staff can find any possible savings beyond those you outlined, I'll get back to you to explore the project further.

The material you were good enough to send along with the proposal is being returned to you separately. Thank you very much for all the obvious effort you have taken in the agency's interest.

cc: H. Columbo
R. Markson

The "positive sandwich" is there. Reason-first is there. And the actual statement of refusal is deemphasized in several ways: it is "buried" in the middle of its paragraph; it is not made to seem absolute; it ends with the softening qualifier "at present;" and it's immediately followed by a positive (though not likely) possibility. Even the memo's distribution is designed to keep Ed Bellow's spirits high: a copy of this memo is openly going to Harold Columbo, Bellow's boss.

Obviously the principles of effective bad-news writing that we've been discussing do not change simply because a communication is internal or because its writer happens to be in a position of authority over its recipient. Another effectively written bad-news memorandum is shown in Figure 27. Its writer, a corporate department head, has been asked for a raise by one of her staff. She is unable to grant it. Her reply, besides being sincere, is designed to keep her employee's morale from breaking down.

The memo quite obviously utilizes a "positive sandwich" structure. The reason for refusal is thoroughly and empathetically developed. Then, in the last sentence of the second paragraph, the refusal is stated. Notice how Fraser, instead of writing "you cannot have the raise," stated her refusal in the most positive way she could: " . . . the entire department must operate for the rest of the fiscal year under a frozen salary structure." It's an effective memo.

Another bad-news communication is familiar to anyone who has tried to write for publication — the rejection notice. Too many manuscripts, submitted with high hopes, get this kind of callous response from editors:

We regret to tell you that your manuscript does not meet our editorial needs.

Yours truly,

Figure 27
An effectively written memo of refusal.

TO: G. Bartholomew DATE: April 5, 19--

FROM: T. C. Fraser FILE # ---

SUBJECT: Your Request of April 2

Greg -- I was glad to get your memo. For one, silence in these matters never helps department morale. And secondly, it gives me some ammunition to carry before the Board of Directors when revisions in salary policy are recommended.

As things stand, any raises must be funded by our department's pro rata share of RI (i.e., Realized Income, the amount left over from net income after capital investments). The company has had a good year in sales, and has moved up over 5% on the Exchange. It has, however, been particularly hard hit by obsolescence of production machinery. The need to replace much of our plant facility has demanded a heavier-than-usual capital reinvestment, in turn bringing down realized income. As a result, the entire department must operate for the rest of the fiscal year under a frozen salary structure.

Along with most of the other department heads, I have hopes that the company's formula-allotment for raises will be adjusted to meet the contingency of abnormally high reinvestment -- such as that necessary this year. The Board meets in nine weeks and the matter is on the agenda. The company's success during the past year makes the likelihood of a policy change quite good. You can bet we'll be in there pitching.

As soon as we're able to, I will be recommending raises for every member of our staff.

Young writers gradually become immune to the cold impersonality of such rejections. But they often don't submit any more writing to the same publisher.

Some publishers, however, believe in encouraging young writers and do their best, when rejecting manuscripts, to stimulate further creative effort. This sense of responsibility is clearly evident in the letter in Figure 28, a rejection letter sent by *The Western Horseman* magazine to a young writer who had proposed submitting an article on the California State Polytechnic University Annual Rodeo. It's a good rejection letter.

Figure 28
A well-written letter of rejection from a publisher.
(Reproduced by permission of Western Horseman.)

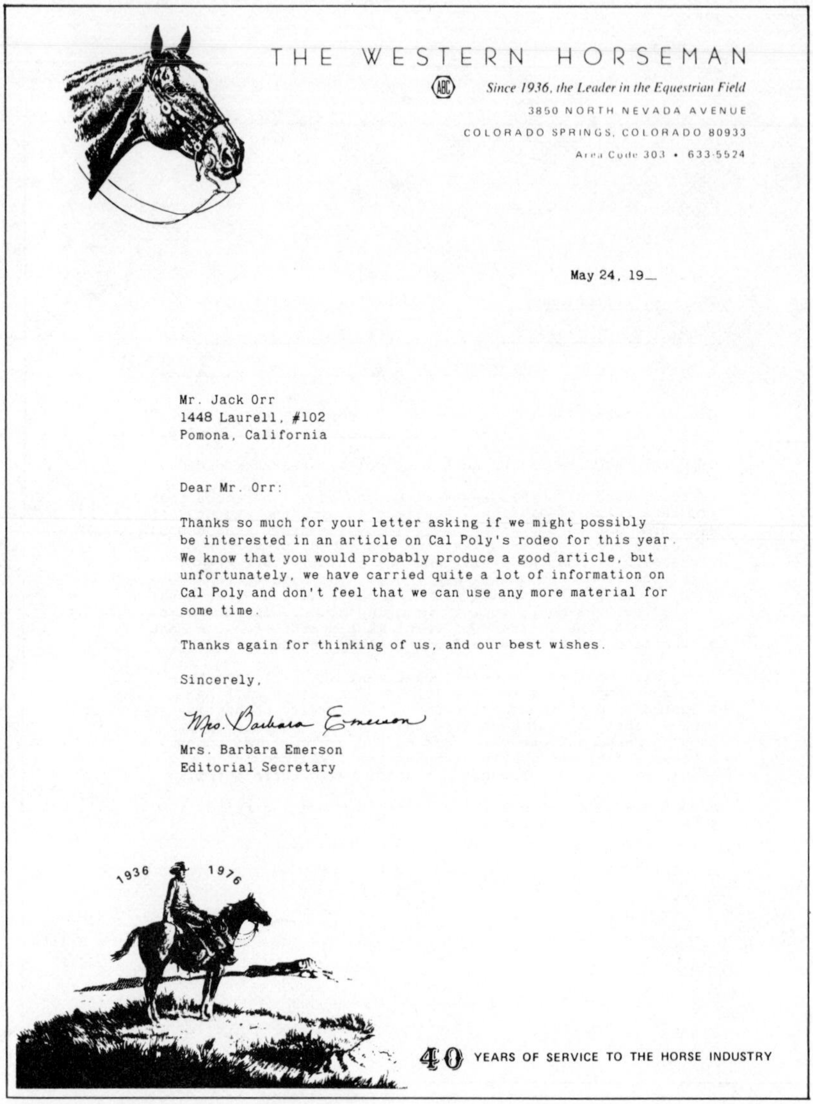

THE WESTERN HORSEMAN
Since 1936, the Leader in the Equestrian Field
3850 NORTH NEVADA AVENUE
COLORADO SPRINGS, COLORADO 80933
Area Code 303 • 633-5524

May 24, 19__

Mr. Jack Orr
1448 Laurell, #102
Pomona, California

Dear Mr. Orr:

Thanks so much for your letter asking if we might possibly be interested in an article on Cal Poly's rodeo for this year. We know that you would probably produce a good article, but unfortunately, we have carried quite a lot of information on Cal Poly and don't feel that we can use any more material for some time.

Thanks again for thinking of us, and our best wishes.

Sincerely,

Mrs. Barbara Emerson

Mrs. Barbara Emerson
Editorial Secretary

1936
1976
40 YEARS OF SERVICE TO THE HORSE INDUSTRY

The bad-news pattern can even be used — in certain circumstances — as a builder of good will. That's the aim of the following "bad-news" letter from the California Department of Fish and Game —to a four-year-old boy:

Master Danny Lundquist
5620 Devonshire Lane
Anaheim, California 92001

Dear Danny,

Thank you very much for entering your eight-ounce rainbow trout in our Fishing Contest. We certainly appreciate your interest and enthusiasm.

During the summer months, we receive many entries in the Trout category. As a result, some of the fish are larger than yours. But, although you did not win one of the bigger prizes for your fish, we are sending you, as a consolation prize, a Department of Fish and Game shoulder patch. We want you to wear it with pride, and keep on angling for bigger and bigger trout in the summers ahead. Keep up the good work.

Your friend,

John Shifflette
Trophy Awards Program

Let's make clear that not every bad-news message must adhere to the suggested pattern. Some refusals and rejections in business just aren't as potentially offensive as others; they need less strategy in the telling. Consider, for example, the Armstrong Cork Company letter in Figure 29. Its job is simply to say "no thanks" to a request that it purchase advertising space. It doesn't bother to wait until its explanation is finished to make its statement of refusal. Nor does it attempt stylistically to soften that actual statement. It does, however, rely heavily on an elaborate "positive sandwich" structure for congenial tone, and its explanation is about as empathetic as it can be.

MORE ON FUNCTIONAL DOWN-SHIFTING

Some business situations call for messages in which the news is neither totally good nor totally bad. A business person may, for example, agree to grant credit to a customer, but wish to put a ceiling on that credit. A claims adjustor may wish to settle a claim for less than the plaintiff wants. A publisher may feel that a manuscript is not yet good enough to publish, but that it will be if it's carefully revised. These are all situations in which the message falls *between* unqualified *yes* and unqualified *no.* How do you handle them?

In such situations, use a *functional down-shift.* (Recall our discussion of functional down-shifting on pages 245–246.) Treat the situation in the most positive way you reasonably can. If you're extending a limited line of credit, don't tell your reader: "We must hold your credit under $1500." Say instead: "We are glad to extend credit to you for any amount up to $1500." Make the letter a good-news message with limitations, rather than a message of bad news. If you can't completely satisfy a plaintiff's demand, don't say: "We can let you have only . . ." but rather: "We will be glad to let you have . . ." — use good-news strategy rather than bad-news strategy; you'll gain a psychological advantage. If you must reject an author's manuscript in its present form, but want to encourage revision, don't write that it isn't yet publishable. Instead write: "It's almost ready for publication and with a few key revisions . . . ."

As a rule of thumb; if you anticipate that the reader will resist the limitation you choose to impose, use bad-news strategy, in which your explanation *precedes* your statement of action; it's your best chance for overcoming that

Figure 29
A congenial and effective refusal letter.
(Reproduced by permission of the Armstrong Cork Co.)

Armstrong
CORK COMPANY

AREA CODE 717 | TELEPHONE 397-0611

LANCASTER, PA. 17604

March 12, 19--

Mr. Frank R. Knox
Advertising Manager
NEWS IN DEPTH Magazine
1566 33rd Street
New York, New York 10010

Dear Mr Knox:

Thank you for your letter of March 10, describing plans for your special "Industry on the Move" issue this October. You are certainly going all out to make this a particularly fine issue, and we appreciate your thinking of us in connection with your plans.

I wish I were able to tell you that we will be placing a corporate advertisement in the "Industry on the Move" number, as you suggest; but after reviewing our advertising schedule for the year, I regret that we will be unable to take part.

Our approach to advertising is based on consistency in reaching our most logical audience. We find that a one-time ad, no matter where it appears, can do little to advance our over-all program. Sometimes this causes us to miss out on a particularly worthwhile issue, as I'm sure yours will be; but in the perspective of our long-range objectives, I believe it is best that we adhere to our present advertising schedule.

Again may I say how much we appreciate your keeping us informed of your plans. I know that your "Industry on the Move" issue will be of real value to your readers, and I wish you the best of success with it.

Sincerely yours,

Norm D. Plume

Norm D. Plume
Manager of Corporate Advertising

resistance. If, on the other hand, you feel the reader will accept the limitation (graciously or otherwise), then let the explanation *follow* your statement of action, as it should in any good-news message.

IN CONCLUSION

Bad-news situations are among the most difficult that business writers must face. Only full-fledged *persuasion* problems equal them in difficulty (as we'll see in the next several chapters). They can be handled, however, and handled successfully if close attention is paid to strategy. The "positive sandwich" and the reason-first principle are both vital. The actual statement of rejection or refusal must be stylistically "de-fused" (by any of several techniques we've looked at). The writer must make a quick and smooth transition from the negative news to some alternate, and more positive, possibility, and develop that as fully as it can be.

Finally, if a message need not be delivered as bad news, it shouldn't be. No business writing problem should ever be treated as more difficult than it really is.

PROBLEMS

1. From some company that sells directly to the general public, obtain a copy of the letter it uses to deny credit to applicants with unacceptable credit ratings. In a memorandum to your instructor, analyze the strengths and weaknesses of this letter. Don't forget to attach the letter you've analyzed.

2. You are the managing director of the Book Cellar, Inc., a large retail and mail-order book dealer. One of your best-selling books lately has been the controversial novel *Ice Cream Every Evening* — at $12.95 a copy.

In this morning's mail, a copy of the novel, which you sent to Homer Jacoby, has been returned, along with a note from Jacoby demanding his money back because, in his words, "It's the most disgusting and obscene book I ever read!!" He's shocked that the Book Cellar would even handle the book. Thumbing through the returned book, you see evidence that at least two-thirds of it has been read; some of the pages are bent, others have smudges on them.

Write a letter to Jacoby, informing him as tactfully as you can that you cannot refund his money. You might explain to him that, as a retail book dealer, you are a provider for the public tastes, not an arbiter of it; that there are a number of books that you feel are of questionable taste, but you don't feel it's up to you to keep them from a demanding public, especially when many literary critics praise them highly. You are returning Jacoby's copy of *Ice Cream* to him; it cannot be resold as a new book and would be a total loss to you. (Incidentally, make sure that the letter of explanation reaches him before the book does.) To keep Jacoby's goodwill, you are inclined to enclose a certificate that would entitle him to two more books "at cost," but you decide against doing this for fear of triggering a wave of such returns.

3. This problem is one that manufacturers occasionally face when they ship their goods to retail dealers. The accounting department at Sorelco, Inc., manufacturers of small appliances, received the following letter one morning from a new customer, Nevins' Home Shop of 711 South Ocotillo Way, Phoenix, Arizona.

Sorelco, Inc.
18880 Wilshire Blvd.
Los Angeles, California

Gentlemen:

Enclosed is a check for $422.50 to cover our invoice #1025 of April 14. We have deducted $16.50 from the invoice price of

$439.00 to cover the cost of the transportation charges we had to pay.

Very truly yours,

Oscar Nevins

The problem is that Nevins should *not* have deducted the $16.50 for shipping charges because the invoice clearly showed, as all Sorelco invoices do, that terms are *f.o.b. Los Angeles* (free on board, Los Angeles) — delivery charges to points outside of Los Angeles are to be paid by the customer.

As the chief correspondent for Sorelco, you now have to write to Nevins disallowing the deduction and asking for a check for $16.50. It's not an easy letter. A blunt refusal and demand for payment would undoubtedly lose Nevins' patronage. Even such explanatory phrases as "you wrongfully deducted" or "you are not entitled to" are likely to offend him. You have to go under the assumption that Nevins' mistake is an honest one. You might explain to him that *f.o.b. L.A.* terms allow you to sell your items at a lower price, and that it would be unfair to your other customers to allow him this deduction even if you could. Write the letter.

4. You are the adjustment manager of the Deb Shop on Main Street in Carlisle, Pennsylvania. Yesterday you received a letter from Mrs. Marshall Creasy of 23 Douglas Road, Harrisburg, Pennsylvania, and she's obviously perturbed. Last week she purchased a white silk crepe blouse at the Deb Shop, marked down on sale from $34.98 to $14.98. When she got the blouse home she noticed a slight tear near the hem of the blouse, so she wants her money back. She says she'll return the blouse as soon as she receives your check.

You've got to write Mrs. Creasy, refusing to refund her money, because the sale was clearly advertised and marked as an "As Is" sale: *all* the items in the sale were slightly soiled or had other small defects. That's why the discount was over fifty percent on her blouse.

Write the letter, making sure to retain Mrs. Creasy's good will if you possibly can.

5. Your employer, Worthington-Bachelor, Inc., the large mail-order house, maintains the following policy: No COD orders of under ten dollars are accepted, because the possibility of the customer's not being at home for delivery, or simply refusing delivery, makes such orders unprofitable. This policy is clearly indicated in the Worthington-Bachelor catalog. In the long run, part of the money saved by this policy is "returned" to its customers in the form of lower prices.

Today, you received a COD order from Mrs. Blanche Goodnoy (18 Elderberry Avenue, Buffalo, West Virginia) for one oak-stained spice rack, model 4A, advertised in the Worthington-Bachelor catalog at $6.49. Your job is to write to Mrs. Goodnoy, explaining your policy and asking that she send a check or money order to cover the price of the spice rack.

Essentially, this is a bad-news letter; you are refusing a customer's request for COD service. But the bad news is not very serious. In fact, a tactful and positive explanation of your policy will probably have the customer agreeing that the policy is a very wise one. Write the letter.

6. Dr. Melvaline Oliver is the Supervisor of the Orange Plains Medical Research Laboratory. Eight weeks ago, she accepted an invitation to give a speech to the Medical Research Seminar being held in New York three weeks from today. She has, in fact, already written her speech and has been putting the final touches on it.

However, just this morning Dr. Oliver received a memorandum from the National Institute of Health (N.I.H.) announcing that the N.I.H. field representatives will be making their annual site-visit to the Orange Plains Lab on the very day of her scheduled speech. And when N.I.H. says they're coming, there's no changing things around! Because the N.I.H. is one of the Lab's main sources of funding (50% of the Lab's research last year was paid for by N.I.H. grants) she realizes that she *must* be on hand that day. She'll have to cancel her scheduled speech to the Medical Research Seminar.

Dr. Oliver must write a letter, right away, to the Seminar's Planning Committee informing them that she's cancelling. She obviously also wants to stay in their good graces — perhaps to be invited again, at some future date, to address the Seminar.

Write the letter for her signature.

7. Back on page 217 the Dean of Admissions at Valhalla University sent a good-news letter of acceptance to a successful candidate for admission. Now he asks you to draft a letter which, without requiring modification for each usage, can be sent to all *un*successful applicants — a rejection letter. It would be quite easy to just say, "Sorry, you've been refused," but Valhalla has a greater responsibility than that to its unsuccessful applicants. Any refusal that tends to completely discourage an applicant can alter the very course of his or her life. So putting all the techniques of effective refusal to work for you, write a good letter of rejection for the dean.

8. Assume that you are in business for yourself, and quite successful. One of the things you have developed a reputation for is the effectiveness of your debt-collection effort. The key to that effort is a series of clever and highly original collection letters. So good, in fact, are these letters that Professor Horace Folsom (of the Business Communications Department at Detroit State College), who is writing a book on communications, has requested permission to use your collection letters as illustrations of effective technique in his book.

Flattered though you are, you feel that to publish your letters would be to weaken their effectiveness. Write to Professor Folsom, tactfully refusing his request.

9. You are the Vice-Chancellor of Employee Relations of the San Sebastian Community College, and have just been alerted to a potential case of personnel grievance. The facts you learn are these:

Two years ago, in July, the college bookstore hired Peter Reeves as a full-time (40 hour-per-week) cashier. His work during the first 18 months of his employment was wholly satisfactory. This past January, Reeves submitted a formal request for an unpaid six-week leave of absence (hopefully to run from January 20 to March 4). The college's business manager, at the advice of the bookstore manager, denied the leave, telling Reeves in writing that the period of his requested leave coincided with the bookstore's "busiest time of the year," and that his services could not be spared.

Reeves needed the time very badly. He was preparing to take the State Bar Exam. So without being granted the formal leave of absence, he stayed home anyway on the 20th of January and called in saying that he was "unable to come to work." He did this every morning for the next two weeks. When he called once more at the beginning of the third week, he was told that he'd been fired. The bookstore manager considered the matter closed, and hired a new cashier.

However, two weeks later (by now it is February 21), the college's Business Manager received a call from the president of the campus collective-bargaining unit complaining that Peter Reeves had been treated unfairly. Leaves of absence, he contended (correctly), were often granted to college personnel provided that adequate notice had been given. Reeves had given more than the two-weeks notice considered adequate. Reeves had been discriminated against, he said. "There's no doubt about it. He should have his job back promptly at the beginning of March!" (Even though he just passed the Bar Exam.)

You consider the facts. It is true that unpaid leaves are often granted to college employees, but the college is under no obligation legally to provide them. In Reeves' case, the leave had been denied for a good reason: the bookstore could not afford to be shorthanded, nor could it get by with an inexperienced temporary replacement. Moreover, a new cashier is already on the job, and there is no reason for removing her. You realize, however, that if you refuse Reeves' demand to be rehired and send him away angry, you will probably be dealing with the matter for months to come.

Your task is this: write a formal letter to Peter Reeves (with a copy to the collective-bargaining president) refusing his request to be rehired, but doing everything possible to avoid a continuing squabble over the matter.

10. Personnel managers must frequently write bad-news letters. Assume that you are the personnel manager at United Foods. Upon receiving a promising application for a management-trainee position from Joanna Rose, a graduating senior at Cerebral College, Amherst, Massachusetts, you invited her in for an interview at company expense. She came, and made a moderately favorable impression on all who spoke with her. However, there are only two trainee positions available, and you and your colleagues decide to offer these positions to two other applicants. They both accept the offers.

Now you must write a letter to Joanna Rose, informing her that she is not receiving an offer. Remember, you want to leave her with the feeling that she has been treated cordially and fairly by United Foods. You also don't want to discourage her to the point that it will adversely affect her search for a job elsewhere.

11. You have graduated. It is mid-August. A friend of yours has mentioned your name to V. P. Perkins, the Executive Vice President at Martindales, Inc. in New York, a very good firm to work for. And Perkins has contacted you about coming to New York for an interview.

Suddenly you learn that you have been admitted to Valhalla University's Masters in Business Administration program, a very desirable graduate program. You must write to Perkins, and tell him that you have chosen to go to graduate school. Obviously, in a year and a half, when you've finished your MBA, you would be very interested in pursuing the possibility of a job at Martindales. Write the letter.

12. You are the manager of the Industrial Engineering Department at Intercontinental Airlines. A position for a Methods Engineer opens up in your

department. The opening is made known to Intercontinental's employees around the world, and thirty-two of them apply for the position.

You interview the ten applicants you feel possess the best credentials, and as a result you narrow the field of candidates down to three, whom you will call in for further interviews. Write a letter that will go to each of the other seven, telling them they are no longer under consideration for the job.

13. Mr. and Mrs. Winston Taylor of 28 Pine Terrace Road, Upland, Michigan, received the following letter one day recently from the bank that holds the mortgage on their home:

November 4, 198_

Dear Mr. and Mrs. Taylor:

We have received your current tax bill showing taxes in the amount of $707.22, an amount which represents a large increase over last year's taxes of $588.54.

Due to the above, an additional payment of $67 into your impound account is required in order for us to pay your taxes before the deliquent date. Therefore, please send us your check for $67.00 in the enclosed envelope so that it will reach us no later than November 30.

Very truly yours,

Janet Ferry

Janet Ferry
Home Loan Officer

It may be true that the surest things in life are death and taxes, but the tone of this bad-news letter really rubs it in! Rewrite the letter, as the bank officer, so that it better protects your own relationship with the Taylors. Some suggestions: it may be a little difficult to open positively in this situation, but it shouldn't be hard to close more positively. You might experiment with the complex-sentence technique and see what ways of actually presenting the bad news you can come up with. Finally, it would seem logical to take the burden of the bad news off your own shoulders (that's probably the major problem in the letter above); after all, it was the county — not you — who raised the Taylor's taxes.

14. The Moon Aerospace Corporation obtains more than half of its business from government defense and space contracts. A key factor in obtaining many of these contracts is the capability of the people who will be working on them. There is little doubt that the company obtained a major contract recently because Dr. Otto Kemp, a very prominent physicist, was to head up the project. Kemp came to the company several months earlier from a major university where he was Research Professor of Astro-Physics. The company gave him a lucrative salary, outstanding research facilities, a staff of highly qualified assistants, a free hand in deciding how to carry out the various phases of the contract assignment, and a very sizable budget.

Kemp's project employs seventeen people, most of them scientists and research engineers with advanced degrees. Unfortunately, the project group has been performing inefficiently: schedules are not being met, and cost overruns have become the rule rather than the exception. The problem seems to be that although Kemp provides brilliant technical leadership, the team is being stymied by normal and routine business procedures, practices, and policies. Kemp finds paperwork and bureaucratic delays especially annoying, and has proven to be a weak coordinator. He communicates ineffectively with other company executives, and is a poor organizer and supervisor.

You, the President of Moon Aerospace, are faced with a dilemma. You realize that Kemp is indispensable to obtaining future contracts for the company, yet the problems that arise with Kemp as Project Head are growing more and more serious. You must pull Dr. Kemp from his supervisorial duties, yet keep him on the job and just as highly motivated as he has been from the start. You decide to put a skilled manager on the project team (a man named Dr. Jack Simpson), a talented researcher himself but hardly in Otto Kemp's league as a scientist.

You must write a formal memorandum to Kemp informing him of the change. Remember that although Kemp has proven not to like administrative duties, he is very proud and probably mistakes his own ability to handle them well. Write the memorandum.

15. Here's a problem in which you might consider the principle of the functional down-shift. It involves handling a customer's demand for adjustment. You aren't going to refuse her demand altogether. But neither are you going to grant her the full adjustment she desires. This kind of problem frequently comes across the desk of the advertising manager of the New York *Herald*. Put yourself in his shoes:

Marissa Handworthy, an advertiser, has written complaining that the ad she placed in the *Herald* the day before yesterday was misprinted, so she wants her bill canceled. The ad was to announce a one-day sale at Marissa Handworthy, Inc., Antique Shop, 12 East 7th Street, New York, N.Y. Her name was misspelled "Marissa D. Worthy, Inc." Everything else in the ad appeared as desired.

The *Herald's* attitude on mistakes of this sort is that some adjustment is deserved, but not total cancellation of a bill unless the ad lost its *full* value. Clearly, Handworthy's ad did *not* lose its full value. It was clear to anyone who read the ad that there was a one-day sale at an antique shop at 12 East 7th Street. Only the shop's name was misprinted. The most you can give Handworthy is a twenty-five percent reduction on the price of her ad.

Write to Handworthy. Give her a twenty-five percent reduction of her bill of sixty dollars, and retain her good will.

16. Your firm, the Landsmere Real Estate Company of Salem, Oregon, today received the following letter from a prospective client:

Gentlemen:

I am very much interested in purchasing a home with at least ten acres of land in Santa Lucia County, somewhere in the $140,000 to $180,000 range. I understand that such properties are frequently available and that you are the outfit most likely to be handling them. Please inform me of appropriate listings. I will reply immediately by phone or in person.

Very truly yours,

Samuel T. Karson

Samuel T. Karson

Obviously, you are interested in the possibility of selling property to Mr. Karson, and you do have several Santa Lucia County listings of over ten acres. Because of a recent boom in land prices, however, none of these properties can be purchased for less than $200,000.

So, your communications problem can be construed as the delivery of "bad news." But it needn't be — and shouldn't be! You *do* have properties available, and even though they're higher priced than Karson would like, their "pluses" far outweigh their drawbacks. The situation can really be treated as a "good-news" situation.

Write a letter to Karson informing him that there *is* property available in Santa Lucia County, and that although the prices are higher than his suggested range, the properties are among the best values still available in the county. The likelihood is that county real estate prices will continue to rise. Tell him, too, that you'd like very much to show him these choice properties.

Your task isn't simple. Consider the reactions you desire from Karson. Your primary objective is to maintain, or even enhance, Mr. Karson's enthusiasm over buying property in Santa Lucia County, in spite of the fact that he underestimated the cost.

CHAPTER 12

THE PRINCIPLES OF PERSUASION

Our final type of direct reaction-evoker is the *persuasive* communication. It's a common kind of message, both in business and elsewhere. For some people, hardly a day goes by in which they don't try to get someone to think or act in a certain way. Yet for all its frequency, the act of persuasion can be quite difficult — especially when you can't exert the strength of your personality face to face. That's the problem business writers face: with words alone, on paper, they must effectively persuade. They must create in the minds of their readers a new way of thinking about something, and often a conviction to act upon it.

Some people feel that *all* business writing is persuasive in nature. "You are always selling when you write," "they say, . . ." selling your ideas or selling yourself." And in one sense they're right. One objective of any reaction-evoking communication is to put the recipient in a receptive frame of mind. But the term *persuasive* in a narrower and tougher sense means creating a brand new state of mind in someone, a desire to believe something or do something not previously believed or done by that someone. That's the sense in which we'll be using the term. The letters, memos, and other documents that we'll examine in the next three chapters will have this kind of start-from-scratch persuasion as their primary goal.

What is persuasion? It is the process of convincing someone to take a certain action or adopt a certain point of view. Sales and promotion letters sent by companies to prospective customers are examples of persuasion put into writing. So are suggestions written by employees, proposals written by companies seeking contracts, budget justifications written by department heads, application letters written by job-seekers — all are business communications that seek to persuade. Despite their obvious differences in approach and attitude, they must all comply with the requirements of the persuasive process —or fail.

Consider the following example of what one expert has called "the most highly specialized form of business writing" — the sales letter. It's persuasion at its toughest. The writer, the President of Georgetown Precision Camera Supply, is addressing real-estate brokers:

SELLING HOMES CAN BE A ''SNAP''

A presumptuous statement . . . but it's true, literally.

In a trial run last month, three real estate brokers – one in Chicago, one in Denver, and one in San Francisco – tried a new sales technique. The technique succeeded, far beyond their expectations.

This is what they did --

Each of the brokers' sales people was given a camera to carry -- a special kind of camera. After showing Mr. and Mrs. John Doe a house, the sales rep would get out the camera and ''snap'' a picture of the Does -- sometimes several pictures -- in front of their prospective new home. <u>Within sixty seconds,</u> the camera -- a new, extra-wide-angle Super Solroid 500 -- developed a large, attractive, full-color photograph. Those photos became the salesman's on-the-spot gift to Mr. and Mrs. Doe, no strings attached.

Psychologists call the technique ''identification'' --

Those photos carried away by the Does were not merely a gift. They were an attractive reminder of exactly what that interesting house looked like -- and what <u>they</u> looked like in front of it. As a result, the prospective buyers identified much more closely with that home than they otherwise would have. And much more closely than with the houses shown them by other salesmen.

That sense of identification paid off for the brokers when the Does and other prospective buyers made their decisions. The three firms that employed the technique reported sales increases of 42%, 48%, and 61% respectively over the corresponding month last year. No other significant variable had changed. The increases could be attributed <u>only</u> to the new Super Solaroid 500.

The technique sounds so simple -- why hasn't it been tried before? Well, the technique <u>has</u> been possible for a number of years. But only <u>now</u> does the new Super Solaroid 500 make it practical.

This is why --

The new 500's extra-wide-angle lens allows you to photograph the whole house while standing within forty to fifty feet of it. The attractive details are not lost because of distance.

The new 500 reproduces colors with extrordinary fidelity. Every color is true -- not washed out, not too intense, as colors often are with less sophisticated cameras.

The new 500's Permaflash attachment allows you the same high-resolution, high-quality color reproductions indoors, without having to carry any bulbs. Those special interior features of a home can now be captured on film and given to the prospects.

The new 500's special 5X Filters allow your sales people to take full advantage of whatever light they have to shoot in. And they're a snap to use.

Finally, the price of the new 500 is low, amazingly low. Here at Georgetown Precision, we are prepared to offer you -- as a licensed broker -- a professional discount of 15% off the regular list price of only $190. And 20% off on the purchase of four or more Super Solaroid 500s for your staff.

The cost of the technique itself is also low. Each photo your salesman presents to Mr. and Mrs. Doe costs only 59¼¢. The three firms who tested this sales technique all confirmed that never had 60¢ been invested so wisely.

Let's be perfectly honest --

The Super Solaroid 500 won't sell every house. Cheap, boxy little houses that have no character tend to look even cheaper and boxier on film. But any house that has a touch of character -- or at least one strong sales feature -- can be sold with the help of the 500. And those strong selling points can be made even stronger by picture takers who know what they're doing.

That's where we go the extra mile for you --

With your order for the new Super Solaroid 500, our photographic consultant, Mr. Roger Maxwell, will at no cost conduct a seminar for your sales staff on the fine points of photographic technique. Your people will learn to take flattering pictures of home exteriors and interiors, and of people as well.

We'd like to give you the complete facts and figures on the three-city test just completed, as well as a demonstration of the Super Solaroid 500 technique. Just give us a call here at 839-7800. We think you'll agree that selling homes can be more of a snap -- if you're snapping the Super Solaroid 500.

Cordially yours,

Niven Campbell, President
Georgetown Precision
Camera, Inc.

This sales letter is a solid piece of persuasive business writing. The first thing one notices about it is its departure from standard business-letter format. It is also substantially longer than the average business letter or memo, with more accumulated detail than the other direct reaction-evokers we've looked at. These differences — like virtually everything else in this letter — are dictated by the demands of the persuasive process. Let's see if we can deduce from it some valid principles about effective written persuasion.

THE CENTRAL APPEAL AND SECONDARY APPEALS

The person you're attempting to persuade must have, or must be given, some motive for thinking or acting as you wish. As a persuader, you've got to *appeal* to this motive in your communication. With as much empathy as you can muster, you must ask yourself: what does (or what should) my reader want? (That's his *motive*.) Then prepare to show the reader (in your *appeal*) how it can be had. The central appeal in the Georgetown Camera letter is, quite obviously, an appeal to increased profits. "Buy the Super Solaroid 500 from us," the letter says in effect, "and your profits will increase." The same appeal to increased profits is at the heart of most sales letters from one business establishment to another.

Sales letters written to consumers usually have different central appeals. A letter from a service station urging customers to come in for an automotive checkup might develop a central appeal to the motive of safety. A letter that attempts to sell home air conditioners would probably appeal to the comfort motive. A letter selling expensive crystalware might aim its central appeal at the reader's pride. One selling fine wines would probably appeal to satisfaction of the taste buds. Here's just a handful of the many motives to which sales letters (as well as other kinds of persuasive message) can appeal:

Making money (profit)
Saving money
Security
Success
Prestige
Protection of reputation
Avoidance of criticism
Popularity
Sex
Ease

The satisfaction of appetites (hunger, thirst)
Curiosity
Humor
Cleanliness
Efficiency
Preparedness
Protection of family and loved ones
Beauty
Style

Ethics	Comfort
Morality	Individuality
The emulation of others	The desire for knowledge and insight
Safety	Generosity
Fear	Romantic enchantment
Pride	Escape
Health	

All persuasive communications, not just sales letters, must develop a central appeal. A memo to your boss justifying a certain action you've taken would have as its goal the boss's approval of that action. Its central appeal might be to his or her desire for efficient operations. A proposal from a public-relations agent to a client might appeal to the client's desire for increased prestige. A persuasive message from a doctor to a patient would probably appeal to the patient's desire for continuing health. In each case, the central appeal is aimed at the reader's predominant motive. A central appeal needs substance. The most noticeable weakness in the persuasive writing of college students and inexperienced business writers is the underdevelopment of their central appeals.

Your first task, then, when faced with writing any persuasive communication is to determine what central appeal you should develop. That central appeal must be clearly defined before you write a single word. Without a strong central appeal, no effort at persuasion can succeed.

Secondary appeals in persuasive communications are appeals used to supplement the central appeal. Any secondary appeal, if it stood alone, would not suffice as a persuasive force. But as a supplement, a secondary appeal strengthens the central appeal by saying, in effect, "Here's just one more reason why you should . . . "

Notice the secondary appeals used in the Georgetown Camera letter. There's an appeal to the practical simplicity of the Super Solaroid 500 technique ("Selling homes can be a snap!" "The technique sounds so simple . . . . But only now . . . [is] it practical"). There's also an appeal to the reader's aesthetic sense ("attractive . . . full-color photograph," "colors with extraordinary fidelity," "Your people will learn to take flattering pictures . . . "). And there's an appeal to economy ("20% off on the purchase of four or more," "Each photo . . . costs only 59¼¢"). No one of these appeals would likely, by itself, persuade the broker to buy. But as secondary appeals they add strength to the central appeal — increased profits — and increase the chances of a sale.

THE PERSUASIVE PROCESS

After deciding what your central and secondary appeals in a persuasive communication will be, you've got to consider the nature of the persuasive process itself — and how to translate it into writing.

To persuade someone to think or act in a certain way, you must lead that person's mind through a series of successive phases. These mental phases must each be fully developed before the next can be reached for, and before the persuasion can be fully achieved. Knowing what these phases are, you can plan your persuasive strategy.

The Necessary Strategy Pattern
for any Persuasive Communication

First, you must *capture* and *maintain* your reader's *attention*;

then,

if the motive you're attempting to satisfy already exists, firmly, in your reader's mind . . .

. . . you must focus his or her mind upon that motive.

if the motive you're attempting to satisfy is *not* yet firmly established in your reader's mind . . .

. . . you must firmly establish it there — even if that means creating it from scratch.

Sometimes these functions can be met simultaneously. But if they cannot, they must both be met separately, and in this order.

Next, once the reader's mind is focused on this motive, you must *fully* develop your *central appeal* and secondary appeals, providing sufficient reason for your reader's taking the action or adopting the frame of mind you want;

finally,

if your persuasive goal is to induce a certain way of thinking . . .

you conclude with a positively phrased statement summarizing the essence of your message.

if your goal is to induce a certain course of action (such as placing an order or calling for a demonstration)

you conclude by suggesting and, if necessary, clearly describing, the action you wish your reader to take.

As we examine this persuasive process in more detail, you'll be able to see how closely the Georgetown Camera letter adheres to it.

Capturing and Sustaining Attention

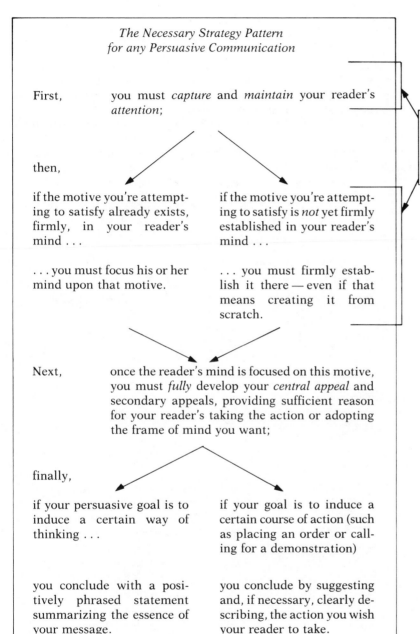

People tend to react skeptically or indifferently to persuasive communications. Every day, sales letters by the thousands are ignored or glanced at briefly and thrown away. Personnel managers receive applications by the score — most of them from people they will not hire. Even executives, who can use better ways of doing things are skeptical about the usefulness of most proposals they consider. So while in some situations persuasive communications are met with enthusiasm by their recipients, much more often they are not.

Therefore, the first thing you must often do when persuading is capture attention. The beginning of the communication must make the reader think: "Now here's a message that might really be worth reading"–and make him or her read on.

If you're putting forth a proposal or a suggestion, you must open as empathetically as possible, with a confident and enthusiastic (yet inoffensive) statement of what you have to offer. Here are several illustrations:

> Mrs. Donohue, I believe we've got a bottleneck in the operation of our steno pool, a slowdown that can be alleviated if we take the right steps.

(A simple opening for a memo that not only gets the office-manager's attention, but also effectively focuses it on an important motive.)

> Gentlemen:
>
> After carefully studying your primary market and your advertising strategy of the past year. . . .

(Here the writer aims to capture and hold the reader's attention with empathetic references to the reader's own interests: *your primary market . . . your advertising strategy* . . . . It's tough to ignore someone who's talking about *you.*)

> Dear Dr. Berger:
>
> I've been thinking carefully about some of the points you made in your talk last Thursday, especially your contention that copper costs must rise 10% if our industry is to survive. In the recent survey made by. . . .

(The rest of this communication will try to persuade its reader to change his mind on a certain point. Yet, notice how, instead of challenging that point in his opener, the writer appeals to the reader's sense of self-importance to gain his attention and an open-minded reading.)

Long ago, one of our greatest business communicators, Benjamin Franklin, advised us how to tailor our language to sustain attention and persuade "those whose concurrence you desire." He repeats that advice for us in Figure 30.

Capturing and sustaining attention is toughest of all for writers of sales and promotion letters. Those letters must overcome not only indifference and human inertia, but the tendency of their recipients to regard anything that looks like a sales letter as "junk mail." Many sales letters dispense with the inside address and salutation, and begin with an interesting claim, an eye-opening statement, or a provocative promise. Even the envelopes of sales letters are designed as attention getters. Conventional letter format gives way to novelty.

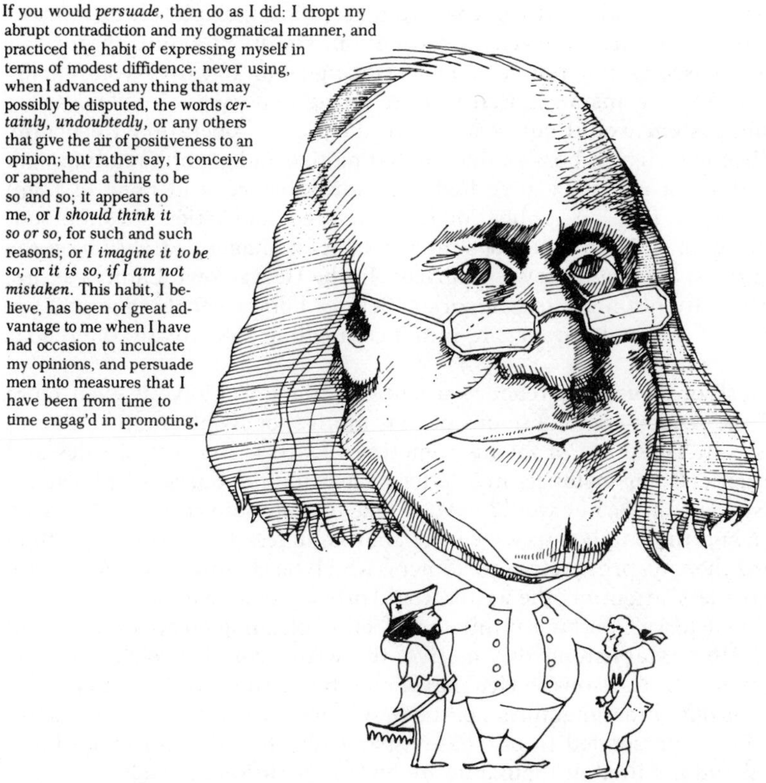

If you would persuade, then do as I did: I dropt my
abrupt contradiction and my dogmatical manner, and
practiced the habit of expressing myself in
terms of modest diffidence; never using,
when I advanced any thing that may
possibly be disputed, the words certainly, undoubtedly, or any others
that give the air of positiveness to an
opinion; but rather say, I conceive
or apprehend a thing to be
so and so; it appears to
me, or I should think it
so or so, for such and such
reasons; or I imagine it to be
so; or it is so, if I am not
mistaken. This habit, I believe, has been of great advantage to me when I have
had occasion to inculcate
my opinions, and persuade
men into measures that I
have been from time to
time engag'd in promoting.

Figure 30
Benjamin Franklin's advice on effective persuasion.

The recipient must be made to start reading. Some of these attention-seeking devices are effective; many are not. In a *mass* mailing, the function of the sales-letter opening is to get as high a percentage of recipients as possible to start reading the letter.

No one rule can tell you the best way of capturing the reader's attention in a sales letter. But there are several helpful guidelines. The opening should stimulate the reader's curiosity. And it should be relevant to the appeal you will be developing. (A startling but irrelevant opening will disgust a reader as soon as he sees it's been just a device for grabbing his attention.) The opening of a sales letter to housewives might well refer to the health and happiness of growing children. A sales letter to executives who depend heavily on credit cards might successfully open with a headline like:

> A single international credit card now offers you all these services . . . .

The writer of the Georgetown Camera letter created a catchy opening — one that appealed to his reader's curiosity, and also invoked his reader's basic motive (selling more homes). That opening also related directly to what he was offering by its play on the word *snap*.

When writing a sales letter, give your imagination full play in creating an opening. But be prepared to apply the guidelines of stimulation and relevance very critically to whatever your imagination comes up with.

Focusing the Reader's Attention Upon Motive

The difficulty of the next phase of the persuasive process depends upon whom you're trying to persuade and what you're persuading that person to think or do. Once you've captured the reader's attention, you must assure that his or her mind is focused on the motive you want to appeal to. If it isn't, your appeal cannot work. Say, for instance, that you are trying to persuade your boss that a new filing system would cut costs; mere mention of operational economy should suffice to focus the boss's mind on that motive and get him reading with interest (unless, of course, you've had such ideas before, and none of them worked). Likewise, in a job application letter, a direct and articulate statement of your reason for writing will focus the personnel manager's attention on the continuing quest for bright new employees. In the Georgetown Camera letter, a provocative attention-getting remark ("Selling homes can be a *snap*!") is transformed, in the first paragraph, into a compelling reason why the reader should continue.

The task of focusing a reader's attention on a key motive is even more difficult if the reader isn't conscious of that motive, or if that motive doesn't really exist yet. These are problems sometimes faced by writers of sales and promotion letters. For instance, in a letter promoting the Carlson Upholstery-Cleaning Service, the writer would have to take into account those readers who have never had their upholstery cleaned (that is, unless this writer is willing to disregard them as prospective customers, which he shouldn't be). After capturing the readers' attention, the writer would provide them with ample motives for clean upholstery — perhaps citing the effects of cleaning on appearance and durability. After establishing this motive, the writer could then develop the reasons why it's the Carlson Service that should be patronized. An even greater problem confronted manufacturers of the first home air conditioners. Consumers could not be persuaded to purchase a particular brand of air conditioner until they'd had instilled in them a desire for air conditioning itself.

So whenever you're writing a persuasive communication, you must ask yourself if the motive you want to appeal to is uppermost in your reader's mind. If it is, you need only mention it, and proceed with your appeal. But if it isn't, you must get it firmly established there before your appeal can work — even if it means creating that motive from scratch. (More on this point later.)

Developing Your Persuasive Appeals

After focusing your reader's attention on the key motive, you're ready to develop your central appeal and secondary appeals. You can develop an appeal in a persuasive communication by using any one, or a combination, of the following techniques:

1. You can give tangible description.
2. You can produce verifiable facts.
3. You can use emotional suasion.
4. You can engage in logical reasoning.
5. You can offer respected opinion.

Tangible description makes clear what a thing looks like or is composed of, or it reveals what a process entails. The Georgetown Camera letter depends heavily on tangible description in developing its appeal — description of both Super Solaroid 500 (extra-wide-angle lens, Permaflash attachment, special 5X light filters, and so on) and the "identification" technique. The sales-letter writer who reveals the vitamin content of a new breakfast cereal, the horsepower and displacement of a new V-8 engine, the ingredients in a new recipe for shish kebab, or the twelve simple steps of a new sewer-cleaning process, is using tangible description to develop his appeal. So is the advertising executive who, in persuading a prospective client to place advertising through the agency, describes the agency's facilities and the capacity of its creative staff. And so is the office manager who compares the functioning of two pieces of office equipment in persuading the boss to purchase the more expensive of the two. Tangible description is a vital element in most persuasive business communications.

Verifiable facts are also used to support your persuasive appeals. People you're trying to persuade obviously won't run right out to verify the facts you put forth. But as long as they feel the facts *can* be verified (and are relevant to their motives), they can be persuaded by your statements. An employment interviewer might urge her company to hire Adam Pierce by citing the details of his college record and his previous work experience: those details are verifiable facts. An architect will persuade his client to use one building material rather than another by citing comparative costs and statistics on comparative durability — again, verifiable facts. The Georgetown Camera letter uses verifiable facts ("The three firms . . . reported sales increases . . . of 42%, 48%, and 61% . . .") and promises more verifiable fact upon request from the reader.

Emotional suasion is an attempt to enlist *feelings* (as distinguished from knowledge) in support of your appeal. The promotion writer who boasts that:

> Senior citizens enjoy glorious and carefree retirement at Sonora Springs Country Club Estates

or the writer who urges:

> For all-round good-news reporting, plus the outspoken opinions that add zest to your own thinking about it — why not try Newsweek . . .

is in no way tangibly describing the offering, nor producing verifiable facts about it (at least not in these passages). Only an emotional aura is being created, in hopes of captivating the reader.

The Georgetown Camera letter also uses emotional suasion in developing its appeal. What difference does it really make that "psychologists call the [Super Solaroid 500] technique 'identification' "? It only adds a scholarly gloss to a straightforward sales idea. Why should a persuasive writer say: "Let's be perfectly honest . . ." — except to try to win over the reader's respect? The businessperson, as well as the average consumer, *can* be won over emotionally.

And there's nothing wrong with emotional suasion. It's a powerful, persuasive tool. Your natural enthusiasm for the action or viewpoint that you're espousing ought to inject at least some emotional suasion into your persuasive communications. What is dishonest is emotional suasion *in the absence of* any tangible description, verifiable facts, or logical reasoning. Sophisticated readers will quickly dismiss any persuasive appeal built on emotional suasion alone.

Logical reasoning in the development of a persuasive appeal can take several forms. The consultant who wants to persuade the Acme corporation that it should forego its planned expansion might base his appeals on *deductive* reasoning (that is, drawing a conclusion from two or more verifiable premises).

He might argue that present funds are insufficient to finance the program, and that all possible sources of new funds have been exhausted; hence, the program should not be started.

The employee at General Products who tries to convince a supervisor to purchase a metered stamp machine might base such an appeal on *inductive* reasoning (basing a general conclusion on specific instances). The employee might cite case after case of other companies with large periodic mailings who switched to metered postage and reduced their costs, and then might conclude that metered postage would probably cut costs for any company with large periodic mailings — General Products included.[1]

Implicit in the Georgetown Camera letter is the inductive assumption that the Super Solaroid 500 technique has been proven effective because it increased sales for all three brokers who tried it. Three cases are hardly enough as reliable inductive evidence (both reader and writer know this), but citing the three cases should get the reader thinking inductively about the effectiveness of the Super Solaroid 500 technique.

A college dean who tries to persuade the trustees to hire a business manager might base his appeal on *analogy* (the kind of logical reasoning that likens one thing to another). The dean might argue that in many respects, especially the financial, a private college is like a business corporation. The strength of this appeal depends, of course, on the validity of the analogy. No analogy is ever perfect proof of a point, but analogy can be a very strong persuasive aid if used conservatively. (Recall the analogy by Antony Jay, on page 106, likening a corporation to a state.)

Respected opinion can also be used to strengthen a persuasive appeal, even though its validity is beyond proof. The bronchial specialist who tells a patient, "If you don't stop smoking, you'll be dead within two years" is persuasive, even though proof of this statement isn't immediately obtainable. The labor relations analyst who tells a company vice-president, "I think you're in for increasing friction between the men in the tooling department and their foreman, Calvin Craig," is similarly persuasive because of his experience and acknowledged expertness.

Persuasive writers who aren't themselves experts often solicit expert opinion to strengthen their persuasive appeals. The department head who tells her boss, "Tom Petersen of our legal staff thinks we've got a good case of unfair practice against Acme and its new promotion scheme" is strengthening her appeal by reporting respected opinion. So is the sales writer who uses a testimonial like this one:

> World-famous beauty expert Rik Danau says:
>
> > No shade of lipstick so entices a man as Verlan's Dusk Coral.

No matter what means you use to develop your persuasive appeal, remember this: developing that appeal is usually a lengthy process. Notice how long the Georgetown Camera letter is, compared with letters we examined earlier. It took the writer over 550 words to develop fully his persuasive appeal,

[1] Deductive and inductive reasoning are both discussed further on pages 419–420.

not counting the opening and closing paragraphs, which are devoted to capturing attention and suggesting action. A persuasive appeal is an attempt to alter the status quo of a human mind. Trying to do the job with a quick, underdeveloped or fragmentary appeal is like trying to move a boulder with a twig.

The Final Phase of the Persuasive Process

After its central appeal has been fully developed and its secondary appeals built in, a persuasive communication must end effectively — lest all your effort go for nothing. The kind of conclusion you write should be determined by the nature of your persuasive goal.

If your goal is to put your reader into a particular frame of mind, you should end your communication with a statement summarizing the essence of your central appeal. For instance, in a memorandum that attempts to justify a new twist in business strategy, you might end by expressing confidence that the new strategy will achieve its objective. A promotion letter from a public utility (whose central appeal has been the inexpensiveness of gas heating) might conclude by summarizing its appeal this way:

> Never before--by comparison with other forms of energy--have so many families profited so cheaply from the benefits of natural gas.

In these situations, no specific response is desired — just a new frame of mind. So conclusion becomes an attempt to drive the point home convincingly.

If, on the other hand, you want the person you're persuading to take a certain course of action (either immediately or soon), your conclusion should directly suggest that action. A letter from a salesman trying to interest a customer in a new product line might end this way:

> Just give me a call and I'll bring over the brochures, a price list, and some samples.[2]

The conclusion of the Georgetown Camera letter makes essentially the same suggestion.

A persuasive memo written by an employee to his boss concluded with this urging:

> Let's go over to the showroom together some day next week and take a look at these new Swiss patterns. I think you'll like them.

— a simple, straightforward request for a specific action.

Sales letters to the general public often don't stimulate action in their readers, even if the persuasive appeal has been well received. It's inertia. People

[2] Notice that the *least* appealing of the three items mentioned in this closing, the price list, is sandwiched between the other two so that it avoids the emphasis naturally falling on the first and last items in any series.

simply tend not to respond. Therefore, these sales letters not only suggest a response, they do all they can to induce it. Here's the way a typical sales letter to the general public might close:

> Find out what Equity Mutual can save you. Just drop the accompanying card into the mail. We'll pay the postage. And there's no obligation on your part whatsoever. No salesman will call.

In very specific terms, the writer of this letter urges the response he desires ("Just drop the accompanying card into the mail"); he provides the means for responding (a stamped self-addressed reply card); he emphasizes that it costs nothing to respond ("We'll pay the postage"); and he assures the reader there are no strings attached ("there's no obligation on your part *whatsoever*. No salesman will call"). All these inducements are built into the closing to overcome the reader's skepticism and natural tendency not to respond.[3]

Sales-letter writers have a whole arsenal of techniques for inducing response from their readers. They can offer trial-purchase terms, gifts, or free pamphlets. They can provide redeemable coupons. They can urge prompt response for a variety of reasons, such as taking advantage of a limited sale offer or ordering in time for Christmas delivery. Any of these techniques, and others, can be used as long as they don't conflict with the letter's purpose or its desired level of dignity. By themselves, these inducements to action would no persuade the recipient of a sales letter to respond. But when used at the end of a letter in which a genuine appeal has been developed, they help complete the persuasive process successfully, by stimulating the actual response.

SOME FURTHER EXAMPLES OF EFFECTIVE PERSUASION

Let's take a look at several more examples of effective written persuasion.

First, a memorandum of justification (with a chart attached) prepared by an office manager for submission to the company comptroller. The office manager wants the comptroller to increase the budget for new office equipment. The message is typical of the kinds of persuasive communications that circulate within an organization. Take a look at it (both the memo and its attachment) in Figure 31.

This carefully written two-part memorandum by Phil Gerlach gives full development to its central appeal — operational efficiency. No secondary appeals are used. Gerlach employs essentially two methods of developing that appeal: he provides verifiable fact, and he relies on respected opinion (his own, as an expert in office operations). His memo also shows a clear awareness of the persuasive process: the need to capture attention, focus on a motive, develop a strong appeal, and close emphatically. The attachment systematically (and with great visual clarity) puts the comparative data side by side to drive home Gerlach's argument. (The memo reappears in Figure 32 where it is analyzed point by point. Take a look at that analysis.)

The next two letters were used recently by a New York firm of management consultants to promote its "Zero Defects" program of employee motivation. The

[3] Many readers, of course, still do not respond. But the costs of sales letters are such that a positive response of two to three percent, or even less, can result in substantial profit on a mass mailing.

Figure 31
A well-written proposal memorandum.

MEMORANDUM

To: T. Fischer, Comptroller   Date: Nov. 29, 19__

cc: F. L. Lucasta   File #: B8
N. J. O'Connor

From: P. Gerlach

Subject: Justification of Recent Budget Request

I wanted you to have, as soon as possible, this justification of my recent budget request for funds to purchase a TBR 930 Automatic Collator.

As you know, the one bottleneck in the operation of our steno pool is in the Duplicating Center, whenever large numbers of mimeographed pages must be collated. As many as four girls are often needed to collate for up to five hours, a situation that not only crowds the duplicating facilities, but leaves the pool severely understaffed. The three new contracts our company has won promise only to increase our work load -- perhaps by as much as 25%. And we just haven't got the capacity. Under present arrangements, our steno pool will be strangled.

This is where the TBR 930 comes in. With only one person operating it, the TBR 930 can collate up to one thousand twelve-sheet documents, and staple them, in sixty minutes. That same job done manually now takes two girls four hours. Assuming that the 25% work-load increase lasts indefinitely, I estimate that this $5325 machine will pay for itself in less than a year -- probably within ten months. Even at our present work load, it would take no more than thirteen months.

Prior to requesting funds for the TBR 930, I fully compared its capacity and characteristics with those of the Korvath 12A Collating Machine, the only comparable competing model. Though the initial cost of the Korvath is lower, I strongly feel (and I think the attached comparison sheet will bear this out) that the TBR 930 is a better value. The data, incidentally, do not come out of manufacturers' brochures. I tested both models personally in factory demonstrations.

I am convinced that the costly bottleneck in the steno pool will disappear with the addition of the the 930 to our facilities.

Phil Gerlach

Attachment

first letter, appearing in Figure 33, was sent (in individualized copies) to major corporations. Read it carefully, and observe its technique.

Immediately noticeable is this letter's style of short paragraphs: it has nine paragraphs in all, five of which are only one sentence long. As we saw back in Chapter 4, ideas tend to stand out more emphatically when given paragraphs of their own. On the other hand, single-sentence paragraphs tend to dissociate ideas from one another. A sense of dissociation is risked in this letter to take advantage of the emphasis the style provides. Here, the risk seems worth it: each idea the writer wishes to emphasize is made to begin its own paragraph.

The central appeal in the letter is obviously aimed at the reader's desire for strong performance from his company's employees. The first paragraph is a bid for the reader's attention, an attempt to draw the reader interestedly into

Figure 31 (continued) The attachment to Phil Gerlach's justification memo.

HOW THE TBR 930 AUTOMATIC COLLATOR COMPARES WITH THE KORVATH 12A

	Korvath 12A	TBR 930
COST		
Basic Collator (no stapler)	$ 3,445	$ 4,200
w/1 stapler	3,840	—
w/2 staplers	3,940	5,325
SIZE OF PAPER	8-1/2 x 11 only	anything from 3 x 5 to 11 x 17
NUMBER OF BINS	8	12
GATHERING METHOD	in ladder sets - -- --- ----	piled sets -- -- -- --
JOG	yes	yes
STACK	yes	yes
SKIP DETECTION	yes (shuts off)	yes (shuts off)
DOUBLE DETECTION	no	yes (shuts off)
COUNTER	yes	yes
PROGRAM	partial	full
FLOOR SPACE	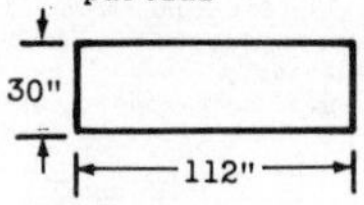 30" 112"	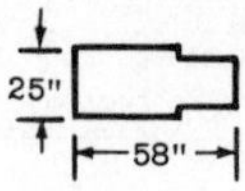 25" 58" 43% of the Korvath
WEIGHT	580 lbs.	?
NO. OF OPERATIONS FROM "LOAD" TO "GO"	approx. 27 to 30	approx. 3 to 5
NO. OF OPERATIONS FROM "STOP" TO NEXT "LOAD"	approx. 9 to 11	approx. 3 to 5
TOTAL NO. OF OPERATIONS	36 to 41	6 to 10
TEACHING TIME	One hour or more	5 to 10 minutes
OPERATOR FREEDOM	little	complete
ANNUAL MAINTENANCE	$ 299	$ 35 to 50
WARRANTY	?	?

the letter by indicating an awareness of PAA's promotional aims. The second and third paragraphs focus that attention on the key motive (which obviously already exists). Then the writer introduces the Zero Defects concept, elaborating briefly on its history. Next, he brings Industrial Motivation, Inc. up front as the means by which the reader can gain the benefits of that concept. Finally, the

Figure 32
Detailed analysis of the effective proposal memorandum.

I wanted you to have, as soon as possible, this justification of my recent budget request for funds to purchase a TBR 930 Automatic Collator.

As you know the one bottleneck in the operation of our steno pool is in the Duplicating Center, whenever large numbers of mineographed pages must be collated. As many as four girls are often needed to collate for up to five hours, a situation that not only crowds the duplicating facilities, but leaves the pool severely understaffed. The three new contracts our company has won promise only to increase our workload – perhaps by as much as 25%. And we just haven't got the capacity. Under present arrangements, our steno pool will be strangled.

This is where the TBR 930 comes in. With only one person operating it, the TBR 930 can collate up to one thousand twelve-sheet documents, and staple them in sixty minutes. The same job done manually now takes two girls four hours. Assuming that the 25% workload increase lasts indefinitely, I estimate that this $5325 machine will pay for itself in less than a year – probably within ten months. Even at our present workload, it would take no more than thirteen months.

Prior to requesting funds for the TBR 930, I fully compared its capacity and characteristics with those of the Korvath 12A Collating Machine, the only comparable competing model. Though the initial cost of the Korvath is lower, I strongly feel (and I think the attached comparison sheet will bear this out) that the TBR 930 is a better value. The data, incidentally, do not come out of manufacturer's brochures. I tested both models personally in factory demonstrations.

I am convinced that the costly bottleneck in the steno pool will disappear with the addition of the 930 to our facilities.

Getting attention is no problem in this memo. Its recipient is awaiting Gerlach's justification. So Gerlach uses his opening sentence primarily to establish a receptive frame of mind in his reader. In effect, he is saying, "I put this justification together for you as fast as I possibly could" — a shrewd opening by Gerlach.

In the second paragraph, Gerlach focuses his reader's attention on the key motive — the need to remedy an operational inefficiency — and he does it in very precise, very specific terms. Generalizations aren't enough for this reader.

In the third paragraph Gerlach begins to develop his central appeal — *efficiency.*

. . . He uses verifiable fact to argue for the TBR 930. . . .

He uses verifiable fact to argue against conceivable alternatives.

He uses respected opinion (his own, as a specialist in office operations) to further develop his appeal. . . .

. . . And he appends additional verifiable fact (the attached comparison sheet) to develop it still further.

Gerlach closes by summing up his appeal and expressing his confidence in it. In this case, no particular response need be suggested by Gerlach. Fischer will respond if, when, and as he chooses.

Gerlach could have written simply "there's a bottleneck in the steno pool." But by suggesting that it's the *only* bottleneck ("the one bottleneck"), he makes his proposed remedy for it seem much more necessary and urgent without being obvious about it.

Notice Gerlach's use of the opening phrase "as many as" which allows him then to describe the worst extent of the bottlenecking.

Two deficiencies are, of course, worse than one.

Gerlach here uses more vivid metaphoric description to drive his point home. He could have written "the pool will be even more severely short-handed," but that lacks style.

Does "sixty minutes" sound shorter than "an hour"?

It's an expensive machine. Notice how Gerlach attempts to de-emphasize cost by making it an adjectival modifier instead of writing "this machine costs $5,325" or "this machine, which costs $5,325 . . . " He gives the price as *little grammatical weight* as he can.

The only purpose of this adverb is for persuasive emphasis . . .

. . . likewise this adverb.

Gerlach attains a confident closing tone by using the definite future tense ("will disappear" instead of "would disappear").

And by writing "with the addition of . . . " instead of "if we add . . . "

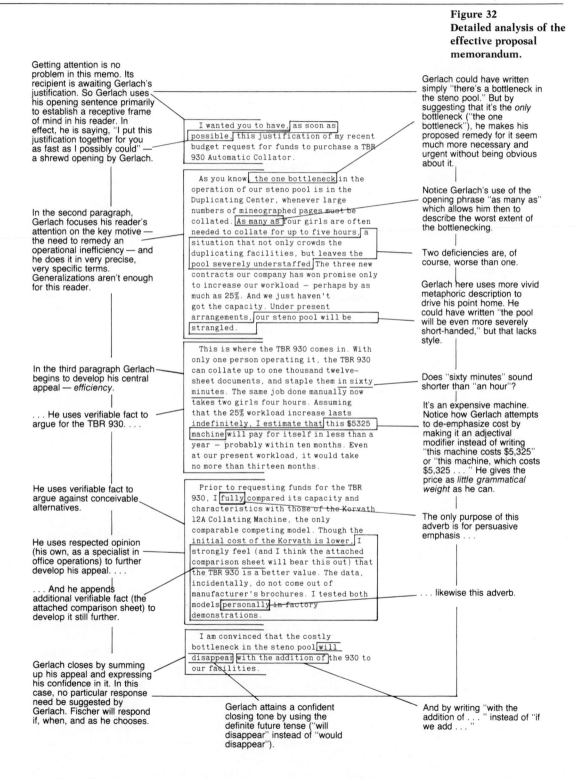

writer sums up his appeal ("It would seem that there are immediate benefits that PAA could gain from being the first to use these concepts . . .") and concludes with a direct request for response.

The letter achieved its persuasive goal: an invitation to speak to PAA's top management.

Several months later, after interest in the Zero Defects program had been generated throughout the United States and Canada, Industrial Motivation scheduled a one-day briefing session about the program for executives in Canadian industry. By explaining the Zero Defects concept in open session, Industrial Motivation hoped to convert interested companies into new clients. The letter and pamphlet in Figure 34 were sent out to announce the session and to persuade Canadian executives to attend. Take a look at them (pages 306–308).

Figure 33
(Reproduced by permission of Industrial Motivation, Inc.)

Industrial Motivation, Inc.

331 MADISON AVENUE
NEW YORK, NEW YORK
Area Code 212 TN 7-3433

February 9, 19--

Mr. Warren L. Morrison, President
Pan Atlantic Airlines, Inc.
345 Fifth Avenue
New York, New York 10091

Dear Mr. Morrison:

We have noted that Pan Atlantic Airline, Inc. is in its current promotion, strongly emphasizaing the "total satisfaction" a prospective passenger can expect when he flies PAA.

Qutie obviously, despite the great improvements being made in airline equipment and facilities, the major responsibility for customer satisfaction still rests with the individual employees, from stewardesses and reservation clerks to mechanics and ramp personnel.

Keeping your employees aware of this key objective and motivating them to continue their commitment to the traveling public is a difficult job.

As you may know, a formalized approach to this problem of employee motivation, an approach called "Zero Defects," was developed at the Martin Company about three years ago, at a time when there was a critical need for superior quality throughout the aerospace industry. We were fortunate enough to have worked on the original program, and later with the Department of Defense, in introducing the ZD concept to the defense industry.

Zero Defects programs have now been initiated in well over 1,000 companies, including such major organizations as General Electric, Lockheed, and General Motors.

Mr. Warren L. Morrison -2- February 9, 19--

Where these programs were soundly conceived and implemented, they have achieved impressive, and in many cases, remarkable results.

Serving as management consultants, we have worked with some leading companies in a number of industries to help develop and implement Zero Defects-type programs. Our clients have included the Pontiac, Buick, and Canadian Divisions of General Motors; General Precision; and International Paper.

Today in the highly competitive airlines industry it would seem that there are immediate benefits that PAA could gain from being the first to use these concepts to upgrade the performance of all its people.

Zero Defects has come a long way since its birth at Martin. It has proven effective in a wide range of activities from general manufacturing to a customer service. I would like to brief you on these recent developments, and suggest some possible applications which might be of interest to Pan Atlantic Airlines.

Please let me know if you would like to pursue this further.

Cordially,

Charles W. Riley, Jr.
Director

CWR/lfb

The two-part persuasive format is used quite frequently by writers who have a business service to offer.[4] The format allows the writer to write a single persuasive description of the offering, and mass-produce that description. Accompanying this description is a relatively brief covering letter which personalizes each communication. The covering letter captures attention and focuses the reader's mind on the key motive — in this case, the need for strong employee motivation. After briefly highlighting the offering, the letter points to the pamphlet, which provides a much more detailed description. Action is suggested in both the letter and the pamphlet, and the pamphlet gives explicit indication of just how response should be made. Two-part formats have long been successful aids to persuasion in business and elsewhere.

Persuasive technique unfolds somewhat more quickly — though still very much in the necessary sequence — in the following *letter of recommendation.* The writer is writing to endorse someone's candidacy for an important position. He seeks to persuade his reader that this is the right person for the job.

[4] The two-part persuasive format is also used — in the form of a covering letter and résumé — by countless job applicants offering their services to industry. We'll examine this use of it in Chapter 14.

Figure 34
Letter and Pamphlet (pp. 307–308) of Industrial Motivation, Inc.
(Reproduced by permission of Industrial Motivation, Inc.)

Industrial Motivation, Inc.

331 MADISON AVENUE
NEW YORK, NEW YORK
Area Code 212 TN 7-3433

June 13, 19--

Mr. William Green, President
Green Electronics Company, Ltd.
202 King Street North
Oshawa, Ontario
Canada

Dear Mr. Green:

Recently there has been a high level of interest throughout Canadian industry in the Zero Defects approach to improving product quality through employee motivation.

As consultants to General Motors of Canada in the development and implementation of their Zero Defects programme, we are aware of the great opportunities (and the problems) that Zero Defects can offer.

We have worked with companies in many industries in the area of employee motivation, and it has been our experience that management understanding of the basic concept behind Zero Defects is the key to developing a successful programme.

On July 11th, Industrial Motivation will conduct a seminar in Toronto on Zero Defects for representatives of Canada's major companies. This seminar will provide participants with a comprehensive understanding of the Zero Defects concept and how it might be applied in their organizations.

A folder outlining this seminar programme is enclosed. We welcome your participation and look forward to the opportunity of seeing you or your representatives at the seminar.

Sincerely,

Charles W. Riley, Jr.
Director

CWR/lfb
Enclosure

Professor George J. Fielding, Acting Chairman
Department of English
Lamont College
Exeter, New Hampshire 08025

Dear Professor Fielding:

I understand that your department is weighing the candidacy of Dr. Patricia Girard for its chairmanship. As a colleague of hers for seven years, and the administrative head of her division, I am pleased to speak a word in her behalf.

Figure 34 (continued)

Registration Fee: Includes meetings, luncheon, coffee break, and hand-out materials:

$75.00 per person

Note: A 10% team discount is available to companies with three or more in attendance.

Attendance Limited: Mail reservation form *today*.

ZERO DEFECTS SEMINAR

Industrial Motivation, Inc.
331 Madison Avenue
New York, N.Y. 10017

Please reserve _____ registration(s) at $75.00 each for your seminar, "Zero Defects and Canadian Industry" to be held in Toronto on July 11, 19-- at The Royal York Hotel.

Check enclosed for sum of $ ____.

Please bill us ____.

Registrants Names (please print)

_____________ Title _____________
_____________ Title _____________
_____________ Title _____________
_____________ Title _____________

Company _____________________

Street Address _________________

City ________________________

Province _____________________

INDUSTRIAL MOTIVATION, INC.
331 MADISON AVENUE
NEW YORK, N. Y. 10017
(212) TN 7-3433

ZERO DEFECTS AND CANADIAN INDUSTRY

A ONE-DAY SEMINAR
FOR MANAGEMENT PERSONNEL
SPONSORED BY
INDUSTRIAL MOTIVATION, INC.

JULY 11, 19--
ROYAL YORK HOTEL
TORONTO, CANADA

Figure 34 (continued)

ZERO DEFECTS

Is it right for your company?

The success of Zero Defects-type employee motivation programmes in the United States has created great interest throughout Canadian business and industry.

Zero Defects has been heralded by many as the *only* truly effective way to achieve and sustain the greatly improved levels of product quality being demanded in today's competitive marketplace.

Results in many cases have been remarkable:

- **Pontiac Division of General Motors reported a 35% drop in customer complaints and a 26% reduction in warranty costs within one year after introduction of Zero Defects.**
- **RCA estimates a $25,000,000 cost saving in one year directly attributed to Zero Defects.**
- **General Electric's programme helped to identify and resolve 3,900 potential causes of error.**

Thousands of similar success stories from companies both large and small indicate that ZD can and does work. The question is, can your company benefit from ZD—and how can you plan an *effective* programme?

This one-day management seminar is intended to give you the background information you need to answer that question, and to help you decide what steps will have to be taken within your own organization to make a Zero Defects programme work successfully.

PROGRAMME

ROYAL YORK HOTEL
Toronto, Canada
July 11, 19--

9:00-9:15 A.M.
INTRODUCTION

9:15-10:00 A.M.
MOTIVATION AS A MANAGEMENT TOOL
- The elements of motivation
- Early studies and recent findings
- Zero Defects as a motivation system

10:00-10:15 A.M.
COFFEE BREAK

10:15-11:15 A.M.
BACKGROUND: ZERO DEFECTS
- History and Concept
- Case studies of programmes in operation

11:15-12:00 Noon
GETTING READY FOR ZERO DEFECTS
- Determining the cost of quality
- Stimulating quality awareness
- Building a motivational environment

12:00-1:00 P.M.
LUNCHEON

1:00-3:00 P.M.
MAKING ZERO DEFECTS WORK
- Steps in programme development
- The Kick-Off
- Goal Setting
- Effective Communications
- Error Cause Removal
- Programmes at the local level
- Sustaining Zero Defects

3:00-3:15 P.M.
COFFEE BREAK

3:15-4:00 P.M.
MANAGEMENT'S ROLE IN ZERO DEFECTS
- Defining organizational objectives
- Creating the climate for action
- Where to place emphasis
- How to insure full participation

4:00-4:30 P.M.
DISCUSSION AND SUMMARY

"Do it right the first time!"

This is the message that thousands of companies have presented to millions of employees in Zero Defects programmes around the world. Find out what's behind this message ... why it has worked ... what Zero Defects can mean to *your* company.

The "Zero Defects and Canadian Industry" seminar is being sponsored and conducted by Industrial Motivation, Inc., a consulting organization which has assisted companies in the manufacturing, aerospace, paper and automotive industries to implement and sustain successful employee motivation programmes.

Recently, Industrial Motivation has been working with General Motors of Canada—first to analyze the potential for applying Zero Defects to Canadian industry, and subsequently on the design, development and implementation phases of GM of Canada's organization-wide Zero Defects programme.

Mr. George Schmidt, President of Industrial Motivation, participated in the development of the first ZD programme at the Martin Company in 1962. Prior to founding his own organization, he assisted the U.S. Department of Defense in presenting Zero Defects to over 1,000 government contractors at seminar meetings in the U.S. He has lectured frequently on the subject of employee motivation, and will be a major participant in the seminar.

During those years, large numbers of students (both graduate and undergraduate) expressed to me their genuine sense of enrichment upon being taught by Dr. Girard. Besides her mastery of several academic specialties, she possesses an intellect of extraordinary scope. Her enthusiasm for meaningful scholarship is contagious. In faculty affairs, her wit and judiciousness have made her, in my estimation, the most respected member of her department. During her fifth year here, she served as president of the faculty senate, and served admirably.

In short, I feel that Dr. Girard is an educator — in the true sense of that much abused word. She possesses the qualities to which I would turn had I to choose someone to chair a first-rate academic department.

Respectfully,

M. Wilson Hodges
Dean of Arts and Sciences
Valhalla University

In Chapter 13 we'll be looking at persuasive letters written by job applicants to companies. But it's a two-way street. Many large companies actively pursue top-ranking college seniors. Among those organizations is The Trane Company of LaCross, Wisconsin. Trane sends these key prospects a well-written recruitment letter persuading them to see the Trane representative when he visits their campus. The letter's central appeal, as you'd expect, is to the graduate's professional future. The appeal is developed with tangible description, verifiable fact, and a healthy dose of emotional suasion to nourish the reader's ego. Take a look at the Trane recruitment letter in Figure 35.

Back in Chapter 8, I suggested that inquiries from the public can often be converted into sales. Realizing this, many companies combine requested information with promotional persuasion in their replies. This kind of persuasion must be subtle and unobtrusive. The inquirer has sought information, not propaganda. A reply that is too high-pressured and blatantly sales-oriented will offend, rather than persuade, the reader. The mildly persuasive reply, however, can turn many an inquiry into profit.

Here's an example of an effectively persuasive answer to a letter of inquiry.

Dear Mrs. Pye:

We're very happy to fill your request for a Cantwell Fund Prospectus and for a copy of our latest investment newsletter with information on the Goldline Plan.

As you will note in the newsletter, the Goldline Plan makes it possible for you to invest from $35 quarterly in whatever combination of securities you choose--with risk at an absolute minimum.[5] We honestly believe the Goldline Plan to be, for the moderate investor, the best plan available anywhere.

When you've had a chance to examine the literature, we will gladly answer any questions you have, with no obligation to you. Just call or drop in. Should you decide to invest in the Goldline, in the Cantwell Fund, or in any other security, we will consider it a privilege to handle the details for you.

Sincerely yours,

Garth Blackman

Garth Blackman
Investment Counselor

Blackman doesn't have to worry about capturing attention because the recipient anticipates the letter. His opening very warmly informs Mrs. Pye that her request is being granted. Nor does Blackman have to be concerned with focusing that attention on the investment motive. It's already there. Blackman's central appeal — to the investment urge — is developed by a brief factual highlighting of the Goldline Plan, and by a professional opinion as to its value. The final paragraph sums up the appeal, and suggests what Mrs. Pye can do to avail herself of the service Blackman is offering. The "sell" in this reply is obviously "soft." Any harder and it probably would have been offensive.

ONE MORE LOOK AT FUNCTIONAL DOWN-SHIFTING

The concept of the functional down-shift, which we looked at earlier when we discussed demands and bad-news messages, can also be effectively applied to persuasion. Sometimes writers will make a letter or memo seem like something other than direct persuasion — in order to make the person more effective. It's done every day.

The intention behind the following letter is as much persuasion as that of any earlier letter or memo we've looked at. But it uses a down-shifted strategy. Cinemakers, Inc., a firm that produces industrial training films for large corporations, has hired a well-known director of TV documentaries to direct its films. The management at Cinemakers decides to build a promotion around its new director, with his reputation as its central appeal ("he's the best in the business, so you should do business with us"). But rather than make a directly persuasive appeal, Cinemakers decides to send out a "mere" announcement:

[5] Style note: The writer could have ended this sentence by writing " — with minimum risk." But instead of having the word *risk* in the emphatic last position, he preferred to emphasize *minimum.* So he wrote " — with risk at an absolute minimum."

MANUFACTURING ENGINEERS OF AIR CONDITIONING • HEATING • VENTILATING AND HEAT TRANSFER EQUIPMENT

THE TRANE COMPANY

GENERAL OFFICES, LA CROSS, WISCONSIN, U.S.A.

September 14, 19__

Mr. John Glover
8660 Cedar Avenue South
Chicago, Illinois 60600

Dear Mr. Glover:

With an educational background such as yours, we would be interested in giving you a little information about our organization. You appear to possess the background and qualifications which make for a success with The Trane Company. We invite you to see our representative when he visits your school on Tuesday, April 20.

The Trane Company designs, manufactures, and markets equipment for the air conditioning, heating, ventilating and heat transfer products markets. In 19__, we set another new record for the company with a total sales volume of $162 million and a profit of $12 million.

Long-term debt of The Trane Company is exceptionally low despite recent major investments in new plants, office expansion and manufacturing equipment. We are opening our sixth new plant since 19__. This new plant is located in Johannesburg, South Africa, for our subsidiary, Clark-Trane.

This continued growth, plus internal promotional policies based on merit, enables young men to advance rapidly to responsible positions. Trane is a growth company in a growth industry. Your placement office has more information on specific job opportunities and more detailed company information. Why not take 30 minutes to investigate with our representative? It would be a pleasure to see you and to learn more about your interests and objectives.

Sincerely,

THE TRANE COMPANY

Dennis C Hood

Supervisor
College Relations

Dennis C. Hood ram

Figure 35
A persuasive letter to recruit attractive job candidates.
(Reproduced by permission of The Trane Company.)

Ladies/Gentlemen:

We would like you, as a major user of corporate training films, to be among the first to receive this announcement:

Cinemakers is proud to have VICTOR CUOSOMANO join its staff as Chief Director.

There's little need writing a long sales talk on Cuosomano. His reputation as a writer and director of serious documentaries for the major television networks amply explains our pride.

Under Cuosomano's supervision, we are putting together a special new catalog of industrial film strategies and techniques. You will be receiving a copy, with our sincere compliments, as soon as it's off the press.

Cordially yours,

Thomas L. Youngblood

Thomas L. Youngblood
President

The thinking behind the announcement is this: to an audience that is always alert to prestige and professional excellence, perhaps the best way to communicate that prestige and excellence is to let Cuosomano's name "speak for itself." Even readers who may not have heard of Cuosomano are likely to think they're learning something ("Hey, this must be a pretty well-known guy!"). This routine "announcement" is really down-shifted persuasion.

The letter in Figure 36, written jointly by two neighbors of the family who live behind the backyard fence, is also down-shifted persuasion — of a different sort. Read it and then let's examine its strategy.

In what way does this letter — which deals with the business of living in a community — down-shift its function for strategic advantage? Well, for one thing, although it's addressed to the Joneses, the Joneses are *not* its primary audience. Finch and Embry have both complained repeatedly to the Joneses about the problems they describe — and their complaints have had little result. Their next recourse is to take their grievance to the Town Council where they would try to demonstrate persuasively that those complaints are justified and ask the Council to threaten legal action against the Joneses unless they keep a tighter rein on their kids and dogs.

Finch and Embry know, however, that Council members (like most other elected officials) dislike making enemies and are often reluctant to take legal action against voting citizens. They prefer to seek compromise — but Finch and Embry do not want to compromise on this matter. They want victory. So instead of presenting their case directly to the Council, Finch and Embry decide to muster all their grievances into one long letter — an apparent "demand" letter — and mail it to the Joneses. Actually, they have little hope that the letter will change the Joneses' behavior. And Finch and Embry do not want to threaten legal action directly against the Joneses because such actions, if legally resisted, end up costing a fortune, win or lose.

So what Finch and Embry have done is build a case in writing, a document that they can, sometime soon, turn over to the Town Council in photo-copy as persuasive evidence of (1) how flagrant the Joneses' violations have been, (2) how very patient Finch and Embry have been in the matter, and (3) how the Joneses (who probably won't even answer the letter) have simply ignored their demands.

With the case put before them in this manner, the Council will find it much harder to suggest compromise, or to find excuses for not taking action against the Joneses. Finch and Embry will have won relief from the problem, and not lost a month's salary or more in legal fees to do so. Their success will have been due to a strategically down-shifted communication: instead of at-

Figure 36
An example of "down-shifted" persuasion.

October 4, 19--

Mr. and Mrs. Harold T. Jones
19441 Trocadero Lane
Sierra, California 92664

Dear Mr. and Mrs. Jones:

We regret having to write this letter, but feel that after much forebearance we must make several neighborly requests of you.

For quite a while now--at least the last year and a half--your children have had a playhouse in the backyard which they obviously, and with good reason, enjoy. As parents ourselves, we certainly have no objection to this, in itself. But the playhouse has given rise to several problems, the consequence of which has been to deprive us and our families of the full enjoyment of our own property, especially our backyards.

Problem #1 is its location. By placing the playhouse immediately adjacent to our common back fence, you've given us a situation in which your children, playing atop it as they usually do, are repeatedly and sometimes for hours on end peering down into our yards within a distance so close as to put them virtually in the midst of anything we choose to do in our own backyards. In fact, both our families, on numerous occasions this past year, elected not to have breakfast or lunch or supper outside, or have adult guests in our yard, <u>solely</u> because the children were looming over us from on top of the playhouse. Admittedly, they are no longer taunting the children on this side from atop their perch (as they did last year), nor are they engaging in profanity up there quite as often as in the past. After complaining of these problems last year, we were grateful that you apparently did something about them. But the fact remains that their frequent presence above the fence--a fence which was made six feet high by the developers precisely to assure us all some privacy--has interfered in a major way with our enjoyment of our own backyards.

Problem #2 is a noise problem. We were both confident last year that the frequent and prolonged hammering from your backyard would continue only until the playhouse was completed. Therefore, we did not complain of it. But now it seems that the hammering (which, as you know, goes on not only during the afternoons and early evenings of the school week, but is sometimes day-long during the weekends) has become part of the general playhouse activity, and is not just a product of its construction. The noise from hammering is present not only in our backyards, but in our houses as well, especially during the summer and fall when our windows, for obvious reasons, must be kept open. It has become a major deterrent to our own quiet enjoyment of our homes, and to the concentration that members of our families must give to the professional work and school homework that we do within them.

tempting to persuade the Council directly, they made their persuasion indirect by building it into an apparent letter of demand.

IN CONCLUSION

This chapter, then, has explored the process of persuasion in business writing. The process is complex, with a number of phases: capturing and sustaining

Figure 36 continued

Mr. and Mrs. Harold T. Jones — 2 — October 4, 19--

Problem #3 is the debris and dog excrement which has, from time to time, been thrown over the fence or brought through it by the dogs using as their passageway the holes in the base of the fence which have been broken through from your side.

Problem #4 is also a noise problem. Owing to the rigors of our work, and a desire to have our children keep a healthy sleep-schedule, we like to be able to retire early and sleep a bit later in the morning when circumstances allow. There have been occasions when your children's shouts and screams have awakened us on this side of the fence--the most recent of which was, of course, just last night when the hollering continued from outside until Mr. Finch's telephone call at 11 p.m., and from inside the playhouse intermittently till 1:30 in the morning.

We said, in the beginning of this letter, that we regretted having to write it. We realize that childhood is a time for exuberance, and that it is the sheer proximity that at times makes that exuberance intrusive. An acre or so between us, and these problems might never arise. With conditions as they are, however, we must make the following requests of you:

1. that the playhouse now adjacent to the back fence be moved elsewhere, so that when the kids are atop it they are not at the same time peering down into our yards and interfering with the privacy we should like to enjoy there;
2. that we be given relief from the hammering noise that has accompanied the children's play in the playhouse for the last eighteen months;
3. that we also be spared the debris from your side of the fence; and
4. that the children's shouts and screams, which we realize are a normal part of their play, be done elsewhere than in the backyard during the evening and early morning hours (that is, preferably not before 9 in the morning, and not past 8 in the evening).

If you feel that further discussion would be helpful in resolving these problems, we would both welcome the opportunity. We have every wish to remain neighbors in the full sense of the word.

Sincerely yours,

Chris Finch — Howard Embry

Christopher Finch
19444 Vista Drive

Howard Embry
19448 Vista Drive

attention, creating a motive (if necessary), focusing upon that motive, and developing to its fullest extent a central appeal–an appeal that satisfies the motive. Each of these phases must be fully achieved before the business writer can genuinely create that new state of mind in readers, or evoke that predetermined response from them — one or the other is the end-point of any persuasive effort.

PROBLEMS

1. Sales letters and promotion letters fill up our mail boxes in great abundance. Take one of these pieces of "junk mail" and analyze it for the persuasive attempt it makes. How does it try to capture attention? How does it focus its reader's attention on a basic motive? How does it develop its central appeal? What *is* its central appeal? Does it have any secondary appeals? Does it attempt to evoke any action from its readers?

Incorporate this analysis into a memorandum to your instructor.

2. Here's a question on the theory of written persuasion: Has the principle of the "positive sandwich" ceased to be meaningful in writing effective persuasive communications or is it still operative? Has the principle perhaps been modified?

3. Assume that you are a sales writer for the Randall Publishing Company. You are planning to write a sales letter, which will be sent to college students, attempting to sell the new edition of the *Randall's Collegiate Desk-Sized Dictionary*.

a. What will be your most effective central appeal?
b. What secondary appeals might you also incorporate into the letter?
c. What kind of emotive claims might you make in developing the central appeal in this letter?
d. That kind of physical description might help develop that central appeal?
e. What kind of verifiable facts might help develop the central appeal?
f. What kind of logical reasoning might help develop the central appeal? Elaborate. (For instance, if you say "inductive," briefly state the inductive argument.)
g. What kind of respected opinion might help to develop that central appeal?

4. Write the sales letter you have so carefully planned in problem 3 above.

5. When you finish this course in business communications, you will—hopefully—be a much improved communicator; so much improved, in fact, that you will be able to advise other business people (those who have never had formal training in communications) on how to improve their letters, memos, and reports.

Assume that, once you graduate, you become an independent consultant in business communications. As one of your professional services, you conduct week-long workshops for companies interested in giving their junior executives and executive trainees expert training in communications. You are interested in expanding the scope of your operations. The way to do this, you feel, would be to compose an effective letter to mail to the executive vice-presidents of corporations in your general area. The letter's objective would be to have as many of these executives as possible call you in to set up communications workshops in their companies.

Remember the nature of your audience. They are sophisticated, top-level executives not likely to be persuaded by any gimmicky, fast-talking appeal. You can, however, count on their already realizing the value of communications skills in business.

Write the letter.

6. Assume that your instructor is the college vice-president in charge of all buildings and facilities. Write the instructor a memorandum persuading him or her to consider some particular change in the utilization of facilities, a change that would result in fiscal savings to the college without compromising its primary function as an institution for learning and teaching.

7.

WAMPUM FEDERAL SAVINGS
AND LOAN ASSOCIATION
6000 North Butte Street Cheyenne, Wyoming 80008

On the above letterhead write a sales letter to easterners, persuading them to bank by mail at the Cheyenne's Wampum Federal. The central appeal you use and the way you develop the persuasive process are entirely up to you.

The Wampum Federal passbook account pays six percent interest, compounded monthly — one of the best rates in the West. The Association has paid sixty-five consecutive dividends since its founding. It has assets of over $55,-000,000. Individual accounts are insured up to $40,000.

Mail depositors are provided with postage-paid airmail envelopes, and (as the Wampum Federal slogan goes) "with friendly same-day service by a friendly institution." (You can either keep or scrap that slogan as you wish.)

As an inducement to prospective new depositors, you can offer to give away some gift (one that would retail for under $10) for all first deposits of $50 or more.

8. You are Olympian Clothiers, Inc., a large retail haberdashery located at 100 Main Street, Sinclair, Indiana. Your store's specialty is clothing for fat men. You carry suits, sportcoats, slacks, shirts, underwear, pajamas, and so forth cut especially for men who ordinarily have great trouble buying clothes that fit well and look good. You also offer expert tailoring service on any garment sold. You are the only store in your area offering this specialty.

In order to promote your new fall line, you have obtained a mailing list of three thousand men in Sinclair and within a thirty-five mile radius who qualify as good prospects for your specialty. They are all fat. Some of them have probably patronized your store in the past but the great majority have not. You want to write an effective sales promotion letter to these three thousand prospects, the desired response to which will be a trip to your store to see your merchandise. Your letter may embody any sales techniques you think appropriate. Consider, also, the necessity for euphemism somewhere along the line. It's very difficult to call a fat man "fat" and still appeal to him in a positive way. Write the letter.

9. Assume that you are the vice-president in charge of personnel at a large professional firm (whatever kind of firm you prefer — engineering, public accountancy, management consultants, market research — whatever). You have

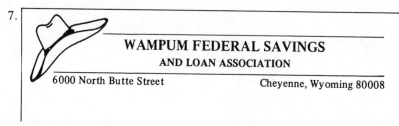

learned from an associate that Mr. Geoffrey Harringsford (a top-flight engineer, or public accountant, or management consultant, or market researcher) from Liverpool, England, is entertaining thoughts of moving to the United States. You would like to have Harringsford join your firm. Write a persuasive "feeler" to Harringsford.

10. Write a promotion letter that will appear in *Holiday Magazine* as an "open letter to all who've never seen California in the fall." The letter will invite readers to the Harvest-Time Open House at the Swiss Mountainberry Winery (Vinoa, California).

The Open House, which is free to all, provides daily tours at the winery, tours on which guests can view the crushing vats, the fermentation chambers, and the bottling line. The Open House also includes wagon rides through the vineyards during harvesting, hours of wine sampling in the Swiss Mountainberry Taste Center, and the general friendly spirit at Swiss Mountainberry.

Your central appeal in this open letter will probably be an emotional one. Select it carefully, and develop it fully.

11. The Snobbe Shoppe is an exclusive boutique in Hyannis Port, Massachusetts. You, as the head buyer, have recently completed a trip to the Middle East where you purchased an unusual collection of women's evening wear and cruise wear. Among the items you purchased are silk stoles and cocktail gowns, lace evening wraps, velvet hostess gowns, embroidered slippers, beaded handbags, hammered-gold bracelets, and mosaic jewelry.

As a special promotion, you wish to invite all the Snobbe Shoppe's regular charge-account customers to a Turkish Coffee and Fashion Show at which your new collection will be displayed before it's put on sale to the general public. Write a persuasive "invitation" to your regular customers, getting them to attend the Turkish Coffee and Fashion Show.

12. Assume that you are a recent college graduate, and that, because of your excellent academic record and business potential, you have been hired to create and manage a collection system for Haljamaar's Department Store in St. Paul, Minnesota. Haljamaar's is an old and reputable store in St. Paul, serving a middle-to-upper class clientele.

Sven Haljamaar, the store's sixty-three-year-old president (and grandson of the founder) has hired you for this newly created position because in the last few years some customers have become "slow" in paying their bills. Mr. Haljamaar is a conservative businessman who tends to distrust people who don't pay their bills on time, yet he realizes the value of maintaining good will. He himself is reluctant to spend "too much money or time" in the collection of overdue accounts, but he also realizes that "times have changed," and that the best thing to do is to hire someone with a good grasp of modern collection techniques (you!) to set up and administer an efficient collection system.

Upon entering the business, you make your evaluation of the credit and collection situation at Haljamaar's and you formulate an appropriate collection-letter series. What you must do now is put your plan into writing in the form of a proposal letter to Mr. Haljamaar (who is vacationing in Stockholm). The letter must carefully describe your plan, its cost, and its projected results. You must justify your proposal and convince Mr. Haljamaar that it will solve the store's collection problem (or at least greatly ease it). You want him to cable you a "go-ahead" on your proposed plan.

13. Here are two communications aimed at the same objective: getting certified life underwriters to renew their memberships in the Long Beach Association of Life Underwriters. The first is a memo from an insurance agency manager that attempts, with some aggressiveness, to persuade its recipients to send in their renewal dues. The second is in the form of a letter to the same agents from the Association's membership chairman: his persuasion is a "softer sell."

Read both communications carefully, and in a memo to your instructor, indicate which of these writers is the more persuasive — and why.

a. February 24, 198_

TO: All District 17 Agents
FROM: L. E. ''Matt'' Madsen, CLU, Agency Manager
SUBJECT: Life Underwriter Membership Renewal Dues

Gentlemen:

Millie Guy, Long Beach Life Underwriters Association executive secretary just advised me that ten out of sixteen of our associates have not renewed their membership.

The importance of your renewal dues getting paid may not be apparent to you. While the reasons 'why' are many, allow me to remind you of a few.

The dues you pay were helpful in getting the U.S. Congress to vote in our products for people buying I.R.A. (Individual Retirement Act). Most of you remember a few years ago when our lobby people in Sacramento (hired by the dollars you put up in dues) got the legislature to exempt insurance from the ''Green River'' law. The most important reason is the fact that you cannot be recognized for M.D.R.T., N.S.A.A., H.Q.A., N.Q.A., and G.A.M.A. ''Man-of-the-year'' awards if you are not a member of your local association.

The dues are payable by the 28th of February. May I remind you that Agency Records will advance the check, and allow you to repay the dues over a five month period through the payroll deduction method.

You all know that my twelve years of membership in the association has been of much value to me. I have had an opportunity to practice leadership through committees served on, as well as taking an active role in the officer ranks within the organization. Much of what I learned about advanced underwriting was directly connected with my friendships in this group. . . . men doing a lot better job than I ever dreamed was possible. These same friends also referred a lot of casualty business to me as they had no outlet for that business.

Won't you please mail your check today, or arrange for the company to advance the funds immediately. No organization can ever succeed unless it retains people like yourselves within its membership.

Matt

Long Beach Association of Life Underwriters, Inc.
100 OCEANGATE, Suite 420 • LONG BEACH, CALIFORNIA 90802 • 213 436-1107

DEAR WHEELHORSE:

It is now February 1 and we only have 28 more days to get membership dues in by the March 1 deadline. After March 1, agents who have not paid their dues will not be eligible for MDRT, NQA, and NSAA awards.

Enclosed is a list of your agency with the agents who have paid their '75 dues as of the 25th of January. The agents who have not paid their dues should be contacted and reminded of the March 1 deadline.

I will be calling you later this week to find out who is going to pay and when, and who is not. So please be ready for my call.

Also enclosed is a membership promotion module for presentation to individual prospects.

Let's all be 100% membership agencies--Goal"400". Best of Luck!

Sincerely,

Tom Pollitt

Thomas M. Pollitt, C.L.U.
Membership Chairman
(213) 595-4405

Affiliated with
National Association of Life Underwriters
California Association of Life Underwriters

14. Here's a problem for discussion. Choosing the central appeal for a persuasive communication can be a very chancy process. Among the riskiest appeals are *negative* ones — appeals to *fear, shame, danger,* and so forth. As we saw earlier (in problem 9, Chapter 7, on page 167) an appeal to safety — that is, to the avoidance of danger — backfired on the airlines in the 1950s. Yet the same appeal has worked very well through the years for manufacturers of blowout-proof tires or safety locks for the home. And appeals to the "avoidance of embarrassment" have long been used to sell correspondence courses in how to speak "proper English." Can you account for the difference?

15. Consider the task of Dale Johnson, the 34-year-old department head who's been on the job only four months. She is faced with a recalcitrant member of her department's staff, 56-year-old Jack Hooper, who's been in the department for 29 years and won't change his way of doing things to comply with Johnson's instructions. In theory, Johnson can fire Hooper — but in practice, Johnson knows it just doesn't work that way. Hooper belongs to the in-house technician's guild, and he's been friendly with most of the people now above him in the corporate hierarchy. It would cause many problems for Johnson simply to try to fire Hooper.

Johnson's problem is similar to the one faced by Chris Finch and Howard Embry in the letter in Figure 37 on pages 313–314. Johnson must make a case to her own bosses that Hooper somehow be removed from the department. Yet she wants to make the case tactfully, and indirectly, so she chooses to write yet another memo of "demand" to Hooper (his third in the last two months) urging his compliance with the instructions she set down. Johnson knows that the chances are slim that another memo will make Hooper shape up. But with Hooper's annual work review coming up in forty days, she hopes to get him removed to some "less critical" spot in the company. She is writing her memo (a copy of which goes into Hooper's work file) with this ultimate objective in mind. Write Johnson's memo for her.

16. Here are some "propositions" for you to write persuasively about, as your instructor directs:

a. Liability insurance (should/should not) be compulsory for all motorists.
b. In general, doctors and dentists (are/are not) overpaid.
c. Police officers and firefighters (should/should not) be unionized.
d. Government (ought/ought not) to subsidize large corporations when bankruptcy threatens them.
e. The United States (should/should not) adopt a system of compulsory national health insurance.
f. Communities (should/should not) enact and enforce anti-noise ordinances.
g. Outdoor billboard advertising (ought/ought not) to be prohibited by law.
h. Companies (ought/ought not) to enforce dress codes for their office employees.
i. Married women, who some people feel pose the risk of moving whenever their husbands have to move (should/should not) be considered for top executive positions.
j. Federal wage and price controls (should/should not) be imposed to aid in the fight against inflation.
k. "Affirmative Action" programs in hiring and promotion (ought/ought not) to be continued.

CHAPTER 13

THE FORMAL PROPOSAL

One of the commonest kinds of persuasive communication in business is the *formal proposal.* Typically, the formal proposal is that communication that takes an idea, presents it formally and in detail to people who possess the resources to turn that idea into action, and persuades them to do it. It's been called the "tall order" communication.

In a sense, of course, every piece of persuasive writing in business proposes something. The Georgetown Camera letter (at the beginning of Chapter 12) proposed a sales idea about a new use for Solaroid cameras. Phil Gerlach's memo (on page 301) proposed an idea for solving an office-management problem that had arisen. But *formal proposals* usually have to go "an extra mile." They're written, typically, in situations where the writer's ability to present the proposal attractively, and to estimate very carefully what it will cost, counts for as much — in the eyes of its recipients — as the ability to carry out the idea being proposed.

A public relations firm presents a new image-enhancement idea to a major corporation and makes a formal bid to be retained by that corporation to carry it out .... A nonprofit group applies to a federal or state funding agency for grant money to carry out an idea it has in the public interest .... An organizational staff member has an idea for advancing the interests of the organization, and presents it formally in writing to the directors .... These are just a few examples of situations that call for the writing of a formal proposal.

The resulting document may actually be called a *proposal,* or a *formal bid,* or a *grant application,* but by any name it's a formal proposal. It must impress as much by its manner of presentation as by the substance of its idea.

A SAMPLE PROPOSAL

The best way, I think, to examine the process of formal proposal writing is simply to look at a good example, then discuss its special characteristics in light of our earlier discussions (in Chapter 12) of persuasive strategy and technique. The example that follows was prepared by Will Tucker & Associates, a Los

Angeles political campaign-management firm. It is a proposal written to a select group of public-spirited business executives and wealthy individuals in southern California who have formed a committee to promote the development of a rapid transit system in Los Angeles.

Once the committee decides to go ahead with its promotion effort, it will be spending a lot of money — probably over a million dollars — to carry out that promotion most efficiently and effectively. Will Tucker & Associates know this, and are attempting with this proposal to have the committee choose them to run the promotional campaign.

The proposal isn't perfect (few are), but it is well written. And, in the real situation on which this example is based, it was well received.

TARGET '82

RAPID TRANSIT IN LOS ANGELES

A CAMPAIGN PROPOSAL

Prepared by

Will Tucker & Associates

for

The Select Committee

on

Rapid Transit in Los Angeles

September 1980

WTA

INTRODUCTION

Rapid transit in the nation's cities . . . no issue more dramatically confronts local governments today. And nowhere, as current conditions make clear, does it confront local government with greater urgency than in Los Angeles. The issue is not a new one. Its rallying cry has been heard almost since the dismantling of the old Red Car system decades ago. But its outlook changes just as surely and steadily as the inadequacy of our present transportation system looms larger each year.

Will Tucker & Associates--after assessing the present economic and political climate, closely studying the recent unsuccessful ballot measures related to mass transit, and projecting likely conditions in the immediate future--conclude that a Rapid Transit ballot measure, though faced with several substantial obstacles, can be passed in Los Angeles in 1982. Toward this end, we have compiled this brief analysis, and here propose a campaign effort aimed at that passage.

Rapid Transit in Recent Local Elections During the last five years, several ballot referenda in support of mass rapid transit in Los Angeles have been put before the voters. Each of them was defeated. Proposition A in 1974, a measure to provide $2.5 billion for construction of a local rapid transit system, was beaten by a margin of 55% to 45%. Two years later, State Ballot Proposition 17, which would have allowed a portion of fuel tax and license revenues to be used by local areas for pollution control and mass transit, also lost out in Los Angeles County by a margin of 54% to 46%. The immediate past thus seems to hold out a warning for those who would try again.

Hindsight however--that handmaiden of most successful second efforts--makes it clear that both these earlier transit-related measures carried serious handicaps into election. Each had the tendency (if only in its drafting) to generate a self-defeating polarization of interest groups about it. There is natural opposition that awaits any transit measure, and both of these earlier measures tended to nourish that opposition. Moreover, both measures were met by a much lower degree of publicly-felt urgency than exists today. Research would show us the precise extent of this change. Finally, both earlier measures were faced with city and county governments oriented substantially toward the status quo--another condition which has obviously changed.

The New Climate for Rapid Transit Past surveys show that Los Angeles voters have long been aware of the city's need for alternative means of transportation. But that usually meant alternative means for the other guy. Rapid transit has long seemed a way to get other people off the freeways and boulevards to make one's own daily drive less irritating and time consuming. This has been a widespread motive, but, as many analysts have argued, a shallow one--not a motive likely to foster endorsement of new billion-dollar expenditures for actual systems.

Times have changed. The public now faces not only growing congestion on the freeways and widespread smog, but staggered increases in the price of gasoline, the prospect of gasoline rationing, and even the possibility of other limitations on auto usage. The Los Angeles motorist-commuter, in a word, faces curtailment of his primary means of transportation. The issue has only recently hit close to home. And it will hit even closer.

The most recent indications (though not the only ones) of the public's growing awareness of the need for rapid transit have been the election of a Mayor who is committed to building a rapid transit system, and the enthusiasm generated by his early efforts with state and federal agencies to facilitate its funding. The Mayor's aggressiveness on the issue will, in turn, only heighten the public's consciousness of the need for rapid transit in the months ahead, and provide the climate for public approval of a well-drawn measure at the polls.

Add to this change in climate the likelihood of the Legislature's lowering the 60% requirement for ballot passage to a simple majority, and the potential for success at the polls becomes even clearer.

The Campaign Outlook Although many a public issue--because of changes in the climate of opinion--has seen its time come at last, seldom does the climate change so propitiously as it has for rapid transit. With November 1982 before us as an electoral target (for reasons touched upon further on), there now exists ample time in which to organize a well-planned, broad-reaching, momentum-building campaign . . . the kind of campaign which, under the circumstances, will be needed to maximize the likelihood of victory. With this lead-time as an asset, a ballot measure can be framed which is aimed not at the throats of potential opponents, but at widely shared interests in what the Governor recently called ''a well-balanced system of transportation.'' And it can be tested for its impact upon allies, potential opponents, and the voting public, and refined for optimum attractiveness and promotability. Then, with a carefully drafted measure in hand, an early campaign can begin the long and complicated orchestration of the various public-interest groups necessary to weld a winning majority around so far-reaching an issue. Although local district campaigns, like those for Congress and the legislature, can successfully be mounted in six months or less, an issue like regional rapid transit, with its multitude of impacts and a constituency of three million voters, requires a campaign calendar at least three times as long.

In proposing the following campaign, we are fully aware of all the factors involved in planning and building a rapid transit system--factors such as the method of financing, the type of system most desirable, advisable routes and corridors, and (in this special case) the role of the existing Southern California Rapid Transit District (SCRTD). Each has political ramifications which could, in a close election, make the difference between victory and defeat. We have felt it advisable, however, in making this initial proposal, to assume that each of these variables can be prudently determined, and to address ourselves to the single question: HOW BEST CAN A BALLOT MEASURE BE PASSED TO ENABLE CONSTRUCTION OF A RAPID TRANSIT SYSTEM IN LOS ANGELES?

THE CAMPAIGN PLAN

In view of the existing circumstances, we anticipate the need for--and hence recommend--the following campaign in three distinct phases:

<u>Phase One: Preliminary Phase</u> Beginning as soon as is practical, and continuing for a period of 60 to 90 days, the following preliminary steps must be taken:

1. The ballot measure must be drafted. It must be framed in a way not only to encourage maximum support at the polls, but to disarm and minimize potential opposition. The key here, we feel, is an appeal centered about rapid transit's role as part of a ''total transportation network'' in southern California--an appeal that would concur with the aims of the recently created State Department of Transportation, rather than any appeal (as has been the case in earlier transit campaigns) which sets rapid transit into opposition against other modes of transportation and their supporters.

2. It must be decided when the measure should go before the voters. (Existing analyses of voter behavior strongly suggest to us that an initiative measure of this nature, requiring a positive vote on a large bond issue, best goes before the voters in the November general election rather than the June primary.)

3. There must be formed a prestigious Citizen's Support Committee, headed by an appropriate Campaign Chairman, and identified by a specially designed logo and letterhead reflecting the breadth of interest groups and geographic areas across Los Angeles

4. The campaign's finance structure must be organized. A local fund-raising base must be established, a finance chairman selected, a budget drawn and approved, and the needed substantial fund-raising effort begun.

5. Public opinion research must be conducted to determine the precise appeals most likely to succeed in the campaign's promotional and advertising phases.

6. Each of the issues affecting rapid transit must be identified and transformed into promotional appeals consistent with the findings of that research. And to embrace those appeals there must be created a campaign theme, a theme which will provide continuous rationale and persuasion throughout the campaign. (We also project a need for additional opinion surveys as the campaign progresses: to test the early effectiveness of the created appeals and to identify any strategic readjustments that might be necessary.)

Phase Two: Educational Phase Beginning approximately 60 days after the start of Phase One, and perhaps overlapping it, a number of organizational and educational activities will be undertaken. They will be sustained straight through to Election Day, and increased incrementally to create a ''bandwagon'' effect.

This second phase will begin with a community-by-community organizing of local task forces throughout the county. Each task force will consist of local government and civic leaders recruited for their support of rapid transit and their willingness to serve as conduits for community education on behalf of rapid transit. The formation of each task force, and the selection of its chairman, will provide occasions for locally publicizing the campaign.

During this second phase, a broad variety of educational activities and instruments will be made available to each community. Communities will be grouped into areas corresponding to the planned rapid transit corridors. Each area will be put under the direction of a full-time Area Coordinator who will be responsible for recruiting further local leadership into the campaign. He will also be responsible for channeling the educational instruments into each community, and for overseeing the activities taking place there.

These educational activities and instruments should, we think, consist of the following:

1. Fact sheets funneled into each community for distribution through local chambers of commerce, service clubs, and allied support groups: This ongoing series of succinct, one-page information sheets will be produced by campaign headquarters. Each will be addressed to a single issue or question regarding rapid transit, and each will provide a persuasive rationale for that issue. On the basis of feedback from Area Coordinators in weekly staff meetings and from ongoing research, each fact sheet will be adapted to the specific interests of the community in which it circulates. Information and explanations contained in them will be frequently updated by new editions.

2. A full-color, sound motion picture highlighting the rapid transit story: specially produced for the campaign, this twenty to twenty-five minute film will be tailored for showing before local community groups, service clubs, business organizations, and the like. The film can be accompanied by commentary from local task force chairmen or by special guest speakers, followed (where meeting formats allow) by question-and-answer sessions. Arrangements for showings will be made by the area coordinators augmenting a program of availability announcements mailed to every service club and community interest group listed in the county.

3. A speakers' bureau: a corps of people, specialists of various kinds qualified to speak on the various facets of rapid transit--technical, environmental, historical, etc.--will be recruited. Forums will be found for them within each community.

4. Endorsements and resolutions: Local organizations and VIPs will be actively solicited to pass or support resolutions that favor construction of a rapid transit

system in Los Angeles County. These resolutions and endorsements can be used as an indication of the growth and magnitude of public support for rapid transit. They will also provide the occasions for press releases to community papers on the activities of local rapid transit chairmen and their committees.

5. Local seminars: Half-day or all-day seminars for local opinion leaders will be sponsored by the campaign. The seminars will feature guest lectures by various experts, slide presentations, and high level question-and-answer opportunities for their select audiences. The seminars will also provide another set of opportunities for campaign publicity.

6. Special activities in the most visible sectors: In areas of greater affluence and/or visibility--e.g. the West Side, San Marino, Palos Verdes, Maravilla, and Watts --certain other mediagenic activities will be conducted on behalf of the rapid transit measure. These activities--including cocktail receptions and dinners, a benefit concert, and a celebrity tennis tournament--will take full advantage of available public personalities and celebrity talent who are already committed to the rapid transit idea.

Phase Three: Election Victory Phase During the four months preceding election, and in concert with increased local volunteer activity, a comprehensive media advertising campaign will be conducted. Its strategies and appeals will be keyed to the findings of the campaign's ongoing research; its intensity will be incrementally increased to peak on election day.

A broad range of advertising media will be used--radio, television, newspapers (including special inserts for the major dailies), billboards, bus cards, and direct mail--commensurate with available financial resources. Built upon the Phase Two groundwork, the campaign's third phase can, we feel, be executed with special effectiveness by the firm's regular advertising talent: the same celebrity talent available for Phase Two's special events will also be available to enhance the campaign's media program.

For general distribution in August, about ten weeks before the election, a prestigiously designed campaign brochure will be produced, summarizing Los Angeles' need for the projected rapid transit system and highlighting the most compelling reasons for a ''Yes'' vote in November.

Then as follow-up to the brochure, a network of campaign ''newspapers'' (of the kind we have used successfully in other local campaigns) each specially adapted to each transit corridor and local community, will be produced for distribution during election week. These quality tabloids will amplify substantially upon the August brochure and reflect the full range of local interests in rapid transit and its local endorsements.

The community activity generated during the campaign's second phase will be brought to focus during these final weeks. Local task forces and support groups will be employed to distribute the campaign brochures and tabloids and to conduct supplemental fund-raising activity to support advertising in the local papers.

During the campaign's third phase, as during the first and second, a broad and ongoing publicity campaign aimed at regional, statewide, and national media will also be conducted by the campaign's central management. Its theme will be ''Greater Los Angeles and Its Leadership in the Vanguard of Rapid Transit Innovation.''

PROJECTED BUDGET

Within the present climate of public opinion, a campaign of the scope we have described should make the chances of victory for a rapid transit measure in 1982 not less than excellent. Modifications of that scope, either upward or down, are of course possible. It would however be unwise, we believe, to project a substantially smaller campaign, lest the energies which latently favor rapid transit in southern California be allowed to dissipate, and voter apathy carry the day.

The campaign as outlined in the preceding pages would require an estimated total budget subdivided as follows into administrative, promotional, and managerial components:

A. Administrative budget includes a full-time campaign communications director; a secretary-researcher; a finance coordinator for all fund-raising activity; a political-labor coordinator; six area coordinators; the necessary support expenses for each; two staff secretaries; a typist-receptionist; and all rent, office equipment, telephone, postage, and miscellaneous office costs. Each of the administrative personnel will be recruited and supervised for the campaign by Will Tucker & Associates.

$240,000

B. Promotional budget includes production of the motion picture tracing the rapid transit story; the August campaign brochure; the network of campaign tabloids; seminar slide production; the series of campaign fact sheets; and all TV, radio, newspaper, special supplement, billboard, bus card, and direct mail advertising. This budget component also includes the ongoing survey research upon which all promotional strategies will be based. It is given as a range to allow for reasonable upward or downward flexibility and for changes in cost.

$800,000 to 1,000,000

C. Managerial budget includes full-time management by an associate of the firm of Will Tucker & Associates as campaign director; supervision of all campaign staff personnel; the additional participation of Mr. Tucker in the entirety of the campaign's policy-making and strategy-shaping phases; the in-house resources of Will Tucker & Associates in specialist personnel, both in Los Angeles and (where necessary) in the Washington D.C. office; and necessary support expenses.

$80,000

TOTAL PROJECTED BUDGET $1,120,000 to $1,320,000

CONCLUSION

Notwithstanding the favorable climate of opinion, there are several obstacles to the ultimate success of a rapid transit measure in 1982. The campaign can count upon, at least initially, the reflexive opposition of certain interest groups which have opposed rapid transit in the past. The campaign must also confront the traditional reluctance of Los Angeles County voters to approve large bond issues of any nature, especially during inflationary cycles.

We do believe though--and that belief is implicit in every stage of this proposal--that a well-financed and professionally managed campaign can overcome these obstacles. By starting early, professional management can help to tailor a measure that will minimize any long-term opposition--a measure that will, in fact, invite a coalition of transportation interests about the building of a balanced transit system in Los Angeles County And with adequate lead time, professional management can design a campaign which, in its appeals and its intensity, will overcome that voter reluctance.

We believe, as well, that the firm of Will Tucker & Associates offers the combination of professional talent, services, and situation best suited to successfully conduct the rapid transit campaign. The firm is one of the few in the nation which provides full-service, full-responsibility management to initiative and referendum campaigns. In addition to recruiting, supervising, and (where necessary) training all of the campaign's full- and part-time personnel and producing all its advertising and promotionalia, the firm accepts responsibility for building, training and orienting all its volunteer committees, for generating all its press and media publicity, for conducting all research, aiding in all strategy development, and assisting in all campaign fund-raising. The firm has, in fact, already ascertained several nationally known availabilities for key administrative posts within the campaign.

Moreover, we are convinced that a campaign like rapid transit, heavily involved as it must be with intergovernmental agency liaison, is best served by a firm like Will Tucker & Associates with fully staffed offices in both Los Angeles and Washington D.C. and best served by a firm which has developed, through past performance, successful working relationships with executive leadership of the incumbent party at both the state and federal levels.

Finally, Will Tucker & Associates offer to the rapid transit campaign an unsurpassed record of recent ballot victories in Los Angeles.

In brief, if rapid transit in Los Angeles <u>is</u> an idea whose time has come, we confidently feel that Will Tucker & Associates is the firm best prepared to bring it home in next year's election. We are ready to assume full responsibility for the campaign, and welcome the opportunity to pursue its various facets in greater detail with all concerned.

FORMAT ANALYSIS

First, let's examine format — which in the case of the "Campaign '82" rapid transit proposal is typical. That format is divided into four major sections:

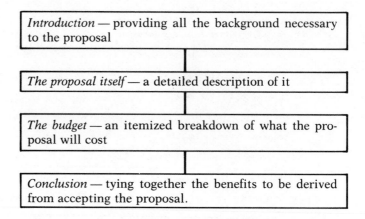

Introduction — providing all the background necessary to the proposal

The proposal itself — a detailed description of it

The budget — an itemized breakdown of what the proposal will cost

Conclusion — tying together the benefits to be derived from accepting the proposal.

The headings given to these sections may differ slightly from proposal to proposal, but essentially they're the same. In "Campaign '82" the second section is called "The Campaign Plan," — for that *is* what's being proposed. The third section is headed "Projected Budget" — so as to allow for the possibility of later modification. The standard four-part format is clearly evident.

Now consider, in terms of this four-part format, the persuasive process itself, that necessary pattern of persuasive strategy that we first analyzed back on page 000.

The "Introduction" aims to capture the attention of the readers (the select committee), and to focus their minds on the central motive: in this case, their desire to get a ballot issue approved by the voters of Los Angeles.

"The Campaign Plan" develops most of the proposal's central appeal — an appeal to the readers' likely appreciation of the expertness with which Will Tucker & Associates would plan and conduct the ballot campaign. Notice the degree of detail to which the writer goes to build this appeal.

The "Projected Budget" section completes the "appeal" phase by making clear what Will Tucker's plan will cost. No expensive proposal ever fully persuades until its potential adopters know what it's going to cost them, and why. A budget breaks down the projected cost so as to justify itself.

The proposal's "Conclusion" summarizes the essence of the appeal, talks specifically of the firm's ability to deliver what has been proposed, and expresses desire to do so. That is to say, the "Conclusion" completes the persuasive process.

You'll note that each page of the proposal is numbered, and that within each of the four major sections of the proposal there are *sub*sections marked off by a system of subheadings. You'll also note that in the second section, "The Campaign Plan," there are numbered *listings* used within several of the subsections (both Phase One and Phase Two of the Campaign Plan show items numbered 1 through 6). We'll discuss pagination, subheadings, and numbered listings later on, in Chapter 18; but if you're ready to write a proposal before you get to that chapter, you might take a look right now at those brief discussions. They're on pages 440–442.

Some Format Options

There are some fairly common additions to, and modifications of, the standard four-part proposal format.

Had the "Campaign '82" proposal been longer than it was, its author would probably have included a *table of contents*. If one were to be built into the proposal as it now stands, it would appear right after the title-cover, and probably would look like this:

Table of Contents

(Tables of contents, as well as covers and title pages, are also discussed further in Chapter 18 on pages 447 and 449.)

Some proposals, either by design of the writer or by request of the prospective funding source, provide a project *summary* at the beginning, usually preceding (sometimes taking the place of) the Introduction. This beginning summary may also be called a *synopsis*, or *abstract*. It's essentially a convenience to the intended readers. It provides a brief overview of the proposed idea and its projected consequences, so that they may more quickly determine whether they're interested in reading the complete proposal. Obviously (if your proposal is well written) it's to your advantage to have the whole thing read. So unless the reader has asked for one, or unless there's some other overriding reason for including a summary up front, my advice is — don't. Persuasion works better when it's allowed to develop fully.

One other section is occasionally added to business proposals. If the writer feels that a vital part of the persuasive appeal is the *expertness* of the people who will be carrying out the idea if the proposal is accepted, there may be a separate section devoted to spelling out their impressive credentials. This section might be headed *Key Personnel, Resource People, Project Staff, Chief Consultants,* or any other suitably pertinent and impressive title. (As always, connotations count.) This section would usually be positioned after the proposal description, before the budget.

TWO-STEP PROPOSALS

A proposal is the effective presentation of an idea whose time — you hope — has come. But sometimes the time isn't right. An idea may be too new to spring, all at once, on an unsuspecting executive — no matter how good a proposal you can write. What then do you do?

What we're talking about here is the classic situation of a non-existent motive. That important early phase of the persuasive process — focusing your reader's mind on the motive you wish to satisfy — obviously can't happen if the motive isn't there. You first have to create it.

In such situations, you are wise to consider turning your proposal into a two-step process:

1. Write a preliminary communication whose primary purpose is to *create* the motive you wish to satisfy. This communication should also candidly state, in the conclusion, that you know how to satisfy it; but it should not itself attempt to do so. The motive must first be allowed to "sink in."

After the recipient has had awhile to contemplate that first communication (and perhaps even asked to talk to you about it), then:

2. Write a thoroughgoing follow-up communication that shows, in full detail, how your idea can satisfy that motive. Once the motive has taken hold (and only then), this second communication can *complete* the persuasive process.

On page 335 is an example of a motive-creating communication, the first part of what, wisely, will be a two-part proposal.

It's a good *first half* of a two-step proposal. Jules Howard has seen, for some time, the need for a separate reference facility; but he does not make the mistake of assuming that his boss, Bill McGaw, sees it. On the contrary, he assumes that nothing is further from his boss's mind.

That being the case — no motive consciously existing in McGaw — Howard wisely chooses *not* to try, all at once in a single communication, to persuade him of the wisdom of his proposal. Rather he devotes this first memorandum to creating the motive. This memo plants the seed.

Howard knows, too, that his boss always wants the Maintenance Division to look good — especially in the eyes of the City Manager and the City Council. (Of course that makes McGaw look good.) So in planting the specific motive he wants to appeal to, Howard ties it to other, more general motives he knows already exist. (Re-examine the memo: you'll see them appealed to from beginning to end.)

Howard already has the "figures" that will make his argument for the new sub-library. But he'll wait a week before submitting them to McGaw —to let the motive sink in and create some positive anticipation in McGaw's mind. It's wise proposal writing.

CONCLUSION

Business proposals are among the most important communications you'll ever write. That's why we devoted a chapter to them (as we also have, immediately following this one, to job applications — another vital kind of writing.)

But looked at functionally, a business proposal (like a job application) is just one more kind of persuasive writing. While its format looks a lot like that of a business report (a format we'll look at in Chapter 18), functionally it follows every step of the persuasive strategy we first examined in Chapter 12. And it draws upon the very same store of techniques and tactics. It must create a new state of mind in its readers, and convince them to take an action that, without the proposal, they wouldn't have taken — and in fact may never have contemplated.

CITY OF CARSONVILLE

INTERDEPARTMENTAL MEMORANDUM

Date: September 4, 197-

To: Bill MacGraw, Maintenance Superintendent

From: Jules Howard, Administrative Aide

Subject: USING THE MATERIAL REFERENCE LIBRARY

At 2:15 p.m. last Thursday, Cliff Black, our Building Maintenance Foreman, received an emergency work order from the City Services Building. He saw that he needed some operations data to perform the job, and it was data that he did not have immediately at hand. Cliff left the office, drove the 2½ miles through our normally heavy midafternoon traffic to the Material Reference Library at City Hall, and once there got in line at the desk.

As Cliff already knew from experience, that trip to the Library was going to cause some problems. Between the trip to City Hall, and the crowd of Public Works Department people using the reference materials, Cliff spent over two hours getting his data. He had to cancel the rest of his afternoon's appointments, postpone the Stevenson Park inspection that he'd scheduled for that day -- and even then, he took some "flak" at City Services for arriving almost three hours "late" on an emergency work order.

Cliff's experience was typical of the complaints we've been hearing from other Maintenance Division foremen. They cannot efficiently use the Material Reference Library at City Hall. And I think there's a remedy. I am convinced, after working out some preliminary figures, that we could be performing more efficiently -- as well as serving the other City departments more satisfactorily -- if we installed a separate Material Reference sub-library here at the Maintenance Division facility.

A small but separate sub-library would accomplish several important things. Emergency work orders would get much faster service. We would also have a valuable tool for speeding the Maintenance Division's contribution to the budget forecasting process, to long range planning, and to work-project preparation. And we'd be providing the City an important back-up facility when the overload at the main Library slows down the work of the other departments -- as I understand has begun to happen.

I will be submitting a formal proposal to you by next Tuesday, the 12th. It will spell out in detail the cost-efficiency figures that I feel demonstrate our compelling need for a separate reference facility. The added costs are small as compared to the advantages; and I think the figures will help to persuade the City Council.

Meanwhile, I'm anxious to get your own response to the proposal, and would like to sit down with you about it as soon as the figures are in your hand.

Jules Howard

PROBLEMS

1. Assume that you are an educational consultant to schools, colleges and universities of various sizes around the country. The chief administrative officer of one of your schools has been encouraged by the trustees to plan "a particular expansion or redevelopment, for the sum of one-and-one-half million dollars, of that school which will most greatly enhance its educational function." (The trustees have recently been promised grants of a million-and-a-half, and they want to learn the best way to spend it.)

You've been retained by top administration to determine what that "expansion or redevelopment" ought to be, and to write a formal proposal to the trustees putting forth the idea.

Come up with the idea, research it (and its costs), and write the proposal.

2. On the job that you now hold (or on a job that you held in the past), come up with a single idea that you believe would improve operational efficiency, develop a budget for it, and propose it formally (in writing) to the people who would be responsible for implementing the idea.

3. In light of the Chapter 12 discussion of persuasive strategy and technique, do a careful page-by-page, paragraph-by-paragraph, sentence-by-sentence analysis of the Will Tucker & Associates proposal in this chapter. Identify the strategy and the persuasive techniques being employed; and, in a detailed memo to your instructor, spell out what you discover in your close analysis of that proposal.

CHAPTER 14

APPLYING FOR A JOB — THE NEED TO PERSUADE

The search for a promising career position can be difficult and highly competitive. Depending on the economic climate, jobs for college graduates may or may not be plentiful. And some industries may have more promising openings than others. But the really good jobs — the "plums" — are always scarce. Those excellent first jobs that students dream about are won only by candidates who have strong qualifications *and* who effectively communicate those qualifications. The same holds true for those advanced jobs that are sought by college graduates with solid work experience. Talent alone doesn't usually land a job; a prospective employer must first learn of that talent.

As you approach graduation, your first good chance to communicate your qualifications to prospective employers will probably be with an *application package* — a persuasive combination of *résumé* and *covering letter* — sent to those prospective employers. The central appeal of this two-part communication will be to the employer's desire for top-quality employees. The "commodity" it offers is *the person best qualified to do the specific job the employer needs done* — namely, you.

SCOUTING THE TERRITORY

Who are those prospective employers? And what jobs, in particular, do they make available to applicants with your background and abilities? No job search can really hope to succeed without these questions being answered at the outset.

Sources of Information

Information about a good job-possibility can come from anywhere, at any time. But wise job-seekers don't wait for Fate to toss up opportunities. They systematically search them out. Where?

Newspaper Ads. Many people think that newspaper ads are the best place to search for job openings. Truth is, many of the best possibilities — even at the starting level — don't need to be advertised to the general public. So while newspaper ads can occasionally provide the lead you seek, most times they're not the best place to begin a job search.

When you do find a promising lead in a newspaper ad, remember that promptness in replying is a key. The first applications received by the employer running the ad are likely to be the most carefully considered.

Professional Journals. Usually a better place to begin (at least with published sources of information) is the professional journal devoted to the industry or the job specialty you're interested in. For example, a journal like *Computerworld,* the newsweekly for computer specialists, will usually carry announcements of job opportunities in that field. (The issue I have before me as I write this has thirty pages of them.)

It almost goes without saying that your education in a given field *must* include knowing where the latest news in that field is being published. Be sure you're familiar with the journals in your field, and use their job announcement pages when your job search begins.

Articles. Apart from their "job announcement" or "help wanted" pages, newspapers, magazines and professional journals will often carry news of corporate expansions, rising government expenditures in certain fields, newly built facilities, forecasted growth in certain industries, or the like. When such activity happens in an area of interest to you, take the initiative and inquire into the employment possibilities that are likely being generated.

A Letter of Inquiry. The best way to inquire into job opportunities is to write a letter of inquiry — the principles of which we discussed back in Chapter 8. And before you write, do everything you can (including picking up the phone) to learn the name and specific title of the person in charge of recruiting and hiring for the organization that interests you. Be sure, as well, to include in your inquiry letter your reasons for inquiring — including whatever you may have learned about recent trends or developments in that company or its industry.

The Telephone. Other kinds of information can also be gotten over the phone. In an extreme case, a student of mine who was interested in becoming an entertainment agent called up a Los Angeles agency (it was a local call) and ended up speaking to one of the partners for almost an hour. The student said she learned more about job opportunities — and obstacles — in the field during that single phone call than she had in her previous year of interest.

If you call, announce your interest and ask to speak to "anyone who might be able to help me." Be prepared though — and express your willingness — to follow up with a thorough letter of inquiry. Most often, prospective employers appreciate a letter.

The College Placement Office. Almost all colleges, universities and professional schools maintain placement offices to help their graduates (as well as ongoing students) get jobs. These placement offices help in several ways: by compiling information about job opportunities; by keeping your credentials on file and sending them out to prospective employers whenever they're asked for; and by arranging interviews for you with representatives of the companies and agencies who are hiring.

No student should approach job-seeking time without being registered with the college placement office.

Teachers. As good as it may be, the placement office isn't the only place on campus that can provide job leads. Many college and university faculty members are active as consultants in their fields. They also attend professional conferences. Both activities will often make them aware of job opportunities that are opening up. Don't hesitate to ask your teachers (at some mutually convenient time) for job-search ideas.

Employment Agencies and Executive Search Agencies. Many employers who seek to hire people — both at entry-level positions and for management spots — turn the task over to personnel specialists, usually employment agencies or executive search agencies. The fee for their services will be borne by either the employer or the person they find to fill the position. In either case, it's obviously to your advantage as a job-seeker to have interviewed and registered your qualifications and job objectives with one or more of the personnel agencies handling the kind of position you're interested in.

The College Library. The library at your school can't get you a job (unless you're an aspiring librarian); but it can be your best source of job-seeking information. Most libraries keep updated directories to corporations and public agencies — *Moody's Manuals, Standard & Poor's,* U. S. Civil Service directories, and the like. They also keep trade and professional journals, and periodicals like *Fortune, U.S. News & World Report,* and the *Wall Street Journal.* Often they have collections of the annual reports of major corporations; and perhaps most useful of all a copy of *Career: The Annual Guide to Business Opportunities.*

Get to know your reference librarians. They can provide valuable help when it's time to look for a job.

Knowing Where You Stand

Knowing where to look for information about the job market is only part of the scouting process. You must also look at yourself — objectively and without self-delusion — and determine where you stand in that job market. Essentially, you've got to ask yourself three questions: "What kind of job do I want?" "What precisely does that job entail?" "And in what ways am I prepared to do that job?"

Let's be realistic. Students approaching graduation don't always know what kind of job they want. (People looking to make mid-career changes aren't always sure either.) What they're looking for is opportunity, attractive pay, perhaps some prestige or excitement. To find such a position, however, you must decide — for appearance's sake — upon some particular job objective, so you can approach the job market looking like a clearheaded, goal-oriented applicant who knows what he or she wants, and is determined to get. (Privately, if you have three or four different job inclinations, you can plan to pursue them all; but each must be prepared for differently.)

And keep in mind that it's not enough to want "a job in advertising," or a "position as management trainee." If it's advertising you want, be prepared to apply for a job in media planning, or copywriting, or ad design, or research, or account liaison. Show your prospective employer that you know the different facets of the business. If you want to be a management trainee, present yourself as one who prefers, and knows a good deal about, a particular industry. Though it won't answer all your questions about job specialty, the *Dictionary of Occupational Titles* (available in the library) can give you some idea of the broad range of possibilities.

Knowing the specific job you want obviously requires knowing what that job entails. Talk with your professional teachers about job specialization in the fields that interest you. Talk to people in the business, and to people who do business with them. Ask specific questions. Get your hands on as much company literature as you can and read it carefully. Read the textbooks devoted to particular fields (even if you haven't taken the course). A good text in advertising, for instance, will survey in detail each of the specialized facets of the advertising industry.

Finally, you have to ask yourself how you're prepared for that particular job you're seeking. On private worksheets (which you'll ultimately turn into one or more finished résumés), lay out all your education and work experience. Then ask yourself, for every bit of it, either one of two questions:

1. How does this show that I'm qualified to do the job?

or

2. How does it show that I'm prepared to *learn* to do it, and to learn it fast and well?

Obviously, experience doing the kind of job you're seeking should not only be noted but described in detail. But there are other kinds of experience — on the job, at school, or elsewhere — that are almost as valuable.

a. Have you ever done work *related* to the kind of position you seek?
(For example, you may not have worked in advertising, *per se*, but perhaps you've sold advertising space in your school prom program, or designed the posters.)
b. Have you ever worked, for pay or not, in the job *environment* you seek to enter?
(One aspiring social-worker I know, though he had never done social work, had volunteered some time to cook and serve meals at a senior citizens' center, and had also spent some free hours sitting in on divorce-court proceedings.)
c. Have you ever supervised the efforts of other people?
(You may have organized a fund-raising drive, been captain of a school team, or officer in a school or social organization.)
d. Have you ever handled the money, or planned the budget, of an organization?
(The "bottom line," as the cliché now has it, of any business organization is the ability to make income exceed expense. In public agencies, they need to balance. *Any* money-experience is valuable experience.)
e. Have you ever started and maintained your own business?
(Any enterprise more substantial than a streetcorner lemonade stand — provided it was legal — is valuable.)

f. Have you had any paid work-experience at all?
(*Any* experience shows an employer you know what it's like to handle job responsibility.)[1]

g. Have you any volunteer experience?
(Volunteer experience implies that you've got *initiative,* as well as a sense of serving others.)

h. Have you graduated, or will you be graduating, from school?
(Then you know how to finish a long-term task.)

j. Have you taken courses in that field?

k. Have you had certain *key* courses, the content of which is valuable in almost any organization?
(Accounting? Statistics? Electronic data processing? Business communications?)

l. Did you get high grades in school?

m. Did you work while you were going to school?

n. Have you had *any* experience (in or out of school, paid or unpaid) with the kind of product or service you seek to work with?

This list of questions isn't exhaustive, but it should give you a good idea of how to learn where you stand in the particular job market you seek to enter.

THE APPLICATION PACKAGE

Now that you've scouted the job market (and looked at yourself in light of it), how best do you enter it? No doubt you could use the telephone to introduce yourself and your desires to an employer, or you could simply show up in person and request an interview. But neither of these approaches is advisable. By showing up in person or calling on the phone unexpectedly, you are probably interrupting someone's busy schedule to talk only about *you,* a topic of absolutely no prior interest to the person you're interrupting. It's not a good way to make a strong first impression.

The *application package* (the combination of résumé and covering letter) is a much better means of introduction. Employers prefer it. With an application package, you needn't worry about nervously stumbling through your opening remarks. You can take as much time as you need to say exactly the right things in the best way you can. You can also, in writing, express yourself completely, without the risk of being interrupted "midstream" as you would be in a face-to-face situation or over the phone. With your communication in hand, your prospective employers get a first impression of you at *their* convenience, when they have cleared the time for the sole purpose of learning your qualifications and desires. And they get the impressions *you* want them to get.

As I said before, you must decide — even if it's only a temporary decision — what kind of job you want; and you must tailor your application package specifically to it. Obviously, if you're applying for an advertised opening, the decision is made for you; but again your appeal must be aimed precisely at that job, if you're to stand a chance of getting it.

[1] Exceptions to this might be jobs like *bartender, night-club bouncer,* or *go-go dancer,* which certain firms might tend to look upon as insufficiently dignified.

Let's take a look at the two components of the application package: first at the résumé, which delineates your relevant background; then at its *covering letter,* which introduces you to the employer and explains specifically why you're writing.

The Résumé

After you decide what kind of job you want, you want to construct an effective résumé, have it reproduced on quality bond stationery, and send it out *with individualized covering letters* to as many prospective employers as you like. But before you write one word of that résumé, you must carefully organize the facts of your background, as they reflect your potential for doing the job you're seeking. Your education, work experience, organizational affiliations, military service (if you've had any), personal interests, and certain personal data — all the facts you've compiled on your worksheet — must be organized for presentation in the résumé. Along with this information, you should have the names of several persons qualified and willing to speak on your behalf. Then you can write the résumé.

When finished, it might look like the résumé in Figure 38. Examine that résumé's makeup and its contents, then consider the following point-by-point discussion of it.

The Heading The heading in our model résumé consists of personal information. The applicant's *name* appears top center in capital letters. Because you want your name to make an impression on the reader, give it both positional and typographical emphasis. Nicknames should be avoided; they seem flippant to some employers. *Address* and *phone number* are naturally important: the employer will want to know where to reach you. *Age* is included on many résumés though some applicants concerned about age discrimination — and aware that such discrimination is illegal — are omitting it these days.

(Let me pause here for a moment to say a word about the résumé-theory that governs much of the advice you'll read in this chapter. In recent years, fair employment legislation has made it illegal for employers to ask certain questions of their job-candidates. Questions about age, marital status, one's housemate . . . are only a few that are now prohibited. Some applicants feel, therefore, that information that cannot be asked for *should not* be volunteered on a résumé. "Legally," they say, "it's none of the employer's business. So why tell him?" It's a point of view with much justification. However, it is not the viewpoint that, in my estimation, produces the most effective résumés. As résumés (and their covering letters) are essentially "selling" tools — designed to make applicants look as good as they possibly can — the decision, in my opinion, to include or exclude any piece of information should turn *only* on whether or not that information will make the applicant look better.)

As for marital status, for jobs that require substantial travel or irregular hours, being single can appear to be an advantage. On the other hand, married applicants are often considered less likely to be "job jumpers." A statement of *willingness to relocate,* if true, can be an advantage when applying to large national companies with regional offices.

Though sometimes seen in résumé headings, indications of religion, national origin, or health need not be included. One's race may or may not be a factor in "affirmative action" hiring: include it or don't, accordingly. Also unnecessary is the date of writing: all a date does is make the résumé seem outdated

Figure 38
A well-written application résumé.

ADAM PIERCE

Demmler Hall
Valhalla University
Kent, Ohio 26780
613 538-7600

Age: 24
Ht: 6-1 Wt: 170
Single
Willing to relocate

Education

B.S. in Industrial Engineering, Valhalla University, June 1980, top 10% of class, with special course work in statistics, motivational psychology, business law, and communications.

Won U.S. Paint Company Scholarship 1978, 1979
Member of Industrial Relations Club
Elected Secretary of the Student Council
On Dean's Honor Roll since 1978

Also attended Colfax College, Colfax, Indiana, 1976-77

Experience

Staff Supervisor, Cleveland Boys' Club Camp, Kiowa, Ohio, summer 1979; responsible for housing, activities scheduling and occasional discipline of fourteen counselors and 110 campers.

Camp Counselor, Cleveland Boys' Club Camp, Kiowa, Ohio, summers of 1977 and 1978.

Personal Interests

Politics, world affairs, camping, chess, junior chamber of commerce member, and volunteer hospital work.

References

Will gladly be provided upon request.

within a few weeks of its composition. Many states prohibit employers from requesting photos of job applicants; but again there is nothing to stop you from providing one without being asked, if you think it will enhance your résumé.

The Education Block If you're a college graduate with no experience in the kind of job you seek, *Education* should be the first block of information on your résumé. Because educational attainment is often considered the best index of a young person's job potential, this information block will usually be your longest and most detailed. Notice what is included in Adam Pierce's résumé: the specific *degree* taken, the *name of the school,* and the *date of graduation* — these are basic facts that any employer wants to know about an applicant's education. A statement of *overall average* (if in the B range or higher) or of *class standing* (if in the top third or better) should also be included here. If you show a grade-point average, a letter-grade translation should accompany it: for example, "Grade-point average: 3.56 (A–)." Specific *courses related to the job,* if they're not implied by the degree, are often included (as on Pierce's résumé); but don't bother to list courses that, as a graduate, you are expected to have taken, and don't list courses that don't relate to the job being sought. *Extracurricular activities* should be listed here too (with emphasis on any offices held in campus organizations), as should any *academic awards, scholarships, certificates,* or *honors attained.* An indication of other colleges you've attended is also necessary. Some applicants include a statement of high-school graduation, but unless your high-school diploma is your highest educational achievement, it's probably unnecessary.

If you begin mailing résumés in the months preceding graduation, as many seniors wisely do, you can use the future tense in beginning your education block (for example, "Will be graduated with a B.S. Degree in marketing from Valhalla University in June,198__").

The Experience Block The résumé's *Experience* block gives the pertinent details of the jobs you have held. It should list those jobs in reverse chronological order — most recent job first. Each listing indicates job title, the name and address of the company, dates of employment, and number of hours per week spent on the job. In addition, any special responsibilities over personnel or budget should be briefly indicated, as Adam Pierce does in his "Staff Supervisor" entry: "responsible for housing, activities scheduling, and occasional discipline of fourteen counselors and 110 campers." If your accomplishments on any past job translated into company profit, be sure to say so on your résumé.

If some of your experience is directly related to the job you seek, and some of it isn't, there's nothing to stop you from creating *two* Experience blocks — e.g., a block called *Advertising Experience* and one called *Other Work Experience.*

Two separate Experience blocks can also be used — to great advantage — if you have two major dimensions to your work experience, both of which pertain to the job you're seeking. A candidate for an aerospace executive's position might well, on the résumé, reserve one block for "Engineering Experience" and another for "Administrative (or Executive) Experience." The brief Taylor Report in Figure 38B suggests another, increasingly frequent double Experience block showing up on résumés written by computer people.

The Personal Interests Block In the sample résumé, Adam Pierce has combined his membership in off-campus organizations with other personal interests and experiences under the combined heading of *Personal Interests* — probably to conserve space. He could have used separate blocks for this information. Activities, interests, and experiences should be included in the résumé to reflect your "well-roundedness" as an individual, a qualification employers are quite interested in.

But be careful! To assure emphasis where emphasis belongs, make sure your personal interests block is smaller than your education block. If you have substantial work experience, your experience block should also be larger than your personal interests block (unless, of course, personal activity bears directly on your ability to perform the job you're seeking, such as private flying if you seek a post as an aeronautical engineer, or ham radio operation if you seek a job in broadcasting or electronics).

Figure 38B

THE TAYLOR REPORT/Alan Taylor

How Do You Write a Computer User's Resume?

How would you write Leonardo DaVinci's resume, assuming that you had to? Would you describe him as a painter? Military defense engineer? Attack strategist? Anatomical artist? Hydraulic designer? What would you choose to emphasize, and what would you ignore?

Leonardo is not the only person who presented this type of difficulty. There were many others — "Renaissance men" we call them, people who could put their hands to many different tasks that nowadays would call for full-time specialists.

Nor was this peculiar multifunctioning ability limited to the Renaissance. Well after that, in the 1700s and 1800s, we find Ben Franklin (diplomat, engineer, writer, inventor), Thomas Jefferson (house and furniture designer, farmer, politician) and, in the computer field, Charles Babbage (postal system designer, "hardware" designer, tidal system mapper and investigator).

Of course, these were all "great men." However, the concept of the Renaissance multifunctioners is now considered something of a more simple, bygone age. Twentieth century complexity has made it more difficult for people to keep up in many different fields.

One exception that comes to mind is the modern computer user. By using computers with many different specialized applications, the user is effectively a specialist in more than one area. How, then, do you write a resume for a computer user specialist?

Accounting Plus

Take an accountant who has been using computerized accounting packages for five or so years. In the precomputer 20th century, an accountant would have been kept in an office, away from customers and other parts of the firm.

In current practice, however, the computer offers the accuracy and single-mindedness that human accounting formerly needed, giving the accountant time for keeping up with the human race — for handling customers and taking on other, nonaccounting duties. Word processing is one area that springs immediately to mind.

The user in this example may be called an "accountant plus." But plus what? It would be altogether inadequate to call him a computer operator, even though he may know enough about hardware, software and maintenance to keep the accounting systems effective and productive.

How would you describe such an individual on a resume? Or, for that matter, if you were a personnel officer, how would you define the position that he held in an organization?

Flexible Position Description

The work that these "accountants plus" are already doing is unique to each individual. Some will be particularly adept at handling machinery matters. A computer system specialist still has to have a "feel" for the equipment, so machine matters are perhaps an important aspect of his position.

Others taking advantage of the additional productivity effected by computers will be able to relate better to management problems or to the handling of customers, suppliers and contractors as well as the corresponding paperwork. The knowledge of the computerized system makes them invaluable in these areas also.

What is now rare, and will be even more rare as systems advance in reliability, is the person who can handle only the computer. Freedom from having to specialize in any one field is already here, thanks to computers.

We should take advantage of this freedom. It is, after all, a renaissance of its own; the computer has created an information-handling revolution of the same magnitude as the one spawned by the printing press long ago.

Clearly, a computer user's resume has to show the strong points. The computer operator capability must be there. The repertoire of computer applications already experienced must be there. But so must the noncomputer abilities: the experience with people, the skills at "butchering" or report writing or both. All should be there, although in any one context many of them may be irrelevant or of no particular value.

This possible irrelevance gives us a key to the nature of the computer renaissance person, inside or outside the computer industry. He is someone who can be totally employed while using only a part of his skills — without the other skills atrophying.

The new generation of resumes will have to be broken down into two separate considerations: first, the flexibility and quality of the person shown by computer-aided work experience; and second, the ability to perform, with or without computers and without previous experience, the major tasks ahead.

And it's best to omit memberships in religious and political organizations. They bear little if any relation to a person's job potential. It is also wise to exclude such hobbies as motorcycle racing, skydiving, or sword swallowing. They tend to create impressions of temperamental irregularity (regardless of how inaccurate those impressions might be).

References There are two schools of thought about personal references on a résumé. One suggests that at the bottom of a résumé the applicant should list the names (with titles and addresses) of three or four qualified "referees"—that is, persons willing and able to speak on behalf of your character and your job potential. Laura Edmondson has done this in her résumé (shown in Figure 39). Others feel that, for the sake of conciseness, all you need include at the bottom of your résumé is a one-line statement that references "will gladly be provided upon request" — as Adam Pierce has done in his résumé back in Figure 38.

Figure 39
A résumé format utilizing a photograph and centered headings.

LAURA EDMONDSON
71 Serendipity Drive
Corona, California 98765
821-2905

PHOTO

EDUCATION

Foothill Junior College San Donaldo, California	A.A. Degree in Legal Stenography

College Course Work in: Legal Stenography, Economics, Typing, Shorthand, Composition, Business Communications, Report Writing, Office Machines, and Principles of Law.

EXPERIENCE

Hernandez-Foster, Inc. Pomona, California	Staff Secretary	Two years
Southwestern Life & Indemnity Company Riverside, California	Personal Secretary to Mr. T. L. Simms, District Manager	Two years

INTERESTS

Theater, painting, travel, collecting Mayan artifacts

REFERENCES

Mr. Marcus Foster Hernandez-Foster, Inc. Pomona, California	Miss Evelyn Winterborn Legal Secretary Beverly Hills, California

Mrs. Dorothy Lyman
Instructor, Secretarial Arts
Foothill Junior College
San Donaldo, California

In either case, when constructing a résumé, you should always indicate that you do have people willing to speak enthusiastically about you. Employers prefer an applicant's references to be teachers and previous employers, rather than family doctors, friends, or members of the clergy. Teachers and employers are usually felt to be more "hardnosed" in their evaluations.

A word of advice: Never give a person's name as a reference without first getting that person's okay. Many a confident applicant has lost a job because someone he thought would write a glowing reference, didn't. No prospective reference writer can object to being asked, "Can you, in good conscience, write a strong reference for me?" If your prospective reference-writer hesitates in answering that question, consider turning elsewhere for the reference you need.

Military Service on the Résumé As of this writing, there is no compulsory military obligation for young American men (though of course, there's no guarantee that this will continue to be so). Employers, therefore, no longer look immediately — as they did several years ago — to see where a male applicant "stands with the draft."

If you have had military service, however, it should be indicated (as in the résumé in Figure 40) in a separate *Military Service* information block on your résumé. In it you want to indicate your service duties *and* emphasize the fact that you have completed active duty. Harper's military service block in Figure 40 shows the dates of his service, his branch of service, and where he served (simply having been abroad or to another part of the country looks good on a résumé). Had he served as a commissioned or noncommissioned officer, this also would have been indicated. The block should also show, as Harper's does, that you've received your military discharge.

Some Other Precautions Just a few other precautions should be taken when preparing a résumé.

For neatness, be sure to maintain a "picture-frame" effect, with one inch or more of white space at top and bottom, left and right.

Be sure, as well, that your headings and subheadings will be clear to the reader *at a glance.*

That a résumé must be physically flawless to be successful goes without saying.

And, unless you have very substantial full-time work experience, be sure to keep the résumé to a single page. Longer résumés, unless they're justifiable at a glance, are considered wasteful of a reader's time.

When you mail out more than one application package, do *not* use photocopies of the résumé. A photocopy carries the implication that the original (more important) copy has gone elsewhere.

Before we move on to the *covering letter,* let's take a look at three other résumés that were written by college-trained job seekers. They appear in Figures 40 to 42. Each is somewhat different from Adam Pierce's and Laura Edmondson's and is, in its own way, as potentially effective.

Figure 40
A résumé prepared by a job applicant with substantial work experience. (Notice that this heavily experienced job applicant wisely places his *Experience* block before his *Education* block.)

ALEX M. HARPER

938 Middle Street
El Segundo, California 90245
(213) 238-9265

Age: 34
Ht: 6-2 Wt: 190
Married, two children

Experience

Department Supervisor, TRW Systems, Manufacturing Engineering and Processes Department, Redondo Beach, California, May 1979 to the present. Responsible for obtaining, scheduling and overseeing work assignments of 30 engineering, planning and administrative support personnel. Also responsible for reconciling Department budgets.

Engineering Writer, TRW Systems, Integrated Logistics Department, Redondo Beach, California, May 1971 to May 1979. Responsible for writing and updating technical manuals on classified spacecraft and military projects. Was granted "Secret" security clearance.

Engineering Writer, Stromberg-Carlson, Technical Publications Group, El Segundo, California, August 1970 to May 1971. Responsible for writing and updating Air Force Technical Orders and the Launch Enabling and Communications Systems on the TITAN II project.

Education

El Redondo Junior College, Torrance, California. Graduated in June 1967. Associate of Arts Degree in Electronics, and Radio Technician's Certificate.

California State University at Long Beach. Electronics major, from September 1967 to June 1968.

California State College, Dominguez Hills. Part-time night student since March 1980. Will be graduated with a B.S. in Business Administration in Spring 1983. (Plan to continue study as a part-time night student at Cal State Dominguez Hills toward the M.B.A. Degree.)

Personal Interests

President of investment club; basketball and softball player; coach in the Bobbysox Softball League.

Military Service

Served two years active duty in the United States Air Force, March Air Force Base, Riverside, California, September 1968 to August 1970. Member of the Air Force Reserve, September 1970 to March 1974. Honorable Discharge, March 1974.

References

Will gladly be provided upon request.

Figure 41
A résumé format employing a headline and an interesting third-person point of view. (Notice that because Maxwell includes a statement of personal objective on her résumé she limits the applicability of the résumé to just one kind of job.)

DO YOU THINK THE FIELD OF MARKETING RESEARCH
NEEDS WOMEN LIKE JANE MAXWELL?

Her Professional Objective:

To begin a career as a market research analyst, and grow into executive status.

Her Education:

Will be graduated from Valhalla University in June with a Bachelor of Science Degree in Marketing and a final cumulative average of A-. With an eye on her future, she has taken courses in:

Advertising Psychology	Statistics
Psychological Testing	Mass Behavior

Her achievements at Valhalla have been:

Dean's Honor Roll 1979, 1980.
Recipient of Industrial League Scholarship 1980.
Chairwoman of University Marketing Club 1979.

Ms. Maxwell plans to attend evening graduate school to work toward a Master's Degree in Economics.

Her Business Experience:

Employed as a clerk for Ruell & Associates, Kent, Ohio, part-time while attending college, 1978 to the present.

Employed as an interviewer for Marston Market Research, Inc., Kent, Ohio, on call from February 1979 to present.

Ms. Maxwell is 22 years old and single. She is free to travel or relocate. Her references will gladly be provided upon request.

If you agree that the record of Jane Maxwell qualifies her for a start in marketing research, and would like to reach her in this regard, please write or call

Jane Maxwell   Izo Hall, Valhalla University   Kent, Ohio
412 346-6500

Figure 42
An alternative format is a "horizontal" résumé. (The standard $8^1/_2'' \times 11''$ sheet is simply turned on its side.)

ALEX M. HARPER

Experience

Department Supervisor, TRW Systems (Manufacturing Engineering and Processes Dept.), Redondo Beach, California. . . . May 1978 to the present. Responsible for obtaining, scheduling and overseeing work assignments of 30 engineering and support personnel. Also responsible for reconciling Department budgets.

Engineering Writer, TRW Systems (Integrated Logistics Dept.), Redondo Beach, California . . . . May 1970 to May 1975. Responsible for writing and updating technical manuals on classified spacecraft and military projects. "Secret" security clearance.

Engineering Writer, Stromberg-Carlson (Technical Publications Group), El Segundo, California . . . . August 1969 to May 1970. Responsible for writing and updating Air Force Technical Orders and the Launch Enabling and Communications Systems on the TRITON III Project.

Education

Bachelor of Science in Electronics, California State University at Long Beach, January 1976. Completed the program at night while working full-time at TRW.

Associate of Arts in Electronics, and Radio Technician's Certificate, El Redondo Junior College, El Redondo, Claifornia, June 1969.

Presently enrolled in California State University, Dominguez Hills "Portal" Program leading to the Master's Degree in Business Administration. Projected date of graduation: December 1981.

Have also taken special courses in data programming and computer applications at the Ramstead Technical Institute, Los Angeles, California.

Personal Data

Born in Cincinnati, Ohio, April 14, 1949. Played high school basketball and tennis, and was elected to student government. Am presently director of the Turtle Rock (Redondo Beach) Community Investment Club; and American Youth Soccer coach.

2384 Del Amo Street   Redondo Beach, California 98761   (213) 912-0027

The Covering Letter

The other half of an application package is the résumé's *covering letter.*

The résumé, if effectively constructed, presents a detailed, factual, and largely impersonal view of your pertinent history. It tells what you have done to qualify for the employment you seek. The function of the accompanying letter is to give your reader a more subjective and personal view by revealing your motives, your goals, something of your personality, and — perhaps most important of all — your ability to express yourself. If résumé and letter effectively complement one another, the reader gets from the application an impressive "total picture" of you as a job-applicant.

More specifically, any covering letter you write must perform these functions:

1. It must introduce you and state your specific reason for writing — your interest in a particular position in the reader's organization.

2. It must highlight your background by mentioning your major qualifications; then relate that background to the job being sought (when possible), and finally invite the reader to consider the details in the résumé.

3. It must ask specifically for the response you desire: *an interview for the job.* Not one employer in a hundred will offer a job without first seeing you; consequently, you would appear naive if you were to ask directly for the job.

The whole thrust of the letter, as well as of the résumé it introduces, must be to explain what you can do for the company.

Although the same résumé can be sent to a number of companies, each application package requires its own individualized covering letter. The letter should be addressed *by name* to the person in the company responsible for screening applicants — either the personnel manager or the head of the department you hope to work in. Letters addressed simply to *Personnel Director* or *Sales Manager* usually won't get the time of day. Specific names and job titles can be found in company pamphlets and directories, or through college placement offices, or simply by requesting the information over the phone or in a letter like the following:

Public Relations Office
Republic Can Company
2121 Terrell Boulevard
Houston, Texas 50011

Gentlemen:

I'd like very much to send a résumé in application for a position with your firm. May I please have the name and title of the officer responsible for selecting new assistants in product research. Your help will be sincerely appreciated.

Very truly yours,

Ted Newman

Ted Newman

I can't stress enough how important it is for the job seeker to do this kind of research. You must know as much as you can, practically speaking, about the company you wish to apply to. And you must, without being flagrant about it, reflect this knowledge in your covering letter. If you show your ignorance about the company you're writing to, you stand little chance of a favorable response.

Remember, too, that your covering letter will show its reader your ability (or inability) to communicate fluently. And the value that executives place on the ability to express ideas dynamically and clearly can't be stressed enough.

Here's an example of a well-written covering letter to accompany the Adam Pierce résumé back in Figure 38.

Demmler Hall
Valhalla University
Kent, Ohio 26780
February 28, 198_

Mr. Carleton F. Goodfellow
Director of Personnel
National Motors, Inc.
5000 Washington Highway
Deerfield, Michigan 30742

Dear Mr. Goodfellow:

As graduation approaches, I would like very much to apply for a position in this year's Executive Training Program at National Motors. My Valhalla degree will be in Industrial Engineering. I will finish in the top 10% of my class.

For the past three summers, I've been employed on the staff of the Cleveland Boy's Club Camp. During the first two years, I served as a counselor. Last summer I became a supervisor responsible for fourteen counselors and their campers. The enclosed résumé will give you fuller details of this experience and the rest of my background.

With my Bachelor's Degree only months away, I see this year as a time of beginning. The career beginning which interests me most is one with National Motors. May I hear from you regarding my qualifications, and come to Deerfield at your convenience for an interview?

Sincerely yours,

Adam Pierce

Adam Pierce

The letter is fairly brief, yet complete. It is articulate, and it seems to reveal a warm and sensible personality. Pierce's letter possesses a delicate balance between *self-confidence* and *modesty*, a balance so many applicants fail to achieve. Had he blatantly proclaimed his qualifications he would have sounded, in writing, like a pompous braggart. These qualifications must be expressed, but with restraint and (at least seeming) humility. One writing specialist has put it this way:

> The man who says, "I have spent fifteen years studying the problems of juvenile delinquency in such cities as New York, Chicago, and Los Angeles," will do more to establish his qualifications than the man who says, "My thoroughgoing studies of the problems of juvenile delinquency in many parts of the country have com-

pletely discredited the half-baked notions of those who have investigated the problems with more zeal than wisdom." The man who jingles his Phi Beta Kappa key usually stirs up more resentment than confidence.

Take a closer look in Figure 43 at the techniques Pierce uses in his covering letter.

Figure 43
A detailed analysis of a good application covering letter.

Pierce follows the recommended pattern for an application covering letter.

Dear Mr. Goodfellow:

As graduation approaches, I would like very much to apply for a position in this year's Executive Training Program at National Motors. My Valhalla degree will be in Industrial Engineering. I will finish at the top 10% of my class.

For the past three summers, I've been employed on the staff of the Cleveland Boy's Club Camp. During the first two years, I served as a counselor. Last summer I became a supervisor responsible for fourteen counselors and their campers. The enclosed resume will give you fuller details of this experience and the rest of my background.

With my bachelor's degree only months away, I see this year as a time of beginning. The career beginning which interests me most is one with National Motors. May I hear from you regarding my qualifications, and come to Deerfield at your convenience for an interview?

Sincerely yours,

Adam Pierce

Adam Pierce

. . . First he indicates his purpose for writing . . .

Here, a really important idea is given its own isolated sentence.

Notice the extra detail to emphasize an attractive fact in Pierce's background, i.e., his supervisory experience.

. . . Then, he highlights his background, making sure to mention its most impressive features. . .

After highlighting his background, Pierce makes explicit reference to the detailed résumé.

Notice how Pierce injects a note of personal aspiration into the letter. Employers do want more than college degrees and experience in their applicants. They want seriously motivated human beings.

. . . And, in closing, he asks for the specific response he desires.

Pierce strikes a nice balance in this letter between *confidence* and *humility*.

One of the difficulties many applicants have in writing covering letters is avoiding beginning every sentence with the pronoun I. Notice that by using opening modifiers, passive construction, and one interrogative sentence, Pierce avoids the "I-opener" in nine of his ten sentences.

Here's another well-written covering letter, this one by Laura Edmondson, who recently completed her associate of arts degree in legal stenography at a junior college. Her résumé accompanying this letter was shown back in Figure 39 on page 346.

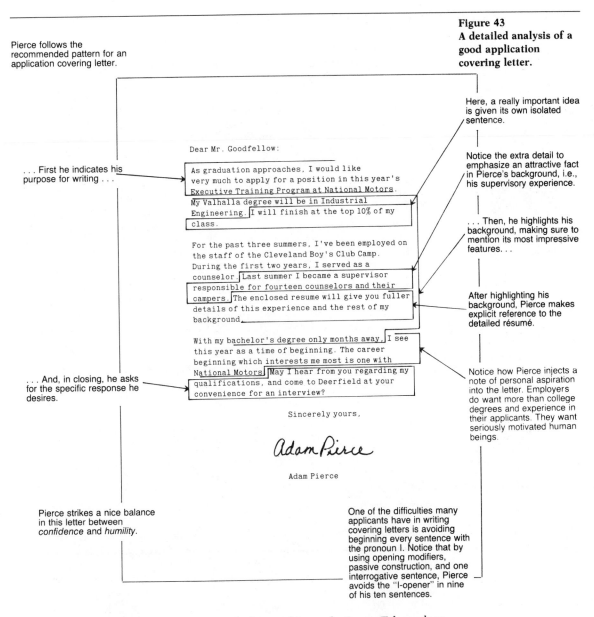

August 25, 198_

Mr. Daniel Levin, Attorney-at-Law
Pearle, Corman, Bishop, Levin & Dilworthy
80 Lomita Canyon Boulevard--Suite 7630
Beverly Hills, California 92025

Dear Mr. Levin:

Edith Winters informs me of an opening in your secretarial staff, a position for which I should very much like to become a candidate.

I understand that you need a legal secretary with rapid stenographic skill and the ability to handle a large volume of correspondence. Along with my degree in legal stenography from Foothill Junior College, I have four years of secretarial experience in retail dry goods and in insurance. My shorthand speed is 145 words per minute. On my present job, I handle between forty and sixty letters every day. Both at Foothill and on the job, I have had training sufficient to prepare me to handle the full range of secretarial responsibilities with minimum supervision.

My present job at Southwestern Life & Indemnity has been quite satisfactory; but, having taken my degree recently, I seek the further challenges and rewards of a top-flight legal firm. Miss Winters' enthusiasm for her work assures me I'd like the job. Hopefully, the enclosed résumé will help interest the firm in me.

I can be in Los Angeles for an interview any afternoon convenient for you. May I look forward to speaking with you about the position you have available?

Yours sincerely,

Laura Edmondson

Laura Edmondson

Once again we have a covering letter that does its job well. It introduces its author by stating her purpose in the first sentence. It highlights her major qualifications for the job. And it makes its request for an interview directly and specifically. The tone of the letter is sufficiently confident, but not overly so.

Several further precautions should be taken in writing a covering letter.

Make sure the letter is neither too long nor too short. Pierce's letter, at 145 words, is concise yet full enough to communicate a personality as well as facts. Miss Edmondson's, at 193 words, is also concise, allowing for her slightly greater experience. Unless you have a lot of relevant work experience, you should keep your covering letter to a maximum of 200 to 225 words. Too long a letter gives the reader a feeling of time's being wasted with details that should have been confined to the résumé. And because a covering letter is about one's self, the longer it is, the more you risk sounding self-centered. On the other hand, too brief a letter will make you seem in a hurry to get just *any* job — not very appealing to a prospective employer.

Avoid the awkward, stiff-sounding opening that mars so many application letters. Your first sentence is just like the first impression you make when you enter someone's office. It requires poise. It should be direct, clear, and positive in tone. And it's this first sentence that applicants generally find hardest to write. Figure 44 catalogs a number of ways in which both inexperienced applicants and experienced job-changers can open an application letter fluently.

Avoid beginning every sentence with the subject pronoun *I*. You've got use to it, of course; after all, you're writing about yourself. But repeating it too often, especially at the front of your sentences, gives it undue emphasis.

Don't ask questions about the job in your letter. Learn as much as you can about the position you seek *before* you write the letter, so that your letter sounds knowledgeable. There's time enough to ask questions when you're interviewed.

Neither should you express a lot of opinion in your letter. As far as its reader is concerned, the letter's purpose is factual: to show how your background qualifies you for the job. Opinions are extraneous, and can be irritating when out of place.

In trying to enhance your apparent job potential, don't make the mistake of proclaiming that you have experience "working with people." It's trite. Almost any job — except perhaps that of night watchman or gravedigger — involves some personal interaction, and employers know it.

Unless you've been asked, it's usually not wise to mention a desired salary in your covering letter. And do not mention any dissatisfaction with a present position (except perhaps to indicate that it provides insufficient opportunity for the professional growth you desire). Confine your letter to statements that will make the most favorable first impression, and wait until the interview or further correspondence to discuss these other matters.

Don't waste space (or the reader's time) by stating things that are self-evident. Such comments as "Because you are the largest company in the industry . . ." or "My experience as a market research analyst is evidence of statistical proficiency" are obvious space wasters. In addition, the first sounds like blatant flattery, and the second implies that the reader can't see the connection for himself.

As always, mechanical errors and sloppiness must be avoided. Most employers quickly discard applications that appear careless, and respond with a polite "Sorry, nothing available."

Do *not,* when you mail an application package, include a self-addressed reply envelope. That device is strictly for sales writers who might otherwise not get replies.

Make no mistake about the purpose of the application package. It is a tool of maximum self-enhancement, an "advertisement for one's self." Everything that you say in the letter and the résumé should contribute to your image as a strong job candidate. Everything that does not contribute should be omitted — unless, of course, the omission would call attention to itself, and imply that you're avoiding something.

Figure 44
Sample openers for application covering letters. With only minor modification, any of these openings could be used in a wide variety of job-application covering letters.

A Catalog of Openers

1. I should like to be considered an applicant for National Motors Executive Training Program.
2. I would like (very much) to apply for a spot as a National Motors Executive Trainee.
3. May I please be considered for a position in the National Motors Executive Training Program this June?
4. I feel that my background and education, as shown on the enclosed résumé, should qualify me for consideration as an applicant to National Motors Executive Training program.
5. I write to inquire into the possibility of a position in National Motors Executive Training Program this coming June.
6. Mr. John Barker of your Product Development Lab has informed me of openings in National Motors Executive Training Program this year. May I apply?
7. My honors degree in industrial engineering and my one year's experience in a supervisory capacity should, I feel, qualify me as an applicant to this year's Executive Training Program at National Motors.
8. A position in National Motors Executive Training Program is my goal. May I, with this letter and résumé, be considered an applicant?
9. Will you please consider my enclosed résumé in application for National Motors Executive Training Program?
10. As a June graduate of Valhalla University with a major in industrial engineering, I should like to apply for a position as a National Motors Executive Trainee.
11. With the scarcity of really good openings for college graduates, I would like to get my application in early for a spot in National Motors Executive Training Program.
12. Should openings exist, I'd like very much to be considered a candidate for this year's Executive Training Program at National Motors.
13. Challenge, and the chance for steady advancement in responsibility are what I seek as an honors graduate in industrial engineering. These prospects seem attainable in the Executive Training Program at National Motors. May I be considered for a position in the Program this June?
14. I am an engineering graduate with a record of achievement, and am eager for the chance to work in an environment where achievement is a daily expectation. Hence this application to National Motors.
15. I am an experienced industrial engineer with a record of achievement, and am eager for the chance . . . (same as above).
16. With both experience and academic training in industrial management, I should like to apply for a position as management trainee at National Motors.
17. Just this week I have read with great interest, in the current issue of Chemical Age, that Dr. James Harmer of your Research and Development Division is conducting research into the problems of Beta-ray refraction and its industrial applications. My senior research project here at Valhalla University has also concentrated upon these problems, under the direction of Dr. Hans J. Neeley. I should like very much to explore the possibilities of coming to work for National Motors in Dr. Harmer's Division after I complete the B.S. degree requirements this coming June.

A WORD TO JOB CHANGERS

The task of preparing an effective application package is not substantially different for an experienced person seeking a change of position than it is for the graduate seeking a good first job. The experienced applicant generally gets "leads" on new job openings from a variety of sources; friends and associates in business often pass along such news by word of mouth. This kind of "inside connection" can often be useful in opening an application letter: remember how Laura Edmondson used her friend's name to break the ice in her letter several pages back.

The résumé of an experienced applicant will also differ somewhat — primarily by showing its experience block first, and carrying more detail than the education block, as Alex Harper's résumé does in Figure 40. Had Harper's experience been much more extensive, he would justifiably have used a two-page résumé.

All the other "rules" we've looked at so far can be applied just as well to applications by experienced job changers as to those of younger college graduates and near-graduates.

SOLICITED APPLICATIONS

As you know, many jobs do come looking for applicants in the daily classified ads, in professional journals, through listings at private and state employment agencies, and through college placement bureaus (one such recruitment effort was illustrated in Figure 35 back on page 311). Responding to these solicitations is, in one sense, easy, because each of the desired qualifications is spelled out; you know just what you have to say in your letter and résumé. But in another sense, a solicited application is difficult, because it invariably faces a lot of competition.

In responding to a job notice, your best tool is still the two-part application package (unless, of course, some other format is requested by the employer). Your covering letter should differ only slightly from an unsolicited one: its first sentence should refer specifically to the employer's solicitation. You might open the covering letter of a solicited application as follows:

> Gentlemen:
>
> Your advertisement in Sunday's Los Angeles Times has prompted me to apply for the position of administrative assistant with your company.

or:

> I believe that my education and experience qualify me for the opening of administrative assistant you advertised in Sunday's Times.

or:

> I feel I can be the aggressive sales representative for whom you advertised in Sunday's Times.

Your covering letter should refer directly to *each* of the requested qualifications. Suppose you found yourself interested in this ad;

An Opening Next Month for
an INTERNAL AUDITOR

Want young college grad with accounting major to train as an Internal Auditor with international corporation based in San Francisco. Excellent opening for a personable young man or woman with ability, ambition, and executive aptitude. Experience helpful, but not essential. Employee benefits highest in the industry. Write stating full qualifications and salary requirements––Times 2R6903

In replying to this ad, you should refer specifically to your accounting degree; your accounting experience (if you've had any); your desire to work for an international corporation in San Francisco; and your ability, ambition, and executive aptitude (unpretentiously, of course). The best way to respond regarding salary requirements is to state a reasonable figure, and add that beginning salary is less important than opportunities for growth and advancement. Of course, if you *do* require some minimum salary — and the solicitation has asked you to state it — you should.

If you don't possess the qualifications requested, you probably won't be considered for the job. But if you're not sure whether you do, your best bet is to apply; you have nothing to lose.

Even if you have a prepared résumé, it's generally wise when writing a solicited application to construct a new one, one in which you stress precisely those qualifications the employer seeks.

FOLLOW-UP COMMUNICATIONS

After a job interview, most applicants go home and quietly await the good or bad news, ignoring the psychological advantage to be obtained from an effective follow-up letter, one which expresses appreciation for having been given the opportunity of an interview, reexpresses a desire for the job, and reasserts the self-confidence necessary to handle it. Here's a good example:

Dear Mr. Goodfellow:

Just a brief note of thanks for the many courtesies shown me during my interview on Monday. Seeing National Motors from the inside has, as I said then, made the Executive Training Program all the more attractive to me.

Incidentally, I located a copy of Michaelson's The Corporate Tempo and found his chapter on training programs as eye-opening as you did.

Needless to say, my fingers are crossed looking forward to hearing from you. After Monday's meeting, I am confident I can bring to the program the energy and ability necessary for success at National Motors.

Sincerely,

Adam Pierce

Both the courtesy and the initiative shown by Pierce in this follow-up letter are bound to impress Goodfellow. And Pierce's attempt in the second paragraph to show that he profited from the interview may give him an edge over competing candidates. It certainly won't hurt his chances.

Whenever you've had an interview with an organization that you'd like to work for, you'd be foolish not to follow up with a well-written letter of thanks.

IN CONCLUSION

Persuasive technique is the key, then, to writing a successful job application. You are trying, in an application package, to persuade its recipients to consider you for a job. The package, as a persuasive communication, must take its readers through the persuasive process just like any other kind of persuasive message.

First, it must capture and sustain attention. Capturing attention is fairly easy; employers are always on the lookout for new talent. Sustaining it, though, is another matter. Sloppy appearance or a dull beginning will quickly make readers uninterested in whatever you have to offer. Hence, the need for a neat, attractive format and a personable style.

The main objective in any application package is making its readers want to see you. They know they will profit from interviewing promising candidates, but they've got to be shown that *you* have that promise. The two-part format of the application package allows them to get, first, a quick view of your potential, by reading the highlights of your background in the covering letter; then, if the letter is impressive, they'll turn to the résumé, not in a neutral frame of mind, but rather looking forward to the detailed description of your background.

If the details in your résumé confirm what the covering letter has promised about your potential, and if an opening exists, you will receive a favorable reply. The employer will probably call you in for an interview, or ask you first to supply further information about yourself. In either case, your letter and résumé have done their job.

Remember that although the application package is your first communication with a prospective employer, it is the *last* one over which you have complete control. If it succeeds, and you become a candidate, all subsequent communications with that employer will involve answering questions put to you. When you write an unsolicited package, no one has asked any questions. You are free to say whatever you want, to make as favorable a first impression as you can.

When you go for the interview, be prepared to let the interviewer do most of the talking at first; be ready to answer any questions that might be asked about your résumé or about you in general. Be prepared also to ask some questions of your own, questions that will further your knowledge of the company, and at the same time reflect your intelligence, your adaptability to new situations, and your prior knowledge of the company and its work. Having accomplished all this, your goal will be in sight — an offer to work for the company. (In Chapter 20, we'll discuss more thoroughly the techniques and pitfalls of the job interview.)

PROBLEMS

1. Decide (tentatively at least) upon some particular kind of job you'd like to get upon graduating. Then, on a worksheet, answer each of the questions about yourself and that job objective that appears on pages 340–341. Be prepared to submit your worksheet to your instructor as he or she requests.

2. Write a personal résumé that would be suitable for inclusion in any job application package you might write upon graduating. If you're not yet in your last year, assume that you are, so that you can offer yourself to a prospective employer as a degree holder. Make sure this résumé is as attractive and as potentially effective as you can make it.

3. Select the kind of job you'd like to be seeking as you approach graduation, and write an effective covering letter to accompany your résumé. Address this letter to the appropriate person in the company you are writing to. (If you are making up a hypothetical addressee, be as specific as you would be if this were a real application package.)

4. Select from the newspaper, or from an appropriate industry periodical, the advertisement for the job that sounds most appealing to you. Write an effective application package in pursuit of that job. As in problem 2, assume that you are in your last year of school. Remember that this is a solicited application. Your résumé *should*, and your covering letter *must*, make specific reference to the job offered.

5. In a well-written memo to your instructor, comment on and evaluate the suggested openings for covering letters in Figure 44.

6. Last Friday you learned that a representative from International Products, Inc. (a firm you'd like to work for) was making an unscheduled visit to your campus placement center. You quickly arranged for an interview; met Mr. Halliburton, the IP representative; and expressed your interest in working for the firm (the specific kind of job is up to you). At the end of what seemed to be a mutually satisfying interview, Halliburton gave you a long application form and asked you to complete it and mail it to him "with an extensive covering letter expressing your plans and your short-range and long-range goals." He indicated that he'd be in touch with you within several weeks of receiving your letter and completed form.

Now your problem is to write that covering letter. Remember, this is not to be an ordinary covering letter. Halliburton wants a good deal of specific information. It's obvious he also wants to see how well you express yourself in writing at length.

7. Assume that it is January, and that you would like to work as a camp counselor this coming summer. You spot an advertisement in *The Herald*, your local paper, which asks for applicants for the position of camp counselor to supervise athletics (or crafts and hobbies, or music, or modern dance, or any other specialty that you like) at a coed camp in the Rocky Mountains. The ad asks all applicants to reply to Box 100, *The Herald*.

Write an effective application package in pursuit of this job.

8. Here's the kind of problem a college senior might confront while seeking a prime first job. Assume that you have sent an application package to the American Corporation seeking a position as ______________(you pick the job) beginning in June after graduation. It is now March. The company's personnel director, Mr. Carter Marvin, has called you in for an interview.

On the designated day, you enter the reception room at American and introduce yourself to the receptionist. You are asked to take a seat. Mr. Marvin's secretary comes out and says that he will see you in twenty minutes. "While you're waiting," she says, "Mr. Marvin would like you to write a brief autobiography, a statement pertinent to your application for a position here. The statement will become part of your application." She hands you pen and paper, smiles, and goes back into the office.

Take a look at the clock and, in no more than twenty minutes, handwrite an impressive autobiographical statement for Mr. Marvin.

9. As the personnel manager for Cooperton & Sons of Minneaplois, you run the following brief ad in the classified section of the *Minneapolis Gazette:*

SECRETARY — Young, ambitious, and capable secretary needed. Apply by mail, stating qualifications. Cooperton & Sons, 860 Park Row, Minneapolis.

One of the first responses you receive is the following letter:

218 S. 48th St.
Minneapolis, Minn.
Oct. 4, 198_

Cooperton & Sons
86 Park Row
Minneapolis

Gentlemen:

I saw your ad in the Gazette and I would like to apply for the position as advertised. I was born in Bimidji, and went to school there. After school I worked for my father who is a public accountant in Bimidji. Then I came to Minneapolis where I took a stenographic position and some junior college courses in secretarial science. I would be prepared to have an interview at any time.

Yours very truly,

Sally Knithouse

What is your reaction to this application? Ascertain all the reasons for your reaction.

10. Here's a job-seeking problem that most college graduates would love to be faced with. Assume that you have applied to five different corporations for a job upon graduation (in whatever capacity suits your background and your preferences). As a result of well-written application packages, you receive invitations for interviews from three of the companies: Larkin-Bell, Inc.; General American; and Consolidated Hoffman. You have the three interviews, and each of them comes off smoothly.

As a result of the interviews and what you know about the companies, you decide that you would most like to work for Larkin-Bell, with General American your second choice, and Consolidated Hoffman a close third. Three days ago, you received a letter from the personnel director at General American offering you the position for which you applied, and requesting that you reply within ten days. Today, three days have passed and you've received no further mail. You would still prefer to work for Larkin-Bell, but you do not want to lose the offer at General American. So you decide to write a letter to Robert Markham, the personnel manager at Larkin-Bell, informing him of your predicament and your preference. Write it.

11. After consulting with an advisor in your major field of study and with your college's placement office, compile a list of at least ten prospective employers to whom you could send a well-written application package as you approach graduation. Try your best to determine that each of them generally has openings for people with your kind of background and professional desires. And make each entry on your list as specific as possible: include not only the name of the company (or organization) but its complete address and the name and title of the person to whom you will be addressing your application.

PART FOUR

REPORT WRITING

CHAPTER 15

PLANNING THE BUSINESS REPORT

One day long ago, it dawned on a man that his business affairs had become too broad for him to keep a constant watch over. He needed help. So he delegated someone, probably his eldest son, to oversee a part of those affairs, and keep him informed about what was happening. This the son did and gradually he came to know as much about that part of the business as his father (maybe more). When the father saw this, he gave his son the added responsibility of interpreting what he observed: of determining how events were affecting that part of the business. When the son proved able to do this as well, he was given the even greater responsibility of recommending the best ways to protect and further those interests. As time passed, these business interests expanded, and the son, like the father, needed help. More assistants were chosen and made responsible for observing, interpreting, and recommending. And somewhere along the line (probably quite early), to ensure accuracy and completeness, these assistants were asked to put their observations, interpretations, and recommendations down on paper (or stone). When this happened, the business report was born.

Reports today still serve the three functions they did long ago. They all convey fact. Some reports also interpret the facts they convey. And some also make recommendations in light of those interpretations.

In all but the smallest of businesses, no one person can do all the work. Others must be enlisted to bear responsibility. And the efforts of these people must be coordinated. Without coordination the business could not run smoothly and meet its objectives. The business report is one of the major means by which those efforts are coordinated.

Consider, for example, the job of Tom Preston, sales manager for a large New York manufacturer. He directs a team of eighty sales people spread across the nation, plus a support staff of forty-five secretaries and stenographers. Each day he must supervise the efforts of these 125 people. And he must coordinate those efforts with the policies, goals, and priorities set by top management, and with the plans of his fellow managers in production, advertising, product development, and accounting (all of whom, of course, have their own large staffs and their own responsibilities to top management). Preston really earns his sixty thousand!

Or consider the job of Marjorie Dietrich, chief administrative officer of a large state agency. Her boss is His Honor, the Governor, a high-powered chief executive who is responsible to four million voters and is constantly hounded by legislators whose interests differ from his own. Marjorie Dietrich has a staff of 173 — administrators, field representatives, secretaries, and maintenance personnel — in seven district offices across the state. Her task of coordination is as large as Preston's — and her salary smaller.

Both Tom Preston and Marjorie Dietrich are "professionals"; they hold their jobs because they're intelligent and have great executive skills. Yet it would be impossible for them to do their jobs without a constant flow of reliable information from other people, and without providing their own share of information to the overall effort. They must write reports. And they must depend upon the well-written reports of other writers.

That's what the next four chapters are all about: the well-written business report. Matters of precision and style, of course, we've already discussed, at length, in Chapters 1 through 4. Good writing is good writing whether you find it in a business document, a TV script, or on the back of a cereal box. But there are special talents that are vital to writing good business reports. Reports, unlike letters, are not primarily intended to evoke reactions; they transmit *facts* (often in great detail) and they frequently give unbiased interpretations of those facts. That isn't easy. Reports, like letters, also perform a variety of functions; but unlike letters they can use a great variety of formats. A business report also entails, on the average, much more preparation than a letter. It's no exaggeration to refer to the writing of a business report as a "project."

So in the chapters that follow, we'll examine the special knowledge required of you when you write a business report — and the special demands that the process makes on you. In this chapter we begin by surveying the vast variety of business reports and looking at the early stages of the report-writing process. Chapters 16 and 17 continue our look at this process. And Chapter 18 examines the finished product — the well-written, well-structured business report.

THE VARIETIES OF BUSINESS REPORT

One of the first problems facing newcomers to business is the confusing variety of report types. There are so many — *progress* reports and *special* reports, *preliminary* and *periodic* reports, *recommendation* reports, *investigation* reports, *initiative* reports, *inspection* reports, and so on. The sheer number can make a trainee's head spin. In truth, however, it's only the terminology that confuses. Once that's learned, it poses no problem, and the early confusion disappears.[1]

Let's look at some of the more important distinctions among reports.

Where Reports Go

Reports, once they leave a writer's hands, can move *up, across, down,* or *outside of* the organization. Those that move within the organization are called *internal* or *administrative* reports. The majority of these move upward, to people like Tom Preston and Marjorie Dietrich who must be kept informed of all work in progress and of any problems that arise within the scope of their authority.

Reports that move across an organizational structure can move at any level — from vice-president to vice-president, from department head to department head, from specialist to specialist, from file clerk to file clerk. The head of accounting might, for example, report to the sales manager on patterns of delinquency in customer payments. The sales manager might report to accounting on special credit provisions being granted to customers to maintain, or increase, the size of their accounts.

Reports directed downward — from executives to their subordinates, or to the staff in general — provide information that subordinates need to perform their jobs, or to keep them abreast of the "larger picture." (More and more executives are seeing this latter function as important to morale and operational efficiency.)

Many organizations also prepare reports for people on the outside. Law firms, advertising agencies, and brokerage houses (to cite just a few obvious examples) must submit reports to their clients. Colleges and universities must compile reports for regional accrediting agencies. Defense contractors like the Rand Corporation or Rockwell International write many reports to the federal government, as well as to their subcontractors. These reports are sometimes referred to as *external* reports.

Periodic and Special Reports

Periodic reports are those written at regular intervals to provide a scheduled flow of information. Hourly stock market reports, daily sales reports, weekly expense reports, monthly payroll or production reports, quarterly reports on committee activities, annual budget reports — these are just a few examples. Hourly, daily, or weekly reports are also called *routine* reports; virtually everyone in business or government must write them.

Equally vital are *special* reports — reports that are written not routinely but whenever a need for information emerges. A problem develops, an accident occurs, a crisis arises — someone in charge needs to know all about it, and a special report is written.

Initiative Reports

Initiative reports are those written because the writer desires to do so (that is, they are written upon the writer's own initiative). An employee detects a bottleneck in the company's operation and, on her own initiative, reports her observations to the executive most immediately concerned. Or a sales representative finds a new technique for getting customers to buy more product, and, without

[1] This initial confusion over terminology can be illustrated by the people who, upon entering business, think a "memorandum" is some kind of a reminder.

being asked, explains his idea in a report to his sales manager. A research chemist discovers a new formula with industrial application; he reports his findings to his project chief in an initiative report.

Although most reports in industry are authorized by someone in charge, or are required by standard company procedure, those submitted at a writer's own initiative are often among the most important.[2]

Reports Classified by Format

Long reports and *short* reports, *formal* and *informal* reports, *memorandum* reports, *letter* reports, and *form* reports — all are terms classifying reports by format. As such, these terms have little to do with the actual content of the report.

The terms *long* and *short* are obviously references to length. How long a report must be to be *long* is really moot, but the length of a report does usually dictate whether or not supplementary sections like indexes or tables of contents are needed. (We'll discuss these elements when we examine report formats in Chapter 18.) Length is also a factor in scheduling a report project (a process we'll discuss later in this chapter).

Closely related to the *long-short* distinction is that between *formal* and *informal* reports. A formal report is one that includes most of the supplementary sections and features we have come to associate with long, important reports: durable bindings, title pages, prefaces, letters of transmittal, tables of contents, bibliographies, and the like. A wise report writer will construct a formal report whenever the report's appearance, as well as its contents, must impress its readers. Informal reports, like those directed to fellow workers or those written on short notice, usually don't have most of these formal, supplementary elements. Don't make the mistake, though, of thinking that informality means a lack of care — it doesn't.

Memorandum reports are usually brief — anywhere from several lines to several pages long — informal in nature, and written in memorandum format. *Letter* reports are reports that employ the business letter format, usually to transmit relatively brief information outside the organization. *Form* reports are reports whose formats are determined not by the writer, but by lines, boxes, designations, and questions imprinted on the paper. Needless to say, though format of a form report is fixed, the writer is no less obligated to complete it accurately and fully.

Reports Classified by Subject Matter and Information Source

Perhaps the most obvious report classifications are those by subject matter. *Engineering* reports, *economic* reports, *sales* reports, *accounting* reports — these are subject matter designations. Within an accountancy firm you will find *budget* reports, *tax* reports, *audit* reports, and *cost* reports — again, subject matter designations.

Reports are also labeled according to where their writers got the needed information. *Field* reports, as the term implies, are based on data obtained on

[2] Among history's most vivid examples of initiative reports was one received unexpectedly by President Franklin Roosevelt in August 1939. Written by Albert Einstein, the report revealed for the first time to Roosevelt the awesome potential of atomic energy as a weapon of war. He heeded the report.

Unheeded in the 1960s and early 70s were a number of initiative reports that warned of increasing American dependence on foreign petroleum, and of the economic leverage this gave to foreign producers.

a job site. *Laboratory* reports carry data derived experimentally in the lab. *Survey* reports or *interview* reports are those based on information obtained by asking questions. And *library* reports, familiar to every college student, are those based on information uncovered in the library.

Procedures and Manuals

A *procedure* (when the term is used to refer to a kind of business document) is a step-by-step explanation of the way to *proceed* in doing a specific task. (There's an example of a well-written procedure on pages 441–442.) Procedures, once written, are often brought together into a *manual* that gives employees a handy one-volume source of answers to the common question: "How do I do this?"

Project Reports

Several kinds of reports arise out of special projects or campaigns. For example, a market research firm doing a survey for a client might submit a series of project reports to that client. First would come a *preliminary* report on how the project is being prepared, what kinds of results it should accomplish, and how the necessary personnel are being recruited and trained. Once the project is under way, a series of periodic *progress* reports (or *status* reports) would follow. At project's end, the firm would submit a *final* report revealing the survey's findings, interpreting those findings, and probably making recommendations.

Investigation and Inspection Reports

After something significant has happened to an organization — perhaps one of its planes has crashed or one of its products has developed a safety problem — someone (usually a task force or an ad hoc investigating committee) will be asked to determine how and why it happened. When their task is complete, their findings will be presented in an *investigation* report.

Organizations also need information on routine, ongoing processes — so as to identify strengths and weaknesses in the process. Anything from the efficiency of a warehouse loading system to the quality and scope of a university curriculum is subject to periodic inspection by the people responsible for its performance. Such findings are compiled into *inspection* reports.

Agenda, Resolutions, Minutes, and Proceedings

Business organizations depend heavily on meetings and conferences to coordinate the efforts of their staff and associates. From meetings, and the necessity for them, arise several types of business report.

One is the *agenda*, a document written prior to a meeting for the benefit of those attending. It lists, in scheduled order, the topics to be discussed at the meeting; in this way it gives structure to the meeting and helps participants prepare for it. Sometimes, an agenda is made "binding" — only topics listed in it are allowed for discussion. More often though, agenda are tentative and open-ended. (A typical agenda for a business meeting appears in Figure 45.)

Resolutions are brief reports which formally announce a consensus or a group intention that was decided upon in a meeting. Those attending a meeting may "resolve" to do any number of things — endorse, condemn, propose, commit a matter to restudy. Resolutions often, but not always, take that unmistakable form: *Whereas* __________, *Whereas* __________, *Whereas* __________; *it is hereby Resolved that* __________. But substance and clarity are more important than any rigid form.

Figure 45
A sample agenda.

CALIFORNIA STATE UNIVERSITY, DOMINGUEZ HILLS
SCHOOL OF MANAGEMENT

SCHOOL FACULTY MEETING, THURSDAY, SEPTEMBER 18, 19--
2:00 - 3:30 ERC B-118 ("LIBRARY THEATRE")

Tentative Agenda

1. Introduction of new faculty
2. School of Management: Plans for the Year
3. New Building Status: Hastings Office Building, Management Lab. Building
4. Faculty Office Changes Made for the New Academic Year.
5. 1980-81 School Budgets as Allocated to Departments:

   OE Budget
   Travel Budgets (In-State, Out-of-State)
   Equipment Budgets
   Student Assistant Budgets
6. Election of Chairpersons of School Committees: Caucuses suggested immediately after School meeting
7. Election of Replacement Member for School Curriculum Committee (Slate to come from Com. on Nominations and Elections)
8. Status Report on Management External B.A. and M.A. Programs (Frances Wilson)
9. Registration and Advisement: Mon., Tues., Wed., Sept. 22 - 24 (Lyle Perkins)
10. Night and Saturday Classes: Night Advisement for Majors and Minors
11. Faculty Research: Rockefeller Fund, NMA Summer Stipends, etc .
12. Summer Session 19--: Proposals for Foreign Travel Study (handout to come)
13. Verification of Class Rosters (End of 3rd Week Census)
14. Announcements by Department or Program Chairpersons

Minutes are the official report of a meeting as it transpired. At their most comprehensive, minutes are a verbatim record of everything said and done at the meeting. Most minutes, though, are less extensive — including only the time, date, place, and purpose of the meeting, and noting all reports submitted to it, all motions made, and how those motions were acted upon. (An example of well-written minutes appears in Figure 46. These minutes are loaded with abbreviations that might be unclear to outsiders; but remember, the minutes are intended for insiders' eyes only.)

More extensive reports of important meetings or conferences are called *proceedings* (not to be confused with *procedures*). *Proceedings* are long reports that include verbatim transcripts of all speeches and papers given at the meeting, all motions, resolutions, a detailed discussion of the purpose and background of the meeting, and sometimes even background information on the

Figure 46
Sample "minutes".

CALIFORNIA STATE UNIVERSITY
DOMINGUEZ HILLS

Academic Senate
Carson, California 90747

Minutes
April 18, 1980

Members Present: Simon, Baldwin, Desberg, Charnofsky, Danis, Dowling, Gray, Groff, Gutierrez, Hart, Hata, Hsuing, Jordain, Kidane, Kuykendall, McCarthy, Milgrim, Ouellette, Pyne, Reeves, Rosenthal, Seely, Wilcox, Schoenwald, Hitchcock, MacPhee, Harris, Wesley.

Members Absent: Bialosky, Cortez, Johnson, Lauerhass, Laws, C. W. Lee, K. Lee, Mahon, Poole, Schoen, Blischke, Gerth, Gilmore, Grenier.

Observers Present: Susan Harris, Jess Overall, Wayne Martin

1. a) Approval of Agenda
The agenda was approved with an amendment to add the following: Discussion of article in the Dominguez News, April 14, titled "Institutional Racism Charged at CSUDH". The item was designated "1-b".

Approval of Minutes - April 3, 1980
Minutes were approved with some editorial changes in Vice-President MacPhee's report.

b) Discussion of article in the Dominguez News, April 14, titled "Institutional Racism Charged at CSUDH".
This item was deferred until after the Time Certain Presentation.

9. Summer Session (Susan Harris, Jess Overall) Time Certain: 10:00 A.M. Susan Harris and Jess Overall were asked to report to the Senate on two aspects of Summer Session: Policies and Procedures for Setting Summer Session Salaries and Clarification of Summer Session Curriculum Approval Procedures.

The Chair stated that in the past there has been no communication between Summer Session administration and the Senate on the structure of summer session salaries. It has been perceived that salary

participants. The format of a *proceedings* report is usually formal, and meant to impress as well as inform.

Summaries and Abstracts

Summaries and *abstracts* are condensations of original reports, frequently only ten percent or less of the original's length. They are usually incorporated into a report at the beginning, to introduce the subsequent, more detailed discussion. But an abstract can also stand alone. Numerous professional journals (like *Chemical Abstracts* and *Economic Abstracts*) exist to publish nothing but abstracts of significant reports which have appeared elsewhere.

Although the distinction between abstracts and summaries is blurred, there is a difference. A summary writer condenses an original report from his

Figure 46 (continued)

-2-

"deals" were made and, seemingly, some schools were treated differently from others. Of particular concern is the issue of balancing salaries. If past practices are going to be changed, faculty would like to know how they are going to be changed and why.

Jess Overall replied that, basically, summer session salaries are set by the Chancellor's office; each professor is paid according to rank and the number of students enrolled in the class. The idea behind it is that summer session is totally self-supporting (no state funding); there is a certain amount of overhead cost involved, and, based on that assumption and the enrollment in the class, the instructor is paid a certain per cent and the rest goes to summer session to pay for administrative staffing. The instructor picks up about 75% of the income generated by a class. This is fairly standard.

Because one particular school not only meets minimum enrollments for faculty to be paid full salary, but also brings in excessive enrollment in many cases, something called "balancing" has been done schoolwide, so that faculty members whose classes didn't make the maximum enrollment were balanced with those whose classes exceeded enrollment. This has not penalized any other faculty member at the University, but it has recognized the fact that this particular school has enrollments far beyond expectations.

The Chair stated that when faculty are paid under the "break-even" rate, they are being paid as piece-work and that violates the principle of what they feel they do in the classroom. The work involved is not related to the numbers of students, except in terms of extremes. Faculty accept the piece-rate because they need the money, but that shouldn't be the driving principle for faculty salaries, even though the program must be self-supporting.

Jess Overall replied that whatever revenue is generated by a class, the minimum a faculty member would be paid would be 75%. Summer session does not arbitrarily close classes; they consult with the faculty member to see if he/she is willing to teach a class with a small enrollment.

The Chair recalled that the Senate approved that option about five years ago and that it was also approved by the Chancellor's office.

Another point raised was that in the case of a graduate seminar, most professors would not want more than 12 or 15 students in the class, yet if that were the total enrollment,

own point of view, while the abstract writer carefully maintains the viewpoint of the original writer. But summaries and abstracts are both written to provide the essence of a longer report to the busy reader — to the executive who hasn't the time or the need to read the original report, or to the interested researcher who wants to know if the full report would be worthwhile reading. (An example of an abstract appears in Figure 59 on page 457.)

Paper, Articles, Monographs, Reviews, Theses, and Dissertations

Papers, articles, monographs and *reviews* are reports intended for wide dissemination. The term *paper* is used most often for a report written by an expert to be read before a body of other experts. An *article* is a report written for publication in a periodical journal, usually offering its readers new data, new ideas, new analyses, or new perspectives on its subject. Like articles, *monographs* are

Figure 46 (continued)

-3-

the instructor would get only 1/2 or 3/5 of his/her salary. This is not the case in the regular session, and there is no reason why the summer session salaries should not be the sàme, which would be fair and equitable if someone were doing a graduate seminar. In addition, the issue of balancing should not be a matter for each individual school. It ought to be a campus-wide policy that all classes or enrollments are tossed in a hopper and professors paid, not according to the number of students in their classes, but on the overall students enrolled in the school for that summer divided by the number of faculty teaching. That would be the most equitable arrangement.

Susan Harris and Jess Overall stated that they realized there are legitimate pedagogical issues involved and also a reality that the program has to be self-supporting. Standards have to be reconciled with the realities of the program.

A motion was approved to form an ad hoc sub-committee of FPC to work with Summer Session administration to study the issues and that the committee report back to the Senate. Persons interested in serving on the committee should give their names to Abe Kidane or Sandy Wilcox. PASSED

In answer to the question regarding approval of summer programs, both Susan Harris and Vice President MacPhee (Chair of COPP) replied that programs which are not in the summer catalogue may not go through all the approval processes that programs do which are in the catalogue, but they do have to have the approval of the school dean. It was the sense of the Senate that there should be some form of standardization in this area, and the issue was referred to the Educational Policies Committee for study.

The issue of payment of faculty summer session salaries was raised, since some faculty reported that checks were not received until the following December. James Harris, Dean of Faculty/Staff Affairs, replied that it takes from four to six weeks after the paper work is in for a check to be issued; if the check has not been received at the end of six weeks, a salary advance may be requested.

Return to Agenda Item 1 (b)

1. (b) Discussion of article in the Dominguez News, April 14, titled "Institutional Racism Charged at CSUDH"

The following statement appeared in the above article and was attributed to a faculty member:

> "Most professors expose students of minority background to constant insults, humiliation, implied and expressed inferiority and grade them down a grade or two."

published reports by experts on particular topics; monographs, however, are usually longer than articles, and are not usually incorporated into journals — more often they take the format of a booklet or short book. A *review* is a report on some other published work, sometimes simply describing the work, at other times evaluating it.

Thesis and *dissertation* are terms that have become almost synonymous in American academic circles. Both refer to the long, formal report that typically culminates work for an advanced degree. In the United States, the *thesis* is commonly submitted for a master's degree while the *dissertation* is required for

Figure 46 (continued)

-4-

Motion was made that the Senate move to a committee of the whole to decide what response, if any, should be made to this article. PASSED

The majority of those present favored sending a letter to the student newspaper. The majority favored having the letter sent by the Senate rather than the Senate Chair. The majority opposed asking the Student Association to endorse the Senate's response before sending it to the paper. The majority favored the Senate's sending its own letter to the paper, then later talking to Otis Jackson, Student Association President, about the students' response.

Motion was made that the Executive Committee draft a response to be presented at the next Senate meeting in two weeks.
Amendment: That a special session of the Senate be scheduled next week to deal with the issue. DEFEATED
Substitute Motion: That the Senate deny the allegations of the specific paragraph and that the Executive Committee prepare an appropriate statement which would be sent to the editor of the Dominguez News.
Suggested change: That the following wording be used: "On April 14 the following statement appeared in the Dominguez News: 'Most professors expose students of minority background to constant insults, humiliations, implied and expressed inferiority, and grade them down a grade or two.' The faculty of CSUDH, through its Academic Senate, denies this unsubstantiated assertion and considers its appearance an affront to its professional standing. We affirm the University's commitment to procedural justice both inside and outside the classroom."

Motion was made that the Senate return to the committee of the whole to vote on the substitute motion. PASSED
Changes suggested and accepted: Substitute "objects" for "denies". Following "The faculty of CSUDH, through its Academic Senate," substitute: "objects to such unsubstantiated and overgeneralized statements and considers them irresponsible and not conducive to faculty/student harmony on campus."

It was the opinion of the Committee of the Whole that the newspaper quotation should introduce the letter.

The following wording was suggested: "The Academic Senate, CSUDH, as a representative of the faculty, objects to this unsubstantiated assertion and finds such unsubstantiated general statements against the faculty irresponsible and disruptive of faculty/student harmony on campus."

a doctorate. Both are intended to demonstrate the author's command of a scholarly subject.

Informational and Interpretive Reports: The Vital Distinction

For all the reports we've been looking at, the single most significant distinction that can be made is that between *informational* and *interpretive* reports. Recall the responsibilities given to the eldest son when his father's affairs began to prosper. First he simply observed, and reported his observations; he provided information that his father could interpret and act upon. Then in time, the son

Figure 46 (continued)

-5-

Substitution:
"The Academic Senate, CSUDH, the representative body of the faculty, notes with both regret and concern the unsubstantiated, irresponsible, overgeneralized, and, indeed, reckless comments in the April 14 edition of the Dominguez News, attributed to a colleague, which charge the faculty as follows: 'Most professors expose students of minority background to constant insults, humiliation, implied and expressed inferiority and grade them down a grade or two.

"The Academic Senate reaffirms the faculty's commitment to equality of educational opportunity for all students regardless of ethnicity, race, age, sex, sexual preference, or ideological convictions, and urges continued efforts by the entire academic community toward that end."

Returning from the Committee of the Whole to the regular Senate session, the Chair asked for a vote on whether or not to propose a motion today and to act on it, using the last substitute wording instead of the original wording. PASSED

Chair asked for a vote accepting this statement of concern, which is to be sent to the Dominguez News, addressed to the campus community. (one abstention, one opposition) PASSED

8. First Reading Items
   a) Academic Master Plan (EPC-80-11) Schoenwald *W
      The Senate was satisfied to let the Educational Policies Committee respond for the Senate at this point in the process.

Meeting adjourned 12:00 noon.

was given the task of interpreting. Such an increase in responsibility is usually the sign of someone's growth on the job. It's a step that a report writer should not take unless the person who authorized the report wishes it. On the other hand, a report writer should never fail to take that step when it is expected of him.

Whenever you begin a report project, be absolutely sure whether the report is expected to be *interpretive* or just *informational*. If your supervisor expects interpretation and gets only information, you will seem to have shirked the most important task. If the supervisor expects only information and gets interpretation he or she will no doubt feel that you've overstepped your bounds. In either case, you will have seriously miscalculated.

Interpretation in a report is a matter of degree. In some reports, only certain data are interpreted. In others, broader conclusions are drawn. Many experienced report writers are even asked to go beyond interpretation and recommend what should be done in light of those conclusions. This kind of report is often called a *recommendation* report or an *advisory* report.

A Summary Word about Definitions

The preceding pages have briefly surveyed the names we give to reports in business and industry. The terminology sometimes varies, but the distinctions are all straightforward and logical. Being aware of these distinctions will not, in itself, make you a better report writer. But it will give you a useful vocabulary and a starting point from which to begin sharpening your skills as a business report writer.

THE REPORT PROJECT: GETTING READY

The failure of many a business report begins at its inception, the moment the writer starts work on it. Careless preparation — sloppy work in the *pre*-writing stages — almost guarantees a faulty report.

For all but the shortest, most routine reports, a series of preparatory steps is vital. The actual writing comes *near the end* of most report-writing projects. The pre-writing steps are these:

1. You must carefully *define* the problem that your report will examine.
2. You must fully *analyze* that problem to determine the scope of the report, the questions it must answer, and the kind of research that will be necessary. This analysis of the problem gives birth to your working outline.
3. You must draw a *work schedule* for the subsequent steps of your report project.
4. You must do the necessary *research* (sometimes a very extensive process).
5. You must *organize* the facts that you've found during research so that they can be interpreted, either by you or (if your report is to be purely informational) by its reader.
6. If the report is to be interpretive, you must *interpret* the facts you've found. And if recommendations are to be made, you must decide what they are.
7. You must prepare whatever illustrations and visual aids you intend to use in the report.
8. Then, you write a first draft of the report.
9. Finally, you do as much proofreading and revising of that first draft as is needed to produce an effective and impressive final draft.

We'll consider the first three of these vital steps in the remainder of this chapter, then move on to the rest in the chapters that follow.

Defining the Report Problem

Defining a report problem means, very simply, deciding what your report will cover, and what it won't. You've got to make that decision systematically.

Except for initiative reports, every report has its genesis in an *authorization*. Your supervisor might ask, either orally or by memo, that you prepare a report. A client might request, by letter or phone, that your firm carry out a project and report your findings. A government agency might, in a formal task order, authorize a project to be done by your company and require that its results be reported back to that agency. Or the responsibilities of your job, as stipulated by company policy, may require that you write reports at certain times. By any of these means — face-to-face or phoned request, memo, letter, task order, or policy statement — the definition of your report problem is usually begun for you. Someone or something tells you what to examine and report on.

But — and it's a big *but* — that authorization by itself is usually not enough to define the problem completely. Most often, you have to go further in determining precisely what your report must cover. Your boss might, for example, call you aside and say, "Find out what happened at last night's arbitration meeting, and give it to me in a memo." Presumably, the boss knows what he expects of you, but has probably given you only the broadest notion of the report he wants. What precisely does the boss want to know? Who was there? What was said? What was decided? Who disagreed? You must go further in defining the problem.

To define a report problem clearly, you must do the following:

1. If there's an authorizing document — a letter, memo, policy statement, or anything else that indicates the desired scope of your report — read it carefully. You might even take pencil in hand, underline the main points, and cross out items that are extraneous to the definition of your problem. In short, make sure you have extracted every bit of definition you can out of that authorization.

2. If you feel that the written authorization doesn't tell you enough, consult with the authorizer (face to face, if possible) and get the necessary clarification. If all you have is a spoken authorization, don't hesitate to seek the necessary clarification right on the spot. If, after several readings, a policy directive remains unclear, go up the chain of command until it's clarified for you.

3. If the problem involves specialized knowledge, be sure to consult the appropriate specialist within your organization — perhaps a member of the legal staff, the project engineer, or the market research director — for help in defining the problem. Or do some preliminary research in the company library. By consulting with specialists or by going to available sources, you can often learn how others have defined similar report problems.

4. Ask yourself the *five W's and an H: Who? What? Where? When? Why?* and *How?* Usually, not all of these questions pertain to a single problem; but by asking them all, you assure yourself that the problem has been completely defined. Let's assume, for instance, that you receive a memo from your boss asking you to "find out what our people think of our new system of staggered lunch breaks." Upon reading the memo, you must ask yourself:

> *Who?* The boss's memo says "our people," but *who* exactly does that include? Does it include executives, or only non-executive staff? Does it include part-timers and summer help, or only permanent full-time employees? Does the boss want opinions from the uptown branch, or only from the home office? Every one of these *who*-questions must be answered if the problem is to be researched accurately.
>
> *What?* The boss wants opinions — "*what* our people think of the new system . . . . " Does he want opinions of the new system only, or ones comparing it to the old system? And does he, besides opinions, want suggestions for further revision of the lunch break system?

What (else)? The "new system of staggered lunch breaks" itself — do you, as report writer, know all the details of the new system? If not, you've got to learn them.

When? This question isn't vital to the definition of the problem, but it should remind you that your report must make clear *when* the opinions are being measured. Presumably, the employees should be given some chance to become accustomed to the new system before their opinions are asked.

Where? In this problem, the answer is self-evident — at your company.

Why? Should your report concern itself with the *whys* — that is, with the *reasons* underlying the opinions you elicit? Or does the boss want only opinions? If the authorizing memo isn't clear on this point, you had better clarify it.

How? The *how* question is, for the most part, irrelevant to this problem, although it does suggest a possible follow-up study on *how* best to satisfy employee wishes about lunch breaks if the new system proves unpopular.

The Test of the Title There's a good test for determining how well you've defined a report problem — *write a title for it.* The title should indicate clearly what the scope of your report will be: it should answer explicitly each of those *five W's and an H* that applies to the problem. Unlike novels or poems, reports need titles longer than one or two words. You simply can't say enough in a word or two to reveal the scope of a report. The "lunch break" problem, for example, might be entitled *Reactions of Acme's Fulltime Employees to the Company's New System of Staggered Lunch Breaks; March, 198_* — a title that clearly indicates the scope of the report.

On the other hand, a title like the following would *not* satisfy the test of a title for a skillful report writer:

Station KRLT's Coverage

This title is obviously incomplete. What kind of station is KRLT? What is meant by its "coverage"? — its programming? its audience? the reach of its signal? This vagueness is remedied when the title is reconstructed to answer the pertinent *five W's and an H:*

The Geographical and Socioeconomic Coverage
of Television Station KRLT
June 198_

Another inadequate report title would be:

The Grapefruit Industry

It doesn't reveal what's to be in the report, just its area of interest. Any "test-title" as vague as this one probably means a vaguely defined report problem. A clearer and more specific test-title might be:

A Survey of the Growth of the Grapefruit Industry
In America Since 1900

or:

A Survey of the Grapefruit Industry's Growth in America Since 1900

Any report problem that's been clearly defined can be clearly titled.[3]

Analyzing the Report Problem

After the report problem has been carefully defined, it must be *analyzed.* (The process is sometimes called *factoring.*) Problem analysis consists of breaking down your well-defined problem into its logical subdivisions (or factors), then breaking down those subdivisions into their own logical subdivisions, and so on, until you have isolated and identified every elemental question the report must answer. The process can be depicted thusly:

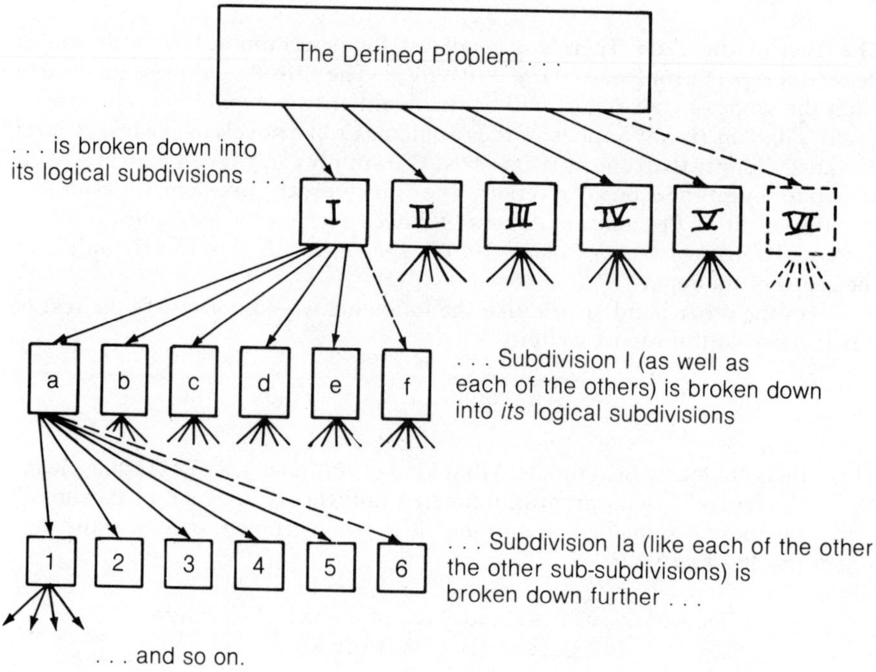

[3] When it's time to draft the final report, the *style* of such a title can be improved by using a subtitle. For example, *The Grapefruit Industry: A Survey of its Growth in America Since 1900.* But style needn't concern you in this early phase; your task here is to *define* the problem. There's also no need to overdo the precision of the title, whether it's just a test-title or a final one. A title like:

Facts and Figures Related to the Growth and Development of Grapefruit Growing, Harvesting, Shipping, Packing, and Distributing in the United States of America since the Year 1900 A.D.

is precise far past the point of redundancy (and a stylistic dinosaur).

A few words of clarification here — problem *analysis* should not be confused with *interpretation.* So far, you've done no research; you've uncovered no information to interpret. That comes later. At this stage, you are analyzing the problem itself (that is, breaking it down) to facilitate that upcoming research and help to organize the findings that result from it. What problem-analysis gives you is a *working outline.*

(It will help, at this point, to look briefly at the two systems of outlining that are widely used: the *number-letter* system and the *decimal* system. Both are illustrated in Figure 47.)

Figure 47
Two main systems of outlining.

The Number-Letter System

THE PROBLEM TITLE

```
I. ________
   A. ________
   B. ________
      1. ________
      2. ________
         a. ________
         b. ________
      3. ________
   C. ________
II. ________
   A. ________
      1. ________
      2. ________
   B. ________
```

The Decimal System

```
1.0 ________
   1.1 ________
   1.2 ________
      1.21 ________
      1.22 ________
         1.221 ________
         1.222 ________
      1.23 ________
   1.3 ________
2.0 ________
   2.1 ________
      2.11 ________
      2.12 ________
   2.2 ________
```

Which of them you use is a matter of preference. The *number-letter* system is more familiar and it appears less complicated, but the *decimal* system has the advantage of explicitly relating every item to the outline's overall scheme.

When using the decimal system of outlining, you must watch out for any heading that is divided into ten or more subheadings. For instance, if item 2.2 were divided into fourteen subheadings, the fourteenth subheading would be numbered 2.2(14)—not 2.214. The latter would erroneously indicate the fourth subdivision of item 2.21 instead of what it should indicate—the fourteenth subdivision of item 2.2.

Now let's look at an example of problem analysis. Joe Roberts is a bright young personnel officer at the Leroy Construction Company, a firm of international building contractors that works under both private and government contract. Joe's boss, the personnel chief, has been asked by the company's financial vice-president, Neville Washington, to hire a new Accounts Director. Joe has been asked to coordinate the talent search. After all the prime candidates have been tested and interviewed, Joe must write a report recommending which of them — Adams, Baker, Carlino, Davis, Edwards or Franklin — ought to be hired.

Joe's report problem was *definable* as follows:

```
Six Candidates for Leroy's Accounts Directorship:
        An Evaluation and Recommendation
```

After defining the problem (and giving it this title), Joe carefully *analyzed* it, looking for its natural subdivisions. Because he had to choose, ultimately, among the six candidates, he used as his primary subdivisions each of those candidates:

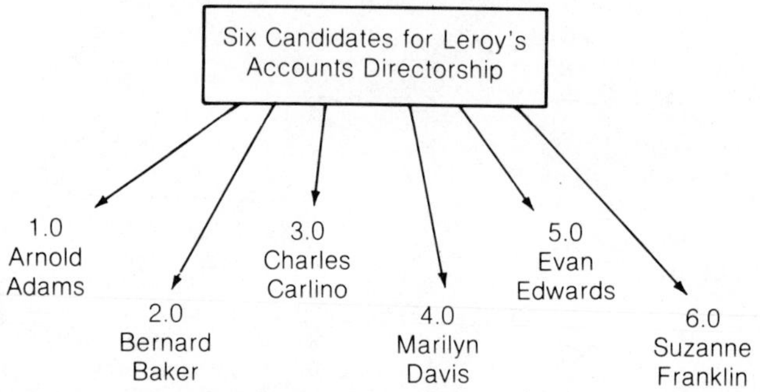

Then, for his next level of analytic break-down, Joe subdivided each candidate into the major areas of qualification for the job:

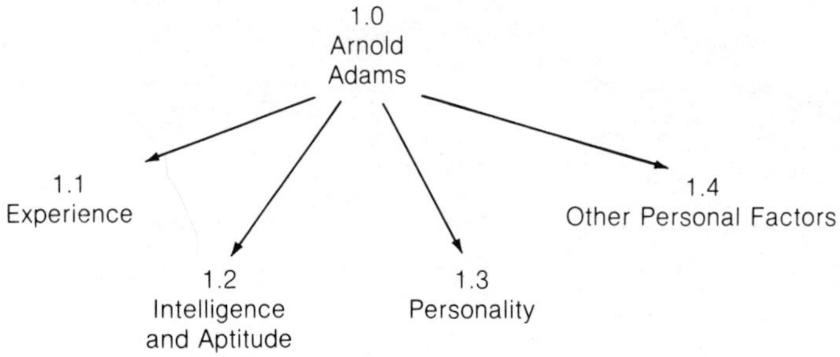

Then each major area of qualification was broken down into its significant components:

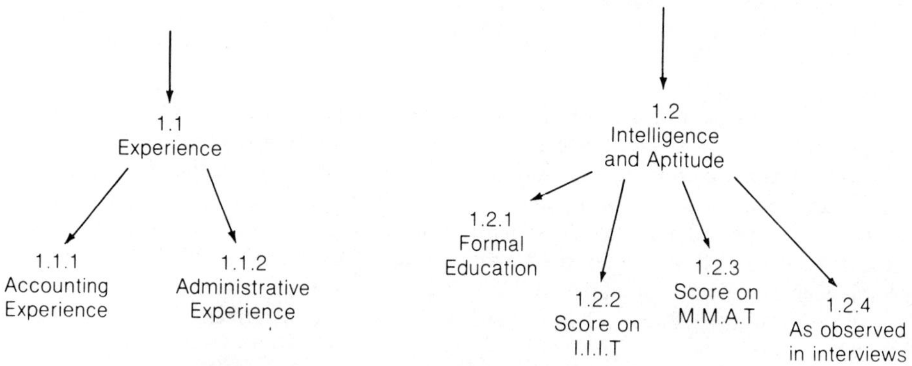

And, where necessary, each of *these* subcategories was further broken down into *its* relevant sub-subcategories. When fully analyzed (and put into outline form), Joe's report problem looked like this:

Six Candidates for Leroy's Accounts Directorship:
An Evaluation and Recommendation

1.0 Arnold Adams's Qualifications
- 1.1 Experience
  - 1.1.1 Accounting experience
    - 1.1.1.1 cost accounting experience
    - 1.1.1.2 international accounting experience
    - 1.1.1.3 other accounting experience
  - 1.1.2 Administrative experience
    - 1.1.2.1 corporate administrative experience
    - 1.1.2.2 governmental administrative experience
    - 1.1.2.3 military administrative experience
- 1.2 Intelligence and Aptitude
  - 1.2.1 Formal education
    - 1.2.1.1 degrees
    - 1.2.1.2 continuing education programs
  - 1.2.2 Score on I.I.I.T. (Indiana Intelligence Index Test)
  - 1.2.3 Score on M.M.A.T. (Measurement of Managerial Aptitude Test)
  - 1.2.4 As observed in interviews
    - 1.2.4.1 in interview with Neville Washington (Vice-President Finance)
    - 1.2.4.2 in other interviews
- 1.3 Candidate's Personality
  - 1.3.1 Results on P.P.S. (Paris Personality Survey)
  - 1.3.2 As observed in interviews
    - 1.3.2.1 in interview with Neville Washington
    - 1.3.2.2 in other interviews
- 1.4 Other Personal Factors
  - 1.4.1 Age
  - 1.4.2 Family status
  - 1.4.3 . . . (here Joe leaves the door open to other criteria that might be added as his evaluation progresses)

2.0 Bernard Baker's Qualifications 3.0 Charles Carlino's . . . 4.0 Marilyn Davis's . . . 5.0 Evan Edwards's . . . 6.0 Suzanne Franklin's . . .	} each of these is broken down exactly as Arnold Adams's section is above

With the problem broken down this way, Joe can see very clearly what data he needs (that is, what questions his "research" must answer) so that he can write this report and make his recommendation.

Alternatively, Joe could have broken down his problem analytically as follows, and gotten just as clear a view of the data he needed to find.

1.0 Experience
- 1.1 Accounting experience
  - 1.1.1 Cost accounting experience

1.1.1.1 Arnold Adams
1.1.1.2 Bernard Baker
1.1.1.3 Charles Carlino
1.1.1.4 Marilyn Davis
1.1.1.5 Evan Edwards
1.1.1.6 Suzanne Franklin
1.1.2 International accounting experience
1.1.2.1 Arnold Adams
1.1.2.2 Bernard Baker
1.1.2.3 Charles Carlino
1.1.2.4 Marilyn Davis
1.1.2.5 Evan Edwards
1.1.2.6 Suzanne Franklin
1.1.3 Other accounting experience
1.1.3.1 Arnold Adams
1.1.3.2 Bernard Baker
. . . . (and so on)

Precisely *how* you break down a problem is less important than making sure to break it down logically, systematically, and completely, so that it can be effectively interpreted.

Other report problems would of course, when analyzed, break down differently. Problems of *fact* would subdivide differently than problems of *valuation*, or problems of *ends*, or problems of *means*. These are, essentially, the four different types of report problems that you'll encounter. Let's look briefly at each of them.

Problems of *fact* require only that certain facts be uncovered, without interpretation. Their natural subdivisions are usually obvious. A report on a new assembly-line process, or one on how a personnel grievance arose, would probably break down *chronologically:*

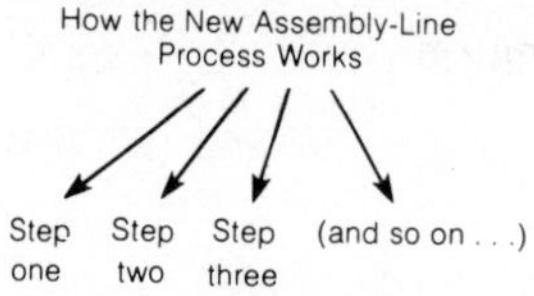

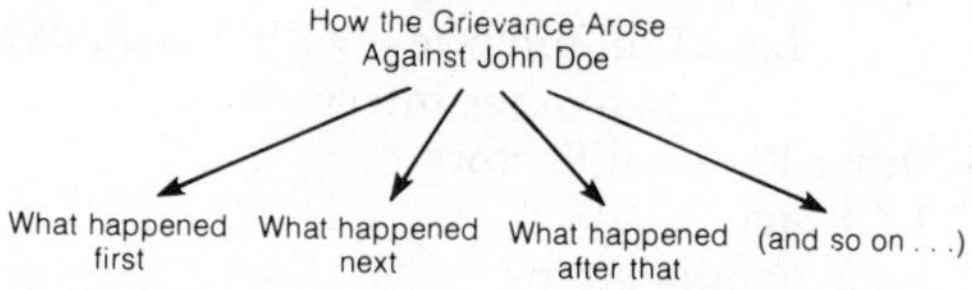

A report describing the scene of an accident would probably break down *spatially* — moving from left to right, south to north, or from "ground-zero" outward, in its major subdivisions. The report that we defined earlier on employee attitudes toward the new lunch-break policy — which was a problem of fact — would no doubt break down *categorically,* and probably into *categories of employee:*

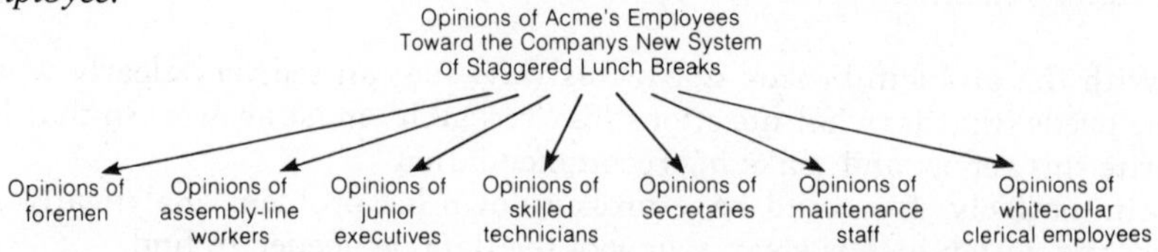

This *categorical* breakdown is probably the most useful, since we know the boss wants to give more weight to the opinions of certain kinds of employees when deciding whether to keep the new system.

Problems of *valuation,* as the term implies, are problems in which you've got to place an accurate value on the facts you present. The valuation can be either *quantitative* or *qualitative.* A report estimating the cost of a proposed construction job, for example, would require *quantitative valuation.* A report measuring the success of a company's public relations program would entail *qualitative valuation.* In either case, the problem ought to break down analytically into the *parts of the whole that must be evaluated.*

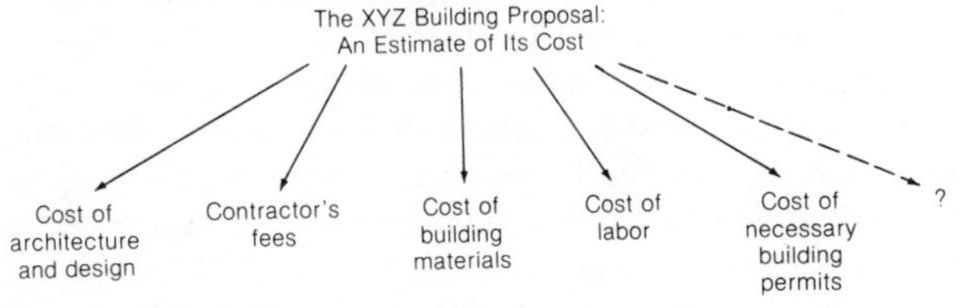

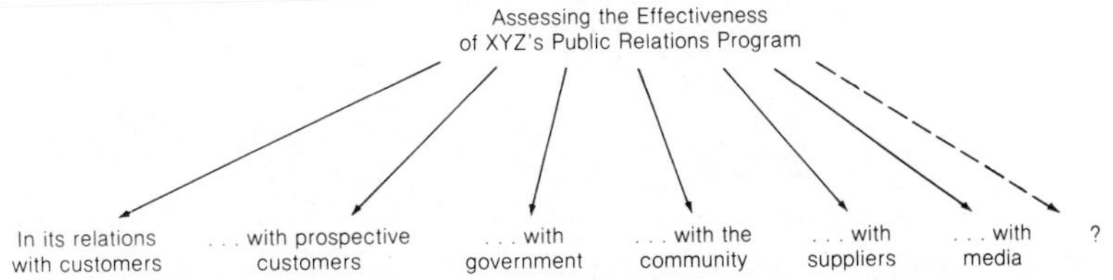

Problems of *ends* require that you examine alternative ends, or results, and determine which of them is the most desirable. Joe Roberts' problem — having to recommend one of the six candidates for the accounts directorship — was a problem of ends. So too is the problem of a company that wants to build a new factory — where should they locate it? Or the manufacturer who intends to spend $100,000 on magazine advertising — in what magazine(s) ought the ads be placed? In a problem of ends, if the alternatives are clearly defined at the start (as they were in Joe Roberts's case — he had six candidates and had to recommend one of them), the first analytical breakdown ought to be *by those alternatives* (as it was in Joe's analysis). If, however, the alternative ends are not clearly identifiable at the outset, the first breakdown of the problem ought to be *by criteria,* the criteria that will be used to make the ultimate choice:

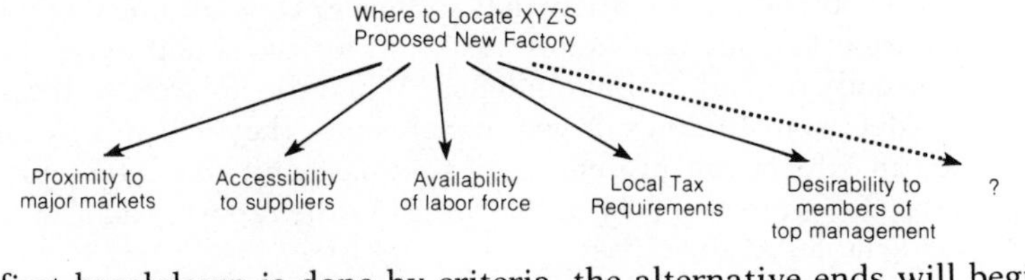

When the first breakdown is done by criteria, the alternative ends will begin to emerge in the second breakdown:

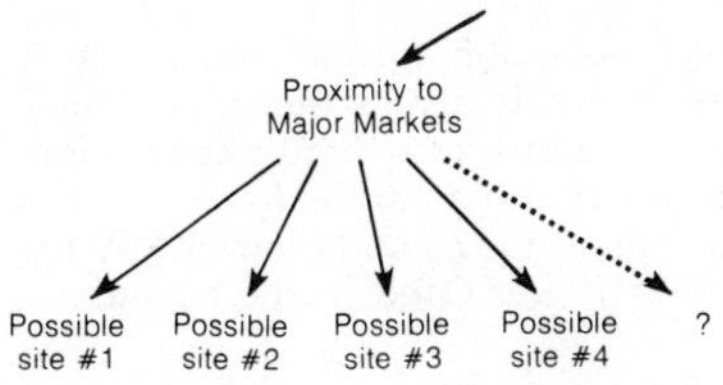

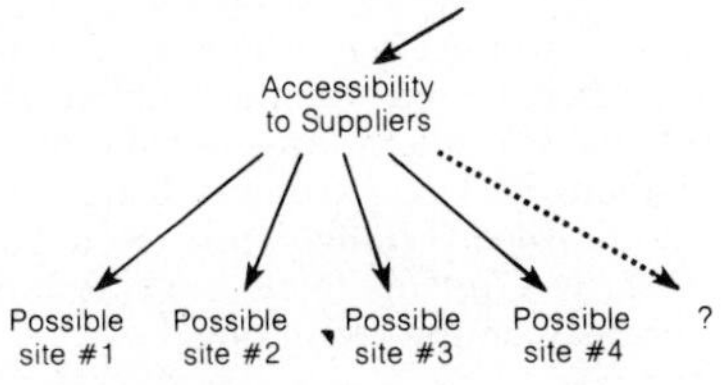

Problems of *means* — usually the hardest kind of report problem you'll face — are problems in which you *have* a desired end, and must find the course of action (that is, the *means*) most likely to bring about that end. Several examples: The XYZ Company must inform its stockholders that prospects for profits next year are bleak — what's the best way to do it? A firm's payroll must be cut by twelve percent — how can it make that cut least destructively? A nation is engaged in war — what's the best way to end it? The most natural analytical breakdown in such problems is by *alternative means.* The difficulty, of course, is recognizing all the feasible alternatives. For this, you've got to turn your imagination loose. Allow it to generate as many ideas about means as it can. Then enlist the aid of others. Ask them how they might achieve the same desired end. And in the beginning, accept every idea — your own and theirs. Only after you've gathered a healthy number of alternative means should you rule out any of them as unworkable.[4] Once all the workable means of achieving that desired end have been isolated, the rest of the analytical breakdown can look like this:

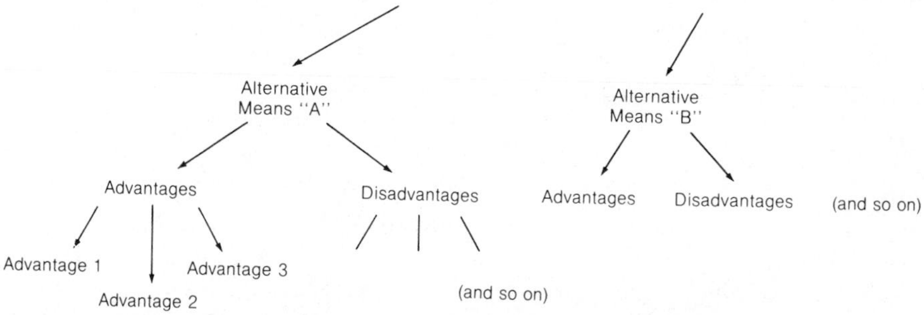

With this kind of systematic view of the report problem, it should be a lot easier to determine the best means of achieving the desired end.

Defining Your Readership and Your Limitations

After you've clearly defined your problem (and proved it by writing a good title), and after you have thoroughly analyzed that well-defined problem, you must, before going on to your research, consider two important variables — your *readership* and *limitations on your resources.*

You must evaluate your readership. Who is your audience? How deeply need you go into your subject to satisfy that audience? How technical or nontechnical must the report be for that audience? What attitudes and biases toward your subject already prevail in that audience? While the answers to these questions will not affect your findings or your conclusions, they *will* affect your style, the sequence in which you present your findings, and the extent to which you explain or elaborate on many of the things in the report. You should be aware of these variables at the outset.

You must also consider limitations on your resources. What restrictions in time, money, or personnel will limit the scope of your report? If you plan your

[4]What I've implied here is closely akin to the technique of *brainstorming.* The technique gathers people together and has them uninhibitedly invent and call out ideas for solving a problem. Anyone who plans a career in business should know something about it. Two excellent discussions of brainstorming can be found in: Alex F. Osborn, *Applied Imagination* (New York, Scribner's, 1957); and Charles S. Whiting, *Creative Thinking* (New York, Reinhold, 1958). It was Osborn who formulated the "brainstorming technique."

report project too ambitiously, you might not have the time, or the money, or the assistance to finish it satisfactorily.

Visualizing the Finished Report

While analyzing your report problem, you should also begin to visualize your finished product. What should your report look like when it's completed? What should its format be? How long, approximately, will it be? And how formal? Report formats vary (as we'll see in chapter 18) from simple handwritten memoranda to thick, permanently bound documents with hundreds of pages and numerous sections.

Drawing a Work Schedule

Before starting research, you should always *schedule* the work that remains to be done, no matter how long or short the project is. Seldom will you have the luxury of writing a report without a deadline.

After defining and analyzing a problem, you will (or should) have a good idea how large the report project will be. And you'll also be aware of limitations in money, assistance, and other resources. Out of this knowledge, you construct a working schedule for the project. Beginning with your *deadline* date and working *backward,* block out on a calendar the amount of time you can allow for each work phase. Working backward makes you focus immediately upon your deadline. If you have a deadline in six weeks (let's say it is now September 1 and your report is due on October 13), and you know you'll have to do all the drafting yourself, you might begin by allowing yourself a full week for this final work phase.

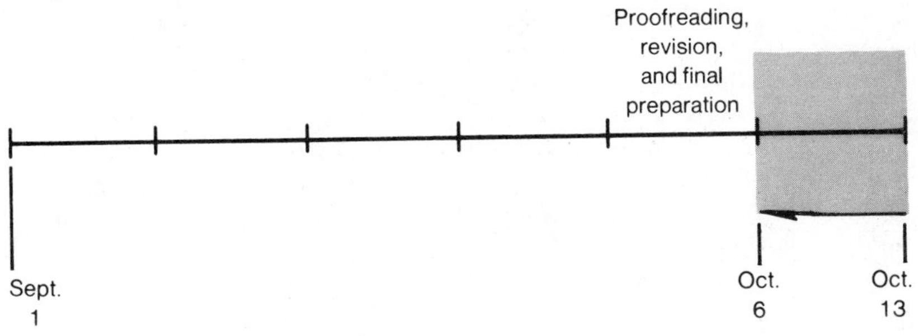

Next, you might allow a week and a half for effectively interpreting your findings.

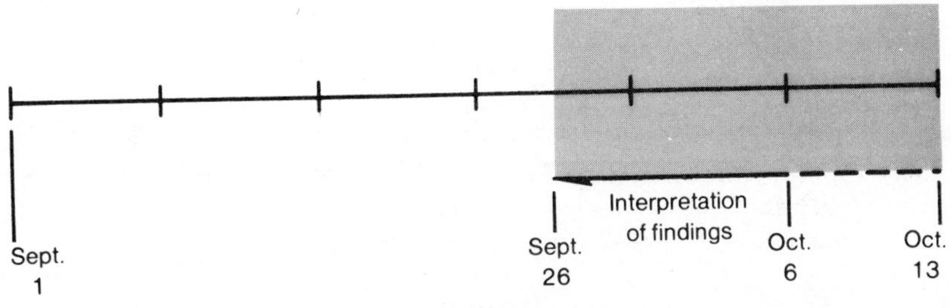

Then, knowing that you'll have to compile and tabulate all the data by hand, without assistance, you might allow a full week for compilation and tabulation. (If you can use the computer, of course, this phase ought to go more quickly.)

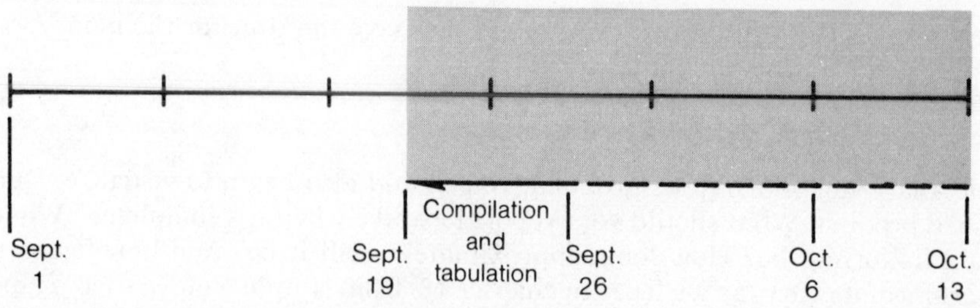

Finally, if you feel that the two-and-a-half weeks at the beginning is sufficient for the necessary research, you have a schedule. Your work schedule for the report project now looks like this:

Research	Sept. 1–19
Compilation and tabulation	Sept. 19–26
Interpretation of findings	Sept. 26–Oct. 6
Proofreading and revision	Oct. 6–13

If you feel that two-and-a-half weeks is not enough time for research, you'd adjust the schedule to allow more time for research and correspondingly less for the other work phases. In fact, many a cautious report writer with a six-week deadline first schedules a safety margin of two or three days preceding the deadline, then blocks out the rest of the schedule.

IN SUMMARY

Definition and analysis — these are the two major steps that mark the beginning of any successful business report project. As the sea captain would never set sail toward a destination without charting the course, neither should the report writer. When you define a report problem, you bring into focus what and where your destination is. When you analyze that problem carefully, you're really determining the best way of getting there. Once the problem is defined *and* analyzed, you can draw up a work schedule to assure that you reach your destination on time.

Only after you've defined, analyzed, and scheduled are you ready to move ahead on your project.

PROBLEMS

1. Arrange and conduct an informal interview with a business executive, and inquire into the role(s) played by written reports in his or her organization. You want to learn about the kinds of reports the organization depends on, how report assignments are made, what steps the organization takes to assure satisfactory reports, what is done with reports after they're written, and anything else your analysis of the problem tells you you ought to know. Key your questions to the various matters discussed in this chapter.

2. Either on your own, or with the help of someone more experienced in business, compile a list of as many different kinds of communications as possible that (a) go *up* the organizational hierarchy, (b) go *down* the hierarchy, (c) cut *across* the organization horizontally, and (d) go *outside* of the organization.

3. Many experts maintain that reports that move horizontally within companies (rather than going up or down the company hierarchy) are usually less complete, less accurate, and less effective than reports that move up, down, or outside. Can you speculate as to why this is probably so? How would you go about proving (or disproving) it.

4. Obtain a copy of an actual business report or government agency report. Study it carefully — its contents *and* its structure. List all those characteristics of the report (no matter how minor) that help to make it clear, easy to understand, and impressive. Then list all the characteristics that in any way hinder its clarity or make it less impressive than it could have been. Prepare your list in a format suitable for submission, along with the report itself, to your instructor.

5. Corporate employers calculate that it costs anywhere between two and three thousand dollars to provide systematic and effective training in report writing for *each* employee they wish to so train. Some companies spend it; others (especially when financial conditions are tight) do not. Based on what you already know about communications in industry and government, what is your feeling about the wisdom of such expenditure? (Be as specific as you can.)

6. Cost is often a factor in preparing a formal business report. Obtain a copy of one, and try to estimate how much it cost the firm to prepare. Be sure that your estimate takes account of each component of that cost.

7. Discuss each of the following propositions thoroughly, and determine whether it's true or false:

a. Since reports are expository rather than reaction-evoking, less attention needs to be paid to precisely who their reader(s) will be.
b. Formal business reports often waste too much money looking pretty — an interested report reader wants facts and interpretations, not gloss and fancy bindings.
c. The report that contains obvious elements of attempted persuasion, in sections other than those expressly set aside for recommendations, is usually not a successful report.

8. From the library or from a company, obtain a copy of an interpretive business report (that is, any report that does more than simply provide information). Read it carefully and, in a memorandum to your instructor, indicate its title, the central problem of the report, and the problem-analysis that is implied by the subdivisions of the report. You might also conjecture on the working schedule that was followed in bringing this report from conception to completion.

9. Sam Baker, a young auto insurance broker, thinks that he has a great idea for a new type of auto insurance company, and he calls you in as a consultant. "I'm going to call it the Young Riskless Club." he says. "You may have noted how high auto insurance premiums are for drivers under age twenty-five. They're much *too* high. Why, those young men and women, especially the men, pay two to five times as much for their insurance as older drivers do. Of course, younger people have more accidents than older people, and they file more

claims. But my idea concerns those young drivers who *don't* get into accidents. They shouldn't have to pay. If I can figure out a set of measures and indexes that would identify the *non*-accident-prone young drivers, I can sell them insurance at less than half of what they now pay. All I have to do is give every applicant a test, check his or her background, and either accept or reject that person's business. My loss rates will be below the industry average, and I can make plenty of money."

As Sam's consultant, carefully *define* and *analyze* the problem before you. Submit your definition and analysis of the problem to your instructor in the form of a memo. (Subsequent phases of this consultant's report problem will be spelled out to you in "Problem 9 in each of the next three chapters.)

10. In a memo to your instructor, propose a major report that you would like to write on some business topic of your own choosing. In your memo, include a precise tentative title for your report, a detailed working outline of its subject, and a proposed schedule for completing the various phases of the project. (Subsequent phases of this report project will be assigned to you in Problem 10 of each of the next three chapters.)

11. Clearly define, and then analyze, whichever of the following report problems your instructor asks you to. (None of them has been stated as specifically as you would like. That's often the case.) Give your instructor a tentative title for the report, and a detailed working outline of the problem as you've analyzed it. Also indicate to your instructor how you arrived at the definition and analysis that you're presenting.

a. Policing the college campus
b. The best washing machine on the market
c. Making paper (*or* long-playing records, *or* books, *or* tennis rackets, *or* surfboards)
d. The services performed by travel agents
e. Using the college library
f. Who patronizes motels?
g. Extracurricular activities at your college
h. Automation — curse or blessing?
i. The commercial implications of space exploration
j. The kind of people who become corporate presidents
k. The aesthetic tastes of American teenagers
l. Should the "Miss America" contest be scrapped?
m. The commercial canning of fruits and vegetables: A description
n. The trend in college enrollments
o. Should our company do something for the arts?
p. Political fundraising in the business community
q. The role of the child day-care center
r. Trends in collective bargaining for public employees
s. Why shoppers don't buy the less expensive store brands of canned foods
t. The 55-mile per-hour speed limit
u. Illegal uses of CB (Citizens Band) Radio

12. As a good exercise in careful expository writing, write (in about 250–400 words) an extended definition, with examples, of one or more of the

following terms (as your instructor directs). Be sure that the intelligent non-specialist will understand your definition(s).

a. mutual fund
b. cost accounting
c. conglomerates
d. affirmative action
e. electronic data processing
f. term insurance
g. management consultant
h. zero-based budgeting

13. One of your old instructors has been appointed editor of a new periodical for business students called *Rules of the Game.* He asks you to become a contributor, and thereby share with students the experience and insight you've gained in handling difficult situations in the working world. (He's also paying good money for your article.)

His memo of authorization to you reads as follows:

I'd like your article to be a detailed description (make it as vivid as you can!) of one or another of the following business situations--

a. a situation in which you did not know what to say, or do,

b. a situation in which you met with some hostility or resentment, or

c. a situation in which you knew what was expected of you but could not do it, or chose not to do it.

Unless you've got a better way of handling it (and please take leeway on this), you might present the situation as follows: First, set the stage for the situation (where it's happening, who the people are, etc.) then, relate the situation as it happened. And finally, summarize by telling the reader what you learned from the situation, or what you resolved to do--or not do--in such a situation in the future. That is to say--what ''rule of the game'' the situation taught you! Don't include anything irrelevant, but don't skimp on important or clarifying details. The more clearly you make your readers see the situation, the more valuable your conclusions are going to be for them.

Write the article.

CHAPTER 16

FINDING THE FACTS

LIBRARY RESEARCH
Libraries Available to Business Report Writers
Using the Library
Gathering Material from your Library Sources
Evaluating Your Sources
Some Concluding Remarks on Library Research
PRIMARY RESEARCH
Research by Observation
Research by Experimentation
Asking Questions: Research by Interrogation
IN CONCLUSION

Your report problem lies before you, clearly defined and analyzed. Now you must uncover the information demanded by the problem. Where do you turn?

Often the information you seek (at least some of it) has already been uncovered and put on paper by somebody else. When you look for it, you're doing *secondary research* (or *library research* since most of the looking is done in libraries). For many report problems — especially those that involve current situations or situations never before examined — you'll find that secondary research is not enough. You'll have to do some form of *primary research: observation, experimentation,* or *interrogation.* In this chapter, we'll examine modes of research — the various ways of finding the facts.

LIBRARY RESEARCH

In researching any problem, turn first to printed sources. The amount of information published every year is staggering. Chances are good that what you need (or something close to it) has already been derived and put on paper. And even if the problem you face is new, studies of related problems can give you valuable insights into your own.

Most people in business keep within reach a shelf of handy reference books containing information likely to be needed on the job. But if the information they need for a report isn't in these books, they turn to a library. Let's briefly survey the kinds of libraries available to you.

Libraries Available to Business Report Writers

Company Libraries The first library to consult is the one closest to you, the library at the company or agency for whom you work. Company libraries typically keep all the material they can lay their hands on that relates to the industry in which the company operates. Libraries at public agencies (like the City Department of Public Works or the County Agency for Commercial Development) also keep materials on subjects of direct concern to that agency.

Public Libraries Within a short distance of virtually anywhere is a public library — often a good source of books, periodicals, and reference works on business and public affairs. Many larger public libraries keep extensive collections of business materials in separate business-branch libraries, branches often located in a city's financial or trade center. At most business branches, trained specialists are on hand to assist researchers in person or over the phone.

College and University Libraries While company libraries and business branches tend to stress current data, for historical background material you are often better off at a university or college library. Though primarily responsible to their students and faculty, these libraries will usually grant access to legitimate "outside" researchers. At larger universities, business materials are often housed in separate facilities. Sometimes an entire specialty library is created to handle a single topic. UCLA, for example, opened a special library on air pollution in 1968, with thousands of items on this one vital topic.

Municipal Reference Libraries In the larger cities, researchers interested in government affairs can use *municipal reference libraries.* Originally intended to serve public officials, municipal reference libraries are now generally available to any legitimate research effort. Usually located in town civic centers, they maintain complete records on city and county departments, as well as books, periodicals, and pamphlets on civic affairs in general, and on topics like accident prevention, city planning, public health, welfare, housing, zoning, cost-of-living, traffic, crime, and law enforcement.

The Libraries of Independent Research Organizations Some of the best libraries for business and public affairs material are those at independent research organizations — organizations like the National Planning Association, the National Bureau of Economic Research, SAM (The Society for the Advancement of Management), and the Institute of Public Administration, to name just a few. While intended primarily to serve in-house research programs, many of these libraries do open their facilities to non-member researchers.

The Libraries of Trade and Professional Associations The libraries of professional and trade associations usually focus on a single industry or profession, but within this narrower focus, their resources tend to be very extensive. The Library of the Bureau of Railway Economics, for example, has the greatest collection of railway information in the world — even broader than the collection on railroading held by the Library of Congress.

Sources of Information on Foreign Countries Some of the best places to get up-to-date information on foreign countries and their economies are the embassies, consulates, or trade commissions of the country in question — provided that you're alert to their possible biases. Information on Austria, for example, can be gathered through the Austrian Embassy in Washington, and through the Austrian Consulate General, the Austrian Information Source, the Austrian Trade Delegate, the Austrian State Tourist Department, and U.S.-Austrian Chamber of Commerce, all in New York. There's a valuable reference book that lists sources of information on foreign countries: James B. Childs' *Government Document Bibliography in the United States and Elsewhere.*

The Library of Congress Foremost among libraries in the United States is the Library of Congress in Washington. It is a copyright library, which means that by law it receives copies of everything published in this country. Your own college and public libraries probably have the Library of Congress Catalog. The Library of Congress Reference Department provides service, in person and by mail, to researchers in all fields except law.

Interlibrary Loans If you can't find the information you need in a library close at hand, turn to the *interlibrary loan system* that ties together a network of American libraries. Through frequently updated "union lists," one librarian can determine which libraries hold the material you need. The librarian can then, on your behalf, submit a loan request, either for the material itself or for copies of it. Two published directories are also useful in locating specialized libraries: *Special Library Resources* (a four-volume guide), and the *Directory of Special Libraries.*

Using the Library

At first glance, libraries with their endless indexes, card catalogs and thousands of volumes on hundreds of shelves can be intimidating. But libraries are all organized pretty much the same way, and they aren't hard to use once you know how. Basically most libraries have four kinds of holdings: *reference works, books in a general collection, periodicals,* and *government publications.* We'll look at each type.

Reference Works When you're searching for published information, turn to reference works first. (Sometimes you needn't go any further.) As any experienced researcher will confirm, the variety of reference books in print is enormous. The following list is intended only to suggest that vast variety. There are:

1. *Encyclopedias,* for broad background information on a subject. There are both general encyclopedias like the *Americana* and the *Britannica;* and specialized encyclopedias like the *Encyclopedia of the Social Sciences* (which provides good coverage in economics, law, government, politics, penology, and social work, among other areas), and the *Encyclopedia Canadiana* (which covers all aspects of Canadian life, economy, history and culture).

2. *Yearbooks,* for information on recent trends and events. Some yearbooks are annual supplements to encyclopedias, like the *Americana Annual* and the *Britannica Book of the Year;* others are annual records of events in specific fields, like the *Sales Management Survey of Buying Power* (an annual supplement to *Sales Management Magazine),* and *The United States in World Affairs* (which surveys America's international involvements during the preceding year). Many other yearbooks are published by professional, trade, and industrial groups, and by foreign nations.

3. *Dictionaries,* helpful in clarifying terminology, definitions, and (yes!) spelling. There are unabridged dictionaries like *Webster's Third* and the *Oxford English Dictionary* (in thirteen volumes); desk dictionaries like *Webster's New Collegiate* and the *American College Dictionary;* and specialized business dictionaries like the *Encyclopedic Dictionary of Business,* and the *Dictionary of Business and Industry* (a work that defines some 45,000 commercial and technical terms.)

4. *Almanacs,* those compendious catchalls of recent and historical facts and statistics. There are general almanacs like the *World Almanac and Book of Facts,* and *Whitaker's Almanac* (a British publication strong on Commonwealth organizations and institutions); and specialized almanacs like the *Economic Almanac* and the *California Information Almanac* (which does for California what *Whitaker's* does for the British Commonwealth).

5. *Handbooks,* for detailed facts and statistics on specialized subjects. For example: the *Accountant's Handbook,* the *Business Executive's Handbook,* the *Corporate Treasurer's and Controller's Handbook,* the *Sales Promotion Handbook,* the *Personnel Handbook,* the *Foreman's Handbook,* and the *Handbook of Industrial Relations.*

6. *Gazetteers,* which are alphabetical dictionaries of data on places large and small. Among the most useful gazetteers are the *Columbia Gazetteer of the World, Webster's Geographical Dictionary,* and the *Directory of Post Offices* (which, for the United States, provides information on the service areas of all the nation's post offices).

7. *Atlases,* the best of which, for American economic coverage, is the *Rand McNally Commercial Atlas* (whose maps and data are updated every year).

8. *Business and trade directories,* for information about people, organizations, and activities in various trades and industries. Among the best known of such directories are *Thomas' Register of American Manufacturers; Kelley's Directory of Merchants, Manufacturers and Shippers of the World;* and the *N. W. Ayer & Sons Directory of Newspapers and Periodicals* (which also provides gazetteer information on every city and town in America in which a newspaper is published).

9. *Biographical registers,* for information about noteworthy people. There are the *Dictionary of American Biography* (covering persons deceased who contributed significantly to American life); *Who's Who in America* (which covers the living); *Who's Who* (which covers important people in other countries); *Current Biography* (a series of monthly reports, bound into yearly volumes, on people newly prominent); various regional registers like *Who's Who in the Midwest, Who's Who in the West, Who's Who in New York;* and registers of important people in various fields, like *Poor's Register of Directors and Executives, Who's Who in Commerce and Industry,* the *Offical Congressional Directory,* and the *American Architects Directory.*

10. *Statistical source books and census reports,* for information on population, manufacturing, housing, transportation, agriculture, and other areas of the American economy and society. The most widely used among these are the annual *Statistical Abstract of the United States,* the annual *County and City Data Book,* and the decennial reports of the United States Census.

11. *Bibliographies and indexes,* which don't provide information *per se,* but do tell you where it can be found.

The General Collection Outside the reference section, the rest of the library's *books* comprise its *general collection.* To locate books in that general collection, you must turn first to the *card catalog,* where books are indexed alphabetically, in three ways — by *author,* by *title,* and by *subject.* Once you've found in the card catalog a book that seems promising, the call-number in the upper left-hand corner of the card is your key to obtaining it. In open-stack libraries you go straight to the shelf with the call-number you seek. In closed-stack libraries, you request the book by call-number at the desk, and await its delivery.

It's not a bad idea, if you have access to an open-stack library, to browse the shelves in the appropriate call-number area to see what books the library holds on your subject of interest. (Ask the librarian to direct you to the call-number area for that subject.)

Periodicals Periodicals are your best source of *current* information, information that hasn't had time to find its way into books. In order to use periodicals — for there are thousands of them! — you must be familiar with the various *indexes to periodicals.*

One kind of index lists periodicals themselves — by title, frequency of publication, and major subject matter. These indexes are most useful when you're unfamiliar with the publications in the field you must report on. Among the best of these are: *N. W. Ayer & Sons Directory of Newspapers & Periodicals* (an annual, already mentioned on page 393, which has extensive lists of trade and professional publications); *Ulrich's Periodical Directory* (a guide to approximately 1400 periodicals published in the Western Hemisphere and Great Britain); and more specialized catalogs like the *World List of Scientific Periodicals.*

The other kind of periodical index is the index to *articles* that have appeared in periodicals. There are generalized indexes like the *Reader's Guide to Periodical Literature* (which indexes articles from popular periodicals by author, title, and subject); and the *International Index to Periodicals* (which indexes articles in the more scholarly publications). And there are the many specialized indexes to periodical literature like the *Accountants Index*, the *Agricultural Index* (which covers agribusiness as well as growing and livestock), the *Business Periodical Index*, the *Engineering Index*, and the *Industrial Arts Index* (which concentrates on articles less technical than those indexed in the *Engineering Index).*

A word about *dailies* — there is no better record of events-as-they-happen than a good daily newspaper. If the report you're working on requires you to trace the day-to-day changes in an important situation, you can consult (either in back issues or on microfilm) the relevant issues of dailies like the *New York Times*, the *Wall Street Journal*, the *American Banker*, *Construction Daily*, the *Daily Freight Record*, the *Oil Daily*, or *Women's Wear Daily*.

There are no general indexes to dailies as such, but several special indexes can be helpful in locating information in them — the *New York Times Index* (which indexes all *Times* articles every two weeks and is bound into annual volumes), *Facts on File* (itself a weekly digest of world news that also directs the reader to broader coverage of events in other publications), and *Keesing's Contemporary Archives* (a weekly diary of important events and statistics which, like *Facts on File*, points to coverage in other publications).

As with books, there are also "union lists" that show which libraries hold certain periodicals. If your own library doesn't have a periodical you're interested in, the librarian can tell you which library does.

Government Publications Most libraries, as an integral part of their holdings, keep government publications — books, pamphlets, reports, periodicals, bibliographies, and reference books published by federal, state, and local governments. Immense in their range of subjects, they provide one of the richest sources of usable information for business people. Get to know the guide books that list and classify these government publications.

For federal publications, there are the *United States Government Publications Monthly Catalog* (whose December editions also list everything published by the government during the year); Hauser and Leonard's *Government Statistics for Business Use;* specialized catalogs like those on labor and on finance, which list all government publications on subjects like unions, collective bargaining, and strikes (in the labor catalog) and banking, securities, and accounting (in the finance catalog); and the catalogs of the various federal departments like the weekly *Business Service Checklist* which lists everything newly published by the Department of Commerce.

The principal guide to state publications is the Library of Congress's *Monthly Checklist of State Publications* (whose listings are arranged by state, and by department within each state).

Publications by municipal governments around the country are too numerous to be listed in any single guidebook; but they are reasonably well surveyed in the U. S. Census Bureau's weekly *Checklist of Basic Municipal Documents,* in *Recent Publications on Governmental Problems,* and in the *Municipal Yearbook.* The best collections of municipal publications are, of course, housed in the various municipal reference libraries, which we discussed back on page 391.

Gathering Material From Your Library Sources.

Once you've located promising sources of information, you want to compile a *working source list,* a list of all books, articles, and other printed sources from which you may be drawing information for your report. Compile the list on 3 × 5 index cards, one source to a card, as shown on the two sample cards below:

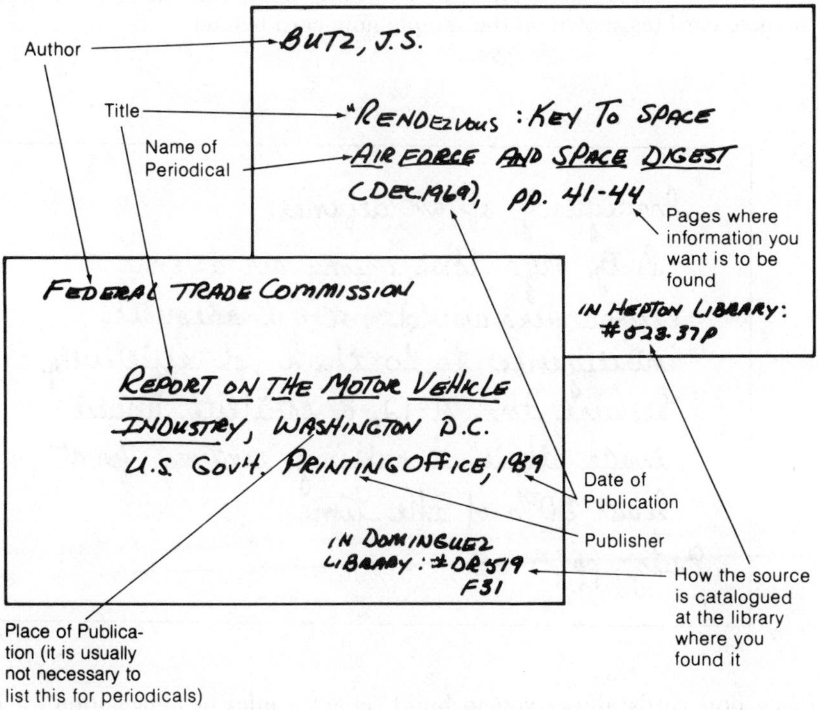

Separate cards are not a must for your source list, but however you compile it, each entry should contain at least the information shown on the samples above.

Such a record will spare you the later annoyance of having to *re*locate a source.

Once you've found your potentially useful sources and listed them, you want to locate the useful information in them, and extract it. Now your ability to *skim read* comes into play. If a book seems promising, turn first to its *preface* or *introduction:* it is here that an author indicates the purpose and scope of the book. Next (if the book still looks useful) scan its *table of contents;* note the chapters. Then turn to the *index* at the rear (if the book has one), and see which pages make mention of pertinent topics; skim those pages as well. If the book has charts, graphs, or illustrations, check its *table of illustrations* at the front and quickly consult those illustrations that seem relevant to your topic. When your promising source is an article in a journal, skim the article, focusing on the opening sentence of each paragraph and reading more carefully only when the contents prove to be "on target."

When you've found what you need, or what you think *might* be useful, extract it. And remember — it's better to take too much than too little. There are several useful methods of extraction.

Most libraries have photocopy machines that aren't expensive unless you copy a large number of pages. Photocopies save you time, spare you writer's cramp, and protect against inaccurate transcription. As soon as you photocopy a page, write its source across the top, circle the pertinent information, and indicate where in the report the information will fit.

If you don't have access to a photocopy machine, use your 3 × 5 cards to take notes from your sources, one note to a card. If you copy verbatim, use quote marks; you may, however, save time by paraphrasing. Be sure that all statistics are copied accurately. Be sure to indicate the source of the note on the note-card (as shown on the sample note-card below):

> Inadequacy of air defense
> Butz says that enemy air defense commanders would not get adequate intelligence to do their job effectively because the A-12-R satellite would evade their tracking systems for at least 80% of the time.
> Butz, pp 63-64

Using note-cards allows you to build separate piles of information for each section of your report. And it allows you to discard notes that later prove to have no value.

Evaluating Your Sources

Not all sources of information will be equally reliable. When extracting data, watch for certain danger signals — tipoffs that the information in the sources may not be perfectly dependable.

1. *Look for some indication of the author's credentials.* Does he or she hold a position of respect in this field? (Beware the "Ph.D." or "Professor" who shows no affiliation with a respected institution — the title is probably to impress the readers.) Has the author written other works in the same field? (You can check this out in biographical registers.) How are this person's writings generally received by other experts in the field? (For this, you can check book reviews in pertinent journals.) Do other writers in the field mention this author as an authority? Do other sources (including bibliographies in the field) refer to his or her writings?

2. *Determine whether the author might be motivated by self-interest.* Does the author stand to gain, financially or otherwise, by expressing certain points of view? (An article by the president of Apax, Inc. praising a new Apax product, would certainly be suspect. So would a book by a known segregationist attacking Affirmative Action hiring programs.)

3. *Beware of the author who depends on sensationalism, or on unsupported generalizations.* The writer who depends entirely on abstractions, purr words and snarl words, and appeals heavily to the reader's emotions is usually *un*reliable as a source of facts. (Remember our discussion of these pitfalls in Chapter 1.)

4. *Distrust the author who depends primarily on a single other secondary source.* The author may be avoiding opinions damaging to his or her own point of view. Back in 1964, a privately published "campaign report," which attacked the then-incumbent President, Lyndon Johnson, made numerous accusations of presidential wrongdoing *and documented all of them.* But most of the footnotes pointed to a single midwestern newspaper which was itself militantly anti-Johnson. Remember, the mere presence of footnotes does not guarantee the reliability of information.

5. *Beware of statistical razzle-dazzle.* Don't automatically accept a statistical analysis. Statistics, as we'll see in Chapter 17, can be used deceptively, both intentionally and unintentionally.

6. *See who published the book you're using.* Is it a well-known and reputable publishing house? The anti-Johnson "report' mentioned above was published by a company previously unheard of — actually by the author himself in a local print shop. While private publication, in itself, proves nothing about a book's quality, chances are good that reputable publishers had a look and decided not to publish it.

7. *Check the date of publication on your source.* While the *latest* word on a subject isn't necessarily the best, older books and articles (especially in scientific and technological fields) do become outdated. Their findings are superseded by newer research.

8. *Don't rely solely upon "omnibus" sources, like encyclopedias, directories, and almanacs.* These sources cover a broad range of topics, so they don't usually provide comprehensive information on any one of them. They are excellent *starting points* in research, but shouldn't be relied upon solely unless all you need are a few broad pieces of information.

9. *Don't depend on summaries, abridged versions, or abstracts of source material,* except to lead you to the originals. The act of leaving out or condensing can result in distortion.

Some Concluding Remarks on Library Research

Learning to use library resources is not a single day's chore. So numerous are these resources that you can learn them only by researching problem after problem. After much trial and error, and a lot of patience, your knowledge of available resources will grow. And let your librarians help you. No group of professionals, generally speaking, is more dedicated than librarians to helping their clientele — that is, you, the researcher. And use this chapter's survey of library resorces as a starting point in learning about them.

Once you've found the information you need, and extracted it for your own use, remember that you've incurred a debt. Some earlier researcher has helped you with your problem. That debt should be repaid through acknowledgment. One reason for carefully compiling your list of sources early on, and for marking the sources of the information you extract, is to help you make your acknowledgments in the finished report. This documentation — we'll discuss its format in Chapter 18 — is not just a matter of form; it's integrity as well. Using someone else's research efforts without acknowledging them — that is, plagiarism — is a form of stealing as unbecoming, and sometimes as illegal, as shoplifting.

PRIMARY RESEARCH

For many reports in business, secondary research — in which you seek information uncovered by someone else — is not enough. Reports on recent situations, unique circumstances, or previously unstudied problems will require that you uncover some new facts of your own. You'll have to do *primary research.*

Essentially, there are three modes of primary research — *observation, experimentation,* and *interrogation.* Though in any one report project you might employ several modes, it's best that we examine them one at a time.

Research by Observation

Observation means, simply to look at something intelligently. Observational research consists of systematically witnessing something and recording the significant facts about it. As a research technique, it can be as complex as charting the orbital eccentricities of the planet Neptune, or as simple as watching a man buy a magazine. And it can involve any of the senses, not just the eyes. The noise abatement inspector, the wine taster, the expert on toxic gases, the buyer of fine cloth — all use observational research methods besides the visual to compile data for their reports.

Nor is observational research limited to the unaided senses, or to what can be recorded with pencil and paper. Modern technology has given researchers a profusion of observational aids — cameras, clocks, thermometers, barometers, rulers, microscopes, telescopes, micrometers, radar, X rays, geiger counters, traffic counters — to help the researcher in systematic observation (provided, of course, that the researcher knows how to use them, or has the help of a specialist).

Observation, like any other kind of research, has its unique strengths and limitations. Done skillfully, observation is perhaps the most reliable — and hence the most convincing — of all kinds of research. Even the best library research must be wary of unreliable secondary sources; the experimenter can have findings distorted by unknown variables; the interviewer can be victimized by unreliable respondents (we'll examine these last two problems in just a moment). But with observation, nothing stands between you and your material. Your findings are as reliable as you are — or as unreliable.

The major limitation of observational research is its inability to probe beyond what can be perceived by the senses. Observation alone, for example, cannot measure attitudes or motives. You can observe that people buy Brand X at the local department store, but you can't observe *why* they buy it.

Another complication arises when a team of observers must pool their observations: uniformity of observation must be maintained. Observing customers at newsstands, one researcher might note that "a man bought a news magazine." Another researcher, his research method uncoordinated with the first's, might note that "a young well-dressed man bought a copy of *Time*." A third might record that "a man first surveyed all the magazines on the rack, then bought *Time*," while a fourth might note that "a man paid for his purchase of *Time* with pennies." Before taking part in any team project that involves observation, be sure that everyone knows precisely the kind of observation to be made.

To observe reliably (as simple as that task may sound!) you must know *when* to observe your subject, *how long* to observe it, and from what *vantage point*. December 15 would not, for example, be the time to observe "normal retail shopping patterns." One week would not be long enough to observe a trend in the Dow-Jones stock average. New York alone would not be sufficient as a place from which to observe new trends in women's fashions. You must always be sure that the observations you make are *representative* of the phenomenon you're researching.

Effective observation can also require *perseverance*, like that of the market-research analyst whose project took him into every supermarket in Bridgeport, Connecticut. He had to determine what percentage of space in each market's display freezer was given over to his client's product, Sealtest Ice Cream. As the study was confidential, the researcher could not reveal his intentions to the market managers. So into each market he went, clipboard and steel tape measure in hand. He measured the length of each display freezer, then measured the portion of it displaying Sealtest to determine the percentage. Several times, the store managers happened by. They asked the man what he was doing. Not getting a satisfactory explanation, two of them ejected him from their store, and two others called the police. Days later, determined to get his data, the researcher (dressed differently) reentered each of these four markets. Without his clipboard, he hurried to the freezers and paced off the measurements he needed. His results were not as accurate, of course, but they were good approximations, and his observational data were complete. He persevered.

Research by Experimentation

Experimentation, long a technique of the sciences, has been used increasingly over the last several decades by business researchers. Essentially, an experiment is nothing more than a well-planned series of observations made while the surrounding circumstances are being controlled and manipulated.

The basic experimental procedure is as follows — you identify the object to be studied, and you measure the characteristic of it that interests you. Then you change one of the important circumstances (or variables) surrounding that object, and remeasure the characteristic, observing how the change has affected it. If all the other surrounding circumstances have been held constant, you can conclude that whatever happened to the characteristic happened *because* that one important variable was changed.

Consider the experiment done by a town government in an effort to relieve southbound traffic congestion at the traffic light at Fifth and Main. Originally, the light was on a three-minute cycle: eighty-seven seconds green, six seconds yellow, eighty-seven seconds red. First, the researcher measured the traffic backup during a succession of red lights, to determine the average backup. Then he altered the length of the light cycle, slowing it down, and speeding it up. He measured the average backup during each of the differently timed light-cycles, and thereby determined the timing that produced the least congestion.

There are pitfalls in this procedure however. Could the researcher, for example, safely assume that the congestion at any one time was wholly attributable to the timing of the traffic light? Perhaps it was affected by the time of day, or by the number of vehicles that were making turns. And on any one day (perhaps the day of the experiment) congestion could have been caused by a department store sale a half-mile north of the intersection. These, and other variables, if not controlled, would have distorted the results of the traffic experiment.

So, to avoid the distortions of these "secondary" variables, the researcher refined his experimental procedure. He used *test units* and *control units* — in this case he made observations on successive days. On the first day, he measured congestion all day long *without* changing the timing of the traffic light. Then on each following day, he made day-long observations with the light newly timed, giving one whole day to each new timing. He had to make sure that no special events were being held nearby on any of the days, or that traffic patterns didn't normally vary on different days of the week (if they did, he would have had to experiment with those days separately). His first day was his *control* day, the day all variables were allowed to operate as usual. Subsequent days were *test* days, days on which all the variables except one — the timing of the traffic light — operated as usual. The researcher could then assume that changes in congestion at different times of the day were probably being caused by the new timing of the traffic light.

Another example: suppose a company wants to measure the public's probable acceptance of a newly designed package for its product. A supply of the newly packaged product is put on sale in a *test* market (probably a single city), while other supplies of the product continue to be sold elsewhere in the familiar old package. The company makes sure that all other marketing factors — advertising, price, availability, the weather, the relative affluence of the immediate consumer market, and so forth — are the same in the test market as in the control markets. If the newly packaged product sells better, the company can conclude that the new package *probably* caused the sales increase. If the experiment is repeated in a different test market, with the same results, the company can safely assume that the new package would result in a nationwide sales increase.

As a general rule, whenever human behavior is being studied, experimentation is risky. There are so many variables that controlling them all is impossible. But with care, and an awareness of the distortion risks involved, experimentation can derive enormously useful results for the business researcher.

Asking Questions: Research by Interrogation

Report writers are often confronted by the need to determine opinions, intentions, motives, recollections, or facts known only to certain people — things that cannot be researched in the library or through observation or experiment. One other type of research remains available: *asking questions*. This kind of research can range from informal discussions with job applicants, to a formal interview with a chairman of the board, to a door-to-door survey of ten thousand people. In each case, the goal is basically the same — to get information from people that is otherwise unobtainable.

Like other kinds of research, asking questions has its difficulties. You (and any assistants you're lucky enough to have) must know *whom* to ask, how to *frame* your questions, what *order* to put them in, and how best to *deliver* those questions to the people you want to answer them.

Whom to Ask If you need only one person's answers, or answers from a small group of people, the matter of *whom* to ask is self-evident. You can pose your questions directly to, say, the corporate Controller, to the members of a select commmittee, or to the witnesses of an accident. But if your report must speak knowledgeably of the attitudes of several thousand company employees, or of many thousands of General Motors stockholders, or many millions of American consumers, the question of *whom* to ask becomes more complicated. Time and cost prevent your asking them all. You have to take a *sampling* of the entire group (of the "universe," as its called), then ask your questions of the sampled individuals, and be assured that their answers accurately reflect the feelings of the "universe" they represent.

How do you assure that their answers are representative? You can never be completely sure, but you can come very close if, besides being large enough, your sample is *random*.

A sample is *random* if all members of the "universe" had an equal chance of being chosen. If they didn't — that is, if some members of the "universe" had a greater chance of being selected in the sample — the results of interrogation will likely be biased toward their kind of response. More of them were likely to have been chosen. In theory, drawing a random sample is as easy as putting every name in a hat, shaking well, and drawing as many names as you need. In practice, though, it isn't quite that simple.

If your "universe" is tightly contained — like the ten thousand employees at a large assembly plant — you could select a random sample of, say, five hundred employees (one-twentieth of the "universe") by using an alphabetized employee list. To give yourself a random starting point on the list, you'd pick a number from one to twenty out of a hat and, from that starting point, choose every twentieth name. (If "twelve" were your randomly chosen starting point, your sample would consist of the numbers: twelve, thirty-two, fifty-two, seventy-two, ninety-two, one hundred and twelve, and so on, down the list.) More difficult is random sampling from a physically scattered universe — like "the American public" or even "all housewives in Los Angeles County." To randomly sample the "L.A. housewives" universe, you would probably engage in *area* sampling. You'd superimpose a grid of numbered squares over a map of Los Angeles County, then randomly select a number of those squares as your sampling areas. In each of the sampling areas, you would then randomly choose among its dwelling units to find the housewives for your sample.[1]

[1] This sample would not be perfectly random because the housewives in the less densely populated squares, once their area was selected, would each have a greater chance of being part of the ultimate sample than the housewives in more crowded sampling areas. But the sample would be *nearly* random, and the method of selecting it is practical and affordable.

In choosing random samples of the public, be wary of using certain convenient lists like the telephone directory or automobile registration lists. People lower on the socioeconomic scale tend to have fewer cars and fewer phones per person than those higher up. Each member of the "public" does not have an *equal* chance of being selected from such lists; so samples drawn from them won't be random.[2]

Framing your Questions Whether you're planning to ask your questions in a single interview or on a questionnaire for a large sampling of respondents, you must carefully prepare the questions you plan to ask. To get full and accurate answers, you've got to ask the right *kinds* of questions, ask them in the right *order,* and avoid various *pitfalls* in asking them.

Essentially there are three kinds of questions you can ask:

1. *Black-or-white* questions (which must be answered by one of two opposite answers) — for example: "Are you married?" "True or false: Baxter is bankrupt." "Does the arrow point left or right?"

2. *Cafeteria* questions (which give the respondent a wider number of possible answers) — for example: "Do you approve of the Alaska pipeline? (a) yes, (b) no, (c) am not sure, (d) don't know about it, (e) don't care." Or "Which of the following uses do you make of your portable tape recorder? (a) to record music from the radio, television, phonograph records or other tapes; (b) to record lectures at school; (c) to record "oral" letters to send to friends; (d) for pure amusement at family or social gatherings."

3. *Open-ended* questions (which allow the respondent to answer in any way, briefly or at length) — for example: "How do you plan to cut next year's budget?" "Why do you prefer to live in Orange County?"

When you're framing questions for a single respondent (like the Corporate Controller), they can all be open-ended; your task of organizing the answers and reporting them poses no special problem. But in a survey that will ask the same

[2] When answers from samples of respondents prove later *not* to have accurately represented their "universe," it's almost never because too few people were questioned. It's because the wrong people were interviewed, or because they were wrongly interviewed. Of course, a sample of two townspeople is less likely to represent their town's opinion than a sample of two hundred. But a sample of one thousand *is* capable statistically of reflecting the opinions of a hundred million people. Very large samples (say, from 10,000 to 50,000 people) aren't much more accurate than samples of 1500 to 5000. The slight statistical advantage of such large samples is hardly ever worth their greater cost.

Formulas of probability, available in any text on basic statistics, reveal probabilities like the following: if, on a question in a survey of 760 randomly chosen people, opinion were to divide 70 percent "yes" and 30 percent "no," the odds are 997 in 1000 that this response reflects, within *five* percent, the feelings of the entire American population on that question. If the sample size were to be increased from 760 to 17,000 (assuming the same 70-30 breakdown of opinion), you'd have the same 997-in-1000 odds of the inaccuracy being less than *one* percent. If opinion were to divide 50-50 instead of 70-30, the sample would have to consist of 900 people (instead of 760) to give you the same 997-in-1000 chance of less than five percent error; and the sample would have to consist of 22,500 people (instead of just 17,000) to reduce your 997-in-1000 chance of error to one percent or less — *as long as the sample is randomly chosen.* You see, then, that twenty times the number of respondents, in this case, reduces the chance of error only from five to one percent — probably not worth twenty times the cost or effort.

questions of many people, you need answers that are not only accurate, but consistent, and easy to tabulate. For this reason, surveys use "black-or-white" or "cafeteria" questions almost exclusively.

In framing your questions, remember that there are a number of pitfalls to avoid:

1. Don't use an inappropriate level of diction. You might ask the board chairman: "For whom do you intend to vote?" But in a public survey, you'd probably want to phrase it: "Who do you intend to vote for?"

2. Avoid *vagueness* in your questions. Questions like "How do you shop?" or "What kind of meals do you prefer?" will leave a respondent groping for clarity.

3. Avoid ambiguity. A simple question like "Why did you buy this car?" can be hopelessly ambiguous. Is the question really asking: "Why did *you* (instead of your spouse) buy this car?" Is it asking: "Why did you *buy* instead of rent this car?" Or is it asking: "Why did you buy *this* car (rather than some other one)?"

4. Don't use undefined relative terms. In questions like "Do you prefer driving fast?" or "Do you visit a physician regularly?" the words *fast* and *regularly* will mean different things in different responses.

5. Don't use undefined abstractions. As with relative terms, they're understood differently by different people. Recall how the writer in the passage on pages 30-31 needed to define what he meant by *insufferable* if he wanted that word to be totally clear.

6. Avoid "hard" words. Instead of asking: "Do you think honesty and generosity are concomitant traits?" scale down your word choice and ask: "Do you think honesty and generosity go together in an individual?"

7. Avoid unnecessary technical terms. Farmers will understand the terms *strip-cropping* and *barn driers.* Anyone who knows anatomy will understand words like *fibula* and *pectoral.* But the average person cannot be expected to know them.

8. Don't ask questions that require much memory. To ask someone when he bought his first TV set, or what she did on her last three New Year's Eves, will get you as many wrong answers as right ones.

9. Don't ask questions about percentages or averages. Most people know how much time they spend in the kitchen each day, but few could tell you *what percentage* of their waking hours they spend there.

10. Avoid direct questions about motives. Most people aren't sure why they buy a certain brand or why they dislike a certain person. The way to uncover motives is to ask a series of "black-or-white" questions. "Do you like the taste of brand X?" "Do you like its package?" and so on, followed by an open-ended question: "What else do you like about it?"

11. Don't ask leading questions, questions that tend to evoke a certain answer. The question: "Would you rather send your son or daughter to Harvard than to any other school?" will get some yeses based solely on a favorable connotation of *Harvard.* If the question were worded: "To what school would you most like to send your son or daughter?" the answers would be different, and more objective.

12. Ask a question indirectly if a more direct phrasing threatens to alter a respondent's thinking. A student researcher I know posed the following question to a sampling of fellow students: "As you know, there has been debate over our college's interdisciplinary curriculum. Some like it. Others think it's a failure. What is your opinion?" Up to that

moment, one student (who was typical of many) had been happy with the curriculum. But upon hearing that some others weren't, the student answered: "Well, I'm not sure." To avoid this influence, experienced researchers would turn that question into a "cafeteria"-type checklist question: "Do you have any objections to the following: (a) The college library facilities, (b) The college cafeteria, (c) The college curriculum, (d) The college parking facilities."

13. Avoid *begging the question*, that is, asking questions that make assumptions that shouldn't be made. You beg the question if you ask someone, "Have you stopped buying pork since the prices went up?" You imply that he or she was buying pork before the prices rose, and that may not be so.

14. Don't ask questions that *pry* unnecessarily. Many people resist direct questions about matters like their income or their age. Such questions are less offensive, and more likely to get accurate answers, if asked in "cafeteria" style. "Into which income bracket do you fall: (a) below $7500, (b) $7500–10,000, (c) $10,000–15,000, (d) $15,000–25,000, (e) above $25,000."

15. Don't ask questions directly that *threaten* a respondent by evoking fear or shame. Some years ago in a study of bums on New York's Bowery, sociologists were asking these men (among other things): "Are you married?" Their answers showed that an unbelievably large number were not married and never had been. The researchers began to doubt these answers. When they changed the question to: "Where is your wife?" the men who had no wives replied: "I'm not married," and the others indirectly admitted they were by saying where she was.

16. Don't ask questions in a way that might stir an irrelevant bias. The question "What is your opinion of Ted Kennedy's plan for a guaranteed annual income?" is more likely to measure Kennedy's reputation than people's opinions about the plan.

17. Don't ask *double-barreled* questions. A question like this one: "Do you feel America should threaten a boycott of Arab goods and a possible military invasion to keep the Arab States from shutting off the oil supply?" is really two questions. They must be asked separately. (Many respondents will feel differently about a *boycott* than a *threatened invasion*.)

18. Don't ask *too many questions*. Don't ask questions whose answers you could learn without asking. Don't ask questions whose answers are clearly implied in other answers. And don't ask the same question twice in different ways (unless you want to double check the validity of earlier answers).

In any plan for interrogational research, bad questions can find their way in. After you've formulated your questions, test them on a few people. See if they're understood as you intend them, and be sure they produce the kind of information you need.

Ordering your Questions The order in which you ask your questions can also affect the answers you get. Encourage free-and-easy replies. Ask your easier questions first; withhold the hard ones, or the more personal ones, until later. If you have no easy questions, make up a few and begin your questioning with them. Ask related questions in a natural order to keep the respondent's interest sharply focused. When questionnaires are to be used by different interviewers, include an opening that cordially "breaks the ice." Notice the positive phrasing of this opening:

> Good morning (afternoon, evening). My name is ____________.
> I'm with the Nebraska State Parks Commission, and we would be pleased to have you tell us your feelings about our state's newly developing roadside parks. May we take just a moment to ask you several questions?

Delivering Your Questions Basically, there are three different ways of delivering your questions to their intended respondent once you've framed and ordered them: *questionnaires, the telephone,* and *face-to-face interview.* Each has its advantages and its drawbacks. Let's look at them:

1. *Questionnaires.* Questionnaires save time — you can distribute a hundred of them much more quickly than you can do a hundred interviews face-to-face or over the telephone. Mailed questionnaires also give you great geographic reach at relatively low cost. A questionnaire in the hands of a respondent allows him or her time to think out the answers, and to look up forgotten data (assuming, of course, that the person is sufficiently motivated to do so). And in the hands of a team of interviewers (who will ask its questions face to face), questionnaires can assure that your questions are posed consistently to each respondent.

On the minus side, it's easier to ignore distributed questionnaires than it is to ignore an interviewer waiting for an answer. They can also be poor tools for obtaining information that is highly personal; unless assured anonymity, people hesitate to put into writing what they will often tell a skillful interviewer. Unless interest in your questions is very high, not all (or even most) of your distributed questionnaires will be returned, even with prodding. And it's not simply a problem of numbers. If only those who feel strongly about your questions respond to them, your answers will not be representative of the random sample at whom you aimed those questions. Here the problem is diagrammed:

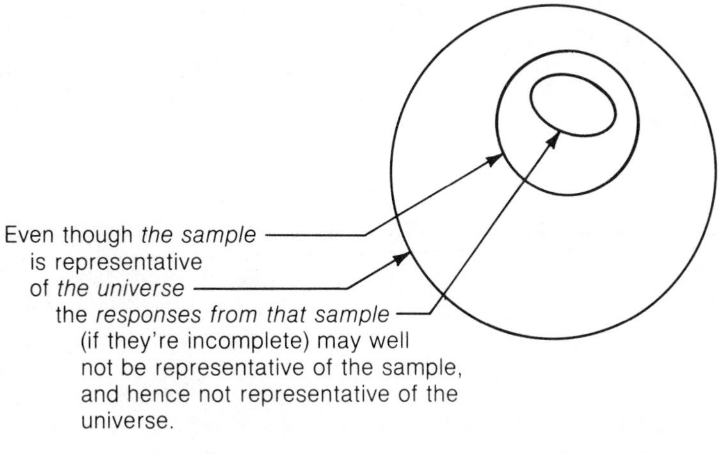

Even though the sample
is representative
of the universe
the responses from that sample
(if they're incomplete) may well
not be representative of the sample,
and hence not representative of the
universe.

2. *The telephone.* The major advantages of the telephone are its speed in reaching people, and its relatively low cost if you have to question quite a few of them. Direct voice contact (as compared to a distributed questionnaire) also makes it harder for potential respondents to ignore your questions.

However, the longer the questioning, the less effective is the telephone as a means of delivery. And people will generally not reveal much personal information over the phone unless they know you. You are also unable to observe your respondents as they make their answers (sometimes that's an important factor). Because so many deceptive sales appeals are attempted over the phone, the public generally distrusts telephone callers who want to ask questions — much to the disadvantage of honest telephone researchers.

3. *Face-to-face interviews.* Face-to-face interviews are obviously the most personal way to ask questions. If you're tactful, you can ask longer, more detailed, and more personal questions face to face than by any other means. You can also (as over the phone) revise your line of questioning as need occurs, and you can clear up any confusion that arises.

The major drawbacks of face-to-face interviewing are its cost and consumption of time. If you have many respondents, or they're geographically widespread, the cost of face-to-face questioning can be prohibitive. (We'll discuss interviewing techniques more fully in Chapter 19.)

IN CONCLUSION

The second half of this chapter, like the first, has been a brief introduction to research method for the student of business communication. The three modes of *primary* research — observation, experimentation, and interrogation (the asking of questions) — are the ways to get the facts when the facts you need have not been previously uncovered and reported on. Our discussion of them here ought to help get you started using any of them in a report project. Sooner or later, you'll want (and need) the detailed discussions that are available in books devoted solely to these research modes. You can find these books in any well-stocked college or business library.

If we've spent a disproportionate amount of time in this chapter on asking questions, it is only because question-asking, unlike observation or experimentation, is a vital addition to reaction-evoking techniques we've been discussing throughout much of this book. Asking questions *is* communication; and because it's sometimes a very difficult kind of communication, it deserves the attention we've given it.

PROBLEMS

1. Assume that you are the Deputy Director of the State Board of Health, and you are put in charge of a research team that has been asked to study and report on the use of marijuana by minors in your state. Your team of researchers consists, for the most part, of college grads between the ages of twenty-two and twenty-seven and many of them have some pretty strong attitudes about the use of "grass." Discuss in detail what you would do to prevent any bias from creeping into the findings uncovered by your researchers.

2. Interrogational research — the asking of questions — must be preceded by careful preparation of the questions to be asked. For each of the following report topics, state *whom* you would interrogate and *what means* of interrogation you would use (face to face, telephone, mailed or distributed questionnaire). Then prepare the questions you would ask (in the order you would ask them).

a. (Your college or university) Ten Years from Now
b. The Occupational Aims of Today's College Student
c. Job Opportunities for ______________ Majors (use whatever academic major you wish)
d. The Perfect Job Applicant
e. The Quality of the College Cafeteria
f. The Cars Preferred by Fleet Operators
g. How Local Employers Feel about Trade Unions

3. Your college (or university) has been selected by Gamma Phi Gamma, the national honorary marketing society, as the site for a survey of students in an attempt to learn why fewer and fewer students seem interested in careers in sales. You have been chosen Project Coordinator, and are responsible for specifically defining and analyzing the problem, and preparing the necessary questioning procedure.

In a cover memo to your instructor, indicate how you are defining and analyzing the problem and what kinds of information you plan to look for. As an attachment to your memo, submit the questions — in their most effective form and format — that you plan to ask.

4. In a memorandum to your instructor, state in detail how you would conduct a business experiment on some problem of interest to you. Assume that you have unlimited time and assistance and whatever funds (within reason) you need. Define and analyze your problem carefully, and reveal your experimental plan clearly.

5. Suppose that you are writing a report to be entitled "Retail Clerks: Good and Bad" — a study of what it takes to be a good retail clerk, and how some people do it much better than others.

A major part of the research on this report will be *observational*. You'll have to make both quantitative observations (how much time is devoted to each phase of the retail clerk's job), and qualitative observations (what manner and technique are used in doing each phase).

Plan a systematic approach to your observation, and apprise your instructor of it in a memorandum.

6. Your company, Hetchy, Inc., is a medium-sized manufacturer of kitchen utensils, whose offices and warehouse are located in a 35,000-square-foot, one-story building on the outskirts of Des Moines, Iowa. The company's president, Harold Dawes, asks you to study the problem of whether Hetchy should continue maintaining its own plant security force, or whether it would be more efficient to contract with an outside security agency.

After defining and analyzing the problem, you now want to prepare a bibliography (or working list of secondary sources) to help provide the information you need. Compile that bibliography and give it to your instructor in a memorandum.

7. Compile a starting bibliography for each of the following topics, or for those among them that your instructor chooses:

a. The Battle Between Margarine and the High-Priced Spread
b. The Uses of TV in Business Education
c. The Failure of the Edsel Automobile
d. The Failure of Xerox's Computer Division
e. Public Relations and the Banking Industry
f. The Boom in Vacation Homes
g. Professional Football Is Big Business
h. Patterns of Child Adoption
i. The Increasing Incidence of Emphysema in America
j. Innovation in Executive Compensation Plans
k. The Future of Supersonic Jet Transport Service
l. The Present State of the Cotton-Growing Business
m. The Preservatives That Are Put into Our Food
n. The Uses of Electronic Data Processing in the Small Firm
o. The Future of Geothermal Energy in the U.S.
p. The Effects of Disarmament on American Industry

8. Using the discussion of *reference works* (on pages 392-393) as a guide, go to your college library and examine its holdings of reference works. In a memo to your instructor, list three or four of each of the twelve types of reference works that the library holds. As part of each listing (unless the title of the reference work makes it clear) indicate the scope of the reference work's coverage.

9. You are once again (as in problem 9 back on pages 387-388) consultant to Sam Baker, the insurance broker who wishes to create the "Young Riskless Club" for drivers under 25 who have good safety records.

Earlier, you carefully defined and analyzed the problem that Sam asked you to solve and report upon. Now, in a separate memo to Sam, you are to set down thoroughly the research plan that you'll be following to solve the problem and write the report.

10. Submit to your instructor a detailed research plan for the report project you proposed in problem 10 of Chapter 14 on page 388. Be sure to indicate the kinds of secondary sources you plan to use, and provide specific descriptions of the observation, experimentation, or interrogation you plan to do. Then, with your instructor's okay, go ahead with the research.

11. In the last decade or so, there has developed (or so it is widely believed) a substantial effort to make corporations more responsive to the "public good," rather than have them simply pursue increased profits. Companies are being pushed to provide broader job opportunities, to protect the environment more effectively, to loosen their hold on the American political process, and in general to make greater social contributions than they have heretofore made.

Select a company (the bigger the better), whose offices are reasonably nearby, and arrange to interview an executive there (the higher up the better) who can speak with authority on the impact this new public mood is having on the company's policies and practices.

Before you do the interview, submit to your instructor a memo that lays out the questions you plan to ask the executive, and the order in which you plan to ask them. Tell your instructor what interviewing strategy you propose to follow to get the most out of the interview.

Then, with your instructor's approval, conduct the interview.

CHAPTER 17

GIVING SHAPE TO YOUR FINDINGS

When research is done, your findings must be systematically organized. And if your report project calls for it, those findings must be interpreted. In this chapter, we'll look at these next two vital phases of the business report project — *organizing* and *interpreting* your research findings.

ORGANIZING YOUR FINDINGS

*Un*organized information (what we call *raw data*) is useless until it's given order. One writer has likened the problem of raw data to that of the house builder who allowed suppliers to dump all the building materials ordered into one big pile in the middle of the construction site. If your report is to convey information only, the findings must be organized for their best presentation. If, on the other hand, the report must also interpret, then the findings must be organized to aid that interpretation. In either case, it's vital that what you found during research be organized.

Actually, the best guide for organizing your findings has been with you from the start: it's your tentative working outline. Prior to research, that outline (and the problem-analysis that went into it) showed you what you needed to know before you could write the report. Now, with research completed, the outline can become the report's very framework, the skeletal structure into which you fit your findings. As you do so, you may find that the outline needs revision. That's no cause for worry. The outline was intended, from the start, to be flexible and accommodate whatever your research uncovered.

Handling Unexpected Information

You may find, for example, that during your research you found important information you didn't anticipate, and weren't looking for. The outline must be adjusted to accommodate it.

As an example, recall the "lunch break" problem we defined back on pages 376–377 and began to analyze on page 382. Assume that while you are surveying employee opinions about the new lunch-break policy, you find that the policy is being implemented differently at each of the company's three plant sites. This is a new and unexpected factor, and an important one. For one thing, it tells you (at the moment you discover it) that you have some extra research to do — to find out *why*. After you find out why, and then finish surveying employee opinions, you will probably alter your original outline. That original outline looked like this:

```
            OPINIONS OF ACME'S EMPLOYEES
         ABOUT THE COMPANY'S NEW POLICY OF
               STAGGERED LUNCH BREAKS

1.0 Opinions of Foremen
2.0 Opinions of Assembly-Line Workers
3.0 Opinions of Junior Executives
                              etc.
```

The new revised outline will probably look like this:

```
            OPINIONS OF ACME'S EMPLOYEES
         ABOUT THE COMPANY'S NEW POLICY OF
               STAGGERED LUNCH BREAKS

1.0 The new policy as implemented at Plant ''A''
    1.1 Opinions of Foremen
    1.2 Opinions of Assembly-Line Workers
                              etc.
2.0 The New Policy as Implemented at Plant ''B''
    2.1 Opinions of Foremen
                              etc.
3.0 The New Policy as Implemented at Plant ''C''
    3.1 Opinions of Foremen
                              etc.
```

With this revised working outline, you've now accounted for the unexpected information, and organized it smoothly into the scheme of the report.

Let's look, as well, at another problem we've seen before: the problem of where to locate the XYZ Company's proposed new factory (which we analyzed, criterion by criterion, on page 383). Perhaps, during your research, you learned about a new federal subsidy for companies who build facilities in depressed rural areas. Your original outline hadn't anticipated this factor; but it can easily be expanded to account for it:

```
            WHERE TO LOCATE XYZ'S PROPOSED
                     NEW FACTORY

1.0 Proximity to Major Markets
    1.1 Possible Site #1
    1.2 Possible Site #2
                           etc.

2.0 Accessibility to Suppliers
    2.1 Possible Site #1
    2.2 Possible Site #2
                           etc.
                            .
                            .
                            .
6.0 Availability of Federal Subsidy
    6.1 Possible Site #1
    6.2 Possible Site #2
                           etc.
```

The new criterion added to the working outline.

The new federal subsidy might even present you with another site possibility — in which case that possible new site would now have to be accounted for under *each* of the criteria (1.0, 2.0, 3.0, etc.). Again the working outline proves flexible. It allows you to organize information that's both expected and unexpected.

Handling Superfluous Information

Some of the information you sought during research may prove superfluous, and unnecessary, once you have it. If it should, don't include it in your report; deadwood is deadwood no matter how hard you worked to find it.

Recall, for example, the problem of assessing the XYZ Company's public relations program (which we analyzed back on page 383.) As you scrutinize your findings under each subheading, and come to subheading 6.0, the company's "relations with the media," you may see that you've learned a lot about XYZ's advertising strategy and about the creation of its radio commercials. Now, these "media" findings may be interesting, but they have little to do with the question at hand: XYZ's image among the media and its working relationship with them. File such findings away for future reference. Keep the body of your report free of anything that isn't central to the problem being reported on.

If you feel that such findings do have a limited, though not a central, bearing on the problem, you can include them in an *appendix*. (More about appendices in the following chapter.)

Discovering Gaps in Your Findings

By using your working outline to organize your findings, you may also discover gaps in those findings, gaps that would otherwise go unnoticed. Consider the problem we began to analyze on page 382. *How the Grievance Arose Against John Doe.* In fitting your findings into that problem's chronological outline, you might discover a missing link between a certain pair of facts. Let's assume that Fact *A* (as you learned during research) was that Doe rejected a customer's request, triggering the episode. Fact *B* might be that Roger Remy, another employee of the company, told Harold Howe, the general manager, about Doe's treatment of the customer. But there's a gap. Your attempt to organize these findings into your working outline reveals that you have at least one more bit of research to do. How did Remy learn of Doe's action? You must find out.

Or consider the problem we outlined on pages 381–382: the evaluation of candidates for Leroy's Accounts Directorship. In fitting your findings about Arnold Adams into that outline, you might discover, when you get to item 1.241, that Adams in his interview with Neville Washington mentioned that he'd once taught accounting. You look back at your 1.1 category (that is, *Experience*) and see that, under it, you have no data on Adams's teaching. So you've got to back up, find out about that experience, and adjust your outline to account for it. If it proves to be true, you need a new subcategory, a 1.1.3 — "Adams's Teaching Experience" or "Other Professional Experience." If it doesn't prove out, then you've got an important new piece of information for your 1.4 category — the fact that Adams lied or exaggerated in his interview. In either case, the gap became obvious when you *organized* your findings.

Editing Your Findings

Ideally, all the information you sought during research gets to your desk in a clear and immediately usable form. But in the real world things don't happen so neatly.

When you're doing all the secondary research or the necessary observation yourself, or when you're conducting an experiment, a survey, or an interview singlehandedly, you can — and obviously ought to — make sure that your findings are accurately and systematically recorded. But when others are helping you, or when you're getting written responses to your questionnaires, you will often have to *edit* the returns. Some responses may be ambiguous or unintelligible. A careless checkmark may fall between two boxes. Someone's handwriting may prove illegible. You may have to scrap not only the unreadable response, but other responses that are closely related to it.

If you stumbled into any of the interrogational pitfalls that we discussed back on pages 403–404, you may not discover it until now when you see that the answers you're getting don't make sense. In such a case you may have to invalidate the question and scrap *all* its responses (a painful decision after you've gone to the effort of getting them).

And, in a survey, if you asked open-ended questions, the answers to them must now be compiled into categories. You might, as a survey team in Montana did several years ago, ask hundreds of people: "What do you think is the most important problem facing your local area at the present time?" When that survey team organized their findings later on, they carefully edited the answers into significant categories of response, as shown in Figure 48. (Note that each category is code-numbered to aid the researchers in interpreting the data by computer; and that each category is shown with a few of its verbatim responses, so that its scope is clear.)

Perhaps there are inconsistencies or contradictions in your findings. These must be resolved before you proceed. Suppose you discover that two authorities (whose opinions you've drawn upon) disagree on a simple point of fact; or that one of your respondents, who claims an annual buying behavior of thirty thousand dollars, earns only twelve. You'll have to stop and check a third (and perhaps even a fourth) authority; you'll either have to clarify the respondent's answers or scrap them as unreliable.

Figure 48
Responses to an open-ended question which has been edited into categories.

QUESTION: What do you think is the most important problem facing your local area at the present time? (open-ended probe)

RESPONSES:

00. Blank / Don't Know / No Response.
01. Taxes — local and state taxes / too many taxes / high property taxes / trying to figure the best way to derive tax revenue.
02. Government Spending — not enough benefits for the money we pay / poor money management / the budget of the city of Butte.
03. Government Corruption — corruption in local government.
04. Urban Renewal — urban renewal should be better organized / doubt the success of urban renewal / reconstruction of Butte / forcing urban renewal on us.
05. Unemployment / General — unemployment / mines all closed down / lack of job opportunities / unemployment among forest product workers since Banner Mill closed down / no jobs for men.
06. Lack of Industry — lack of industry / need to get some industry payrolls in here / should open up the mines.
07. Anaconda Company / Unemployment / Transfers — Anaconda selling out causing unemployment / Anaconda transfers / Anaconda buying property elsewhere — relocating families elsewhere.
08. Economy / General — lack of money / the economic problem / people go out of town to buy.
09. Inflation / High Prices — inflation / high prices / the high cost of living / retired person's area so prices are higher here.
10. Education — education / our schools need improving.
11. Drugs — young people have access to drugs.
12. Crime / Law Enforcement — crime / laws not enforced / teenage crime.
13. Moral Decay — people don't respect one another / not enough people have their lives centered on God.
14. Population Growth — people coming into the area too fast / influx of people causing land values to soar / Missoula growing too fast.
15. Inadequate Housing — no houses for old people / a lot of the housing needs to be cleaned up.
16. Zoning / Land Development — zoning too strict / zoning won't allow trailers inside city limits / can no longer build what we want to / the need for land use planning.
17. Ecology — environmental / development versus preservation / have to preserve the wilderness better.
18. Pollution / Water / Land — pollution of rivers and streams / littering / location of dumps / pollution of Flathead Lake.
19. Streets — streets are our most important problem / street care and maintenance.
20. No Problems — none / no problems.

In every case, editing your findings requires keen judgment. If you feel, in a given project, that your judgment is not experienced enough, you'll want to consult with someone whose judgment is.

Tabulating Your Findings

Tabulation is the process of putting your findings, where possible, into *tables*. Tables are simply devices for making your findings more *visual*. They allow the findings to be easily scanned and their inner relationships more easily compared. (If your research was observational or experimental you probably put your observations straight into tables as you recorded them.)

Take, for example, the responses to that Montana survey question. To prepare them for interpretation, they (along with the responses to the survey's other questions) must first be tabulated — as shown in Figure 49.

Figure 49
Table of responses to a question.

TABLE OF RESPONSES TO THE QUESTION:

What do you think is the most important problem facing your local area at the present time?

Response Code	Response Category	Number of respondents indicating this as the major problem
00	Don't Know / No Response	30
01	Taxes	20
02	Government Spending	15
03	Government Corruption	2
04	Urban Renewal	13
05	Unemployment (General)	91
06	Lack of Industry	71
07	Anaconda Company	83
08	Economy (General)	104
09	Inflation / High Prices	55
10	Education	2
11	Drugs	3
12	Crime / Law Enforcement	24
13	Moral Decay	14
14	Population Growth	17
15	Inadequate Housing	12
16	Zoning / Land Development	19
17	Ecology	15
18	Pollution	28
19	Streets	2
20	No Problems	21

Although tables lend themselves best to *numerical* data, they can sometimes be used to help visualize *verbal* data, and make it easier to interpret. That's what the table in Figure 50 does. It brings together the opinions of five well-known economists who were asked to judge a new five-point plan for economic growth that had been proposed by the President's Council for Economic Advisement. The table summarizes their feelings about each point, and about the plan as a whole.

Figure 50
Putting verbal data into tabular form.

Summary of the Opinions of Five Economists on the
Five Point Proposal of the President's Council for Economic Advisement

	Point # 1	Point # 2	Point # 3	Point # 4	Point # 5	Overall Opinion of the Proposal
Economist #1 Dr. Millard Levering Harvard College	strongly approves "best part of the proposal"	sees as unimportant	approves (with a single reservation about its cost efficiency)	approves (though sees this item as less important than the rest)	mixed opinion "will work if it's publicized—but that's expensive"	Generally optimistic "Program is worth trying."
Economist #2 Dr. Kenneth Patch Rand Corp.	approves	disapproves	tentatively approves (wants to see labor union reaction to it)	mildly approves	mixed opinion (sees results as "unlikely"—but thinks the item is a sop to some supporters of the plan)	Proposal should be accepted "...though we should proceed carefully and in measured increments."
Economist #3 Dr. Mildred Ewart Valhalla Univ.	mixed opionion "problems may outweigh the benefits"	strongly disapproves	strongly approves	tentatively approves	approves	Would vote that proposal be implemented as long as point #2 were deleted.
Economist #4 Dr. Quentin Nicholls Colman Research Institute	strongly approves	disapproves	strongly disapproves "cost will far outweigh the benefits"	disapproves	approves	Feels proposal is generally inadequate. "But it may cure spot problems, and give us a starting point for next year's council deliberations."
Economist #5 Dr. Lev Pearlman Stanford Institute	indifferent	indifferent	strongly disapproves (feels this is the central point in the "whole wishy-washy" proposal)	indifferent	mildly approves (feels this one could work if other steps were in line)	Strongly objects to the "cosmetic" nature of the plan. "Where it is substantive, it is backward in its approach."

Whenever possible, tabulate your findings. They are easier to interpret that way. You will often find yourself bringing those same tables into your final report as visual aids (a matter we'll discuss in the following chapter).

A Word About Electronic Data Processing

In counting and tabulating business data, the old "one-two-three-four-slash" method (𝍸) and the ten-key adding machine are now pretty much relics of the past. *Data processing* (that is, the organizing and interpreting of data) has been largely taken over by electronic computers. During the research phase, information is entered directly onto computer cards and processed electronically, resulting in print-out sheets of information that are as detailed and sophisticated as the "programming" that went into them. Electronic data processing (EDP) has made the task of the business report writer easier, and at the same time allowed for interpretations more complex and more reliable than in the past.

Every few years, a "new generation" of computers comes to the fore, dramatically increasing the capacity to organize, store, and interpret data. Even the most experienced handlers of business information find themselves constantly striving to "keep up with their new computers."

Any lengthy discussion of electronic data processing (EDP) is beyond the scope of this text. But you won't really be prepared for a career in modern business until you've taken at least an introductory course in EDP — and, preferably, a few advanced ones.

INTERPRETING YOUR FINDINGS

No doubt your first reports on the job will be (or were) purely informational. You'll be asked to uncover some necessary facts and present them on paper, clearly and in good order. But before very long (if those first assignments are handled skillfully) you'll be asked to do more than just report the facts. You'll be expected to *interpret* them. That's a crucial point in one's career. One's ability to interpret findings — to make sense out of them, and show what they mean to the organization — is the clue that bosses look for. To them, it spells talent and the capacity for even greater responsibility. For you, it means promotion and job success.

The First Question: How Far to Interpret

Once you know that you're expected to interpret the facts you've found, make sure how *far* that interpretation should go. Are only specific parts of your data to be interpreted? Or should overall conclusions be drawn as well? And if conclusions are called for, should you take the additional step and turn them into recommendations?

Suppose, for example, that your boss, the corporate sales manager, asks you for a report interpreting current sales trends. Should you limit yourself to identifying sales trends as *up* or *down* on a territory-by-territory basis? Or should you draw overall conclusions — perhaps by evaluating the company's overall sales condition based on your territory-by-territory data? Should you, moreover, recommend steps to be taken to improve the current sales picture — perhaps greater effort in certain territories, maybe the abandonment of others, perhaps the hiring of more sales people or the firing of others? (A lot of toes that can be stepped on.) No doubt your first interpretive efforts should stop well short of making recommendations — maybe they should even withhold overall judgments. Only your feeling for the relationship between you and your boss can let you know. As time goes on, though, and your responsibility grows, your interpretations *will* become broader and broader.

Keeping an Objective Frame of Mind

Before you begin interpreting your findings, it's vital that you purge yourself of any *preconceptions* or *wishful thinking* about what they will or should prove. If you are smugly confident that your findings will substantiate a certain viewpoint, or if you strongly hope they will, a poor interpretation is almost guaranteed. People tend to find facts and arguments that support what they've believed from the start, and tend to overlook or undervalue the rest. The report writer who starts out to "prove" that Philadelphia's economy is in bad shape will no doubt see the falling profits of the city's five largest companies as proof of the point. The writer who believes the city is economically sound, will no doubt view the same falling profits as unreliable indicators. Truth probably lies somewhere in between: those falling profits aren't proof in themselves, but they do suggest an economic "softness" in the city. Both writers were led to view the facts unclearly because they each wanted to show a certain outcome, rather than write an objective report.

Quantifying Data for Interpretation

No single chapter — no whole book, for that matter — could catalog all the possible ways of interpreting information. Every problem has its own best way of handling the data. It's your job, as a report writer with growing experience, to find that best way. A few rules-of-thumb are possible, though. The most general is this: Information is most easily interpreted when it is accurately reduced to numbers. That's why most report writers seek to *quantify* their information, to give it numerical value.

In problems that involve distances, time periods, dollar values, or the like, the numbers are already there. A problem like: *Will It Be Profitable for the OK Corporation to Expand into the Hawaii Market?* shouldn't be difficult to interpret soundly (once the data are in). With an accountant at hand, we could determine the *cost of expansion* into Hawaii, the *fixed costs* of doing business in Hawaii, and the *variable cost* of selling each item of OK's product there. From these figures, we can determine what OK's *break-even point* would be (that is, how much of its product the OK Corp. would have to sell in Hawaii not to lose any money there). We can also measure, in terms of dollars, the existing *market* in Hawaii for OK's product, and what the *up-trends* or *down-trends* in that market are. We can determine what *percentage* of that market OK would have to capture to reach its break-even point, and calculate how long it should take (with a given amount of advertising expenditure) to reach it. All these factors are quantitative. If we account for each of them, we ought to be able to interpret the data, and answer the central question, without too much difficulty.

Quantification becomes less certain in a project like the Montana opinion survey, which (like all such surveys) runs the risks of sampling error and unrepresentative responses. Nonetheless, because the survey team must quantify in order to interpret, it tabulates the responses to each of its questions (as in Figure 49), turns those numbers into percentages, and bases its campaign appeals on the problems that worry the greatest percentage of people. (If 200 people responded to the survey, then the twenty who felt that "Taxes" were the major problem would represent 10% of the total; the twenty-eight who said "Pollution" would be 14%; and so on.)

The survey team will also perform numerous *cross-tabulations* to identify internal relationships among its findings. (For example, only twenty-eight people, or 14% percent, of the Montanans interviewed thought "Pollution" was their major local problem; but what is the percentage of those who live in Butte, the state's mining center, who feel that way? A cross-tabulation of responses, city by city, would reveal this more specific information.)

Other kinds of report problems are even more difficult to quantify, and hence interpret. Consider a problem like "Assessing the XYZ Corporation's Public Relations Program" (which we looked at on page 383), or "Evaluation of the President's Council's Plan for Economic Growth" (the responses to which were tabulated in Figure 50). They are both problems of *qualitative* evaluation, not easily assigned numerical values. But some kind of rough quantification will be tried nonetheless, to provide a basis for interpretation. (For example, in the latter problem, none of the five experts disapproves of point 1 of the plan, none approves of point 2, they split almost evenly on point 3, and so on. So point 1 will probably be judged one of the plan's better points, and point 2 one of its worst.)

Realizing how useful numbers are in interpreting, report writers plan to quantify their data even before they research it. This planning becomes part of their problem analysis.

Inductive and Deductive Reasoning

Drawing general conclusions from specific data (as was done in interpreting the opinions of the five economists) is called *inductive reasoning,* or *induction.* It's a method of reaching conclusions that is used all the time, no matter how accurately quantified the data are. If *most* of the specific instances that make up your evidence point in a certain direction, you can draw a conclusion — and hedge it as the evidence warrants. Here's the inductive process illustrated:

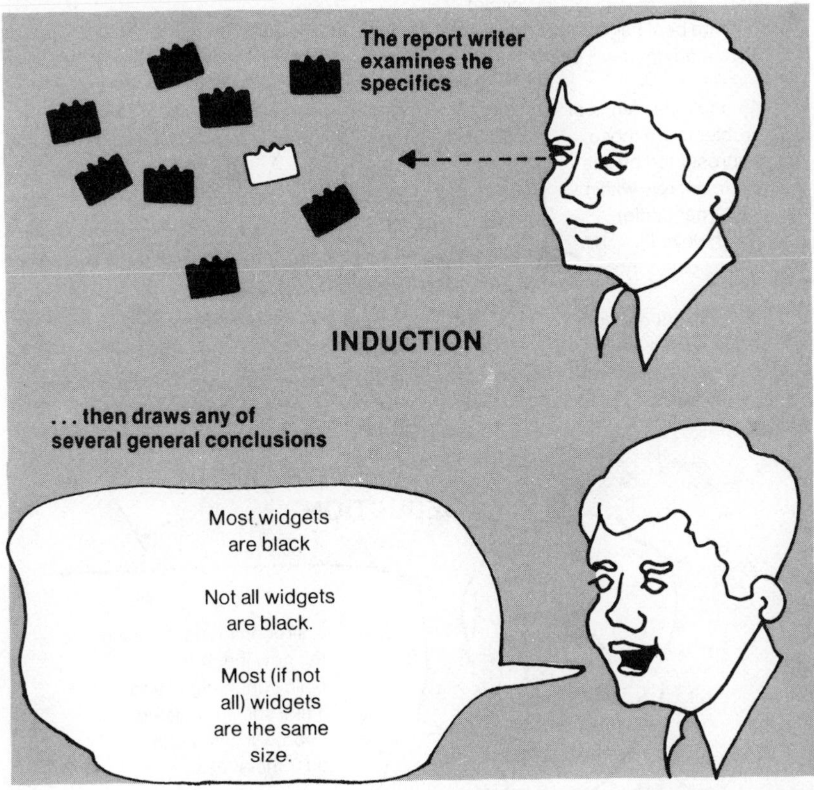
The report writer examines the specifics
INDUCTION
. . . then draws any of several general conclusions
Most widgets are black
Not all widgets are black.
Most (if not all) widgets are the same size.

Deductive reasoning, or *deduction,* is the process of drawing a specific conclusion from facts (or *premises)* we already know. Recall, for example, the problem in which a researcher was asked to measure employees' attitudes toward the company's new lunch-break policy, and to make a recommendation on the basis of what was found. Let's assume that through interrogation it is learned that employees don't really like the new policy, but that it is not a major complaint of theirs. Having examined the various theories of personnel management, the researcher also knows that, as a general rule, most cases of employee discontent that don't involve wages or safety are best handled by letting the offending policy remain in force, and making some other, unrelated goodwill gesture to the employees. Knowing what he does, then, the researcher will reason deductively, as follows:

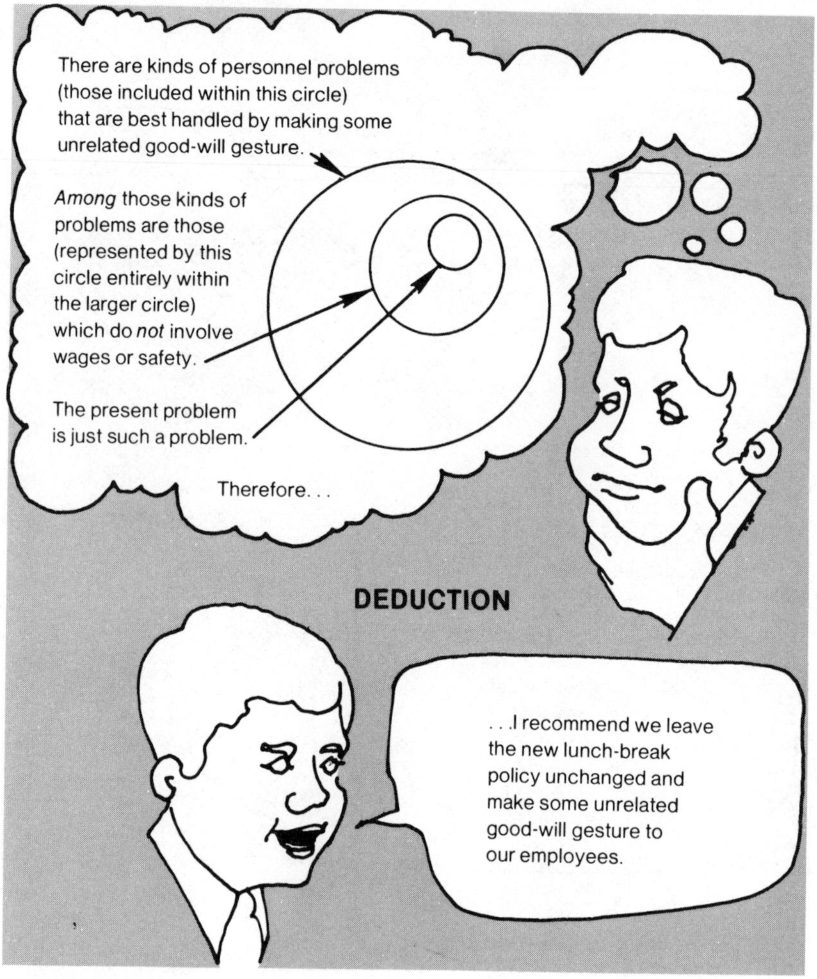

Interpretive Pitfalls

Besides requiring clear, sound thinking, the interpretive process is beset with pitfalls that must be avoided if a report is to do its job. Let's examine some of these pitfalls.

1. *Hasty conclusions.* The more eager the report writer, the more likely he or she is to leap at the first interpretation the evidence allows. More evidence often shows the first conclusion to be the wrong one. Sometimes, even with complete evidence, no firm conclusion is possible.

2. *Faulty premises.* Deductive reasoning can be sound, and still *wrong* if one of the premises is faulty. If, for example, the theory that "certain personnel problems are best solved with an unrelated good-will gesture" is *not true*, the conclusion reached in our "lunch break" problem will be erroneous. Always distinguish among *facts* (which are provable), *inferences* (which are conclusions based on facts), and *opinions* (which often aren't based on anything) — and treat them accordingly in your deductive interpretations.

3. *Misleading statistics.* To say that "the average income of a neighborhood is almost $38,700" implies that it is a neighborhood of well-to-do families. It does not reveal — it even hides — the fact that in the case at hand twenty of its families average only $14,500 a year while the other two average $200,000.

4. *Meaningless percentages.* Percentages are useful only when their base-numbers are large enough to justify their use. It would be grossly misleading to say that "employment at the Kahn Can Company fell by over fourteen percent last month" when, in fact, the company had only seven employees and one of them quit.

5. *Wrongly assumed causes.* Just because the latest wave of inflation was preceded by large pay increases to labor unions does *not* mean that the new inflation was *caused* by those raises. They may have been the cause, or one of several causes, but we can't merely assume that they were.

6. *Neglected variables.* A study not long ago reported (among other things) that graduates of Harvard University earned, on the average, eight thousand dollars more per year than graduates of Valhalla University. It concluded, therefore, that a Harvard education was worth that much more than a Valhalla education. What it neglected when it made that interpretation, however, was the fact that Harvard students were much more likely to come from wealthy homes, and would have made more money than Valhalla graduates even if they never went to college.

7. *Incomparable data.* Some data can't reasonably be compared with other data, even if they look comparable. You cannot, for example, use the fact that bread cost 19¢ a loaf in 1945 to show that times were better then. People didn't earn as much in 1945, and in fact it took more minutes of work to earn the price of a loaf then than it does now.

Adapting Your Interpretations to Your Readers

The final part of the interpretive process is your willingness — and ability — to adapt your findings and conclusions to your reader's ability to understand them. Different audiences require different explanations and differently adapted presentations.

If your report includes quantitative data, you must determine whether your readers will grasp the significance of the large numbers, decimals, ratios, averages, or statistical distributions you include; or whether you must interpret their significance for these readers by relating them to ideas more commonly understood. Certain readers will understand the magnitude of the national budget better if they are told, not only that it is $500 billion per year, but that the figure breaks down to over $2200 a year for every man, woman, and child in America. Or if you wish to point out that the distance to the moon is 239,000 miles, you might also state that it would take a jet airliner about seventeen days and nights of continuous flight to make the trip (if it could), or that it would take a train about six months.

If your report involves objects, concepts, or processes unfamiliar to your reader, you must decide how much definition or explanation to include. Writing to an audience of bankers, you would not have to define terms like *municipal bonds* or *credit rating*. They know the terms well. But if writing instead to potential investors (many of whom might be financially unsophisticated), you would probably include elements of definition and explanation:

> Municipal bonds--that is, bonds issued by states, counties, cities or special taxing districts--come in a wide range of credit ratings. The safest are rated ''triple-A'' while the riskiest are rated ''C'' or ''D.''

Remember, writing a report is not a self-indulgent process. It is communication. You must know, or at least make every attempt to estimate, your readers' grasp of your subject and what you're saying about it — and you must adapt your interpretations to it.

IN SUMMARY

Your research findings, once you have them, must be put into order. They must be *organized;* and in the majority of cases, they must be *interpreted* to some degree. Top executives complain all the time that the reports they get from their subordinates are disorganized and deficient in showing what their findings mean. One chapter in a textbook like this won't solve the problem, but it ought to alert you to the need to work as hard with your findings *after* you've found them as you did in getting them. Realize that a well-organized report, a report that highlights the logical relationships between its subtopics, also reflects — in unmistakable ways — its writer's capacity to impose logical order on his material. And know, too, that your ability to interpret what you've found is, probably, the most fundamental sign of your worth to an organization.

PROBLEMS

1. During the next week or two (however long your instructor directs) collect all the examples of faulty interpretive thinking you can find. Get them from the daily newspaper, magazines, books (including textbooks), from listening to the radio and watching TV, and from conversations with other people. Present them in a memorandum to your instructor, with a brief explanation of the faultiness in each.

2. Prepare a detailed checklist of the factors that editors of data should be concerned with as they edit the returns of a mail questionnaire.

3. Consult a standard textbook on statistics, and find out from it the tools of data analysis that would be useful to the Savoy Manufacturing Company in analyzing its personnel turnover in 1980. Here are the pertinent figures:

Unit	*Workers 1/1/80*	*Workers 12/31/80*	*Workers Hired in 1980*	*Workers Resigned in 1980*	*Workers Fired in 1980*	*Workers Short 12/31/80*
Plant:						
A	1,825	1,715	336	425	21	185
B	1,832	1,650	425	540	67	236
C	1,850	1,601	456	689	16	91
D	910	890	165	182	3	16
Office:						
1	82	88	21	13	2	5
2	110	62	6	13	41*	0

*Reduction in force associated with installation of new equipment and closing three branches.

4. Figures from the *Annual Assessment of American Advertising* show that the percentages of the "total dollar" spent on advertising in America have shifted in the last several decades, as shown in the following table:

	1960	1970	1980
Newspapers	36.3%	31.0%	29.9%
TV	3.0	13.3	18.3
Direct Mail	14.1	15.3	13.7
Magazines	9.4	8.2	7.2
Radio	10.6	5.8	6.5
Business	4.4	5.1	3.7
Papers	2.5	1.7	1.0
Outdoor	19.7	19.6	19.7
Misc.	100.0%	100.0%	100.0%

Based on what you know about the shifts in American society and the growth of various media during the last quarter century, account as best you can for these trends. Report your interpretations in a memorandum to your instructor.

5. The following report is a superb example of business writing adapted to its audience — intelligent newspaper readers who are interested in learning something about the complexities of investing in municipal bonds. Read it carefully. In a memo to your instructor, identify *all* the things its author does to *adapt* his fairly technical material to his nontechnical audience. (If you see any weaknesses in presentation, note them too.)

How to Make Your Nestegg Grow in the Bond Market

BY JOHN GETZE

Are you tired of earning 5 or 6% on your nest egg?

If you have enough cash in a savings institution to tide you over life's little emergencies, and if your job or income prospects look good for the foreseeable future, you may want to consider bonds.

With relative safety, you can begin earning up to 9 or 10% immediately.

Basically, bonds are IOUs that earn interest. The issuer — a corporation, the U.S. government or a municipality — agrees to return your money (principal) at a future date, and in the meantime, pay you annual or semiannual fees (interest).

Unlike stockholders, you cannot expect to receive anything more than what you originally agreed to.

If the issuer goes bankrupt, however, the claims of the bondholders are satisfied before any amount is paid to the stockholders.

Of the three major categories of bonds, "governments" are easily the safest. U.S. bonds are backed by the full faith and credit of the United States government, and if it goes bankrupt, we're all going to be in deep trouble anyway.

"Municipal" bonds rank second in safety, although, like "corporates" (the third category), they come in a wide range of credit ratings. The best are rated "triple-A," while the worst are rated "C" or "D."

Municipal bonds are issued by states, counties, cities or special taxing districts. They are backed by the taxing provisions of that entity's government.

Corporate bonds are, of course, issued by corporations, and thus are backed by the faith and credit of that company.

In all three categories, there are "short-term" bonds and "long-term" bonds, and even "intermediates." These terms refer to the length of maturity; in other words, how long it will be before the bondholder gets his principal back.

In the government sector, short-term can mean anything from 90 days (Treasury bills) to three or four years (Treasury notes). Intermediates generally refer to bonds in the five-to-10-year maturity range, and long-term means anything over that.

Municipal bonds usually are offered with maturities ranging from one to 25 or 30 years, while corporates can most often be found in 5-to-25-year maturities.

Picking the right maturity for your needs is very important, according to investment advisers. The vast majority of bonds purchased by individuals are kept until maturity, and there's a good reason.

If you should have to sell your bond before it matures, there's no way of telling what you'll get for it. Some of your prinicipal could be lost, or, if you're lucky, you might make a profit. It all depends on what has happened to interest rate levels since the time of purchase.

Let's say a company sold bonds several years ago with a yield of 5%. Today, that same company wants to sell a new bond issue, but finds that, because of changed economic condition, it must offer 8% in order to attract investors.

It's obvious that you and everyone else would rather have the new bond paying 8% than the old one paying 5%. Thus, the market price of that old, 5% bond must move downward so that its yield to a new buyer is comparable to the new bond's rate of 8%.

This is why investment advisers say that, for most individual investors, bonds are no substitute for a savings account. With your money in a bank or a savings and loan, the cash is there if and when you need it. With a bond —if you must sell before maturity —you never know how much of your principal will be realized.

Here are two examples of different maturity needs:

Michael is in his mid-30s. He and his wife recently received a large lump sum —about $18,000. He doesn't need the money to live on, but he's pretty sure he's going to need it in 1982 when his first son reaches college age. Michael buys $17,000 worth of seven-year corporate bonds. He'll be earning 8% interest for the next seven years, and he'll have all of his money back in 1982 — just in time to pay for his son's education.

Margaret is in her late 60s and reasonably wealthy. She wants to leave all the money she can to her daughter and son-in-law, but she also wants to live comfortably — including travel — while she's still alive. She decides to invest several hundred thousand dollars in 25-year government bonds. She knows she probably won't be around when they mature, but so what? The long-term bonds pay higher interest than short-term bonds (because of the extra years of risk) and all she wants is the income. The principal she'll leave to her children.

The persons in both examples are in modest income tax brackets — Michael because he's a teacher, Margaret because she's retired. (Margaret may have $200,000 in the bank, but her only source of taxable income is interest and dividends, which amounts to less than $20,000 annually.)

Had Michael or Margaret been in higher tax brackets, they might well have chosen municipal bonds.

That's because municipal bonds offer varying degrees of tax exemption. Almost all municipal bonds are free from federal income taxes. State income taxes can also be avoided.

Here in California, for example, an investor pays no income tax — state or federal —on the interest earned from a bond issued with the state. That includes State of California bonds, Los Angeles Department of Water & Power bonds, California school district bonds, and others.

You must be a resident of California and the bond you buy must be issued by a district or local government within California to earn both state and federal tax exemption.

Sheldon Wolk, a vice president and bond specialist with Stern, Frank, Meyer & Fox Inc., Beverly Hills, says tax-exempt municipal bonds are best for people in higher tax brackets — generally 40% or more.

That's because municipal bond yields are much lower than taxable corporate bond yields. You must be in a high bracket before the tax advantage of municipals can make up the difference.

Here's an example: top-quality municipals are now yielding about 6%; top-quality corporates about 9%. If you're in a 50% tax bracket, however, that 6%, tax-free yield is equal to a taxable (or corporate bond) yield of 12%.

Counselors like Wolk have tax tables on hand to make this type of calculation simple.

(U.S. government bonds also offer a tax advantage, although nothing like municipals; i.e., you don't have to pay state income taxes on government bonds, but you do have to pay the federal.)

The best place to buy corporate or municipal bonds is from an investment firm. There are dozens in the phone book under "Investment." Most participate in new bond offerings and also have a ready supply of older bonds.

Most important, they have people like Wolk who are trained to help pick the right issue, yield and maturity for your needs. Commissions generally average less than 1% of the principal amount, except on very small orders.

Investment firms will also purchase government bonds for you, but most individuals buy their government bonds from major banks. It is generally the banks which have the large inventories of older U.S. government issues, and only a handful of investment firms deal in new government bond offerings.

Also, many new government bonds can be purchased directly from the Federal Reserve System. In Los Angeles, there's a branch of the San Francisco Federal Reserve Bank where you can order Treasury bills and many other new government securities.

Despite its advantage for many people, the world of bonds was not designed for individuals. On a good day, the dollar volume of all bond transactions can total $10 billion, and more than 99% of that is carried on among big institutions — banks, insurance companies, pension funds and hundreds of investment firms dealing for themselves.

The small investor can get lost. The bulk of most bond salesmen's income comes from dealing with $500,000, $1 million or $10 million orders, so when you call up and order $5,000 worth, he's not going to get overly excited.

That's why the bond market is no place for individuals to be "trading." Compared to stocks, bond prices don't fluctuate enough to provide much of an opportunity for big profits. And besides, the small investor will always be at a disadvantage in terms of price.

When you buy five bonds, you're not going to get as low a price as the insurance company portfolio manager who's buying 500. And when you sell, you won't get as high a price.

For individuals, bonds are something to keep, not trade.

6. Write a simple statement of something you firmly believe to be true (about the economy, a political belief, some psychological, social or sexual behavior, etc.). Then, in separate lists beneath the statement, list (a) as many ways as you can possibly think of to document that belief and (b) as many ways as you can find to discredit it.

7. Back in problem 8 on page 387, you got hold of an interpretive business report from a company or from your college library. (If you haven't yet, then do so.) Using that report, read carefully through it and

a. Indicate each of the *interpretations* it makes of the data it has uncovered,
b. for each of these interpretations, indicate the interpretive process that was followed to arrive at the interpretation (if you can't be sure, infer it as best you can),
c. comment upon the validity of each of those interpretations.

8. For one week, keep careful notes on all the interpretations-of-fact that you encounter in your day-to-day living — in conversations with friends, in school, in the newspaper, on radio or TV, etc. For each example you come up with, indicate in a memo to your instructor: (a) the facts that were being turned into an interpretation, (b) the kind of interpretation that was being made, and (c) the validity of the interpreter's interpretation(s).

9. You are continuing your work as a consultant to Sam Baker and his "Young Riskless Club." (See problem 9 on pages 387–388 and on page 408.) You have completed your research and now are ready to organize and interpret your findings.

In a progress report to your instructor (which should include a revised working outline), indicate the kinds of interpretations you'll be making and the kinds of recommendations you plan to put forth in your final report to Sam Baker.

10. In a progress report to your instructor, indicate in summary form the information you've uncovered in the report project you began back in problem 10 on page 388 and continued in problem 10 on page 408. You should include the revised working outline that you now see giving shape to your final report. And you want to describe the kinds of interpretations that you will be performing on the information you've found (and the recommendations, if any, you will be making).

11. You've been promoted by the new president to the position of Associate Dean of the School of Business at Valhalla University. One of the tasks regularly carried out by the holder of that position is an analysis — every term — of the grading practices of the various departments and faculty members in the school. The prime copy of each report goes to the head of the department in question. In some respects, it's a delicate task (academic freedom being what it is), but it has to be done to help the School maintain its standards, its top accreditation, and its strong reputation.

At the end of your first term on the job, your computer printout of grades given by members of the Marketing Department during the term reads as follows:

Course & section	Instructor	A	B	C	D	F	I*
Basic Marketing (1)	Aaron	8	4	11	3	0	3
(2)	Aaron	11	9	7	0	0	4
(3)	Cummings	1	3	16	5	1	1
(4)	Dickens	3	6	10	6	3	0
(5)	Dickens	2	7	9	5	1	0
Principles of Advertising (1)	Budofsky	3	7	8	0	0	0
(2)	Dickens	2	5	8	3	1	0
Elements of Retailing (1)	Cummings	2	6	6	5	0	2
Sales Management (1)	Eamons	5	5	6	0	0	3
Sales Promotion (1)	Cummings	0	4	11	4	2	0
Marketing Psychology (1)	Budofsky	4	8	5	0	0	2
Market Research (1)	Eamons	8	10	4	0	0	2
Advanced Advertising (1)	Foster	1	4	11	3	1	0

*Incomplete (work to be completed)

The head of the Marketing Department (for the last seven years) is Dr. Lizette Foster, a nationally renowned advertising psychologist. Drs. Aaron and Budofsky are senior professors, both very popular with their students. (Budofsky was department head before choosing to step down seven years ago.) Professor Cummings (an assistant professor with a Ph.D from Harvard) is a second-year man in the department. Professor Dickens (a first-year assistant professor with a Ph.D from Stanford) has just completed her first term of full-time teaching. Professor Eamons (an associate professor, five years in the department) is a dynamic personality, well known as a lecturer and consultant, with a reputation for spellbinding his students by recounting his own exploits in multimillion-dollar sales management.

Top administration at Valhalla has long advocated a general "bell-shaped" distribution of grades, throughout the University, of 10% As, 30% Bs, 50% Cs, and 10% Ds and Fs — but has never tried to make the rule binding. Policy within the School of Business (whose Dean is himself a very forceful fellow) has been "Hands off" — with instructors grading their students entirely as they see fit. There is also a general (but unstipulated) practice — throughout the University and in the School of Business — that basic courses that are required of all students be graded a little harder than advanced elective courses. In the Marketing Department, only "Basic Marketing" is a required course.

As part of the report to each department head, it has been the practice of your predecessor to include a summary of grade distributions throughout the School of Business. This past term, the distribution looks like this:

A: 230	C:793	F:28
B: 356	D:136	I:45

In memorandum format, prepare the term's report on the Marketing Department's grading. Make whatever analyses you feel are pertinent (or that your instructor asks you to make), whatever conclusions you feel are called for, and whatever recommendations you think you should. And write well.

12. In a recent study, statistics showed (let's assume) that there was a direct correlation between grades earned in public four-year colleges in Texas and the heights and weights of the students making the grades. Taller, heavier students were doing better than shorter, lighter ones. So, the report concluded, statistically, bigger people are also smarter people, at least in the 18-24-year-old range. Comment in detail on the validity of that conclusion.

CHAPTER 18

THE FINISHED REPORT

After completing your research, organizing your material, and (when necessary) interpreting that material, you are ready (at last!) for the final phase of your report project — the actual writing. It's a crucial phase. No matter how good your work has been up to this point, your report can still be ruined by poor presentation. The objectives now are those of *style, structure,* and *format:* how to put your findings into words, how to develop the shape of your report, and how to put that report into finished form.

STYLE

In Chapters 1,2,3, and 4 the question of *style* in business writing was gone over thoroughly. We discussed the use of words, the avoidance of bad style habits, and the means of achieving effective style. Here we need make only a few final points about style in business reports.

Keeping the "Human Element" in Business Reports

You can get most businesspeople to agree that letters should show some life and sound as though they've been written by human beings. But when it comes to reports, many of the same people (especially in the technical and engineering fields) write as though the human element were something alien, to be kept out or silenced for the sake of "objectivity." They fall back on jargon and unnecessarily formal diction, slip into wordy constructions, pile up their adjectives, and addictively turn every fact and idea into nouns and noun-phrases. They end up writing sentences like: *The immediate effectuation of policy is desired* instead of *We want to enforce the rule.* They apparently believe that all these traits — in a word, CorpSpeak — make reports more accurate and impressive, which isn't so. It takes live human beings to formulate report problems, and human beings to research, organize and interpret data intelligently (or to program the computer that does the organizing and interpreting). The only result of removing the human element is a slow and boring style that makes reports harder to read. (If you think it might be helpful, you might review the discussion of Corp-Speak on pages 39–52.)

Consider the memorandum report in Figure 51. It was written by Chris Allen as the first of the daily reports his boss requested in the memo on pages 179–180. Allen's report is a gem of lively style, impressive for its directness and the clarity of its detail.

Even in more formal reports, style can be crisp and lively, as it is in the Bank of America's public-information report on gold investment in Figure 52. First read it through. Then go back and consider the marginal comments on its style.

These two examples of report style (Chris Allen's and the Bank of America's) ought to demonstrate that business reports can be lively, personalized, and (of all things!) interesting to read — at no expense to the writer's desired objectivity or impressiveness.

Creating a Lively Opening

One other factor of report writing style must be looked at here — the wisdom of imaginative and interest-grabbing *openings*. Even though a report aims at strict objectivity, you want to get your readers reading with enthusiasm. You can often do that with a good opening sentence or two, something out of the ordinary, something which by its liveliness reaches out and grabs your readers' attention and promises them that your report will be a pleasure to read.

"Adam Smith," the stock market expert, begins his essay on the commodities market in cocoa with this sentence: *The world is not the way they tell you it is.* Given this opening, it's hard *not* to want to read on. Describing an accident that took the lives of two prominent people, another writer opens his account with the sentence: *Eileen's watch stopped at 2:55 on the afternoon of December 22.* Again, the opening makes you want to continue reading.

Another dependably good way to open a report (or some major section within a report) is with a *question.* Here's the opening sentence in a recent report on business in the black community:

> How badly were blacks hurt by the high inflationary levels of the 1970s?

Like any other question-opener, it virtually forces the reader's mind to become engaged, and read on. Questions demand our attention. When's the last time you ignored someone asking you a question?

Or you might open by focusing on a single human being whose plight reflects the topic of your report. That's what the author of a report on "starting a small business" did when he began:

> Every working day at 5 p.m. James Felton joins a herd of thousands of men and women packed onto the Cleveland Rapid Transit System, going home. He works on an assembly line at the Ford Motor Company plant out near the airport.

Figure 51
A well-written report memo.

CONFIDENTIAL

M E M O R A N D U M

T O : Tony Rowan   D A T E : April 10, 19--

F R O M : Chris Allen   F I L E : 612

S U B J E C T : Obereddy Project -- Field Report #1

On this first day of the project, I had a rough time shaking free from Mr. Art Wayne, the Plant Manager down here. He welcomed me to his office at eight this morning, and insisted on escorting me around the plant. I had been hoping to circulate freely among the plant people, but instead took advantage of the chance to get to know Wayne. He's an outwardly easygoing, but strong-willed man who seems to know production like he was born to it. As we walked through the various plant departments, he'd pick a piece off the assembly line here and there and point out its technical characteristics. He almost always gave credit for its quality to one or two men in each department, loud enough for them to hear him, and they seemed to love it. But I thought I noticed a number of workers looking coldly at me, as though they thought I might be appointed their new supervisor. Then when Wayne introduced me as a "consultant," they grew even more suspicious, as though I were there to do a time-and-motion study on their work.

The plant seems very well kept, and I complimented Wayne on having the aisles well marked and the machinery so well protected. "I'm an old Navy man," he replied," and like to keep things shipshape." Back in his office after the tour, we talked about morale in the plant -- which did seem reasonably high to me. He said morale was really the easiest thing to build, if you knew what you were doing. When I asked him about cooperation between managers in the plant, though, his mood changed. "There's room for a lot of improvement there," he said, and added that there were "a couple of empire builders" who needed watching. I didn't ask him to name them. He might have refused and thought me nosey. Or he might have told me, and established a more confidential relationship between the two of us than I think would be wise for now.

Wayne took me to lunch at a small restaurant near the plant where a lot of Obereddy's supervisors eat. He was greeted repeatedly, but with deference and respect. Almost everyone calls him "Mr. Wayne," except for Alan Beekman, the traffic manager, whom we both joined for lunch. Beekman was affable enough, but clearly more suspicious of me than Wayne was. And when Wayne said jokingly, "You ought to have a real good look at Alan's department," Beekman didn't laugh. I'm going to try to visit Beekman's department tomorrow.

While Wayne and I walked back to the plant (Beekman had left before we did), a big, blue Cadillac drove past us, the driver waving to Wayne. "Well, there's our number one hotshot!" Wayne said after the car went by. It was Mike Older, whom you prepared me for in our conference last Thursday. His great sales record as a district sales chief is no secret to anyone down here. Wayne obviously does not like him. After leaving Wayne at his office, I tried to see Older, but he was rushing off on a sales trip, so I spent an hour or so with his assistant, Ann McCallum. While I was with her, she made a few calls to department heads, reminding them that the starting time for Older's meeting with them on Wednesday was 9:13 a.m.! "That's the way he schedules his conferences," she told me, " . . . it keeps people real conscious of starting times." She gave me a rundown of her responsibilities for Older, but nothing too revealing about the man. I'm on his schedule for a conference on Thursday morning. At 8:53.

At about four, I left the plant and spent most of the next three hours doing some reading on "group work." Augusta rolls up the sidewalks at about eight in the evening as far as I can tell; but the pecan pie in the hotel dining room at least partly makes up for it. I'll report again tomorrow evening.

CA

> Usually he is tired, like most of the other passengers who stream onto the train at one of the stops between the airport and downtown. He is tired not just from the day's work. He is tired of working for someone else. As the train shakes along, he sits dreaming that one day he will have his own business and work for himself.

One more example of effective opening: take the routine and (let's face it) dull way the writer of the left-hand excerpt below, describing the commercial applications of solar energy, opens a section of his proposal, and compare it with the way the writer at right handles the same section opening. Which would you rather keep reading?

> There is a fourth prevailing misconception that the purported energy shortage is fallacious. Skeptics believe that there are still substantial quantities of oil and coal available to meet our energy needs, and that the availability of nuclear energy is virtually without limit.
>
> This belief can be shown to be a misconception by examining the declining production statistics of oil in this country. In spite of the fact that oil prices have almost quadrupled since . . . .

> Misconception #4. There's plenty of oil, a huge coal reserve, and limitless nuclear energy.
>
> Well, the country used to be overrun with buffalo too, and look what happened. The difference is—buffalo can reproduce themselves.
>
> Despite the quadrupled price of oil, production in this country is actually falling. Huge discoveries . . . .

Good openings don't always come easy. Never slow yourself down in drafting a report because you can't immediately find a good way to open. But, before you complete your final draft, remember how helpful those imaginative opening sentences can be, and devote some effort to creating them.

STRUCTURE

The problem of structure boils down to this — you must make a final decision about the order in which the elements of your report will be presented. And you must decide what structural and visual aids you will use to help your reader understand your findings. Let's look at these problems of structure.

Giving the Text Its Final Sequence

The *text* of your report is where its findings are fully presented to the reader. But in what order or sequence? Again, the answer begins with your working outline. You formulated that outline at the very beginning, when you defined and analyzed the problem; after that you probably revised it as you organized your findings to give you a better look at what you'd found. Now shift your

Figure 52
This public information report has a lively style.
(Reproduced by permission of Bank of America.)

GOLD:

Notice the TITLE: Subtitle format. It allows more drama to the title without sacrificing clear indication of what the report is about.

Facts you need to know before you buy gold.

December 1974

It's no longer illegal to possess gold in the United States. Effective December 31, 1974, the government lifted restrictions on gold ownership and trade in the United States.

Notice the contraction: establishes an informal tone at the outset.

For the past 42 years, Americans who owned gold have been restricted by law to old or foreign coins, jewelry, dental work, gold mining stocks, and supplies for scientific and industrial use. Now you may buy, sell, and own gold as you can any other commodity.

The linking word *now* is put into a position parallel to the phrase it links with (*for the last 42 years*). The sentence could have begun: *You may now buy* — but the clear transition would then be weakened.

Buying gold may seem like a good idea. But there are important facts about buying, owning, and selling it that you need to know before deciding to enter today's gold market.

This could all have been a single sentence, but the note of warning is more emphatic with the second sentence beginning with *But*.

Throughout history, gold has had a unique glamor amounting to mystique. It has intrinsic value as a metal. It is regarded by many as protection in times of rampant inflation. Through turbulent periods — for instance, in the midst of a depression or when a government falls — it has tended to retain some value. The free market price has risen from $42.50 per ounce as recently as three years ago to about $190 an ounce in December, 1974.

Notice, in this sentence, that if the modifier "Throughout history" had been put at the end instead of the beginning, initial and terminal emphasis would have been less effectively employed.

In this paragraph, the writer uses parallel sentence structures: *It has . . . It is . . . It has* . . . to emphasize, by accumulation, the factors that have, in combination, given gold its mystique.

In today's market, however, gold may prove an overpriced commodity. It is certainly a highly risky purchase. It earns no interest, pays no dividends — and actually costs money to store and handle. As a buyer, you can take a significant loss if you purchase gold without studying all the facts carefully.

The connective *however* need not begin the sentence. Here the writer opens with the phrase he wishes to contrast with the phrase that opened the preceding paragraph. *History* is one thing; *today* is another matter.

The recent rise in the price of gold is attributed to speculative buying, which means that the price can go down just as easily and quickly as it went up.

In this sentence, notice the abstract phrase (*speculative buying)* being followed by concrete elaboration.

Critics say gold must be bought on the "bigger fool" theory: You buy gold at one price and hope that a bigger fool will buy it from you later at an even higher price.

Notice that in these 2 paragraphs (and the 3 which follow them), the writer is attempting to emphasize, by isolation into separate paragraphs, ideas which could have been incorporated into a single paragraph.

Gold is being promoted as a sound investment. Yet any promotions involve a degree of hucksterism and gimmickry.

Gold is often regarded as financial protection against disaster. But buying gold today may involve more risk than protection.

Figure 52 (continued)

In this series of 3 descriptive adjectives, does it make a difference what order they're in? Try rearranging them, and see what you think.

Notice how the word *carefully* is given terminal emphasis here.

Notice how the phrase *Four nations* gets 4 different kinds of emphasis here:
1. subject emphasis
2. by initial position
3. by isolation
4. by successive stressed syllables (fóur nátions)

. . . and how the names of those nations are put into an interruptive structure—to give them their own separate sentence.

The writer here has taken pains to avoid "splitting the infinitive"—which he would have done if he had written: *to ostensibly influence . . .*

In this paragraph, note how the general assertion is followed by specific example. (This is a *must.*)

Notice how the colon (:) is used to introduce an explanatory phrase.

The price of gold is determined by worldwide supply and demand. Its price trend is uncertain, complicated, and volatile.

If you're thinking about buying gold in any form, consider each of the following facts carefully:

Producers' Influence. Four nations — South Africa, the Soviet Union, Canada, and the United States —produce 90 percent of the world's gold. South Africa alone accounts for more than 60 percent of the world's production. The producing nations can exert a heavy influence on the price of gold by altering their production and sales.

In a move ostensibly to influence gold prices, South Africa recently said it would withhold two million ounces from the market. The move came after the U.S. government said it was prepared to sell that much to curb a potential surge of gold imports. In fact, reduced production by all the major producers except the Soviet Union may have been responsible for much of the rise in gold prices since 1970.

Such concentration of production leaves the future supply of gold vulnerable to adverse political and economic developments in the producing nations.

Market Changes Abroad. Market developments in the United States could be more than offset by developments abroad. For example, any increase in the demand for gold in the United States (and potential price rise) might be completely offset by increased sales of gold from foreign holdings that were acquired in anticipation of the increased American demand.

Government Influence. Gold is widely used as a monetary standard and reserve. Governments can buy or sell gold from their very large stocks. When the United States said it was prepared to sell two million ounces, the impact on gold prices was immediate: a drop of about $9 an ounce.

Industrial Demand. Gold is also a raw material used in electronics, jewelry, and dentistry. Since 1970, while speculation has been driving up gold prices, industrial users have readily switched to substitute materials. The amount of gold sold for industrial uses has declined. Any further rise in gold prices probably will not stem from basic industrial demand but from more volatile speculative demand — now including the added demand of private American citizens.

Figure 52
(continued)

The Costs. The cost of buying and holding gold is likely to be substantial. You may have to pay as much as 20 to 30 percent over the quoted market price of gold. These additional costs include charges for fabrication, packaging, shipping, handling, storage, insurance, state sales taxes, and distributor and seller commissions.

If you take possession of gold and later decide to sell it, you may also have to pay assaying fees for an independent laboratory analysis to determine its purity. Fees may range from $30 to $175, depending on the amount to be assayed. Also, a discount of 4 to 6 percent from the quoted market price may be charged at resale.

The charges for buying and selling gold are likely to vary among dealers and retailers. The reliability of some sellers and dealers may command a higher commission than others. The unsophisticated nature of the market, at least in the beginning, could also result in nonuniform prices for gold.

The Returns. Gold yields no dividends or interest. You make a profit only if the price goes up. This is true whether you take possession of the gold yourself (together with the responsibility for storage, insurance, and authenticity) or whether your supplier stores the gold for you and issues you a receipt.

Buying a Little. The less gold you can afford to buy at a time, the less likely you are to break even. What you'll have to pay above the quoted market price to cover all the costs of buying, holding, and selling gold will vary with the amount you buy. These costs are proportionally higher for small purchases. If you buy less than, say, 50 ounces, the quoted price of gold bullion probably will have to rise 25 to 35 percent for you to recover your total buying and selling costs.

That means that if you buy gold when the quoted price is $180 an ounce, the price will probably have to rise to the range of $225 to $240 — an increase of $45 to $60 an ounce — before you can recover all your costs of buying and selling.

If you buy more, the buying and selling costs will be proportionally lower, and you probably will be able to recover your costs with a smaller increase in the quoted price. The less you buy, the greater the drawbacks of gold as an investment.

Owning very small quantities can hurt you another way — you have no guarantee of a ready market should you decide to sell.

Throughout this report, even though the general tone and dictional level are semi-formal, the writer is not at all reluctant to address his readers *directly*.

Notice how the word *also* is put at the beginning of the sentence and set off with a comma. It's an important word here: the writer is stressing *cumulative costs* of buying gold—so he does what he can to emphasize the "cumulating" word.

Notice how a key modifying idea is rephrased as a sentence *interrupter* (pages 81–82).

Notice the way the conversational interrupter, *say*, is used here.

The writer is careful to adapt his interpretation of the economics of gold ownership to his audience of non-specialists: he provides a tangible dollars-and-cents example of the principle he is discussing.

Again, we see a very important idea—here a warning—isolated in a short paragraph all its own, for emphasis.

Figure 52
(continued)

Have you been noticing the writer's use of frequent *headings* in this report? Do you think these headings are effectively used?

Fraud. Now that trading is legal, there could be a wave of counterfeiting and "fool's gold" schemes. Gold can easily be molded over cheaper metals or mixed with other metals to form cheaper alloys.

The best protection against fraud is to deal with a local firm or a financial institution of excellent reputation. Be wary of unsolicited correspondence, calls from strangers, promises of spectacular profits, and pressure to make hurried decisions. Obtain complete information about costs, purity, terms of purchase, and how you can sell what you buy. Be wary even of gold in sealed packages bearing the insignia of reputable dealers if there is an unknown intermediary in the sale, for insignia are easily forged.

Storage and Theft. You pay a lot for a little gold. The theft of small amounts can mean heavy financial loss. Gold is easily stolen, easily transformed, and hard to trace. If you own gold, you should make sure you have secure storage as well as insurance against theft and other loss.

Hedge Against What? Gold is widely portrayed as a hedge against inflation. But in fact, over the last 175 years, gold has been a better hedge against deflation than inflation. In times of deflation, gold prices didn't fall with other prices. Only since 1971 have gold prices risen faster than other rising prices. However, it should be noted that a gold commodity market with freely fluctuating prices determined by supply and demand is a recent phenomenon.

Notice how repetition of key words is used here to insure smooth connection and flow from sentence to sentence.

The Futures Market. You are now also permitted to buy and sell gold futures. In buying futures, you pay a given price now for delivery of gold in the future. If the price of gold rises in the meantime, you come out ahead. But if the price falls — as it may — you lose.

Purity. The quoted market price is established for gold that's at least 99.50 percent pure. Most reputable dealers handle bullion that pure or purer. But not all gold bullion is that pure, nor is all gold in other forms.

Again the writer makes a general statement of fact . . .

. . . then follows it up with concrete and specific examples to assure that his readers will understand the general fact.

Gold is alloyed with other metals to make it harder and better-suited for jewelry and other industrial uses. The purity (or fineness) of these alloys is measured in karats. Twenty-four-karat gold is 99.90 percent pure. Eighteen-karat gold is only 75 percent as pure as that, and 14-karat gold is 58.27 percent pure. The difference in purity should be reflected in the price.

Determine both the purity and weight of any gold you might buy. Getting a written guarantee is best, of course. To estimate the value of the gold content of your purchase (not counting the other buying and selling costs), mul-

Figure 52 (continued)

tiply its percentage of purity times its weight in troy ounces times the quoted market price per ounce.

(Gold is always measured in troy ounces. A troy ounce is 1.097 common ounces or about 31.1 grams. One troy pound is 12 troy ounces.)

As you consider buying gold, keep these factors in mind: the market's volatility, the costs, the risks of fraud and theft, and the return.

A realistic appraisal of future gold price movements requires a thorough investigation of many supply and demand factors, including the size of unmined reserves, prevailing and probable production costs; the level of hoarding by governments and individuals, potential industrial demand, the general economic outlook, and international and domestic political developments. Individual buyers are at a serious disadvantage in analyzing these complicated factors.

Notice how a carefully constructed parallelism allows a sentence to get lengthy without getting clumsy.

Lifting the ban on gold ownership increases both freedom and risk for buyers and sellers. Striking changes in the structure of the market are likely to occur in the future. Buying gold from a reputable source at a fair price provides no guarantee of selling at a profit — or breaking even.

Here is an apparent parallel structure, but is it actually a parallelism? Does it have any effect on the paragraph's readability?

Gold is available in a number of forms and several methods of purchase from some banks, brokerage houses, and retail stores.

But before you buy, you will want to weigh all the risks carefully.

If you do decide to buy gold, a Bank of America officer can assist.

Only here does this report betray its underlying promotional interest. It has up till now faithfully maintained its objectivity.

focus to your reader. You may, or may not, have to revise the outline one more time to give you the order in which your reader can best partake of your findings. What are your alternatives?

Chronological Sequence This sequence presents facts in the order of their occurrence. Starting with the earliest fact (or event), you merely follow the clock or the calendar in your presentation. Chris Allen's memo-report in Figure 51 is built essentially on chronological sequence. It traces the day's events from morning till evening. Chronological sequence is also the most convenient sequence to use when you describe a process; it makes the process easy for the reader to follow.

Occasionally, you'll find it useful to employ a *modified* chronological sequence. You can reverse time by covering the most recent event first and working backward, thereby accommodating the reader who might be most interested in what happened recently. Or you can use a *broken* chronology (sometimes called *flashback*), by beginning at a critical point in time, working forward to the most recent event, then "flashing back" to the earliest point and working back up to the critical point. Flashback allows you to emphasize the most interesting point in your chronology by locating it at both the beginning and the end.

Spatial Sequence If your report describes something tangible (perhaps a piece of equipment, a newly fashioned garment, a contemplated convention facility, or the results of a controlled destruction test), you would probably use a spatial sequence. You'd use some convenient pattern of eye movement — from left to right, from top to bottom, from east to west, from large to small, from inside out — and follow that order in your presentation. Here's an excerpt from Admiral Byrd's report on his expedition to Antarctica; it uses spatial sequence to describe the hut that served as headquarters at the Pole:

> My bunk, fastened to the north wall, was about three feet off the floor, with the head flush against the eastern wall. At the foot of the bunk, on a small table, was the register, a glass-enclosed mechanism of revolving drum and pens which automatically recorded wind direction and velocity as reported by the wind vane and anemometer cups to which it was electrically connected. The dry cells powering the pens and driving the drum were racked underneath. Across the room, in the southeast corner, was a triangular shelf holding the main combination radio transmitter and receiver, with a key fastened near the edge. The transmitter was a neatly constructed, 50-watt, self-excited oscillator which Dyer had assembled himself, and which was powered by a 350-watt, gasoline-driven generator weighing only 35 pounds. The receiver was a superheterodyne of standard make. Above this shelf was a smaller one holding the emergency radio equipment, consisting of. . . .

Categorical Sequence This is the sequence that moves from one parallel category to another, making it well suited to a discussion of parallel ideas. If, for example, you're writing that report on the six candidates for the company's accounts directorship, you would use the categorical sequence that was generated by your earliest working outline: devoting one major section to each of the candidates being considered.

When using a categorical sequence, make sure that (1) you choose the categorization most useful to your purpose, (2) you maintain those categories consistently, (3) those categories do not overlap, (4) all essential categories are included, and (5) the categories are in approximate balance. (As an example of this last, if you wrote a report on the religions practiced in America, you would not devote a separate category to every one. You would probably construct *four* major categories — *Protestant, Catholic, Jewish,* and *Others* — the last of which is roughly balanced with the other three by including all those religions which, in America, are comparatively underrepresented.)

Within a categorical sequence, some dramatic effect can be achieved by *climactic order* — that is, by putting the categories into ascending order of importance. A sense of relative priorities can be implied by *anticlimactic order,* arranging the categories in their descending order of importance, the most important one first, the least last. Also useful is the order that sees the two most important categories put one at the beginning and one at the end (the two positions of natural emphasis). Finally, if you wish *not* to imply any relative importance or priorities, you can put your categories into *alphabetical order* (and make clear that you're doing so).

Combining Sequences In a long report, different sections of the report may require different kinds of sequences. There is nothing wrong with using different sequences as long as each section of the report, internally, is ordered logically and consistently.

The Body of Your Report

The text is the heart of your report, the full presentation of your findings. But, except in the briefest reports, the text does not stand alone. Usually added to the text are separate sections that introduce the report, reveal the research methodology (if it isn't obvious), state the writer's conclusions (if conclusions are drawn), and make recommendations (if the reader expects them). These various sections, along with the text, constitute the *body* of the report.

The Introduction The *introduction* in a report can be several sentences, several paragraphs, or several pages long, depending on the size and the scope of the text that follows it. The introduction spells out the purpose of the report, the background of the problem considered, the criteria used for evaluating the findings (if the report is evaluative), and the methods used in researching the problem. In effect, the introduction says: "Here's what this report is all about." Most report writers don't compose the introduction until they've finished writing the text.

Materials and Methods In a long report, a description of the materials and methods used in compiling the information is often removed from the introduction and given a separate section preceding the text — a "Materials and Methods" section. With intelligent readers, you must earn their faith in your findings by showing them how those findings were derived. So you describe in detail, and even show, the *materials* you used: documents, experimental equipment, questionnaires, and so on. And you describe precisely how they were used and the logic behind that usage; in short, you discuss your *method.*

Conclusions and Recommendations In longer interpretive reports, you should also construct a separate section to state your conclusions — and recommendations if you're making them. This concluding section usually appears *after* the text and draws on the information the text reveals. But sometimes, for the sake of readers who want conclusions and recommendations first, this section is placed *before* the text. You should not introduce any new data (that is, data not considered in the text) in this section. If your conclusions are lengthy and your recommendations numerous or complex, you should construct two separate sections: one for conclusions, one for recommendations.

The body of a typical report might be structured like this —

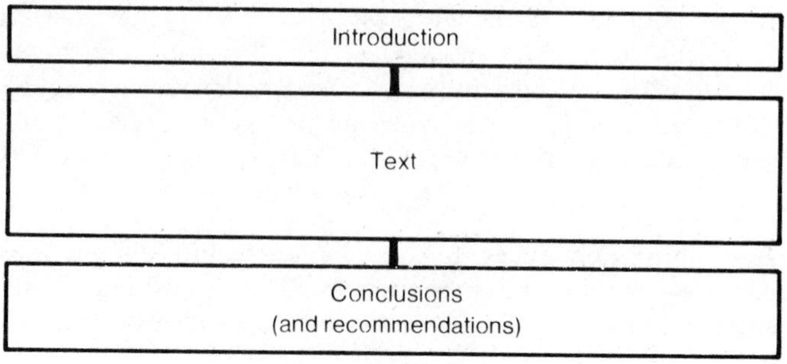

The body of a more extensive report might be structured like this —

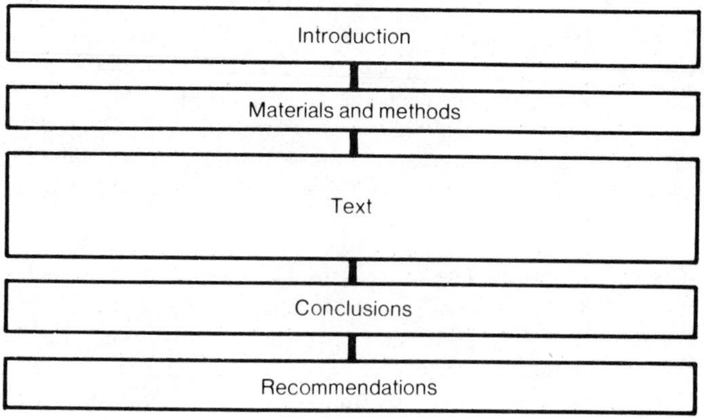

Structural Aids for the Reader

Novelists plan the structure of a novel in great detail, then work very hard to camouflage that structure for artistic effect. But report writers don't aim at art. They are interested less in effect than in getting their facts and interpretations to their readers, totally and unmistakably. To assure this clear transmission of details, report writers work just as hard to expose and make visible the structure of their reports, as novelists do to camouflage theirs. They do it in several ways.

Numbering For one thing, report writers often carry the numbering system of their working outline right into the report (revised, of course, into the most effective order of presentation). Each section and subsection is *numbered* to correspond to the outline (which itself has become the table of contents).[1]

Headings Report writers also use formalized systems of headings and subheadings to identify their sections, subsections, and paragraphs.

We ll discuss *tables of contents* on page 449.

This is a typical system of headings:

A FIRST-DEGREE HEADING

Generally, there's only one first-degree heading in a report. It's used for the title of the report at the top of page one. The title heading is typed entirely in capitals and centered over the page, as shown here.

A Second-Degree Heading

This kind of heading is used for the major subdivisions of the report. Capital letters begin each word, and the heading is underlined. If a five-degree breakdown (the system shown here) is unnecessary for the scope of your report, this kind of heading can be dispensed with and third-degree headings used for the major subdivisions.

A Third-Degree Heading

Third-degree headings are typed just like second-degree headings, but they are brought over to the left-hand margin.

A Fourth Degree Heading. Fourth-degree headings are dropped down onto the first line of the paragraph, as shown here.

A fifth-degree heading is incorporated right into the opening sentence, and the capitals (except for the first one) are dropped. Underlining is sufficient to make the opening words stand out as a heading.

Listings At times, when describing a step-by-step process, writers will impose a *listing* structure upon their entire description. That's what I've done in introducing the report-writing process back on page 375, and it's what the writer of the following memo of procedure does:

TO: All Department Heads
FROM: T. Hargrave, Executive Vice-President
SUBJECT: Procedure for Requesting New Facilities for Your Department

Responsibility of	Action
Requester	1. completes Form 99 (''Facilities Request'') in three copies;
	2. sends two copies to Facilities Engineering.

```
Facilities           3. assigns a job number
Engineering             to both copies of the request,
                        indicating when preliminary
                        action on the request will be taken;

                     4. returns one copy of Form 99
                        to the Requester.

Requester            5. in case of inquiry,
                        refers to the request by
                        its job number.

Facilities           6. reviews all requests;
Engineering
                     7. determines priorities
                        among the facility needs
                        of the various departments;

                     8. allocates available funds
                        in accordance with those
                        priorities.
```

Where the subject matter allows for them, listings can greatly aid the reader's grasp of new or complicated processes being described.

Pagination The pages of a report should be numbered so that a reader always knows approximately where he is, and has a convenient way of referring back to parts of the report. Some writers put their page numbers in the upper right-hand corner because that's the first part of a page the reader sees. Others center their page numbers at the top of the page, to give the page a more formal look.

Wherever you put them, begin your page numbers with the first page of the report's body, and omit the actual number from page one. Pages that precede the report's body (we'll discuss these supplementary pages in a moment) should be numbered with lower-case Roman numerals, as the first few pages of this book are.

Footnotes Footnotes are used in business reports for either of two purposes: (1) to identify the source of a piece of information (as the footnote on page 443 does), or (2) to elaborate on something said in the text if that elaboration would be digressive *in* the text (that's what most of the footnotes in this book have done: see, for example, the footnotes on pages 248, 269, 402). In either case, footnotes are a convenience for readers who want the information they provide. If cost and time permit (says one school of thought), footnotes belong at the *foot* of the page, where a reader can refer to them at a glance. Others feel that, to save time in preparing the report, footnotes should be gathered at the end, right after the body. I personally prefer them at the bottom of the page.

In either case, certain rules of format should be followed when preparing footnotes in a typed report. These rules are set out in the arrowed comments in Figure 53. Take a look at them.

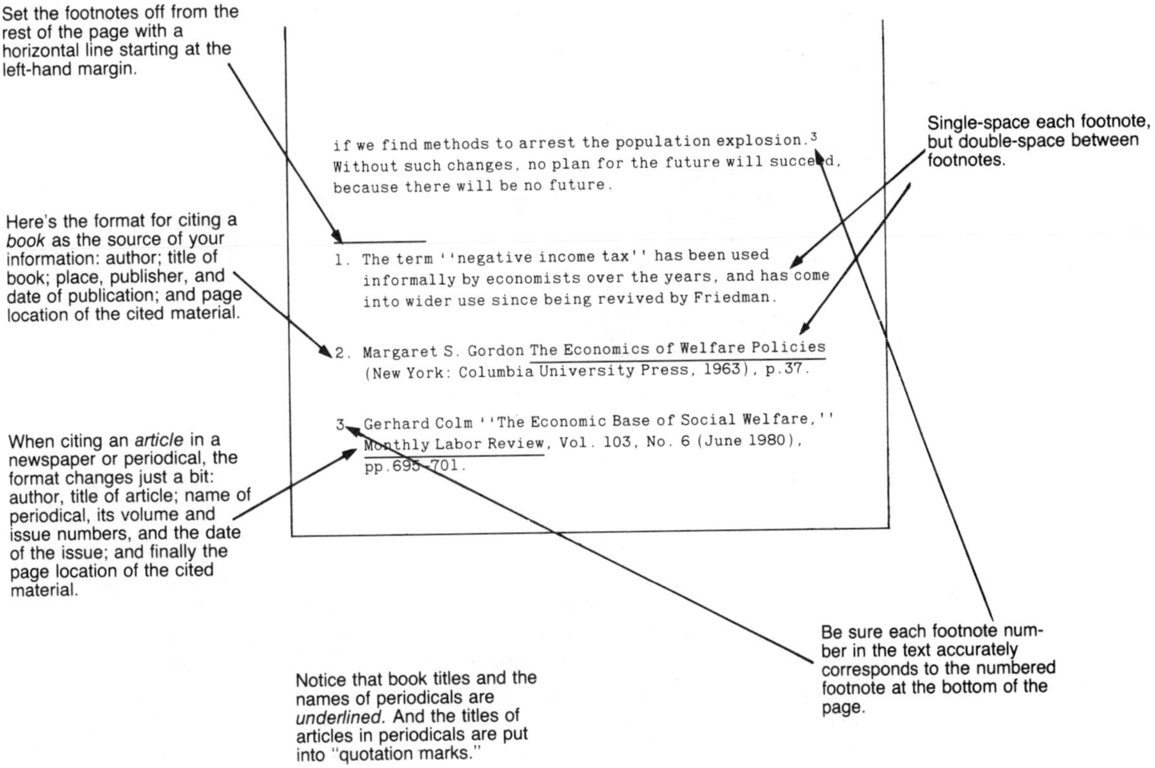

Set the footnotes off from the rest of the page with a horizontal line starting at the left-hand margin.
if we find methods to arrest the population explosion.3 Without such changes, no plan for the future will succeed, because there will be no future.
1. The term ''negative income tax'' has been used informally by economists over the years, and has come into wider use since being revived by Friedman.
2. Margaret S. Gordon The Economics of Welfare Policies (New York: Columbia University Press, 1963), p.37.
3. Gerhard Colm ''The Economic Base of Social Welfare,'' Monthly Labor Review, Vol. 103, No. 6 (June 1980), pp.695-701.
Here's the format for citing a book as the source of your information: author; title of book; place, publisher, and date of publication; and page location of the cited material.
When citing an article in a newspaper or periodical, the format changes just a bit: author, title of article; name of periodical, its volume and issue numbers, and the date of the issue; and finally the page location of the cited material.
Single-space each footnote, but double-space between footnotes.
Be sure each footnote number in the text accurately corresponds to the numbered footnote at the bottom of the page.
Notice that book titles and the names of periodicals are underlined. And the titles of articles in periodicals are put into "quotation marks."

Figure 53
The Format of Footnotes in a Report.

Illustrative Aids The written text of a report must, of course, communicate its contents with total clarity. But to help the reader grasp the significance of those contents — and to make the report livelier and more physically interesting — you can supplement the text with various kinds of illustrative aids. Graphs, tables, charts, photographs, diagrams, and maps can all — in their own special ways — help illustrate a report.

Graphs are visual representations of quantitative data. If well drawn, they give readers a vivid picture of significant statistical relationships. Below, you'll see rudimentary examples of the four types of graphs: the *line graph,* the *bar graph,* the *pictograph,* and the *pie graph. Line graphs* are used to represent changes that occur at short intervals (such as daily changes in the stock-market average or monthly fluctuations in profits). *Bar graphs* are used to illustrate

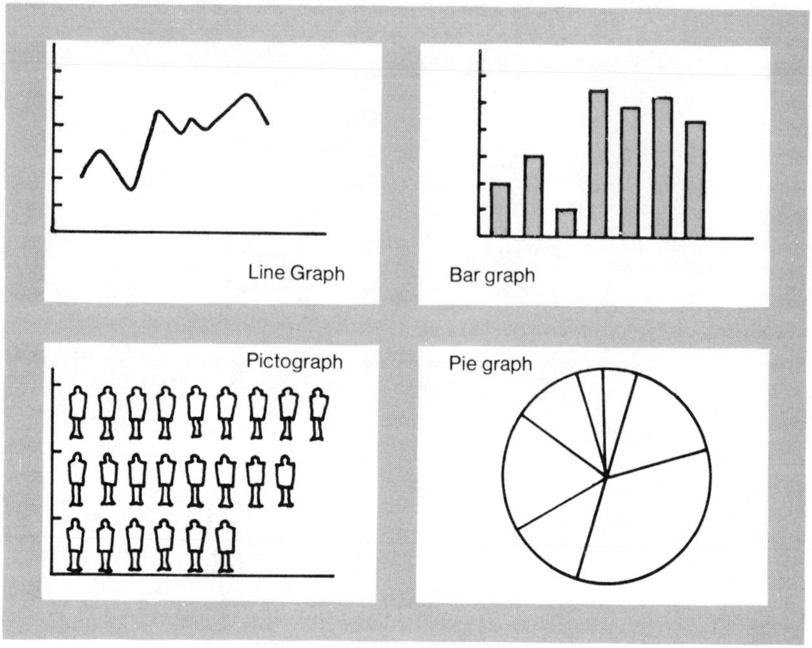

comparative values (such as company profits for each of the last five years, or the total raw material exports for each of seven countries last year). *Pictographs* are graphs that use pictorial symbols drawn in appropriate proportions (such as a stack of coins to represent money, little human figures to represent every one-thousand workers, or little automobiles to represent each ten thousand cars produced) in place of the standard bars or lines. *Pie graphs* are used for the portion-by-portion breakdown of some whole entity (such as the number of cents in each tax dollar going for education, welfare, defense, and so forth). The circle represents the whole; each wedge the appropriate portion.

The variety within each of these basic types of graphs is enormous — and limited only by a writer's imagination and awareness of the kinds of graphs readers will understand. Vital to the effectiveness of *any* graph is uncluttered simplicity, and clear identification of its purpose and all its parts. Remember that clear captions, like clear report titles, answer all the relevant questions: *Who? What? Where? When? Why?* and *How?*[2]

Tables, as we've seen in earlier chapters, don't exactly illustrate data. Rather tables help to illustrate the data by putting them into logically organized and clearly labeled columns. When incorporated into the final report, tables make data "scannable," giving the reader's mind quicker access to the data. Here's an example of a well-drawn, well-labeled, well-captioned *table:*

[2] A more detailed yet very readable discussion on preparing basic graphs (and flow charts and maps) for business reports is in Cecil Meyers, *Handbook of Basic Graphs* (Belmont, Calif.: Dickenson Publishing Co., 1970).

TABLE 12

A Comparison of the Annual Cost per Employee of Health Insurance Policies Submitted by Eight Companies March 1, 1980

Company	*Plan "A" $10,000 Maximum Annual Coverage*	*Plan "B" $15,000 Maximum Annual Coverage*
Chicago General	$375.00	$492.50
Chesapeake	325.00	450.00
D & Z Life	385.50	485.60
Equitable	312.50	443.50
Landover Mutual	415.00	502.00
Moneywell	309.45	404.31
New England	350.00	475.00
White Mountain	406.50	597.00

Charts are used to indicate relationships among nonquantitative items. Though the variety of charts is infinite, there are essentially two types: the *static chart* and the *flow chart.* Typical of *static charts* are the many organization charts that show lines of authority between boxes representing the different jobs within a company. Typical of *flow charts* is a chart that shows how a bill progresses through Congress, or one that shows the movement of a piece of raw material through a manufacturing process. The flow chart on page viii of this text shows optional ways of using this textbook in a communications class.

Photographs naturally provide the most realistic kind of illustration (especially color photos), but they *don't* necessarily provide the best illustration for your purposes. And they're expensive to reproduce. Consider using a photo only when you want to illustrate the external appearance of an object in all its surface detail.

Diagrams and line sketches are often used instead of photographs because they can omit extraneous detail and shadows, showing only what the reader needs to see. A diagram or a sketch can also be used to provide a look *inside* an object (how, for instance, could a writer illustrate the human circulatory system or the cooling system in a car if limited to photographs?).

Maps are simply geographical diagrams. They make good illustrations for virtually anything that has geographical implications: distances, routes and movement between places, and geographical distributions. On the next page is an example of a distribution map.

Any kind of illustration you use is potentially effective if you keep several general principles in mind. Don't use any illustration for its own sake; make sure it contributes to the worth of the report. And make sure that the text of the report directs the reader's attention to the illustration at the appropriate point. Make any illustration as simple as it can be to serve its purpose. Be sure to label all relevant parts of your illustration clearly. And, again, remember to give it a precisely written caption.

STATE-BY-STATE DISTRIBUTION
OF THE TOP 100
BLACK-OWNED BUSINESSES IN AMERICA
1980

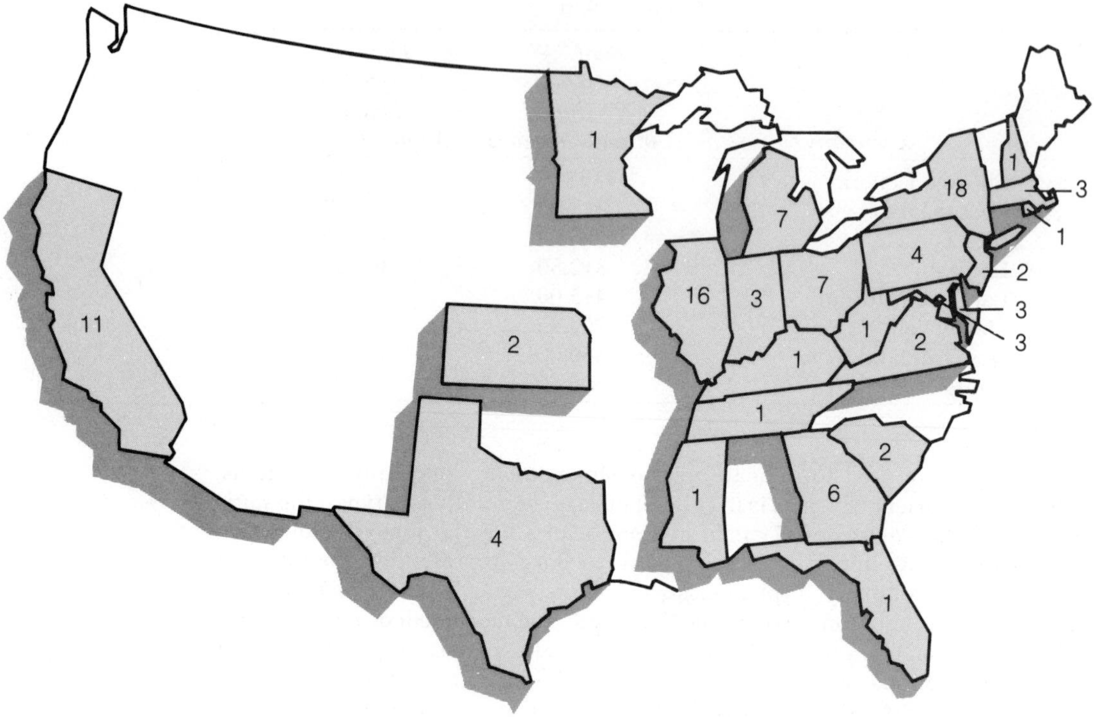

FORMAT

After you've written the body of a report, you must still put it into a finished format, the format you probably decided on during the planning stages of the report. To the *body* of many reports you must add certain component sections to make the format complete. (Form reports are, of course, an exception; their formats are predetermined.)

Reports that employ a business-letter format (that is, *letter reports*) require a heading, inside address, salutation, and signature block, just like any other letter.

Memo reports are prepared on memorandum stationery. The heading on page one of that stationery provides the necessary format; all subsequent pages are plain, bearing only a page number, and what you've written on them.

Reports that aren't written in letter or memo format need various preliminary and terminal sections (called *front sections* and *back sections*). As a general rule, the longer the report, and the more formal it is, the greater the number of front sections and back sections you will use.

Title Page and Cover

All reports except letter, memo, and form reports should have a separate *title page*. The standard title page contains four pieces of information: the complete title of the report, the name of the person or organization for whom the report is written, the name of the writer and his or her position, the date of submission. A typical title page is shown in Figure 54 (page 452).

On a short and comparatively informal report, the title page can also serve as the *cover*, no separate cover being needed. But for added formality, as well as durability, you should add a *cover*. Unless the cover is transparent, or has a window onto the title page, it should carry at least an abbreviated form of the report's title, for ready identification. Title page, cover, and the body of the report are joined together as shown in this worm's-eye view.

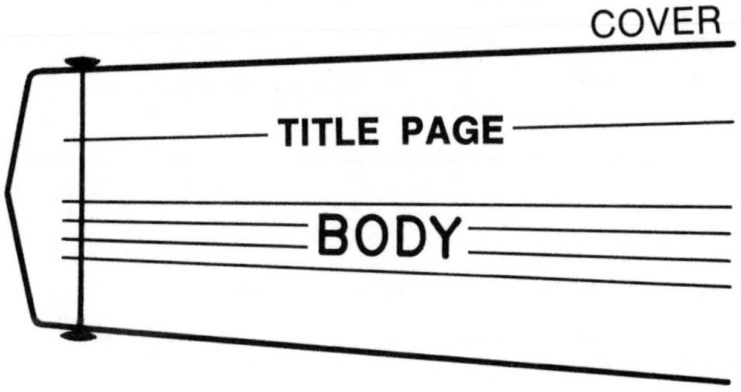

Bibliography

A *bibliography*, or list of sources, like the one shown in Figure 60 (page 458), should be added as a back section to any report for which you needed to consult at least several published sources. Your reader will probably be interested in these sources too. The following rules and examples ought to be followed in preparing a report bibliography:

1. List the items in the bibliography alphabetically by author's last name.

2. Type the heading BIBLIOGRAPHY, or LIST OF SOURCES, in first-degree form at the top.

3. Triple-space between the heading and the first reference. Single-space within each reference, and double-space between references. If a reference requires more than one line, indent the second line (and each succeeding line) five spaces.

4. If an author has written more than one of your sources, type a five-space line in place of his or her name for each item after the first.

5. When the author is unknown, alphabetize the reference by its title.

6. End each reference to a magazine, journal, or other multi-articled source with page indicators.

On the following page are a few sample bibliography entries in acceptable form (and in alphabetical order):

Newspaper column with author

Donnelly, Richard A., "Commodities Corner," Barrons, August 13, 1973, pp. 31-32.

Magazine article without author

"Electronic Calculators," Changing Times, July, 1973, pp. 39-41.

Article in professional journal

Humphrey, Susan R. and Gerald F. Williamson, "Make Your Technical Reports 'People Oriented,' "American Business Communication Association Bulletin, 35, December, 1971, pp. 27-31.

Book, one author

McCready, Richard R., Solving Business Problems With Calculators, 3rd Ed., Wadsworth Publishing Company, Belmont, California, 1969, 148 pp.

Another book, same author

———, Business Mathematics, Wadsworth Publishing Company, Belmont, California, 1973, 243 pp.

Book, two authors

Phillips, E. Bryant and Sylvia Lane, Personal Finance, 2nd Ed., John Wiley & Sons, Inc., New York, 1969, 536 pp.

Magazine article with author

Rose, Sanford, "Multinational Corporations in a Tough New World," Fortune, August, 1973, pp. 52-56.

Government publication

Statistical Abstract of the United States, U.S. Bureau of the Census, Washington, D.C., 1972, 973 pp.

Abstract (or Synopsis)

Many longer reports also have an *abstract* (or *synopsis*) added as a front section—immediately preceding the body of the report. An abstract, like the one shown in Figure 59, is an abbreviated version of the whole report with an emphasis on the conclusions. You write an abstract only after finishing a report. Its length is usually somewhere between five and ten percent of the report's length. Its purpose is to save time for those readers who want to scan the report and for those who, at a later date, must refer back to it. (It is for these reasons that an abstract is sometimes called an *Executive Summary*.) One precaution, however: If you feel that your reader will accept your conclusions *only* after seeing the complete interpretation of data in the report body, do *not* provide an abstract at the beginning where it will meet only biased resistance.

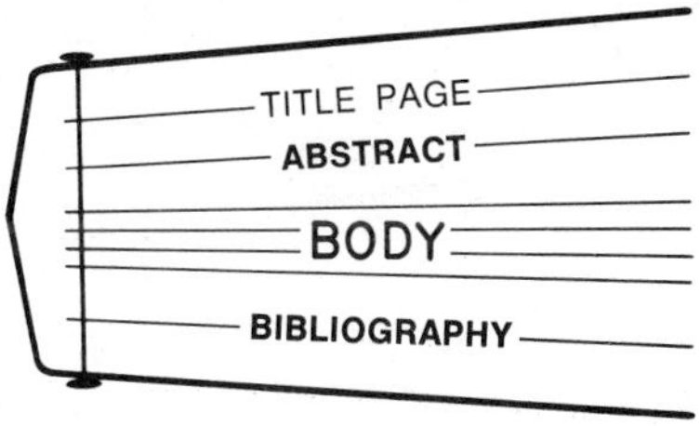

Table of Contents

The longer a report, the more it needs a *table of contents*. A table of contents helps a reader to refer back to your report later on. For the first reading, it serves as an initial look at the report's structure. Actually a table of contents is little more than your final working outline transposed onto a fresh sheet of paper and keyed to the page numbers of the report. The table of contents shown in Figure 58 is constructed in good form. Notice that it shows only the first- and second-level breakdowns of the report; this is sufficient in most cases. The titles of sections and subsections shown in the table of contents should be identical to the headings and subheadings in the body. The table of contents should be inserted into the report immediately preceding the abstract (or, if you don't have an abstract, immediately preceding the body).

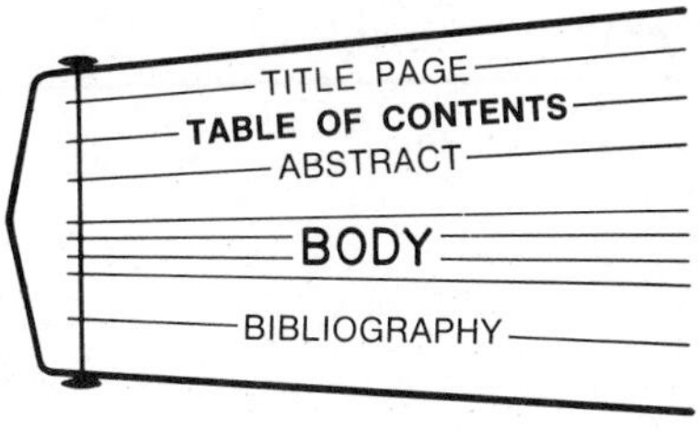

Table of Illustrations

A *table of illustrations* is also sometimes included — on a separate page, immediately following the table of contents — if the graphs, diagrams, or other illustrations in the report might later be referred to independently (that is, without reference to the textual discussion relating to them). A table of illustrations lists the number of each illustration (Figure 1, Figure 2, and so on), and gives its caption, and the number of the page on which that illustration appears.

Index

Another component section in long reports is an *index*. It helps readers later on to refer back to specific items. An index, like the one at the end of this book, is an alphabetically ordered key to significant names and items in the report, giving the page numbers on which those items are discussed. When an index is included, it becomes the very last section in a report. It cannot be composed until the rest of the report is in final draft with its pages numbered.

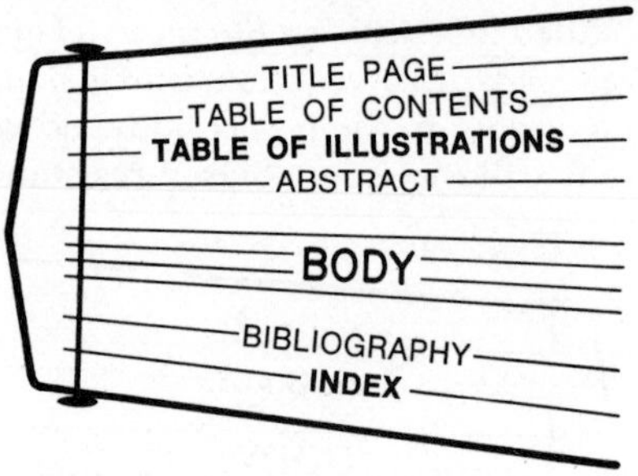

Letter of Authorization

A highly formal report — one which sets out to be as impressive as it is informative — usually includes, as a front section, a copy of the document that authorized it. If, for instance, an outside organization commissioned you to do a study, their request for the report would be given to you in writing. This document is called a *letter of authorization* (an example appears in Figure 55). You would include a copy of this authorization letter, or the original (keeping a duplicate copy of yourself, of course) in your formal report. It would follow the title page and precede the table of contents.

Letter of Transmittal

You should also include, in a formal report, your *letter of transmittal* — a letter which, in essence, says "Here's the report you requested." A letter of transmittal can have as little as two or three sentences, or it can synopsize the report (eliminating the need for a separate abstract or synopsis). A letter of transmittal is inserted into the report after the letter of authorization. A good one is shown in Figure 57.

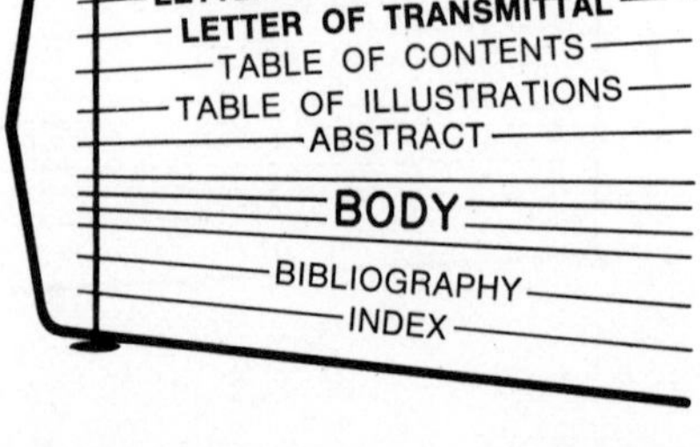

Letter of Acceptance

A third letter is sometimes included as a front section in a formal report: a copy of the *letter of acceptance.* The letter of acceptance (a typical example of which is shown in Figure 56) is the letter you write to answer the letter of authorization. Together with the authorization letter, the acceptance letter constitutes the agreement between you and the authorizer for you to write the report. They should appear next to each other in the report, preceding the letter of transmittal.

The attributes of effective letters of authorization, transmittal, and acceptance are those of any well-written *routine* letter, though they are usually written at a more formal level than most routine letters.

Appendixes

One other component section sometimes included in long reports is an *appendix* (or *annex)* — sometimes several of them. An appendix should be used to provide information that is unnecessary to the readers' understanding of your report but that will probably interest them because of its relevance. Detailed statistical computations, background discussions, maps, diagrams, and other illustrations not essential to the clarity of the report are all materials that can be included in appendices. Each appendix (like each one in this book) should be assigned a letter (A,B,C) and carefully titled. The titles should appear in the table of contents. Appendices are inserted into the report following the bibliography and preceding the index.

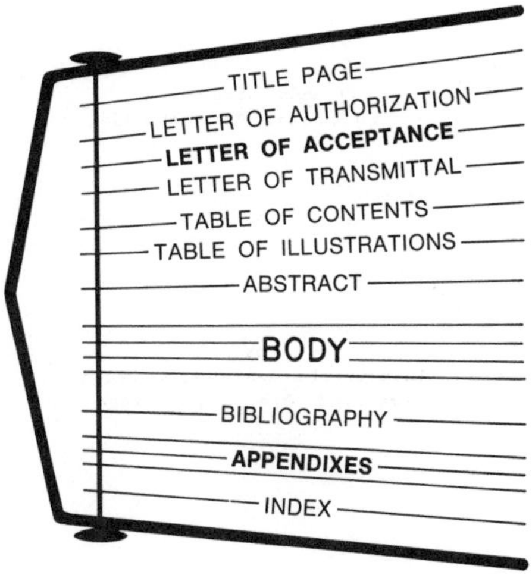

REPRODUCTION OF REPORTS

Always produce *at least* two copies of a report, one to submit and the other to keep — and only rarely will two copies even be enough. If, for example, you must submit a report to your company vice-president, you should produce a copy for everyone directly in the line of authority from you to him. If you're submitting a report to a board or a committee, you must produce at least one copy for each member.

The photocopy process is now the virtually universal means of copy-making in American business. Highly formal reports, however, are often produced by more attractive and expensive means — when budget permits.

You must consider how durable each copy must be, how attractive it must be, how each copy is going to be bound (making sure you've left room at the left side of each page to attach that binding), how much you can spend on reproducing each copy, and what kind of illustrations are being reproduced (photocopying for example, usually will not reproduce photographs very

Figure 54
Sample of a title page in a business report.

THE FUTURE OF SINCLAIR
A Study of the Potential Industrial Expansion
of Sinclair, Indiana

submitted to
The Sinclair City Council

by
Industrial Research Associates
Marvin L. Bierce, Director

June 11, 19__

clearly). Being aware of these problems is three-fourths of the solution.

Figures 54–60 are samples of the format components of a long, formal business report.

Figure 55
Sample of a letter of auhorization.

THE CITY COUNCIL
OF THE CITY OF SINCLAIR, INDIANA

March 10, 19--

Mr. Marvin L. Bierce, Director
Industrial Research Associates, Inc.
545 Lakeshore Drive
Chicago, Illinois 45390

Dear Mr. Bierce:

The City Council of the City of Sinclair hereby requests that your firm conduct a study, in accordance with requirements discussed in recent conferences with us, of the potential for industrial expansion in this city.

We request that you report the findings of this study to this Council no later than June fifteenth of this year.

Respectfully yours,

Homer Immerman

Homer Immerman
President

Figure 56
Sample of a letter of acceptance.

INDUSTRIAL RESEARCH ASSOCIATES
545 LAKESHORE DRIVE
CHICAGO, ILLINOIS 45390

Marvin L. Bierce,
Director

March 12, 19--

The City Council
Sinclair, Indiana 33303

Ladies and Gentlemen:

We are glad to undertake the study requested by the City Council of Sinclair on the potential for industrial expansion in Sinclair.

The Council can be sure that the Staff of Industrial Research Associates will make a thorough study of the question, and submit to the Council a written report of its findings not later than June 15.

Sincerely,

Marvin L. Bierce

Marvin L. Bierce

MLB:ct

Figure 57
Sample of a short letter of transmittal.

INDUSTRIAL RESEARCH ASSOCIATES
545 LAKESHORE DRIVE
CHICAGO, ILLINOIS 45390

Marvin L. Bierce,
Director

June 11, 19--

The City Council
Sinclair, Indiana 33303

Ladies and Gentlemen:

We are pleased to sumbit to the City Council this report on "The Future of Sinclair."

Industrial Research Associates has studied all the factors it believes pertinent to the question of industrial expansion in the city. Very definite conclusions arise from this study, conclusions which we believe will be vital to the process of city planning in the years ahead.

We are happy to have had the opportunity to serve the City of Sinclair in performing this study.

Sincerely,

Marvin L. Bierce

Marvin L. Bierce

MLB:ct

Figure 58
Sample of a table of contents in a business report.

CONTENTS

Figure 59
Sample of an abstract in a business report.

ABSTRACT

After an extensive study of the pertinent factors and all available data, Industrial Research Associates concludes: (a) that Sinclair's most likely source of industrial expansion is the attraction of existing corporations seeking new branch locations; (b) that certain "light" industries are the most likely to be attracted, and (c) that as a result of such attraction, economic conditions in Sinclair will improve sharply. We recommend that a reputable public relations firm, one specializing in industrial expansion and relocation, be retained by the City Council to implement these conclusions.

Figure 60
Sample of a bibliography in a business report. In this bibliography the different kinds of publications are given separate alphabetical listings. This is an optional format. Alternatively, all sources might be indicated in a single list.

SOURCES CONSULTED

Books

Dormann, Robert P., An Industrial History of Central Indiana, Indianapolis, Dowling Press, 1974. 291 pp.

Gerber, Philip M., Industrial Relocation, New York, Hruger, 1980. 340 pp.

Government Publications

Indiana State Auditor's Office, Guide to City and State Taxes, Indianapolis, 1979. 33 pp.

U.S. Bureau of the Census, 19th Census of the United States: Census of Population. Washington, U.S. Government Printing Office, 1981, 4 vols. 2187 pp.

Periodicals

Morris, Alex D., "Light and Heavy Industry in the Medium-Sized City," Harvard Business Journal, Vol. 62, No. 3 (October 1978), pp. 231-278.

IN SUMMARY

By this point in the text, it comes as no news that written communications impress people almost as much by how they look as by what they say. Of course the two characteristics can't be completely separated: the report's physical construction — when it's well done — actually helps to clarify and make more accessible its contents. So whether for clarity's sake, or for appearance's, this chapter's discussion on the "finished report" is vital.

Every element of a report's style, structure, and format is intended to serve a purpose. We've looked at the purposes they serve, and at how those elements are built to best serve them.

When all the planning stages of a report project are done, when the research has been completed, the findings organized and interpreted, and the last draft written, a skillful report writer works just as intently on the final product as he did on those earlier stages. Good report writers know that it is their reports *in final form* that show those around them the job they are capable of doing.

PROBLEMS

1. What kinds of illustrations would you use to illustrate each of the following in a report, and why?

   a. The new habits being worn by nuns
   b. The operation of a sewing machine
   c. The new routes being added by Pan-National Airways next month
   d. The five largest companies in America and their relative sizes
   e. The organizational structure of the (your city) government
   f. The number of suicides per year in San Francisco since 1900
   g. Sources of the highway construction dollar in (your state)
   h. The acceleration (that is, the increasing speed) of a manned space rocket as it leaves the launching pad
   i. The movement of a bill through the state legislature
   j. The relationship between job performance and temperature, humidity and noise level in a factory or office.

2. Here's a problem in straightforward expository writing: Write a carefully structured paragraph aimed at college freshmen explaining the difference between *salary* and *wages*, or *a partnership* and a *corporation*, or a *holding company* and a *conglomerate.*

3. Select some major company of interest to you and investigate its methods of recruiting employees from colleges and universities. When you've concluded your study, write a report revealing your findings.

   If your instructor requests it, submit first a detailed preproject report revealing your plan of attack.

4. You are asked to write a report on how the ____________ Company (any large company of your choice) trains its letter writers.

   a. Submit to your instructor a memorandum indicating the company whose letter-training program you wish to examine, an analysis of the

report problem as you see it, and a statement of the kinds of research that will be necessary.
b. Write the report.

5. From any business journal, select an article that interests you, and after reading it carefully, prepare a 150–200 word abstract of it.

6. Write an abstract of the article "How to Make Your Nest Egg Grow in the Bond Market," which appears on pages 423–426.

7. Using observational research to derive your data, and library and interrogational research to establish criteria, write a report entitled "Bulletin Boards at (your college): Well- or Ill-Used?"

8. For some organization to which you belong (club, team, fraternity, residence hall, labor union, company, standing committee, and so on), assume that you are responsible for submitting monthly reports to the head of that organization detailing the organization's activities and achievements during the past month.

Write such a report and submit it to your instructor.

9. After making all of your structural and format decisions (or following the requirements set down by your instructor), prepare an impressive final report to be submitted to Sam Baker — bringing to a conclusion the report project you've been pursuing in Problem #9 on pages 387–388, 408, 426–427.

10. Complete and submit the report project you have been working on in problem 10 (page 388), problem 10 (page 408), and problem 10 (page 427).

11. Obtain a copy of an existing business report and read it carefully. Then, in memorandum format, prepare an evaluation of the report, commenting specifically and critically on its organization, its style, its format components, and the value of its contents. Keep in mind that the techniques of effective report writing we've been discussing are *ideals;* you are unlikely to find any report that you can praise unqualifiedly. Submit this evaluative memo report to your instructor.

12. Discuss each of the following propositions:

a. Conciseness is not as important to a business report as it is to a letter.
b. The general level of diction in a business report should be higher than in a letter or memo.
c. Fluent writing and attractive format in a report can go a long way in camouflaging deficiencies in its findings.

13. Here's an exercise in report-writing conciseness and the elimination of CorpSpeak. The following paragraph, which typifies the style of many business report writers, suffers from noun-heaviness and an overload of words. What it takes 142 words to say in this paragraph took one of the best reporters of his generation only 81.

> It became standard operating procedure, during the night hours, that small patrols were dispatched surreptitiously into the area immediately between the two opposing armies. Once they obtained the designated locations, the members of the patrol party would sequester themselves in excavated

```
portions of the terrain and proceed to monitor sounds
emanating from objects like bugles, motor cars, and similar
implements, which in turn would be an indication of activity
in Huesca. Our own intelligence could thereby deduce
confirmation of various movements in the Fascist
encampment; and the size of Fascist deployments were
measurable, in approximation, through calculations drawn
from reports by our patrol personnel. A standing order was
operative that any sounds issuing from church bells be
reported forthwith. It had been earlier demonstrated that
preceding any battle action on the part of the Fascists,
church services were conducted for their combat personnel.
```

14. Write a report on vehicular accidents in your state during the last twenty years, using published data to obtain your facts and interrogational research to find out what is being done about the accident rate.
If your instructor requests, submit a research plan for his or her evaluation prior to performing your research.
See if you can match this reporter in conciseness, retaining all the paragraph's facts and ideas and getting rid of only the static language and the dead wood.

PART 5

THE ARTS OF SPEAKING AND LISTENING

CHAPTER 19

EYES, EARS, AND MOUTH IN BUSINESS

We've devoted almost an entire text to the principles and strategies of effective writing in business, and to the human factors that determine those principles and strategies. Obviously, though, not all communicating in business is done on paper. While almost everything of substantial importance finds its way onto paper, the greater part of all communicating in business is done orally — in speaking, and in listening to others speak.

As we saw back in Chapter 3, the two forms of communication — writing and speaking — have a lot in common: many of the same situations and states of mind, many of the same principles, strategies and tactics. Yet, speaking and writing are not the same. So in order to cover the field of business communications with anything approaching completeness, we must finally turn our attention to oral communication — its varieties, its strengths and pitfalls.

In this chapter and the next, we'll look at the different modes of oral communication in business. This chapter will examine *listening* (for who can speak well without first listening?); then the *telephone* (where so much of our daily business is transacted); then *nonverbal communication* (those messages we get and send by means other than words); and finally *face-to-face speaking* situations (conversation, meetings and group discussion, and interviews). The next chapter will examine the techniques of *formal presentations.*

LISTENING

You don't speak well in business — maybe you speak quickly, or glibly, but you don't speak well — unless you first know how to listen and to learn from what you hear. One expert puts it this way: "Almost everyone in business is a talker. The problem is getting them to listen." And the higher up in an organization you go, the worse the problem can become.

Poor listeners generally lose out in two ways. They fail to get the insights and the early-warning signals that the talkers (even when they are one's own subordinates) can provide. And they fail to satisfy the need of the talkers (especially when they are one's own subordinates) to feel that they are being listened to.

How hard is it to improve one's listening skill? Unlike the writing skill, which can take quite awhile to develop fully, better listening can be developed within a matter of days, once you set your mind to it.

The Requirements of Effective Listening

What does effective listening entail? A number of things. Let's examine some of the requirements.

Listening for Purpose as Well as Details Obviously, as a good listener, you listen for facts — whether you intend to respond to them immediately, or to store them in mind for future reference. And listening for facts is more than just listening to details, as important as those details may be.

You want to listen, as well, for a sense of where the speaker is going. You want to listen ahead. If John Doe is speaking to you, he may state his purpose clearly and openly as he begins — but not always. He may not wish to reveal his purpose right away, or may just assume you can see it. In such case, you have to interpret the direction of his remarks and infer his purpose from them. Or he may simply be unorganized, forcing you to work hard mentally to get a sense of the direction in which he's moving.

As soon as you're sure what Doe's purpose is, you're in a position to help or hinder him in achieving it (whichever you wish) by how you respond. And you know how long to let him speak before you offer a reply. Knowing his purpose, you not only hear the details he's stating, but you're able to weigh those details as the instruments with which he's attempting to achieve his purpose. And you're able to see what kinds of details, if any, he's leaving out or ignoring.

Listening for Bias Recall our lengthy discussion of *connotation* back on pages 21-26. Careful listening requires that you listen for connotations, as well as for literal meanings. The words a speaker chooses to transmit information will very quickly reveal any biases that he or she feels about that information. This is probably even truer for speakers than writers, for writers have a chance to reconsider and change their words while speakers (at least those who are speaking extemporaneously, or "off the cuff") generally use the first words that come to mind. Or, they'll evidently fumble around for substitute words. In either case, their bias shows.

Bias can also show up in the evidence that a speaker provides — or doesn't provide — to back up an argument. The various "interpretive pitfalls" that we looked at in our discussion of report writing (pages 420–421) will show up just as often in speaking as in writing. You want to listen for them.

Encouraging the Speaker to Open Up The good listener isn't merely a sensitive receiver of details and a perceiver of biases and purposes. He also encourages a speaker to express himself or herself more freely and more fully, thereby learning as much as possible from the speaker. When someone is talking to you, give him or her your complete attention. That's what the speaker wants, and he'll be flattered to have it. Establish eye contact with the speaker and maintain it as best you can. Be sure that your posture and facial expression imply that what you're hearing is important to you: you may, in fact, be able to listen very well from a slouch or with a blank look on your face, but the speaker will feel that such a manner betrays a lack of interest on your part — and be more likely to "clam up" than "open up."

Pitfalls in Listening

Learning to be a good listener also means avoiding the numerous pitfalls into which so many people in business stumble. What are these pitfalls?

Preconceptions You may have some preconceived opinions or biases regarding the matter being put to you by a speaker. Your opinions may even be more valid than the speaker's (or at least seem to be at the outset). But, always hold open the possibility — for it's very real — that the speaker has a new slant on the matter, or some new information that hasn't yet reached you. Assume that he does. Set aside your preconceptions while he speaks, and make yourself as free of your own biases as you possibly can.

Getting Turned Off by Dryness or Dullness Many people, when confronted by a speaker, listen carefully for a minute — then, if the subject seems dry, or the speaker clumsy, they get turned off. They continue listening, if at all, through a filter of their own disapproval. And through such a filter, you don't hear very well. Good listeners, when they find themselves trapped by dry subjects or dull speakers, remind themselves that even the driest presentations can yield some fertile facts or ideas. They also remember that there is little relationship between the quality of a person's mind and the fluency of his tongue; the most tongue-tied speakers can put forth valuable information and insight.

Becoming Distracted Because we can think, and hence receive information, at a much faster rate than a speaker can give it to us, there is always the risk that we'll allow something else to enter our field of attention and distract us from what a speaker is saying. You've got to protect yourself against this. Work hard to improve your power of concentration. Forget what the speaker looks like, or is wearing. Shut the door or the window if necessary. Turn off the radio or the intercom. Move closer to the speaker. Use that faster thinking rate to anticipate where the speaker is going, to mentally summarize where he's been, to assess every nonverbal signal (we'll be discussing these in just a moment), and to determine the speaker's motives and purposes.

Posturing There's a bad habit some students learn in school and carry with them into business. They try so hard to *look* attentive when a teacher addresses them — and to impress a teacher with that attentiveness — that they actually fail to hear some of the things being said to them. Their attention is really on themselves and the impression they're creating. Ironically, this kind of posturing impresses only those speakers who need to have their egos stroked. More predictably, it turns off most business supervisors — and most job interviewers.

Note-Taking as a Pitfall Though you can think more quickly than a speaker can speak, you cannot (unless you're a master of shorthand) write as fast. As a consequence, listeners who take notes when a speaker speaks — and who try to get down *everything* the speaker says — usually fall behind and lose track of the central idea being developed. Tests have shown that only one out of four people listening to formal speeches is able to grasp the central idea. (And people speaking extemporaneously to you are usually even less organized than formal speakers!) In spite of good intentions, therefore, the copious note-taker often distracts himself more than he helps himself by trying to get everything down on paper. If you do take notes, put down only major ideas and direction signals — and any questions you want to ask when the speaker is done. Listen carefully and jot down statements of purpose, patterns of idea development, and recapitulations — and let the rest sink in without the distracting effort of a pencil losing its race for time against a speaker's words.

Fatigue Listening, like most other human activities, consumes vital energy. Careful listening is actually marked by a faster heartbeat, quickened pulse, even a small rise in body temperature. The lesson is clear then: when you've got to be at your listening best (in an important conference or during an interview) do anything you can to avoid entering the situation in a state of fatigue or divided interest.

A number of years ago, Ralph G. Nichols and Leonard A. Stevens wrote a book called *Are You Listening?* (New York, McGraw-Hill, 1957). It's still an excellent guide to the fine (and often underestimated) art of listening in business.

USING THE TELEPHONE

So vital has the telephone become to the conduct of modern business, that one has to wonder how business was ever transacted before Alexander Graham Bell. We so take the telephone for granted as an instrument of business, that we sometimes neglect to consider what its real advantages and disadvantages are. It does have both. Let's briefly consider them.

The Telephone's Advantages

Most obvious among the telephone's advantages are its convenience and its time efficiency. You can be in contact with the person you need (if you're lucky) within a minute. By using the phone, you can reach any number of people during a working day with virtually no time spent in moving from conversation to conversation.

The telephone is also quite cost-efficient. Telephone bills are rising less rapidly than the total costs (including secretarial time) of preparing business letters. Only when long-distance calls become lengthy do telephone charges exceed those of letters — and even then sometimes, the speed and direct voice contact are worth the added cost.

A telephone call — especially a long-distance one — can also help give a sense of urgency to your message. In addition to its actual speed, the call implies that you couldn't wait for any of the slower means of communication. And the telephone is a relatively inexpensive way to express *frequent* concern. The salesman who follows up on a sale with several calls to his customer probably could not afford to make several follow-up visits, but the calls help to generate the same good will.

On the telephone, you can combine the spontaneity and personableness of direct voice-to-voice contact (which we'll discuss in the next section) with the wisdom of having an outline or even written remarks or questions in front of you to make sure that you say everything you have to, and say it in precisely the right way. That — along with not having to get dressed up — is the major advantage of being heard without being seen.

With the telephone and a little preplanning, you can also arrange *conference calls,* linking three or more parties at different places — even different cities — into the same conversation.

The Telephone's Disadvantages

Among its drawbacks, perhaps the most serious is that it does not allow a message to be transmitted uninterruptedly. In Chapters 10-12 we examined a number of difficult reaction-evoking situations, all of them demanding that the writer very carefully construct, from beginning to end, a message that would in some way reshape the thinking of its recipient. Those messages sought to make the reader receptive to a demand, to conciliate anger, to convey bad news successfully, or to persuade someone to do something not previously contemplated. If the recipient of such a message had gotten it by phone instead of by letter or memo, he or she would undoubtedly have interrupted the message a number of times to ask questions, raise objections, or offer a different viewpoint. The carefully structured message would have been forced into tangents and sudden quarrels, and had its structure broken down. This is why business people often decide against the phone, and instead write or dictate their reaction-evoking communications.

When it's imperative, because of time, to use the telephone for such a message, the wise communicator will adjust the strategy to compensate for these disadvantages. Let's reconsider the bad-news message back on page 271 as a case in point:

Conrad Jones must refuse Ray Rilling's request for credit, yet at the same time retain Rilling's patronage "C.O.D." Part of the strategy — in writing — was to explain the reason for the refusal *before* actually stating the refusal — which can be done well on paper. Over the phone, though, it's unlikely that Rilling would remain attentively silent while Jones spelled out that reason. He'd probably interrupt and say something like, "Well, get to the point . . . do I get the credit or not?" So Jones would change his strategy. After introducing himself and referring back to Rilling's request, he would probably state the refusal *before* detailing the reason. But, he would preface his refusal statement with a phrase that would at least help to focus Rilling's mind on the reason:

> ''Because of market conditions in Carthage, Mr. Rilling, we're not able, at present, to offer you credit terms.''

That way, Rilling is less likely to say:

> ''What do you mean you can't offer me credit?''

and more likely to ask:

> ''What market conditions in Carthage do you mean?''

Jones will have kept the give-and-take of conversation moving in the direction he wants it to move: focussed on Rilling's plight in Carthage rather than on Jones's refusal to grant the credit. He will have minimized the telephone disadvantage.

As compared to face-to-face contact, the telephone is also a less personal means of initiating communication with someone. The importance of some communications — presentations, proposals, interviews — demands that they be made face-to-face. The telephone can be used to schedule them, but not to conduct the actual conversation. Your insistence on doing it all over the phone will strike some business people as self-serving expediency, and not as the right way to do business. The telephone also doesn't allow visual feedback from the person you're talking to. And it's easier for someone to break off a phone conversation than a face-to-face conversation.

Unless a person has secretarial protection to fend off telephone calls when he or she is busy, your call may interrupt at a busy time. If it does, the recipient will surely be less receptive to your message, especially if it seems self-interested. Many people dislike — even detest — unexpected sales calls, especially when the caller calls at dinnertime.

These many disadvantages certainly do not diminish the value of the telephone as a business tool, but they do warn you to think twice about the nature of your message before you pick up the telephone to convey it.

NONVERBAL COMMUNICATION

A vital part of careful listening (when you're not on the telephone) is careful looking. People will communicate as many things to you nonverbally — that is, *without* words — as they will verbally. You must keep a watchful eye for these nonverbal messages.

Those Nonverbal Messages That Accompany Speech

Even when they speak to you, people always use a number of nonverbal signals — some they're not even aware of. These nonverbal signals sometimes reinforce, often add to or modify, and at times even contradict what the words are saying. If you're sensitive to these nonverbal components of a person's speech, you'll receive the "complete" communication — at times more complete than the speaker intends.

The Handshake One of the most obvious, and most looked for, nonverbal messages in business is the *handshake*. The man who extends a limp or weak hand to an associate may be conveying a sense of weakness or untrustworthiness to his new acquaintance. The "bone-crushing" handshake is usually taken as a sign of overbearance or a desire to dominate. A golden mean, therefore, is advisable for those in business: make the handshake firm, but only as strong as necessary to reciprocate the firmness of the other person's grasp. The woman who extends her hand first is usually understood to be saying, "I wish to be treated without regard to my sex . . .", while the woman who adheres to the older etiquette and shakes only the hand that is offered her may be signaling that she sees her femininity as one tool in her business dealings.

Vocal Quality *Vocal quality* is also a sign — more precisely, a combination of signs — pointing to a speaker's state of mind. Varied *voice-pitch* (a natural mixture of high and low tones) implies genuine interest and spontaneity — although too much obvious alteration in high and low tones will convey a sense of well-oiled artificiality. An unvaried monotone implies a lack of interest, or, if accompanied by body tenseness, a sense of nervousness. The *volume* of one's voice will also reveal state of mind: a loud talker conveys a sense of either annoyance or bluster, depending on other signals that accompany the loudness; the too-soft speaker implies either nervousness or a desire to establish confidentiality. The *speed* of oral delivery also reflects a speaker's attitude toward listeners: unvarying rapidity suggests that the speaker is more interested in getting done than in transmitting information; frequent pauses or a halting hesitancy often signify indecision, resistance, or some other tension.

Body Movements *Body movements* also provide significant cues that reinforce, or contradict, a verbal message. (The study of this relationship between words and body movements is known as *kinesics*.) Postures or gestures that close off part of the body — arms folded across the chest, legs tightly crossed, a fist clenched — usually betray some "defensiveness" in a person. Sustained eye-contact conveys a sense of self-assuredness. While we're still a long way from an exact science of kinesics, an awareness of the more obvious relationships between body and speech will undoubtedly enhance your ability to communicate. (We'll look further at body movement and posture in Chapter 20.)

Space and Distance *Space* and *distance* are also nonverbal factors that communicate meaning. The distance around or across a conference table, even the shape of the table, have been shown to affect dramatically the amount of personal interaction at business meetings. The interviewer who pulls a chair up alongside you conveys a different attitude toward you than the interviewer who stays behind a desk. The size of that desk, and the presence or absence of paperwork on it, also convey meaning; as does the size of the interviewer's office and the vista out the window.

Nonverbal Messages By Themselves

Many nonverbal messages are transmitted independently of speech. Some experts say that *everything* we do constitutes a message to other people. Certainly we convey a sense of businesslike efficiency by being punctual for appointments;

lateness implies carelessness, and arriving too early can imply that you haven't much else to occupy your time. The clothes you wear, the car you drive, the home you live in, the address of the place you work — all, for better or worse, are felt to say something relevant about your success or your temperament, and hence about your business ability.

Consider the matter of *dress* alone. Unquestionably, part of the nonverbal message that people get from you, every time they look at you, comes from the clothes you wear. This may or may not please you; but it's a fact of professional life, a fact that only the most independent (and brilliant) business people can treat lightly. The old adage isn't true: clothes do not, in any complete way, make the man. But they can *un*make him, fast, if they're inappropriate to the position he — or she — holds or aspires to.

Not being a fashion expert, I won't pretend to advise readers — men or women — what to wear on the job. I do ask you to note, however, that one recent book on men's fashions (Egon Von Furstenberg's *The Power Look*) devotes five full chapters to dressing for business. Considering everything from suits and shirts to shoes, socks, coats, ties, gloves, wallets, jewelry, and briefcases, Von Furstenberg puts it this way: "Dressing incorrectly can jeopardize financial and even job security. Fortunately, it is easy to dress well for business. Because the standards for corporate America are fairly strict, the rules are fairly simple. And as the code is very slow to change (for men, at any rate) the right clothes are good long-term investments."

An equally useful treatment of the subject, from the woman's point of view, can be found in John T. Molloy's *The Woman's Dress for Success Book*, published in paperback by Warner Books (New York, 1977).

Even many things you *don't* do convey messages to other people. Your failure to acknowledge the presence of another person in a business or a social situation, your failure to be at your desk or work station at starting time, your forgetting to express thanks when the situation calls for it, your silence when someone expects or hopes to hear from you — all these, too, are signals that convey messages to people about you. Consider well the advice that if you want to get ahead, always be at your desk and busy at work by the time your boss arrives in the morning — and, if possible, still be there when he or she leaves in the evening.

FACE-TO-FACE SPEAKING

During the course of an average workweek, the experienced business person is likely to handle a wide variety of face-to-face situations each requiring well-developed skills in speaking. Let's look here at two of the most common of them — extemporaneous conversation and group or conference situations.

Extemporaneous Conversation

Because extemporaneous speaking is an almost instantaneous process — we convert our thoughts almost immediately into language and immediately transmit that language to our listeners — there's no way of knowing precisely where a conversation is going (try as we may to control it). There is almost no opportunity to ponder the best way of saying something, and none whatsoever to reconsider something we've already said. Unlike writers, speakers are "on the firing line" the moment they open their mouths. What writers can carefully plan to do, speakers must *condition* themselves to do reflexively — that is, say the right things, the right way, the first time—to achieve the reactions they seek.

What should you do to condition yourself to become a better extemporaneous speaker? Here are a few suggestions.

Keep Your Mind on Your Purpose You often speak in business for the same reasons you write — to initiate routine contact with someone, or make a routine reply, to create goodwill, to transmit good news, to make demands, to conciliate bruised feelings, to transmit bad news, or to persuade people to do things they weren't planning to do. In short, you do all those things we examined in Chapters 8-14. To achieve each of those functions, a writer has to take the reader through a series of mental phases. (Remember the recommended strategy patterns for each of those purposes.) The speaker must also take the listener's mind and feelings through those same phases. The difference, of course, is that the speaker has the listener in front of him. The speaker gets verbal and nonverbal *feedback* from a listener, and can tell — if sensitive to that feedback — when each phase of the strategy is satisfied, and when it isn't.

Control Your Intensity Be sure that your conversational speech shows a *balanced enthusiasm*. Avoid, on the one hand, any tendency to become too intense — to speak too loudly or too fast, to use heavily connotative language, to "talk with your hands." These traits will actually distract your listener, and cause him or her to focus on your intensity rather than your message. On the other hand, if you fail to show *some* feeling for what you're saying, you can hardly expect your listener to develop any feeling for it. It's a matter of balance.

Avoid Tangents If you have a specific purpose in mind in a face-to-face discussion, don't let the discussion get off on a tangent. Tangents develop when one idea reminds you of another, then that other reminds you of a third, and so on. You can't stop yourself from thinking tangentially (it's the sign of an active mind), but you *can* resist expressing those tangents when they do come to mind. When the person you're speaking to goes off on a tangent, pursue it only as far as courtesy dictates, then graciously guide the discussion back on the track.

Keep Your Speech Appropriate to Situation As in writing, so too in speaking: the language and mood appropriate to one situation may not be appropriate to another. Informal diction, joking, a laying-on of hands, some four-letter expletives — all of these can be helpful in some conversations, but destructive in others. When a listener, whether because of upbringing, sex, professional position, or self-assumed status, construes what you've said, or how you've said it, as *inappropriate*, you're not communicating, but rather building a barrier against communication.

Work on the Quality of Your Voice Whenever you can find the chance, listen to your own voice on a tape recorder. Speak extemporaneously into it, talk with someone while the microphone is on, read a page of your favorite book into it. Chances are if the voice you hear coming back to you is pleasing to you, it will be pleasing to other people. If it isn't, you have some self-improvement to do. Try to rid your voice of any inclination toward harsh or nasal tones. Make sure that enthusiasm doesn't cause your voice to lose its resonance. You should also overcome any tendency to fragment your speech with meaningless *uhs, likes,* and *you knows.* If you have a strong regional or cultural accent, don't try to purge it entirely, but work on softening it; make it less pronounced. Make sure you enunciate all your words and syllables clearly, but without assuming a clipped or overly formal tone (again, it's a matter of balance). Work on building as pleasing a quality as possible into your voice, even if that means taking a course in elocution. There's no escaping the fact that people are moved not only by what you say, but by how you say it — and that "how" includes the quality of your voice.

Meetings and Group Discussions

Group discussions, formal and informal meetings, conferences, and round table exchanges of ideas are frequent in business, and very useful. It may even be true that the clearest sign of your growth and success within an organization is the number of meetings you must attend.

Too often, though, these discussions and meetings are conducted inefficiently. They waste time and frustrate their participants — usually because the chairperson lets control of the meeting slip away. A delicate problem of *balance* confronts the leader of any meeting. On the one hand, control must be maintained, lest the group go off on unproductive tangents. On the other hand, every member of the group must feel free to contribute ideas and opinions. If some do not, then the group's basic purpose — the free exchange of facts and ideas — is defeated.

The Role of the Chairperson or Discussion Leader The first tool in preparing for a group discussion is an *agenda* of the kind we looked at back on pages 368–369. The leader or chairperson must decide when the meeting is to be held, what the meeting should (and shouldn't) deal with and in what order, and what should result. The agenda reflects these objectives. The chairperson should not, however, dominate the meeting.

Once the group convenes (with everyone hopefully there on time) the discussion leader must meet a number of responsibilities. He or she must congenially but persuasively call the group to order, getting members to set aside their individual concerns to face the matters at hand. The leader must — and this requires preparation beforehand — describe clearly and concisely the nature of each issue and problem confronting the group. If the chairperson also has the authority to decide the issues being raised, he should be very circumspect in stating his own views, lest the others become reluctant to state opposing ones. Participants should be encouraged to take the initiative in offering their views, and called on specifically only if no one in the group takes this initiative.

If group discussion veers off on a tangent, the leader must gently steer it back on course, reminding the group of the agenda if necessary. He or she must keep any one participant or group of participants (the "floor hogs") from dominating the meeting — yet do it inoffensively. The leader should also try to restate, for the group's benefit, any idea that is unclear — but should do so without offending the author of the idea. And the leader should, at certain junctures, summarize what has already been said: by so doing, he gives the group a clearer sense of its own progress, while reasserting control over the meeting.

The more heated the debate becomes in group discussion, the harder the chairperson must work to assure equal opportunity for all viewpoints. And when the leader notices gaps in the group's information, he or she should take immediate steps to fill them, even if it requires temporary recess while the information is found. As debate begins to move toward some consensus (or as consensus begins to prove impossible), the chairperson must help to consolidate that consensus by stating it clearly (or to isolate the points of disagreement for later resolution). Finally, it's a chairperson's task to close the meeting and send its participants off with a sense that their time has been productively spent.

The more formal a business meeting is, the more a chairperson will want to depend on the long-established rules of parliamentary procedure, the rules for offering and voting on motions, and the techniques for channeling discussion and debate. Parliamentary procedure lends order to a meeting, and creates a feeling among participants that every issue and every contribution is being treated fairly. Obviously, a chairperson must first learn parliamentary procedure in order to depend upon it. Various guidebooks on the subject are widely available: the best known, of course, is *Roberts' Rules of Order*.

The Role of the Participant in Group Discussion Like the chairperson, each participant should come prepared to discuss each item on the agenda, and to follow the rules for discussion that are in force. When you receive an agenda prior to a meeting, make notes on the points you wish to raise, and jot down any questions you want to ask. Bring with you, too, an attitude that allows you to raise those points in a congenial and unargumentative manner. Let the *substance* of your remarks, and not the passion with which you offer them, make its mark on the group. Each of the principles of good face-to-face conversation that we discussed earlier pertains as well to effective group discussion.

Be a good listener too, and show tolerance for the contributions of others, even if you disagree with them, or if they're presented more aggressively or more fumblingly than you would prefer. Your tolerance of others will likely be repaid you when you need it most.

INTERVIEWS

An *interview* — the very word sends shudders up some people's spines. And the fear is quite unnecessary, for an interview is really only a formalized conversation, usually conducted for some specific purpose — to get answers from someone who has them, to probe the reasons behind a situation, to brief someone in preparation for a task, or to measure a person's qualifications for a job opening. All the qualities of extemporaneous speaking we've discussed come into play, *plus* some additional preparations and strategies that we ought to consider.

Both interviewer and interviewee must *prepare* for an interview. Too many interviews bog down — to the disadvantage of both parties — because neither participant had a clear idea of how the interview should proceed. They knew what they wanted from the interview, but didn't know precisely how to get it. Let's consider first the interviewer's role; then shift our focus to the interviewee.

From the Interviewer's Standpoint

Experienced interviewers, those who know how to get the most from their time, will (like a careful writer starting a report project) carefully define what they hope to achieve in an interview, and prepare their questions directly toward that end; this keeps the interview from "straying" once it starts. They plan a brief several minutes to establish a friendly climate: both to get the interviewee talking freely, and to assess the interviewee's personality, his nervousness, and the like. Skillful interviewers do all the "homework" necessary to have pertinent data at their fingertips during the interview. And they prepare their questions in the way most likely to evoke full responses from the interviewee — usually by asking easier, less open-ended questions first, and only later moving into the more complex, open-ended ones like, "How then would you reorganize the department?" or "What specific talents can you bring to the firm?"

In recent years, various "fair employment practices" laws — passed to protect job-seekers against unfair discrimination — have complicated the task of the job interviewer. Where these laws apply, it can be illegal to ask an applicant: "With whom do you live?" "Do you plan to have children?" "What kind of work does your father do?" and numerous other questions. Today's job interviewer must be able to stimulate discussion without straying into people's private lives. It's made the task — though justifiably — even tougher than it used to be.

The interviewer's objective is not to dominate the interview, but to get interviewees to make responses and reveal themselves. Though probably doing most of the talking in the early stages, the interviewer should become primarily a listener once the interview is in full swing. When all has been learned that the interviewer wishes to learn, he or she graciously brings the interview to an end — never letting it just "peter out," or end with some outside intrusion like a telephone call or a secretary's interruption. If a resolution is possible at the end of a job interview — that is, if the interviewer has decided what action to take or what the next step should be — the interviewee should be told, and not kept "hanging."

The Well-Prepared Interviewee

Things look a little different from the other side of the desk, from the viewpoint of the interviewee. But careful planning and preparation are just as necessary. Let's consider the interviewee's role in one of the most difficult interviews of all: the job interview. If you can handle this interview successfully, you won't have many problems with other kinds.

As your interview date approaches, you've got to take one more long look at yourself from the employer's point of view. (Presumably you've been doing this all along or you wouldn't have gotten to the interview — so don't stop now.) You must be prepared! All of your scouting, planning, resume preparation, letter writing, and pavement pounding has led you to this critical meeting. Advance preparation is the only way you're going to carry it off successfully. Be sure you've carefully gone over every bit of information you can lay your hands on about the organization. And make doubly sure that you know what you want and what you've got to offer, because that's precisely what the interviewer — more likely several interviewers — will be looking for. When an organization hires you, it's making an investment of many thousands of dollars (considering salary, fringes, payroll taxes, training costs, and the like). You can't blame them for wanting a quality product.

When "zero hour" arrives, remember the following advice:

1. *Arrive early.* Be sure you know how to get to the place of the interview, and approximately how long (considering traffic) it will take to get there. Arrive about fifteen minutes early to give yourself time to relax, take in the surroundings, and think over your strategy. (And if you're nervous, brush your hand unobtrusively across your pants leg or skirt: you want your handshake to be dry.)

2. *Open pleasantly.* Exchange pleasantries and brief small talk at the beginning, and allow yourself to be put at ease by the interviewer. Most interviewers aim to do this, and you're ahead of the game if you show them they've succeeded. Don't jockey for position. Let the interviewer take the lead, at first. Later on, you'll be taking it over.

3. *Handle the questions wisely.* Here's where preparation begins to pay off. There are some questions almost always asked at job interviews. You ought to come with ready answers to them: "Why do you want to work for us?" "Tell me about this experience you've had." "Where do you see yourself five years from now?" "What kind of salary do you require?"

Whatever the question, try to strike a balance in answering it. Don't limit yourself to *yes* or *no* answers (you'll seem defensive); but yet don't answer too lengthily (and seem like a "wind bag" — some people try to explain all they know about clock design when someone asks them what time it is). You also want to balance your enthusiasm in your responses. Show by your answers and your manner that you are greatly interested in the company. Yet don't be so effusive, so "gushy" that you seem more like a puppy dog than a self-respecting human being. Dignity counts.

One experienced job interviewer suggests that, if possible, young job seekers accept one or two interviews *prior to the ones they're most interested in* just for the practice. The advice is ethically questionable: you're wasting a lot of somebody's valuable time and money if you're not really interested in what they offer. But the practice is probably quite widespread.

During the early part of the interview, you can get clues from the interviewer's questions about the kinds of problems the organization has — problems you might help to solve. You're better prepared for the next phase of the interview if you've listened carefully for such clues.

4. *Now "sell" yourself.* As the interview progresses, you'll spot the point at which you should begin to "sell." Once you've sized up the situation, you'll want to — in fact you'll be expected to — make a case for yourself as a valuable new addition to the staff. At this point, you assume a gentle dominance of the interview. That's what the interviewer wants (most of them do, anyway). You dominate not by interrupting the interviewer, but by explaining in detail why and how you can help the organization. Use every technique of effective face-to-face conversation that we discussed earlier. If appropriate, pull out some of the work from your briefcase to demonstrate what you can do — as long as the documents aren't confidential. (If you violate someone else's confidentialities, the inter-

viewer will assume you'd violate this company's too.) In as many ways as you can, show your interest in the job, and your interest in doing the kind of work the job promises.

5. *Close confidently*. A lot of sales are lost because of careless closing by the salesperson. What kind of carelessness? Usually a simple failure to ask the customer to buy. So be sure to ask. You want some kind of commitment at the end of the interview, even if it's rejection. It can be quite painful to be left hanging because the interviewer has to "talk to a few more people." Asking might even help the interviewer make up his mind. If you're willing to be left hanging, you encourage the interviewer to want to look further. If, however, you put the question forthrightly, the interviewer can hire you and save all that extra time. If others in the company must be consulted before a decision is made (as is often the case), try at least for a commitment on when you might phone for a decision. Suggest a date and a time, and make sure it's a morning call — 9 a.m. may be best. You want to get him before all the hectic problems of the day have settled in. Ideally it will be you who will initiate the "closing" phase of the interview —after you're satisfied you've done all you could to sell yourself. Quite often, however, the interviewer will give some sign (or come right out and say) that he's heard what he wants to hear. Or he may just glance at his wristwatch. When you pick up this cue (whether the interviewer has given it intentionally or not), that's the time to move into your close.

After the interview, drop the interviewer a thank-you note like the one on pages 358–359, and add anything you may have forgotten to say at the interview. If the interviewer has withheld a decision, be congenial but persistent in your follow-up. In preserving your own self-respect you'll enhance the interviewer's respect for you. In many companies, coming up with a firm salary offer requires time and a lot of paperwork, so have patience. If you've followed these suggestions, and have the qualifications a company needs, you should soon find yourself at work on a job to your liking.

Stress Interviews

Some interviewers — not a great number of them, but some — believe in "stress interviews" — interviews in which the job candidate is put under stress so that the interviewer can see how well the candidate handles it. Sometimes the stress is applied by aggressive questioning, like "What makes you think you can do this job?" At other times, it's applied merely by disagreeing with what the candidate has said. In either case, the tactic is best handled by staying cool and confident (it is, after all, only a game). The aggressive question should be answered exactly as though the same question had been asked unaggressively. The disagreement can be tactfully fended by replying, "You've got a point, but the way I see it. . . ." (Remember the advice given by Ben Franklin back on page 295.)

Stress interviewers may also try to set you against yourself — perhaps by asking you to discuss "your own worst shortcomings." How would you handle it? It's really a snap if you're prepared for it. Answer by citing traits that, while imperfect, can be seen as signs of potential strength rather than weakness — "Well, I have a tendency toward impatience, which I'm getting better at controlling." "Sometimes I'm compulsive, and find I'm unable to relax before a job is done." "I can be too much of a perfectionist, which plays havoc with deadlines, and makes me unable to accomplish everything I want to do."

Whatever comes at you, if it's designed to cause stress, keep in mind that the interviewer is merely testing the way you handle difficult situations. Don't get upset; don't show frustration, or anger, or confusion. Stay cool, and you're bound to impress the stress interviewer.

CONCLUSION

In this chapter, then, we've looked at almost every kind of non-written communication you'll have to engage in on the job — all but one in fact (the *formal presentation*, which we'll look at in the final chapter). Above all else, you want to remember that the word communication means not only *talking* but *listening*, and *watching* (for those telltale nonverbal messages).

The businessperson who can impressively communicate both on paper *and* in person is almost guaranteed a successful climb up the organizational ladder . . . or, in the case of the small entrepreneur, increasingly frequent and pleasurable trips to the bank.

PROBLEMS

1. Conduct a brief interview with a business executive or administrator about the inflow and outflow of communications on his or her job.

Learn what percentage of incoming messages is written, and what percentage is oral. Find out what different expectations the executive has for each form of incoming message; and what his or her frustrations are with each form.

Also ask the executive about the relative percentages of oral and written communications that are outgoing: whether he or she prepares differently for the two forms of message; and when he or she would rather speak than write, or write than speak.

Report on your findings to your instructor.

2. It's one of the oldest party games we have, but still tremendously useful as a reminder of the distortions that intrude into oral communications as they pass from person to person — the message whispered into one ear, then whispered by the recipient into someone else's ear, and in turn whispered by each recipient into someone else's ear. In spite of our good intentions, we tend to hear what we want to hear, rather than what's been actually told us. And we tend to pass along what we want to pass along, rather than what we've actually heard.

Get together a group of at least six people. Write the first version of a paragraph-long message, and whisper it, verbatim, into the first ear. After the message has been whispered down the line, use a tape recorder to recapture the message as told by its final recipient. Transcribe the final version, and submit it to your instructor with an assessment of what was gained along the way, what was changed, and what was lost.

3. Excluding your business communications instructor, make a list of the instructors you have this term, but give each of them a fictitious name. (If you're presently taking fewer than three other courses, list the instructors you've had during the past year.)

Be completely honest and assess the impressions you get from the way each of those instructors dresses. And be specific in referring to that manner of dress.

In a memo to your business communications instructor (whom you've exempted from your analysis), spell out these impressions and their causes, using the fictitious names you've assigned to your subjects.

4. On a selected "typical" day in your life, make a descriptive list of all the nonverbal messages you receive during that day, and indicate specifically what those messages told you.

5. As one way of measuring the importance of nonverbal messages, do the following: tape-record a lecture or a speech at which an audience is present, and make careful notes on the nonverbal components of the lecturer's presentation. Then, after gathering one or more people (who were *not* at the lecture), play your tape back for them. Have them tell you, as the tape is playing, what nonverbal behavior they believe the speaker is projecting. Then, on your own, analyze the discrepancies between the real and the imagined nonverbal messages, and determine how much, if at all, those nonverbal messages contributed to overall communication in the lecture.

6. Write a brief memo-report detailing the kinds of questions that it is now illegal — under the Fair Employment Practices laws that pertain in your state — for an interviewer to ask a job candidate.

You may get your research leads from any of several sources: (a) your instructor in personnel management, (b) a professional job interviewer, (c) an employment agent, (d) a counselor at your school's placement office, or (e) your reference librarian.

7. As your instructor directs, prepare to stage a series of simulated job-interviews in class.

a) Those of you who are to be job applicants will prepare a resume (and hopefully a covering letter) to be submitted prior to the interview; and prepare in all the other necessary ways for a strong interview.
b) Those of you who are to be the interviewers will prepare your interview strategy, including the questions you plan to ask the interviewee; and come prepared to recommend either hiring or rejection, depending upon your assessment of the candidate(s).

At the appointed hour, under the critical scrutiny of not only your instructor but your classmates, conduct the interview.

8. The next time you are part of a formal group discussion or committee meeting, take careful notes on the chairperson's conduct of the meeting, on the roles and behavior of each of the participants, and on the results of the meeting. Use the discussion back on pages 473–474 to direct your note-taking, and to help you write a brief memo-report analyzing group communication at the meeting.

9. Here's a problem to ponder. Put yourself in the shoes of John L. Jones, the sales manager who wrote the letter on pages 247–248, (analyzed in detail on page 250). You've received the stinging complaint from Carl Teasdale (on page 247), and you must respond with conciliation and the same adjustment offer that Jones makes in his letter. However, instead of writing, you decide to phone Teasdale, because it's quicker. Will your effort be just as satisfactory? More so? Less so? More importantly, why?

As you think through this problem, play out the telephone scenario in your mind. What will Teasdale's response to you be when you identify yourself? Will you have the opportunity to apologize as effectively? to explain as fully? to offer your adjustment as clearly and persuasively?

Some people feel the telephone is the best way to handle a problem like this one. What do you think?

10. Read carefully the situation and letter on pages 265–266. You are the credit manager, and you have to turn down Ray Rilling's request for credit; yet you want to retain his patronage on a cash basis.

However, instead of writing him a letter, you decide to do it by phone. Carefully plan your phone call. Then, with a classmate, simulate the phone call, achieving the same results the problem asks you to achieve.

After the call, discuss (or write a memo regarding) the advantages and the disadvantages of using the telephone to convey this bad-news message.

CHAPTER 20

"SPEECH . . . SPEECH . . ."

We come, in the final chapter of this book, to a situation many people hope they never come to — the stand-up speech.[1] The prospect of getting up in front of an audience and effectively communicating ideas to them — perhaps even persuading them — is enough to send chills down the sturdiest of spines. And yet success in business, or in any other kind of public enterprise, requires that it be done. Public speaking is necessary in climbing up the ladder; and it's necessary for asserting the authority one must assert at every rung on the way up. In truth, it's not really difficult, once a few obstacles are gotten out of the way.

The greatest of these obstacles (at least at the beginning of one's career) is nervousness. Almost everyone who stands before an audience, for the first time or the thousandth, feels it. (As one of my students put it, "that's why they call our human wiring the 'central nervous system.' ") The beginning speaker is not alone.

That nervousness before the speech can be minimized, but never totally gotten rid of. You want to accept it for what it is — Nature's way of assuring alertness and top performance when it's most needed. (The gazelle or zebra who isn't nervous when the lions are near isn't long for the herd.) Your task — whether they're lions or lambs out there in your audience — is to turn that nervousness into productive tension.

For one thing, you almost always appear more confident to listeners than you feel inside. Next time you make a speech in class or on the job, check this out with members of your audience afterwards. Nerves don't show through nearly as much as inexperienced speakers think they do. So, at the least, you ought not to be nervous about looking nervous. You won't.

Furthermore, nervousness is almost always most intense before things begin. "Butterflies" tend to diminish once the speech — or anything else that's

[1] This chapter was prepared for the Third Edition of this text by Mr. Dan Meier of the El Camino College Writing Center, Via Torrance, California.

made you nervous — gets under way. Only a sense of utter failure midway will increase anxiety, and if you're prepared for your speech (we'll talk about preparation in a moment) utter failure is impossible. With your factual material in front of you (or well implanted in your mind because you've worked with it and wrestled with it) the worst you can expect is disagreement from your audience. If you've prepared you simply cannot look bad.

PRELIMINARIES

First let's examine a few vital preliminary matters: choosing a *subject* and *purpose*, and assessing your *audience*. Sometimes, subject, purpose and audience are all known quantities to the speaker — as, for instance, when a corporate V.P. periodically addresses a gathering of division managers to keep them fully apprised of new company policy and planning. But at other times, either the subject and purpose, or the audience, can be a variable that the speaker has to resolve. You may, for example, have developed or invented some new process or machine, and be required to explain it to different groups of people (some of whom are going to be harder to teach than others). Or perhaps you're a company rep who has to sell a product or service to different groups of prospective buyers (not all of whom will be equally easy to sell). In each case, you know what your subject and purpose are, and must decide how best to present that subject to the particular audience in order to achieve the purpose. Alternatively, you may know who your audience is and have to select the right subject to present to them. If you're a well known figure (say, the President, or a corporate chairman of the board, or a well-known consumer advocate) and have been asked to address the monthly meeting of Rotary, or the Young Republicans, or a college commencement — what should your subject be? More likely you're a student in a communications class; you have to make a speech and must decide what you're going to talk about.

So let's look at these potentially important variables: deciding upon a subject and purpose,[2] and assessing your audience.

Choosing a Subject and a Purpose

Wisely choosing a subject and purpose for a speech requires that you consider at least five important factors. Let's examine them.

Deciding the Subject Itself. For one thing, the subject you choose to talk about should be one that interests you. This might seem a self-evident rule, but it's often ignored: speakers choose topics they think their audiences will like, then show up at speechtime lacking the enthusiasm that's necessary to communicate

[2] A note on terminology here: It would be more concise, rather than referring to *subject* and *purpose*, simply to talk about the *topic* of a speech. *Topic* means that combination of subject and purpose you mean to pursue. But for our purposes, I think it's better to refer to *subject* and *purpose* — as a constant reminder that you have to decide upon, and keep your mind on, both.

well. You have to like the subject yourself — or at least feel strongly about it in some other way — before you can make your audience like hearing about it from you.

Considering Your Audience. Of course the audience must be interested in that subject too — or at least be curious enough to "warm" to it once you interestingly present it to them. (More on audience assessment in just a moment.)

Determining Your Authority to Handle the Subject. The subject you choose should also be within your ability to talk about with confidence — so that you can project a sense of *authority* in presenting it. The subject should come either from what you already know, and need only to organize for effective presentation; or from what you can (and have the time and the resources to) find out about with some research. What *do* you already know that might make a good subject? If you're like most other people (though they often don't realize it), you possess a wealth of information that you've derived from your education, your earlier research projects, your work experience, your hobbies, your travel, your interests, your outside reading. Tap that experience. Turn that knowledge into some new awareness for your prospective listeners. And what kinds of subjects can you research? The possibilities are as numerous as they are for written reports — the research for which we discussed at length in Chapter 16. Any subject for which library material is accessible to you, or any subject within your ability to observe, experiment with, or ask questions about of those who know, can make good subject matter for a speech if all the other conditions are met.

Nothing turns off an audience more quickly than an apparent lack of authority in a speaker — that feeling that they're trapped having to listen to someone who knows less (or seems to) about a subject than they do. Some advisors will say: "Never accept an offer to speak on a subject with which you're not entirely familiar." If you do, though, make sure you can quickly immerse yourself in the subject; then do not pretend to expertise — only to an educated interest — in that subject once you stand before the audience.

Making the Subject Specific. In selecting your subject, remember: you can't retell the history of the world in an hour, nor can you usefully discuss "the uses of the wheel" in even twice that time. Selecting too broad a subject (that is, failing to narrow it sufficiently, as we discussed in Chapter 15) is virtually to guarantee a superficial and unsatisfactory speech — a boring speech.

A warning is in order here: audiences who make general requests of their prospective speakers often have more specific expectations and will be disappointed if those unvoiced expectations are not satisified. I was once asked to address an audience of insurance people about "communications problems in the insurance industry." I (foolishly) prepared a general survey of such problems as I saw them, went before my audience . . . and laid the proverbial egg. When it was over, I asked a member of that audience why there was so much obvious dissatisfaction with my speech. "Because you didn't really talk about our major problem," he said. I asked what that was, and he said, "how to communicate well enough to overcome buyer resistance to more insurance." (I needn't tell you what murderous and uninsurable thought I briefly entertained.)

Assuring That Your Subject Has an Obvious Purpose. As someone once said, "a topic isn't really a topic until it has a point of view." There's a valuable lesson in that advice. For speakers even more than writers (remember, speakers are face to face with their audiences) the subject of a speech does not exist separately from the mind of the speaker who is speaking about it. (Writers can sometimes "hide" behind a pose of anonymous objectivity; but speakers, who have to look their audiences in the eye, simply cannot separate their subjects from themselves, and ought not to try.)

Essentially, your motive in presenting a subject will be either expository or reaction-evoking (the distinction around which most of this book has been built). A third purpose may be to entertain — but unless you're an acknowledged stand-up comic, this can be an empty motive (as far as your listeners are concerned) if it isn't attached to one of the other two.

Unless you've got some reason for masquerading it, you want to be sure your motive shows through in your speech. (If you want to conceal it — as might be the case for the speaker who really wishes to persuade but can only appear to be "giving the facts" — then you want your *ostensible* motive, instead of the real one, to show through clearly.) In a purely expository speech, the purpose you should show is your strong belief that the subject is worth examining, and that it's worth your audience's time to listen. That may mean showing them why. And unless it's potentially offensive to your audience, you should also make clear where you stand on your subject, even if you don't seek to win the audience to your point of view. When, on the other hand, you're seeking specific reactions with your speech — building good will, placating anger, relating bad news, persuading your audience to a new belief or a new course of action —you should use the appropriate strategy-patterns provided in Chapters 9 through 12.

Can You "Billboard" Your Speech? Apply the "billboard" test to see if the scope of your proposed speech is clearly in focus. Write a "billboard" for the speech that spells out its subject, its audience, its purpose, and your authority to speak on that subject — as these two "billboards" do:

Subject:	Methods of Harvesting Wheat in Kansas
Audience:	Students of economics at New York University
Purpose:	To explain to these students, most of whom are urban dwellers, how wheat, which is fundamental to our national diet, is harvested economically
Authority:	I'm a graduate student in agriculture at Kansas State University, and have worked summers as a harvest hand and supervisor.

Subject:	Direct Election of the President
Audience:	Members of the local Rotary Club
Purpose:	To show citizens how their influence in national affairs would be diminished by direct election of the President (rather than by the Electoral College)
Authority:	I have studied the question closely for over a year, and interviewed a number of federal officials and members of Congress.

If you can write this kind of billboard for your speech, chances are excellent that your subject and purpose have been well defined.

Assessing Your Audience

You also want to know as much as you can about the audience you'll be addressing, so that your speech — in both its preparation and its delivery — can be specifically adapted to them. If you're not familiar with the group, you might try to speak to a few of its members informally beforehand — especially the member who invited you to speak. You can also learn a lot from other speakers who have addressed the same audience, or otherwise dealt with them. If the group is publicly visible, information about them might also be available in the local press, or in publications the group itself puts out.

What, specifically, do you want to know about your audience? Here are the questions you should be asking:

What do they already know about the subject? Your speech should be designed to build upon your audience's pre-existing knowledge. In planning a speech on legalizing marijuana, for example, it would make a difference if the audience were college students, doctors, regular churchgoers, senior citizens or the local Toastmasters Club. The amount and the kind of knowledge they possess would likely differ for each group. That doesn't mean you'll take a different viewpoint; but it does mean you'll probably want to use a different starting point, and perhaps different examples, statistics, emphases, and the like.

What do they feel about the subject? Regardless of how much your audience knows about the subject, they may *feel* strongly about it from the outset. Again, you won't tailor your viewpoint to satisfy theirs; but you do want to plan your speech so that its viewpoint doesn't clash with theirs before they've had a chance to hear the information or the insights you're bringing them. If the group has taken a public stand on the subject — either for or against — you want to plan to acknowledge that stand early in your speech, and perhaps even use it as your starting point.

What, if anything, do they feel about you? Does your audience know you — personally or by reputation — and have some predictable bias for or against your presumed point of view? Or perhaps they're inclined toward, or against, the organization you represent (as minority groups sometimes distrust state government agencies, and conservationists often suspect large corporations). Unless you like confrontation, you probably want to plan your speech so as to soften, even overcome, this initial bias — or strengthen it if it's in your favor. At another level, you might engender some feelings toward you the moment you stand up to speak. There might, for example, be some initial doubts about your "expert's" view on physical fitness if you show up short of breath at five-foot-five and over two hundred pounds.

Is there a common occupation or activity among the members of your audience? If they consist mostly of aerospace engineers, or accounting students, or tennis players, you might be able to build your speech upon that common background — or at least be able to view your subject through their eyes.

What is their economic status? While this variable may not make a difference for some subjects, it certainly will for others. If you plan to speak on the necessity for federal tax reform, or on the wisdom (or folly) of a national health plan, the economic status of your listeners is almost guaranteed to present some biases you'll have to deal with.

What is their educational background? When you address younger audiences, the extent and the kind of education they've had — as well as their ages — can play an important part in shaping your speech. (With older people, education matters less because their experiences in life have had a chance to supersede it.) College students and young graduates can obviously be expected to be more worldly than high-school dropouts. Tenth-graders will usually know more than fifth-graders. But even amongst the "better educated," you'll want to know (if possible) *what* your audience has studied. Undergraduates in business administration, for example, tend to know more about management principles than do Ph.D. candidates in art or English (and conversely less about cultural affairs).

How large is the audience likely to be? The size of your audience should help you decide how formally or informally you wish to speak to them, how much interaction with your audience you should plan for, and what kinds of visual aids you can use.

Besides the audience itself, there is the *setting* in which your speech will be delivered. You must, as far as possible, know what it's going to be like. Be sure to ask —

What is the purpose of the meeting you're addressing? Is that audience going to be there solely to hear your speech, or is your speech part of a larger meeting? If it's a business occasion, is the occasion routine, or are there some special circumstances — even emergency circumstances — underlying it? Is there something being celebrated, or lamented, at the meeting? — an anniversary, holiday, or some other happy or sad event? Your speech ought to show that you're fully aware (even as an outsider) of the purpose behind the meeting. Your presence makes you a part of it.

Where is the meeting being held? Like the size of the audience, the nature of the site will affect the impact of your speech. Is it a small conference room, a medium-sized meeting hall, a large auditorium . . . perhaps a classroom? And is that speech site — or has it ever been — the site of some other notable activity? If it's in a gymnasium where the home team has just won the state championship, or in a meeting room where an important charter was signed a century ago, your speech might effectively be able to make note of it.

What are the speech-making facilities? At the practical level, you also want to know what facilities are available at the site. Is there a public address system? (And is the microphone mobile or fixed?) Is there a podium or lectern? A chalkboard or easel large enough for charts. What kind of seating is there likely to be? (Will the audience be at tables? in rows? — how wide? how deep?) How are the acoustics? Is the place air conditioned? (And is the air-conditioning noisy?) It isn't easy to learn all of this, but ideally you'd like to know.

How much time will you be allotted? Many an otherwise excellent speech-subject has been destroyed by trying to squeeze it into too brief a time slot. Never plan a speech before you've gotten some idea of how much time you'll be allowed — or how much time, practically speaking, your audience will want to listen to you. If, after you've prepared your speech, you're not sure how long it will take, devote at least one simulated run-through to timing it and adjusting it to fit the allotted time.

What is your scheduled place on the program? Whatever takes place at the meeting *prior* to your speech can affect the mood of the audience and the way it listens to you. Will there be routine business conducted, or problems debated, or matters settled? Maybe entertainment? Will there be other speakers speaking before you (either invading your subject, or making remarks that you can take note of and exploit in your own speech)?

And what about *after* your speech? Are there other speakers who can "have the last word"? Is there something scheduled (like the drawing of a prize, some prime announcement, or simply departure at the end of a long day) that will make the audience eager for you to be done? Will you have the opportunity (under favorable circumstances) to handle questions from the audience on your speech. If so, your planning may be a little different (and necessarily more thorough). Some speakers, when circumstances permit, even "plant" a question or two in the audience to assure they'll look good when they knowledgeably answer them.

PREPARATION

Once you've chosen your subject (or had it chosen for you by circumstance), defined your purpose, and assessed your audience, you're ready to *prepare* the speech you'll be delivering. This preparation consists of: finding your information (to the extent you don't already have it at hand); organizing that information (along with your interpretations and other remarks you plan to make) into the best sequence for presentation; "writing" the speech; and preparing whatever visual aids you plan to use.

The first two of these steps — research and organization — have already been thoroughly discussed (in the report-writing context) in Chapters 16 and 17. The principles and pitfalls we looked at in those chapters pertain, just as well, to preparing a speech. You might want to refer back to them. What differs is the way a speech is "written" — and, to some extent, the preparing of visual aids. So in this section we'll assume a grasp of research and organizational techniques, and turn straight to the "writing."

"Writing" a Speech

I've been putting the word "writing" into quotation marks because the majority of speeches are not, in the strict sense, written — that is to say, they are not written out word for word. More often, a speech is delivered from a prepared outline, or off the top of a speaker's head.

There are, in fact, four different ways in which speeches are prepared for delivery:

1. impromptu
2. from notes
3. by memory
4. from verbatim script

Let's look at each of them.

The Impromptu Speech. To talk about "preparing" an impromptu speech may seem a contradiction of terms. An impromptu speech is a spur-of-the-moment speech, given when you (as the speaker) didn't know you'd be called on to speak — or at least were presumed not to know. Upon being asked, you stand up and deliver — without benefit of notes — an intelligent set of remarks on the subject at hand. Your ability to do this impresses everyone, and pretty soon you find your reputation and your job responsibility on the rise.

But can an impromptu speech really be prepared? To a substantial extent, it can. First of all, you're not very likely to be asked to speak on a subject you know nothing about. People want to hear from you when they've got reason to believe you know more about a subject than they do — maybe even just a little more. And while they sometimes expect specific facts from you, more often they want to hear your opinion, your ideas, or your suggestions. You can always apologize for not having specific data at your fingertips. Just promise to supply it, and go on to say, "Based on what I've been able to learn, . . . "

Moreover, there are steps you can take to avoid the surprise, and the consequent unpreparedness, of being asked to make an impromptu speech:

Learn to anticipate when you might be called upon. Certain situations make it fairly likely that someone will ask you to speak. You're the only experienced computer programmer in your marketing class, and the class is scheduled to discuss the handling of market research data. Or you're the mother of two high-school students who has returned to college to resume your degree work, and tomorrow night your local P.T.A. will be discussing how parents can keep up educationally with their kids. Your political action group on campus is examining America's dependence on imported oil, and the group's chairperson knows you've traveled extensively in the Middle East. In any of these situations, it would be folly *not* to assume you'd be called on. You must be alert to them.

Stay current on recent developments. Don't get lazy and let developments — in your area of specialization or the world at large — slip by without your knowing about them. Read the newspaper every day, and at least one weekly newsmagazine. And be sure to read — preferably subscribe to — the professional journals that keep abreast of current happenings in your field of interest.

Keep a ready supply of anecdotes, witty remarks, and "impressive" facts in mind. Realize that, in business, it won't be long before someone asks you to make an impromptu speech

— perhaps just a brief one. Knowing this, you have an extra incentive to search out, and commit to memory, those relevant tidbits that can be used to begin or enliven your impromptu remarks.

Speaking from Notes. Sometimes called the "extemporaneous" speech, this is the kind of speech most often given by businesspeople, public officials, advocates for various causes, educators and other professionals. It's delivered from *notes:* sometimes a fairly thorough outline, sometimes just a list of items the speaker wants to be sure to mention in a certain order. During the speech, the notes are glanced at when necessary. But for the most part the speaker speaks directly to the audience, creating the language of the speech "off the cuff."

"Writing" an extemporaneous speech means:

(a) gathering all your material (facts, statistics, interpretations, anecdotes, etc.) together in raw form;

(b) arranging it into the sequence best designed to satisfy the purpose of your speech;

(c) being sure you know the material (or at least most of it) "by heart"; and then

(d) putting on paper only as much of an outline, or as many notations, as necessary to keep you "on track" as you make the speech.

Some speakers put their notes on a series of 3" x 5" or 4" x 6" note cards. Personally, I prefer one or two larger sheets of paper so that I have in front of me not only my specific notes but, at a glance, an overview of my entire speech. (You'll see an example, in Part A of Figure 61, of a speech-outline used as notes in a recent address to a regional P.T.A. meeting. In Part B you'll see a more informal list of points-to-be-made that could have been used as "notes" — provided the speaker had completely mastered the information beforehand.)

There are several dangers in speaking from notes alone. Inexperienced speakers may suddenly "freeze" and forget what they wanted to say at a certain point. And if the material hasn't been thoroughly mastered, a speech from notes can consist of a lot of hemming, hawing, "and-uhing," and awkward silences.

Generally speaking, though, most speakers feel the advantages of the extemporaneous speech outweigh the potential problems. Better "eye contact" is possible with the audience. The language of the speech will sound more conversational, and can be adjusted on the spot to fit the particular audience. Additions or deletions can be comfortably made in the speech — and relevant tangents taken — if need arises. And the speaker speaking from notes simply seems more confident, and often more sincere, than the speaker who is obviously reading a speech.

Speaking from Memory or from a Script. The main alternative to preparing notes and speaking from them "extemporaneously" is to write out your speech, in its entirety, word for word. This gives you a script to work from. It also gives you two alternatives for delivery. You can either memorize the speech and deliver it "by heart," or bring the script with you and read it to your audience. Let's consider both those possibilities.

Figure 61A
An outline used as notes for a speech to persuade the audience that schools should be made to "guarantee" their instruction.

I. Introduction (inc. comment re: PTA's concern for ''accountability'')

   A. Would you buy a new Plymouth (or Datsun, or Chrysler) if you knew that half of them were breaking down within a year?

   B. Would you buy an educational system that had an even poorer performance record than this?

   C. Schools should be made to <u>guarantee</u> their ''product.''

II. The Argument

   A. Why we need guaranteed learning
      1. 1/2 of students who start college don't become sophomores
      2. many graduate from h.s. with 4th or 5th grade reading ability
      3. we spend (in this state) more than $1400/yr. per student, with no assurance of what results we'll be getting

   B. How guaranteed learning works
      1. parents, teachers, administrators, community-at-large set broadly defined learning goals
      2. teacher (with approval of admin.) establishes specific (i.e. measurable) objectives
         a. what, specifically, the student must learn
         b. what ''tests'' must show at end of learning period
      3. Teacher designs the instruction to meet these specific objectives
      4. Teacher measures effectiveness of that instruction, and redesigns for ever greater efficiency.

   C. Can it work?
      1. Results in Des Moines: K–6, over 500 students
      2. Results in Newark, N.J. Grades 4–8, 1200 students
      3. Results in San Diego County District pilot program, 5000 students
      4. Over 100 other successful projects across the country
      5. No reported failures

   (See separate data sheets)

III. Conclusion

A. Guaranteed learning is a must
   1. it's systematic, it's verifiable, it works
   2. detailed proposals must be made to school boards

B. If you don't like the cantaloupe, you take it back to the market. If the plumber doesn't fix your toilet, you don't pay him. Can we say the same about our educational system?

Figure 61B
Informal "notes" for the same speech.

What if half the new cars broke down?
Public education performs even more poorly!

Guaranteed learning a "must"
Cite failures: ½ don't make soph; h.s grads can't read;
#14K/yr @ no guarantee.

Who sets the broad goals
Teacher sets narrow goals, and determines testing —
then designs instruction to meet
then re-designs for greater effic.

see data sheets

Results: Des Moines, Newark, San Diego Co., 100+ elsewhere
No failures!

We need guar-learning — need to propose to school boards
Cantaloupes?... Plumbers?... Educ. system???

Most teachers of "speech" are quick to discourage formal speaking from memory — for several reasons. Memorized speeches tend to sound like . . . memorized speeches. Sincerity and spontaneity — two important qualities of an effective speech — are usually lacking. Moreover, the consequences of sudden "stage fright" can be even more disastrous than in an extemporaneous speech being given from notes. One "memory block" and the show is over — to your lasting embarrassment.

However, if your memory is good, *and* the speech is not too long, *and* you have dramatic training or a flair for the stage — the memorized speech can serve you well. Especially if you have plenty of time to rehearse it, and can bring a prepared script with you, just in case.

If you do choose to write your speech word for word and deliver it verbatim (either from memory or from a script), be sure to build into it those qualities of language that distinguish speaking from written prose. (In spite of what you may have heard, most people do *not* speak the way they write.) Consider which of these two passages "sounds" more like spoken language:

> An imaginative but honest painting of a contemporary consumer would likely depict a perplexed figure standing before a backdrop of accounting forms, gross national product data, and computer printouts, holding a comparatively small pay envelope in one hand and a larger price tag in the other. Toward the edge of the frame, standing in even deeper perplexity, would be another figure, an economist. Were such a picture to be painted, I should make every attempt to procure it for display amongst my other examples of artistic realism.

> If someone were to let his imagination go, and paint a picture of the contemporary consumer, that consumer would probably be shown in front of a background of accounting forms, economic tables and graphs and charts, and computer printouts. That consumer in the painting would probably have a little pay envelope in one hand, and a big price tag in the other hand. Off to the side (maybe hiding behind a rock) there'd be this little economist, even more confused looking, and wiping the sweat from his brow. If someone painted this picture tomorrow, I'd buy it (if I could afford it) and hang it on the wall at home--the wall I've reserved for examples of artistic realism.

There's no question, I think, that the second of these passages sounds more like ordinary, spontaneous speech than the first — though it is just as carefully written. The second contains more of the characteristics of spoken language. Its diction is more informal (even to the use of contractions). It has a greater number of sentences, and a shorter average sentence length. It uses the conjunction *and* more frequently. Its style is less "nominal," more "verbal," with fewer noun phrases and less adjectival pile-up (remember our discussions of these qualities back on pages 47–50). There is also a greater use of interruptive structures (especially the parenthetical asides), structures which, as we saw on pages 81–82, are more common to speech than to writing. All in all, the second passage has been carefully tailored to "sound" more like spoken English — and will, as a result, make a better verbatim speech, whether it's memorized *or* read.

There's one other thing you can do to achieve a greater feeling of spontaneity, and make better eye-contact with your audience — if you plan to read your speech rather than memorize it. You can lay out the language of your speech on the page so that it reflects your patterns of phrasing and is easier to read at a glance. (The less time you spend with your eye on the script, the more you can spend looking at your audience.)

Instead of making a script that looks like regular prose on a page (with every line stretching from left-hand margin to right-hand margin), you can make it look something like this:

```
If someone
     were to let his imagination go,
and paint a picture
     of the contemporary consumer,
that consumer would probably be shown
     in front of a background of
            accounting forms,
            economic tables,
            graphs, and charts,
            and computer printouts.

That consumer in the painting
     would probably have
            a little pay-envelope in one hand,
     and,   a big price-tag in the other hand.

Off to the side
     (maybe hiding behind a rock)
     would be this little economist
            (looking even more confused)
            wiping the sweat from his brow.

If someone painted this picture tomorrow,
     I'd buy it
            (if I could afford it)
            and hang it up on the wall at home . . .
                 the wall I've reserved for examples
                      of artistic realism!
```

There's no magic to the way these lines are divided. I've simply broken them up so that each phrase or clause (each unit of thought and intonation) is a separate unit that I can spot at a glance. With the speech laid out this way, and with the words that I want to stress underlined, I'll probably need to spend less than 30% of the time with my eyes on the script. (Try it. You'll see what I mean.) With the ordinary prose layout, I'd probably spend 75% or more of my speechtime with my eyes glued to the script — and make some inflectional errors besides. Why make the job more difficult by using a format intended to save space on the page, when what I need is an instant guide to effective reading aloud?

Preparing the Opening and the Closing

As we saw in our discussions of reaction-evoking letters and memos (especially in Chapters 7 through 12), skillful writers very carefully construct the opening and the closing of any message. What is said first, and last, leaves strong impressions upon readers — and (when one is speaking) upon listeners as well. Experienced speech-makers — even if they plan to speak only from notes —

carefully plan and rehearse their openings and closings to leave strong impressions at beginning and end.

You can open strongly by stating an unusual (but relevant) fact, by telling an interesting (and relevant) anecdote, or by asking a thought-provoking (and relevant) question. (Need I advise any more persistently that your opening, whatever it is, be relevant to the subject on which you're speaking?) Or you might open by quoting some impressive source, by referring to some historic event related to your subject, or even by telling a joke (as long as it's not potentially offensive). One other good way to open is to focus upon the audience and either refer to the purpose of the meeting, point to some belief or opinion you share with them, compliment them on some action they've taken, or describe the importance of your subject to them (as long as it's not self-evident).

Be sure, in opening your speech, *not* to apologize for anything (like your raspy voice, or your failure to prepare as thoroughly as you might have). Don't open by saying, "Today I'm going to talk to you about . . ." (it's boring); or by saying anything your audience is likely to resist. (If you want to challenge them, you can do it later on, after you've got them listening.) And be sure your opening is not long-winded (you want to get to the heart of your speech fairly quickly).

In closing your speech, you may want briefly to summarize, or even repeat, your main points. You can also, as a closing strategy, return to the theme of your opening; you can look to the future; or you can (if it's appropriate) issue a call for action.

However you close, be sure not to end abruptly (without an obvious conclusion). Don't introduce any new points and leave your audience "hanging." Don't let your closing drag on. And don't apologize for any inadequacies of your speech. These problems are marks of the amateur, of the inexperienced public speaker. They are not impressions you want to leave with your audience.

Preparing Visual Aids

Visual aids of one sort or another — charts, graphs, pictures, models, diagrams, maps, and the like — are used by speakers for two reasons: either to *clarify* information for an audience, or to *strengthen the impressions* being made by the information.

Most *statistical* information requires a graph or a table for its significance to be fully clear. Without a chart or a table, by the time you've gotten to a third or fourth number (or percentage figure), the audience will already be forgetting the first one and losing track of whatever trend you're attempting to demonstrate. Numerical values are hard for most people to hold accurately in mind for very long.

Spatial information (that is, movement through space, like the pattern of movement of the burglars who made away with the diamonds, or the three-pronged attack by the army on a strategic town) also requires visualization to be totally clear. It should be presented with the aid of a diagram or a map.

Even when your facts are easily grasped without a visual aid, a well planned chart or picture — or series of them — can help to strengthen the impressions those facts make upon your audience. Psychologists long have known that messages received by more than one of the senses — in this case, both by ear and by eye — are more thoroughly remembered than those received by one sense alone.

As a general rule, the only kinds of visual aid you should *not* consider using are those that might (by their content or their number) *distract* the audience's attention from the speech itself, or those that might insult them because they're so elementary. (If I announce that my subject is nutrition, then write the word "nutrition" on the blackboard, I'm probably insulting a good part of the audience.)

You must also make sure that the visual aids you prepare — or plan to draw as the speech goes along — are large enough to be seen at the back and the extreme sides of your audience. The chart that looks large to you in your study or living room can look awfully puny from the 14th row in an auditorium.

(Remember, there is further discussion on visual aids and illustration back on pages 443–445.)

PRESENTATION

The moment arrives. Your speech is about to begin. Hopefully, you're as prepared as you can be. Even if you're an experienced speechmaker, you're at least a little nervous. (The less experienced, the more nervous you probably are.)

Once the speech begins, there are relatively few things you can concentrate on: the unfolding information in your speech, your audience's reactions to it, and perhaps the visuals you have them looking at. Yet there are many things you must do to make the speech as effective as it can be. So you want to be sure to consider each of the following points closely *before* each speech — then consider them closely again in self-evaluating each speech *after* you've given it.

Delivering a Speech

1. *Approach the moment of your speech with confidence and authority.* You're prepared, and you know your subject. Be sure that your demeanor exudes it! Look confident as you await your turn to speak, and as you approach the rostrum when the moment arrives. People will be watching you in those minutes before your speech (as well as during it). What they see should impress them.

2. *Get set before you begin.* Whether you're speaking from behind a rostrum, or more informally in front of your audience, be sure that you're comfortably into position, with your notes and your visuals in place, before you start to speak. If you begin, and then have to straighten a microphone, take a drink of water, or arrange your notes — your opening remarks will be lost in the resulting distraction.

3. *Begin without looking at your notes.* Memorize your opening remark. The audience will understand why you must glance at your notes during the course of the speech; but they're likely to doubt your sincerity, or your preparedness, if you have to consult your notes in order to begin.

4. *Establish eye contact and maintain it throughout the speech.* Whether you're speaking from notes, from memory, or from a script, spend as much of your speech time as possible in direct eye contact with your audience. Catch the eye of one, then another, then yet another member of your audience. Move your attention around from side to side, from front to back, from the middle to the extreme corners of your audience — not in any set pattern, but randomly. Make your remarks directly to people, not just to an audience *en masse.*

5. *Avoid sloppy language habits.* If you're speaking extemporaneously from notes, or from memory, avoid those *and-uhs* and *you-knows* that so often fill the spaces in talk that we hear. Listen to tape recordings of yourself; note the sloppy habits you have (if

you have them); and commit yourself to not making any sounds that aren't a part of your well-considered flow of language.

6. *Avoid careless posture.* You can rest your hands on the rostrum if you wish (you have to put them somewhere), but don't give your audience the impression that you're "holding on for dear life." Don't lean, slouch, cross your legs, or in any other way allow your "body language" to suggest a sloppy approach to your subject or your audience.

7. *Use gestures and facial expressions effectively.* Using your hands freely and naturally (like the figures below) will aid your delivery in several ways. It will help to relax you. Your obvious relaxation will help to relax your audience. And you'll be able more effectively to emphasize your main words as you speak them. Naturalness is the key. Don't wave your arms about wildly; but don't lock them at your sides either, or glue them to the rostrum or into your pockets. And as your hands gesture freely, let your facial expressions also reflect your feelings about the things you're saying. The lively personality is simply more enjoyable to listen to than the rigid Stoneface. And the hands and face are largely what convey liveliness.

8. *Avoid distracting habits with your hands.* If your hands are at work supplementing your words, they won't have time for those distracting habits we often see in speakers — repeatedly brushing the hair from their eyes, playing with a pencil, scratching their elbows, stroking their beards, and the like. These gestures, unrelated to the content of the speech, inevitably distract listeners from that content.

9. *Dress with respect for your audience.* In the previous chapter we discussed business dress. The need to look impressive is, if anything, even greater when you're standing before an audience who await your authoritative remarks on your subject. You ought to *look* authoritative too. And look as though you have respect for the audience who, after all, have invited you, and are devoting their time to listening to you.

10. *Speak up!* Obviously your speech won't move the audience if it's mumbled at them. But more than this, you have to realize that the larger the audience, and the larger the room, the more energy it requires for your voice to be heard clearly at the rear. You must also be sure to vary the pitch and volume of your voice — don't drone. Even while your eyes are making contact with people up front, your voice should be reaching the person furthest away. And if you're speaking into a microphone, be sure your mouth is precisely that optimum distance away for it to amplify most clearly.

11. *Move around, if it's feasible.* If you're not glued to a microphone, or to your notes on the lectern, and if your speech is informal, you might even move away from your starting point and station yourself for several moments at various points in the front of the room. (Some speakers even work the aisles.) As long as your mobility is relaxed, that freedom of movement will also help to relax your audience.

12. *Convey enthusiasm.* Even if your subject is serious, you want to exude a sense of enjoyment at the opportunity to speak about it — *and* pleasure that those particular people out there are the ones who are listening to you. Make your subject seem special to you; make your audience seem special to you.

13. *If you goof, stay cool.* Even the most experienced speakers will fumble a word or phrase here or there. But when they catch themselves in a goof, they make light of it — often even ignore it. They do *not* go back and emphasize the error by re-enunciating it (unless clarity requires it), and they *don't* get flustered and speed-up the speech as though escaping from the scene of the blunder. They stay cool, knowing that coolness is not only most impressive, but also the best way to avoid other blunders.

14. *Don't begin "packing" until you're done.* Even though you know you're approaching the end, don't start gathering your notes together until you've finished and the audience *knows* you're finished. If you do, your audience will also, psychologically, start looking for the exits — and your well-developed conclusion will fizzle out.

15. *When you're finished, move off confidently.* Even if you feel the speech didn't go well (and who doesn't sometimes feel that things could have gone better?), leave the rostrum confidently — just as you approached it, taking pride in what you have offered your audience. If your departure reflects disappointment or frustration, you virtually assure that your audience will be disappointed too. They'll take their cue from you. Your confidence will, to a certain extent, increase their confidence that they've heard a speech worth hearing.

CONCLUSION

In a nutshell, then, the process of making an effective speech is three-phased. There are *preliminaries* that must be carefully attended to: you must determine (unless the situation determines it for you) an appropriate subject and purpose, and then assess the audience you'll be addressing. After the preliminaries, there is the necessary *preparation* — a lot of it. You've got to decide what form of speech you want to give (whether impromptu, from notes, from memory, or from full script), and "write" the speech accordingly. You must also prepare the opening and closing of your speech for maximum effect; and prepare your visual aids as well. Finally, after the preliminaries and the preparation, there is the *presentation* itself — and the number of things you must be sure to do (and to avoid) in delivering your speech to the audience.

This chapter, the last of the book, has tried to provide a ready reference to each of those three phases. Let it conclude by wishing you the best of luck in your next hundred business speeches. (After that, you won't need any.)

PROBLEMS

1. It will be an impromptu speech, but you know it's coming. Your instructor, who wishes to examine techniques of effective speaking, is going to ask you (as surely as you're sitting there) to deliver a brief "unprepared" speech — probably no more than three minutes long — introducing yourself to the class, and giving them some salient facts about yourself. Prepare yourself.

2. Write out completely a five-minute speech on any topic you wish. (Make it a topic you know well.) Then prepare a topic/subtopic outline of the same speech.

Get yourself an audience (either your class, if classroom time can be spared, or a smaller group of classmates outside of class), and deliver the speech twice to that audience — once using the complete script you've written, and once using only the outline.

Then get your audience's candid evaluation of both forms of your speech: their opinions on the strengths and weaknesses of each method of presentation.

3. Prepare to deliver to the class a short, formal presentation (of whatever length your instructor directs) on one of the topics listed in problem 11 on page 388.

4. For delivery to your business communications class, prepare a ten-minute speech on some business subject of your own choosing, solely for the purpose of informing your audience.

5. For delivery to your business communications class, prepare a ten-minute speech on some business subject, a speech whose purpose is to persuade your audience to adopt your point of view. (Be prepared, at its conclusion, to see how well you've met your persuasive objective.)

6. Without making specific reference to the discussions in Chapter 20:

(a) prepare a list (with very specific descriptions) of the traits you most appreciate in speakers and lecturers you have to listen to. The list ought to describe at least a half-dozen traits, more if you wish. Be prepared to discuss these preferred traits with your fellow students, whose lists may of course be quite different from your own.

(b) prepare a similar list of the half-dozen traits that most displease you in a speaker.

7. Attend a formal speech or lecture, and go prepared not only to learn from the speech, but to *evaluate the speaker's delivery*. Using the third part of

Chapter 20 as a guide, take notes on how well the speaker presents the speech. Then, in a detailed memo to your instructor, write a critique of the speaker's delivery — assessing both its strengths and its weaknesses.

8. On a given day during one of your other classes (one in which the instructor depends on lectures) assume the role of "analytic listener," and take notes on the various characteristics you want to learn to listen for — that is, overall purpose as well as details, any biases, and the pitfalls you either do or don't manage to avoid when listening to a lecture.

Compile your notes into a brief memo-report and submit it to your instructor.

9. Here's what one teacher has to say about "memorized" speeches:

> The disadvantages of the memorized speech are greater by far than its advantages. A memorized speech is very difficult to deliver with a feeling of sincerity and spontaneity--two characteristics you always want in a speech. In addition, speakers-from-memory always run the risk of memory block, of forgetting what they have memorized and making fools of themselves as a result. My advice on the memorized speech is simple: don't do it.

In a memo to your instructor, prepare a response to this advice based upon your own experiences and observations.

10. As you've seen in Chapter 20, speeches, at their best, employ a slightly different language than good writing does. They must register effectively upon the ear, not the eye. So no matter how good a piece of business prose is, it would require at least some (maybe not much, but some) modification if you wished to turn it into an effective speech.

Take the article by John Getze (on pages 423–426 of this text) entitled "How to Make Your Nestegg Grow in the Bond Market," and convert it into a speech that you could present before the monthly meeting of a local community-service club.

As your instructor directs, prepare the speech either:

(a) into notes for extemporaneous delivery
(b) into a speech-script to be read verbatim to the club
(c) into a speech-script that you can memorize and deliver without benefit of notes.

11. Think carefully about — and come to class prepared to discuss — how you would handle a heckler whose snide comments were interrupting your speech.

APPENDIX A

DICTATION

To save time, the business person learns to *dictate* communications. By dictating, he or she hands over the most time-consuming part of communication, the mechanical acts of writing and typing, to someone else. Besides saving time, dictation also frequently results in a more effective style; the communication tends to be more conversational, without the stodgy overformality that creeps into so much business writing.

Like most valuable shortcuts, dictation isn't as easy as it might seem. The person who can sit in front of a stenographer or a dictation machine and dictate a fluent, well-organized communication has had to work long and hard to develop the skill. One's first attempts at dictation are usually marred by an apparent paralysis of the vocal cords. The presence of a stenographer with pencil poised, or a machine with a live microphone, can be intimidating. Even after the initial "stage fright" is overcome, dictated communications still tend to ramble, lacking conciseness, unity, or any other semblance of effective style. A good deal of practice is necessary. Also necessary is a firm grasp of the principles of effective communication, the principles to which this book has been devoted. In time, after many frustrating attempts, the dictating skill takes shape. From then on, the skill reaps dividends.

The ability to dictate is becoming increasingly imperative in business and industry. Many companies insist that their employees dictate their communications; work loads are just too heavy to allow for pencil and paper. And the requirement that you dictate in no way lessens the expectation that *your* communications will be fluent, well organized, and effective.

Effective dictation is a process of three phases: preparation, actual dictation, and post-dictational responsibility.

Preparation

You cannot dictate effectively unless you do some planning.

1. Be sure that you've clearly defined the purpose of the communication to be dictated. If it's a letter or a memo, determine precisely what reactions you want from its recipient, and keep those desired reactions uppermost in your mind.

2. With your purpose clearly in mind, determine the order in which your facts and ideas should be presented. You may even want to jot down a brief outline to help you in

dictating longer letters and memos. When evoking reactions, remember the strategy patterns provided in Chapters 8-12. When dictating a report, you will surely want an outline to guide you.

3. If your communication is in answer to one you've received, reread the communication you are answering. If you're dictating a report or a memo at the written request of someone, reread that request. If the request was oral, recall its details as clearly as you can.

4. Visualize your intended reader. A communication is always more effective when written with its specific audience in mind.

5. If, as you go through these steps, a key phrase — the right way of saying something — pops into mind, don't trust yourself to remember it when you need it. Jot it down right away.

Dictation Itself

Only after these preparatory steps are you ready to dictate effectively. Effective dictation is pretty much the result of good habits. So —

1. Relax. Your prose will sound unnatural unless you feel natural dictating it.

2. Speak in your natural voice at a fairly constant speed, a little slower than your normal rate. (Average speech is about 120 words per minute; slow down to about 90 for dictation.)

3. Enunciate clearly, even to the point of sounding artificial when you have to distinguish between words that sound very much alike — such as *affect* (say *aah-fect*) and *effect* (say *ee-fect*).

4. Spell out anything that might confuse the person doing the transcribing — the names of persons, companies, and places, for instance, and words that sound the same as other words, such as *cite, coarse,* and *through.*

5. Dictate all but the most obvious punctuation marks. At the end of a sentence, say *period* (or *question mark* or *exclamation point*). At the end of a paragraph, say *new paragraph.* Wherever you want a semicolon, a dash, or quotation marks, say so. (But do trust the stenographer to insert the most obvious punctuation marks, such as commas in a series or between city and state. You don't want to insult the stenographer's intelligence.)

6. When you catch yourself making a mistake, stop to correct it immediately. If you don't, you'll probably forget it until you see it in type, then you'll have to waste time revising it.

7. Be sure to dictate any instructions regarding attachments, enclosures, and carbon copies, and any special instructions about format that aren't obvious to the stenographer.

8. Do not hesitate to stop for a readback (or a playback if you're using a machine) at any time during dictation if you think you could have said something more effectively, or if you want to hear the "flow" of what you've already dictated.

A short letter might sound like this when dictated by an executive into a dictating machine for a secretary:

```
Jean type the following letter please with two copies  the
extra copy going to Paul Martin our eastern regional
consultant The letter goes to Mister Anthony Rowan that's
```

r-o-w-A-n 501 Fifth Avenue New York New York 10026 Dear Mister Rowan It is with great pleasure that we add your name to the list of patrons whose contributions correction Jean make that generous patrons whose contributions have kept alive the work of our foundation period new paragraph At eight thirty on the evening of October 4 no correct that it's October 5 our executive staff will be meeting at the Centurion Plaza that's capital C-e-n-t-u-r-i-o-n capital P plaza in New York period I would be pleased no strike pleased Jean I would be delighted to have you attend as my guest so that we may discuss comma among other things comma our plans for the park site s-i-t-e in Texas period A late supper will be served colon pheasant under glass I believe period new paragraph Again let me express our thanks for your thoughtful support comma and our hope of seeing you in New York period Very truly yours Jean please get this out as soon as possible I should have gotten to it last week thanks that's all

After Dictation

It's the secretary's job to transcribe your dictated communication into final form; but it's *your* responsibility to see that the secretary does it well. The communication goes out over your signature, not the secretary's. The impression it makes on its reader will be attributed to you. The faith you have in your secretary's ability will, of course, determine how closely you check a final draft; but you should always make the following checks:

1. Read the transcribed draft carefully.

2. Insist on accuracy, neatness, and mechanical excellence. Do not hesitate to have an unacceptable draft retyped, whether the mistakes are the transcriber's or your own. Set your standards high; any good secretary will respect you for them.

3. When an acceptable final draft is ready, sign it. Your signature signifies your responsibility for the document.

The letter dictated to Anthony Rowan in New York should look like this in final draft:

September 2, 19--

Mr. Anthony Rowan
501 Fifth Avenue
New York, New York 10026

Dear Mr. Rowan:

It is with great pleasure that we add your name to the list of generous patrons whose contributions have kept alive the work of our foundation.

At 8:30 on the evening of October 5, our executive staff will be meeting at the Centurion Plaza in New York. I would be delighted to have you attend as my guest so that we may discuss, among other things, our plans for the park site in Texas. A late supper will be served: pheasant under glass, I believe.

Again let me express our thanks for your thoughtful support, and our hope of seeing you in New York.

Very truly yours,

Foster Carmichael
Assistant Director

FC:jw
copy Paul Martin

Some Don'ts about Dictating

Dictation is a process involving two individuals. When you dictate, have consideration for that other person. *Don't* waste time with your own poor planning. *Don't* assume that the other person can read your mind or will understand all the technicalities about which you may be dictating. And *don't* neglect to praise your secretary for work well done.

Dictation is a process of economy, employing the talents of two specialists working as a team. All the rules of effective team effort must be in force if the team is to be successful.

PROBLEM

1. Obtain a dictaphone recorder. Turn to page 163 in Chapter 7 of this book, and carefully read problem #3 on that page. Keeping in mind all you've learned about the writing of routine letters, dictate your improved reply to Doris Caswell onto the tape. Have someone else (if possible) transcribe your dictated letter into finished form, ready for your signature.

APPENDIX B

RECOMMENDED FORMS OF ADDRESS AND SALUTATION IN FORMAL BUSINESS LETTERS

The following list shows the proper form of address and salutation for specific addressees. When the addressee is a woman, substitute one of the following for the salutation shown:

> "Madam" for "Mr." before formal terms such as "President," "Vice-President," "Chairman," "Secretary," "Ambassador," and "Minister."
>
> "Ms.," "Miss," or "Mrs." for "Mr." before the name of a member of the House of Representatives, a senator-elect, a representative-elect, or a lesser official.

Addressee	*Address on Letter and Envelope*	*Salutation*
The President	The President The White House Washington, DC 20500	Dear Mr. President
Wife of the President	Mrs. (full name) The White House Washington, DC 20500	Dear Mrs. (surname):
Assistant to the President	Honorable (full name) Assistant to the President The White House Washington, DC 20500	Dear Mr. (or Ms.) (surname):
The Vice-President	The Vice-President United States Senate Washington, DC 20510	Dear Mr. Vice-President:
The Chief Justice	The Chief Justice of the United States The Supreme Court of the United States Washington, DC 20543	Dear Mr. Chief Justice

Forms Of Address And Salutation In Formal Business Letters

Addressee	*Address on Letter and Envelope*	*Salutation*
Associate Justice	Mr. Justice (surname) The Supreme Court of the United States Washington, DC 20543	Dear Mr. Justice:
United States Senator	Honorable (full name) United States Senate Washington, DC 20510	Dear Senator (surname):
	or	
	Honorable (full name) United States Senator (local address) 00000	
United States Representative (Member of Congress)	Honorable (full name) House of Representatives Washington, DC 20515	Dear Mr. (or Ms.) (surname):
Cabinet Members	Honorable (full name) Secretary of (name of department) Washington, DC 00000	Dear Mr. (or Madame) Secretary:
	or	
Deputy Secretaries, Assistants, or Under Secretaries	Honorable (full name) Deputy Secretary of (name of department) Washington, D.C 00000	Dear Mr. (or Ms.) (surname):
	or	
	Honorable (full name) Assistant Secretary of (name of department) Washington, DC 00000	
	or	
	Honorable (full name) Under Secretary of (name of department) Washington, DC 00000	

Addressee	*Address on Letter and Envelope*	*Salutation*
Head of Independent Offices and Agencies	Honorable (full name) Comptroller General of the United States General Accounting Office Washington, DC 20548	Dear Mr. (or Ms.) (surname):
	or	
	Honorable (full name) Chairman, (name of commission) Washington, DC 00000	Dear Mr. (or Madame) Chairman:
	or	
	Honorable (full name) Director, Bureau of the Budget Washington, DC 20503	Dear Mr. (or Ms.) (surname):
American Ambassador	Honorable (full name) American Ambassador (City), (Country)	Sir: (formal) Dear Mr. (or Madame) Ambassador: (informal)
American Consul General or American Consul	(Full Name) American Consul General (or American Consul) (City, Country)	Dear Mr. (or Ms.) (surname):
Foreign Ambassador in the United States	His Excellency (full name) Ambassador of (country) (local address) 00000	Excellency: (formal): Dear Mr. (or Madame) Ambassador: (informal)
Governor of State	Honorable (full name) Governor of (name of state) (City), (State) 00000	Dear Governor (surname):
Lieutenant Governor	Honorable (full name) Lieutenant Governor of (name of state) (City), (State) 00000	Dear Mr. (or Ms.) (surname):
State Senator	Honorable (full name) (name of state) Senate (City), (State) 00000	Dear Mr. (or Ms.) (surname)

Addressee	*Address on Letter and Envelope*	*Salutation*
State Representative, Assemblyman, or Delegate	Honorable (full name) (name of state) House of Representatives (or Assembly or House of Delegates) (City), (State) 00000	Dear Mr. (or Ms.) (surname):
Mayor	Honorable (full name) Mayor of (name of city) (City), (State) 00000	Dear Mr. (or Ms.) (surname)
Protestant Clergy	The Right Reverend (full name) Bishop of (name) (local address) 00000	Right Reverend Sir: (formal) Dear Bishop (surname): (informal)
	or	
	The Very Reverend (full name) Dean of (name of church) (local address) 00000	Very Reverend Sir: (formal) Dear Dean (surname): (informal)
	or	
	The Reverend (full name) (Title), (name of church) (local address) 00000	Dear Reverend (surname): Dear Mr. (surname):
Catholic Clergy	His Eminence (given name) Cardinal (surname) Archbishop of (diocese) (local address) 00000	Your Eminence: (formal) Dear Cardinal (surname): (informal)
	or	
	The Most Reverend (full name) Bishop of (city) (local address) 00000	Your Excellency: (formal) Dear Bishop (surname): (informal)
	or	
	The Right Reverend Monsignor (full name) (local address) 00000	Right Reverend Monsignor: (formal) Dear Monsignor (surname): (informal)

Addressee	*Address on Letter and Envelope*	*Salutation*
	or	
	The Very Reverend Monsignor (full name) (local address) 00000	Very Reverend Monsignor: (formal) Dear Monsignor (surname): (informal)
	or	
	The Reverend (full name) (add initials of order, if any) (local address) 00000	Reverend Sir: (formal) Dear Father (surname): (informal)
	or	
	Mother (name) (Initials of order, if used) Superior (name of convent) (local address) 00000	Dear Mother (name):
Jewish Clergy	Rabbi (full name) (local address) 00000	Dear Rabbi (surname):
Chaplain	Chaplain (full name) (rank, service designation) (post office address of organization and station) (local address) 00000	Dear Chaplain (surname):
President of a College or University (Doctor)	Dr. (full name) President (name of institution) (local address) 00000	Dear Dr. (surname):
Dean of a School	Dr. (full name), Dean School of (name) (name of institution) (local address) 00000	Dear Dean (surname): or Dear Dr. (surname):
Professor	Professor (full name) Department of (name) (name of institution) (local address) 00000	Dear Professor (surname):

Addressee	Address on Letter and Envelope	Salutation
Physician	(full name), M.D. (local address) 00000	Dear Dr. (surname):
Lawyer	Mr. (full name) Attorney at Law (local address) 00000	Dear Mr. (or Ms.) (surname):
Widow	Mrs. (husband's first name, last name) (local address) 00000	Dear Mrs. (surname):
	or	
	Mrs. (wife's first name, last name)* (local address) 00000	Dear Mrs. (surname):
	or	
	Ms. (wife's first name, last name) (local address) 00000	Dear Ms. (surname):
Service Personnel	(full grade, name, and abbreviation of service designation) (Retired is added if applicable) (title and organization) (local address) 00000	Dear (grade) surname:

*This form is also used for a woman who is separated or divorced from her husband or for a married woman who has so signed.

APPENDIX C

A FEW WORDS ABOUT INTERNATIONAL BUSINESS COMMUNICATIONS

International business messages pose some special problems for business writers — primarily problems of empathy. People raised in different cultures have different values. No matter how universal the business impulse may be, people in other cultures react differently to business language and behavior. You must be prepared to bridge that culture gap. To a French businessman, for example, money is usually second in importance to power and prestige. "Profitability," says Alonzo MacDonald, Paris chief of McKinsey & Company, "simply isn't the driving force *here* that it is in the U.S." In dealing with the French, you ought to be aware of this.

Naturally the best way to correspond with a foreign customer is to use his or her language, if you can. Write Dutch to a Dutchman, Arabic to a Saudi, Spanish to a Spaniard, Mexican or Peruvian businessman, and British English (as opposed to American English) to a Briton. (Notice, for instance, the spelling of *programme* in the letter written *by* an American to Canadian readers on page 306.)

But if you can't use the appropriate foreign language and must communicate in English, there are still special precautions you want to take. Richard Lurie, a foreign trade expert, tells of the export manager who had to explain a rise in prices to three of his foreign distributors. To his German distributor, the exporter was straightforward and came right to the point (without, of course, being discourteous). To his Lebanese distributor, he was much less direct and much more detailed in his explanation. To his Peruvian distributor he took pains to be as polite as possible and highly formal; he didn't get around to the reasons for the price increase until the second page of his letter.

Nonverbal signals can be just as important — and just as troublesome — as using the right words. Habits that are quite conventional here can offend foreign nationals. One American executive recently insulted a Saudi Arabian official when he casually reached out and squeezed the official's arm to emphasize a point. In Saudi society, it's simply not done. Other Americans have offended Saudis by crossing their legs while sitting. "Among Saudis," says a Commerce Department advisory, "it is offensive to allow the soles of one's shoes to be seen by others." And the problem cuts both ways. Upon arriving for an appointment with a Saudi official, an American corporate president may find the meeting room filled with Saudi citizens and other foreign businessmen —

all waiting to talk to the same official at the same time. Our Commerce Department advises Americans not to take offense at this, nor to worry that business secrets may be compromised. "A first meeting," say the Commerce advisory, "is only a warming up period." Once the seriousness of the visit is determined, the visitor will be invited to "call again the next day to discuss the matter at hand."

In American business correspondence (as you'll remember from Chapter 2) we generally avoid using cliches and stale adages. By contrast, Iranian business writers (both before and since the recent revolution in that country) will often go out of their way to use one. In Persian culture, an adage or proverb — with its presumably timeless wisdom — is often the *best* way to wind up a persuasive argument.

Even so simple a matter as the date on a document, if numeralized, can cause problems internationally. The date 4/11/81 (April 11, 1981 in America) is written 11/4/81 in Britain (where dates are commonly written 11 April 1981). Their April 11th looks like our November 4th. Or consider the word *billion.* In America, *billion* means "one thousand millions" (1000 × 1,000,000). In Britain, *billion* means "one million millions" (1,000,000 × 1,000,000). What the London accountant calls *two billion,* we call *two trillion.* What we call *two billion,* they call *two thousand million.* Got it?

You can do a lot to earn the respect of foreign nationals simply by addressing and saluting them correctly. If you encounter a hyphenated name — for instance, John Peter Billings-Blake — in corresponding with an Englishman, you'd address him as *Mr. J. P. Billings-Blake* (the British prefer initials in place of given names) and salute him *Dear Mr. Billings-Blake.* A hyphenated name in Spanish — for example, Juan Hernandez-Gomez — would be addressed *Sr.* (for *Señor) Juan Hernandez-Gomez,* but you'd salute him simply *Dear Señor Hernandez.* In Chinese names, the family name usually comes first. So if you addressed a letter to *Mr. Chen Yee Song,* you'd salute him *Dear Mr. Chen* (not *Mr. Song).* A Chinese with an Americanized name like *Betsy Ling* would obviously be saluted *Dear Ms. Ling* (or *Mrs. Ling* or *Miss Ling).* French lawyers use the title *Maître* preceding their names, in the same way that doctors use *Dr.* instead of *Mr.* So if you addressed *Maître Pierre DuPrey,* you would salute him *Dear Maître DuPrey.* The average Frenchman is addressed like this — *M.* (for *Monsieur) Jean Valjean* and saluted, simply, *Monsieur.* In Arabic, the word *Bey* in someone's name is a title, not actually a name. *Gamal Kaldun Bey* would be saluted *Dear Mr. Kaldun* (not *Mr. Bey).*

This sampling of international variables is by no means exhaustive. It's simply meant to alert you to the problems that can arise in international business communication.

APPENDIX D

ABBREVIATIONS COMMONLY USED IN BUSINESS

acct., a/c	account
agt.	agent
amt.	amount
ans.	answer
approx.	approximate
assn.	association
asst.	assistant
Atten., Attn.	Attention
atty.	attorney
Ave.	Avenue
bal.	balance
bbl.	barrel
B/L	bill of lading
bldg.	building
Blvd.	Boulevard
bu.	bushel(s)
C.	centigrade, (Celsius), center, hundred
cat.	catalogue
cc, c/c	carbon copy
C/D	Certificate of Deposit
c/o	in care of
c.o.d., C.O.D.	cash on delivery
dept.	department
dis., disc.	discount
ea.	each
e.d.p.	electronic data processing
e.g.	for example
enc.,	enclosure,
e.o.m.	end of month
et al.	and others
etc.	and so forth
exc., exch.	exchange
ff.	following (pages)
Fig., fig.	figure
f.o.b., F.O.B.	free on board
frt.	freight
ft.	foot, feet
fwd.	forward
gal.	gallon
hr.	hour(s)
ibid.	in the same place
i.e.	that is
in.	inch, inches
Inc.	incorporated
ins.	insurance
inv.	invoice
kt.	carat, karat
kw.	kilowatt
lb., lbs.	pound, pounds
mdse.	merchandise
memo.	memorandum
Messrs.	messieurs, Gentlemen
mfg.	manufacturing
misc.	miscellaneous
mi.	mile(s)
min.	minute(s)
mkt.	market
mo.	month
MS	manuscript
N.B., n.b.	note well
No., Nos.	number, numbers (before figures only)
O.R.	operations research
oz.	ounce
p., pp.	page, pages
pat.	patent, patented
payt.	payment
PBX, P.B.X.	Private Branch Exchange (telephone)
pd.	paid
pfd.	preferred (stock)

pkg.	package
p.m., P.M.	after noon
p.p.	parcel post
pr.	pair, pairs
P.S:, p.s.	postscript
qt.	quart, quantity
R&D	research and development
R.F.D.	Rural Free Delivery
recd.	received
retd.	returned
Rev.	Reverend
R.N.	Registered Nurse
RSVP, r.s.v.p.	respond, if you please
Rte., Rt.	Route
Ry.	railway
Sec., secy	secretary
sect., sec.	section
s.o.p.	standard operating procedure
sq. ft.	square foot (feet)
Sr.	Senior
St.	Street, Saint, Strait
supt.	superintendent
u.c.	upper case
viz.	namely
vol., Vol., vols.	volume, volumes
vs., v.	versus
whsle.	wholesale
wk.	week
wt.	weight
yd.	yard, yards
yr.	year

APPENDIX E

Glossary of Terms Frequently Used in Business

absentee ownership ownership of property by persons living elsewhere than where the property is located

account payable a debt that is owed *by* an enterprise to someone else, and which hasn't been paid yet

account receivable a debt that is owed *to* an enterprise, on which payment hasn't yet been received

actuary a mathematician who calculates insurance risks and the premiums based on those risks

ad valorem Latin phrase meaning "according to value" — that is, not according to weight or number of units

agent one who acts in another's behalf, such as an advertising agent or an independent sales representative

amortization reduction in a debt by periodic payments of the principal and interest

arbitration a method of settling disputes by having them mediated by an impartial third party

attachment a legal document authorizing the sheriff to seize a debtor's property for non-payment of a debt

balloon payment a lump sum, usually large, payable at the end of a loan period after the periodic payments have been made

bankruptcy a legal means by which a debtor relinquishes claim to his assets and relieves himself of his financial obligations

bear market the stock market when prices are falling

bid the price offered by a willing buyer

blue chip a stock-market term for a stock whose products and financial record are of a high quality

boycott a refusal to have commercial dealings with someone or some organization

bull market the stock market when prices are rising

cartel an agreement between companies of various countries to fix the world price on a commodity and thereby control the world market in that commodity

caveat emptor Latin phrase meaning "let the buyer beware"

chattel any property or right except real estate property

closed shop a business firm within which all wage-earning employees are required to be union members

compound interest interest that is due, calculated by adding to the principal the interest already earned

cooperative a type of corporation set up to gain the benefits of large-scale operation, in which every member, regardless of the size of his or her investment, has a single vote
creditor one to whom a debt is owed by another (by the *debtor*)
debtor one who owes a debt to another (to the *creditor*)
demand the amount of a good that buyers are ready to buy at a specified price at a given time
demography the study of population and its characteristics — for example, age distribution, birth and death rates, percentages of married/single, urban/suburban/rural, and so on
depletion the decreasing value of an asset that's being reduced by being converted into a saleable product — like oil in the ground
dividend the earnings that a corporation pays out to its stockholders in cash, property, more securities, or any combination of these
domicile in law, a person can have many *residences*, but only one *domicile*, the place he or she declares to be home
efficiency ratio the ratio of ends produced (that is, output) to the means used to produce it (that is, input)
encumbrance a claim — a mortgage, a lien, and so on — against a specific piece of property
entrepreneur originally a French word, meaning "an enterpriser," or owner and operator of a business
equity the amount of one's actual ownership in a piece of property — for example, one's equity in a $50,000 property may be $10,000
escalator clause a provision in an agreement for adjusting a price if the cost of living or some other index rises
escrow an arrangement by two parties to clear their transaction through a designated third party (the escrower), so that neither of the two can take unfair advantage of the other or jeopardize down-payment monies before the transaction clears
estate the total of one's property left at death
exclusive agent an agent who has sole rights to handle a product or service within a designated market area
extrapolation estimating a future value by projecting the curve of past and present values into the future
featherbedding practices by labor unions to maintain or increase artificially the number of jobs at a company
Federal Reserve System a system of twelve central banks, created in 1912 and controlled by a Board of Governors in Washington, to which national banks must belong and in which they must keep certain percentages of their assets to assure the security of their depositors
fee simple absolute *or* fee simple an old term from Anglo-Saxon law meaning the full and unconditional ownership of a piece of land
fiduciary anyone who holds a position of trust or confidence in the eyes of the law — for example, trustees, executors of estates, corporate directors, and so on
fiscal adjective that means "pertaining to financial affairs"
fixed asset any property used in operating a business, which won't be consumed or converted into cash during that business's operation
foreclosure the legal procedure by which a mortgage holder forces the sale of property in order to recover the money owed him or her

franchise a right granted by a corporation, or by the government, to someone to carry on a certain kind of business in a certain location — for example, utilities companies are public franchises; your local McDonald's is a corporate franchise
frequency distribution a distribution determining how many of each item have the same value — for example, the frequency distribution of grades in your class may be: 7 As, 12 Bs, 8 Cs, and so on
futures contracts whose fulfillment by delivery of the goods is not required until a specified time in the future; most commodity exchanges — wheat, coffee, pork bellies, etc. — work on the basis of "future delivery" contracts, or "futures"
gold standard the monetary system under which money can be converted into gold, and gold into money, at specified fixed rates
goon slang term for a person hired by a company to intimidate its workers and hold their demands in check
Gresham's Law "Bad money drives out good" — when two kinds of money circulate in the same economy, people hoard, melt down, or export the more valuable of the two, thereby keeping the less valuable money in circulation
gross national product money value of the total output of goods and services in a national economy during a given period of time, usually a year
head tax a tax per person
hidden asset assets carried on a company's books at less than their fair market value; the value of the "hidden asset" is the market value of the asset *minus* its book value
implied warranty a warranty that a buyer can assume to exist when nothing to the contrary has been said by the seller
impounds the money required to be put into an account to assure later payment (usually of taxes) when payment is due
inflation a period when the purchasing power of one's money is falling
interest the price paid for using someone else's money — usually stipulated as a percentage of the money being used (the principal)
interpolation determining an intermediate value by plotting along a curve between two already determined points
inventory all the saleable goods on hand at a company, *or* a list of those goods
jobber same as "wholesaler" *or* one who buys in relatively small (that is, "job") lots for resale to a retailer
joint venture a business transaction or project carried out by individuals who join together for that purpose
judgment the decision a court makes in a law suit
Keynesian economics a school of economics based on the thoughts of John Maynard Keynes (1883-1946); the school basically disagrees with classical economics in holding that an equilibrium (position of rest) can be reached even though some economic resources are unemployed; the remedy advocated is government intervention in one form or another
kickback payment by someone of part of his or her earnings to assure himself or herself favorable treatment or to evade some requirement
lease *or* leasehold a contract to possess something for a fixed period of time in return for payment of a certain sum of money
letter of credit a letter authorizing that credit be extended to the bearer of the letter and assuring that the signer will pay the resulting debt
liability a valid claim by a creditor against one's assets
line position a line position in a company is any position — from president to laborer — whose job it is to operate or get out production, as distinguished from a staff position (*see* staff position)

liquidation turning one's assets into cash by selling them off
local option the right of local communities (as provided by state constitution or legislative act) to regulate certain activities as they see fit
lockout the closing of a plant by an employer to enforce demands against employees or to avoid the employees' demands against him
manifest a shipping document that records the value, count, point of origin, and destination of each item of cargo the ship is carrying
margin in commercial transactions, the difference between the purchase price paid by someone and the price he or she gets for it when it's resold
mats short term for "matrices" — printing devices that serve as dies from which printing plates are made
maturity date the date on which an obligation is due
maturity value the amount that must be paid on the date the obligation is due
mean* the "average" that is computed by adding all the pertinent numerical items, and dividing by the number of items
median* the "average" that is calculated by identifying the middle value in a group of numerical values — that is, there are the same number of items above the median as below it
mediation the process by which a third party (the mediator) attempts to bring two disputing parties into agreement
mixed economy a national economy that has some characteristics of free enterprise and some socialism (that is, governmentally determined)
mode* the "average" in a series of items that is determined by identifying the value that occurs most frequently
monopoly sufficient control of an industry or a commodity to be able to control or regulate its price
mortgage a legal claim on a property, derived from having loaned money to the purchaser of that property
mutual fund an investment trust whose managers decide which securities to buy and sell
nationalization the acquisition and operation by the government of a business that was previously owned and operated privately
net sales the total of all sales *minus* returned sales
nonprofit corporation a corporation organized for charitable, educational, humanitarian, or other purposes not primarily aimed at making a profit
notary public an official appointed by a state to administer oaths, certify documents, and perform similar functions
obsolescence the decrease in value of something because of lessened demand or new invention, but not because of wear and tear
open-end contract a contract that allows a buyer to order additional units, on same terms, without additional consent by the seller
operations research ("o.r.") a term embracing all research that aims to quantify and analyze business data by scientific method and thereby guide the decision-making process
option a contract that gives someone rights with respect to property, usually the right to buy it or sell it at a stipulated price
overdraft a draft (or check) drawn in excess of the amount a person has on deposit in the bank

*If we have the following values in a group: 2,4,4,4,5,7,9,9,10, the *mean* is 6, the *median* is 5, the *mode* is 4.

over-the-counter market name applied to security transactions that take place outside an organized stock exchange, usually through local brokers

partition in law, the division of property among co-owners; where division in kind is impractical, the whole is sold and the proceeds divided

par value the value printed on the face of a stock or bond certificate, the *stated* value

patent the exclusive right to "any new and useful art, machine, manufacture, or composition of matter, or any new and useful improvement thereof. . . ."

peak load in public utilities, refers to the time of the week during which the greatest consumption of electricity or gas occurs

per capita Latin phrase meaning "by the heads" or "per individual"

perquisite compensation or privileges over and above one's regular salary; now usually called "perks"

personal property *or* personalty all one's property other than interests in real estate

petty cash a cash fund kept on hand for small disbursements

piggyback service the loading of motor-truck trailers onto railroad flat cars

portfolio a term used to refer to all the securities held by one person or institution

power of attorney a written instrument empowering someone else to act as your agent and signatory

prima facie Latin phrase meaning "at first sight," or "on the face of it" — prima facie evidence will carry a legal verdict if nothing valid is presented in rebuttal

pro rata Latin phrase meaning "in proportion"

proxy a written authorization designating someone else to cast your vote

quick asset assets that can be turned into cash immediately with a minimum loss

quitclaim deed a deed in which the grantor (the person giving the deed) signs away whatever rights he or she has in a property, but without guaranteeing what rights, if any, he or she has

quorum the number of persons legally necessary (in person or by proxy) to conduct a valid business meeting

rationing any arrangement, usually under governmental regulation, limiting the quantity of product that can be purchased by a given class of buyers

real estate an interest in land or things attached to land

rebate a return of some part of the charges that have been paid out for a service or commodity

receivership the court's appointing a person to administer the affairs of a person or firm unable to meet its debts when they are due

registry the flag a ship flies, designating the country whose laws the ship is governed by

rescind in law, to revoke an action or an agreement

residence *see* domicile

retainer the fee charged by a professional person for services in a matter

right-to-work laws laws that outlaw closed shops (*see* closed shop)

riparian rights the rights of an owner whose land abuts water to the land under the water

rolling stock in transportation, movable property such as trucks, locomotives, freight and passenger cars, and so on

royalties the money paid out per unit of good sold, to the person or company who owns or holds rights to that good

salary money paid to an employee at a fixed weekly or monthly rate (*see* wages)

scab derogatory slang term for a "strikebreaker": someone who takes employment at a company when its regular employees are on strike

secondary boycott a boycott (*see* boycott) of someone who uses or sells the product made by the company who is the primary object of the boycott — for example, a boycott against supermarkets who sell grapes in order to harm their suppliers, the grape growers

securities collective term applying to all kinds of written instruments of investment value: mortgages, stocks, bonds, certificates of ownership, and so on

seniority giving preference solely on the basis of how long someone has been on the job

slow-down a form of strike in which workers stay on the job but deliberately reduce their efficiency

solvency a business is "solvent" when its assets exceed its liabilities, and it can pay its debts as they become due

staff position a position in the company whose holder does not work directly in management, production, or distribution but gives specialized assistance to "line" employees (*see* line position)

stock split the issuance of a number of new shares to replace each share of stock now outstanding

subcontract an agreement by which the party who has contracted to do a job gets someone else to do part or all of the work on that job

subsidy money granted, usually by the state, to support an enterprise or a program felt to be in the public interest

subvention a grant or subsidy

supply the amount of a good that sellers are ready to sell at a specified price in a given market at a given time

surcharge a charge imposed in addition to another charge

surtax a tax levied in addition to another tax

syndicate any combination of persons or corporations joined to achieve a common business purpose

tariff a customs duty or tax levied on goods as they enter (or leave) a country

title evidence of ownership in something of value

trading down action by a merchandiser in buying and selling cheaper goods in an effort to increase sales volume (*see* trading up)

trading up handling goods of higher price in an effort to increase the profit margin per item (*see* trading down)

underwriter anyone who guarantees to furnish a definite sum of money by a definite date to a business or government in return for an issue of bonds or stock; in insurance, one who assumes somebody's risk in return for a premium payment

unlawful detainer legal device by which a landlord can have a tenant evicted when the tenant has overstayed the tenancy or broken the terms of the lease

value added the difference between the purchase price of raw materials and the sale price of the product; in some places, value added is now subject to taxation — a value-added tax

vendee the buyer of something

vendor the seller of something

vested a legal term to identify a right of immediate enjoyment or future enjoyment that cannot be allotted without consent of the party having that right

wages the money paid to those who render their work on an hourly or daily basis (*see* salary)

waiver voluntary abandonment by a person of some or all of his or her right to something

wildcat strike a strike called suddenly without the preliminary procedures called for by the union's contract with the company
windfall gain a gain which was not foreseen
writ a written order by the court directing a court officer to perform an act — for example, seizing a property

APPENDIX F

A REVIEW OF MECHANICS: GRAMMAR, SPELLING, AND PUNCTUATION

The grammar of the English language — of any language — is the system of word structures and word arrangements with which we organize our meanings and accurately relate them to one another. Knowing grammar doesn't guarantee effective writing, but the correlation between good grammar and good writing is high. Even if it weren't, a knowledge of grammar would be necessary to help avoid errors that automatically label any writer a dunce in the eyes of the reader. Hence this brief review of English grammar.

THE SENTENCE

A sentence is, quite simply, *something being said about something*. That something, which is *spoken about* in the sentence is the *subject* of the sentence. Whatever is being said about the subject is called the *predicate.* (To *predicate* means to *assert* — a sentence is an assertion about a subject.) For example:

```
The computer                    is broken.
```
(subject) (predicate)

```
Those four large packages
which Sherman brought
down from Sacramento            were stolen yesterday.
```
(subject) (predicate)

The predicate always contains a key word, a word that triggers the assertion in that sentence. This trigger word is called the *verb.* Watch this sentence unfold:

Carson
(the subject)

Carson gives
(the verb, which triggers an assertion)

Carson gives Spanish lessons
(the *direct object,* the thing directly affected by the action of the verb)

Carson gives Spanish lessons to his friends.
(the *indirect object,* the thing that receives the action established by the verb and the direct object)

Often, the indirect object precedes the direct object in a sentence:

Carson	gives	his friends	Spanish lessons.
(subject)	(verb)	(indirect object)	(direct object)

Not all sentences have objects. Some verbs make the entire assertion about the subject:

Baxter thinks. The bell tolls.

Anything that appears in a sentence besides these four components is there to modify the subject, or the verb, or one of the objects, or the entire assertion; or it's there to connect several of the elements.

THE PARTS OF SPEECH

Our traditional English grammar distinguishes eight parts of speech: *verbs, nouns* and *pronouns, adjectives* and *adverbs, prepositions* and *conjunctions,* and *interjections.*

Verbs

There are three kinds of verbs: *transitive* verbs, *intransitive* verbs, and *linking* verbs. A *transitive verb* triggers an assertion, then takes a direct object to complete the assertion.

Thomas opened the confidential document.

An *intransitive verb* not only triggers but completes the assertion by itself.

Maxwell and I left.

Most verbs can be used either in a transitive or an intransitive role. One common exception is the verb *lie,* which functions only intransitively. A *linking verb* is a verb that triggers some description, rather than an active assertion, about the subject:

Harwood was outraged by Orr's behavior.

The pie smelled delicious.

A number of everyday verbs can function as linking verbs: *be, appear, become, feel, sound, look, taste, smell.*

Verb Auxiliaries and Verb Phrases A verb can consist of more than one word. A multiword verb is called a *verb phrase.* A verb phrase consists of the essential verb word plus *auxiliary* words which round out the meaning of the verb. For example: *will speak, may be learning, had taken.* Words commonly used as verb auxiliaries are *am, is, are, were, be, been, has, have, had, do, did, does, used to, going to, ought to, have to, about to, could, should, would, shall, will, can, cannot.*

The words of a verb phrase are sometimes separated in a sentence:

Baxter may, of course, resist your suggestion.

She does not always reveal what she's thinking.

A verb auxiliary is sometimes combined into one word with *not* (or its contraction *n't*):

I cannot understand his argument.

Isn't it raining out?

Number and Person Verbs have *number* and *person:*

I speak tomorrow night.
(first person singular verb)

Perkins speaks tonight.
(third person singular verb)

Perkins and Leventhal speak tonight.
(third person plural verb)

Tense Verbs have tense. There are six verb tenses in English; that is, six ways of indicating the time relationship between the writer and the action or description the verb is triggering. They can be plotted on a time line, as shown on page 524.

Related to the future tense is the *conditional* tense, used to express a contingent future action:

I should write to my rich brother.

Carson would rather call than write.

Voice There are two verb voices in English: the *active* voice and the *passive* voice. In the active voice, that which is performing an action is the subject of the sentence:

Mr. Bigelow fired Joe Hebberson for laziness.

In the passive voice, the subject is that which is being acted upon. The passive verb takes on some form of the verb *to be* as an auxiliary:

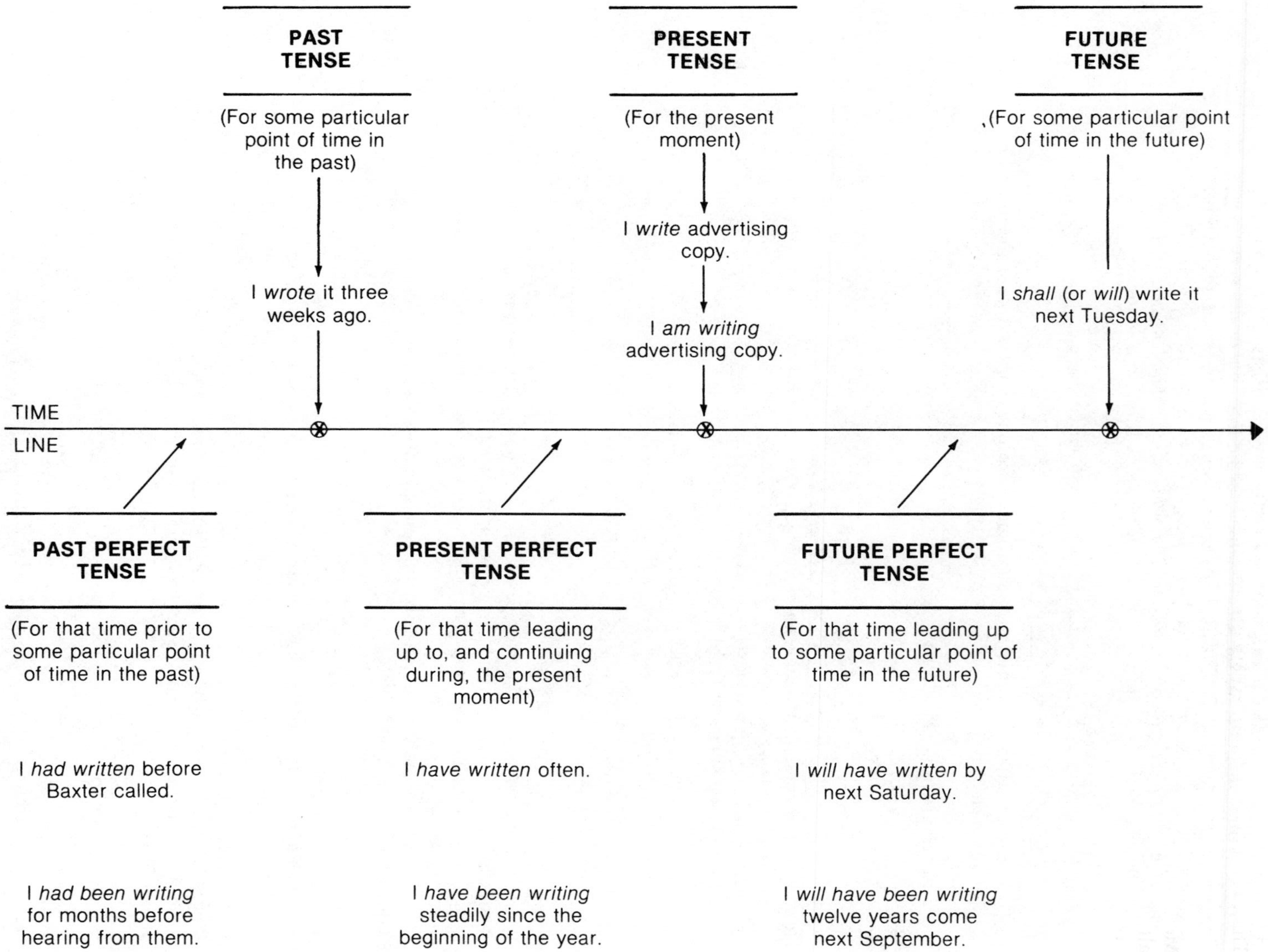
PAST TENSE
(For some particular point of time in the past)
I *wrote* it three weeks ago.
PRESENT TENSE
(For the present moment)
I *write* advertising copy.
I *am writing* advertising copy.
FUTURE TENSE
(For some particular point of time in the future)
I *shall* (or *will*) write it next Tuesday.
TIME
LINE
PAST PERFECT TENSE
(For that time prior to some particular point of time in the past)
I *had written* before Baxter called.
I *had been writing* for months before hearing from them.
PRESENT PERFECT TENSE
(For that time leading up to, and continuing during, the present moment)
I *have written* often.
I *have been writing* steadily since the beginning of the year.
FUTURE PERFECT TENSE
(For that time leading up to some particular point of time in the future)
I *will have written* by next Saturday.
I *will have been writing* twelve years come next September.

Joe Hebberson was fired by Mr. Bigelow for laziness.

The style ramifications of verb voice are discussed on page 77 in the text.

Mood The *subjunctive mood,* which is used to state conditions contrary to fact, alters the form of some verbs.

Indicative mood (present tense)	Indicative mood (past tense)	Subjunctive mood (present tense)
Baxter is here.	Baxter was here.	If only Baxter were here.
I have a good idea.	I had a good idea.	I wish I had a good idea.

Agreement A verb must agree in number with its subject ("A letter *is* . . .," "Letters *are* . . ."), even if

1. an intervening noun is of different number:

The advent of two-hour transatlantic flights is imminent.

2. the predicate noun is of different number:

Baxter's primary liability is his table manners.

3. a parenthetical element intervenes:

The foreman, along with his crew, is going before the grievance board.

4. the subject follows the verb:

There are seven prime candidates for the comptrollership.

Exceptions:

1. A compound subject which refers to a single person takes a singular verb.

My best friend and advisor, Jim Jackson, is leaving the firm.

2. A compound subject which is generally considered to be a unit takes a singular verb.

Bacon and eggs is a typical American breakfast.

3. A plural subject which is being treated as a unit also takes a singular verb.

Five thousand cartons is an exceptionally large shipment.

4. When used as a subject, *everybody* or *everyone* takes a singular verb.

Everybody is here.

5. When used as subjects, *all* and *none* take either singular or plural verbs, depending on the sense of the sentence.

None of them is aware of his deficiencies.

None of them are aware of their deficiencies.

All is well. All are present.

Verbals Verbs, in certain forms, can perform the substantive function of nouns and the modifying function of adjectives, and adverbs. A verb performing such a function is called a *verbal.* A verbal cannot function as the verb in a sentence.

The infinitive form of a verb can function as a verbal:

To speak as a minority of one is not an easy task. (The verbal here functions as a noun.)

He had a job to do. (Here the verbal functions as an adjective, modifying *job.*)

Baxter hurried over to read the will. (Here the verbal functions as an adverb, modifying *hurried.*)

The participial forms of a verb can function as verbals:

Shouting at the top of his lungs, the chairman called the convention to order. (Here the present participle verb [functioning as a verbal] is used to introduce an adjectival phrase, modifying *chairman.)*

Defeated, the Giants walked slowly from the field. (Here a past participle, functioning as a verbal, modifies *Giants.*)

The gerund is a third kind of verbal. It takes the form of a present participle, but functions as a noun in a sentence.

Watching others very carefully has been the key to Zuckerman's success. (Here the gerund functions as a subject noun.)

Baxter prefers drinking alone. (Here it functions as an object noun.)

Nouns

Nouns are words we use as labels for things (or groups of things or types of things), so that we can refer to those things. Nouns are generally classified as either:

1. *Proper nouns* — the labels given to particular things, such as people (*Dwight Eisenhower, Ida Schultz*), places (*Tahiti, Brooklyn*), brand products (*Cadillac, Del Monte*), books (*The Grapes of Wrath*).

2. *Common nouns* — all other nouns.

Number Nouns are either *singular* (*man, desk, knife, mouse*) or *plural* (*men, desks, knives, mice*). Some groups of things are given singular names — called *collective nouns* (*army, congregation, group, staff, faculty*). The importance of *number* in nouns is apparent in our discussion of agreement.

Gender In other languages, almost every noun is masculine or feminine. In English, only nouns like *woman, boy, waiter,* and *comedienne* have gender. All the rest are neuter.

Uses A noun can be used in different ways in a sentence.

1. As a *subject* — the thing about which an assertion is made or a question asked:

`The computer ran wild.` `Did Peters see it?`

2. As a *direct object* — the thing directly affected by a verb's action:

`Jackson pulled the alarm.`

3. As an *indirect object* — the thing which receives the action triggered by the verb:

`The boss gave Baxter a raise.`

4. As a *subject complement* — the thing which completes the sense of a linking verb or a passive transitive verb by referring to the subject of the sentence:

`Michaels is a lawyer.`

`I was elected chairman for the third time.`

5. As an *object complement* — the thing which completes the sense of a transitive verb by referring to the direct object:

`Jennie Marx called Mr. Dixon a clown.`

`He considered her remark a joke.`

6. As a *possessor:*

`This document is the property of the Guild.`

7. As an *appositive* — a noun injected parenthetically to explain or elaborate on another noun:

Mr. Joseph T. Pender, the noted international banker, will address the meeting.

8. In *direct address:*

Men, I want your attention.

Good morning, Mr. Levine.

Pronouns

Pronouns are words that substitute for nouns to avoid a tiresome repetition of nouns. The noun to which a pronoun refers is called the *antecedent* of that pronoun.

Kinds of Pronouns Eight kinds of pronouns are usually distinguished in the traditional grammar of English.

1. *Personal pronouns:*

	SINGULAR			*PLURAL*	
	masculine and feminine				
Subjective case	I			we	FIRST PERSON
Objective case	me			us	
Possessive case	mine			our	
	masculine and feminine				
Subjective case	you			you	SECOND PERSON
Objective case	you			you	
Possessive case	yours			yours	
	masculine	*feminine*	*neuter*	*all genders*	
Subjective case	he	she	it	they	THIRD PERSON
Objective case	him	her	it	them	
Possessive case	his	hers	its	theirs	

2. *Relative pronouns* — pronouns that introduce subordinate clauses by referring back to antecedents. The relative pronouns in English are *who, which* and *that*. *Who* refers only to animate things (people and animals). *Which* refers to inanimate things and sometimes animals (never people). *That* can refer to animate or inanimate things. In an informal sentence, if something inanimate (a *jail* for example) is a possessor, you can, at an informal level of diction, use the animate relative pronoun *whose* to refer to it. You can write

This is the jail whose inmates rioted last year.

To be formally correct, however, you'd have to write

This is the jail the inmates of which rioted last year.

3. *Interrogative pronouns* — pronouns used to introduce a question: *who, which, what, whoever, whichever, whatever.*

4. *Indefinite pronouns* — pronouns that do not refer to definite or specific antecedents. The language has many indefinite pronouns: *any, anybody, anyone, anything, each, either, every, everybody, everyone, everything, neither, nobody, none, one, some, somebody, someone, something.* The main problem with indefinite pronouns is their *number;* see the earlier discussion on *agreement.*

5. *Demonstrative pronouns* — pronouns that point to something: *this, that, these, those.*

6. *Reflexive pronouns* — pronouns that serve as direct objects in a sentence while referring back to the subject:

I hate myself.

Keep yourselves out of harm's way. (Here the reflexive pronoun refers back to the implied subject *you.*)

7. *Intensive pronouns* — an intensive pronoun, although not necessary to complete the sense of the sentence, is used to emphasize (or intensify) the subject. It takes the same form as a reflexive pronoun but does not act as a direct object.

I'll type the report myself.

Do it yourselves if you want it done.

8. *Reciprocal pronouns* — pronouns used to relate two antecedents: *each other, one another.*

Whenever a pronoun is used (except for indefinite pronouns)there should be *no* doubt as to its antecedent.

Special Problems of Pronoun Case: *I* and *me, he* and *him, she* and *her, we* and *us, they* and *them.* The subjective case (*I, he, she, we, they*) should be used (1) in the subject of a sentence, (2) after *than* or *as*:

He is wiser than I.

I am as successful as he.

and (3) in the subject complement, when following a linking verb:

That well-dressed group over there may be they.

One exception to rule (3): Informal usage approves of *It is me* as well as *It is I.*

The objective case (*me, him, her, us, them*) is ordinarily used in the object of a sentence.

The pronoun immediately preceding a gerund (a verbal noun) is ordinarily in the possessive case:

Bigelow approved of my flying to Chicago.

His begging for a raise didn't appeal to the boss.

Adjectives and Adverbs

Adjectives and adverbs are modifiers — that is, they clarify, qualify, limit, add meaning to, or make more specific other parts of a sentence. Adjectives modify substantives (nouns, pronouns, gerunds, and noun phrases). Adverbs modify verbs and other modifiers.

The form of an adjective or adverb is varied only to indicate whether it is noncomparative, comparative (used in comparing two things), or superlative (used in comparing three or more things).

	Noncomparative	*Comparative*	*Superlative*
Adjectives	large	larger	largest
	friendly	friendlier	friendliest
	delicious	more delicious	most delicious
	good	better	best
Adverbs	far	farther	farthest
	consistently	more consistently	most consistently
	well	better	best
	badly	worse	worst

Prepositions and Conjunctions

Prepositions and conjunctions are *function words*, their primary purpose being to indicate relationships and connections between other elements in a sentence.

A *preposition* is used to show the relationship of a substantive to some other word in the sentence.

`The computer is on the twenty-seventh floor.`

(The preposition *on* indicates the relationship of its object, *the twenty-seventh floor*, to the verb *is;* that verb having triggered an assertion about the subject, *the computer*.)

Words most commonly used as prepositions are *over, under, through, between, at, before, after, during, across, above, below, up, to, with, near, by, for, from, of, in, into, on.*

A *conjunction* is used to connect words, phrases, clauses, or sentences; and, in connecting them, to show the relationship between them. There are two kinds of conjunctions: *coordinating* conjunctions and *subordinating* conjunctions.

A *coordinating conjunction*, such as *and, or, nor, but,* connects parallel elements.

`Timmons, McCarthy, and Baxter were laid off.`

(Here the conjunction *and* connects nouns.)

`You can come with me or stay here at the office.`

(Here the conjunction *or* connects clauses.)

A *subordinating conjunction*, such as *if, because, while, since, whenever, although,* connects a subordinate clause to a main clause.

`Piedmont intimidates his staff whenever he looks at them.`

The stylistic ramifications of conjunctions are discussed on pages 102–103 in the text.

Interjections

An interjection is an utterance that is grammatically independent of the rest of an assertion. It is followed by either a comma or an exclamation point.

`Congratulations, I just received the good news about your contract.`

`Never! No amount of money would cause me to blackmail Baxter.`

SPELLING

Spelling can be quite a problem in the English language, our words having come historically from so many different sources. But in business very few allowances are made for the poor speller. Misspelling on letters and reports generally marks the writer as a person going absolutely *nowhere*. And there's really no shortcut to spelling competence. If your spelling is weak, you must commit yourself to the task of improving, and word by word learn the right way to spell all the words you now make mistakes on.

The following few pages contain two lists — one a list of words whose spellings are frequently confused with one another, and the other a general list of frequently misspelled words.

If spelling is ever a problem for you, you might keep these lists nearby for ready reference.

Words Frequently Confused with One Another

accept except	adapt adopt	affect effect	aid aide
aisle isle	all ready already	all together altogether	allusion illusion
altar alter	angel angle	appraise apprise	ascent assent
bare bear	baring barring bearing	berth birth	beside besides
biannually biennially	born borne	bough bow	breath breathe
bridal bridle	canvas canvass	capital capitol	censor censure
cite sight site	climactic climatic	clothes cloths	coarse course
complement compliment	consul council counsel	corps corpse	credible creditable

dairy	decent	deduce	desert
diary	descent	deduct	dessert
	dissent		
device	die, dying	diner	dual
devise	dye, dyeing	dinner	duel
elegy	emigrant	eminent	equable
eulogy	immigrant	imminent	equitable
facetious	fair	faze	flaunt
factious	fare	phase	flout
factitious			
formally	forth	hear	heard
formerly	fourth	here	herd
hoard	holly	idle	imply
horde	holy	idol	infer
	wholly	idyll	
ingenius	instance	its	later
ingenuous	instants	it's	latter
lead (metal)	lessen	loose	mantel
lead (verb)	lesson	lose	mantle
led			
marital	metal	moral	naval
martial	mettle	morale	navel
ordinance	passed	peace	perquisite
ordnance	past	piece	prerequisite
persecute	personal	plain	populace
prosecute	personnel	plan, planned	populous
		plane, planed	
pore	practicable	precede	precedence
pour	practical	proceed,	precedent
		procedure	president
presence	principal	profit	prophecy
presents	principle	prophet	prophesy
quiet	rain	respectably	right
quite	reign	respectfully	rite
	rein	respectively	write
road	rout	seams	shone
rode	route	seems	shown
sole	stationary	statue	steal
soul	stationery	stature	steel
		statute	
straight	suit	tale	than
strait	suite	tail	then

their	threw	till	to
there	through	until	too
they're			
vain	venal	waist	waiver
vein	venial	waste	waver
weak	weather	which	who's
week	whether	witch	whose

Words Frequently Misspelled

absence
absorption
accelerate
acceptable
accessible
accidentally
accommodate
accompanying
accomplish
accumulate
accustom
achievement
acquaintance
acquire
acquitted
across
additionally
address
adequate
advertisement
aggravate
aggressive
agreement
alcohol
allege
all right
almost
although
always
amateur
among
analysis
analyze
annual
answer
apiece
apologize
apology
apparatus
apparent

appearance
appreciate
approach
appropriate
arctic
arguing
argument
arising
arithmetic
around
arouse
arrangement
article
artillery
assistant
association
asylum
athletic
attendance
audience
auxiliary
awful
awkward

bachelor
background
balance
balloon
banana
barbarous
battalion
beautiful
becoming
before
beggar
beginning
belief
believe
beneficial
benefited

biscuit
blasphemous
boundary
bourgeois
brilliant
Britain
bureau
burglar
bus
business

calendar
candidate
career
carriage
category
ceiling
cemetery
certain
changeable
chauffeur
choice
choose
chosen
college
collegiate
colonel
column
comedy
coming
commission
committed
committee
comparatively
compelled
competent
competition
completely
concede
conceivable

conceive
concrete
condemn
conferred
confidentially
conqueror
conscience
conscientious
conscious
consistent
conspicuous
continuously
controlled
controversial
convenient
counterfeit
courteous
cries
criticism
criticize
curiosity
curriculum
customer
cylinder

dealt
deceive
decide
decision
defendant
definitely
definition
democracy
dependent
descendant
describe
description
desirable
despair
desperate
destroy
develop
development
different
disagree
disappearance
disappoint
disastrous
discipline
discussion
dissatisfaction
dissipation
divide
divine
doctor
dormitory
drunkenness
duly

easily
ecstasy
efficient
eighth
eligible
eliminate
embarrass
encouraging
enemy
engineer
enthusiastic
entirely
environment
epitome
equipment
equipped
equivalent
erroneous
especially
etc.
evidently
exaggerate
excellent
exhausted
exhilarate
existence
expense
experience
extremely

familiar
fascinate
February
fiery
finally
financially
financier
foreign
fluent
forty
forward
fourteen
friend
fundamentally

generally
ghost
goddess
government
governor
grammar
grateful
gratuitous
gratuity
grievous
group
guarantee
guard
guidance

handkerchief
happiness
harass
height
heroes
hierarchy
hindrance
hoping
huge
humorous
hurriedly
hurrying
hypnotic
hypocrisy

ignorant
image
imaginary
immediately
immensely
impossible
impromptu
incidentally
incredible
incumbent
independent
indispensable
inevitable
instead
intellectual
intelligent
intentionally
interest
intramural

irrelevant
irresistible

jargon
jaundice
jewel
journey
journalism
justice

khaki
kinetic
knowledge
knead

laboratory
laborer
laid
laissez-faire
language
languorous
legitimate
leisure
length
library
lightning
likely
loneliness
loveliness
lying

maintenance
manual
manufacturer
marriage
mathematics
mattress
meant
medicine
medieval
Mediterranean
merely
metaphor
millionaire
miniature
minute
mischievous
misspelled
monotonous
mortgage
murmur
mysterious

naturally
necessary
neither
nickel
niece
nominal
normal
noticeable
nourish
nowadays

oblige
obstacle
occasion
occurred
occurrence
off
omission
omitted
opinion
opportunity
optimist
ordain
originally
orthodox

pamphlet
parallel
paralysis
parliament
particularly
pastime
peaceable
perceive
permanent
permissible
perseverance
personnel
perspiration
persuade
pertain
pertinent
petition
physically
picnicking
playwright
poisonous
politician
possess
possibly
practically
practice
predominant
preference
preferred
prejudice
preparation
presumption
prevalent
prisoner
privilege
probably
procedure
professor
prominent
pronunciation
propaganda
proportion
prove
psychology
purpose
pursue
pursuing

qualm
quantity
quizzes
quotient

really
recede
receipt
receive
recipe
recognize
recollect
recommend
refer
reference
referred
regard
relevant
relieve
religious
remembrance
repetition
representative
resemblance
reservoir
resistance

restaurant
rhythm
ridiculous
roommate

sacrifice
sacrilegious
safety
scent
schedule
secretary
seize
sentence
separate
sergeant
severely
Shakespeare
shepherd
shining
shriek
siege
significant
similar
simultaneous
sincerely
skis
smooth
sophomore
source
specimen
sponsor

stopping
strenuous
stretch
strictly
studying
succeed
sufficient
superintendent
supersede
supplies
suppress
surely
surprise
syllable
symmetry
sympathize

temperament
temperature
tendency
terminal
therefore
thorough
thought
through
together
toward
tragedy
tremendous
tries
truly

typical
tyranny

unanimous
unequivocal
undoubtedly
unnecessary
using
usually
usury

vacuum
valuable
variable
vegetable
vengeance
view
village
villain
vulnerable

warring
Wednesday
weight
weird
welfare
writing
written

yield

Capitalization

Here are the standard conventions of capitalization in written English.

1. Avoid all unnecessary capitals.
2. Capitalize:
   a. proper nouns — Indonesia, Boeing, Clarence Baxter.
   b. words derived from proper nouns — American, Californian, Turnerite — except when the derivative has become a term in general use — malapropism, roentgen.
   c. abbreviations, if the word being abbreviated is usually capitalized — CIA (Central Intelligence Agency), mph (miles per hour).
   d. titles which precede proper nouns — Judge Jackson, General Knox, Mr. Lowell.
   e. the titles of books, stories, plays, reports, etc. (except short conjunctions, prepositions, and articles) — *Seven Days in May, How to Succeed in Business Without Really Trying.*
   f. the pronoun *I*.
   g. the first word of every sentence, including statements quoted within a sentence and questions.

PUNCTUATION

Punctuation in our written language is partly logical and partly arbitrary. Some of the rules of punctuation help us clarify what we write. Other rules are just habits that all literate writers share. It is obviously to the advantage of the business writer to know these rules, for by putting them to work correctly, he or she can add to the clarity of the message and enhance its character.

The standard punctuation marks in written English are the *period,* the *question mark,* the *exclamation point,* the *comma,* the *semicolon,* the *colon,* the *apostrophe, quotation marks, underlining* (or *italics*), the *dash,* and *parentheses.*

The Period

The period is used	Example:
1. at the end of a sentence (except when that sentence is a question or a strong exclamation).	Baxter is a careful writer.
2. at the end of a rhetorical question.	Won't you give us a call today.
3. after abbreviations (but beware, certain abbreviations, such as RCA, CIA, mph, and IBM, do not take periods).	Pres. Ph.D. Mrs. Calif. C.O.D.
4. in an ellipsis (those periods used to indicate an omission from a quotation). Three periods are commonly used. When the omission is at the end of a sentence, a fourth period is added.	The October Consumer's Digest says, ''The new Cougar . . . is a superb automobile!''

The Question Mark

The question mark is used	Example:
1. after a question (but beware, a question mark is *not* used in a declarative statement about a question — for example, "I asked Baxter if he's a careful writer").	Is Baxter a careful writer?
2. to indicate that a statement of fact is open to question.	Nicholas de Wisker: born Dec. 12(?), 1883, Omaha, Nebraska

The Exclamation Point

The exclamation point is used	Example:
1. to bring out the emotion in a statement (surprise, joy, anger, wonder, frustration, admiration, or whatever).	Harley's report is a truly great piece of work! I don't see how we'll ever finish on time!
2. to inject emphasis or authority into a command.	Your supervisor expects you here at 8 o'clock sharp!

Beware of overusing the exclamation point. It is a device of emphasis, and like everything used for emphasis it can grow stale with overuse. Also keep in mind the childishness of the double or triple exclamation mark.

The Comma

The comma is used	Example:
1. to separate independent clauses in compound sentences of substantial length, if the second clause is introduced with a conjunction (the comma is unnecessary when the compound sentence is short — for example, "Smith flew and Martin took the train").	Electronics firms have had their troubles on Wall Street this month, but they still look forward to a prosperous year.

The comma is replaced by a semicolon when the conjunction is omitted from the compound sentence or replaced by a transitional phrase or conjunctive adverb, for example: "Jones likes Conroy's work; Conroy thinks Jones is a fool." "Electronics firms have had their troubles on Wall Street this month; nevertheless, they look forward to a prosperous year."

2. to set off introductory phrases.	In the weeks that followed, Mason devoted himself to learning the new code.

(Without the comma, the reader would be misled into reading, "In the weeks that followed Mason . . .")

3. to set off introductory subordinate clauses.	Just as he picked up the telephone, Baxter came in.
4. whenever else it is necessary to help avoid ambiguity.	I told Peters to visit the doctor now, and again the following month.

Without the comma, the sentence would read, "I told Peters to visit the doctor now and again . . .")

5. to set off mild interjections and words of direct address at the beginning of a statement.	Why, this report will take months to complete. Gentlemen, this concludes our demonstration.
6. in pairs, to set off	
a. nonrestrictive clauses.	Mr. Ewell, who has observed the new system, thinks it will work at Acme.
b. appositives.	Our pension plan, one of the nation's best, is responsible for our low turnover.

c. transitional words and phrases.	It is true, however, that we must strengthen our department. The doctors predicted that, as a matter of course, the epidemic would subside shortly.
d. commentary which interrupts dialogue.	"You've got to admit," he said sadly, "the evidence proves us wrong."
e. other interrupters.	You are not, if I understand your explanation, prepared to accept this contract.
7. to separate words, phrases, or clauses in a series.	Ira's report was neat, concise, and perceptive. His new assistant will provide stenographic aid, mathematical proficiency, a good telephone voice, and the ability to make visitors comfortable. We went to Detroit, saw the production lines, and came away amazed at their efficiency.
8. to separate day and year in writing the date.	April 1, 1936
9. to separate place names in addresses.	Pomona, California Paris, France Lowndes County, Alabama
10. to separate names from degrees or titles.	David B. Rankin, Ph.D. Charles Sumner, Treasurer Orville S. Thompson, Jr.
11. after the salutation in a friendly, informal letter.	Dear Jim,
12 after the complimentary close in any letter.	Sincerely yours,

The Semicolon

The semicolon is used	Example:
1. To separate independent clauses in a compound sentence when the conjunction is either omitted or	Davis not only denied seeing the accident; he doubted it ever happened.

	replaced by a conjunctive adverb (as shown in usage 1 of the *comma*).	We don't usually work on week-ends; however, this project must be ready by Monday morning.
	2. as a "big comma" to separate phrases or clauses in a series when the phrases or clauses contain internal commas.	Carson arose from his seat, pointer in hand; walked over to the display board; and pointed out to Miller, our sales manager, exactly where the losses were affecting the company. Her itinerary will take her to Pueblo, Colorado; Kankakee, Illinois; and Shreveport, Louisiana.
The Colon	The colon is used	Example:
	1. to introduce something which immediately follows, such as	
	a. an illustration.	Too many supervisors share a common failing: they dislike losing their best workers through promotion.
	b. an explanation.	The street corners are heavily populated this year: jobs for high school dropouts are harder to come by.
	c. a formal series.	At closing time, the following steps must be taken: the vault must be secured, the burglar alarm must be set, and the door must be triple-locked.
	d. a quotation.	In a 1967 article, Martin Luther King said: Negroes will have to learn to refuse crumbs from big city political machines and steadfastly demand a fair share of the loaf.
	2. in the salutation of a formal business letter.	Dear Mr. Brown: Gentlemen:
The Apostrophe	The apostrophe is used	Example:
	1. to signify possession (if a singular noun ends in *s*, add an *'s* or just an *'*, depending on the desir-	Martin's job Sullivan's difficulties man's plight

able pronunciation — for example, Jones's or Jones').	nobody's fault the butchers' salary demands
2. to substitute for the omitted letters in contractions.	didn't we've she's o'clock (literally *of the clock*)
3. to form the plural of	Not knowing her abc's or her p's and q's, Terry had mostly D's and F's on her record.
a. letters.	
b. numbers.	Fred owned several .32's back in the 1940's.
c. words as words (words being talked about, not used as vehicles of meaning).	Stevens uses too many if's, and's, and but's.

Quotation Marks

Quotation marks are used	Example:
1. to enclose words taken directly from someone's speech or writing (the quotation must be verbatim to take quotation marks. This sentence would *not* take quotation marks: "Then the boss told them not to let it happen again." Note that quoted material taking four or more lines is written in a separate, indented paragraph, without quotation marks).	Then the boss told them, ''Don't let it happen again.'' Newton Minow called television ''a vast wasteland.''
2. to distinguish the title of an article in a magazine or newspaper, an essay, a short story, or a poem.	Did you read Henry Hazlett's article ''Retarding Growth'' in last week's issue of Newsweek? (The title of the periodical is underlined.)
3. to distinguish words that are being talked about.	The word ''socialism'' has widely varying connotations. Would you rather be called a ''huckster'' or a ''drummer''?
4. to distinguish terms that are obviously unfamiliar to the reader, or that would strike the reader as slanglike (thereby showing that you know they would be out of place in your context).	For three months, he attended a school for ''grease monkeys.''

Rules for the position of quotation marks: Frequently, closing quotation marks appear at the same point in a sentence as another punctuation mark.

Which comes first? Though there is some disagreement, most authorities suggest the following rules:

1. Always put closing quotation marks *outside* the *period* and the *comma.*

2. Always put closing quotation marks *inside* the *semicolon* and *colon.*

3. Put closing quotation marks either outside or inside the question mark and exclamation point, depending on context.

Underlining

Underlining is used	Example:
1. to distinguish all titles of written works except those of magazine articles, news articles, essays, short stories, and poems (these take quotation marks).	The entire text of Gore Vidal's play <u>The Best Man</u> has been printed in <u>Theater Arts</u>.
2. to distinguish foreign words and phrases not yet completely a part of the English vocabulary.	Cranston's promotion campaign is <u>fait accompli</u>.
	The ambassador's daughter cannot attend the reception without her <u>dueña</u>.
	He spent last summer on a <u>kibbutz</u>.
3. to give emphasis.	I fear his government's actions <u>might</u> lead to war.

As a device for emphasis, underlining should be used sparingly.

The Dash

The dash is used	Example:
1. to break off an unfinished sentence for dramatic effect.	If this bill goes through, our imports will cease, our profits will fall, our loans will be called in, and then--
2. to set off a climactic (or anticlimactic) thought.	Underlying most dating habits in our society is one motive --conquest.
3. in informal writing, to introduce a series (in more formal writing, a colon is used).	Farsightedness was a trait possessed by virtually all the early automotive inventors--Selden, Duryea, Leland, Durant, Ford.
4. to gather up the elements of an introductory series.	The sharpness of Baxter's insights, the scope of his imagination, the richness of his wit--all contribute to his success.

5. to isolate a parenthetical element for emphasis.	War is often an intentional and calculated--albeit an insane--political maneuver.

Note that a dash is typed as *two* hyphens.

Parentheses

Parentheses are used	Example:
1. to set off a parenthetical element as an aside.	Senator Wilson's speeches (most of them ghostwritten) have set the tone of civil rights debate in the northern states.
2. to enclose dates.	The American Civil War (1861-1865) marked the end of an era.
3. to enclose numbers or letters which introduce parts of a series.	A satisfactory definition should (a) include everything the word refers to, (b) exclude everything the word does not refer to, and (c) avoid using the word itself.

INDEX